THE ANNALS OF THE FOUR MASTERS

Winner of the 2011 Irish Historical Research Prize,
awarded by the National University of Ireland

FROM SOME REVIEWS

'This important study not only makes a vital contribution to source criticism and understanding of the interrelationships of extant manuscripts, and the nature of historical learning and collaborative scholarly networks that transcended confessional boundaries to include Protestant scholars, such as James Ussher, Church of Ireland archbishop of Armagh, and Sir James Ware, but equally importantly elucidates the ideological milieu in which the Annals of the Four Masters were compiled between 1626 and 1636', Marie Therese Flanagan, *Journal of Ecclesiastical History*.

'The sheer intellectuality of this book, the overt depth of its learning was itself a pleasure ... fascinating and accessible ... an exceedingly handsome book', Joe Horgan, *Books Ireland*.

'*The Annals of the Four Masters* is one of the most formative books in Irish history. Bernadette Cunningham here provides an exhaustive resumé of the modern research, by herself and others, on the composition, content and context of the work of the Four Masters. This is a book which every library with a serious interest in Ireland will want to have and, though written for an academic audience, it will also prove enlightening for the ordinary reader about the emergence of the very idea of a Catholic Gaelic Ireland, which has dominated the consciousness of the country down to a recent date ... This is a scholarly tribute to a set of exceptional scholars. Bernadette Cunningham has provided a valuable and important book, which enables the reader to gain a perspective on the early modern period and its scholars, as well as on its idea of its own past', Peter Costello, *Studies*.

'Cunningham's work is a labour of love that deploys the best resources of professional scholarship and personal enthusiasm ... in its understanding of the sheer central importance of its subject, this masterly book is unique', Mícheál Mac Craith OFM, *Irish Economic and Social History*.

D1572331

The Annals of the Four Masters

*Irish history, kingship and society
in the early seventeenth century*

Bernadette Cunningham

FOUR COURTS PRESS

Typeset in 10.5 pt on 12.5 pt Ehrhardt by
Carrigboy Typesetting Services for
FOUR COURTS PRESS LTD
7 Malpas Street, Dublin 8, Ireland
www.fourcourtspress.ie
and in North America for
FOUR COURTS PRESS
c/o ISBS, 920 NE 58th Avenue, Suite 300, Portland, OR 97213.

A catalogue record for this title is available
from the British Library.

ISBN 978–1–84682–538–5

Printed in Ireland by
SPRINT-Print, Dublin.

Contents

LIST OF ILLUSTRATIONS 6

PREFACE 7

ACKNOWLEDGMENTS 9

LIST OF ABBREVIATIONS 10

1 Introduction: Mícheál Ó Cléirigh's Irish annals 13

2 Irish history and ideology: the Louvain dimension 26

3 The late medieval Irish historical tradition 41

4 Form and structure of the Annals of the Four Masters 74

5 The methodology of the Four Masters: new annals from old 102

6 Scribes at work 136

7 Heroes, historians and political memory 176

8 Holy men and holy places 215

9 Scholarly networks and patronage 244

10 Conclusion: making history 301

APPENDIX – Annals of Lecan. Extract for the years 1451–60 305

BIBLIOGRAPHY 316

INDEX 335

Illustrations

6.1   Scribal hand **A**. RIA MS C iii 3, fo. 117v.   140

6.2   Scribal hand **B**. RIA MS C iii 3, fo. 311r.   140

6.3   Scribal hand **C**. RIA MS C iii 3, fo. 231r.   141

6.4   Scribal hand **D**. RIA MS C iii 3, fo. 387r.   141

6.5   Scribal hand **E**. RIA MS C iii 3, fo. 160v.   141

6.6   Scribal hand **1**. UCD–OFM MS A 13, fo. 3r.   144

6.7   Scribal hand **2**. UCD–OFM MS A 13, fo. 414r.   144

6.8   Scribal hand **3**. UCD–OFM MS A 13, fo. 382r.   145

6.9   Scribal hand **4**. UCD–OFM MS A 13, fo. 301r.   145

6.10   Scribal hands **5 & 6**. UCD–OFM MS A 13, fo. 448r.   146

6.11   Scribal hand **7**. UCD–OFM MS A 13, fo. 231.   146

6.12   Scribal hand 8. UCD–OFM MS A 13, fo. xxiii.   146

6.13   AFM entry for AD1438. TCD MS 1301, fo. 767r.   150

6.14   AFM entry for AD1438. RIA MS 23 P 6, fo. 175r.   151

6.15   AFM entry for AD457–9. UCD–OFM MS A 13, fo. 235r.   162

6.16   AFM entry for AD457–9. RIA MS C iii 3, fo. 222r.   163

6.17   AFM entry for AD1428. RIA MS 23 P 6, fo. 166r.   172

6.18   AFM entry for AD1428. TCD MS 1301, fo. 758r.   173

8.1   Proportion of secular and ecclesiastical entries in AFM and AU.   216

9.1   Signatures appended to autograph copy of AFM. UCD–OFM MS A 13, fo. xxiv.   275

9.2   Signatures of Four Masters appended to *Genealogiae regum et sanctorum Hiberniae*, 1630. UCD–OFM MS A 16, fo. x verso.   275

CREDITS

6.1–6.5, 6.14, 6.16–6.17 © RIA; 6.13, 6.18 © Board of TCD; 6.6–6.12, 6.15, 9.1, 9.2 © UCD Archives.

Preface

This book explores the making of the Annals of the Four Masters in early seventeenth-century Ireland. The 'Four Masters' – Mícheál Ó Cléirigh OFM, Cú Choigcríche Ó Cléirigh, Fearfeasa Ó Maoil Chonaire and Cú Choigcríche Ó Duibhgeannáin – were all trained historians from Gaelic learned families from south-west Ulster and north Connacht. The lengthy annals they compiled in the 1630s covered the history of Ireland from the biblical flood down to their own day. There was something about the form and substance of the Annals of the Four Masters that, read or unread, allowed them to become accepted as an authentic, reliable and comprehensive record of Gaelic society. They became recognized as an important element of the cultural capital of a community that valued its Gaelic heritage. In later centuries this reputation made a national hero of its chief compiler, Mícheál Ó Cléirigh, whose work was deemed to have captured the essence of what was worthy of remembrance from the Irish past.

This study of the historical annals of Ireland compiled by the Four Masters surveys the scholarly context, both Irish and European, that inspired the annalists. The Four Masters worked in an era of rapid cultural transition, where old and new networks of professional expertise and patronage combined to generate a renewed interest in the Irish past and to facilitate historical scholarship on an ambitious scale. Questions about why the annals took the form that they did, and how the compilers went about the task of producing a new account of the Irish past from the sources available to them, are addressed here in an analysis of the original manuscripts. The source texts consulted by the annalists, in so far as they can be identified among extant manuscripts, are used to throw light on their working methods and their understanding of history. A comparison of the two sets of autograph manuscripts illuminates how the annalists collaborated in the day-to-day production of their *magnum opus*, and how they planned, executed and revised their work.

Two in-depth case studies, one secular and one ecclesiastical, are used to explore the extent to which the Four Masters' perceptions of the world in which they lived can be discerned from their historical writing. The ecclesiastical values they espoused are contextualized in a study of the manner in which ecclesiastical material is handled. The complexity of the political ideas that are contained within the text is discussed in the context of the historical representation of the Uí Dhomhnaill. The tensions within the text, which allow the expression of contradictory political values, are highlighted by this case study. Respect for the memory of the achievements of past generations permeates the annalists' approach to the historical record. Similarly, their approach to making their own annals clearly conveys their high regard for the written records that had preserved for them, in manuscript, the history of their ancestors.

Acknowledgments

I am grateful to the Royal Irish Academy for allowing me a three-year career break which gave me time to research and write this book. In particular, I thank Siobhán Fitzpatrick and Paddy Buckley for keeping the process simple, Petra Schnabel for her willingness to take my place, and all at the Academy library for their support, and not least their generous assistance on my return visits there as a reader. Among the other libraries I have had reason to use in the course of this research I wish to acknowledge the assistance of the staff of UCD Archives and the UCD James Joyce Library, the manuscripts department and library of Trinity College Dublin, the Bibliothèque Royale, Brussels, the British Library, and the National Archives of Ireland. The microfilm collections of the National Library of Ireland, the John Paul II library at National University of Ireland, Maynooth, and the Dublin Institute for Advanced Studies library were of special importance in making available copies of manuscript materials from other institutions that were otherwise difficult to access. Also invaluable were the CELT (University College Cork) and ISOS (Dublin Institute for Advanced Studies) projects, which provided free on-line access to texts and images of core sources.

This book is based on research carried out for a doctoral thesis in the Department of Modern Irish at University College Dublin under the joint supervision of Caoimhín Breatnach and the late Alan Harrison, whose advice and guidance is acknowledged. I enjoyed the support of the Mícheál Ó Cléirigh Institute for the Study of Irish History and Civilisation at University College Dublin, and also benefited from the facilities of the Humanities Institute of Ireland at University College Dublin.

Scholars who shared information, resources or advice on particular points include Edel Bhreathnach, David Dumville, Joseph Flahive, Anthony Harvey, Seamus Helferty, Patricia Kelly, Eoin Mac Cárthaigh, Dan McCarthy, Mícheál Mac Craith, Megan McGowan, Con Manning, Vincent Morley, Kenneth Nicholls, Meidhbhín Ní Úrdail, Breandán Ó Buachalla, Colmán Ó Clabaigh, Ailbhe Ó Corráin, Maura O'Gara-O'Riordan, Nollaig Ó Muraíle, Margaret Ó hÓgartaigh, Pádraig Ó Riain, Salvador Ryan and Katharine Simms. For exceptional hospitality during my visits to libraries abroad, I thank Virginia Davis and John McLoughlin in London, and Clodagh and Gerry Moran who were living in Brussels at the appropriate time. I thank all at Four Courts Press for making possible the publication of books of this kind. Finally, I thank my husband, Raymond Gillespie, for his enthusiastic encouragement of my brief return to full-time research.

Abbreviations

AClon	Annals of Clonmacnoise
AClon	Denis Murphy (ed.), *Annals of Clonmacnoise from the earliest period to AD1408, translated into English by Conell Mageoghagan, AD1627* (Dublin, 1896)
AConn	Annals of Connacht
AConn	A.M. Freeman (ed.), *Annála Connacht: the annals of Connacht, AD1224–1544* (Dublin, 1944)
AD	*Anno Domini*
Add.	Additional
AFM	Annals of the Four Masters
AFM	John O'Donovan (ed.), *Annála ríoghachta Éireann: annals of the kingdom of Ireland, by the Four Masters, from the earliest period to the year 1616* (2nd ed., 7 vols, Dublin, 1856)
AI	Annals of Inisfallen
AI	Seán Mac Airt (ed.), *Annals of Inisfallen (MS Rawlinson B 503)* (Dublin, 1951)
ALCé	Annals of Loch Cé
ALCé	W.M. Hennessy (ed.), *The Annals of Loch Cé: a chronicle of Irish affairs from AD1014 to AD1590* (2 vols, London, 1871)
ALec	Annals of Lecan
ALec	*[Annals of Lecan]* John O'Donovan (ed.), 'The annals of Ireland from the year 1443 to 1468, translated from the Irish by Dudley Firbisse, or as he is more usually called, Duald Mac Firbis, for Sir James Ware in the year 1666' in *Miscellany of the Irish Archaeological Society* 1 (Dublin, 1846), pp 198–302.
AM	*Anno mundi*
ATig	Annals of Tigernach
ATig	Whitley Stokes (ed.), *The Annals of Tigernach* (repr. from *Revue Celtique* in 2 vols, Felinfach, 1993)
AU	Annals of Ulster
AU	W.M. Hennessy and B. MacCarthy (eds.), *Annála Uladh: Annals of Ulster from the earliest times to the year 1541* (4 vols, Dublin, 1887–1901)
BARUD	'Beatha Aodha Ruaidh Uí Dhomhnaill' by Lughaidh Ó Cléirigh
BARUD	Paul Walsh (ed.), *Beatha Aodha Ruaidh Uí Dhomhnaill* (2 vols, ITS XLII, XLV, London, 1948, 1957)
BL	British Library, London
Bodl.	Bodleian Library, Oxford
BR	Bibliothèque Royale, Brussels
Cat. Ir. mss in BL	S.H. O'Grady and Robin Flower, *Catalogue of Irish manuscripts in the British Library* [formerly *Museum*] (3 vols, London, 1926–53)
Cat. Ir. mss in Bodl.	Brian Ó Cuív, *Catalogue of Irish language manuscripts in the Bodleian Library at Oxford and Oxford College Libraries* (2 vols, Dublin, 2001–3)

Cat. Ir. mss in FLK	Myles Dillon, Canice Mooney and Pádraig de Brún, *Catalogue of Irish manuscripts in the Franciscan Library, Killiney* (Dublin, 1969)
Cat. Ir. mss King's Inns	Pádraig de Brún, *Catalogue of Irish manuscripts in King's Inns Library, Dublin* (Dublin, 1972)
Cat. Ir. mss in RIA	T.F. O'Rahilly, Kathleen Mulchrone et al., *Catalogue of Irish manuscripts in the Royal Irish Academy*, Fasc 1–27 (Dublin, 1926–70)
CS	Chronicum Scotorum
CS	William Hennessy (ed.), *Chronicum Scotorum* (London, 1866)
d.	died
DIAS	Dublin Institute for Advanced Studies
DIB	*Dictionary of Irish biography* (9 vols, Cambridge, 2009)
DIL	E.G. Quin et al. (eds), *Dictionary of the Irish language based mainly on Old and Middle Irish materials* (Dublin, 1913–76)
DNB	*Dictionary of national biography*, ed. Leslie Stephen et al. (63 vols, London, 1885–1900)
FLK	Franciscan Library Killiney
GRSH	Paul Walsh (ed.), *Genealogiae regum et sanctorum Hiberniae, by the Four Masters, edited from the manuscript of Michél Ó Cléirigh* (Maynooth, 1918)
HMC Franciscan mss	Historical Manuscripts Commission. *Report on Franciscan manuscripts preserved at the Convent, Merchant's Quay, Dublin* (Dublin, 1906)
IAS	Irish Archaeological Society
IMC	Irish Manuscripts Commission
ITS	Irish Texts Society
MDon	J.H. Todd and W. Reeves (eds), *The martyrology of Donegal: a calendar of the saints of Ireland: Féilire na naomh nErennach* (Dublin, 1864)
MP	Member of Parliament
MSS	manuscripts
NAI	National Archives of Ireland, Dublin
NLI	National Library of Ireland, Dublin
n.s.	new series
NUI	National University of Ireland
OFM	Order of Friars Minor
Oxford DNB	*Oxford dictionary of national biography* (60 vols, Oxford, 2004)
Rawl.	Rawlinson
repr.	reprint/reprinted
RIA	Royal Irish Academy
s.a.	*sub anno*, under the year
ser.	series
s.n.	*sub nomine*, under the name
s.v.	*sub verbo*, under the word
TCD	Trinity College Dublin
TNA	The National Archives, Kew
trans.	translation/translated by
UCD	University College Dublin
UCD–OFM	Franciscan Manuscripts, UCD Archives
ZCP	*Zeitschrift für Celtische Philologie*

CHAPTER ONE

Introduction: Mícheál Ó Cléirigh's Irish annals

The compendium of Irish history known as the Annals of the Four Masters (AFM) is an example of a cult text that is rarely read. The annals compiled in the 1630s are still consulted by local historians and archaeologists seeking specific details regarding people and places in the past, but the most usual approach to the text is probably through the index to John O'Donovan's mid-nineteenth-century edition.[1] Indeed, the average researcher is just as likely to resort to the information contained in O'Donovan's extensive topographical footnotes as to read the text of the annals themselves. The history of the kingdom of Ireland compiled by the Four Masters is rarely read as a work of history, and to date there has been little systematic analysis of the content of the annals. This study of the Annals of the Four Masters seeks to rectify that omission, and to situate the historical writings of the early seventeenth-century annalists within the cultural and political world of Ireland and Europe in their own day.

Perhaps the most extraordinary aspect of the story of the Annals of the Four Masters is the way in which the text has long been regarded not merely as a source that still retains some value for the history of Ireland, but also as representing something more than that. From the end of the nineteenth century, in particular, commentators have seen AFM as one of the enduring achievements of native Irish scholars before the disappearance of the Gaelic world. The significance of the work of the Four Masters is described in the colourful prose of Aodh de Blácam, who in 1929 concluded that:

> Nothing, perhaps, in our history is more piteous or more dramatic than the sitting down of these heirs of an immemorial tradition to rescue and set in order what could be recovered, in a land of blood and ashes, of the names and titles and deeds of the great men of Éire. Their vast compilation is justly famous, although it is somewhat fantastically supposed by many folk to be the prime, if not the only, monument of Irish letters. ... Be it remembered that the Masters laboured in the cold belief that the Irish nation was dead, and that nothing remained to be salved save its memory. They succeeded in their task. They saved great tracts of the Irish past from oblivion. Were it not for them our knowledge of mediaeval Ireland would

---

1 John O'Donovan (ed.), *Annála ríoghachta Éireann: annals of the kingdom of Ireland, by the Four Masters, from the earliest period to the year 1616, edited from mss in the library of the Royal Irish Academy and of Trinity College Dublin, with a translation and copious notes* (1st ed., 7 vols, Dublin, 1848–51; 2nd ed., 7 vols, Dublin, 1856; repr. New York, 1966; Dublin, 1990).

be largely a picturesque tradition that could not be related easily to fact. In their vast work we see an immemorial civilization, as it were Atlantis with all its towers and temples, looming out of the dim backward of time.[2]

More soberly, but with a similar degree of reverence, Douglas Hyde, writing in 1899, described Mícheál Ó Cléirigh's scholarly endeavours in heroic terms. Commenting on Ó Cléirigh's researches on hagiographical manuscripts, Hyde noted that:

> Up and down, high and low, he hunted for the ancient vellum books and time-stained manuscripts whose safety was even then threatened by the ever-thickening political shocks and spasms of that most destructive age. These, whenever he found, he copied in an accurate and beautiful handwriting, and transmitted safely to Louvain. ...
>
> Before O'Clery ever entered the Franciscan Order he had been by profession an historian or antiquary, and now in his eager quest for ecclesiastical writings and the lives of saints, his trained eye fell upon many other documents which he could not neglect. These were the ancient books and secular annals of the nation, and the historical poems of the ancient bards. ...
>
> There is no event of Irish history from the birth of Christ to the beginning of the seventeenth century that the first inquiry of the student will not be, 'What do the "Four Masters" say about it?' for the great value of the work consists in this, that we have here in condensed form the pith and substance of the old books of Ireland which were then in existence but which – as the Four Masters foresaw – have long since perished.[3]

Describing a visit to Louvain in the late 1880s, journalist and poet Eugene Davis recalled for *Evening Telegraph* readers the particular connection with Ó Cléirigh:

> St Anthony's College will live chiefly in history as the institution where Brother O'Clery, the leading light of the Four Masters, matured that remarkable talent of his, and that untiring capacity for intellectual research, thanks to which we owe the 'Annals'. It was in these cloisters, under the shade of these trees in the courtyard, that he paced up and down often and often, dreaming of the 'magnum opus', sketching its proportions with his mind's eye, or lost in enthusiasm at its scope and grandeur.[4]

Tomás Ó Cléirigh's 1935 study of the Irish college at Louvain incorporated a succinct version of the Ó Cléirigh myth, affirming the Franciscan scholar's status as Ireland's greatest chronicler.[5] In the same year, Brendan Jennings's

2 Aodh de Blácam, *Gaelic literature surveyed: from earliest times to the present* (Dublin, 1929, repr. 1973), pp 233–4. 3 Douglas Hyde, *A literary history of Ireland, from earliest times to the present day* (London, 1899, rev. ed. 1967), pp 574–80. 4 Eugene Davis, *Souvenir of Irish footprints over Europe* (Dublin, 1889), p. 9. 5 Tomás Ó Cléirigh, *Aodh Mac Aingil agus an scoil Nua-Ghaedhilge i Lobháin*

meticulously researched book on Ó Cléirigh likewise focused on the career of Ó Cléirigh rather than specifically on his historical writing. He placed the annals in the context of the whole corpus of Ó Cléirigh's writings, sifting through the almost incidental material for evidence of the environment in which the work was produced, but refraining from analyzing the work as history. Jennings was keen to stress the status of Ó Cléirigh as one of Ireland's most important historians, concluding that:

> this humble Brother, who hid himself so completely while accomplishing so much for Ireland, has fulfilled one of the noblest ambitions man can have. He has written his name large across the history of his country, and has left it engraved indelibly on the hearts of all his countrymen.[6]

The passage of the twentieth century has seen more muted enthusiasm. Máirín Ní Mhuiríosa, in an Irish translation of J.E. Caerwyn Williams's 1958 survey of the Irish literary tradition, offered a measured contextualization of Ó Cléirigh's world, drawing on the researches of Brendan Jennings.[7] The account of Ó Cléirigh's researches was subsequently re-romanticized in Patrick Ford's reworking of Caerwyn Williams' text for an English edition. Discussing Ó Cléirigh's researches on saints' lives undertaken for John Colgan's hagiographical project, Ford quoted from Charles Plummer:

> There is, indeed, hardly to be found in the history of literature a more pathetic tale than that of the way in which Colgan and his fellow workers ... strove amid poverty, and persecution, and exile, to save the remains of their country's antiquities from destruction.[8]

The degree of adulation traditionally accorded Mícheál Ó Cléirigh is somewhat curious. Earlier generations of annalists and their compilations, such as the Annals of Ulster (AU), the Annals of Connacht (AConn) or the Annals of Loch Cé (ALCé), have not attracted the same kind of eulogistic comment. However, the special character of AFM is not difficult to discover. Alone among the extant annals in the Irish language, AFM is surrounded by its own romantic myth of a struggle against the odds to rescue the ancient lore of the Irish past from oblivion. The traditional story of the circumstances of the work of the Four Masters takes the form of a heroic tale comparable to that told of another seventeenth-century Irish historian, Geoffrey Keating, reputedly, if improbably, writing his work while hiding in a cave in the Glen of Aherlow.[9] Secondly, the

(Dublin, 1935, repr. 1985), pp 10–14.   6 Brendan Jennings, *Michael O Cleirigh, chief of the Four Masters, and his associates* (Dublin, 1936), p. 174.   7 J.E. Caerwyn Williams and Máirín Ní Mhuiríosa, *Traidisiún liteartha na nGael* (Dublin, 1979), pp 240–1; rev. trans. of J.E. Caerwyn Williams, *Traddodiad llenyddol Iwerddon* (Cardiff, 1958).   8 Cited in J.E. Caerwyn Williams and P.K. Ford, *The Irish literary tradition* (Cardiff, 1992), p. 209.   9 For discussion of this latter myth, see Bernadette Cunningham, *The world of Geoffrey Keating: history, myth and religion in seventeenth-century Ireland*

Four Masters, and in particular Mícheál Ó Cléirigh, found ready champions in early twentieth-century Ireland in the Franciscan Order. Membership of the Franciscan community did Ó Cléirigh's scholarly reputation no harm. As Peter Burke has demonstrated, it was much easier to become a saint in sixteenth- and seventeenth-century Europe if one had the institutional backing of a religious order.[10]

Not having been martyred for the faith, Ó Cléirigh was never among the lists of those seventeenth-century Irish Catholics whose cause for canonization was promoted in early twentieth-century Ireland.[11] Instead, he represented the epitome of scholarly sainthood in the newly established Free State, in which the Irish language and Irish history were central to its sense of the core tenets of Irishness. As the scholarly hero credited with having rescued the records of the Gaelic past from oblivion, the Franciscan lay brother, Mícheál Ó Cléirigh, became the focus of celebrations of Irish national identity.[12] Thus, in 1944, commemorative events were organized to mark the tercentenary of his death. Specially commissioned postage stamps were issued in his honour, designed by an Irish artist, R.J. King. The Minister for Posts and Telegraphs emphasized that the stamps were being printed in Ireland using Irish paper. It was noted that 'The stamp is a tribute not only to the great chronicler, Michael Ó Cléirigh, but it recalls to the minds of the present generation the very ancient traditions of our Nation and our civilization'.[13] These were not merely commemorative stamps issued for a short period, but became part of the definitive series that remained in use until 1969.[14]

On Sunday 25 June 1944, a gala celebration of Ó Cléirigh's life and work was held in the Gaiety Theatre in Dublin. The event honoured the memory of the lay brother 'whose labours in the cause of Irish history, literature, and language, saved our country's records from obliteration and our native tongue from extinction'.[15] The commemorative programme produced on the occasion included a special apostolic blessing from Pope Pius XII, addressed to:

> His eminence Cardinal MacRory, primate of all Ireland, an Taoiseach Eamon de Valera, and other leaders of Church and State, together with many persons

(Dublin, 2000), pp 59–60. 10 Peter Burke, 'How to be a Counter-Reformation saint' in Kaspar Von Greyerz (ed.), *Religion and society in early modern Europe, 1500–1800* (London, 1984), pp 45–55. 11 Patrick J. Corish and Benignus Millett (eds), *The Irish martyrs* (Dublin, 2005), passim. 12 For further discussion of the twentieth-century context, see Bernadette Cunningham, 'Remembering Mícheál Ó Cléirigh' in Edel Bhreathnach and Bernadette Cunningham (eds), *Writing Irish history: the Four Masters and their world* (Dublin, 2007), pp 76–81. 13 *Comóradh i n-onóir Mhichíl Uí Chléirigh, bráthair bocht, ceann na gCeithre Máistrí* (Dublin, 1944), [p. 15]. On the importance attached to the promotion of Irish history in the Irish Free State, see Philip O'Leary, *Gaelic prose in the Irish Free State, 1922–1939* (Dublin, 2004), pp 245–343. 14 The stamps, issued on 30 June 1944, were in denominations of ½d. and 1s. They remained in general use until 1969. M. Don Buchalter, *Hibernian specialised catalogue of the postage stamps of Ireland, 1922–1972* (Dublin, 1972), pp 50–1. 15 *Comóradh i n-onóir Mhichíl Uí Chléirigh*, [p. 16].

prominent in the religious, civil, educational, and cultural life of the Irish nation, assembling in Dublin to commemorate the tercentenary of the death of Ireland's great annalist, and historian, the Franciscan lay-brother, Michael Ó Cléirigh, known as 'The Chief of the Four Masters'.[16]

In the same year, the Assisi Press published a collection of academic essays in memory of Mícheál Ó Cléirigh, under the editorship of Sylvester O'Brien, OFM.[17] While representing a major contribution to the academic evaluation of the researches of Ó Cléirigh and other Franciscan scholars, that volume, too, contained more by way of eulogy of Ó Cléirigh's achievement than it did analysis of his historical annals. None of the twenty academic contributions in the volume dealt specifically with AFM, the historical annals merely receiving passing mention in Canice Mooney's contribution under the title 'The Golden Age of the Irish Franciscans, 1615–50'.[18] Having largely ignored the historical text for which Ó Cléirigh was remembered, the volume concluded with an epilogue in verse, in praise of the scholar himself:

> Lo! He who saved from deep oblivion
> The chronicle of saint and king and bard
> Through gathering menaces of war and strife
> Went not all unremembered, for upon
> One white memorial war hath not marr'd
> His name stands written – on the Book of Life.[19]

In short, by the mid-twentieth century, Ó Cléirigh had become not merely a cultural icon of Irishness, but was hailed as the saviour of the Irish past.

In post-1922 Ireland, as Philip O'Leary has shown, there was a strong belief in the importance of history in promoting loyalty to the Irish nation. The emphasis on Irish history, written by Irish people, was all the more important in view of the decline of the Irish language.[20] An editorial in the *Irish Independent* in August 1924, headed *Uaisleacht na hÉireann*, stressed the 'national' value of history:

> It is from history will come to us again the confidence and that national hope that were alive in Ireland when the national language was commonly spoken in our country. Let us give our young students accurate knowledge of the golden age of

---

16 *Comóradh i n-onóir Mhichíl Uí Chléirigh*, [p. 3]. It seems that Jennings's work, which had as its subtitle 'Chief of the Four Masters', was a particular influence on these 1940s perceptions of Ó Cléirigh. The term had also been used by O'Curry a century earlier. O'Curry, *Lectures on manuscript materials*, p. 142.   17 Sylvester O'Brien (ed.), *Measgra i gcuimhne Mhichíl Uí Chléirigh: miscellany of historical and linguistic studies in honour of Brother Michael Ó Cléirigh, OFM, chief of the Four Masters, 1643–1943* (Dublin, 1944).   18 O'Brien (ed.), *Measgra i gcuimhne Mhichíl Uí Chléirigh*, p. 29. 19 Liam Brophy, 'Epilogue' in O'Brien (ed.), *Measgra i gcuimhne Mhichíl Uí Chléirigh*, [p. 243]. 20 Philip O'Leary, *Gaelic prose in the Irish Free State, 1922–1939* (Dublin, 2004), pp 252–71.

faith and learning, when our native land was respected throughout Europe. For the salvation and the uplifting of the nation today are in the revival of the spirit that was alive in Ireland at that time.[21]

However, there were many in post-civil war Ireland for whom the Four Masters' record of kings and battles and dates was not the kind of history deemed appropriate for the new state. Many cultural commentators supported a move away from the kings and battles of 'traditional' history, towards a history of the 'ordinary people' of the Irish past. Writing in March 1922, Myles Dillon observed that:

> Until recently, history as it was taught was the story of the kings who came to rule the country, about the battles they fought, the day of their birth, the day of their death, and so on. But usually an attempt is now made to interpret for the new world the old world, both noble and common, their customs and deeds and their thoughts, affairs of war and affairs of peace.[22]

O'Leary has documented the growth in interest in folklore and in local history as a way into a different, more balanced view of the Irish past. But yet, although AFM with its origin legend, its chronologies of kings and battles, its narratives of death and loss, was not the kind of history desired by some in the new Free State, the cult of Mícheál Ó Cléirigh was nonetheless well-established, and celebrated by church and state.

The standard edition of AFM, edited by John O'Donovan, had been published in 1851.[23] That edition was primarily the product of the antiquarian researches of George Petrie and Eugene O'Curry as well as O'Donovan. Petrie had been responsible for the acquisition by the Royal Irish Academy of a set of autograph manuscripts of AFM covering the period from 1170 to 1616.[24] His published article on the annals, which was extracted at length in the introductory remarks to O'Donovan's edition, concentrated on the provenance and authenticity of the manuscript that he had purchased.[25] Eugene O'Curry devoted two lectures to the researches of Mícheál Ó Cléirigh and his associates in his *Lectures on the manuscript materials of ancient Irish history* delivered at the

---

21 *Irish Independent*, 5 Aug. 1924, cited in O'Leary, *Gaelic prose in the Irish Free State*, p. 259.
22 *An Reult*, March 1922, 57, cited in O'Leary, *Gaelic prose in the Irish Free State*, p. 254.
23 O'Donovan (ed.), *Annála ríoghachta Éireann: annals of the kingdom of Ireland, by the Four Masters, from the earliest period to the year 1616.*   24 The term 'autograph' manuscripts is used here to denote the original manuscripts of the annals written by members of the Four Masters team, as distinct from later transcripts by other scribes. The manuscripts purchased by Petrie are now RIA MSS 23 P 6 and 23 P 7. They were purchased for the Academy at the sale of the library of Austin Cooper (T. Ó Raifeartaigh (ed.), *The Royal Irish Academy: a bicentennial history, 1785–1985* (Dublin, 1985), p. 323); according to a priced sale catalogue, the sum paid was £53 (William O'Sullivan, 'The Slane manuscript of the Annals of the Four Masters', *Ríocht na Mídhe* 10 (1999), 78); *AFM*, I, p. xv.   25 George Petrie, 'Remarks on the history and authenticity of the Annals of the Four Masters', *Transactions of the Royal Irish Academy* 16 (1831), 381–93.

Catholic University in Dublin in the mid-1850s. Introducing the annals as 'the most important of all in point of interest and historic value', he commented:

> In whatever point of view we regard these annals, they must awaken feelings of deep interest and respect; not only as the largest collection of national, civil, military, and family history ever brought together in this or perhaps any other country, but also as the final winding up of the affairs of a people who had preserved their nationality and independence for a space of over two thousand years, till their complete overthrow about the time at which this work was compiled. It is no easy matter for an Irishman to suppress feelings of deep emotion when speaking of the compilers of this great work and especially when he considers the circumstances under which, and the objects for which, it was undertaken.[26]

O'Curry, following the lead of John Colgan's 1645 preface to *Acta sanctorum Hiberniae*, devoted more space to discussing Ó Cléirigh and his assistants than to the historical annals they produced. Aside from offering an opinion as to why the annals devoted so much space to the period from the twelfth to the seventeenth centuries, and a statistical assessment of the relative attention devoted to the Uí Bhriain of Thomond and the Uí Dhomhnaill of Tír Conaill, O'Curry offered little analysis of the annals as history. Concerned to introduce Ó Cléirigh's work to a student audience, he concentrated on the introductory material that had accompanied the autograph annals, letting that evocative evidence speak for itself.[27] He concluded his discussion of the annals by drawing attention to O'Donovan's standard edition of the text, 'which must form the basis of all fruitful study of the history of Ireland'. O'Curry exhorted his students to use this newly available edition 'to study the great events of your country's history in the time-honoured records collected by the O'Clerys'.[28]

O'Donovan's edition has been rightly hailed as a major achievement, and his notes to the text are unsurpassed. Yet, as even O'Curry felt obliged to observe, it was merely the standard edition 'in the present state of our knowledge' at the time of its publication in 1851. The edition had one very serious flaw. Working in Dublin in the 1840s, O'Donovan did not have access to either of the extant autograph manuscripts of AFM for the period before 1171, though he and O'Curry were aware of their existence.[29] Both O'Donovan and O'Curry were blissfully unaware that the eighteenth-century transcripts on which O'Donovan relied had entirely omitted hundreds of entries relating to the pre-Christian and early Christian periods.[30] Yet, over one hundred and fifty years later, at the

---

26 O'Curry, *Lectures on manuscript materials*, p. 140.   27 O'Curry, *Lectures on manuscript materials*, pp 140–61.   28 O'Curry, *Lectures on manuscript materials*, pp 160, 161.   29 The 'Stowe' manuscript (now RIA MS C iii 3) was then in the collection of Lord Ashburnham and unavailable to Irish scholars (O'Curry, *Lectures on manuscript materials*, p. 155). The Franciscan manuscript (now UCD–OFM MS A 13) was then in St Isidore's College, Rome, and was returned to Ireland in 1872.   30 See below,

beginning of the twenty-first century, that incomplete and unsatisfactory edition remains un-revised, still attracting vague adulation if not much in-depth interest. Perhaps more significantly, in contrast to the work of Geoffrey Keating, AFM remained out of print from the late nineteenth century until 1966. The original, expensive, seven-volume edition lay locked away in the libraries of the gentry and national institutions. The older, partial and quite inaccurate, edition by Rev. Charles O'Conor, comprising the third volume of a four-volume collection entitled *Rerum Hibernicarum scriptores*, was a similarly expensive production designed for gentry libraries.[31] By contrast, Keating's *Foras feasa ar Éirinn*, a prose history of Ireland from creation to the twelfth century, written about the same time, was available in print in cheap pocket editions, in English translation, from 1820, and partly in Irish from 1880. Substantial extracts of Keating's Irish text were widely disseminated in school textbook format, and from the first decade of the twentieth century, a scholarly dual language edition published by the Irish Texts Society satisfied the demand for a full edition of the work.[32]

By the mid-twentieth century, therefore, for all the adulation heaped on AFM, and despite the publicity surrounding the life of Ó Cléirigh, encouraged in particular by Brendan Jennings's book published in 1936,[33] AFM was not a readily accessible text. Not only were the annals generally unavailable to purchase, except as an expensive antiquarian collector's item, they also failed to attract any significant academic scholarship up to the 1980s, with the notable exception of the indefatigable Paul Walsh.[34] Despite the Franciscan enthusiasm for Mícheál Ó Cléirigh, of over four hundred books and articles listed in the bibliography of the work of Irish Franciscan scholars at the Killiney house of studies, 1945–95, only one article was devoted to AFM: a lecture by Cathaldus Giblin commissioned for a 1964 radio broadcast designed for a general

pp 75–6. **31** Charles O'Conor (ed.), *Quatuor Magistrorum annales Hibernici* in Rerum Hibernicarum Scriptores III (Buckingham, 1826). Both O'Curry and O'Donovan were openly critical of the shortcomings of O'Conor's edition (O'Curry, *Lectures on manuscript materials*, p. 159; *AFM*, I, p. vii). Owen Connellan had also produced an English translation of the post-1171 section of AFM, published under the title *The annals of Ireland translated from the original Irish of the Four Masters* (Dublin, 1846), a more modest production quickly overshadowed by the appearance of O'Donovan's authoritative dual language edition. **32** The first cheap edition in English designed for wide circulation was [Geoffrey Keating], *The history of the ancient Irish from their reception of Christianity till the invitation of the English in the reign of Henry the second, translated from the original Irish* (Newry, 1820); P.W. Joyce (ed.), *Foras feasa air Éirinn ... History of Ireland, book 1 part 1* (Dublin, Gaelic Union Publications, 1880); Osborn Bergin (ed.), *Sgéalaigheacht Chéitinn: stories from Keating's history of Ireland, edited with notes and glossary* (1st ed., Dublin, 1909); David Comyn and P.S. Dinneen (eds), *Foras feasa ar Éirinn: the history of Ireland* by Geoffrey Keating (4 vols, ITS IV, VIII, IX, XV, London, 1902–14). **33** Jennings, *Michael O Cleirigh and his associates*. **34** Paul Walsh, 'The dating of the Irish annals', *Irish Historical Studies* 2 (1940–1), 355–75; Paul Walsh, 'The Four Masters', *Irish Book Lover* 22 (1934), 128–31; Paul Walsh, 'Manuscripts of the Four Masters, RIA 23 P 6 and 7', *Irish Book Lover* 24 (1936), 81–3; Paul Walsh, 'Slips in O'Donovan's Four Masters, vol. V', *Irish Book Lover* 25 (1937), 100–2; Paul Walsh, 'Travels of an Irish Scholar', *Catholic Bulletin* 27 (1937), 123–32; Paul Walsh, *The Four Masters and their work* (Dublin, 1944).

audience.[35] Giblin's article followed a now well-established pattern, telling the story of Ó Cléirigh's overall research-undertaking, rather than analyzing AFM itself in any detail.

In some ways, the lack of scholarly attention devoted to AFM is unexceptional, as there has been a paucity of published historiographical research on all late medieval Irish annals until very recently. It is also the case that the text of AFM presents certain palaeographical and diplomatic challenges, because there is no single authoritative autograph manuscript. Rather, the text now survives in five manuscript sections which, when taken together, appear to make up one complete and one near-complete set. It is only in recent years that it has been reasonably confidently established that the extant manuscripts probably constituted two sets, a patron's set and a compilers' set, though the question may still be revisited.[36] Moreover, as will be discussed below, each of the extant manuscripts resembles a working draft rather than a final polished version. Each manuscript has been subjected to layers of editorial revision, and none could be described as a fair copy.[37]

While some of the technical problems with the text have begun to be elucidated, the more fundamental questions of the motives for compiling AFM and their function within the scholarly world from which they emanated have received little attention. As part of broader surveys of Irish literature in the early modern period, J.J. Silke and Mícheál Mac Craith have discussed one element of the background context for this investigation, which can be broadly termed the Irish Renaissance.[38] Breandán Ó Buachalla, by focusing more specifically on AFM and building on the insights of publications such as D.R. Kelley's *Foundations of modern historical scholarship* (1970), J.G.A. Pocock's *The ancient constitution and the feudal law* (1957), and Peter Burke's *The Renaissance sense of the past* (1969), has contributed the only systematic analysis of the intellectual

---

35 Anthony Lynch, 'Scríbhinní foireann taighde Dhún Mhuire, 1945–95' in B. Millett and A. Lynch (eds), *Dún Mhuire Killiney, 1945–95: léann agus seanchas* (Dublin, 1995), pp 14–36; Cathaldus Giblin, 'The annals of the Four Masters' in Liam de Paor (ed.), *Great books of Ireland: Thomas Davis lectures* (Dublin, 1967), pp 90–103.   36 For the most convincing statement on this issue, see Nollaig Ó Muraíle, 'The autograph manuscripts of the Annals of the Four Masters', *Celtica* 19 (1987), 75–95. His findings support the suggestion initially made by Paul Walsh. The principal advocates of an alternative view were the Killiney Franciscans, notably Cathaldus Giblin and Canice Mooney. Mooney's views are incorporated into the catalogue description of OFM-UCD, MS A 13 in *Cat. Ir. mss in FLK*, pp 24–7, while Giblin's Thomas Davis lecture in *Great books of Ireland*, pp 97–8, likewise favours what is now a minority view. More recently, Daniel Mc Carthy has put forward a new hypothesis of successive 'initial', 'formalized' and 'final' drafts, but the findings presented in chapter 6 below contradict that hypothesis in respect of the extant manuscripts. For his argument, see Daniel Mc Carthy, *The Irish annals: their genesis, evolution and history* (Dublin, 2007), pp 300–1. However, the possibility that there were more than two sets of the annals cannot be discounted. It is certainly conceivable that the learned families of Ó Maoil Chonaire and Ó Duibhgeannáin retained copies as a reward for their involvement.   37 See below, chapter six. 38 J.J. Silke, 'Irish scholarship and the Renaissance, 1580–1673', *Studies in the Renaissance* 20 (1973), 169–206; Mícheál Mac Craith, 'Gaelic Ireland and the Renaissance' in Glanmor Williams and Robert Owen Jones (eds), *The Celts and the Renaissance: tradition and innovation* (Cardiff, 1990), pp 57–89.

context of AFM as a historical text that has been attempted to date.[39] Making the case that AFM needs to be viewed in a wider continental context of European historical writing, Ó Buachalla surveys a range of contemporary English and European authors with which AFM might usefully be compared.[40] In particular, Ó Buachalla addresses the role of historical debate in the ecclesiastical controversies of the age, and the link between that debate and the growth of interest in national histories. He notes that the Reformation had sparked competition between nations over the interpretation of ecclesiastical history, raising historical questions over whether the Reformation was a return to the basic principles of the early church, or whether the church had changed over time. Both views were in parallel in that they relied on a return to basic historical sources and attached importance to distinguishing between primary and secondary sources.[41] His observation that the much-lauded phrase *Do chum glóire Dé agus onóra na hÉireann* ('for the glory of God and the honour of Ireland'), used by Mícheál Ó Cléirigh in AFM, was in fact an adaptation of a phrase used also in other countries, is the kind of comment that might have fallen on deaf ears among the Free State enthusiasts for Ó Cléirigh's heroic achievements.[42] Ó Buachalla also discusses the political stance of the compilers of AFM, focusing on the material that the annalists include from within living memory at the time of composition. He places particular emphasis on the royalist ideology expressed in the closing section of the annals.[43]

This wider cultural and political context within which Irish history came to be written in the early seventeenth century – not least the desire to produce a national history such as other countries had – has only begun to be explored in an Irish context. A case for the importance of the European dimension in the writing of Keating's *Foras feasa ar Éirinn* has recently been argued.[44] However, it is important to realise that the world of Geoffrey Keating was not that of the Four Masters. Some of the differences are obvious. Keating was a secular priest, and an active preacher; Ó Cléirigh was an unordained member of a religious order, and his scholarly collaborators were laymen. Keating was a trained theologian, having attained the degree of Doctor of Divinity; Ó Cléirigh was a lay brother, lacking a university education. Keating was of Anglo-Norman

39 Breandán Ó Buachalla, '*Annála ríoghachta Éireann* is *Foras feasa ar Éirinn*: an comhthéacs comhaimseartha', *Studia Hibernica* 22–3 (1982–3), 59–105; Breandán Ó Buachalla, *Aisling ghéar: na Stíobhartaigh agus an t-aos léinn, 1603–1788* (Dublin, 1996), pp 90–8; D.R. Kelley, *Foundations of modern historical scholarship: language, law and history in the French Renaissance* (New York, 1970). 40 Matthew Parker, John Bale, John Foxe, William Camden, Polydor Virgil, Caesar Baronius, Henri Lancelot du Voisin de la Popelinière, François Baudouin and others. 41 Ó Buachalla, '*Annála ríoghachta Éireann* is *Foras feasa ar Éirinn*', 70–1; A. Momigliano, *Studies in historiography* (London, 1966), pp 1–39. 42 Ó Buachalla, '*Annála ríoghachta Éireann* is *Foras feasa ar Éirinn*', 74; Ó Buachalla, *Aisling ghéar*, p. 92. 43 Ó Buachalla, '*Annála ríoghachta Éireann* is *Foras feasa ar Éirinn*', 94–6; see also Gerard Murphy, 'Royalist Ireland', *Studies: an Irish Quarterly Review* 24:96 (1935), 589–604. 44 Cunningham, *World of Geoffrey Keating*.

descent, a member of the community who in the early seventeenth century described themselves as the 'Old English' in Ireland; Ó Cléirigh was of Gaelic descent, and a member of a hereditary learned family of professional historians. Keating wrote his history of Ireland as a continuous flowing narrative, in elegant modern Irish; Ó Cléirigh and his associates opted for a simpler and more traditional annalistic format, sometimes using deliberately archaic language.[45]

This book seeks to understand the historical writing of Ó Cléirigh on its own terms, and as an example of how history was used by Irish Catholics in the early seventeenth century. It examines the compilation of the annals not as an example of 'the backward look' – Frank O'Connor's term for what he perceived to be the tendency of the Irish literati to retreat into the past[46] – but rather as a creative product of 1630s Ireland. History, like literature, tends to reflect the concerns of its compilers, perhaps in more ways than its practitioners would readily concede, and the analysis of historical writing to provide insights into a cultural world is a well-established practice.[47] Given the importance of the study of the past as an interpretive tool, it seems clear that a study of the underlying values given expression in AFM can shed light on the cultural and political world of Ireland in the 1630s. As a product of hereditary professional historians, AFM is a key text in understanding the way history was viewed in the Gaelic world on the eve of its transformation, and the kind of history that the annalists chose to write is indicative of their priorities. The background context in terms of the continental connections of the Franciscans is outlined in the next chapter. This is followed by an overview of the Irish annalistic tradition as a prelude to a detailed investigation of the Four Masters' approach to the past. The nature of their project, in terms of ideology and methodology, is then evaluated by way of analysis of the form and structure of the text, comparison and contrast with the content of earlier collections of annals, and attention to the evidence of the autograph manuscripts themselves. As will become clear, the text was not the exclusive product of one set of cultural influences. In addition to the indigenous annalistic tradition, the socio-religious context of the Counter-Reformation – of which the Franciscans were an important channel in Ireland – provides another dimension to the analysis of the text, and this is one of the themes explored in a case study of the ecclesiastical material in the annals.

45 For discussion of the language of the Four Masters, see Pádraig A. Breatnach, 'Irish records of the Nine Years War: a brief survey with particular notice of the relationship between *Beatha Aodha Ruaidh Uí Dhomhnaill* and the Annals of the Four Masters' in Pádraig Ó Riain (ed.), *Beatha Aodha Ruaidh: The life of Red Hugh O'Donnell, historical and literary contexts* (London, 2002), pp 124–47. 46 Frank O'Connor, *The backward look: a survey of Irish literature* (London, 1967). 47 Some recent examples close to home include D.R. Woolf, *The idea of history in early Stuart England* (Toronto, 1990); Annabel Patterson, *Reading Holinshed's Chronicles* (Chicago, 1994); Chris Given-Wilson, *Chronicles: the writing of history in medieval England* (London, 2004); Joep Leerssen, *Remembrance and imagination: patterns in the historical and literary representation of Ireland in the nineteenth century* (Cork, 1996); Clare O'Halloran, *Golden ages and barbarous nations: antiquarian debate and cultural politics in Ireland, c.1750–1800* (Cork, 2004); Cunningham, *World of Geoffrey*

The altered political circumstances of west Ulster following the ending of the Nine Years War in 1603, and the implementation of the English government-sponsored plantation scheme for the province in the early seventeenth century, influenced the writing of history in a variety of ways. The declining fortunes of the professional historians and their traditional patrons, changing perspectives on monarchy, more pragmatic perceptions of power and authority, all influenced the way the past as well as the present was perceived by contemporaries, and AFM offers intriguing insights into that rapidly evolving world. Among those most affected were the dominant traditional elite of Tír Conaill – the Ó Domhnaill kin group[48] – and a case study of their representation in AFM illuminates significant political and cultural values in a period of transformation. These case studies allow for a close reading of the text to highlight key aspects of society as perceived by indigenous historians in the 1630s, and are the first in-depth analyses of how specific themes are dealt with in AFM.

The constraints on how historians could function, in terms of scholarly standards, access to sources, the sanctions of the profession and the expectations of contemporaries, all have a bearing on how a work such as AFM was conceived and brought to completion. The scholarly networks within which the Four Masters operated are examined in some detail in the final part of the book to situate the work within the appropriate professional environment, and to understand the nature of the choices open to the compilers when making their annals.

One aspect of the value of AFM to later historians is that it preserves data not otherwise extant, drawing as it did on source texts of which many are now lost. Thus, for instance, when John Lynch used AFM as a source of information on Irish bishops in his *De praesulibus Hiberniae*, he was able to extract a considerable quantity of evidence from that source that had not been available to Sir James Ware from other annals.[49] But in addition to this role as channel for the transmission of information from older sources, AFM has its own intrinsic value as representing part of the scholarly output of a team of Irish historians trained in the traditional schools of history, and applying their learning to the task of providing a comprehensive set of annals of Irish history at a time of political and social change in the 1630s. While the chapters that follow give due attention to the sources from which AFM derives, the main focus is on the particular

Keating; Ó Buachalla, '*Annála ríoghachta Éireann* is *Foras feasa ar Éirinn*'; Ó Buachalla, *Aisling ghéar*. 48 The older *Clann Dálaigh* or *Síol nDálaigh* names for the kin group are not used here; the surname Ó Domhnaill is preferred throughout (Tomás Ó Máille, *An béal beo*, ed. Ruairí Ó hUiginn (Dublin, 2002), p. 16). 49 J.F. O'Doherty (ed.), *De praesulibus Hiberniae potissimis Catholicae religionis in Hibernia serendae, propagandae, et conservandae authoribus*, 2 vols by John Lynch (IMC, Dublin, 1944); Aubrey Gwynn, 'John Lynch's *De praesulibus Hiberniae*' [review article]. *Studies: an Irish Quarterly Review* 34:133 (1945), 37–52; Sir James Ware, *De praesulibus Hiberniae, commentaries a prima gentis Hibernicae ad fidem Christianem conversione, ad nostra usque tempora* (Dublin, 1665).

interests and priorities of the Four Masters themselves as they engaged with the task of preserving for posterity what they valued most about the Irish past. Their contemporaries were aware that the memory of the past was a contested issue,[50] and an undertaking on the scale of AFM was an important attempt by chroniclers from the Gaelic tradition to assert their claim to ownership of the Irish past. While there is an understandable tendency, even among professional historians, to regard history written in the form of annals as simply a 'straightforward recitation of dates and what happened',[51] the Four Masters did not operate in an ideological vacuum, and they well understood that history had a propaganda value. Their consciousness of the nature of their role as preservers of the memory of the past is a strand of enquiry throughout this exploration of the cultural world within which the Annals of the Four Masters took shape.

50 Cunningham, *World of Geoffrey Keating*, pp 105–21; B. Cunningham, 'Colonized Catholics: perceptions of honour and history in Michael Kearney's reading of *Foras feasa ar Éirinn*' in V.P. Carey and U. Lotz-Heumann (eds), *Taking sides? colonial and confessional mentalités in early modern Ireland: essays in honour of Karl S. Bottigheimer* (Dublin, 2003), pp 150–64. Michael Kearney, a Munster Catholic, writing a preface to his translation of Geoffrey Keating's *Foras feasa ar Éirinn* in 1635, was conscious of countering 'a malignant and envious nature undeservedly borne to Ireland's inhabitants for endeavouring to preserve a memory of their ancient right thereunto' (RIA MS 24 G 16, fo. 25v).   51 Alan Ford, 'James Ussher and the invention of Protestant history', seminar paper, Mícheál Ó Cléirigh Institute, UCD, 8 April 2005.

CHAPTER TWO

Irish history and ideology: the Louvain dimension

Introduction

In the Four Masters' formal dedication of their work to their patron, Fearghal Ó Gadhra, the chief compiler, Mícheál Ó Cléirigh, explained the purpose of the history they had just completed:

> *As ní coitchend soilleir fon uile domhan in gach ionadh i mbí uaisle no onoir in gach aimsir da ttainicc riamh diaidh i ndiaidh nach ffuil ní as glórmaire, 7 as airmittnighe onoraighe (ar adhbharaibh iomdha) ina fios sendachta na senughdar, 7 eolas na naireach, 7 na nuasal ro bhádar ann isin aimsir rempo do thabhairt do chum solais ar dhaigh co mbeith aithentas, 7 eolas ag gach druing i ndeadhaidh aroile cionnas do chaithsiot a sinnsir a ré 7 a naimsir, 7 cia hairett ro battar i tticcernas a nduithce, i ndignit, no i nonoir diaidh i ndiaidh, 7 cred i an oidheadh fuairsiott.*
> (It is a thing general and plain throughout the whole world, in every place where nobility or honour has prevailed in each successive period, that nothing is more glorious, more respectable, or more honourable (for many reasons), than to bring to light the knowledge of the antiquity of ancient authors, and a knowledge of the chieftains and nobles that existed in preceding times, in order that each successive generation might possess knowledge and information as to how their ancestors spent their time and life, how long they were successively in the lordship of their countries, in dignity or in honour, and what sort of death they met.)[1]

According to Ó Cléirigh, therefore, the annals upheld the nobility, honour and dignity of the Irish by remembering the earlier generations of chieftains and nobles from whom the present inhabitants of the country were descended. It was to promote the honour and dignity of the Irish, he said, that he had compiled a formal history such as other nations had. Ó Cléirigh made no claim to uniqueness; rather he placed his history of Ireland firmly in the context of other similar histories elsewhere. It was composed, he told his patron, *do chum glóire Dé 7 onora na hÉireann* ('for the glory of God and the honour of Ireland'). This was the fourth occurrence of the word 'honour' in Ó Cléirigh's short dedication, mainly focused on the honour of the nobility of Ireland.[2] This belief that history brought honour to God and man was not exclusive to Ó Cléirigh or to Ireland.

---

1 *AFM*, I, pp lv–lvi; based on the text in the misplaced vellum section of RIA MS 23 P 6, fos 35r–36v, containing the dedication to the patron, Fearghal Ó Gadhra.   2 *AFM*, I, p. lvi.

Breandán Ó Buachalla has noted sixteenth-century writers from other countries who expressed similar sentiments, including Charles Dumoulin in France, *reipublicae Franciae ornandae causa: pour le bien et honneur du peuple francois* and John Bale in England 'to the honour of God, beauty of the realm'.[3]

The characteristics Ó Cléirigh claimed for his annals of Irish history correspond well to the aspiration for such a history voiced by Patrick Fleming, another Franciscan scholar, in a letter to Hugh Ward, in the summer of 1624: *quid restat amplius, nisi facere unam historiam cum temporam de regibus Hiberniae, sicut et caeterae habent nationes* ('what more remains, other than to make a history of the kings of Ireland with their reigns such as other nations have').[4] Fleming and Ward were among the chief instigators of Franciscan research into Ireland's past and they undertook extensive archival work in search of relevant manuscript materials on the lives of Irish saints.[5] Their scholarly endeavours are particularly associated with the Irish Franciscan college of St Anthony, founded at Louvain in 1607,[6] and it was there that Mícheál Ó Cléirigh encountered them when he joined the Franciscan order about the year 1623. His prior expertise in dealing with Irish manuscript materials was sufficient to ensure that, although never ordained a priest, he was nonetheless an active participant in the collaborative Franciscan scholarly research into the surviving hagiographical manuscripts of Irish interest. As is well known, this research was prompted in part by the publications of Thomas Dempster claiming early Irish saints as Scots, but even more fundamentally there was a desire to promote a positive image of Ireland's Christian heritage among European readers, and the lives of saints were a key element in that objective. As Fleming envisaged in his letter to Ward quoted above, the next step in presenting an appropriate version of the Irish past was to prepare a secular history of the kingdom to complement the ecclesiastical work embodied in the lives of saints. Here, too, the example of other nations was reason enough in itself to write a history of Ireland. Conscious of the need to assemble the source material necessary for all aspects of their research, Fleming continued the letter by urging Ward, who was then in St Anthony's College,

3 Cited in Ó Buachalla, *Aisling ghéar*, p. 92, from Kelley, *Foundations of modern historical scholarship*, p. 181.   4 Patrick Fleming to Hugh Ward, 24 August 1624, printed in Brendan Jennings (ed.), 'Documents from the archives of St Isidore's College, Rome', *Analecta Hibernica* 6 (1934), 216; quotation translated from Latin in Pádraig A. Breatnach, 'An Irish Bollandus: Fr Hugh Ward and the Louvain hagiographical enterprise', *Éigse* 31 (1999), 11.   5 Richard Sharpe, *Medieval Irish saints' lives: an introduction to Vitae Sanctorum Hiberniae* (Oxford, 1991), pp 46–57; Breatnach, 'An Irish Bollandus', 1–30; Bernadette Cunningham, 'The culture and ideology of Irish Franciscan historians at Louvain, 1607–1650' in Ciaran Brady (ed.), *Ideology and the historians: historical studies XVII* (Dublin, 1991), pp 11–30, 222–7; Edmund Hogan, 'Irish historical studies in the seventeenth century, II: Hugh Ward, *Irish Ecclesiastical Record* n.s., 7 (1870–1), 56–77; Edmund Hogan, 'Irish historical studies in the seventeenth century, III: Patrick Fleming, OSF', *Irish Ecclesiastical Record* n.s., 7 (1870–1), 193–216.   6 Patrick Conlan, *St Anthony's College of the Irish Franciscans, Louvain, 1607–1977* (Dublin, 1977), pp 1, 7, gives 3 April 1607 as the official date of foundation with the first members of the community arriving in May 1607.

Louvain, to proceed with a plan – which they had evidently discussed on a previous occasion – to send Mícheál Ó Cléirigh to Ireland to conduct research.[7]

Among the Louvain Franciscan scholars in the early seventeenth century, the history of early Christian Ireland was the main area of interest because it provided the broader context necessary to substantiate the material they were in the process of collecting on the lives of Irish saints. Thus, for example, when Patrick Fleming mentioned to Hugh Ward the history that had been written by Peter Lombard at the height of the Nine Years War,[8] he was somewhat dismissive about the material on recent history contained therein.

> *Habeo in manibus commentaria ipsius Primatis nostri de rebus Hyberniae, et praeter historiam ultimorum saeculorum nil pene habet quod ante non vidi; copisior tamen est in nomenclatura quam alii, quia fuse id ex historia Bedae probat.*
>
> (I have in my possession the commentary of our Primate [Peter Lombard], on the affairs of Ireland; but if you except the history of the last centuries, he has scarcely anything that I had not seen before. He is more full, however, than others on the question of the nomenclature, as he illustrates it copiously from Bede and other writers.)[9]

For those like Fleming and Ward whose interest in conducting research in Irish history was closely linked to their concern to promote research on the lives of Irish saints, the polemical prose of Lombard was of limited appeal. Fleming's comment also highlights the fact that he was already well versed in the sources for the early history of Ireland, but was keen to probe further into the kind of sources that Lombard had left untouched. Fleming wanted no half measures, and he knew that Hugh Ward was of like mind.[10] While a comprehensive history of Ireland, secular as well as ecclesiastical, was a long-term objective, their immediate concern was to proceed with the publication of Irish hagiographical material. When Patrick Fleming received news in July 1624 that the Franciscan

---

7 The story of the hagiographical researches of Ward, Fleming and their associates has been well researched by others, and will not be rehearsed at length here. The most extensive treatment of the topic, and one which extends beyond the Franciscan context to recognize the importance of scholars such as the Jesuit Stephen White, is Sharpe, *Medieval Irish saints' lives*, pp 39–74. 8 Lombard's historical polemic on the kingdom of Ireland, originally written in 1598–1600, was eventually issued in print in Louvain in 1632, and reissued in the mid-nineteenth century (P.F. Moran (ed.), *De regno Hiberniae sanctorum insula commentarius*, by Peter Lombard (Dublin, 1868)). Prior to being issued in print, it evidently circulated in manuscript copies and was available to Fleming in Rome in that form. There are two copies of the manuscript, each dated 1600, in the Bibliotheca Apostolica Vaticana, Barberini Lat. MS 2466 and Lat. MS 6386. A copy of part of the text made in 1601 is in UCD–OFM MS B 27. A partial translation of Lombard's work is available in M.J. Byrne (ed.), *The Irish war of defence, 1598–1600: extracts from the De Hibernia insula commentarius of Peter Lombard* (Cork, 1930); Thomas O'Connor, 'A justification for foreign intervention in early modern Ireland: Peter Lombard's *Commentarius*' in T. O'Connor and M. Lyons (eds), *Irish migrants in Europe after Kinsale* (2003), pp 14–31. 9 Fleming to Ward, 27 July 1623, printed in Jennings (ed.), 'Documents from of St Isidore's', 204; translated in Hogan, 'Irish historical studies in the seventeenth century, iii, Patrick Fleming, OSF', 195–6. 10 Breatnach, 'An Irish Bollandus', 1–30.

archbishop of Dublin, Thomas Fleming OFM, was prepared to fund the publication of a volume of lives of Irish saints, he was dismayed that the task was being entrusted to a priest named Gallagher. Patrick Fleming's reaction was that 'this Father, though qualified for the task by his memory, and his style, is deficient in the knowledge of our ancient histories'.[11] If the work was to be done at all, it was to be done properly, and would require 'a great deal of leisure, and a good supply of books'.[12] Patrick Fleming was in no doubt that Hugh Ward himself was the best qualified for the task of publishing the lives of Irish saints, though he was unspecific as to who might ultimately complete the project by writing a secular history.

As an interim measure, he suggested that Ward should content himself with translating the Irish lives of saints he already had to hand at Louvain and drawing also on the Latin lives in his possession, to publish, in Latin, 'a compendium of all in one small volume, *De viris illustribus Hiberniae*'. This would not be an elaborate or detailed work, but would simply record details of each saint's place of birth, followed by 'his manner of life and his death'.[13] With an eye to the practicalities of the project, Fleming suggested that this could be published without great expense and could be used to announce plans for a more substantial publication. He suggested that the work should be modelled on that of the English writer John Pits. This approach, he advised, would not offend Thomas Messingham and the naming of so many Irish saints would impress continental readers.[14] The letter is particularly revealing of Fleming's thinking and of the cultural context within which his concern to promote research on early Irish saints originated. The intended audience for the published work was an educated continental one, identified explicitly here as an audience that would read works in Latin. The example of similar work done in respect of other countries was also an important factor. There was a quiet confidence that the sheer number of Irish saints' lives would impress. This view was shared by other Irish scholars with experience of European universities, not least Geoffrey Keating, who claimed a few years later:

> *agus an mhéid bheanas re naomhaibh Éireann, ní rachadh d'á mhaoidheamh créad a líonmhaire do bhádar, do bhrígh go bhfuilid úghdair coigcríche na hEorpa ag a admháil, agus go n-abraid gur líonmhaire Éire fa naomhaibh ioná aoin-chríoch i san Eoraip.*

11 Fleming to Ward, 27 July 1624, translated in Hogan, 'Irish historical studies in the seventeenth century, iii, Patrick Fleming, OSF', 199 (*Pater quidem ille et stylo et memoria ad rem illam censeri posset idoneus, sed peritia in historiis volvendis ipsi deest*); Jennings (ed.), 'Documents from St Isidore's', 213.   12 Fleming to Ward, 24 August 1624, translated in Hogan, 'Irish historical studies in the seventeenth century, iii, Patrick Fleming, OSF', 200 (*multam petunt lectionem et copiam librorum*); Jennings (ed.), 'Documents from St Isidore's', 214.   13 *Omnibus collectis compendiose in unum, inscribe librum de viris illustribus Hiberniae, descripto tantum loco nativitatis, conversationis, et obitus cujuslibet sancti*, Jennings (ed.), 'Documents from St Isidore's', 214.   14 Fleming to Ward, 24 August 1624, Jennings (ed.), 'Documents from St Isidore's', 214–15; English adaptation in Hogan, 'Irish historical studies in the seventeenth century, iii, Patrick Fleming', 200.

(and forasmuch as regards the saints of Ireland, it needs not to boast what a multitude they were, because the foreign authors of Europe admit this, and they state that Ireland was more prolific in saints than any country in Europe.)[15]

There was a clear sense of satisfaction detectible in the comments of both Keating and Fleming that the reputation of the saints of the early Christian period could be relied on to do Ireland proud. While Keating himself was not concerned to undertake further research on the lives of saints, Fleming clearly believed that a Latin publication on the lives of Irish saints, however modestly produced, would be worthwhile because it would take its place among a range of similar publications produced by other nations. As far as he was concerned, it was not a matter of researching the past for its own sake; it was the propagandist value of the past for Ireland's modern reputation among the learned elite in Europe that was invaluable.[16]

The matter had become urgent following the publication of the work of the Scottish author, Thomas Dempster, whose descriptive catalogue of Scottish saints and writers propagated the false view that those early Christian saints who were Scoti were Scottish rather than Irish.[17] It was not just the nationality of many early saints that was called into question, but also that of a major Franciscan philosopher, John Duns Scotus. Aodh Mac Aingil was a major authority on the works of John Duns Scotus and believed, erroneously as it turned out, that he was of Irish descent.[18] Dempster's claims concerning the origins of Irish saints were refuted by the Irish Jesuit, Henry Fitzsimon,[19] David Rothe, bishop of Ossory,[20] the rector of the Irish College in Paris, Thomas Messingham,[21] and Peter Lombard, but ultimately it was the Louvain Franciscans who did so most

15 Comyn and Dinneen (eds), *Foras feasa ar Éirinn*, I, pp 78–9. 16 For an overview, see Cunningham, 'The culture and ideology of Irish Franciscan historians at Louvain', pp 11–30, 222–7. 17 Thomas Dempster, *Scotorum scriptorum nomenclatura* (Bologna, 1619), reissued in a revised edition as *Historia ecclesiastica gentis Scottorum* (Bologna, 1627). Another volume, Thomas Dempster, *Scotia illustrior, seu mendicabula repressa, modesta parecbasi Thomae Dempsteri* ([Lyon], 1620), was a reply to a work entitled *Brigida thaumaturga* written by David Rothe. See also Ulrike Morét, 'An early Scottish national biography: Thomas Dempster's *Historia ecclesiastica gentis Scotorum* (1627)' in L. Houwen, A. Mac Donald and S. Mapstone (eds), *A palace in the wild: essays on vernacular culture and humanism in late medieval and Renaissance Scotland* (Mediaevalia Groningana, 1) (Leuven, 2000), pp 249–70. 18 Ó Cléirigh, *Aodh Mac Aingil*, pp 55–7. Scholars are now agreed that John Duns Scotus was born at Duns in the Scottish Borders (*Oxford DNB*, s.n.). 19 P. Grosjean (ed.), 'Édition du *Catalogus praecipuorum sanctorum Hiberniae* de Henri Fitzsimon' in John Ryan (ed.), *Féilscríbhinn Eóin Mhic Néill* (Dublin, 1940), pp 335–93. See also Richard Sharpe, 'The origin and elaboration of the *Catalogus praecipuorum sanctorum Hiberniae* attributed to Fr Henry Fitzsimon SJ', *Bodleian Library Record* 13:3 (1989), 202–30; Pádraig Ó Riain, 'The *Catalogus praecipuorum sanctorum Hiberniae*, sixty years on' in Alfred P. Smyth (ed.), *Seanchas: studies in early and medieval Irish archaeology, history and literature in honour of Francis J. Byrne* (Dublin, 2000), pp 396–430. 20 David Rothe, *Hibernia resurgens sive refrigerium antidotale, adversum morsum serpentis antiqui in quo modeste discutitur, immodesta parechasis Thomae Dempsteri a Muresck Scoti de represis mendicabulis* (Rouen, 1621). 21 Thomas Messingham, *Florilegium insulae sanctorum, seu vitae et acta sanctorum Hiberniae* (Paris, 1624); Thomas O'Connor, 'Towards the invention of the Irish Catholic *Natio*: Thomas Messingham's *Florilegium* (1624)', *Irish Theological Quarterly* 64 (1999), 157–77.

comprehensively in the two folio volumes of Irish saints' lives edited by John Colgan in the 1640s.[22]

In planning a systematic refutation of Dempster's propaganda, the specific example selected by Fleming as a model for a catalogue of Irish saints was the work of the English Catholic author John Pits, which had been published posthumously in 1619.[23] It was a substantial volume of 990 pages, containing entries on 1,635 persons. Following a lengthy introduction, the second and principal part of the volume contained a dictionary of English writers, and bore the running head *De illustribus Angliae scriptoribus*.[24] Among the entries included in Pits' work that would have caught the eye of the Irish Franciscans was a lengthy one for John Duns Scotus.[25]

The particular emphasis placed on the work of Dempster and Pits provides evidence that national rather than confessional issues were of key importance to Irish scholars on the continent. It is true that the work of Pits was far from being the only example that the Franciscan enthusiasts for research into the Irish past would have known. Moving in university and ecclesiastical circles in Louvain, Rome, Paris and Salamanca, Ward and Fleming would have encountered scholars and clergy of many nationalities, and they would have been well aware of the kind of ecclesiastical and secular histories of other nations that had been published. Many of them had been published in the course of the sixteenth and early seventeenth centuries, when the emphasis was on writing the history of individual nations, in contrast to earlier universal chronicles.[26]

Examples to follow: histories of other nations

The general histories of Scotland by John Mair (1521), Hector Boece (1527), and George Buchanan (1582), all originally issued in Latin, had no Irish equivalents in print.[27] In England, books such as William Camden's *Britannia*, first published in

---

22 John Colgan, *Acta sanctorum veteris et majoris Scotiae, seu Hiberniae sanctorum insulae* (Louvain, 1645) (facsimile reprint with introduction by Brendan Jennings, Dublin, 1948); John Colgan, *Triadis thaumaturgae, seu divorum Patricii, Columbae, et Brigidae … acta* (Louvain, 1647) (facsimile reprint with introduction by Pádraig Ó Riain, Dublin, 1997); Canice Mooney, 'Father John Colgan' in T. O'Donnell (ed.), *Father John Colgan, OFM* (Dublin, 1959), pp 13–21. 23 John Pits, *Relationum historicarum de rebus Anglicis*, ed. William Bishop (Paris, 1619, repr. Farnborough, 1969). John Pits (Pitseus) had died in 1616. 24 Pits, *Relationum historicarum*, pp 62–818. It presented brief biographies of English writers in chronological order, beginning with Brutus Troianus, under the year AM2879, and ending with an entry for Pits himself. The volume also contained a series of elaborate indexes, which classified the ecclesiastical entries by hierarchical status, beginning with cardinals and then archbishops, scholastics, graduates of Oxford, Cambridge and Paris, and the members of various religious orders, beginning with the Benedictines and ending with the Jesuits (pp 939–87). 25 Pits, *Relationum historicarum*, pp 390–4. 26 May McKisack, *Medieval history in the Tudor age* (Oxford, 1971), pp 99–124; Burke, *Renaissance sense of the past*. 27 John Mair (Major), *Historia majoris Britanniae tam Angliae quam Scotiae* (Paris, 1521); Hector Boece, *Scotorum historiae* (Paris, 1527); George Buchanan, *De rerum Scoticarum historia* (Antwerp, 1582). The Palesman, Richard Stanihurst's small volume, *De rebus in Hibernia gestis* (Antwerp, 1584), was written from a

Latin in 1586 and in English in 1610, and John Speed's *History of Great Britaine* (1611), were impressive works, consciously designed to enhance the image of Britain. Camden's foray into near-contemporary history in his *Annals of Queen Elizabeth* (1615) was a sophisticated work too, one in which he reminded his readers that 'if you take out of history why, how, and to what end, and what is done, and whether the actions answer the intents, that that remains is rather a mocking than an instruction; and for the present may please but will never profit posterity'.[28] Sir John Hayward's *Lives of the three Normans, kings of England* (1613), was dedicated to Charles, prince of Wales, and was explicit about the usefulness of history. The author recalled the wish of Henry, prince of Wales (d. 1612), to have a history of English kings 'for his own instruction'. The prince, it was reported, had 'desired nothing more than to know the actions of his ancestors because he did so far esteem his descent from them as he approached near them in honourable endeavours'.[29] Polydor Virgil's *Anglica historia*, commissioned by the Tudor king, Henry VII, had been in circulation from 1534,[30] and prompted a reply from a Welsh humanist writer, Sir John Prise, whose *Historiae Brytannicae defensio* was published posthumously in 1573.[31]

While numerous early national histories such as Florian de Ocampo's history of early Spain (1541), Francesco Guicciardini's more contemporary history of Italy written in the 1530s, and Carlus Sigonius's history of the kingdom of Italy (1574) were published on the continent through the sixteenth century;[32] of more immediate relevance here, perhaps, are those that date from the opening decades of the seventeenth century. Works such as André Du Chesne's *Les antiquitez et recherches de la grandeur et majesté des roys de France* (1609) and its companion volume *Les antiquitez et recherches des vielles, chasteaux, et places plus remarquables de toute la France* (1609) and Étienne Pasquier's multi-volume *Recherches de la France* (1607),[33] each used history to promote the honour of the kingdom in question.[34] The Spanish Jesuit, Juan de Mariana's *Historia general de España*, which had been first published in 1592 also emphasized the significance of the Spanish monarchy in both Latin and Spanish editions. Jérôme Bignon's

political perspective unacceptable to many of Gaelic origin or allegiances, though it was much more moderate than his earlier contributions to Raphael Holinshed's *Chronicles of England, Scotland and Ireland* (London, 1577). Colm Lennon, *Richard Stanihurst: the Dubliner, 1547–1618* (Dublin, 1981), pp 88–98.   28 William Camden, *Annals of Queen Elizabeth* (1615), preface, cited in Peter Burke, *The Renaissance sense of the past* (London, 1969), p. 128.   29 Sir John Hayward, *The lives of the three Normans, kings of England* (1613), The epistle dedicatorie, sig. A 3.   30 Denis Hay (ed.), *The Anglica historia of Polydore Virgil, AD1485–1537* (London, 1950).   31 Ceri Davies, 'Latin literature' in Philip Henry Jones and Eiluned Rees (eds), *A nation and its books: a history of the book in Wales* (Aberystwyth, 1998), p. 69.   32 Florian de Ocampo, *Crónica general de España* (Zamora, 1541); Francesco Guicciardini, *History of Italy*, trans. C. Grayson (New York, 1964); Carlus Sigonius, *Historiarum de regno Italiae libri quindecem* (Venice, 1574; Frankfurt, 1591).   33 George Huppert, *The idea of perfect history: historical erudition and historical philosophy in Renaissance France* (Urbana, 1970), pp 28–71; Orest Ranum (ed.), *National consciousness, history, and political culture in early-modern Europe* (Baltimore, 1975), p. 16.   34 For further discussion of early modern French historiography, see Orest Ranum, *Artisans of glory: writers and historical thought in seventeenth-century France*

historical tract, *De l'excellence des rois, et du royaume de France* (1610) was a defence of the French monarchy in response to claims by Diego Valdez that Spanish kings took precedence over all others. As with others of his contemporaries, Bignon wrote to impress foreign readers as well as his own countrymen:

> I have sought to show the truth of the matter, not only to cause the French to understand what they are, their advantages and how much they should esteem and revere their kings, true creatures of heaven, the dearest children of God and the first-born of his Church, but also to show foreign peoples, who recognize Your Majesty for the greatest and worthiest of all who hold sceptres, that [your precedence] is as much by right of your crown as by your own virtue and valour.[35]

The Danish historiographer, Johannes Pontanus, published the first volume of his *Rerum Danicarum historia* in 1631, with a second volume completed, but not published, at the time of his death in 1639. Contemporaneously, the work of a Dutch author Johannes Meursius, also on Denmark, and entitled *Historia Danica*, was published in two parts, the first in 1630 and the second in 1638. The publications of both these authors on Danish history were formally dedicated to the king, Christian IV.[36]

It was secular national histories of this kind, but particularly those relating to England and Scotland, that Geoffrey Keating had in mind when he undertook to write his history of Ireland, *Foras feasa ar Éirinn*, in the 1620s, and when Ó Cléirigh's address to the patron of AFM placed the annals in a context that embraced a world larger than Ireland, he too demonstrated that he was aware of the trends in historical writing then current outside Ireland. His concern with researching the secular history of Ireland, in tandem with his work on the lives of Irish saints, is evidence that he had absorbed the intellectual culture of exiled scholars of many nationalities on the European mainland who were concerned to enhance the reputation of their own particular homeland.[37] In Ó Cléirigh's case the immediate source of that influence was the community of Irish Franciscans established at Louvain since 1607.

Irish scholars in continental Europe

A combination of circumstances had prompted the scholarly endeavours of individuals attached to the various Irish colleges in Europe in the early seventeenth century. Trends that had a direct bearing on the Irish Catholic educational and intellectual endeavours included first, the impetus to education

(Chapel Hill, NC, 1981). **35** Printed in translation in William F. Church, 'France' in Ranum (ed.), *National consciousness* (1975), p. 50. **36** Karen Skovgaard-Petersen, *Historiography at the court of Christian IV* (Copenhagen, 2002), pp 44–58, 68–74. **37** Evidence that Ó Cléirigh was collecting source material on the secular history of Ireland as early as 1627 is to be found in RIA MS B iv 2, which comprises transcripts of relevant secular material that he made during the years 1627 and

arising from the decisions of the Council of Trent, which had established new standards for the seminary education of clergy. Secondly, for Irish Catholics this initiative was combined with the enforced exile from Ireland and England of Catholics pursuing higher education, a situation that led to the establishment of colleges or residences in many European university towns where Irish students came to live while they pursued their studies. A third factor which helped mould the scholarly interests of some members of these colleges was the crisis in lay patronage in Ireland prompted by the decline in political influence of the Gaelic elite who had previously supported professional poets and historians. That vacuum in scholarly patronage in Ireland was partially filled by the Catholic Church overseas with some of the offspring of hereditary learned families benefiting from higher education within the church and opting for ecclesiastical careers. In turn, patronage from the O'Donnells, O'Neills and O'Rourkes among the Irish military community in Spanish Flanders helped to support the Irish religious communities there.[38]

Aided by access to print, the study and interpretation of history became an important element of the intellectual ferment of Reformation and Counter-Reformation Europe in the sixteenth and seventeenth centuries. Christianity being a historical religion, the divisions within the church, usually termed the Reformation and Counter-Reformation, prompted propagandists on both sides to use history to justify particular confessional allegiances. Throughout western Europe, rival interpretations of ecclesiastical history were put forward by each side in the debate over which was the true church.[39] The availability of print technology facilitated this development, which came on top of the earlier cultural movement termed the European Renaissance, which had itself prompted a renewed interest in the writing of history.

In Ireland, as is well known, James Ussher, Church of Ireland bishop of Meath and later archbishop of Armagh, devoted much scholarly effort to arguing the historical case for regarding the Established Church in Ireland as the legitimate successor of the early Christian church. His tract entitled *A discourse on the religion anciently professed by the Irish and British* comprised a lengthy presentation of the relevant historical evidence, and his particular interest in the historical evidence associated with St Patrick was directed towards the same objective.[40] In 1639 his major work on the history of the early Irish church was

1628 (*Cat. Ir. mss in RIA*, pp 3021–9). **38** Gráinne Henry, *The Irish military community in Spanish Flanders, 1586–1621* (Dublin, 1992), pp 107–8, 129–33. **39** Gordon Bruce (ed.), *Protestant history and identity in sixteenth-century Europe, volume 2: the later Reformation* (Aldershot, 1996); Momigliano, *Studies in historiography*, pp 1–39; Ó Buachalla, 'Annála ríoghachta Éireann is Foras feasa ar Éirinn', 59–105. **40** James Ussher, *A discourse of the religion anciently professed by the Irish and British* (Dublin, 1631), first appeared in 1622 as an appendix to Sir Christopher Sibthorp's *A friendly advertisement to the pretended Catholickes of Ireland* (Dublin, 1622). See also C.R. Elrington and J.H. Todd (eds), *The whole works of ... James Ussher* (17 vols, Dublin, 1847–64), IV, pp 235–381. James Ussher, *Veterum epistolarum Hybernicarum sylloge, quae partim ab Hibernis, paratim ad Hibernos, partim de Hibernis vel rebus Hibernicis sunt conscriptae* (Dublin, 1632), edited by Elrington

published, a work which drew extensively on the Irish manuscript sources to which he had access.[41] While Ussher's polemical writings on Irish church history display an enthusiasm for refuting the arguments of Catholic writers, historians such as Geoffrey Keating who had read his work were less concerned to be seen to respond explicitly to Protestant authors. Rather, Keating was among those Irish Catholic historians who were sufficiently confident of their readers' loyalty to Catholicism to deem superfluous the need for a polemical response to the historical arguments of Ussher or other Protestants.[42] Most Irish Franciscans, likewise, showed relatively little interest in pursuing this kind of intellectual debate on matters of confessional allegiance. They did, however, sporadically embrace print technology for their own catechetical purposes. A further exception can perhaps be found in the work of the Louvain Franciscan Robert Rochford, whose dedicatory epistle prefacing the abridged lives of Saints Patrick, Brigit and Colum Cille, published in English in 1625, can be read as a reply to the 1622 edition of James Ussher's *Discourse on the religion anciently professed*.[43]

Among Irish Franciscans on the continent, Donagh Mooney at Louvain and Luke Wadding at Rome were actively involved in recording the history of the Franciscan order. Mooney concentrated on the history of Irish Franciscan foundations,[44] while Wadding made a name for himself as historian of the order internationally.[45]

Utilizing the technology of print, the Franciscans at the college of St Anthony in Louvain became involved in producing catechisms in Irish for use both at home in Ireland and also among Irish soldiers serving in the Spanish Netherlands.[46] In a study of the emergence of the political concept of 'faith and fatherland' in Counter-Reformation literature in Irish, Mícheál Mac Craith has highlighted the political overtones of the catechetical and devotional texts produced by the Louvain Franciscans.[47] The official English response to the re-

and Todd, *The whole works of … James Ussher*, IV, pp 383–572. See also Ute Lotz-Heumann, 'The Protestant interpretation of history in Ireland: the case of James Ussher's Discourse' in Bruce (ed.), *Protestant history and identity in sixteenth-century Europe*, vol. 2, pp 107–20; Ford, 'James Ussher and the creation of an Irish protestant identity', pp 185–212; Hugh Trevor-Roper, 'James Ussher, Archbishop of Armagh' in Hugh Trevor-Roper, *Catholics, Anglicans and Puritans: seventeenth-century essays* (London, 1989), pp 120–65.   41 James Ussher, *Britannicarum Ecclesiarum Antiquitates* (Dublin, 1639).   42 Cunningham, *World of Geoffrey Keating*, p. 120.   43 *The life of the gloriovs bishop S. Patricke apostle and primate of Ireland, togeather with the lifes of the holy virgin S. Bridgit and of the gloriovs Abbot Saint Colvmbe patrons of Ireland* (St Omer, 1625), pp iii–xvi; John McCafferty, 'From manuscript to print: early modern receptions of the Patrician life', unpublished lecture, Muirchú conference, UCD, 24 April 2004.   44 Brendan Jennings, 'Brussels MS 3947: Donatus Moneyus, de Provincia Hiberniae S. Francisci', *Analecta Hibernica* 6 (1934), 12–138.   45 Gregory Cleary, *Father Luke Wadding and St Isidore's College, Rome* (Rome, 1925), pp 12–18, 53–9.   46 Thomas Wall, 'The Catechism in Irish: Bonaventure O'Hussey OFM', *Irish Ecclesiastical Record* 5th ser., 59 (1942), 46–8; John Brady, 'The catechism in Irish: a survey', *Irish Ecclesiastical Record* 5th ser., 83 (1955), 167–76; Anselm Ó Fachtna (ed.), *Parrthas an anma*, by Antoin Gearnon (Dublin, 1953) (originally published Louvain, 1645); Salvador Ryan, 'Popular religion in Gaelic Ireland, 1445–1645' (PhD thesis, 2 vols, NUI Maynooth, 2002), II, pp 23–5.   47 Mícheál Mac Craith, 'Creideamh agus athartha: idé-eolaíocht pholaitíochta agus aos léinn na

issue of Ó hEodhasa's *Teagasg Críosdaidhe* in 1614 was to criticize 'the unworthy proceedings of the Irish friars at Louvain in printing and publishing those seditious libels, and that in their own language'. King James lobbied the ambassador of the Spanish Netherlands to request that 'all copies of such books should be called in and publicly burned'.[48] The concern was not so much about the religious doctrine being disseminated, but that the catechetical publications of the Louvain Franciscans were part of an attempt 'to reconcile their countrymen in their affections and to combine those that are descended of the English race and those that are mere Irish in a league of friendship and concurrence against your majesty and the true religion now professed in your kingdom'.[49]

In addition to the catechisms, longer devotional prose tracts, some of them adaptations of continental works, were also translated into Irish and published by the Louvain Franciscans. Flaithrí Ó Maoil Chonaire's *Desiderius*, also known by its alternative title of *Sgáthán an chrábhaidh*, was published in 1616.[50] Viewing the Irish as persecuted Catholics, Ó Maoil Chonaire was concerned not just with the spiritual dimension of the text, but also with ensuring that it offered appropriate guidance to Irish Catholics. It advocated strength in the face of the coercive demands of a government that supported a heretical church. It advised against becoming embroiled in polemical battles, recommending instead reliance on the articles of faith as expounded in the Creed, and offering guidance on how to use the teachings summarized in the Nicene Creed as a means of refuting Protestant doctrines.[51]

The Down-born Franciscan, Aodh Mac Aingil, also compiled a devotional tract for Irish readers, *Scáthán shacramuinte na hAithridhe*. In his preface to the reader, he outlined his reasons for preparing the work, making clear that it was the example of other nations that prompted the publication of vernacular devotional texts:

Bid leabhráin mar so ag gach náision Chatoilic eili, 7 atáid do riachdanas ar an náision dá bhfuilmídne go speisialta, do bhríogh go bhfuil gan maighistre gan prealáide gan seanmóntuidhe, leath amuigh do bheagán bhíos a bhfholach d'eagla bháis nó phríosúin, mar do bhídís na habsdail tréis bháis Chríosd d'eagla an chinidh Iudaidhe.

[Every other Catholic nation has books like this, and they are essential for our nation especially, on account of it being without masters without prelates without preachers, apart from a few who are in hiding for fear of death or imprisonment, as the apostles were after the death of Christ for fear of the Jews.][52]

Gaeilge i dtús an seachtú haois déag' in M. Ní Dhonnchadha (ed.), *Nua-léamha: gnéithe de chultúr, stair agus polaitíocht na hÉireann, c.1600–c.1900* (Dublin, 1996), pp 7–19. **48** Mac Raghnaill (ed.), *An Teagasg Críosdaidhe*, pp xiv–xv. **49** Cited in Mac Craith, 'Creideamh agus Athartha', p. 11. **50** T.F. O'Rahilly (ed.), *Desiderius, otherwise called Sgáthán an chrábhaidh*, by Flaithrí Ó Maoil Chonaire (Dublin, 1955) (originally published Louvain, 1616). **51** O'Rahilly (ed.), *Desiderius*, 163; Ryan, 'Popular religion in Gaelic Ireland', II, pp 119–20. **52** Cainneach Ó Maonaigh (ed.), *Scathán shacramuinte na hAithridhe*, by Aodh Mac Aingil (Dublin, 1952) (originally published Louvain, 1618), pp 4–5, with my translation.

Tadhg Ó Dúshláine has drawn attention to the fact that English Catholic authors had been preparing English translations of similar texts as early as the 1570s,[53] while Mícheál Mac Craith has assessed the political context from which the text emerged. Mac Craith argues that Mac Aingil's work, like that of Ó Maoil Chonaire, offers evidence of a connection between the world of Irish learning, the Louvain Franciscans, the king of Spain and ongoing support for Aodh Ó Néill.[54] However, he also notes that after the death of Ó Néill at Rome in 1616, it appears that the Irish exiles from Gaelic backgrounds began to adopt a political position closer to that of the Catholic Old English at home. Thus, Mac Aingil's repeated use of the term *náisiún* in this work can be interpreted as evidence of the politicized world in which the exiled Irish learned community lived, and an expression of the coming together of all Catholic Irish regardless of ethnic origin.[55] The exiled Gaelic Irish came to accept the Stuart king as their own, as the Old English both at home and abroad had already done.[56] By the 1630s, the writings of the Four Masters provide a clear acceptance of this new political orthodoxy, though they stopped short of dedicating any of their works to the monarch.[57] There are instances in the prefaces to the various works completed by Mícheál Ó Cléirigh and his lay associates where Charles I is expressly recognized as the legitimate king, a feature that has been particularly emphasized by Breandán Ó Buachalla.[58]

Mac Craith notes that some passages in Flaithrí Ó Maoil Chonaire's *Desiderius* discuss the distinction between spiritual and temporal authority, drawing on the political ideas of Robert Bellarmine and Francisco Suarez.[59] Bellarmine rejected the concept of the divine right of kings and argued that the pope could refuse to recognize the authority of a heretical king. In Ó Maoil Chonaire's adaptation of this idea, he asserted that the people of Ireland had the authority to determine the conditions under which they would offer loyalty to James I as their king.[60] Salvador Ryan has argued in the case of Ó Maoil Chonaire's *Desiderius* that his main concern was to 'counsel and support Catholics suffering oppression in Ireland'.[61] Ryan also

---

53 Tadhg Ó Dúshláine, *An Eoraip agus litríocht na Gaeilge, 1600–1650* (Dublin, 1987), pp 82–3. 54 Mac Craith, 'Creideamh agus Athartha', p. 13; Mac Craith, 'Scáthán shacramuinte na haithridhe: saothar reiligiúnda nó saothar polaitíochta', *Irisleabhar Mhá Nuad* (1993), 144–54. 55 Mac Craith has traced the earliest instance of the use of the word 'nation' in Irish to Tadhg Ó Cianáin, *Teicheamh na nIarlaí* (1609) (Mac Craith, 'Creideamh agus Athartha', pp 13–14); Paul Walsh (ed.), *The flight of the earls*, by Tadhg Ó Cianáin (Dublin, 1916), p. 42. For this political outlook in the work of the Old English Catholic historian Geoffrey Keating, see Cunningham, *World of Geoffrey Keating*, pp 112, 127–8. 56 Breandán Ó Buachalla, 'James our true king: the ideology of Irish royalism in the seventeenth century' in D.G. Boyce, Robert Eccleshall and Vincent Geoghegan (eds), *Political thought in Ireland since the seventeenth century* (London, 1993), pp 7–35; Ó Buachalla, *Aisling ghéar*, pp 3–98. 57 For evidence of the controversy engendered when one Fr Malone dedicated a book to the king of England, see Brendan Jennings (ed.), *Wadding papers, 1614–1638* (Dublin, 1953), p. 274. 58 Mac Craith, 'Creideamh agus Athartha', pp 13–16; Ó Buachalla, *Aisling ghéar*, pp 88–90; for further discussion of the Four Masters' treatment of the theme of kingship, see below, chapter five. 59 Mac Craith, 'Creideamh agus Athartha', p. 12. 60 Mac Craith, 'Creideamh agus athartha', p. 13. 61 Ryan, 'Popular religion in Gaelic Ireland', II, p. 121.

makes the point that the stories reaching Louvain may have painted a bleaker picture than the everyday reality at home.[62]

While these catechetical and devotional works were small volumes in the vernacular, designed for personal or small-group use as aids to piety, the major hagiographical works published by St Anthony's College were aimed at a more cosmopolitan audience. The two large folio volumes of saints' lives in Latin published in 1645 and 1647 under the editorship of John Colgan represented the coming to fruition of the hagiographical project conceived by Fleming and Ward some twenty years earlier. They were on a scale equivalent to the volumes being produced by the Bollandists at about the same time. The Bollandists' programme of research and publication of the sources for the lives of saints had been initiated by a Belgian Jesuit, Heribert Rosweyde in 1607, the year St Anthony's College was founded at Louvain.[63] The work brought to fruition by Colgan matched the scholarship of the Bollandists and enhanced the reputation of Ireland as an island of saints and scholars. Colgan's first volume, published in 1645, dealt with the extant lives of Irish saints whose feast days fell in the months from January to March.[64] The second volume, published two years later, concentrated on Ireland's three best known saints, Patrick, Brigit and Columba, and brought together all the lives of those saints then known to be extant, together with Colgan's extensive annotations.[65] Ultimately, the project remained unfinished, and although the volume for April to June had apparently been completed by Colgan, it remained unpublished at the time of his death and his manuscript is now lost.

Colgan's hagiographical publications are relevant to the historical endeavours of Mícheál Ó Cléirigh in so far as they provide evidence of the variety of ways in which members of the Irish learned class and other scholars who found themselves in exile on the continent responded to the intellectual environment they encountered in European university towns. Furthermore, Colgan specifically acknowledged in the preface to his work that he drew extensively on AFM in the course of editing the lives of Irish saints, and devoted more space in his preface to acknowledging the scholarship of Ó Cléirigh than any other researcher associated with the project.[66] He cited the Annals of the Four Masters frequently in his annotations on the lives of saints, often referring to them as the Annals of Donegal.[67] But, while the usefulness of the annals for the Louvain hagiographical project was an important part of their original rationale, and while AFM can be unequivocally placed in this context, that is not the full story. Although the inspiration may have come from Louvain, the annals were researched and

62 Ryan, 'Popular religion in Gaelic Ireland', II, p. 120. 63 David Knowles, *Great historical enterprises* (London, 1962), pp 1–32; Ó Riain, 'John Colgan's *Trias thaumaturga*' in facsimile reprint of John Colgan, *Trias thaumaturga* (Dublin, 1997), [p. 3]. 64 Colgan, *Acta sanctorum Hiberniae*. 65 Colgan, *Trias thaumaturga*. 66 Colgan, *Acta sanctorum Hiberniae, praefatio ad lectorem*, sig. b2v–b3v; Ó Riain, 'John Colgan's *Trias thaumaturga*', [p. 5]. 67 For example, Colgan, *Acta sanctorum Hiberniae*, pp 437, 439, 453, 455, 456, 464, 465, 466.

written in Ireland. These annals were not the work of Mícheál Ó Cléirigh alone, but of a team of professional chroniclers whose cumulative experience in interpreting the past was overwhelmingly Irish rather than European. Indeed, Ó Cléirigh's own qualifications for the task had been acquired in Ireland, not continental Europe. Without his formal training in Ireland within the traditional mould of a hereditary family of historians, he would never have been selected by Hugh Ward to undertake systematic research into sources for the history of early Christian Ireland.

Nor was the Irish Franciscan community to which he returned in Donegal an intellectual backwater compared to the world of the continental seminaries. Although residing in temporary accommodation close to the Drowes River in the extreme south of Co. Donegal, following the destruction of the original monastery buildings in 1601,[68] the Donegal Franciscan community was a vibrant one in the 1620s and 1630s. That it contained a library of historical works is evident from extant library lists from Louvain.[69] The religious community included Fr Bernardinus Ó Cléirigh, an older brother of Mícheál, whose seminary education had been at Salamanca and Louvain,[70] Fr Muiris Ulltach, son of Seaán, a former provincial of the Franciscan order in Ireland, and a man who was able to supply Ó Cléirigh with Irish translations of Latin texts,[71] and another Fr Muiris Ulltach, son of Donnchadh, who, along with Flaithrí Ó Maoil Chonaire, had been at the deathbed of Aodh Ó Domhnaill in Spain in 1602.[72] In 1624, some two years prior to Mícheál Ó Cléirigh's return from Louvain to Donegal, one of the Donegal Franciscans, Muiris Ulltach son of Seaán was already employing the services of Cú Choigcríche Ó Cléirigh to conduct hagiographical research for the Donegal community.[73] This connection is particularly significant because it provides a clear indication that the community that Mícheál Ó Cléirigh joined in Donegal after his time in Louvain was fully in sympathy with the objectives of the Louvain hagiographical research project that he had been instructed to undertake. The principle of collaboration with lay professional historians was already established, and the need for scholarly use of the most authoritative manuscript sources was clearly recognized.

There is no indication from the surviving sources that any member of the Four Masters team other than Mícheál Ó Cléirigh had ever lived or studied outside Ireland. But they enjoyed direct ongoing personal contact with people

---

68 *AFM*, VI, p. 2253.   69 Ignatius Fennessy (ed.), 'Printed books in St Anthony's College, Louvain, 1673 (FLK MS A 34)', *Collectanea Hibernica* 38 (1996), 93–6.   70 Listed as Moylerus Clery in D.J. O'Doherty, 'Students of the Irish College, Salamanca (1595–1619)', *Archivium Hibernicum* 2 (1913), 28; listed as *Fr Milerus Cleri, nunc dictus Fr Bernardinus a Sancta Maria, dioecesis Rapotensis* in Brendan Jennings (ed.), *Louvain Papers, 1606–1827* (Dublin, 1968), p. 55.   71 Joseph Moloney (ed.), 'Brussels MS 3410: a chronological list of the foundations of the Irish Franciscan province', *Analecta Hibernica* 6 (1934), 192.   72 *AFM*, VI, p. 2297; J.J. Silke, 'The last will of Red Hugh O'Donnell', *Studia Hibernica* 24 (1984–8), 51–60.   73 BR MS 4639, fos 2–2v. The Donegal Franciscan context is discussed further in chapter 9, pp 282–93 below.

who had done so, and the inspiration provided by the knowledge that there was a potential international readership for a comprehensive history of the ancient kingdom of Ireland was part of the motivation for the work of the Four Masters team. The projects they undertook will be analyzed in detail below, but first, the indigenous *seanchas* tradition on which they modelled their annals of the kingdom of Ireland will be considered in the next chapter.

CHAPTER THREE

The late medieval Irish historical tradition

Introduction

In the 1620s, as discussed in the previous chapter, Irish Franciscans such as Hugh Ward, Patrick Fleming and Mícheál Ó Cléirigh, as well as the secular priest Geoffrey Keating, influenced by their continental perspective on Ireland and on historical scholarship, judged that Ireland did not have a history such as other nations had.[1] Yet, they well knew that an abundance of historical texts, old and new, existed in manuscript form in Ireland. None of these manuscript sources, in themselves, however, were regarded as meeting the requirements of the kind of history appropriate to Ireland in the early seventeenth century, and research was undertaken to produce a new version of Irish history, appropriate to the modern age. That new history, it was anticipated, would assist the Louvain project of making available scholarly editions of the lives of Irish saints, by providing a comprehensive record of the historical context. It was also intended that the annals would circulate in print, probably in Latin,[2] and therefore needed to be tailored to the overseas readership for whom they were intended.[3] Although the existing manuscript sources available in Ireland were not generally accessible to non-specialists, and did not tell the story of Ireland as the early seventeenth-century Irish scholars on the continent would wish it to be told, those sources were the essential precursor of the kind of history of Ireland it proved possible to compile in the early seventeenth century. The pre-existing compilations of annals provided a general guide to the structural framework for, and some but not all of the contents of, the annals which Mícheál Ó Cléirigh and his fellow historians compiled. The Four Masters did not confine themselves to annalistic sources. Rather, they drew on a broad range of sources from the *seanchas* tradition, while adhering to a formal annalistic framework. The fact that they had

---

1 *AFM*, I, pp ix, lvi; Jennings (ed.), 'Documents from St Isidore's', 216; Comyn and Dinneen (eds), *Foras feasa ar Éirinn*, I, pp 6, 76.   2 That Latin was the language envisaged can be inferred from the intention to translate the *Genealogiae regum et sanctorum Hiberniae* into other languages mentioned in the dedication to Toirrdhealbhach Mac Cochláin (Paul Walsh (ed.), *Genealogiae regum et sanctorum Hiberniae* (Maynooth, 1918), pp 5–6, 142), as well as the choice of Latin as the language for the published saints' lives issued from Louvain under the editorship of John Colgan. The ecclesiastical approbations to AFM are provided in Latin only, and are of a kind usually found in published works of the Counter-Reformation era (*AFM*, I, pp lxx–lxxi).   3 The content of the Latin approbation by Baothghalach Mac Aodhagáin, bishop of Elphin, prefixed to UCD–OFM MS

earlier prepared new recensions of other texts of historical importance suggests that they did not perceive their task as merely creating new annals from old. Rather they were weaving together a new and comprehensive historical compilation, encompassing origin legends, genealogies of saints, and king lists, as well as annals.[4] Perhaps it was conceived as a new 'Book of Donegal' in the manner of the great medieval miscellanies, but now addressed to a wider readership because of the potential of access to print.

Named manuscript sources

The crucial element in the preparations made for the compilation of AFM was the gathering together in one place of a range of source texts from which the new set of historical annals could be extracted. Mícheál Ó Cléirigh assured his patron, Fearghal Ó Gadhra, that:

> do cruinniccheadh lem na leabhair Annáladh as ferr 7 as lionmhaire as mó do beidir lem dfághail i nErinn uile (biodh gur dhecair damh a ttecclamadh go haoin ionad) do chum an leabhairsi do sccriobhadh.
>
> (there were collected by me all the best and most copious books of annals that I could find throughout all Ireland (though it was difficult for me to collect them to one place), to write this book.)[5]

From his particular experience in working on Irish manuscript sources for the lives of saints, Mícheál Ó Cléirigh was familiar with the range of source texts available, and had established sufficient contacts with their owners or keepers in different parts of Ireland to ensure that he could obtain the use of those manuscripts.[6] He also pointed out that those he selected were the best and most copious available, implying that inferior source materials were disregarded. Little detail survives of the circumstances in which treasured manuscripts would have been given on loan by their owners to scholars such as Mícheál Ó Cléirigh, but it appears that such loans were not unusual.[7] At any rate, it appears that the Four Masters successfully gathered in one place an impressive range of manuscripts containing annals and other historical materials, out of which a new set of annals was compiled.

Like any work of history at this period, the Four Masters were keen to make clear to their readers that their historical annals were based on reliable and authentic sources.[8] This practice was in line with the broader European

A 13, makes this clear.   **4** For discussion of the medieval concept of 'weaving' a text, see Chris Given-Wilson, *Chronicles: the writing of history in medieval England* (London, 2004), pp 14–20.   **5** *AFM*, I, p. lvii.   **6** For discussion of the network of scholars from whom manuscripts were obtained, see below, chapter nine.   **7** For the case of loans of manuscripts by James Ussher, see Bernadette Cunningham and Raymond Gillespie, 'James Ussher and his Irish manuscripts', *Studia Hibernica* 33 (2004–5), 81–99.   **8** For similar statements regarding sources in the work of their

Renaissance interest in primary sources.[9] For this reason, their finished manuscript was accompanied by a *testimonium* which outlined the authorities on which their history was based. The *testimonium* was presented as a statement by the Franciscan order, and was signed by the guardian of the Donegal friary and other respected members of the community as witness to the authenticity of Ó Cléirigh's scholarship.[10] In detailing the source manuscripts consulted, a distinction was made between the sources of the first part of the annals down to the year 1207, transcribed in the year 1632–3,[11] and those used in the second part, which was compiled in 1635–6.[12] The sources used in the first part were named as:

> *Leabhar Cluana mic Nóis in ro bhennaigh NaoimhChiarán mac an tsaoír, Leabhar Oiléin na Naemh for Loch Ribh, Leabhar Shenaidh mec Maghnussa for Loch Erne, Leabhar chloinne Uí Maoílconaire, Lebhar muintere Duibgeandáin Chille Rónáin, 7 leabhar oirisen Leacain meic Firbisicch fríth chuca iar scriobhadh urmhoir an leabhair, 7 as ro scriobhsatt gach lionmhaireacht da bfuairsett (Rangator a les) nach raibhe is na céitt leabhraib bátor aca, ar ní bhaoí i Leabhar Cluana, ina fos i Leabhar an Oiléin acht gus an mbliadhain si daois ar ttigherna 1227.*

(the book of Cluain mic Nois,[13] [a church] blessed by Saint Ciaran, son of the carpenter; the book of the Island of Saints, in Loch Ribh; the book of Seanadh Mic Maghnusa, in Loch Erne; the book of the Clann Ua Maelchonaire; the book of the O'Duigenans, of Kilronan; the historical book of Lecan Mic Firbisigh, which was procured for them after the transcription of the greater part of the book [work], and from which they transcribed every copious matter they found which they deemed necessary, which was not in the first books they had, for neither the book of Cluain, nor the book of the Island, were [carried] beyond the year of the age of our Lord, 1227.)[14]

contemporary, Geoffrey Keating, see Comyn and Dinneen (eds), *Foras feasa ar Éirinn*, II, pp 78–81; III, pp 32–3.   9 Burke, *Renaissance sense of the past*, pp 7–13.   10 *AFM*, I, pp lxiii–lxvii. 11 According to the *testimonium*, the first phase of the work of compilation terminated with the entry for the year 1207. This early portion of AFM is now represented for the most part by RIA MS C iii 3 (AM2242–AD1171) and UCD–OFM MS A 13 (AM2242–AD1169).   12 The second part contained annals from the year 1208 down to the year 1616 (now partially represented by TCD MS 1301 (AD1334–1605) and RIA MS 23 P 6–23 P 7 (AD170–1616).   13 The very similar citation of sources in the Martyrology of Donegal refers to a famous book of 'Cluana Mic Nóis .i. na hUidhri' (J.H. Todd and W. Reeves (eds), *The martyrology of Donegal* (Dublin, 1864), p. xxxviii), and a more complete version of *Leabhar na hUidhre* than now survives may be the book intended in the AFM listing also.   14 *AFM*, I, pp lxiv–lxv. Charles O'Conor's translation of the very similar list from RIA MS C iii 3 differs only in minor details, though his use of the word 'annals' to translate '*leabhar*' is misleading. The assumption that the sources cited were all necessarily in the form of annals is unfounded. 'The annals of Clonmacnoise, an abbey founded by Holy Kiaran, son of the Carpenter; the Annals of the Island of Saints, on the Lake of Rive; the Annals of Senat Mac Magnus, on the lake of Erne [now called the Ulster annals]; the Annals of the O'Maolconarys; the Annals of Kilronan, compiled by the O'Duigenans. These antiquarians had also procured the Annals of Lacan, compiled by the Mac Firbisses' (*AFM*, I, p. xii, citing O'Conor (ed.), *Quatuor Magistrorum annales Hibernici*).

It can perhaps be surmised that the suspension of the work once the year 1207 had been reached might have been to allow the acquisition or consultation of additional source material before proceeding to complete the later portion of the work. The first phase of the work had commenced in January 1632, and may have continued into the summer of the following year.[15] Work was resumed on the later portion of AFM late in the year 1635 when the annals for the years 1208 to 1616 were compiled, possibly in two phases with a break after the year 1333 had been reached.[16] The sources named for the second part were:

> *an leabhar cetna sin Chloinne Uí Maoilconaire go míle cuicc ced a cúig, 7 as í sin an*
> *bliadhain deidhenach baoi and, leabhar na muintire duibhgendán tar a ttangamar o thá*
> *naoí ccéd go míle cúicc céd seasccatt a trí, Leabhar Seanaidh mec Maghnusa ina raibhe*
> *co míle cuicc céd triochat adó, bladh do leabhar Choncoiccriche meic Diarmatta mic*
> *Taidhg caimm uí Clerigh on mbliadhain si Míle da chéd, ochtmhoghatt a haon, co mile*
> *cuicc céd triochatt a Seacht, Leabhar Mec Bruaideadha Mhaolín óicc on mbliadhain si*
> *Míle, cúic céd, ochtmoghat a hocht, go mile Sé chéd a tri, Leabhar Lughach uí Clerigh,*
> *ó Mhíle, cuicc céd, ochtmoghat, a Sé, go Míle, Sé chéd a dó.*
>
> (the same book of the O'Mulconrys, as far as the year one thousand five hundred and five, and this was the last year which it contained; the book of the O'Duigenans, of which we have spoken, from [the year] nine hundred to one thousand five hundred sixty-three; the book of Seanadh Mic Maghnusa, which extended to one thousand five hundred thirty-two; a portion of the book of Cucogry, the son of Dermot, son of Tadhg Cam O'Clerigh, from the year one thousand two hundred and eighty-one, to one thousand five hundred and thirty-seven; the book, of Mac Bruaideadha (Maoilin Og) from the year one thousand five hundred eighty-eight, to one thousand six hundred and three; the book of Lughaidh O'Clerigh, from one thousand five hundred eighty-six, to one thousand six hundred two.)[17]

One inference that can be drawn from the *testimonium* is that the sources known to the Four Masters as the Book of Clonmacnoise, and the Book of the Island of Saints were used for the pre-1208 compilation only, while the Book of Cú Coigchríche Ó Cléirigh, the Book of Maoilín Óg Mac Bruaideadha and the Book of Lughaidh Ó Cléirigh were relevant to the later sections of the annals only. The *testimonium* indicates that three major source manuscripts were drawn on for

15 Jennings, *Michael Ó Cléirigh and his associates*, p. 125. Two of his principal collaborators, Fearfeasa Ó Maoil Chonaire and Cú Choigchríche Ó Cléirigh, were in the convent of Donegal in August 1633 when Mícheál Ó Cléirigh completed his transcript of the Martyrology of Gorman. This may possibly imply that they were still working on the annals while Mícheál Ó Cléirigh devoted himself to transcribing further ecclesiastical sources (Jennings, *Michael Ó Cléirigh and his associates*, 136).   16 Mc Carthy, *The Irish annals*, p. 335, where he points out that the extant preface signed by five of the six 'Masters' referred to a terminal date of AD1333. This fits with the statement by Fearfeasa Ó Maoil Chonaire that only the Ó Cléirigh scholars worked on the entries relating to events after AD1333 (*GRSH*, p. 150). However, it does not necessarily follow that a set of annals that terminated in 1333 went into circulation, and it is clear that the Ó Cléirigh historians continued to work on the project after the departure of the other annalists.   17 *AFM*, I, pp lxvi–lxvii.

both the first and second parts of the work, namely the 'Book of Seanadh Mic Maghnusa', the 'Book of the O'Duigenans of Kilronan', and the 'Book of the O'Mulconrys'. In addition to these source manuscripts, named in the testimony of the Donegal friars as having been seen 'in the hands of the antiquaries, who have been the compilers of the present work', there were also assembled there 'other documents, too many to be mentioned'.[18] The precise scope of those additional sources must remain a matter for speculation, though it is known that Cú Choigcríche Ó Cléirigh himself was reputed to have owned a library of relevant material, and the Donegal friary also contained a library.[19] Newly compiled material such as their source for the foundation of Franciscan monasteries[20] as well as the Four Masters' new recension of the *Leabhar gabhála*[21] and their own version of the *Genealogiae regum et sanctorum Hiberniae*[22] would also have been among the 'other documents' consulted.

One point to note concerning this list of sources is that it appears to be arranged chronologically according to the antiquity of the sources, beginning with the oldest material. Secondly, not all the items listed are necessarily annals and thirdly, as noted above, it is not a comprehensive list of the manuscript sources used in the compilation of AFM. Modern scholars have debated the likely identity of each of the major source manuscripts named by the Four Masters, but without systematically establishing connections with extant manuscripts in modern repositories, with the probable exception of AU.[23] Each of the sources will be considered in turn here. The analysis commences with AU, as the largest compilation of medieval annalistic material, though, as will be seen later, AU cannot actually be regarded as the principal annalistic source used in

---

18 *AFM*, I, p. xii.   19 Pádraig A. Breatnach, 'The methodology of *seanchas*: the redaction by Cú Choigcríche Ó Cléirigh of the chronicle poem *Leanam Croinic Clann nDálaigh*', *Éigse* 29 (1996), 14–16; Fennessy, 'Printed books in St Anthony's College', 93–6.   20 Printed in Brendan Jennings (ed.), 'Brevis synopsis Provinciae Hiberniae ff Minorum', *Analecta Hibernica* 6 (1934), 139–91, from a manuscript in St Isidore's College, Rome. The list of Irish Franciscan foundations in BR MS 2324–40, fos 1–8, is a transcript of Muiris Ulltach mac Seáin's Irish translation of the 'Brevis Synopsis', which asserts that it was drawn '*as leabhraibh 7 as gnathcuimhne bhrathar*' (from books and from the recollections of monks).   21 The fragmentary RIA MS 23 M 70 is now recognized as Mícheál Ó Cléirigh's working copy of this work (Rolf Baumgarten, 'Kuno Meyer's Irish manuscript', *Newsletter of the Dublin Institute of Advanced Studies* 1 (1987), 23–5), while RIA MS 23 K 32 is an expanded version believed to be in the hand of Cú Choigcríche Ó Cléirigh. The latter formed the basis of the partial published edition by R.A.S. Macalister and John Mac Neill (eds), *Leabhar gabhála, the book of conquests of Ireland, the recension of Mícheál Ó Cléirigh*, part 1 (Dublin, 1916). The dedication to the patron, Brian Mág Uidhir, is not found in RIA MS 23 K 32 but a copy is included in TCD MS 1286.   22 UCD–OFM MS A 16 printed in *GRSH*. A second contemporary copy of the text is found in RIA 24 P 33. For convenience, the Latin title assigned this work by its twentieth-century editor, Paul Walsh, is used here.   23 Walsh, *The Four Masters and their work*, pp 3–5; Paul Walsh, *Irish men of learning* (Dublin, 1947), pp 22–3; Nollaig Ó Muraíle, 'Annála Uladh: the Annals of Ulster, Introduction to the 1998 reprint' in *Annals of Ulster* (4 vols, Dublin, 1998), I, [pp 1–40]; Mc Carthy, *The Irish annals*, pp 328–34. Katharine Simms has raised questions about the broad acceptance of the idea that the manuscript of AU available to the Four Masters was the 'A' text now represented by TCD MS 1301 (Katharine Simms, 'Additional Ó

the compilation of AFM, since the source now represented by the Annals of Connacht appears to have been equally influential.[24]

Annals of Ulster

Writing in 1958–9, Aubrey Gwynn presented the case for identifying the copy of AU now preserved in TCD MS 1282 as the actual manuscript consulted by the Four Masters.[25] It is believed to be the manuscript known to them as 'the book of Seanadh Mhic Mhaghnusa', though this cannot be said to have been proven conclusively, and Katharine Simms has drawn attention to some contrary evidence.[26] The Irish text of AU now survives in two vellum manuscripts, TCD MS 1282, which covers the years 431 to 1504, with a separate pre-Patrician section spanning the years AM4034 to 4523, and Bodl. MS Rawl. B 489, which commences with the year 431 but contains entries down to the year 1541 with a few sporadic later entries ending in 1588. The first full edition of the text was published in the years 1887–1901. The edition was based on TCD MS 1282, the 'A' text, with parallel readings supplied as appropriate from the 'B' text in Rawl. B 489.[27] As has been observed by Aubrey Gwynn, where the 'A' and 'B' texts differ, the relevant entries in AFM are generally closer to the 'A' text.[28] In the 1630s, when consulted by the Four Masters, the text of AU evidently continued

---

Domhnaill entries in the D version of the Annals of Ulster', unpublished typescript supplied by the author).   **24** See pp 104–12, below.   **25** Aubrey Gwynn, 'Cathal Mac Maghnusa and the Annals of Ulster, part 1', *Clogher Record* 2:2 (1958), 230–43; part 2, *Clogher Record* 2:3 (1959), 370–84. **26** Aubrey Gwynn, *Cathal Óg Mac Maghnusa and the annals of Ulster*, ed. Nollaig Ó Muraíle (Enniskillen, 1998), pp 39, 51; J.F. Kenney, *The sources for the early history of Ireland: ecclesiastical: an introduction and guide* (New York, 1929, repr. Dublin, 1979), p. 23. John Colgan similarly refers to these annals in the Latin form as [*Annales*] *Senatenses* in his *Acta sanctorum Hiberniae* (Louvain, 1645), pp 6, 439, 466; Ó Muraíle, 'Annála Uladh: the annals of Ulster, introduction to the 1998 reprint', [19–20]; Simms, 'Additional Ó Domhnaill entries'.   **27** William M. Hennessy (ed.), *Annála Uladh: Annals of Ulster, otherwise Annala Senait, Annals of Senat, a chronicle of Irish affairs from AD431 to AD1540* (4 vols, Dublin, 1887–1901). Hennessy's edition was reissued in 1998 with a lengthy introduction by Nollaig Ó Muraíle. A new edition and translation of the first half of the text was produced in 1983: Seán Mac Airt and Gearóid Mac Niocaill (eds), *The Annals of Ulster (to AD1131), part 1: text and translation* (Dublin, 1983). Mac Airt and Mac Niocaill's edition includes the pre-Patrician annals for the years AM4034–AM4523 contained in TCD MS 1282.   **28** Gwynn, *Cathal Óg Mac Maghnusa and the annals of Ulster*, pp 29, 39. Instances where the Four Masters' appear to follow the 'A' text rather than the 'B' text of AU include AFM 1468.28, 1469.5, 1469.6, 1471.9, 1471.15, 1475.11. In other cases, the extent of the verbal differences are such that it is not possible to conclude that 'A' rather than some other set of annals was the source, but yet the text of AFM corresponds more closely to 'A' than to 'B'. Examples where, despite revision, a possible reliance on 'A' rather than to 'B' can be discerned include AFM 1456.2, 1457.3 and 1460.6. Conversely, for the year 1468, AFM includes five entries that have corresponding items in the 'B' rather than the 'A' text of AU. However, AFM has much more detail than AU in four of these five instances, making them sufficiently different to assume that AU was almost certainly not the Four Masters' source. It is noteworthy that Ó Muraíle, in 'Annála Uladh: the annals of Ulster, introduction to the 1998 reprint', 19, is careful to maintain the distinction between the 'A' and 'B' versions of the text and the extant manuscripts that reflect those versions, leaving open the

to the year 1532,[29] which means that if TCD MS 1282 was the actual manuscript used it is now incomplete. The title used by the Four Masters for the copy of AU available to them, *Leabhar Sheanadh Mhic Mhaghnusa*, associates the manuscript with the territory at the northern end of upper Lough Erne, in Co. Fermanagh.[30]

The original manuscript (TCD MS 1282) was prepared, for the most part, during the lifetime of and under the direction of Cathal Óg Mac Maghnusa, *nech ro chumdaigh 7 ro theglaim 7 ro thinoil an leabur so a leabhraibh ilímdai[bh] ailibh* ('one that projected and collected and compiled this book from very many other books').[31] According to the palaeographical analysis by Gearóid Mac Niocaill, it was transcribed by Ruaidhrí Ó Luinín as far as the year 1489, and continued thereafter by other scribes, including Cathal Óg Mac Maghnusa himself.[32] More recently, Daniel Mc Carthy has emphasized the significance of Ruaidhrí Ua Caiside's role as principal compiler of the text transcribed by Ó Luinín, arguing that Mac Maghnusa's role was probably confined to 'supplying the MS sources, furnishing the physical resources and presumably remunerating Ua Caiside and Ua Luinín'.[33] TCD MS 1282 was in the possession of James Ussher no later than 1619, so if it is the actual copy used by the Four Masters then it must have been returned to west Ulster no later than 1632.[34] The alternative explanation is that the Four Masters used a different, now lost, copy of AU, perhaps one then still in west Ulster in the possession of the descendants of Cathal Óg Mac Maghnusa, whose death is recorded by both AU and AFM under the year 1498.[35] As Aubrey Gwynn noted, it is only in the fifteenth-century entries that AU has a particularly pronounced focus on Ulster, and then predominantly on Fermanagh and the Méig Uidhir.

It is now accepted that Bodl. MS Rawl. B 489 is the later of the two extant copies of AU, and that it was copied from TCD MS 1282.[36] Additions continued to be made to it through much of the sixteenth century, the latest entry being for the year 1588. Aside from these additions, there are other relatively minor variations in this 'B' text, as compared with TCD MS 1282. Brian Ó Cuív's analysis of the scribal hands in Rawl. B 489 revises the earlier findings of Aubrey

---

possibility that the actual manuscript of AU used by the Four Masters may not have been either of those now extant. **29** *AFM*, I, pp lxvi–lxvii. **30** Gwynn, *Cathal Óg Mac Maghnusa and the Annals of Ulster*, ed. Ó Muraíle, pp 18–20 and map on p. ix. The place is now identified in English as Belleisle, in the parish of Cleenish. John O'Donovan noted on the basis of information collected in the course of his work for the Ordnance Survey that the place was traditionally called Ballymacmanus or Mac Manus's Island. Writing from Tempo, Co. Fermanagh, 17 Nov. 1834, O'Donovan noted that this 'corroborates the tradition in Kinnawley parish that it was the ancient territory of the Mac Manuses' (RIA, Ordnance Survey letters, Fermanagh, pp 87–8). **31** *AU*, III, pp 430–1. **32** Mac Airt and Mac Niocaill (eds), *The Annals of Ulster (to ADI 131)*, p. ix. **33** Daniel Mc Carthy, *The Irish annals: their genesis, evolution and history* (Dublin, 2007), p. 35. **34** William O'Sullivan, 'Correspondence of David Rothe and James Ussher, 1619–23', *Collectanea Hibernica* 36–7 (1994–5), 16, n. 48; O'Sullivan, 'Ussher as a collector of manuscripts', *Hermathena* 88 (1956), 54; Daniel Mc Carthy, 'The original compilation of the Annals of Ulster', *Studia Celtica* 38 (2004), 69–95. **35** *AFM*, IV, pp 1240–3. **36** Mac Airt and Mac Niocaill (eds), *The Annals of Ulster (to ADI 131)*, pp viii–ix.

Gwynn as to the contributions of the various scribes involved.[37] Ó Cuív indicates that this transcript of AU was made by Ruaidhrí Ó Caiside as far as the entry for the year 952, and by Ruaidhrí Ó Luinín, the main scribe of the earlier copy of these annals, from the year 952 to 1506. Two unidentified scribes then wrote the section from 1507 to 1535, with up to ten scribes adding further entries down to the year 1588.[38] The later contributors to the sixteenth-century portion of these annals included Matha Ó Luinín, grandson of one of the original scribes, who lamented the untidy contribution a member of the Ó Caiside family had made to the last five or six folios of his grandfather's manuscript:

> *Ni maith lem olcus sgribhus mac hi Caiside na cuig duilleoga no se so ar dered in leabhuir si do sgrib mo shenathair .i. Ruaidhri O Luinin. Misi Matha O Luinin. Ocus tabradh in ti leighfes bendacht air ar nanmuin araon. AD1579.*
>
> (I regret how badly the son of Ua Caiside wrote these five or six folios at the end of this book which my grandfather, namely Ruaidhri O Luinin, wrote. I am Matha O Luinin. And let him who reads bestow a blessing on the souls of both of us. AD1579.)[39]

A seventeenth-century English translation of part of AU survives in BL Additional MS 4795, with a further section in BL Additional MS 4789. Taken together, these comprise the 'C' text, while a Latin rendering of most of the thirteenth-century section of AU is found in BL Additional MS 4784 – the 'D' text.[40] In the case of both the 'C' and 'D' texts, the translations contain some items not found in either 'A' and 'B'. It has been pointed out by Katharine Simms that some of this additional material in the 'D' text is also in AFM, but in no other extant annals. Simms has discerned a pattern in the additional material in the 'D' text of AU that is also found in AFM: all but two of the items concern Tír Conaill or the Uí Dhomhnaill; the remaining two relate to St Francis and the Franciscan Order. This points to the intriguing possibility of a lost 'Donegal' version of AU, the source of the 'D' translation, to which the Four Masters may have had access.[41] That such a manuscript might have expanded the coverage of the Uí Dhomhnaill and simultaneously lessened the coverage of the Méig Uidhir is entirely plausible, but also entirely speculative.[42] Such a manuscript, however, if it existed, might not have been termed the 'Book of Seanadh Mhic Mhaghnusa'. An alternative explanation also offered by Simms is that both the AU 'D' version and AFM made independent use of a common source which contained more detailed material on the Uí Dhomhnaill than now

---

37 For Gwynn's assessment, which also formed the basis of the summary provided by Nollaig Ó Muraíle in the 1998 reprint of AU, see Gwynn, *Cathal Óg Mac Maghnusa and the Annals of Ulster*, pp 29–31. 38 *Cat. Ir. mss in Bodl.*, I, pp 156–61. 39 *Cat. Ir. mss in Bodl.*, I, pp 160–1; the quotation from Matha Ó Luinín is in Bodl. MS Rawl. B 489, fo. 125, and is printed in Ó Cuív's catalogue description of the manuscript at p. 160. 40 *AU*, IV, pp vi–vii. 41 Simms, 'Additional Ó Domhnaill entries', p. 4. 42 On the treatment of the Méig Uidhir in AFM, see below, pp 234–5.

survives outside AFM. The likely existence of historical manuscript sources, no longer extant, focusing on the Uí Dhomhnaill is discussed further below in a case study of the treatment of the Uí Dhomhnaill in AFM.[43]

The nature of the correspondence between the fifteenth- and early sixteenth-century entries in AFM and AU will be examined in some detail in a later chapter, where it will be shown that the entries recorded in AU formed one among several significant sources from which material was evidently selected and edited for inclusion in AFM. Since AU is a significant source, extant in a form close to that consulted by the Four Masters, even if TCD MS 1282 should prove not to have been the actual manuscript used, a comparison between it and AFM provides important evidence of the methodology of the Four Masters.[44] The conclusions of this comparison are strengthened by the analysis of other extant annalistic sources that derive ultimately from manuscripts to which the Four Masters also had access. Chief among these other source texts is the collection of annals now known as the Annals of Connacht (AConn). These annals are the nearest approximation that now survives to the collection known to the Four Masters as the 'Book of the O'Duigenans of Kilronan'. The closely related text now known as the Annals of Loch Cé (ALCé) is also relevant to the discussion.

Annals of Connacht and Annals of Loch Cé

It has sometimes been suggested that the source known to the Four Masters as the 'Book of the O'Duigenans of Kilronan' might be identified as the manuscript now known as the Annals of Connacht (RIA MS C iii 1), a manuscript of Ó Duibhgeannáin provenance.[45] However, that tentative identification is quite problematic, and it appears more appropriate to conclude that the manuscript now known as AConn is probably *derived from* the Book of the O'Duigenans of Kilronan. The unique surviving autograph manuscript of AConn, RIA MS C iii 1, is a sixteenth-century vellum manuscript containing annals for the years 1224 to 1544. There are a number of gaps in the text owing to the loss of folios in the manuscript, so that material contained in these annals for the years 1378–84 and 1393–8 has been lost. Another gap in the text occurs for the years 1427–32, but A.M. Freeman has argued that in this instance there is no loss of a folio, but

---

43 See below, chapter seven.   44 It will be shown, however, that for the opening years of the fifteenth century, for instance, AFM did not derive its chronological framework from either AU or the Annals of the Island of Saints. The latter source is believed to be 'Fragment III' in Séamus Ó hInnse (ed.), *Miscellaneous Irish annals (AD1114–1437)*, (Dublin, 1947), pp 142–85, and is discussed further below.   45 A.M. Freeman (ed.), *Annála Connacht: the annals of Connacht, AD1224–1544* (Dublin, 1944, repr. 1970); RIA MS C iii 1; *Cat. Ir. mss in RIA*, pp 3274–6; Walsh, *The Four Masters and their work*, 3. Among the other manuscripts with Ó Duibhgeannáin associations in circulation was the exemplar seen at Ard Coill (Co. Clare) in 1585, from which a variety of texts, including a poem and a genealogy, were copied (see Maynooth, MS R 70, fos 505–512). The same manuscript also cites a range of other manuscript sources including one *Leabhar Uí Maolchonaire* (Pádraig Ó Fiannachta, *Lámhscríbhinní Gaeilge Choláiste Phádraig, Má Nuad*, fascúl IV (Maynooth, 1967), p. 78).

rather that there was a hiatus in the source text from which the scribes were working.[46] There is general acceptance for Gearóid Mac Niocaill's view that AConn, like ALCé, derives ultimately from 'a text compiled by a member of the Ó Maoilchonaire family, probably in the mid-fifteenth century'.[47]

Mac Niocaill's conclusion that the 'Book of the O'Duigenans of Kilronan' derived ultimately from an Ó Maoil Chonaire source is based on the extent to which AConn 'is centred essentially on the doings on the Ó Conchubhair family, to whom the Ó Maoilchonaires were hereditary historians'.[48] The earliest entry in the extant manuscript of AConn relates to the death of Cathal Crobderg Ó Conchobhair in 1224, a date and event of special significance within the Ó Maoil Chonaire school of history. The commencement date can only have been deliberately chosen, and the eulogistic tenor of the opening entry sets the tone for the entire text, though it is noticeable that the number of entries relating to the Ó Conchobhair family declines significantly from the mid-fourteenth century.

The entries in the closing section of AConn, however, recording events later than the presumed mid-fifteenth-century source, can probably be ascribed to the Ó Duibhgeannáin school of *seanchas*, and Gearóid Mac Niocaill has noted that the early sixteenth-century entries in AConn 'may be treated with confidence as a contemporary record'.[49] The manuscript concludes with one later entry, dated 1562, in a different hand and ink 'though very much the same type as the last scribe', according to Freeman, and presumably added some years after the bulk of the manuscript had been completed.[50] No precise date of writing has been suggested, although Freeman was of the opinion that the greater part of the manuscript should be assigned to a date 'at least 75 years earlier than the oldest part of ALCé',[51] a comment based on his overall palaeographical assessment of the extant manuscript.

Kathleen Mulchrone's description of the AConn manuscript (RIA MS C iii 1) included in the published *Catalogue of Irish manuscripts in the Royal Irish Academy* identifies the scribes as Paitín Ó Duibhgeannáin, Seán Riabhach Ó Duibhgeannáin, and a third scribe who was probably also a member of the Ó Duibhgeannáin family.[52] Mulchrone also tentatively suggests that the manuscript might be the 'Book of the O'Duigenans of Kilronan'. Although Freeman does not formally reject this suggestion in his introductory comments to his edition of AConn, it seems that the identification cannot be sustained.[53] The Four Masters are specific about stating that their Ó Duibhgeannáin source extended as far as the year 1563; yet this appears never to have been the case with AConn, which end with the year 1544, with one stray entry for the year 1562. That 1562 entry follows immediately after the entry for 1544, with no intermediate loss of

---

46 *AConn*, p. ix.   47 Gearóid Mac Niocaill, *The medieval Irish annals* (Dublin, 1975), p. 32. 48 Mac Niocaill, *Medieval Irish annals*, p. 34.   49 Mac Niocaill, *Medieval Irish annals*, p. 37. 50 *AConn*, p. ix.   51 *AConn*, p. xx.   52 *Cat. Ir. mss in RIA*, no. 1219, pp 3274–5.   53 *Cat. Ir. mss in RIA*, no. 1219, p. 3276; *AConn*, p. xiv.

text; the closing entry for 1562 relates to the death of Brian Ó Ruairc, and its slightly incongruous inclusion points to the possibility of Ó Ruairc patronage. The AConn manuscript, RIA MS C iii 1, does however have strong Ó Duibhgeannáin associations and was still in Ó Duibhgeannáin hands in 1727.[54] Freeman's discussion of the identity of the scribes outlines the alternative case for identifying the scribes with members of the Ó Maoil Chonaire family, though on balance he seems to accept the conclusion that the manuscript was the work of Ó Duibhgeannáin scribes. The latter view was also that favoured by John Brady and Paul Walsh, and has most recently been confirmed by Daniel Mc Carthy.[55]

The close relationship between many entries in AConn and AFM for this period supports the conclusion that the manuscript now known as AConn derives from an annalistic source to which the Four Masters had access. Given its associations with the Ó Duibhgeannáin family, it seems reasonable to conclude that AConn probably derives from the source known to the Four Masters as the Book of the O'Duigenans of Kilronan.[56] The extent of the correspondence between the two sets of annals will be explored in more detail in the discussion of methodology, where it will be shown that there is a strong if inconsistent correlation between AConn and AFM in respect of entries relating to the fifteenth and sixteenth centuries.[57]

Annals of Loch Cé

The Annals of Loch Cé (ALCé) in their extant form were compiled in 1588–9 under the direction of Brian Mac Diarmada of Moylurg, and they have a predominantly north Connacht focus.[58] Like AConn, they show evidence of the influence of both the Ó Maoil Chonaire and the Ó Duibhgeannáin schools of history, in their emphasis on the activities of the Uí Chonchobhair and Clann Mhaolruanaidh, the group that included the families of Mac Diarmada, Mac Donnchadha and other north Connacht families in the late medieval period. There is a very close similarity between AConn and ALCé from 1014 to 1316 and again from 1479 to 1544, and it is clear that they derived largely from a common source.[59] In contrast, Gearóid Mac Niocaill has pointed out that the section of

---

54 *AConn*, p. x. There is an annotation by 'Domnick Diggenan' dated 1727 indicating that he owned the manuscript at that date (RIA MS C iii 1, fo. 15r). The manuscript was acquired by Charles O'Conor in or before 1744. 55 John Brady, Review of Freeman's edition of the *Annals of Connacht*, in *Irish Ecclesiastical Record* 5th ser., 65 (Jan. 1945), 64–5; Paul Walsh, 'The book of the O Duigenans' in *Irish men of learning*, ed. Colm O Lochlainn (Dublin, 1947), pp 23–4; Mc Carthy, *The Irish annals*, pp 44–6. 56 *AFM*, I, p. lxvi. 57 The correlation is clearest for the years 1400– 21, 1460s, 1470s and 1530s. For discussion see below, chapter six. 58 W.M. Hennessy (ed.), *The annals of Loch Cé: a chronicle of Irish affairs from AD1014 to AD1590* (2 vols, London, 1871). 59 The similarities are so close that in his edition of ALCé William Hennessy thought it appropriate to use the text of AConn to supply the lacunae from 1316 to 1412 (*ALCé*, I, pp 584–end, and II, pp 1–145). See also Hennessy's preface to *ALCé*, I, pp lii–lv, and Freeman's introduction to *AConn*, p. xxi.

ALCé covering the years 1413 to 1461 has no close textual connection with AConn, but rather presents traces of a text that was also incorporated into AU.[60] Significantly, the relatively strong correspondence between AFM and AConn for much of the fifteenth and sixteenth centuries is not sustained for the years 1422 to 1460, another indication that AConn as now extant was not the Four Masters' Ó Duibhgeannáin source.[61] This section of ALCé displays a south-west Ulster focus, before resuming its north Connacht focus after 1462.

The principal surviving manuscript of ALCé is TCD MS 1293, which contains entries for the years 1014 to 1577 with significant lacunae from 1138 to 1170, and 1317 to 1412. Another portion of ALCé, containing entries for the years 1568–90 is preserved within BL Add. MS 4792, and Mc Carthy considers that this section represents Brian Mac Diarmada's earliest work on these annals.[62] Mac Diarmada then wrote the section covering the years 1413–61, on paper rather than vellum. The main scribe of the vellum sections of ALCé for the years 1014 to 1316, and 1462 to 1577 was Pilib Ballach Ó Duibhgeannáin, and much material relating to the Ó Duibhgeannáin family is preserved through the text.[63] However, the emphasis on the Ó Maoil Chonaire family, noticeable in AConn, is also a feature of the earlier sections of ALCé.[64] It has also been noted by Mac Niocaill that the thirteenth-century portion of ALCé, and also AConn, incorporates a detailed narrative of events in Connacht, dealing mainly with the Anglo-Norman invasion of the province, and written from a north-Connacht perspective, the writer probably being based in the area of Boyle or Lough Key.[65] Not surprisingly, almost half of the fifteenth- and sixteenth-century obituaries in ALCé relate to Connacht families and most of these pertain to families in the north-east of the province. The next largest portion relates to families from west and south-west Ulster, which traditionally had close associations with north Connacht, and it was the dynastic politics of this region that dominated the historical record preserved in ALCé.

A further Ó Duibhgeannáin complication in seeking to identify extant manuscripts that may represent the sources used by the Four Masters is introduced by similarity between the manuscripts itemized in AFM and those named by the same scholars in their list of the sources consulted when preparing their new recension of *Leabhar gabhála* in 1631. Given that the same team of scribes were at work, and that the work was undertaken between 22 October and 22 December 1631 – just a month prior to their commencing on AFM, it seems reasonable to speculate that they probably used some of the same source manuscripts. As in other instances, the scribes asserted that they had consulted

60 Mac Niocaill, *Medieval Irish annals*, p. 35.   61 Neither is AU a significant source for AFM entries for these years.   62 Mc Carthy, *The Irish annals*, pp 49–50.   63 *ALCé*, I, pp 630, 632, 652; *ALCé*, II, pp 10, 16, 20, 56, 58, 72, 112, 130, 154, 192, 226–8, 252, 336, 380, 424, 436, 456, 462, 496, 516.   64 *ALCé*, I, pp 306, 310, 454, 468, 482, 454, 510; *ALCé*, II, pp 56, 62, 74, 90, 108, 112, 168, 170, 184, 206, 230, 278, 338, 358, 468, 496.   65 Mac Niocaill, *Medieval Irish annals*, p. 33.

a range of manuscripts in preparing their recension of *Leabhar gabhála*. They itemized the versions of *Leabhar gabhála* available to them as:

> *Leabhar Baile Ui Maoil Conaire, do scriobh Muirghes mac Paidin Uí MaoilConaire*
> *as Leabhar na hUidre, do scriobhadh hi Cluain Mac Nois ind aimsir Noimh Ciaráin:*
> *Leabar Baile Uí Cleirigh, do sgriobhadh ind aimsir Maoil(sh)eachloind Moir meic*
> *Domhnaill, Ri Erenn: Leabar Muintire Duibhgendáin o Senchuaich ua nOilella, da*
> *ngoirther Leabhar Glinde da Lacha: et Leabar na hUac[h]ongbala: maille re*
> *leabraibh gabala et senchusa oile cenmothátt.*
>
> (The Book of Baile Ui Maoil-Chonaire, which Muirghes, son of Paidin ua Maoil-
> Chonaire, wrote out of the Book of the Dun Cow, that was written in Clonmacnois
> in the time of S. Ciaran: the Book of Baile Ui Cleirigh, which was written in the
> time of Maol-Shechlainn Mór, son of Domhnall, king of Ireland: the Book of
> Muinter Duibhghenain, from Senchua of Ui Oilella, which is called the Book of
> Glendaloch, and the Book of the Uachongbhail: together with other books of
> conquests and of history besides.)[66]

The coincidence of listing source manuscripts pertaining to the Ó Maoil Chonaire, Ó Duibhgeannáin, and Ó Cleirigh families both in the preface to the 1631 recension of *Leabhar gabhála* and in the *testimonium* which prefaced AFM does not necessarily imply that identical manuscripts were being referred to in both instances. Indeed, the list appears to indicate that the source manuscripts consulted for the *Leabhar gabhála* were rather older compilations than was the case with some of the manuscripts itemized in the AFM list of sources. In this case the coincidence might be best explained simply by reference to the fact that the three families named as the owners of the source manuscripts were the same three families who comprised the team of scholars at work on both *Leabhar gabhála* and AFM. It seems logical to assume that the historical sources in the possession of those families formed an essential core of the material from which the Four Masters worked. That the sources in the possession of each of those three families of professional historians should include both a text of *Leabhar gabhála* and a set of historical annals extending over much of the medieval period would be unexceptional. In such circumstances it is unnecessary to argue for the equivalence of the *Leabhar Muintire Duibhgendáin o Senchuaich ua nOilella, da ngoirther Leabhar Glinde da Lacha*,[67] which contained a version of *Leabhar*

---

66 Macalister and Mac Neill (eds), *Leabhar gabhála*, pp 4–5. As explained below, a book of Baile Uí Mhaoil Chonaire survives in fragmentary form in RIA MS D iv 3.   67 For further discussion of the identification of this source see Pádraig O Riain, 'The book of Glendalough or Rawlinson B 502', *Éigse* 18 (1981), 161–76; Caoimhín Breatnach, 'Rawlinson B 502, Lebar Glinne dá Locha and Saltair na Rann', *Éigse* 30 (1997), 109–32; *Cat. Ir. mss in Bodl.*, I, pp 163–200; Ó Riain, 'Rawlinson B 502 alias *Lebar Glinne Dá Locha*: a restatement of the case', *Zeitschrift für Celtische Philologie* 51 (1998), 130–47; Caoimhín Breatnach, 'Manuscript sources and methodology: Rawlinson B 502 and *Lebar Glinne Da Lacha*', *Celtica* 24 (2003), 40–54. Caoimhín Breatnach has suggested to me that this may be a reference to the *Leabhar gabhála* text in Bodl. Rawl. B 512, fos 75Br–90v, where *Leabar gabála Glind dá Locha* is named as the source of the text (*Cat. Ir. mss in Bodl.*, I, p. 233).

gabhála, with the manuscript described as *Leabhar muintere Duibgendáin chille Rónáin*, which contained a set of historical annals for the years 900 to 1563.[68] Given the Ó Duibhgeannáin commitment to supporting the historical researches of Mícheál Ó Cléirigh, it is probable that Cú Choigcríche Ó Duibhgeannáin's involvement with the project would have facilitated access to more than one manuscript in the possession of the Ó Duibhgeannáin school of history.[69]

Book of Cú Choigcríche son of Diarmaid Ó Cléirigh

No extant manuscript has been identified as *Leabhar Choncoicccriche meic Diarmatta mic Taidhg caimm Uí Clerigh* ('Book of Cucogry, the son of Dermot, son of Tadhg Cam O Clerigh').[70] However, the precision of the dates assigned to it by the Four Masters, 1281–1537, implies that it too was in the form of a chronological arrangement of annals. This Cú Choigcríche Ó Cléirigh son of Diarmaid son of Tadhg Cam Ó Cléirigh should not be confused with the Cú Choigcríche Ó Cléirigh who was one of the Four Masters, and son of another Diarmaid. Rather, the compiler of the Ó Cléirigh source text used by the Four Masters was the paternal grandfather of Lughaidh Ó Cléirigh, author of *Beatha Aodha Ruaidh Uí Dhomhnaill*.[71] In all probability, these two Ó Cléirigh sources came to the Four Masters through Muiris, son of Lughaidh Ó Cléirigh, with whom Mícheál Ó Cléirigh is known to have had contact when transcribing saints' Lives.[72] Given the association of the Ó Cléirigh historians with the Ó Domhnaill family over many generations, it is probable that the 'Book of Cú Choigcríche Ó Cléirigh' would have placed particular emphasis on the exploits of the Ó Domhnaill leaders. It is certainly possible that many of the significant narratives relating to members of the Ó Domhnaill family recounted at length in AFM could have been drawn from such a source.[73]

Book of Ó Maoil Chonaire

The source known to the Four Masters as *Leabhar Chloinne Uí Maoílconaire* ('Book of Clann Uí Mhaoil Chonaire') evidently contained a set of annals ending

68 Macalister and Mac Neill (eds), *Leabhar gabhála*, pp 4–5; *AFM*, I, pp lxiv–vi. Of course, it is also possible that a composite Ó Duibhgeannáin manuscript might have contained both the *Leabhar gabhála* and a late medieval chronicle in the form of annals. 69 The nature of the scholarly networks that allowed access to manuscripts is considered further in chapter nine, below. 70 Paul Walsh, *The Ó Cléirigh family of Tír Conaill* (Dublin, 1938), p. 12, merely mentions the fact that the manuscript is now lost. 71 Walsh, *The Ó Cléirigh family of Tír Conaill*, pp 11–12, 21. Tadhg Cam Ó Cléirigh was a renowned historian whose death was recorded in AFM under the year 1492, *AFM*, IV, pp 1194–5. 72 Jennings, *Michael O Cleirigh and his associates*, p. 96; Paul Walsh, 'The travels of Mícheál Ó Cléirigh', repr. in Nollaig Ó Muraíle (ed.), *Mícheál Ó Cléirigh, his associates, and St Anthony's College Louvain* (Dublin, 2008), p. 136. 73 This is not to suggest that they were preserved exclusively in such a source, and some were certainly also preserved in AU. The Ó Domhnaill material will be considered in more detail below. See also Bernadette Cunningham,

in 1505. It is not known whether the book also contained other historical sources. This Ó Maoil Chonaire source used in AFM is probably, though not certainly, to be distinguished from the manuscript referred to by Mícheál Ó Cléirigh and his fellow historians in the preface to their recension of *Leabhar gabhála* as *Leabhar Bhaile Uí Mhaoilchonaire do sgríobh Muirghios mac Paídín Uí Mhaoilchonaire as Liobhar na hUidhre.*[74] This Ó Maoil Chonaire manuscript survives in incomplete form as RIA MS D iv 3. A vellum manuscript dating from the early sixteenth century, it now contains an incomplete text of *Leabhar gabhála*. It does not now contain any annalistic material, nor could a manuscript derived from *Leabhar na hUidhre* contain annalistic entries extending to 1505.[75] This was not the original *Leabhar na hUidhre*, RIA MS 23 E 25, but rather a manuscript that included a transcript by Muirgheas Ó Maoil Chonaire of material from that earlier source. This appears to fix the date of the Four Masters' exemplar of *Leabhar gabhála* to the early sixteenth century. Muirgheas son of Páidín Ó Maoil Chonaire is known for his manuscript compilations, not least of which is the Book of Fenagh, a work dated to 1516.[76] It is known that Mícheál Ó Cléirigh had access to the hagiographical texts in the Book of Fenagh,[77] and thus it would not be surprising if he also had access to a set of historical annals and a version of *Leabhar gabhála* from the same school.

Book of Clonmacnoise

The manuscript known to the Four Masters as the 'Book of Clonmacnoise' evidently did not contain material later than the year 1227. It therefore cannot be equated with the 'Annals of Clonmacnoise' now preserved in an English translation made by Conall Mac Eochagáin in 1627. Conall Mac Eochagáin's text commences with the creation of the world and continues to the year 1408.[78] An alternative identification was put forward by William Hennessy, who argued that the annals now known under the title *Chronicum Scotorum* might represent at least some of the material known to the Four Masters as the Book of Clonmacnoise. Hennessy pointed out that many entries common to AFM and

O'Donnell histories: Donegal and the Annals of the Four Masters (Rathmullan, 2007), pp 19–43. 74 The preface to Ó Cléirigh's recension of *Leabhar gabhála* is printed in O'Curry, *Lectures on manuscript materials*, appendix LXXIV, p. 555. 75 *Cat. Ir. mss in RIA*, no. 1224, pp 3307–13. These two source manuscripts are conflated in Paul Walsh, *The Four Masters and their work*, p. 4, n. 12; this may be an error by Walsh, or it may have been deliberate, since he points out that the extant material in RIA MS D iv 3 is a mere fragment. 76 W.H. Hennessy and D.H. Kelly (eds), *The Book of Fenagh, in Irish and English* (Dublin, 1875; repr. 1939). Muirgheas died in 1543 (AFM *s.a.*). Yet another historical book of the Uí Mhaoil Chonaire is alluded to in TCD MS 1292, fo. 13b, as having been a source for the *Seanchas Búrcach*. 77 Jennings, *Míchael O Cleirigh and his associates*, pp 94–5; and colophon printed from BR MS 2324–40 at p. 200, n. 5; Cunningham and Gillespie, 'Muirgheas Ó Maoilchonaire of Cluain Plocáin'. 78 *AFM*, I, p. lxv; *AClon*. Gearóid Mac Niocaill had suggested that the lost original of Mac Eochagáin's Annals of Clonmacnoise might have been the Four Masters' Clonmacnoise source (*Medieval Irish annals*, pp 28–9).

Chronicum Scotorum 'are not found in any other volume of Irish annals now known to be in existence'.[79] This view has been reiterated by Aubrey Gwynn and Nollaig Ó Muraíle, who argue that TCD MS 1292, now known as *Chronicum Scotorum*, comprises a seventeenth-century abridgment of the annals alluded to as the Book of Clonmacnoise by the Four Masters. The reference to this Clonmacnoise source is not confined to the preliminary statement of sources consulted by the Four Masters. Nollaig Ó Muraíle has drawn attention to the fact that the source is also cited within the text of AFM, and that the references correspond to material found in *Chronicum Scotorum* for those years.[80] However, a more cautious view is presented by David Dumville, who settles for the conclusion that the Four Masters' Clonmacnoise source is now lost.[81] Daniel Mc Carthy argues that as far as the year AD1207, *Chronicum Scotorum* and AFM 'share a common Mac Fhirbhisigh annalistic source which was known to both Mícheál Ó Cléirigh and Dubhaltach as *Leabhar Airisin [Lecain] Meic Fhirbhisigh*.' Thus, in Mc Carthy's view, the seventeenth-century *Chronicum Scotorum* is simply Mac Fhirbhisigh's abridgment of an older set of annals in the possession of the Mac Fhirbhisigh family.[82]

The earliest extant manuscript of *Chronicum Scotorum* is that prepared by Dubhaltach Mac Fhirbhisigh for John Lynch, now forming part of TCD MS 1292, a manuscript that contains fragments from several Irish language texts.[83] It contains a set of annals for the years AM1599 to AD1135 with lacunae in the years 723–804. These annals have sometimes been attributed to Gillachrist Ua Maeileoin, abbot of Clonmacnoise.[84] The pre-Christian section is in narrative form, a characteristic it shares with Conall Mac Eochagáin's translation of the Annals of Clonmacnoise (AClon). The extant text is accompanied by a prefatory note which records that the early section of the work has been much abbreviated, most likely by Mac Fhirbhisigh himself.

> *Tuig, a lécchtóir, fa adhbar áiridhe, et go follus do secna eimealtais, gurab edh as áil linn tagha et tráctad athcumair do denum ar airisin na Scot amain san coipse, ag fagbháil listacda na leapur airisin amuigh, conidh aire sin iarrammaid oirbsi gan ar n-increachadh trid uair d'fedamamar gurab adhbal an teasnamh he.*

79 William Hennessy (ed.), *Chronicum Scotorum* (London, 1866) [*CS*], p. xxxviii. 80 Gwynn, *Cathal Óg mac Maghnusa and the Annals of Ulster*, ed. Ó Muraíle, p. 39; Nollaig Ó Muraile, *The celebrated antiquary: Dubhaltach Mac Fhirbhisigh, c.1600–71: his lineage, life and learning* (Maynooth 1996), pp 100–1; The correspondence between AFM and CS in entries for the years 1005 and 1022, for which the 'Book of Clonmacnoise' is cited as a source, is suggested by Ó Muraíle as strong evidence that the exemplar of CS was among the sources consulted for AFM. 81 David Dumville, 'Where did the "Clonmacnoise chronicle" originate? The evidence of the Annals of Tigernach and *Chronicum Scotorum*, AD974–1150' in Grabowski and Dumville (eds), *Chronicles and annals of medieval Ireland and Wales* (1984), p. 166, n. 46. 82 Mc Carthy, *The Irish annals*, pp 311, 312. 83 Previously TCD MS H 1 18, and occupying fos 16–27 of that manuscript. 84 *CS*, p. xxxix. Hennessy prints a translation of a description attached to a late transcript of these annals, preserved in RIA MS 23 O 8. 'The *Chronicum Scotorum*, i.e. the Annal of the Scotic Race, written at first at Clonmacnois, sometime in the twelfth century, by Gilla Christ O Maeileoin Abbot of Clonmacnois,

(Understand, Reader, that for a certain reason, and plainly to avoid tediousness, what we desire is to make a short Abstract and Compendium of the History of the Scoti only in this copy, leaving out the lengthened details of the Books of History; wherefore it is that we entreat of you not to reproach us therefor, as we know that it is an exceedingly great deficiency.)[85]

It seems clear, therefore, that Mac Fhirbhisigh's *Chronicum Scotorum* can no longer be considered to represent the Four Masters' Clonmacnoise source. The annalists specifically say that the manuscript they consulted was *Leabhar Cluana mic Nóis in ro bhennaigh Naoimh Chiarán mac an tsaoír*, implying that their source was a book old enough to have been blessed by St Ciaran himself. The manuscript with that reputation in the seventeenth century was none other than *Leabhar na hUidhre*[86] and, as already noted, a copy of part of that manuscript is known to have been available to Mícheál Ó Cléirigh. Indeed, R.I. Best and Osborn Bergin, the editors of the diplomatic edition of *Leabhar na hUidhre*, have interpreted the statement of sources attached to AFM as referring to that manuscript.[87] The transcript from that source now preserved as RIA MS D iv 3, already mentioned, indicates that *Leabhar na hUidhre* contained a version of *Leabhar gabhála* at one time, and since the opening section of AFM derives essentially from *Leabhar gabhála*, the notion that *Leabhar na hUidhre* was a Clonmacnoise source used by the Four Masters is a valid one. The fragmentary state of the *Leabhar na hUidhre* manuscript, as now extant, cannot be taken as a guide to what that source contained in the seventeenth century. Best and Bergin also draw attention to the fact that *Leabhar na hUidhre* was specifically cited in AFM at the year AD266, and that Ó Cléirigh had earlier cited material drawn from the same manuscript in the Martyrology of Donegal at the entry for 23 September.[88] It should be pointed out here, however, that the explicit reference to *Leabhar na hUidhre* is part of a marginal annotation in both sets of autograph manuscripts of AFM.[89] Similarly, in the 1630 manuscript of the Martyrology of Donegal, the reference to *Leabhar na hUidhre* is part of an addition to the text, written vertically in the margin of the entry for 23 September.[90]

Leabhar na hUidhre's long history as a prestige manuscript prized by the Uí Dhomhnaill, taken together with the explicit statement in AFM that their Clonmacnoise book had been blessed by St Ciaran, and the fact that they give pride of place to this manuscript in their list of sources, all point to *Leabhar na*

in which is contained an account of a great many valuable affairs, particularly the affairs of Ireland, from Adam to the Age of Christ, 1150'. **85** *CS*, pp 2–3, translation by Gearóid Mac Niocaill (digital edition only), www.ucc.ie/celt consulted 23 November 2004. **86** That reputation is explicitly repeated in the preface to Ó Cléirigh's *Leabhar gabhála* in the form: *Leabhar na hUidre do scríobhadh hi Cluain Mac Nois ind aimsir Noimh Ciaráin* (Macalister and Mac Neill (eds), *Leabhar gabhála*, pp 4–5). **87** R.I. Best and O.J. Bergin (eds), *Lebor na Huidre: Book of the Dun Cow* (Dublin, 1929), pp xi–xii. **88** *Amhail atá a bFhis Adhamhnain do sgriobhadh as Leabhar na Huidhre* ('as contained in the Vision of Adamnan, which was copied from the *Leabhar na hUidhre*') (*MDon*, pp 256–7). **89** RIA MS C iii 3, fo. 196v; UCD–OFM MS A 13, fo. 209v. **90** BR MS 5095–6, fo. 48.

hUidhre rather than some other manuscript containing a text similar to *Chronicum Scotorum* as their 'Clonmacnoise' book.[91]

The Four Masters' Lecan source

At first glance it seems perverse not to equate the *Leabhar oirisen Leacain meic Firbisicch* ('Historical Book of Lecan Mic Firbisigh'), listed by the Four Masters as one of their authorities, with the compilation now usually referred to simply as the Book of Lecan.[92] The reference to the Lecan source cited specifically states that they gained access to it when they had almost completed their annals – implying 1636 – and it is known that a copy of the Book of Lecan was available to the Four Masters, through Conall Mac Eochagáin, in that year, and that lengthy poems such as the *Naoimhshenchus naoimh Innsi Fáil* were transcribed by Mícheál Ó Cléirigh from that source sometime prior to 28 April 1636.[93] The principal scribe of the Book of Lecan was Gilla Ísu Mac Fir Bisich,[94] and while the source does not now contain annals, it does contain much relevant genealogical material, king lists, historical poems and other matter pertinent to the work of the Four Masters. The revisions to the autograph manuscripts of AFM reveal that the insertion of additional genealogical information was a particular concern to the Four Masters in the final stages of their editorial revision of their annals. The evidence is inconclusive, however, and it is likely that the annalists drew on a wide range of genealogical sources.

While the evidence in favour of identifying the Book of Lecan alongside *Leabhar na hUidhre* among the authoritative sources cited by the Four Masters is thin, it is important to remember that these were prestige manuscripts, the kind of sources chroniclers would like to claim their compilations had utilized. There is contemporary evidence that the high-status dimension to these manuscripts would have enhanced the likelihood of their being listed as sources even if the level of use of other less prestigious manuscripts was in fact of greater practical significance.[95]

There is, however, another contender for identification as the Four Masters' Lecan source. A small portion of a set of Annals of Lecan, for the years 1443–68, survives in an English translation prepared by Dubhaltach Mac Fhirbhisigh at the request of Sir James Ware in 1666, and it reflects a source used extensively,

---

91 Mac Fhirbhisigh makes reference in *Leabhar na nginealach* to material that Lughaidh Ó Cléirigh copied from *Leabhar na hUidhre* (Ó Muraíle, *Celebrated antiquary*, p. 234).   92 RIA MS 23 P 2.
93 BR MS 5100–4, fos 239–244, colophon dated 28 April 1636 (the date of a transcript by Ó Cléirigh of a text he had already extracted from the Book of Lecan), cited with translation in Ó Muraíle (ed.), *Mícheál Ó Cléirigh, his associates*, pp 101–2.   94 *Cat. Ir. mss in RIA*, p. 1552.   95 For Keating's embellishment of his list of authoritative sources, see Cunningham, *The world of Geoffrey Keating*, pp 63–4; for exaggerated claims about sources made by Brian Mág Uidhir in his 'Book of Knockninny' in the 1630s, see Bernadette Cunningham and Raymond Gillespie, 'The purposes of patronage: Brian Maguire of Knockninny and his manuscripts', *Clogher Record* 13:1 (1988), 44.

if selectively, by the Four Masters.[96] It is certainly possible that these Lecan annals were derived from the more extensive work alluded to in the Four Masters' list of sources as *Leabhar oirisen Leacain meic Firbisicch*. Thus, for example, the two narrative passages concerning Niall Ó Domhnaill added to AFM for the years 1422 and 1434, which have a strong Sligo interest, might plausibly derive from a Lecan annalistic source.[97] Likewise a marginal note in TCD MS 1301 makes clear that the Ó Conchobhair Fáilghe entry at AFM 1421.12 was found in a 'book of Lecan'.[98]

Roderic O'Flaherty's late seventeenth-century annotations and additions to TCD MS 1301 offer further clues about now lost 'Lecan' annals. When annotating the work of the Four Masters he had access to three additional sets of annals containing fourteenth- and fifteenth-century entries. He referred to these sources by the abbreviations 'MSL', 'Mac Firbh' and 'Cod. Cl.' It is clear from the extent of the annotations that 'Mac Firbh' must refer to a set of Mac Fhirbhisigh annals that continued into the fifteenth century, while 'MSL' must have been a similar annalistic source because O'Flaherty frequently cited the two in tandem, noting any discrepancy in dates between them.[99] The last of O'Flaherty's three additional sources has been tentatively identified by Daniel Mc Carthy in a different context as being Conall Mac Eochagáin's Annals of Clonmacnoise, the Armagh transcript of which was also annotated by O'Flaherty, but the Mac Fhirbhisigh annals he consulted are apparently no longer extant.[100] His additions from 'MSL' span the years 1334 to 1418, while he commences citing 'Mac Firbh' at the year 1361. His additions from all annalistic sources effectively cease after 1418.[101]

As well as inserting new material from his supplementary annals, O'Flaherty occasionally indicated where material found in those sources had already been incorporated by the Four Masters. Thus, for example, at the year 1370 in TCD MS 1301, he indicated that the last six entries for that year were recorded under the year 1371 in 'MSL' and under the year 1370 in 'Mac Firbh'.[102] This is important, because those entries are among the additions in an editorial hand in

96 BL Additional MS 4799, fos 45–70v; John O'Donovan (ed.), 'The Annals of Ireland, from the year 1443 to 1468, translated from the Irish by Dudley Firbisse … for Sir James Ware, in the year 1666', *Miscellany of the Irish Archaeological Society* (Dublin, 1846), 198–302.   97 RIA MS 23 P 6, fos 162, 171v.   98 TCD MS 1301, fos 752v–753r.   99 For example, TCD MS 1301, fos 710v–712. Nicholls interprets MSL as meaning a Lecan manuscript (Nicholls, 'Introduction' to 1990 reprint of *AFM*).   100 Mc Carthy, *The Irish annals*, p. 26; his identification is of O'Flaherty's 'Cod. Cluan.' in the TCD MS 1292 text of *Chronicum Scotorum*. As noted above, Mc Carthy categorizes the Mac Fhirbhisigh source as an annalistic one, and relates it specifically to the source of *Chronicum Scotorum* (Mc Carthy, *The Irish annals*, p. 311). However, this does not adequately explain the late medieval 'Lecan' material as the extant version of *Chronicum Scotorum* ends in 1150, whereas the Four Masters considered their Lecan source particularly valuable to them for the period after 1227.   101 TCD MS 1301, fos 687–749v; O'Flaherty may have drawn on pre-1333 material also, but that portion of TCD MS 1301 is now lost; it would be unwise to regard 1418 as a confirmed terminal date for his 'Lecan' annals.   102 TCD MS 1301, fo. 712.

the Four Masters' autograph manuscript, and provide clear evidence that some of the late additions made by the Four Masters were derived from annals associated with the learned family of Mac Fhirbhisigh of Lecan.[103]

It is evident, therefore, that the annalists had access to more than one historical manuscript associated with the Mac Fhirbhisigh: they had a now lost set of Lecan annals which they used extensively for fourteenth-and fifteenth-century material, while at about the same time Mícheál Ó Cléirigh is known from other work to have had access to the manuscript now commonly known as the 'Book of Lecan'. Besides the internal evidence of the manuscripts, this conclusion is further supported by evidence noted by Nollaig Ó Muraíle where Dubhaltach Mac Fhirbhisigh cited a *Leabhar Mór Leacáin Mec Fhirbhisigh* in the context of texts not now present in the manuscript generally known as the 'Book of Lecan'.[104] Clearly, there was more than one major medieval historical manuscript associated with the Mac Fhirbhisigh learned family still in circulation in the seventeenth century.

Book of the Island of Saints on Lough Ree

The vellum fragment of annals, known to Sir James Ware as *Annales Prioratus Insulae Omnium SS in Loghree*,[105] survives in Bodl. MS Rawl. B 488, fos 29–34. It is now part of a composite manuscript that was bound in its current form in the seventeenth century.[106] The surviving fragment relates to the years 1392 to 1407. It was in the possession of Sir James Ware by 1636, and he recorded that he had received it in 1627 from Muiris Ó Maoil Chonaire: *dono dedit Mauritius Conry 25 Augusti 1627*.[107] The manuscript was the work of Auguistín Magraidhin, one of the monastic community of Saints' Island, who died in 1405, and was continued after his death by another unnamed scribe who was probably also a member of the same monastic community.[108] The obituary of Magraidhin describes him as:

> *suígh gen rasabhra i nd-eagna dhiadha 7 domhanta etir léghend 7 shenchas 7 eladhnaibh imdha ele archeana, 7 ollamh daeirlabhra iarthair Eorpa, fear tecair in liubhair-sea 7 liubhar imdha ele etir beathaidh naemh 7 shenchas.*
> (an undisputed master of the sacred and secular wisdom, including Latin learning, history, and many other sciences, *ollamh* of eloquence for Western Europe,

---

103 See below, chapter 6, for discussion of the phases of writing and revision engaged in by the scribes. 104 See also Ó Muraíle, *The celebrated antiquary*, pp 178–9. For loss of sections of the Book of Lecan, see *Cat. Ir. mss in RIA*, pp 1551–2. 105 The description is found among Ware's notes from this manuscript in TCD MS 804, pp 327–30. 106 The fragment has been published in full with an English translation as 'Fragment III' in Ó hInnse (ed.), *Miscellaneous Irish annals*, pp 142–85. The preface to the edition contains Ó hInnse's discussion of the provenance of the fragment, and its ownership in the seventeenth century (pp xiv–xviii). 107 Bodl. MS Rawl. B 488, fo. 34; see *Cat. Ir. mss in Bodl.*, I, p. 148. 108 Ó hInnse (ed.), *Miscellaneous Irish annals*, pp xiv–xv.

compiler of this book and many other books, including Lives of the saints and histories.)[109]

The extant portion of the Annals of the Island of Saints contained in Bodl. MS Rawl. B 488 gives a snapshot of the geographical scope of those annals in the late medieval period. Though the surviving late fourteenth-century vellum fragment is an uncertain indicator for the earlier period, it is possible that an earlier portion of these annals might account for many of the early north Leinster entries in AFM.

However, it must be noted that although there are occasional overlaps, there is little indication that these annals, as now extant, were used by the Four Masters for the years for which they survive. It seems clear that the annals from Lough Ree preserved in Rawl. B 488 were already in a fragmentary condition in the early seventeenth century, when they came into the hands of Sir James Ware. The editor of the published version, Séamus Ó hInnse, has shown that these annals were more extensive in Sir James Ware's lifetime than is now the case, since Ware made notes from them concerning events down to the year 1441.[110] The Four Masters may have had an earlier fragment from the same manuscript or alternatively they may have had access to a different historical compilation produced or owned by the monastic community on Saints' Island in Lough Ree. It is known that the Franciscan John Goulde made a transcript of hagiographical material from a vellum manuscript associated with the same Saints' Island in 1627,[111] and it is possible that Mícheál Ó Cléirigh similarly either transcribed an annalistic source from the same location containing entries down to 1228 or borrowed all or part of such a manuscript from the monastery at the Island of Saints either then or subsequently.

Beatha Aodha Ruaidh Uí Dhomhnaill

The Book of Lughaidh Ó Cléirigh is now better known under the title *Beatha Aodha Ruaidh Uí Dhomhnaill*. The autograph manuscript of the Book of Lughaidh Ó Cléirigh is not extant, but the material it contained on the life of Aodh Ruadh Ó Domhnaill has been preserved in a seventeenth-century transcript believed to be in the hand of Cú Choigcríche Ó Cléirigh, one of the Four Masters.[112] The work is now usually identified by its published title of

109 Ó hInnse (ed.), *Miscellaneous Irish annals*, pp 176–7.   110 Ó hInnse (ed.), *Miscellaneous Irish annals*, pp xvi–xvii.   111 FLK MS F 1. This was the *Insulensis* source used by Ó Cléirigh in preparing his Martyrology of Donegal; it consisted of a transcript of material from Bodl. Rawl. B 485 or Rawl. B 505, the latter being a transcript of the former. The same source was later used by John Colgan (Sharpe, *Medieval Irish saints' lives*, pp 247–8; Charles Plummer, 'On two collections of Latin Lives of Irish saints in the Bodleian Library, Rawl. B. 485 and Rawl. B. 505', *Zeitschrift für Celtische Philologie* 5 (1904–5), 429–54).   112 RIA MS 23 P 24; *Cat. Ir. mss in RIA*, pp 396–7.

Beatha Aodha Ruaidh Uí Dhomhnaill.[113] Its form differs from the annalistic compilations that comprised most of the source material for entries in AFM prior to the 1540s. Though arranged by calendar year – the dates being supplied as an afterthought in the margin of the earliest extant copy – the narrative focuses on the career of one man, eulogising his heroic exploits on the battlefield in the course of the Nine Years War. As well as recording his actions, it contextualizes and explains them. Its account of the life and achievements of Aodh Ruadh is presented in discursive prose, and employs artificially archaic language.[114] Being partially reliant on this source, the form and content of the entries in AFM from 1587 to 1602 reflect the very different nature of the sources available to them. Yet, despite their extensive use of Lughaidh Ó Cléirigh's narrative biography, the material in AFM is far from being a simple transcript of that source. Pádraig A. Breatnach has examined in detail the editorial method of Cú Choigriche Ó Cléirigh, one of the Four Masters, who is identified as the compiler of an abridged version of *Beatha Aodha Ruaidh*, now preserved in an eighteenth-century transcript in NLI MS G 488.[115] It can be argued that a very similar editorial process was undertaken in adapting the *Beatha Aodha Ruaidh* narratives for inclusion in AFM.

The biographical narrative preserved in *Beatha Aodha Ruaidh* and selectively incorporated into AFM, though by far the most extensive, was not the only Ó Domhnaill narrative material incorporated into AFM. From the latter half of the fifteenth century, AFM abounds with short narratives in which the military exploits of prominent members of the Uí Dhomhnaill are recounted. The extent of such entries is very considerable, they are usually by far the longest annalistic entries recorded for the years in which they occur. While a number of them can also be found, in quite similar form, in AU, in other instances the Uí Dhomhnaill narratives in AFM are not found in any other extant annals. Given the rise in political prominence of the Uí Dhomhnaill in this period, it should come as no surprise to find that their military exploits were recorded and praised by the learned class.[116] This material will be considered in more detail in the case study of the representation of the Uí Dhomhnaill in a later chapter.

Annals of Maoilín Óg Mac Bruaideadha

The source described by the Four Masters as the book of Maoilín Óg Mac Bruaidheadha, was clearly a recent compilation. It contained annals relating to

113 Paul Walsh (ed.), *Beatha Aodha Ruaidh Uí Dhomhnaill [BARUD]* (2 vols, ITS, London, 1948, 1957).   114 *BARUD*, II, pp 18–19. A comparative analysis of the language of BARUD and AFM is provided in Pádraig A. Breatnach, 'Irish records of the Nine Years' War: a brief survey, with particular notice of the relationship between BARUD and the Annals of the Four Masters' in Ó Riain (ed.), *Beatha Aodha Ruaidh* (2002), pp 124–47.   115 Pádraig A. Breatnach, 'A seventeenth-century abridgement of *Beatha Aodha Ruaidh Uí Dhomhnaill*', *Éigse* 33 (2002), 77–172.   116 See Katharine Simms, 'Niall Garbh II O'Donnell, king of Tír Conaill, 1422–39', *Donegal Annual* 12:1

the years 1588 to 1603. Although it is no longer extant, some of its contents can be deduced from the entries relating to Thomond incorporated into the Annals of the Four Masters for those years.[117] Their concise entries look somewhat out of place juxtaposed with the longer more discursive narrative material from the life of Aodh Ruadh Ó Domhnaill, which was the annalists' principal source for these years. The inclusion of a Munster source here may hint obliquely that the Four Masters were aware of the anti-Uí Bhriain dimension to Lughaidh Ó Cléirigh's life of Aodh Ruadh. Read in this way, it provides evidence of the Four Masters' concern that their annals should bring together Leath Cuinn and Leath Mogha.[118]

Other sources

Even if all the manuscript sources consulted by the Four Masters could be identified as still extant, it is probable that they would not record every detail contained in AFM. Although their work was carefully prefaced with an itemization of the authorities on which it was based, it is likely, particularly for the period from the mid-sixteenth century, that material other than that recorded in earlier annalistic compilations was included. It is clear that the Four Masters had no reservations about incorporating recent compilations, including the work of some of their own contemporaries. This was clearly the case in respect of Lughaidh Ó Cléirigh's biographical narrative (which may have been written as late as 1627),[119] and also the annals of Maoilín Óg Mac Bruaideadha. They may also have included information derived from non-written sources, recording information that came to hand from *lucht sgailte na scél 7 chuartaighthi na cuan* ('the folk who spread news and frequent ports'),[120] to supplement the information available to them from manuscript sources. Their Franciscan sources, too, were derived in part from the personal recollections of members of the community, and provide evidence that the annalists were willing to draw on eye-witness accounts of some events recorded in the closing section of their text.[121] None of the annalistic sources named by the Four Masters cover the middle years of the sixteenth century, from the mid-1530s to 1587, yet AFM contains a substantial range of entries for these years. Since they showed no reluctance in naming the very recently compiled sources that they used for the years after 1587, it seems unlikely that they would have neglected to mention their source for the decades

(1977), 7–21 for the evidence available on one prominent Ó Domhnaill leader. **117** Bernadette Cunningham, 'The historical annals of Maoilín Óg Mac Bruaideadha, 1588–1603', *The Other Clare* 13 (1989), 21–8. **118** For a similar argument concerning AFM, using different evidence, see Joep Leerssen, *Mere Irish and Fíor Ghael* (2nd ed. Cork, 1996), p. 268. **119** Mícheál Mac Craith, 'The *Beatha* in the context of the literature of the Renaissance' in Ó Riain (ed.), *Beatha Aodha Ruaidh* (2002), p. 53. **120** *AU*, III, pp 538–9. **121** See, for instance, the material evidently supplied by those Franciscans resident in the Donegal community who had been at the death-bed of Aodh Ruadh Ó Domhnaill in 1602, as discussed below, pp 186–7.

prior to 1587 if such material had already been written down as a coherent historical compilation in any of the schools of history with which they had contact.

Neither their list of sources, nor the extant manuscripts that can be traced reach anything approaching the full spectrum of sources utilized by the Four Masters in the compilation of their annals, and this reality places constraints on the kind of analysis of their methodology that can be undertaken.[122]

Among the more recent source materials available to the Four Masters to assist in the compilation of their chronicle was a series of texts they had themselves prepared. These included a new recension of the *Leabhar gabhála*, prepared in 1631, complete with its own prefatory material and dedication, the Martyrology of Donegal, of which two versions had been compiled by 1630, and a summary of the genealogies of Irish kings and saints, which included chronological information that facilitated its use as a framework for the annals.

Leabhar gabhála

For any historian in the Gaelic tradition writing a comprehensive history of Ireland, the inclusion of the origin myth of the peoples of Ireland as traditionally recorded in the *Leabhar gabhála* was a necessary element. Thus, for example, Geoffrey Keating's *Foras feasa ar Éirinn*, written contemporaneously with AFM, accepted the series of invasions of Ireland as an integral part of its narrative framework.[123] The Four Masters likewise adopted the *Leabhar gabhála* material as the basic framework of the pre-Christian section of their annals. For this reason, Paul Walsh has described the opening section of AFM as essentially comprising a recension of the *Leabhar gabhála* presented in the form of annals.[124] However, the annalists did not merely adopt the *Leabhar gabhála* tradition without revision. Rather, they began their work on the secular history of Ireland by creating an entirely new recension of the *Leabhar gabhála*.[125] Their prose version of the text differs significantly from the versions found in older manuscript sources because it omitted the biblical elements that were normally part of the text. Their new version, bereft of biblical allusions, provided much of

---

122 In a review of the *Annals of Connacht*, for example, Aubrey Gwynn has discussed the source of some of the early Leinster material in AFM, which he speculates probably originated at Clonenagh, but the source appears to be no longer extant (*Studies: an Irish Quarterly Review* 33:131 (1944), 416–19). **123** Comyn and Dinneen (eds), *Foras feasa ar Éirinn*, I, pp 138–237; II, pp 2–63. **124** Walsh, *The Four Masters and their work*, p. 5. **125** The draft of this work predominantly in the hand of Mícheál Ó Cléirigh is now RIA MS 23 M 70, the opening part being now fragmentary (though the manuscript has been restored and rebound). An unfinished edition of the work, based on the enhanced version in the hand of Cú Choigcríche Ó Cléirigh (RIA MS 23 K 32), already mentioned, was published as Macalister and MacNeill (eds), *Leabhar gabhála*. Parts 2 and 3 of this proposed edition were never published. Ó Cléirigh's dedication to Brian Ruadh Mág Uidhir, together with the address to the reader, survive in another transcript of the text, now TCD MS 1286, and were published, with translation, in O'Curry, *Lectures on manuscript materials*, pp 169–73,

the essential framework for the opening pre-historic section of AFM. Drawing on *Leabhar gabhála* in combination with its continuation in the *Réim ríoghraidhe*, the Four Masters arranged the material within a rigidly chronological framework defined by the reigns of kings. They named the four source manuscripts on which they principally relied, three of them associated with the Four Masters' own families, the fourth text being the Book of Leinster.[126] Versions of the *Leabhar gabhála* were widely available and, as noted above, the Four Masters made clear that they had constructed their version of the *Leabhar gabhála* from a range of authoritative sources. While a detailed analysis of their recension of *Leabhar gabhála* does not form part of this book, their attitude to the source manuscripts from which they derived their recension is relevant. Far from being a rescue mission to preserve a particular text of the *Leabhar gabhála* from loss, it is clear that the Four Masters departed radically from the versions available in the authoritative and quite early sources available to them. They prepared a quite distinct recension, probably intended for eventual publication. Their objective was not the transcription or preservation of earlier sources, but the creation of an appropriately revised account of the remote Irish past.

Genealogiae regum et sanctorum Hiberniae

Even before the Four Masters prepared a new recension of *Leabhar gabhála*, the same four chroniclers had collaborated on another historical project to produce a work which they entitled rather cumbersomely *Seanchas ríogh Érenn: Genealuighi na naomh nÉreannach*. The more generally known Latin title of the published edition is used here.[127] The autograph manuscript is partly in the hand of Mícheál Ó Cléirigh, but there are layers of later annotations in a variety of other hands. It is now preserved as UCD–OFM MS A 16, and that manuscript formed the basis of the edition published by Paul Walsh. The prefatory material indicates that the genealogies of saints were the main focus and that the reigns of kings were ancillary to the primary purpose of making the saints of Ireland better known.

The work itemized the genealogies of the kings of Ireland, beginning with Sláinghe, and followed by his brothers Rudhroighe, Gann, Geanann and Seangann. It moved through the various phases of invasions, providing separate chapters for the kings of the Fir Bolg, the kings of the Tuatha Dé Danann, and the kings of the Clann Mhíleadh up to the coming of Christianity.[128] The text then commenced a new section devoted to the genealogies of the kings of Ireland

552–7; see above, chapter three.   **126** In respect of the Book of Leinster, it is known that while working on collecting lives of Irish saints, Mícheál Ó Cléirigh had access to the Book of Leinster or a copy of it in Kildare in October 1627 (Jennings, *Michael O Cleirigh and his associates*, pp 57–8). **127** Paul Walsh (ed.), *Genealogiae regum et sanctorum Hiberniae by the Four Masters* [*GRSH*] (Maynooth 1918).   **128** *GRSH*, pp 11–29.

after the advent of Christianity, beginning with Laoghaire, who reigned for thirty years before his death in AD458, and ending with Maoilsechlainn who died in 1022. Finally, this first part of the *Genealogiae regum et sanctorum Hiberniae* contains a short section recording the genealogies of six kings of Ireland 'with opposition', ending with Ruaidhrí Ó Conchobhair in the twelfth century.[129]

While the date 1630 is clearly stated as the date of compilation in the dedication to this work, it can be seen from the autograph manuscript (UCD–OFM MS A 16) that various scribes added further details to the text. Not least among these additions was the insertion of *Anno mundi* and *Anno Domini* dates for the reigns of each king, a feature that greatly enhanced the work's usefulness as a framework for the annals. Since these dating elements are mentioned in the preface to the reader, they were probably among the very first additions to Ó Cléirigh's basic text.[130] It is unclear whether the Four Masters already had access to an annalistic source from which these dates were derived or whether they are based on their own calculations about chronology derived from their *Réim ríoghraidhe* sources.[131] Unlike the earlier sections, no AD dates are supplied for the reigns of five of the six kings 'with opposition',[132] perhaps indicating that this closing section was of less interest than the earlier parts of the work as a source for the framework of the annals. That the chronological detail found in this recension of the *Réim ríoghraidhe* closely resembles the framework of the reigns of kings as preserved in the Annals of the Four Masters is beyond doubt. The reigns of kings cease to be systematically itemized in AFM after the year 1022. It is also notable that the sense that the year 1022 marked the termination of a major phase in the history of the kingship of Ireland is echoed in the scribal treatment of that year and the subsequent year 1023 in one of the autograph manuscripts of AFM.[133]

Unlike in the case of the *Leabhar gabhála* and the annals themselves, the Four Masters did not specify their sources for the *Genealogiae regum et sanctorum Hiberniae*, though the text is prefaced by a general list of authorities on Irish history.[134] Given that the compilation was done in Co. Westmeath, under the patronage of Toirrdhealbhach Mac Cochláin and with the cooperation of Conall Mac Eochagáin, it seems reasonable to assume that the manuscripts on which

129 *GRSH*, pp 30–6.   130 *GRSH*, pp 7–8, 144. The preface itself is not explicitly dated, but it is signed by each of the Four Masters and probably dates from the time of completion of the original draft of the work on 4 November 1630.   131 The dates for the kings of the Fir Bolg and the Tuatha Dé Danann are in a different hand and ink from the rest, and so may have been added at a different time. Curiously, in the later transcript of the text in TCD MS 1348, the *Anno mundi* and *Anno Domini* dates appear to have been calculated independently from those in UCD–OFM MS A 16. The TCD manuscript is in two volumes and was transcribed by Maurice Gorman, *c*.1770 from a manuscript written by Pól Ó Colla in 1644.   132 *GRSH*, p. 36.   133 The heading for the year 1023 is written in extra large lettering, on a new page, in UCD–OFM MS A 13, fo. 410(a) r, as though it were intended as the opening page of a new volume of the annals. The same is not true of the other autograph manuscript, RIA MS C iii 3.   134 UCD–OFM MS A 16, fo. xvi.

they principally relied could have been in the possession of Conall Mac Eochagáin. His approbation affixed to the autograph manuscript attested that he had seen the sources from which the work of the Four Masters derived:

> *Ataimsi Conall mac Neill Meg Eochagáin o Lios Maighne a gCinel Fhiachach a gcundae iairthair Midhi, dhuine uasal, admhalach go bhfhaca me na leabair chruthaighthe do bhi ag an leabar sa, agus dfhiaghnuisi ar sin do cuir me mo lamh an ceathramhadh la do mhí Nouembir anno Domini 1630.*
>
> (I Conall son of Niall Mac Geoghegan of Lios Maighne in Cineal Fhiachach in the county of Westmeath, gentleman, testify that I have seen the source books of this book, and as witness thereto I set my hand the fourth of November Anno Domini 1630.)[135]

While the availability of patronage may have been a significant factor, the availability of a particular manuscript source or sources is probably the best explanation for the Four Masters' presence in the neighbourhood of Lismoyny while executing this work. Mc Carthy has put forward the hypothesis that the manuscript in question is now part of BR MS 2569–72, containing a transcript of the poem *Éire árd, inis na ríogh*, which he tentatively identifies as being in the hand of George Dillon, OFM, guardian of Athlone.[136] However, neither the list of poems on fo. 16 of BR MS 2569–72, which Mc Carthy attributes to Ó Cléirigh,[137] nor the annotations in the lower margins of fos 94r, 95r, 97v and 99r, are in the hand of Mícheál Ó Cléirigh.[138] Instead, the list at BR MS 2569–72, fo. 16 is in the same hand and compiled for the same purpose as the index pages that now precede the annals text in RIA MS 23 P 6, fos 1–8. These crude indexes post-date the compilation of the annals.

Mc Carthy also suggests that Conall Mac Eochagáin might have supplied the exemplar from which the text of the poem was copied.[139] The poem was a particularly well-known one, found in many manuscripts to which Ó Cléirigh could have had access, and he had already transcribed this poem in 1627–8 from the Book of Leinster.[140] However, Mc Carthy rightly emphasizes that the variant dating found in the poem as transcribed in BR MS 2569–72, fos 94r–99r, of the time that elapsed between the various 'invasions' of Ireland, corresponds to that adopted by the Four Masters.[141]

As in other instances, the task undertaken by the Four Masters clearly involved far more than simple transcription of a single older text. The preface to

135 *GRSH*, pp 9, 145.   **136** Mc Carthy, *The Irish annals*, pp 294–5, where the MS is cited by the Van den Gheyn catalogue entry number 4640.   **137** The index is found at BR MS 2569–72, fos 16–16v.   **138** Mc Carthy may have derived this identification of the hand from J.H. Todd's account of the manuscript (*PRIA* 3 (1845–7), 482), but Todd was clearly mistaken. For a refutation of a separate instance of Todd's misidentification of Ó Cléirigh's hand, see Breatnach, 'An Irish Bollandus', 28.   **139** Mc Carthy, *The Irish annals*, pp 295–7.   **140** RIA MS B iv 2, fos 101–107v; the transcript ends at fo. 107v, followed by the words '*sliocht Liubhair na hUa Chongbala*' [extract from the Book of Leinster].   **141** Mc Carthy, *The Irish annals*, p. 296, figure 42.

the reader of the *Genealogiae regum et sanctorum Hiberniae*, signed by each of the Four Masters, conveys the sense of a more complex engagement with the available sources than that. Having described Ó Cléirigh's four years of research on hagiographical manuscripts, the preface explains the coming together of the Four Masters and the thinking behind this, the team's first collaborative project:

GRSH

Tangadar na pearsonna rémhraitte go hénionadh 7 iar ttorrachtain do chinnsead na cceathror rémenna rioghraidhe na hEreann do sccriobhadh i ttosach an liubhair do tionnsgainsiod ar dá ádhbhar. An céd adhbhar, uair nír fédadh seancas na naomh do breth isin raon díreach go a mbunadhas gan seanchos na riogh do bheth reampa, ar as uatha ro shiolsad. An dara hadhbar, ionnas go madh móide dúthracht 7 devotion na ndaoineadh uasal da naomhaibh da ccomharbaibh 7 ceallaibh fios a ccairdis 7 a ccaradraidh do beth aca re a bpátrúnaibh beannaighthe 7 re duthchasnaomhaibh na fremhe da mbeth gach craobh diobh 7 fós fios nuimre naomh na craoibhe cédna. 'Oir atá gach aicme do naomhaibh na hErenn, don mhéd fríth iar nurd a seanchas díbh, diaidh a ndiaidh gan tréchomascc sleachta for aroile, acht amhail ro ghabhlaighsiod 7 ro sgaoilsead ó a mbunaidhfremhaibh. Gibé tú, a léghtóir, legmíd a mheas ad leth fén go bfuil tarbha effeacht eolas 7 athcuimriocht isin saothar so, óir atá rém na riogh guna ngluinibh genealaighe go bunadh ann, do rér mar do ghabhsat rioghacht iar nurd, guna naireamh bliadhan, go naois an domhain a bforbhadh flatha gach rígh díobh, 7 go naois ar ttigearna 'Iosu ó a ionchollnughadh go hécc Maoileachloinn mhóir; 7 na naoimh do rér uird aibghitre 7 do rér a mbunadhais mar do raidheamar romhainn.

(These men came together in one place, and when they came, the four agreed that they should insert a list of the kings of Ireland in the beginning of the book they had commenced, for two reasons: the first, because it was impossible to trace the descent of the saints directly to their origins without first setting down the descent of the kings, for it is from these that the saints sprung; the second, that the reverence and devotion of the nobility for their saints, comharbs and churches might be increased by knowledge of their connexion and kinship with their holy patrons and with the tribal saints of the stock to which each family belonged, and by knowledge of the number of saints connected with each family. For each group of the saints of Ireland, in so far as they have been found traced to their origins, is set down in succession without mixing one with another, but as they branched off and separated from their original stocks.

Whoever thou art, reader, we leave it to thy judgment whether there be profit, advantage, knowledge and brevity in this work, for it contains the Succession of the Kings with the genealogy of each to his origin, the number of the years and the Age of the World at the conclusion of his reign, and, from the Incarnation to the death of Maoilsheachloinn the Great, the Age of Christ also; and the saints' names in alphabetical order according to their descent as we have said above.)[142]

The compilers drew the attention of readers to the particular manner in which the entries were arranged, and indeed this feature distinguishes their version

142 *GRSH*, p. 8; with trans. pp 143–4.

from earlier texts containing similar genealogical material. The preface also made clear that the genealogies of saints were the principal focus of attention for the compilers and suggested that the inclusion of the genealogies of kings was of secondary significance. However, the material on the origins of kings proved to be of key importance as part of the framework of AFM.

Daniel Mc Carthy has demonstrated that the chronology of kings devised for the *Genealogiae regum et sanctorum Hiberniae* corresponded exactly with that subsequently used in the Annals of the Four Masters.[143] He also notes that the detail of this chronology up to the year 1022 was derived by Ó Cléirigh not from the *Leabhar gabhála*, but rather from the historical poems of Gilla Cóemáin.[144] The poems *Éire árd, inis na ríogh* and *Atá sund forba feasa*, attributed to Gilla Cóemáin, are among the lengthy historical poems transcribed by Mícheál Ó Cléirigh in RIA MS B iv 2, a miscellany assembled in 1627 and 1628 partly from the Book of Leinster when Ó Cléirigh was also engaged on transcribing saints' Lives.[145] Peter Smith has shown that while there is a close relationship between *Éire árd, inis na ríogh* and the *Leabhar gabhála*, the poem has been preserved independently in the manuscripts from at least the twelfth century.[146] As noted above, Mc Carthy has argued that another Franciscan transcript of the poem *Éire árd, inis na ríogh*, now preserved in BR MS 2569–72 may have been the working draft used by Ó Cléirigh and his team as the basis of their chronological calculations in the *Genealogiae regum et sanctorum Hiberniae*.[147] Smith has drawn attention to other copies of what may be an Ó Cléirigh recension of the poem, including that incorporated in the Four Masters' revision of the *Leabhar gabhála*. He posits that the redactor may have been Mícheál Ó Cléirigh, but holds that some subsequent revisions were the work of Cú Choigcríche Ó Cléirigh.[148]

A second contemporary copy of the Four Masters' *Genealogiae regum et sanctorum Hiberniae* is preserved in RIA MS 24 P 33. This copy appears to post-date 1636, since it includes not just the transcripts of approbations provided by Conall Mac Eochagáin in 1630 and Flann Mac Aodhagáin in 1632, but also one by Conchobhar Mac Bruaideadha dated 2 November 1636, copied into the text ahead of that of Conall Mac Eochagáin.[149]

143 D.P. Mc Carthy, 'Collation of the Irish regnal canon', www.cs.tcd.ie/Dan.McCarthy/chronology/synchronisms/annals-chron. accessed November 2008. 144 Mc Carthy, *The Irish annals*, pp 193–4; See also Peter J. Smith, *Three historical poems ascribed to Gilla Cóemáin: a critical edition of the work of an eleventh-century Irish scholar* (Münster, 2007). 145 *Cat. Ir. mss in RIA*, pp 3021–9; for an edition of the Book of Leinster version of these poems see R.I. Best, M.A. O'Brien and A. O'Sullivan (eds), *The Book of Leinster, formerly Lebar na Núachongbála* (6 vols, Dublin, 1957–83), iii, pp 471–95. 146 Smith, *Gilla Cóemáin*, p. 26; see also John Carey, '*Lebor gabála* and the legendary history of Ireland' in Helen Fulton (ed.), *Medieval Celtic literature and society* (Dublin, 2005), pp 44–5. 147 Mc Carthy, *The Irish annals*, p. 294. 148 NLI MS G 131, RIA MS B iv 2, RIA MS C iv 3, BR MS 2569–72. RIA MS 23 K 32, pp 164–73 contains the text incorporated into the Ó Cléirigh recension of *Leabhar gabhála*; for a preliminary discussion, see Smith, *Gilla Cóemáin*, pp 37–9, 55–6; for analysis of another such redaction of a historical poem, see Pádraig A. Breatnach, 'The methodology of *seanchas*: the redaction by Cú Choigcríche Ó Cléirigh of the chronicle poem *Leanam Croinic Clann nDálaigh*', *Éigse* 29 (1996), 1–18. 149 RIA MS 24 P 33,

The genealogies of saints in the Four Masters' compilation have been briefly discussed by Pádraig Ó Riain in the preface to his *Corpus genealogiarum sanctorum Hiberniae*.[150] Ó Riain has shown that the Four Masters treated the version of the text found in the *Leabhar Breac*[151] as their basic authority, occasionally supplementing it by reference to other versions. His further assertion, however, that they also had access in 1630 or earlier to the metrical version of the *Naomhsheanchas* as found in the Book of Lecan might require modification. Most of the evidence he cites for the influence of the Book of Lecan text on particular readings found in the Four Masters' prose version of the *Naomhsheanchas* is contained in the annotations added to OFM–UCD MS A 16, and was not part of the basic text as originally penned by Mícheál Ó Cléirigh.[152] It could well have been added as late as 1636.

While Ó Riain's basic argument for the influence of the Book of Lecan source on the completed text inclusive of later annotations is not disputed here, the dating he suggests in arguing that the Lecan text was available to the Four Masters in or before 1630 is not accepted on the basis of the evidence offered. Rather, the evidence of the autograph manuscript indicates that the features to which Ó Riain draws attention concerning the influence of the Book of Lecan on the Four Masters' *Genealogiae regum et sanctorum Hiberniae*, when seen for what they are as revisions to the text rather than as part of the original draft prepared in 1630, supports the evidence discussed elsewhere that the Book of Lecan only

pp 43–98; the Irish-language approbations are on p. 45. Although the catalogue description identifies the hand of the manuscript as 'almost certainly' that of Mícheál Ó Cléirigh (*Cat. Ir. mss in RIA*, p. 3005), the characteristic curled ascenders of Ó Cléirigh's hand are not in evidence. The copy signature of Mícheál Ó Cléirigh on p. 45 includes diacritics and underlining that are not characteristic of his actual signature. The words *cóip fhirinneach* ('authentic copy') appear twice on the page containing the Irish approbations (p. 45). It is possible that the date given in this transcript, 2 November 1636, was a misreading of 11 November 1636 as Ó Cléirigh was with Flann Mac Aodhagain in Tipperary on 2 November 1636.   150 Pádraig Ó Riain (ed.), *Corpus genealogiarum sanctorum Hiberniae* (Dublin, 1985), pp xlii–xlv.   151 RIA MS 23 P 16.   152 Ó Riain, *Corpus genealogiarum sanctorum Hiberniae*, p. xlv. *GRSH*, chapter 12, entry 9: in UCD–OFM MS A 16, fo. 34v, the reference to Dallán Forgaill in Eochaidh mac Colla's pedigree is interlined; *GRSH*, chapter 9, entries 1, 7, 16: in the Four Masters' autograph manuscript only the saint's name is in Ó Cléirigh's hand in each of these three entries, the remainder of the entry is a later addition in another hand, and thus could have been added from the Book of Lecan source as late as 1636 (UCD–OFM MS A 16, fos 29r–31r). These additions to UCD–OFM MS A 16 are not found in the other seventeenth-century version of the text in RIA MS 24 P 33 (pp 69–70), a fact that lends support to the suggestion that they were later insertions in UCD–OFM MS A 16. On the question of influences of the first prose recension of the *Naomhsheanchas* from the Book of Lecan, Ó Riain cites as an example *GRSH*, chapter 22, entries 19 and 20. In entry 19, the genealogy of *Muirgen*, the qualification *.i. :Liban* is an interlineation in UCD–OFM MS A 16, fo. 73v, possibly added later as in the above cases. The detail in entry 20, the genealogy of Senan, contains no later amendments, but appears to resemble that in the Book of Leinster (LL, 352d) more closely than that in the Book of Lecan (Lec 1, 37v b c) in that it includes *Laithrigh Briuin* (UCD–OFM MS A 16, fo. 74r). Thus it seems that it is not necessary to assume the influence of the Book of Lecan version in this example either. The one remaining piece of evidence for the influence of the metrical *Naomhsheanchas* from the Book of Lecan on the Four Masters' recension, the coincidence of the name form *Modichu* in both texts (Ó Riain, *Corpus genealogiarum regum Hiberniae*, pp xliv–xlv), seems too insubstantial to

became available to the Four Masters after 1634 when Conall Mac Eochagáin borrowed it from James Ussher.[153] This detail highlights yet again the approach of the Four Masters to their sources. They sought out the most authoritative sources available, and in this case they evidently included, amongst others, the *Leabhar Breac* and the Book of Lecan. They made selections as required from those sources to create not a transcript but a new text, quite distinct in its arrangement from the sources from which it derived. Even after an initial draft was completed, they continued to work on their recension of the *Genealogiae regum et sanctorum Hiberniae*, supplementing it as additional material of relevance became available. The incremental nature of their work is indicated not merely by the evidence of a variety of scribal hands but in this instance also by the approbations. In addition to the testimonies of George Dillon and Conall Mac Eochagáin supplied on 4 November 1630 when the initial phase of work was completed, two other approbations were added much later. Flann Mac Aodhagáin's approbation is dated 31 August 1632, while that of Conchobhar Mac Bruaideadha is dated 2 November 1636.[154] The latest approbation is that of Thomas Fleming, which is dated 6 February 1637.[155] The date-range of these approbations provides evidence that a copy of the text remained with Ó Cléirigh in Ireland until at least February 1637, by which time the work on AFM was completed, and that *Genealogiae regum et sanctorum Hiberniae* may have continued to be augmented during those years.

Martyrology of Donegal

The Annals of the Four Masters are generally built around secular rather than ecclesiastical sources, but nonetheless saints' obits are integrated into the text. Two seventeenth-century compilations were used by the Four Masters as a source for this material. The most significant was Ó Cléirigh's earlier work known as the Martyrology of Donegal.[156] The second recension of that work, which includes a comprehensive index also in the hand of Mícheál Ó Cléirigh, was completed on 19 April 1630 in Donegal.[157] That martyrology was partly derived, in turn, from the Martyrology of Gorman.[158] There is a sufficiently

---

be of relevance when the other pieces of evidence are removed from consideration. 153 Walsh, *Irish men of learning*, p. 107; a scribe writing in 1660 refers to Conall Mac Eochagáin having obtained the Book of Lecan from James Ussher in 1634 (King's Inn's Gaelic MS 4, p. 55; *Cat. Ir. mss in King's Inns*, p. 10), while Pól Ó Colla, writing in 1644, mentions Conall Mac Eochagáin having transcribed the Book of Rights from the Book of Lecan on 4 August 1636 (RIA MS 23 D 9, p. 1; *Cat. Ir. mss in RIA*, pp 416–17). 154 *GRSH*, p. 146; this Mac Bruaideadha approbation is found in RIA MS 24 P 33, p. 45. It is possible that this date is a mis-reading of 11 November in the original manuscript. See below, chapter nine, p. 278 (n. 163). 155 RIA MS 24 P 33, p. 47. The manuscript reads '1636', but if the year is taken as beginning on 1 January rather than 25 March then the year in question in 1637. 156 J.H. Todd and W. Reeves (eds), *The martyrology of Donegal: a calendar of the saints of Ireland: Féilire na naomh nErennach* (Dublin, 1864). 157 BR MS 5095–6. The index occupies fos 66–100v, and the date of completion is given at fo. 100v. 158 The twelfth-

close correspondence between the dates given for individual saints in AFM and in the Martyrology of Donegal to be confident that it was systematically consulted in the course of compiling the annals.[159] Indeed, Pádraig Ó Riain goes further and suggests that the two works may have proceeded in tandem, arguing that a preliminary draft of AFM may have been available to the compilers of the Martyrology of Donegal as early as 1628.[160] When this suggestion is considered together with the evidence of Ó Cléirigh's transcripts of secular historical sources in RIA MS B iv 2, it emerges that significant preparatory work on the Annals may have been underway from about the time Ó Cléirigh first returned to conduct research in Ireland in 1626.

Other contemporary source compilations

The Four Masters also took care to include the foundation dates of numerous Franciscan monasteries in their chronology of the Irish past. Their principal source for this material was a recently compiled work by a former Franciscan provincial, Francis O'Mahony, entitled *Brevis synopsis Provinciae Hyberniae FF Minorum*,[161] an Irish translation of which was prepared in Donegal by the Franciscan Muiris Ulltach mac Seáin for the use of the Four Masters.[162] The Ó Cléirigh book of genealogies, a version of which is now preserved as RIA MS 23 D 17, a manuscript that also contains notes on Franciscan matters and is believed to be in the hand of Cú Choigcríche Ó Cléirigh, should probably likewise be regarded as a working document originally prepared by the same group in connection with the compilation of the annals.[163] However, Mícheál Ó Cléirigh's transcript of *Cogadh Gaedhel re Gallaibh* seems not to have been utilized by the annalists, though John Colgan later cited it in his annotations on the lives of saints.[164]

century source now survives in Mícheál Ó Cléirigh's 1633 transcript, BR MS 5100–4, fos 124–97v. The published edition of Ó Cléirigh's transcript is William Stokes (ed.), *Félire Húi Gormáin: the Martyrology of Gorman* (Henry Bradshaw Society XI, London, 1895). **159** Pádraig Ó Riain, *Feastdays of the saints: a history of Irish martyrologies*, Subsidia Hagiographia 86 (Brussels, 2006), 281–313. **160** Ó Riain, *Feastdays of the saints*, 301. **161** Jennings (ed.), 'Brevis synopsis', 139–91. Their use of this source is discussed in the ecclesiastical case study in chapter eight below. **162** Jennings (ed.), 'Brevis synopsis', 142. **163** The date of compilation of this set of genealogies has not been satisfactorily established. The extant manuscript, RIA MS 23 D 17, is in the hand of Cú Choigcríche Ó Cléirigh, one of the Four Masters, but Ó Muraíle notes that it was assembled 'at some time, as yet undetermined, in the period c.1630–64' (Nollaig Ó Muraíle (ed.), *Leabhar mór na ngenealach: the great book of Irish genealogies* (5 vols, Dublin, 2003), i, p. 12). The text of RIA MS 23 D 17 has been edited in Séamus Pender, 'The O'Clery book of genealogies', *Analecta Hibernica* 15 (1951), xi–xxxiii, 1–198. **164** J.H. Todd (ed.), *Cogadh Gaedhel re Gallaibh. The war of the Gaedhil with the Gaill, or the invasions of Ireland by the Danes and other Norsemen.* Rolls series (London, 1867); Mícheal Ó Cléirigh's transcript (BR MS 1569–72, made in November 1635 from a copy he had made some years earlier at Multyfarnham) is now the only complete version of this work (Jennings, *Michael O Cleirigh and his associates*, p. 60); Colgan, *Acta sanctorum Hiberniae*, p. 106.

Conclusion

In the light of the evidence discussed in the final section of this chapter, it is clear that the research on Irish manuscripts that underpinned the work of the Four Masters ranged well beyond the pre-existing annalistic compilations that undoubtedly served as their model. It is clear that they had access to an extensive range of source manuscripts, old and new, in prose and verse, and that the annals they produced were quite different in scope and content from those that had previously existed. Thus, AFM records much unique material on Irish history not simply because the compilers drew on annalistic sources no longer extant, but also because they consulted a much broader range of source materials than just annals.[165] The following chapters will explore in more detail the form and structure of the annals that they produced and will consider the working methods of the Four Masters as they engaged with the variety of sources available to them.

---

165 Walsh, *The Four Masters and their work*, pp 8–9.

CHAPTER FOUR

Form and structure of the Annals of the Four Masters

Introduction

The Annals of the Four Masters open with the year AM2242 and end with the year AD1616. While not every year is itemized by the annalists in the opening part – from the year of the flood, which they date to AM2242 (as in the Septuagint),[1] down to the year AM3266 – there is continuous annual coverage once the year AM3266 is reached. That year marked the opening of the reign of the first king, Sláinghe. The text continues thereafter, itemizing each regnal year down to the year AM5199. The opening year of the Christian era, AD1, follows immediately on from AM5199, though the scribes start the year AD1 on a new page in each of the two autograph manuscripts. After that, every year of the Christian era from AD1 to AD1616 is itemized, though the closing section, after the year 1605, is fragmentary in both manuscripts. This is particularly the case with TCD MS 1301, in which the fragmentary surviving entry for 1616 is misplaced, though the manuscript contains annual headings for most years up to that date. The unbound, damaged condition of RIA MS 23 P 7 prior to its acquisition and conservation by the Royal Irish Academy means that it is not possible to discern the number of leaves that may once have existed between the entry for AD1611 and that for AD1616.

The two sets of autograph copies of the annals are on laid handmade rag paper of uniformly good quality,[2] apart from two vellum leaves containing Mícheál Ó Cléirigh's dedication to his patron, Fearghal Ó Gadhra.[3] In each manuscript, the text is laid out in single column, with clear annual headings, in a planned and consistent manner throughout, though the initial pages of RIA MS C iii 3 are less carefully presented. There are generous margins and spaces for the insertion of additional material. Three parts of the autograph manuscripts are in generally good condition; the remaining two, RIA MSS 23 P 6 and 23 P 7,

---

1 That equates to the year 2957BC. For the use of the Septuagint dating system in medieval chronicles, and for the Four Masters' adoption of this system, see Mc Carthy, *The Irish annals*, pp 119–22, 297. 2 RIA MS C iii 3 (AM2242–AD1171); UCD–OFM MS A 13 (AM2242–AD1169); TCD MS 1301 (AD1334–1605), RIA MS 23 P 6 (AD1170–1499), RIA MS 23 P 7 (AD1500–1616). 3 These vellum leaves are currently misplaced, being bound into RIA MS 23 P 6, between the entries for AD1207 and AD1208, the point that marks the beginning of the second volume as conceived by the annalists. The dedication on vellum was presumably intended to be placed at the beginning of the first volume of one complete set. A variant version of the dedication on paper is incorporated into RIA MS C iii 3, fos [vi]r–v.

were comprehensively restored in the nineteenth century.[4] None of the current bindings dates from the seventeenth century, but a former binding of UCD–OFM A 13, of probable seventeenth-century date, has been preserved.[5] The mid-eighteenth-century bindings of the Ó Gadhra set of autograph manuscripts (RIA MS C iii 3 and TCD MS 1301), are currently in need of repair.[6]

The description of the outline contents of the annals, together with the overview of form and structure presented in this chapter, is based principally on the two sets of extant autograph manuscripts, because the standard printed edition, edited by John O'Donovan from later copies, is misleading in respect of the fundamental issue of the content of the autograph manuscripts for the years from AM2242 down to AD653. O'Donovan's edition, following the example of O'Conor's earlier printed version, omits approximately 88 per cent of the annual entries contained in the autograph manuscripts for the pre-Christian period. The omitted entries are those that are repetitive and uninformative, containing little or no information other than the regnal year. Thus of the 1,948 years itemized in the autograph manuscripts up to the year AM1599 (1BC), just 219 are printed in O'Donovan's edition. For example, where O'Donovan's printed text skips from AM3371, the first year of the reign of King Eochaidh Ollathair, to AM3450, the year of his death some eighty years later, each and every one of the intervening years from AM3372 to AM3449 is itemized in the two autograph manuscripts.[7] The same pattern of selective omission of entries from the O'Donovan edition is evident from the year AM3266 right through to AM5199, and to a lesser extent in the entries for the Christian era down to AD549, and more occasionally thereafter down to the year AD653.[8]

It is well known that O'Donovan did not have access to either of the extant autograph manuscripts, now UCD–OFM MS A 13 and RIA MS C iii 3 and it would appear that O'Donovan may have been unaware that the copies he worked from were abridged. Neither he nor Eugene O'Curry made mention of the extensive omissions from the text as published. O'Donovan relied in part, for his edition, on the Irish text printed in Charles O'Conor's 1826 edition of the pre-

4 George Petrie had them bound in two volumes by George Mullen, a well-known Dublin binder (O'Sullivan, 'The Slane manuscript of the Annals of the Four Masters', 78).   5 The former binding of UCD–OFM MS A 13 was transferred to UCD archives in 2007, where it was examined by consultant conservator John Gillis and dated to the seventeenth century.   6 RIA MS C iii 3 was bound at the expense of Dr John Fergus in 1735 (noted on the opening page of the manuscript). No marks of any earlier binding are visible, and the worn condition of the paper in the opening and closing pages of the manuscript suggests that it may have lain unbound for a considerable time. For discussion of the differences between the Louvain set of autograph manuscripts and the set presumed to be associated with Ó Gadhra, see below, chapter six.   7 RIA MS C iii 3, fos 11–16v; UCD–OFM MS A 13, fos 13r–19v; *AFM*, I, pp 22–3 (the date AM3520 printed by O'Donovan is a misprint for 3529. The Irish text is correctly printed, except that it consistently omits the date heading given in arabic numerals in the manuscript.)   8 The AD years 549, 575, 578, 599, 603, 621, 626, 629, 632 and 653, omitted from O'Donovan's text, are all to be found in RIA MS C iii 3. In most instances the content is not significant, being merely a statement of the regnal year; an exception is AD626, where seven lines of text in the manuscript are omitted (note that there is a

1171 material, which was apparently based on the autograph manuscript now known as RIA MS C iii 3.[9] For the years to 1171, O'Donovan also used a transcript made in 1781 for Chevalier Thomas O'Gorman, and a copy made for John Fergus in 1734–5.[10] The Fergus copy is abridged in much the same fashion as O'Conor's printed edition. In the O'Gorman transcript, the Irish text begins only with the year AD76, and again like the O'Conor edition, the entries for the pre-Christian period are only very selectively presented. There is no extant transcript of the text of AFM that would have been accessible to O'Donovan that reproduces the full text as given in the autograph manuscripts, and the transcripts that do survive give no specific indication that the text has been abridged.

Overview of scope and content of AFM

The Annals of the Four Masters were more ambitious in scope than any of the other extant annals from medieval Ireland. Using the simple measure of the number of words in the Irish text of the printed edition, they are over twice as long as the next longest set of annals that extends beyond the year 1200.

Table 4.1: Word-count of Irish language text of annals[11]

AFM	396,848[12]	CS	33,500
AU	184,010[13]	AI	47,178[14]
ALCé	150,250	ATig	44,575
AConn	112,880		

In terms of the time period covered, likewise, the closest comparable set of annals is AClon, which begins with Creation and ends with the year AD1408.[15] The Annals of Inisfallen similarly open with an outline of the six ages of the world, and contain entries as late as AD1450, although its post-1200 contents are fragmentary.[16] In

misprint in O'Donovan's translation of the entry for AD625 so that it is incorrectly identified as AD626, in the English translation.) **9** *Cat. Ir. mss in RIA*, no. 988, p. 2830 makes passing reference to omissions in O'Donovan's edition but does not elaborate. **10** RIA MSS 23 F 2–23 F 3, had been transcribed at the house of Charles O'Conor, Belanagare, for the use of Chevalier Thomas O'Gorman in 1781; the first volume, to AD946, includes an English translation (*Cat. Ir. mss in RIA*, no. 988, p. 2830); the two-volume transcript in TCD MS 1300, made for John Fergus in 1734–5, is similarly abridged. **11** These figures are derived from the calculations published on the CELT website in respect of the digitized version of the Irish language texts of the various annals (www.ucc.ie/celt, accessed 23 November 2004). AClon is omitted from these calculations because the Irish text does not survive and a word-count of the English text would not provide a valid comparison. **12** This figure for AFM is an under-estimate, because it is based on the published edition, which omits over 1,720 skeleton entries contained in the autograph manuscripts for years prior to AM5199. **13** Excludes the pre-Patrician section printed in Mac Airt and Mac Niocaill (eds), *The Annals of Ulster (to AD1131)*, pp 2–37. **14** Includes pre-Patrician section of AI text. **15** Denis Murphy (ed.), *Annals of Clonmacnoise from the earliest period to AD1408, translated into English by Conell Mageoghagan, AD1627* (Dublin, 1896). **16** Seán Mac Airt (ed.), *Annals of*

contrast, AU commences with the year AD431, and the coming of Christianity to Ireland, though a preliminary section covering the years from AD81 to AD431 in TCD MS 1282 is now regarded as part of the same text. The later of the two extant manuscripts of the Ulster annals ends with AD1541, with occasional later entries down to 1588.[17] The Annals of Loch Cé (ALCé) open with the year 1014 and contain entries as late as 1590.[18] The Annals of Connacht (AConn) have one of the narrowest time-frames of the annals that survive more or less intact. They open with an account of the death in 1224 of a prominent thirteenth-century king, Cathal Crobderg, and end in 1544, with one later entry for 1562.[19]

In terms of conceptual scope, therefore, and particularly in terms of coverage of the pseudo-historical material, AFM most closely resembles AClon and to a much lesser extent the *Chronicum Scotorum* and the Annals of Inisfallen. However, in contrast to the 1627 translation of AClon, and to some extent the *Chronicum Scotorum*, the Four Masters present their pre-Christian material in annalistic form rather than as a prose narrative. Thus, the material derived from the *Leabhar gabhála* tradition is processed in quite a different form in AFM than in AClon.

The most striking feature of the opening section of AFM when compared with AClon is the conscious secularization evident in the Four Masters' account of prehistory. The biblical context that pervades the older recensions of the *Leabhar gabhála* is almost entirely omitted.[20] The focus of AFM is exclusively on the non-biblical material outlining the sequence of 'invasions' of Ireland, beginning with Ceasair, and then Parthalon and his followers and descendants.[21] No background information is supplied in AFM on who Ceasair was, not even the traditional assertion that she was a daughter or niece of Noah.[22] The text opens by simply stating the date of her coming:

AFM [AM2242]

Aois Domhain gus an mbliadhoinsi na dileand, da mhile da chéad da fichet 7 da bhliadhoin. Ceathracha la ria ndilinn tainig Ceasoir go hEirinn, go ccaogaid ninghen, 7 go ttriar bfer, Bioth, Ladhra, 7 Fiontoin a nanmanna.

(The Age of the World, to this Year of the Deluge, 2242. Forty days before the Deluge, Ceasair came to Ireland with fifty girls and three men; Bith, Ladhra and Fintain, their names.)[23]

Inisfallen (MS Rawlinson B 503) (Dublin, 1951).   **17** TCD MS 1282 and Bodl. MS Rawl. B 489, the earlier of the two being the TCD manuscript; Hennessy and MacCarthy (eds), *Annála Uladh*. For the pre-Patrician material see Mac Airt and Mac Niocaill (eds), *The Annals of Ulster (to AD1131)*, pp 2–37.   **18** Hennessy (ed.), *The Annals of Loch Cé*.   **19** RIA MS C iii 1 is the only extant manuscript. The standard edition is Freeman (ed.), *Annála Connacht*.   **20** This omission of biblical allusions is also characteristic of the Four Masters' new recension of *Leabhar gabhála*. RIA MS 23 M 70; 23 K 32; Macalister and MacNeill (eds), *Leabhar gabhála*.   **21** *AFM*, I, pp 2–9.   **22** As is claimed, for instance, in *AClon*, p. 12: 'This Kessar was neace unto Noeh, his Brothers Daughter'.   **23** *AFM*, I, pp 2–3.

The annals then record the places of death of the four named persons, but offer no further discussion of this first 'invasion'. The next entry simply proceeds to record the number of years from the deluge until the arrival of Parthalon.[24] This is in contrast to the much longer, more discursive, account of the same material presented in AClon, which opens with Adam himself, and includes much genealogical detail of the kind recorded in the Old Testament:

> AClon
> Adam in the 130 yeare of his age Begatt Seth, and afterwards Adam Liued 800 yeares & in all he liued 930 yeares. Seth in the 105th yeare of his age Begatt Enos, and liued afterwards 137 yeares, Enos in the 90th yeare of his adge Begatt Cainan and liued after his Birth 815 yeares. Cainan in the 70th yeare of his age Begatt Malalle and liued himself after 840 yeares. Malalele in the 65th yeare of his age Begatt Jareth and liued after 830 yeares. Jareth in the 62nd yeare of his adge begatt Enoche and liued after 800 yeares. Enoche in the 65th yeare of his age Begatt Methusalem, after whose Byrth he walked with God. Methusalem in the age of 187 yeares Begatt Lamech and liued himself after 782 yeares. Lamech in the yeare of his adge 182 Begat Noah and liued after 595 yeares. This yeare of Lamech's age came the woman called Cesarea or Keassar accompanied onely by three men and 50 Women to this Land which was the first habitacon of Ireland, though others say yt this land was first Discouered and found by three fisher men who were sayleing in these parts of the world, and Because they made noe Residence in the Land I will make noe mention of them.[25]

The opening section of the Annals of Inisfallen is incomplete, but enough survives to indicate that it too derives ultimately from the biblical account of Abraham and his descendants.[26] In contrast, Dubhaltach Mac Fhirbhisigh's recension of the *Chronicum Scotorum* omits most of the biblical material and outlines the six ages of the world with conscious brevity, and skims over the various invasions of Ireland prior to the arrival of the Clann Mhíleadh with the briefest of mentions. Although the *Chronicum Scotorum* and the Annals of Inisfallen have quite skeletal, if different, opening sections, the biblical dimension is predominant in both, in a manner that contrasts starkly with AFM. The decision to omit the Old Testament material from AFM was a conscious one. It was specifically alluded to in the preface to the new recension of the *Leabhar gabhála* that Mícheál Ó Cléirigh and his collaborators had earlier prepared:

> *Leigtmít dhín labhairt ar na hoibrighthibh selaithe. robudh gnáth hi ttosach gach sein-*
> *liubhair ghabhála oile, do brigh co bfuil isin scriobtuir dhiadha ní as ferr, et gorab dona*
> *diadhairidhibh as córa trachtadh orra, et nach dona daoinib oile; aga mbeith co lor le a*
> *trachtadh, et le a scriobadh aca ina éccmais.*

24 *AFM*, I, pp 4–5. 25 *AClon*, p. 11. 26 *AI*, pp 1–5.

(We forbear from the discussion of the six days' work, which was usual in the beginning of every other old Book of Conquests, because they are related better in the Holy Scripture, and because it is more right for divines to treat of them and not for other men; who may have enough to treat of and to write without it.)[27]

This astute editorial decision was implemented not just in Ó Cléirigh's recension of the *Leabhar gabhála* but in AFM also. It allowed the Four Masters to present a very considerably condensed version of the *Leabhar gabhála* material in their annals. This approach may have enhanced the credibility of the text for European audiences familiar with the Old Testament by avoiding the discrepancies between the *Leabhar gabhála* account and that of the Bible.

From the very earliest entry, for AM2242, right through to the closing year AD1616, AFM consistently adheres to a formal annalistic format, albeit in the early part a very condensed one. In this it contrasts with the pre-Christian section of AClon which, in its extant form in English translation, is presented as a continuous narrative, drawn from *Leabhar gabhála*, much closer in form to Geoffrey Keating's *Foras feasa ar Éirinn* than to AFM.[28] Although this pre-Christian material was not the primary concern of the Four Masters, they appear to have included it simply because such material, drawn from the *Leabhar gabhála*, was still regarded as an essential element of the origin legend of the Gaeil. In the early part of the text the annalists did not generally leave blank spaces for the missing years. Thus the opening entry for AM2242 is immediately followed by an entry for AM2527 and then AM2530. The annalists would have been thoroughly familiar with the nature and extent of the information available from the *Leabhar gabhála* for this period and clearly they did not anticipate that any additional material would be encountered that might need to be added later.

Occasionally, their attempt to reduce the contents of *Leabhar gabhála* to a precise annalistic format defeats the annalists and thus under the year AM2550, for example, they admit the vagueness of the sources:

AFM [AM2550]
Aois domhain, da mile cuig céd caoga. Parthalon décc for Senmoigh elta Eadair isin mbliadhoinsi. A naimsir gabhala Parthaloin ro slechtoit na muighesi: acht na ma ni feas caite bliadhna áiridhe in ro slechtoid.
(The Age of the World 2550. Parthalon died on Sean Magh-Ealta-Eadair in this year. In the time of Parthalon's invasion these plains were cleared [of wood]; but it is not known in what particular years they were cleared.)[29]

Rather than omit material they judged worthy of inclusion – on the formation of the plains of Ireland – they chose to deviate slightly from the annalistic form in this instance, content that it was fixed chronologically within the Parthalonian

---

27 Macalister and Mac Neill (eds), *Leabhar gabhála*, pp 2–3. 28 *AClon*, pp 11–69. See, in particular, Comyn and Dinneen (eds), *Foras feasa ar Éirinn*, I, pp 138–237; II, pp 1–117. 29 *AFM*, I, pp 6–7.

era. Generally, however, they admitted no such uncertainty. They had no reservations about including in the annals the series of invasions of Ireland that were at the core of the *Leabhar gabhála*. These were synchronized with precise *Anno mundi* dates. Thus, the arrival of Parthalon was dated to AM2520, Nemed AM2850, the Fir Bolg AM3266, the Tuatha Dé Danann AM3303 and finally the arrival of the sons of Míl was dated to AM3500.[30] The year AM3500 was deemed a particularly significant one by the scribe of one of the autograph manuscripts, RIA MS C iii 3, the opening words being written in extra large lettering.

Kings

From the year AM3266 forward, the annalists recorded the reigns of kings, commencing with Sláinghe, first king of the Fir Bolg, material that was also available in their *Leabhar gabhála* source and its continuation, the *Réim ríoghraidhe*.[31] Their practice was to itemize each year of the reign of each king even where no additional information other than the name of the king was available, and they itemized every year from AM3266 forward. This approach projects back into prehistory the idea of a kingdom of Ireland, an interpretation that these annals share with Conall Mac Eochagáin's similarly royalist Annals of Clonmacnoise.[32]

In general, the pre-Christian entries in AFM are very perfunctory statements of the regnal year but, following some rather tentative opening pages adapted from the *Leabhar gabhála*, they are invariably carefully transcribed with a heading for the year followed by the available details about the king's reign. The entries recording the death of each king and the accession of his successor are slightly more substantial, but the annalists appear to have been working primarily from the *Réim ríoghraidhe* and historical poems emanating from the *Leabhar gabhála* tradition, and presenting the available details in the form of annals. Their immediate source is not difficult to identify. The Four Masters had already completed their own comprehensive king-list in 1630, now UCD–OFM MS A 16, which they entitled *Seanchas riogh Ereann, ar na leanmain go a mbunaidh-fremhoibh accas an aimsir ro chaith gach rí diobh a cceannas 7 a ccumhachtaibhhh Erenn ina righe*. ('The pedigrees of the kings of Ireland, traced to their tribes of origin, together with the period each spent in his reign of the sovereignty of Ireland').[33] When this work was completed in 1630 under the patronage of Toirrdhealbhach Mac Cochláin, the Four Masters drew attention to the fact that their recension included *Anno mundi* and *Anno Domini* dates for the reigns of kings, a feature which they regarded as an innovation in their text. As noted above, this annotated king-list supplied the basis from which the Four Masters calculated the chronology of the annals.[34]

---

30 *AFM*, I, pp 4–25.   31 Commencing in the autograph manuscripts of AFM at RIA MS C iii 3, fo. 3v; UCD–OFM MS A 13, fo. 3v.   32 *AClon*, pp 11–63.   33 UCD–OFM MS A 16, fo. viii; *GRSH*, pp 3, 141.   34 The *Genealogiae regum et sanctorum Hiberniae* of the Four Masters is

In the case of some very early kings, the events of a lifetime are conflated into a single year, as in AM4169 when the events that occurred during the reign of Siorna Saoghlach mac Déin are all recorded in AFM under the year of his death. The nearest preceding date for which they could claim to have information was some century and a half earlier, in AM4020.[35] The annalists' outlining of each individual year within those dates was, in one sense, merely a technical exercise. They had no way of knowing how to allocate events to specific years within that time-span. Yet their method of presenting an account of Ireland's ancient past had a very clear purpose. Itemizing every regnal year in chronological order was an effective way of emphasizing the exceptional antiquity of the kingdom of Ireland. This was one of the great advantages of the annalistic format. The form in itself conveyed a message about the Irish past, even when short on factual detail. While more utilitarian later transcripts of AFM tended to abbreviate the early part of the text, thereby reducing the reigns of kings to a mere record of succession and death, the Four Masters had deliberately shunned such an approach. For them, every year for which it could be stated that a king had ruled in Ireland was a year worth recording.

Despite the skeletal nature of the information available on most of these early kings, there is clear evidence that the Four Masters chose not to include all the information they had to hand in their sources. In writing of Sétna, who died in AM4290, Gilla Cóemáin's historical poem, *Éire árd, inis na ríogh*, recorded that:

> *Sétna Indarraid arsaid*
> *do-rat chrod do chétamsaib*
> *certfichi blíadan cen brón*
> *coro ríagad la Símón.*
> (Venerable Sétna Indarcaid
> gave payments in cattle to the first mercenaries,
> for exactly 20 years without sorrow
> until he was put to death by Símón.)[36]

The Four Masters itemize each year of the reign of this king from AM4271 to 4290, but omit any reference to cattle and mercenaries in their account. It is also clear that they drew on sources other than Gilla Cóemáin. Thus, for example, in their account of the reign of Munemón who died in AM3872, they record that he died of plague, as is also mentioned in *Éire árd, inis na ríogh*. However, they also note that the making of the first chains of gold in Ireland occurred during his reign, a detail not found in *Éire árd*.[37] Thus, in this early part of the annals, as

discussed above, pp 65–71. The *Anno mundi* and *Anno Domini* dates in UCD–OFM MS A 16 are interlineations by two different scribes. For further discussion of the dating system as applied in both *GRSH* and AFM, see now Mc Carthy, *The Irish annals*, pp 293–8. **35** RIA MS C iii 3, fo. 67v; UCD–OFM MS A 13, fo. 79v; *AFM*, I, pp 56–9. **36** Smith, *Gilla Cóemáin*, pp 130–1. **37** Smith, *Gilla Cóemáin*, pp 122–3.

elsewhere, it is clear that the Four Masters are synthesizing a diverse range of sources, and arranging the selected material according to the precise chronology they have devised.

The pre-Christian section of AFM occupies the first 164 folios of the autograph manuscript RIA MS C iii 3. The text continues to AM5199, which was designated as the seventh year of the reign of Crimhthann Niadhnair, son of Lughaidh, as sovereign of Ireland (here O'Donovan's edition, relying on an incomplete manuscript transcript together with O'Conor's abridged edition,[38] is particularly misleading, because the last entry of the pre-Christian era in the printed edition is AM5194, the years 5195–9 being omitted in his exemplar because nothing particularly significant was recorded in them).[39]

The transition from the age of the world (AM dating) to the age of Christ (AD dating) is almost seamless, distinguished in the autograph manuscripts merely by commencing AD1 on a new page.[40] No elaborate lettering is used in either RIA MS C iii 3 or UCD–OFM MS A 13 to mark the opening of the Christian era. The style of the AM era is continued with each calendar year being itemized in the autograph manuscripts, even when no information other than the regnal year was available. Throughout this part of the annals, the information on the dates of the reigns of kings continues to correspond to the information itemized in the *Genealogiae regum et sanctorum Hiberniae*, compiled by the Four Masters in AD1630. In the 1630 text there were two major watersheds in the record of the succession of kings. The first division came with the coming of Christianity. Thus Dathi mac Fiachrach, who died in AD428, was accorded the dubious honour of being the last king of Ireland before the coming of Christianity.[41] For him, as for many of his royal predecessors, the entry in the genealogical list is as informative as the AFM entry.

GRSH

Dathí m Fiachrach m Eathach moighmedóin tri bliadna fiched go ttorcair do shoighitt gealáin ag Sléibh Ealpae. AM5627, AD428.
[Dathi son of Fiachra son of Eathach Muighmheadhain, twenty-three years, was killed by a flash of lightening at Sliabh Ealpa, AM5627, AD428.][42]

38 O'Conor, *Quattuor Magistrorum annales Hibernici*, p. 68, ends the pre-Christian era with the year AM5193; a similar pattern of abridgment is followed in RIA MS 23 F 2, which was available to O'Donovan, but that manuscript contains only an English translation for the years prior to AD76. The English translation ended the pre-Christian era with AM5194. Thereafter, an Irish text is interleaved with the English translation. Both text and translation of RIA MS 23 F 2 are abridged throughout, in much the same way as the edition subsequently published by O'Conor, though there are occasional differences in respect of the years omitted. 39 RIA MS C iii 3, fo. 164; *AFM*, I, pp 92–3. 40 UCD–OFM MS A 13, fo. 177v; RIA MS C iii 3, fo. 164v. 41 *GRSH*, p. 29. 42 *GRSH*, p. 29, with my translation.

AFM 428

Aois Criost, ceithre céd ficht a hocht. Iar mbeit tri bliadhna fichet i righe nEreann do Dathí, mac Fiachrach, mic Eathach Moighmheadhoin, torchair do saighit gealain ag Sleibh Ealpa.

(The Age of Christ, 428. After Dathi, son of Fiachra, son of Eochaidh Muighmheadhoin, had been twenty-three years in the sovereignty of Ireland, he was killed by a flash of lightening, at Sliabh Ealpa.)[43]

Throughout AFM, the content and arrangement of such entries owe more to their own earlier work on genealogy and chronology, *Genealogiae regum et sanctorum Hiberniae*, than to any annals now extant, and it seems unnecessary to presume that their pre-Christian material was based on an annalistic exemplar.

A new era commenced with the coming of Patrick, and the regnal lists began anew itemizing the reigns of kings after the coming of Christianity.

GRSH

Do Rioghaibh Érenn iar ccredeamh.
Laoghaire m Néll naoighiallaigh deich mbliadhna fichet go nerbailt etir Érinn 7 Albain .i. ainm da cnoc filet a nUíbh Faoláin a ttaobh Caise. AM5657, AD458.[44]
[Of the kings of Ireland after the faith.
Laoghaire son of Niall Naoighiallach thirty years until he died between Ireland and Scotland, i.e. the two hills which are in Uíbh Faoláin beside Caise. AM5657, AD458.][45]

The autograph manuscripts of AFM itemize each year of the reign of Laoghaire beginning with the year AD429, and ending with the year AD458.[46] As could be expected, these years are interspersed with narrative detail about the coming of Patrick. The Patrician material is one of the few instances where the contents of the autograph manuscripts deviate significantly from one another. Thus, it appears that whereas the basic framework of the reigns of kings was readily available and essentially unproblematic, the material on Saint Patrick had to be assembled by the annalists from a range of sources. Unusually, one of the autograph manuscripts, UCD–OFM MS A 13, was subject to further revision and addition at this point that was not replicated in RIA MS C iii 3.[47]

The year 1022 was a particularly significant one from the perspective of the annalists. This was the year in which the regnal lists and historical poems of 'kings of Ireland' came to an end, to be replaced by token lists of 'kings with opposition', commencing with Toirrdealbhach Ó Briain and ending with Ruaidhrí Ó Conchobhair.[48] The scribes marked the year 1022 as a watershed in

---

43 *AFM*, I, pp 128–9.   44 *GRSH*, p. 30.   45 My translation.   46 UCD–OFM MS A 13, fos 231r–5r; RIA MS C iii 3, fos 218r–222r. As in many earlier instances, O'Donovan's edition omits the entries for the years in which no information other than the regnal year is available. Thus in the reign of king Laoghaire the entries for AD429, 439, 441, 442, 443, 445, 446, 450, 451, 452 and 455 are omitted from the printed edition of AFM.   47 See below, pp 159–68.   48 *GRSH*, pp 35–6;

one of the autograph manuscripts, by commencing the following year, 1023, with an extra large heading so as to indicate the beginning of a new era.[49]

From this point onwards, the regnal years are generally dispensed with in AFM, though there are occasional occurrences such as in the opening description of AD1156 as *An chéd bhliadhain do Mhuirchertach Ua Lachlainn uas Erinn* ('The first year of Muircheartach O Lochlainn over Ireland'.)[50] There is some confusion in the detail regarding these kings, so that despite the chronological overlap, Muircheartach Ó Briain who died in 1119 and Domhnall Mac Lochlainn who died in 1121 are both described by the Four Masters in their obituaries and elsewhere as 'king of Ireland', without the qualification 'with opposition'.[51] As regards the overall chronological structure of AFM, however, the opening and terminal points of their reigns do not have the same significance as was allowed to the reigns of kings prior to AD1022.

The year AD1022 was also marked as a particular watershed in AClon. Having reached that year the compiler (or translator) of AClon inserted a section summarizing the preceding text with its 48 kings of Irish blood and 615 years since the coming of St Patrick.[52] AClon then named the families descended from the various kings, before commencing a new section of text headed 'Hereafter followeth a discourse of the Kings of Ireland that lived without a crown & of certaine accidents happened in theire raignes'.[53] This standard conceptual distinction regarding the nature of Irish kingship was also used in AFM, even though the transition from the era of 'kings of Ireland' to 'kings with opposition' was not marked by an analytical narrative interlude such as is found in the translation of AClon.

Those two events, the coming of Christianity and the ending of what was deemed the unopposed kingship of Ireland following the death of Maoilseachlainn in 1022, were the two major watersheds in Irish history from the AFM perspective. Thereafter, the annalistic formula is continued, taking in its stride such events as the coming of the Normans in the late twelfth century. Given the function of the annals as a chronological outline of Irish history designed to accompany other texts already compiled on the lives of saints and the genealogies of saints and kings, a terminal date coinciding with the death of Ruaidhrí Ó Conchobhair in 1198 might have been expected. In fact, the first phase of compilation of AFM concluded instead with the entry for the year 1207, a year without any apparent significance as a terminal date.

Mc Carthy, *The Irish annals*, p. 294, summarizing the evidence of Mc Carthy, 'Irish regnal canon', shows that the Four Masters used Gilla Cóemáin's historical poems as a source for the reigns of kings down to AD1022, and used the *Leabhar gabhála* from AD1023 for the 'kings with opposition'.
49 UCD–OFM MS A 13, fo. 410(a)r; the scribe of RIA MS C iii 3, fo. 408v, however, gives no indication of a watershed at the years 1022–3.   50 *AFM*, II, pp 1010–11.   51 *AFM*, II, pp 1008–9, 1112–13. The presentation of Connacht kings 'with opposition' was the source of controversy with Tuileagna Ó Maoil Chonaire after the annals were completed. For discussion of this debate, see pp 263–7 below.   52 *AClon*, pp 171–2.   53 *AClon*, p. 173.

When work resumed in 1635, after an interval, the second part of AFM commenced at the year 1208 and continued down to 1333, after which the Ó Cléirigh members of the team alone continued the work to the close of the annals in 1616. The entries for the early thirteenth century are now extant in only one of autograph manuscripts, RIA MS 23 P 6. In that manuscript, elaborate scribal lettering indicated a 'new beginning' at the year 1208, not because of its significance in the history of Ireland, but simply because it marked the beginning of the second volume of the text as planned by the annalists. It is also noticeable that the staining on the paper on the page which ends with the entry for 1207 and the page which opens with the entry for 1208 is consistent with those having been the outer pages of unbound volumes.[54] The year 1333 marked the end of another phase of the work. Recalling the project in retrospect, Fearfeasa Ó Maoil Chonaire observed that the team of four worked on the Annals as far as the year 1333 only. He outlined that he, together with Mícheál Ó Cléirigh and the two Cú Choigcríches, compiled:

> urmhór Naoimhshenchuis Eirionn go na Réim Ríoghraidhe Gábhaltus Eirenn go hiomlán ó bheagán daimsir ria ndílinn go flaithes Ruaidhrí mheic Toirrdhealbhaigh Mhóir I Chonchubhair (rí Eirionn go bhfreasbhra) agus leabhair Annála agus Irisi Éirionn ón mbliaghoin do chéadaois an domhain tionnsguintear ann gusan mbliadhainn 1333 agus gan bheith go coitchionn dhúinn an cearthrar sa dfiaghnuibh ar éinní dár tráchtadh isin leabhar Irisi ó sin síos.
>
> (the greater part of the Pedigrees of the Saints of Ireland together with the Succession of the Kings; the whole Book of Invasions from a little before the Flood to the reign of Ruaidhri, son of Toirrdhealbhach Mor, O Conchubhair, King of Ireland with opposition; the book of Annals and Chronicles of Ireland from the year which begins the first age of the world to the year of our Lord 1333; and that the whole four of us are not jointly responsible as authorities for anything that is treated of in the Annals from that year onwards.)[55]

It is also the case, as Mc Carthy has emphasized, that the short preface attached to UCD–OFM MS A 13 is worded as a preface to a work ending in 1333.[56] The

---

54 RIA MS 23 P 6, fo. 34v, fo. 1r. The sequence in which the leaves are now bound in RIA 23 P 6 dates from the mid-nineteenth century. The page which opens with the text for AD1208 is now immediately preceded by two vellum leaves containing the dedication to the patron, Fearghal Ó Gadhra (fos 35r–6v). The older ink foliation is missing from some leaves due to the condition of the manuscript, but in so far as an older set of numbers survives they do not account for all of the extant paper folios, and disregard the two vellum leaves. A modern pencil foliation begins again at fo. 1 with the entry for AD1208, and this modern foliation has been used in the digitized edition of the manuscript (www.isos.dias.ie) and is the foliation cited here (the corresponding section of the other autograph manuscript, TCD 1301, is now lost). 55 *GRSH*, pp 134, 150. 56 The 'short' preface is printed from UCD–OFM MS A 13, fos xxiii–xxiv, in Paul Walsh, *Gleanings from Irish manuscripts* (2nd ed. Dublin, 1933), pp 74–6, and is discussed in Mc Carthy, *The Irish annals*, pp 58, 334–5. Mc Carthy builds an elaborate but flawed hypothesis about 'initial' 'normalized' and 'final' drafts of the annals starting from the existence of this 'short' preface. Mc Carthy's hypothesis of an 'initial', 'normalized' and 'final' draft rests on the mistaken assumption that the six named chroniclers

signatures of three of the Four Masters, together with two scribal assistants, are attached to this short '1633' preface (figure 9.1), whereas none of the scribes signs the long '1616' preface, now preserved on the second of two vellum leaves bound into RIA MS 23 P 6.[57] That the signatures of the team are attached only to the '1333' preface is consistent with Fearfeasa Ó Maoil Chonaire's later assertion that only the Ó Cléirigh members of the group were responsible for the final portion of the annals (after 1333). However, as the witness of both extant autograph copies makes clear, the annals were nonetheless continued to the year 1616. While TCD MS 1301 now commences midway through AD1334, the layout of RIA 23 P 6 gives no indication of a break around AD1333.

Perhaps in an attempt to continue the framework of the reigns of kings as a key element of the structure of the annals, the dates of accession of English kings were added to the annals, commencing with the appointment of Henry II as 'king over the Saxons' dated here to 27 October 1154.[58] Each successive English monarch's accession was similarly recorded in AFM, right down to the seventeenth century.[59] This was an innovation by the annalists, and the evidence of the autograph manuscripts reveals that most of this data was added at a late stage in the compilation of the manuscripts, all the additions being made by a single scribe. Thus, whereas for the early medieval period, prior to 1022, the reigns of kings were an integral part of the structure of the annals, from the mid-twelfth century they were less central to the structure of the work.[60] In most instances, the accession of English monarchs was inserted towards the end of the entry for a given year. One exception to this was the Catholic queen, Mary, whose accession on 6 July 1553 was the first entry recorded in AFM for that year.[61] The names of some monarchs were given in extra large letters, suggesting that they were regarded by the annalists as particularly significant.[62]

The addition of this basic data on reigns of kings and queens from Henry II to James I was apparently regarded by the Four Masters as a necessary element of a history that aspired to be an inclusive record of the kingdom of Ireland.

worked simultaneously on equal tasks (p. 336). A very different scenario regarding how the work on the autograph manuscripts progressed is presented in detail in the chapters that follow below. 57 The 'long' preface (RIA MS 23 P 6, fos 36r–36v), which incidentally intimated incorrectly that the work ended with the year 1608, is signed by various members of the Donegal Franciscan community but not by any of the 'Four Masters' or their scribal assistants. In both cases the preface is preceded by a dedication to Ó Gadhra, signed by Mícheál Ó Cléirigh alone (UCD–OFM MS A 13, fo. xxii; RIA MS 23 P 6, fo. 35v). 58 *AFM*, II, pp 1114–15. 59 Henry II (AFM 1154 [i.e. 1155]); Richard I (AFM 1189); John (AFM 1199); Henry III (AFM 1216); Edward I (AFM 1272); Edward II (AFM 1307); Edward III (AFM 1326 [i.e. 1327]); Richard II (AFM 1378); Henry IV (AFM 1399); Henry V (AFM 1412 [i.e. 1413]); Henry VI (AFM 1422); Edward IV (AFM 1460 [i.e. 1461]); Edward V (AFM 1483); Richard V (AFM 1483); Henry VII (AFM 1485); Henry VIII (AFM 1509); Edward VI (AFM 1546 [i.e. 1547]); Mary (AFM 1553); Elizabeth I (AFM 1558); James I (AFM 1602 [i.e. 1603]). 60 For further discussion of kingship, see below, chapter five. 61 *AFM*, V, pp 1528–9. 62 For example, RIA MS 23 P 7, fo. 79v. In TCD MS 1301, the 1553 entry on Queen Mary is deleted from the end of the year and inserted in slightly different wording at the beginning. It is uncertain whether this amendment was done so as to re-order the sequence of

Their inclusion was also a tacit acknowledgment of the reality that the continuity of kingship in the kingdom of Ireland was now represented by those English monarchs whose jurisdiction extended over the island of Ireland.[63] They were not presented as kings, queens or lords of Ireland, however, but as kings or queens of England, and there was no change in terminology in this regard following the implementation of the 1541 Act for the Kingly Title.

Ecclesiastical material

Despite the deliberate secularization of the opening prehistoric section of the annals, there is a strong emphasis on ecclesiastical matters throughout. References to saints are particularly prevalent in the entries for the early Christian era, reflecting the content of the available sources, though the annals are not used as a forum in which to present detailed accounts of the lives of individual saints. Key saints are fitted into the secular chronological framework, however, and in some cases the availability of a written life of the saint is alluded to. Thus, for example, in the entry on St Brigit's death and burial recorded under the year 525, there is specific reference to the evidence about her contained in her Life, and in the Life of St Brendan of Clonfert.

> AFM 525
> *S. Brighit ogh, banab Chille dara [décc]. As disidhe cetus ro hiodhbradh Cill dara, 7 ba lé conrodacht. Así Brighit tra ná tucc a meanmain ná a hinntheifimh as in coimdheadh eadh naonuaire riamh acht a siorluadh, 7 a siorsmuaineadh do grés ina cridhe 7 menmain, amhail as errderc ina bethaidh fein, 7 i mbethaidh naoimh Brenainn, espucc Cluana ferta.*
> (Saint Brigit, virgin, Abbess of Cill-dara [died]. It was to her Cill-dara was first granted, and by her it was founded. Brigit was she who never turned her mind or attention from the Lord for the space of one hour, but was constantly meditating and thinking of him in her heart and mind, as is evident in her own Life, and in the Life of St Brenainn, Bishop of Cluain-fearta.)[64]

This entry contrasts with the AU account of the death of St Brigit, where the date of her death is recorded variously at AD523, 525 and 527, presumably from three different sources, and without any of the additional detail on the life and character of the saint contained in the AFM account.[65] It is clear from such entries that the Four Masters had a much greater interest in saints than was the case with the compilers of earlier secular annals such as AU, but nonetheless the Four Masters remained focused on the purpose of the annals as the secular chronological framework within which to fit the hagiographical material already being assembled.

entries within the year, or to correct an inadvertent duplication of information. 63 See also Ó Buachalla, *Aisling ghéar*, pp 96–8. 64 *AFM*, I, pp 170–3. 65 *AU*, I, pp 40–3.

The relationship between the annals and an earlier Ó Cléirigh compilation, known as the Martyrology of Donegal, is a close one.[66] There is a definite correspondence between the dating of obituaries of saints in both texts, so that it can be concluded that the Four Masters drew on hagiographical material contained in the Martyrology but did not seek to include all of the information on particular saints available in that source. Rather than seeking to replicate the contents of the Martyrology of Donegal in AFM, the annalists were producing a text designed to complement that hagiographical work. Indeed, Pádraig Ó Riain's examination of the Martyrology of Donegal has led him to conclude that the compilers must have had access to a draft set of AFM by the year 1628.[67]

Even after the medieval golden age of saints had come to an end, the continued significance of saints was documented through reference to their direct influence on secular affairs. Thus, in secular episodes of a political nature, such as the account of Rotsel Piton in 1197, the miracles of saints are liberally invoked.

AFM1197
Sluaigheadh lá Iohn Do Cuirt co nGallaib Uladh co hEss cCraibhe, 7 do-rónsatt caislén Cille Sanctáin. Ró fásaigheadh 7 ro folmhaigedh triocha céd Cianachta leó. Ro fhágaibh Roitsel Phitún co sochraide moir immaille fris isin ccaistiall hísin, 7 ro ghabsat ag indradh, 7 occ argain tuath 7 ceall as. Tainig iaromh Roitsel Phitun ar creich co port Doire, 7 ro airg Cluain Í, Eanach, 7 Dergbruach. Rug dna Flaithbeartach Ua Maoil Doraidh tighearna Conaill 7 Eóghain co nuathadh do Chlandaibh Néill an tuaiscirt forra. Ro fighedh iomaireg eatarra for traigh na hUachongbhála, 7 ro cuireadh a nár im mac Ardgail Mhéc Lochlainn tria mhíorbhail Colaim Chille, Caindigh, 7 Breacain isa cealla ro airccseatt.

(John De Courcy and the English of Ulidia marched, with an army, to Eas-Creeva, and erected the castle of Kilsanctan, and wasted and desolated the territory of Kienaghta. He left Rotsel Pitun, together with a large body of forces, in the castle, out of which they proceeded to plunder and ravage the territories and the churches. Rotsel Piton afterwards came on a predatory excursion to the harbour of Derry, and plundered the churches of Cluain-I, Enagh, and Dergbruagh. But Flaherty O'Muldory, lord of Kinel-Owen and Kinel-Conell, with a small party of the northern Hy-Niall, overtook him; and a battle was fought between them on the strand of Faughanvale, in which the English and the son of Ardgal Mac Loughlin were slaughtered, through the miracles of SS. Columbkille, Canice, and Brecan, whose churches they had plundered.)[68]

However, in terms of the overall form and structure of the early Christian and medieval sections of AFM, the essential framework is a secular, regnal rather than an ecclesiastical, hagiographical one.

---

66 BR MSS 4639 and 5095–6.   67 Ó Riain, *Feastdays of the saints*, p. 312. This date, of course, is earlier than the date of commencement given by the Four Masters in their own preface. It remains a distinct possibility that working notes towards the annals were already to hand some years prior to the stated commencement date of January 1632.   68 *AFM*, III, pp 106–9. For multiple examples

Verse

The Four Masters had access to a considerable range of historical poems, not least those assembled in BR MS 2569–72, which includes some transcripts in Mícheál Ó Cléirigh's own hand. However, their use of this material appears to have been quite limited, with a few notable exceptions. The manner in which the Four Masters drew on the historical poems *Éire árd, inis na ríogh* and *Atá sund forba feasa*, attributed to Gilla Cóemáin, as a source for the chronology of the annals has already been mentioned.[69] However, AFM is essentially presented as a prose history, and Gilla Cóemáin's compositions are not preserved in verse form in the work. In some instances, however, other verse extracts are occasionally cited as evidence, particularly in entries for the early Christian period.[70] In general, just one stanza is cited in an annal entry, and it is typically used to substantiate a point already alluded to in the preceding prose. Three themes emerge from the verse extracts cited in the early Christian section of the work of the Four Masters. Firstly, there are records of particular battles, and these have a strong place-lore element. Secondly there is material on the lives of saints, typically recording the age of the saint at the time of death. Thirdly there are verse accounts of the deaths of kings, a theme that virtually ceases after 1022.

Some of the early verse passages on kings and battles are cited in a similar way in ATig (fragment 3), and also in *Chronicum Scotorum*.[71] This material is not replicated in AU, and very rarely in the Annals of Inisfallen. It seems that, while the annalists were well aware of historical verse sources, the use of verse in AFM was primarily influenced by the contents of an earlier annalistic compilation of Clonmacnoise origin, for the period down to the eleventh century. The precise annalistic source cannot be confirmed,[72] however, and the Four Masters' use of verse is very selective as compared with ATig and *Chronicum Scotorum*. Thus, in an instance where ATig and *Chronicum Scotorum* each cite multiple stanzas in one entry, as in the account of the death of king Muircheartach, who was burned in his house at Cletty, after having been drowned in wine, the Four Masters select just two stanzas for their account.[73]

from AU, see *s.a.* AD1201.   **69** See above, p. 69; Mc Carthy, *The Irish annals*, pp 294–6; Smith, *Gilla Cóemáin*, pp 104–87.   **70** A similar methodology is employed, on occasion, by James Ussher in his work on Irish ecclesiastical history where, for example, he quotes verse relating to St Declan and to *sean Phádraig* (C.R. Elrington and J.H. Todd (eds), *The whole works of … James Ussher* (17 vols, Dublin, 1847–64), VI, pp 428, 458).   **71** For example, stanza on the death of Patrick, *AFM*, I, pp 158–59; *ATig*, I, p. 121, *CS*, *s.a.* 488 (489); on bishop Erc, *AFM*, I, pp 168–9; *ATig*, I, p. 126, *CS*, *s.a.* 511 (509); on the four battles in AD526, *AFM*, I, pp 174–5; *ATig*, I, p. 132, *CS*, *s.a.* 530 (529); on the teeth of Mochta, *AFM*, I, pp 176–9, *ATig*, I, pp 134–5, etc. The dates in brackets for CS entries cited here are taken from the re-dated English translation of the text by Gearóid Mac Niocaill, published in an online version only (www.ucc.ie/celt, consulted 23 April 2003).   **72** See Grabowski and Dumville, *Chronicles and annals of medieval Ireland and Wales*, p. 166.   **73** *ATig*, I, pp 132–3; *AFM*, I, pp 174–7; *CS*, *s.a.* 531.

The first verse passage in AFM occurs at AD106, where two separate un-attributed verses on Tuathal Techtmar, who had been king for thirty years, are cited, recording the name of the place where he was wounded and the place where he died.[74] There are similar entries on the death of Ferghus Duibhdhedach at AD226, which is also an account of the battle of Crinna,[75] and king Laoghaire at AD458. The latter item gives a reason for the king's death as well as identifying the place where he died.[76] Many of the verses cited are unattributed. Named authors of poems include Ceannfaeladh, whose verses generally relate to battles or the deaths of kings;[77] Becc mac Dé, whose poem records the battle of Ocha (AD478);[78] and Patrick, whose praise of the judgments of Bishop Erc are recorded in an obituary dated AD512.[79] The stanza cited in AFM on Saint Darerca, whose death is dated to 6 July 517, is also found in the Martyrology of Donegal. However, a second stanza used about the same saint in the same Martyrology is not included in AFM.[80] Indeed, many of the verse passages recorded in the Martyrology of Donegal are omitted from the corresponding obituaries of saints in AFM. Conversely, the stanza cited in AFM on Bishop Erc, mentioned above as having been written by St Patrick, is not contained in the entry for the bishop at 2 November in the Martyrology of Donegal.[81]

The various scribes differed in their approach to transcribing these verse extracts, some scribes using punctuation to indicate the end of each line of verse,[82] others making no obvious distinction between verse and prose.[83] Overall, the verse passages cited appear relatively unimportant, being in the nature of miscellaneous adjuncts to the prose text, occasionally confirming a statement given in prose, but rarely adding much new information. The poets concerned are not usually named, and are thus not being invoked as authorities. Verse extracts dealing with secular topics can almost all be accounted for by the availability of the same material in older annals. Some of the hagiographical passages are likewise to be found in ATig, such as, for example, the verse account of the battle of Cúil Dreimhne recorded in AFM at AD555.[84]

In the late medieval section of the annals, the use of verse is much less common. There are, for example, no occurrences of verse at all in the section of AFM covering the fifteenth century. On the extremely rare occasions where verse is used in the later sections of the text, it is used to good effect. Thus, in 1567, on the occasion of the death of Seaán Ó Néill, one stanza is inserted which effectively places the death of the prominent leader in a clear historical perspective. Aside from the reference in the verse to the birth of Christ, the clear

74 *AFM*, I, pp 98–9.   75 *AFM*, I, pp 110–11.   76 *AFM*, I, pp 144–5.   77 *AFM*, I, pp 166–7 (AD507), 174–7 (AD526 and AD527).   78 *AFM*, I, pp 150–1.   79 *AFM*, I, pp 166–9; c.f. *ATig*, I, p. 126.   80 *MDon*, pp 186–9; *AFM*, I, pp 168–9.   81 *MDon*, pp 292–3.   82 For example, RIA MS C iii 3, fo. 177v, entry for AD106; RIA MS C iii 3, fo. 230r, entry for AD512; RIA MS C iii 3, fo. 230v, entry on St Darerca, AD517.   83 For example, RIA MS C iii 3, fo. 191r, entry for AD226; RIA MS C iii 3, fo. 227, entry for AD493.   84 *AFM*, I, pp 194–5; *ATig*, I, p. 143.

echo of the style of verse used in relation to the early Christian kings of Ireland must have been deliberate.

> *Secht mbliadhna Sesccatt cúicc céd,*
> *míle bliadhain is ní brécc,*
> *co bás tSeain mic mic Cuinn*
> *ó thoidhecht Críost hi ccolainn.*
> (Seven years, sixty, five hundred,
> And a thousand years, it is no falsehood,
> To the death of John, grandson of Con,
> From the coming of Christ into a body.)[85]

In this instance, the scribe transcribed the passage in such a way that it was immediately discernible as verse.[86]

There was a deliberate use of verse also in the annalistic commemoration of Aodh Ruadh Ó Domhnaill entered at the year 1602. In adapting Lughaidh Ó Cléirigh's account, the Four Masters incorporated a verse that recounted a specific prophecy in respect of the Ó Domhnaill leader. The annalists adopted *Beatha Aodha Ruaidh*'s allusion to Aodh Ruadh as *tairrngeartach tinghealltach* ('a promised and prophesied one'), and confirmed this by citing a stanza that Lughaidh Ó Cléirigh had used in another place, saying:

> *... 7 co sainredhach las an naoimh érlamh Colaim Cille mac Feilim dia nébairt*
> *Ticfa fer an éngha aird*
> *do bhéra golmaircc in gach tír,*
> *budh é sin an donn diadha,*
> *is biadh .x. mbliadhna na rígh.*
> (... and particularly by the holy patron, Columbkille, the son of Felim, who said of him:
> A noble, pure, exalted man shall come,
> Who shall cause mournful weeping in every territory.
> He will be the pious Don,
> And will be ten years King.)[87]

The Four Masters' attribution of this verse to Colum Cille is not derived from *Beatha Aodha Ruaidh*. The same verse, which is part of the poem *Atá sunn lecht Conuill cruaidh*, is also found, however, in a much older source, the Book of Fenagh, compiled by Muirgheas Ó Maoil Chonaire in 1517, where it is attributed to St Caillín.[88] In Muirgheas's abbreviated version of the Book of Fenagh, prepared in 1535, the same poem is attributed to Colum Cille.[89] Mícheál

---

85 *AFM*, V, pp 1620–1. For further discussion of the historical context of this annalistic entry, see below, pp 204–5.   86 RIA MS 23 P 7, fo. 106.   87 *AFM*, VI, pp 2298–9.   88 RIA, MS 28 P 8, fos 15v–16v.   89 Hennessy and Kelly (eds), *The Book of Fenagh*, pp 152–3, and 142–3 note. The abbreviated version of the Book of Fenagh is BL Cotton Vespasian MS E II, where the poem is

Ó Cléirigh, having transcribed texts from the Book of Fenagh, would have been familiar with the poem, and as a historian of the Uí Dhomhnaill, would have favoured the attribution to their patron, Colum Cille.[90] The use of prophecy, in such a context, was designed to enhance the status of the person commemorated, and it appears that the verse form was employed to emphasize further the significance of the deceased leader. Aodh Ruadh had indeed been ten years 'king', as lord of Tír Conaill, having been officially inaugurated in 1592, as the annalists recorded.[91]

While there are these rare exceptional instances of the use of verse in the annalistic portrayal of leading personalities whose careers were within living memory, the Four Masters do not appear to have normally sought out poetical sources for the late medieval period. In almost all the instances in the pre-twelfth-century period, the secular verse extracts cited were already present in earlier annalistic sources. The hagiographical material in verse form was to hand in the Martyrology of Donegal, material they occasionally, though not system-atically, incorporated also.[92] It remains the case, however, that the essential chronological framework of the reigns of early kings echoes that of the historical poems of the eleventh-century poet, Gilla Cóemáin, yet without specific attribution to him. Rather, the recension of his work embedded in the Four Master's new recension of *Leabhar gabhála* appears to have been the immediate source used.[93]

Structure and outline contents of the late medieval section of AFM

As the annals of the Four Masters progress through the thirteenth to sixteenth centuries, the entries become progressively longer, and with greater emphasis on the lives and exploits of secular leaders within the context of lordship society. The entries include both obituaries and narratives of military exploits, with

given on fos 114–115 (older foliation, fos 6–7). See R.A.S. Macalister (ed.), *The Book of Fenagh: supplementary volume* (Dublin, 1939), p. 7, for a description of the abbreviated manuscript of the Book of Fenagh that revises the interpretation of Hennessy and Kelly. 90 Extracts from the poem are also liberally used in Maghnus Ó Domhnaill's Life of St Colum Cille (1532). A. O'Kelleher and G. Schoepperle (eds), *Betha Colaim Chille* (Illinois, IL, 1918), p. 23; see also the manuscript of that work transcribed by Giolla Riabhach Ó Cléirigh, now Bodl, Rawl. B 514, commencing at fo. 5r, where the poem in question is attributed to Caillín. 91 *AFM*, VI, pp 1928–9; the verse prophecy was modified by the Ó Cléirigh historians to read '10' rather than '9' years, so that it would fit the career Aodh Ruadh Ó Domhnaill. For the older form see BL Cotton Vespasian MS E II, fo. 117 (older foliation 7), line 19. 92 It should be noted here that the verse passages attributed to Flann Mainistreach and Dallán Forgaill printed in AFM in the entries on Saints Patrick and Colum Cille must be disregarded in the present discussion since they are late interpolations in the hand of Henry Burc (RIA MS C iii 3, fos 218v, 244). However, they are interesting in that they provide evidence that such verse passages had a special attraction to early readers of the annals, enough to prompt one such reader to attempt to enhance the work by adding more verse from well-known sources. 93 Mc Carthy, *The Irish annals*, pp 283–4, 294–6; Gilla Cóemáin was not accorded an obituary in AFM, but the Four Masters were thoroughly familiar with his work having made several

occasional records of a more miscellaneous nature, including references to serious outbreaks of disease and observations of unusual natural phenomena. The annalists generally made no attempt to group entries on related topics together.[94]

For example, in the year 1486, there are numerous distinct entries on closely related individuals. Thus, among the forty-four items recorded for that year, there are four separate Mág Mathghamhna entries, six separate Mág Raghnall entries, and four Ó Néill entries, two of which are grouped together.[95] The decision to accord each a separate entry was primarily dictated by the nature of the sources from which each element was derived. In some instances, as in the Uí Néill material, the entries are matched by equivalent passages in AU, where they are similarly presented as distinct items. In other instances, such as the Mág Raghnall entries, only three of the six had AU as their potential source,[96] one is found in AConn, while the source of the remaining two is untraced. Of the four Mág Mathghamhna entries, two are found in AU; the likely source of the remaining two is untraced. Since the annals were compiled by piecing together material from a diversity of sources, it was far simpler to present the material as discrete entries rather than to attempt a synthesis.

The format had other advantages besides simplicity. The Four Masters may have deliberately preserved the annalistic format so as to accord each individual actor his own distinct entry in recognition of his role as a distinct political operator. To integrate their stories would have been to deny their perceived status as autonomous actors in the political world of the time. The annals treated their actions as worthy of mention for their own intrinsic worth, and not simply as part of a grand narrative. This, then, was another advantage of the annalistic format: it allowed recognition of a wide array of persons of varying political influence each to have their own presence in the historical record in a largely non-analytical, non-judgmental context. It could be argued that this characteristic of the annals, where many relatively minor political figures are recorded separately from their peers, was an apt reflection of late medieval lordship society where many minor contenders for political status within local lordships, or in inter-lordship rivalries, strove to make their mark. Remembering their efforts and escapades was an important dimension of the whole political process. The entries in AFM must have emanated from some such process of politicized record-keeping, and the annalists' decision to preserve the essence of individual entries in preference to creating a synthesis in which many of those minor actors might have no place must be presumed to have been a deliberate one. In this sense, the composition of annal entries can be seen as reflecting the political

transcripts of his poems with some additions (Smith, *Gilla Cóemáin*, pp 37–9, 41–2, 44).   94 The exception is the ecclesiastical material, for which see chapter eight, below.   95 *AFM*, IV, pp 1138–45.   96 AFM 1486.2, 1486.9, and possibly 1486.12, though the latter is related from a different perspective in AU.

processes of lordship society. There is a particular abundance of annalistic material for the late fifteenth century, particularly the 1480s and 1490s. Whether this marks a high point of this kind of historical record-keeping to which the Four Masters had access or whether it merely represents an accident of survival is difficult to say.

Down to the middle of the sixteenth century there were other extant annals available on which the Four Masters could draw, and unsurprisingly the form and structure of those sections were largely determined by the contents of those other annalistic sources. The manner in which the annalists used material from these other sources will be discussed in the following chapters. While the Four Masters continued to record many very short entries on minor individuals and events throughout their coverage of the thirteenth to sixteenth centuries, the increasing number of lengthy narratives of military exploits, especially relating to the Uí Dhomhnaill, is noticeable, particularly from the fifteenth century onwards. This transition from short individual entries to long discursive narrative is never total, however, and even in the distinctively different final section of the annals, after 1587, some short individual entries are intermingled with long narrative passages.

As has already been noted, the bulk of the AFM entries from 1587 to 1602 are derived from Lughaidh Ó Cléirigh's biography of Aodh Ruadh Ó Domhnaill.[97] The annalists generally shorten the material they adopt from that source, and divide it into discrete entries, dispensing with the connecting passages that gave the original text its narrative coherence. Their decision to intersperse discursive passages from that source with very short entries taken from the annals of Maoilín Óg Mac Bruaideadha,[98] illustrates their conscious policy of adhering to the annalistic format throughout, whatever the style and form of the sources from which they derived their material. The abrupt transitions that occur in the annals for the closing years of the sixteenth century appear incongruous at times, because of the contrasting nature of the sources they attempt to weave together. The AFM entries for the year 1596, for example, commence with a miscellany of seven short entries ranging in geographical scope from south Munster to north Ulster, to north Leinster and back to Munster. A discursive narrative condensed from the portion of *Beatha Aodha Ruaidh* relating to 1596 then forms the basis of a very lengthy section of the Four Masters' account of that year.[99] This is followed by a further six Munster and Leinster entries, in a more typical short annalistic style.[100]

Although the Four Masters state that the source known to them as the 'Book of Lughaidh Ó Cléirigh' came to an end in 1602,[101] there is evidence in the closing years of the annals that they were able to continue on with the same kind

97 Their use of this source is discussed in more detail in the case study of Ó Domhnaill material in chapter seven, especially pp 209–12, below.   98 Cunningham, 'The historical annals of Maoilín Óg Mac Bruaideadha', 21–8.   99 *AFM*, VI, pp 1997–2005.   100 *AFM*, VI, pp 2005–7.   101 *AFM*, I, p. lxvi.

of narrative for a few years after that date.[102] There are two ways of explaining this. The first scenario is that one or more of the Four Masters themselves composed the later material, and did so in the style of *Beatha Aodha Ruaidh*.[103] An alternative explanation is that there was more written source material available to them on the activities of the Uí Dhomhnaill in the early seventeenth century than is preserved in Cú Choigcríche's transcript of Lughaidh Ó Cléirigh's narrative biography. Either way, it seems reasonable to suggest that the seventeenth-century material on the Uí Dhomhnaill recorded in AFM was probably the work of Ó Cléirigh historians, and given that the annals incorporate new details such as the name of the chaplain to Aodh Ó Domhnaill in 1602,[104] the Four Masters' account was written by someone who had access to information from eyewitnesses to some of the events described. This, of course, means that the entries for the closing section of the annals should probably be regarded in a different light to the earlier portions of the text compiled from sources with which the Four Masters had no direct personal association. Although they continued to adhere to the same annalistic form as was used in earlier sections of their annals, in reality this near contemporary material had little enough in common with what had gone before.

For the Four Masters, however, all that had gone before may have been leading up to this present-centred conclusion. The structural imbalance between the long prehistory with which the annals open and the short time-span but enormous level of detail of the episodes on the life of Aodh Ruadh Ó Domhnaill, which dominates the final portion of the text, might perhaps be read as having a biblical parallel. The opening section with its origin myth and its itemization of the genealogies of kings over many generations echos elements of the format of the Old Testament, while the detailed narrative of the life and tragic death of Ó Domhnaill can perhaps be read as an echo of the New Testament Gospel story, a story that gives meaning to, and is contextualized by, all that has preceded it, while also offering hope for the future. Although there is no hint that Lughaidh Ó Cléirigh conceived of his biographical narrative in this way, it can be argued that the manner in which the narrative is contextualized in AFM gives it a significance in the story of the Irish past that it would not otherwise have achieved. In particular, the Four Masters' citation of a verse prophecy attributed to Colum Cille, which made a direct reference to a ten-year reign as king, in their account of the death of Aodh Ruadh Ó Domhnaill in 1602[105] contains strong echoes of the verse passages on early kings of Ireland recorded in the pre-Christian and early Christian sections of the annals.

---

102 The extant manuscripts of BARUD come to an end in 1602. 103 For Cú Choigcríche Ó Cléirigh's potential skill in this regard, see the discussion of NLI MS G 488 in Breatnach, 'A seventeenth-century abridgement of *Beatha Aodha Ruaidh Uí Dhomhnaill*', 77–172. 104 *AFM*, VI, pp 2296–7. 105 *AFM*, VI, pp 2998–9. The verse is quoted above, p. 94. The verse passage is integral to the autograph manuscript RIA MS 23 P 7, fo. 273, and is not an interpolation.

At any rate, recording the exploits of those who had gone before was a form of the cult of ancestry, a means of claiming ownership of the dead of many generations.[106] In the end, the story was not allowed to conclude with the death of Aodh Ruadh Ó Domhnaill, but was extended to 1616 to record also the death of Aodh Ó Néill. This may, perhaps, have been in recognition of the fact that his departure, and his subsequent death in exile, no less than that of Ó Domhnaill, symbolized the declining fortunes of the Gaeil in the early seventeenth century.

The final few years covered by the annals are not coherently presented. After 1605, the entries are confined to a few major obituaries. There is no longer an attempt at a consistent year-by-year treatment of events, though the presence of annual headings but without anything else entered for the year suggests that the finished product was not concluded quite as intended.[107] The obituary of Aodh Ó Néill in 1616 now provides an appropriate conclusion to the text in one autograph manuscript only,[108] though a misplaced fragment of the same obituary is still present in the other autograph manuscript, indicating that both autograph manuscripts originally terminated at the same date.[109]

Dating system of annals

The traditional annalistic form of AFM should not blind us to its glaringly obvious character as an exercise in chronological calculation. As has already been noted, the calculation and recording of dates in Ó Cléirigh's various works, the Martyrology of Donegal and the *Genealogiae regum et sanctorum Hiberniae* as well as AFM, are all interlinked in respect of the formal business of recording the dates of death of saints and kings.[110] Thus, a concern with matters of chronology, with placing the records of all people of significance in Ireland's past in their appropriate place in the chronicle of Irish history, permeated the thinking of the compilers in their approach to each of these works. The system of dating annual entries adopted by the Four Masters was a simple one of using AM and AD dates only. They dispensed with the Kalends system of indicating the commencement of a new year, such as had been used in earlier compilations like the Annals of Inisfallen and AU. Paul Walsh has deduced from the alterations to the system of dating used in the later parts of the Annals of Loch Cé that knowledge of complicated calculations of dates, taking account of ferial numbers, epacts and leap years, was obsolete by the sixteenth century. It is probably because the Four Masters, or their intended readership, did not fully understand such dating that they opted to use *Anno mundi* and *Anno Domini* dates only.[111]

106 For the particular Franciscan dimension to this, associating various Franciscan friaries with the burial places of particular families, see pp 186–7, below.   107 It can hardly have been deliberate, but the disintegration of the annalistic structure in these closing years unwittingly conveys to the modern reader a sense of the disintegration of the traditional Gaelic world that the annals had chronicled.   108 RIA MS 23 P 7.   109 TCD MS 1301, the surviving fragment of the 1616 entry is now bound in between fos 997–998.   110 See above, chapter three.   111 Walsh, 'The dating of

Occasionally, a stray reference to this system of dating survives in the text as at AD1471 where an obit records that *Aodh mac Briain mic Pilip na Tuaighe Meguidhir decc .16 calainn Marta*. 'Hugh, the son of Brian, son of Philip-na-Tuaighe Maguire, died on the 16th of the Kalends of March'.[112] This appears to have been copied verbatim from AU, where that older style of dating was standard.[113] Ó Cléirigh's Martyrology of Donegal retained references to Kalends as its basic system of dating, perhaps because it was easier to follow the style of the Martyrology of Gorman from which Ó Cléirigh's work derived, than to apply systematically an alternative style of dating.

A comparison of the dating system used in the AU obituary of Ceallach (AD1129) and that in AFM illustrates how AFM simplified references to specific dates.

AU 1129

Ceallach ... rofhaidh a anmain a n-ucht aingel 7 archaingel, i n-Ard-Patraic, isin Mumain, i Kalainn April, in secunda feria 7 isin cethramadh bliadhain fichet a abdaine 7 isin cóicatmadh bliadhain a aisi. Rucadh tra a chorp hi tert Non April co Les-mór Mochutu, do reir a timna fadhéin 7 rofrithairedh co salmaibh 7 ymnaibh 7 canntaicibh. Ocus rohadhnaicedh co honórach i n-ailaidh in[n]a n-epscop i prid Non April, in quinta feria.

(Ceallach ... sent forth his spirit into the bosom of angels and archangels, in Ard-Patraic in Munster, in the Kalends [1st] of April, on the 2nd feria, and in the 24th year of his abbacy and in the 50th year of his age. His body was then carried on the 3rd of the Nones [3rd] of April to Lis-mor of Mochutu, according to his own will and it was waked with psalms and hymns and canticles. And it was buried with honour in the tomb of the bishops, on the 2nd of the Nones [4th] of April, on the 5th feria).[114]

AFM 1129

Ceallach ... ro fhaidh a spirat do cum nimhe in Ard Pattraicc isin Mumhain an céd lá dApril dia luain do shonnradh isin caeccatmhadh bliadhain a aoisi. Rugadh tra a chorp dia adhnacal isin ccédaoin ar ccind go Lios mór Mochúda do reir a thiomna budhdein, 7 ro friothairedh co psalmaibh, 7 imnaibh, 7 canticibh, 7 ro hadhnaicedh co honorach i niolaidh na nepscop Dia Dardaoin arnabharach.

(Ceallach ... resigned his spirit to heaven, at Ard-Padraig, in Munster, on the first day of April, on Monday precisely, in the fiftieth year of his age. His body was conveyed for interment, on the Wednesday following, to Lis-mor-Mochuda, in accordance with his own will; it was waked with psalms, hymns, and canticles, and interred with honour in the tomb of the bishops on the Thursday following.)[115]

As has been seen, the Four Masters simply dated pre-eleventh-century events by regnal year, and they used the calculations outlined in their own version of the

the Irish Annals', 373.   112 *AFM*, IV, pp 1076–7.   113 *AU*, III, p. 243.   114 *AU*, II, pp 120–3. 115 *AFM*, II, pp 1032–5.

Genealogiae regum et sanctorum Hiberniae in respect of both AM and AD dates.[116] Daniel Mc Carthy has detailed how the Four Masters modified the chronological evidence found in source poems in an attempt to synchronize it with the chronology of a Clonmacnoise chronicle. The result was that AFM 'inherited most of the anachronistic regnal chronology of Gilla Cóemáin, modified only by Ó Cléirigh's adjustments needed to adopt Septuagint chronology, and to synchronize Patrick's venit with AD432 and Brian Borúma's death mistakenly with AD1013.'[117] In some instances in the sixth century, the difference between the chronology of AFM and that in the 'Clonmacnoise chronicle' can vary by as much as seventeen years.[118] For later centuries, the variation is less pronounced, but as Paul Walsh observed, the AD date is almost uniformly wrong down to 1020.[119] For the years AD913 to 977, the correct date may usually be calculated by adding two years to the AFM date. Events of the year 980 are entered under 978 and 979 in AFM. Then, from AD980 to AD1018 the AFM dates are generally one year out. This means, for instance, that the AFM account of the Battle of Clontarf is recorded under the year 1013 rather than 1014. For years between AD980 and AD1018, therefore, one year should be added to the AFM date to arrive at the correct date. Events of the year AD1020 are placed under 1019 and 1020.[120] Thereafter, the dating of events in AFM is generally in agreement with other sources, though the dates of accession of English kings are sometimes inaccurate. In recording the reigns of English kings, the annalists evidently drew on an external source that treated the year as beginning on 25 March, so that the entries for those monarchs whose accession fell on dates between 1 January and 24 March were recorded under the preceding year. Only in respect of the accession of James I do the annalists make reference to the different systems of dating, when they record:

AFM 1602
King Semus do ríoghadh i nionad na bainríoghna Elizabeth an cethramhadh lá fichet do mharta, 1602, do réir airmhe na Saccsan 7 do reir rímhe na romhan as 1603.
(King James was proclaimed King in the place of the queen, Elizabeth, on the 24th of March, 1602, according to the English computation, or in 1603, according to the Roman computation.)[121]

While the autograph manuscripts of AFM have no formal title page, and no *finit* to mark a definite end to the work, the annals form a coherent whole. That they were deemed to be complete is clear from the preliminary material in the way of dedicatory epistle and letters of approbation that accompany the manuscripts.

116 For the Four Masters' annotations regarding dates of the reigns of kings see UCD–OFM MS A 16, passim. 117 Mc Carthy, *The Irish annals*, p. 298; for a comprehensive survey of the data see Mc Carthy, 'Collation of the Irish regnal canon'. 118 Mc Carthy, *The Irish annals*, p. 299, figure 43. 119 Walsh, 'The dating of the Irish Annals', 357. 120 Walsh, 'The dating of the Irish annals', 373–4. 121 *AFM*, VI, pp 2322–3.

There is a lengthy address to the patron, Fearghal Ó Gadhra, which, among other things, traces his pedigree back to Míl and beyond.[122] There are letters of approbation from two hereditary historians, Flann Mac Aodhagáin and Conchobhar Mac Bruaideadha, and four senior Irish bishops.[123] The approbations of the historians are in Irish, while those of the bishops are in Latin. Most important, perhaps, is the preface signed by four members of the Donegal Franciscan community itemizing the authentic manuscript sources on which the new compilation is based.[124] While older collections of annals, such as AU, made reference in passing to the fact that they were drawn from many earlier sources, this formal itemization of particular manuscript sources is an innovation. However, the brief statement of manuscript authorities falls far short of the detailed citation of sources found in the works of their contemporaries, not least Geoffrey Keating's *Foras feasa ar Éirinn* and James Ussher's *Britannicarum ecclesiarum antiquitates*.[125] Although the prefatory material in AFM has no parallel in any older set of Irish annals, it closely resembles the kind of preliminary approbations that accompany printed theological works from this period, including those issued in print from the Irish Franciscans at Louvain.[126]

Conclusion: the value of the annalistic form

The annalistic form suited the disparate nature of the available material; it allowed the coherent contextualized presentation of episodes that were local and immediate. The secular events they describe took place within a local context and the impact and relevance were primarily local, but yet it was possible to record them within a larger historical framework. The annalistic format allowed the combination of separate episodes into a logical structure, the arrangement being dictated by chronology. It was generally left to the reader, however, to make the connections between separate events. On occasion, stories that must have originated as single narratives were broken up and entered in sections under separate years. This is the case, for instance, in a story about a raid on Clonmacnoise recorded under the year AD 1129. The stealing of precious objects is described in some detail, and the entry ends by noting *Ciarán dan ó rugaitt dia ffoillsiuccadh iaramh* ('But Ciaran, from whom they were stolen, afterwards revealed them').[127] Then, in a quite separate entry in the following year, the sequel is provided where the fate of the thief is documented and St Ciaran again featured:

---

122 *AFM*, I, pp lv–lxi.   123 *AFM*, I, pp lxviii–lxxi.   124 *AFM*, I, pp lxiii–lxvii.   125 Comyn and Dinneen (eds), *Foras feasa ar Éirinn*, passim; Ussher, *Britannicarum ecclesiarum antiquitates*, passim. 126 Colgan, *Acta sanctorum Hiberniae*, sig. b 5–5v; Fearghal Mac Raghnaill (ed.), *An teagasg Críosdaidhe*, by Bonabhentura Ó hEodhasa (Dublin, 1976), p. 1; Ó Maonaigh (ed.), *Scáthán shacramuinte na haithridhe*, 219; Ó Fachtna (ed.), *Parrthas an anma*, p. 200.   127 *AFM*, II, pp 1032–3.

AFM 1130

Seóid Cluana mic Nóis d'foillsiughadh for Ghallaibh Luimnigh iar na ngoid do Ghiollachomhgáin. Giollacomhgáin féissin do chrochadh i nDún Cluana Bhriain lá ríg Mumhan, iar na thairbert la Conchobhar Ua mBriain. Ro shir tra an Giollacomhgáin soin Corcach, Lios mór, 7 Portláirge do dhol tar muir. In long i raghbhadh ionadh ní fagbhadh gaoith sheolta, 7 fo gheibhdís na longa ele archeana. Deithbhir ón ar no fhostadh Ciaran an luing i ttrialladh somh teacht tairis, 7 do rádhsomh ina coibhsenaibh frí bás co naicedh Ciarán co na bhachaill ac fosttadh gacha luinge ina ttrialladh. Ro moradh tra ainm Dé 7 Ciaráin de sin.

(The jewels of Cluain-mic-Nios were revealed against the foreigners of Luimneach, they having been stolen by Gillacomhgain. Gillacomhgain himself was hanged at the fort of Cluain-Bhriain, by the king of Munster, he having been delivered up by Conchobhar Ua Briain. This Gillacomhgain sought Corcach, Lis-mor, and Port-Lairge, to proceed over sea; but no ship into which he entered found a wind to sail, while all the other ships did. This was no wonder, indeed, for Ciaran used to stop every ship in which he attempted to escape; and he said in his confessions at this death, that he used to see Ciaran, with his crosier, stopping every ship into which he went. The name of God and Ciaran was magnified by this.)[128]

The annalists made no attempt to tell the story as an integrated episode, but nonetheless each element of the story was assigned a place in the overall structure. For them, as for medieval chroniclers elsewhere, recording the material in its proper chronological place was usually sufficient. The raw material was made available; in cases where there was conflict of evidence, readers could draw their own conclusions.

The annalistic form suited the Four Masters' purpose of providing a detailed outline of the historical record that would complement their work on the lives of the saints. The straightforward chronological arrangement ensured that the available historical evidence was readily accessible. The form was sufficiently flexible to incorporate both the outline of the reigns of kings and also the description of local secular and ecclesiastical events and personalities. The resultant history gave the impression of objectivity and therefore reliability. Alternative viewpoints in the sources were dealt with by the simple device of recording variant accounts as found in the sources. The historian functioned as reporter rather than as judge of events. The reader was not openly addressed, and unlike in the case of polemical narrative history, the personal opinions of the chroniclers were not easily discerned.

And yet, the overall form and structure of AFM presented a powerful message concerning the antiquity of the kingdom of Ireland and the richness of the historical record preserved within its pages. At a fundamental level, retaining the form of annals was, perhaps, itself part of the process of memorialization, part of the Four Masters' homage to tradition, acknowledging what was of value

128 *AFM*, II, pp 1034-5.

in the world of their ancestors. The imitation of the form of medieval annals, along with the use of archaic linguistic forms,[129] preserved a sense of continuity even within change, leading to what Nancy Struever has described in the Florentine Renaissance context as 'a productive sense of anachronism'.[130]

The pre-Christian section of the Annals of the Four Masters opened with a largely artificial structure dictated as much by the compilers' ideology of kingship as by the nature of the available sources. It was presented in a tediously repetitive manner which later copyists of the text chose to condense because of the paucity of historical data actually recorded. The historical data presented in the central portion of the annals, from the coming of St Patrick in the fifth century down to the mid-sixteenth century, were much better adapted to the annalistic format used, not least because the contents were largely derived from pre-existing annalistic compilations. In the final portion of the text, the discursive narratives on which the annals are based strain to fit the annalistic form superimposed on them. Yet, although the annalistic form is somewhat tested at the beginning of the text for lack of data and at the end of the text because of the wealth of accessible, familiar detail for the closing years, the integrity of the text is maintained throughout. The rigid adherence to a chronological arrangement is the key to the success of the work. By this simple device for presenting movement through time, the text conveys a clear sense of the continuity of the Gaelic world from the creation of the world to the compilers' own day. Along the way, the annals fill the story of the Gaelic past with the achievements of the illustrious ancestors of the annalists' contemporaries whose history they were.

---

129 Damian McManus, 'The language of the *Beatha*' in Ó Riain (ed.), *Beatha Aodha Ruaidh*, pp 54–73; Pádraig A. Breatnach, 'Irish records of the Nine Years War: a brief survey with particular notice of the relationship between *Beatha Aodha Ruaidh Uí Dhomhnaill* and the Annals of the Four Masters' in Ó Riain (ed.), *Beatha Aodha Ruaidh*, pp 124–47.   130 Nancy S. Struever, *The language of history in the Renaissance: rhetoric and historical consciousness in Florentine humanism* (Princeton, NJ, 1970), p. 193.

CHAPTER FIVE

The methodology of the Four Masters: new annals from old

Introduction

The Four Masters drew the attention of their readers to the availability of earlier annalistic sources on which they relied in their work.[1] Adhering to the format of those older annalistic compilations, the team of chroniclers who assembled AFM opted to present their record of the past as short discrete entries, arranged in chronological sequence by year of occurrence. Yet, there is ample evidence in the work of the Four Masters to show that the annalistic framework allowed innovation in content and prioritization to be introduced in a systematic if subtle way. It is possible to use the extant manuscripts to examine the manner in which the Four Masters selected, revised and restructured the historical material available to them in their source manuscripts. Their work on the fifteenth century is particularly revealing, being a period for which numerous other annalistic sources are extant, and their approach conveys the sense of Ireland they nurtured through their remembering of the past.

It should be noted at the outset that there is little evidence that the Four Masters favoured making verbatim transcripts of older sources. Given the extent of rewriting in which the annalists engaged, general equivalence of subject matter is sufficient to postulate a possible link or influence between texts. For the late medieval period, as Gearóid Mac Niocaill has observed, 'where two sets of annals recount the same event in different terms, one cannot safely assume that they are independent, for one simple reason: they are concerned primarily with events, not with the formulae or phrases in which they are recorded'.[2]

Among the major extant sources available to the Four Masters when compiling their fifteenth- and early sixteenth-century entries was AU, known to them as *Leabhar Seanaidh mec Maghnusa*. Although AU cannot be regarded as their principal source, the many similarities and differences between AU and AFM are an indicator not just of the Four Masters' approach to their source texts, but also of how they chose to portray the Irish past. The nature of the parallels between AFM and the extant portions of ALec and AClon, each of which now survives only in seventeenth-century translations, will also be

---

1 *AFM*, I, pp lxiv–lxvii. 2 Mac Niocaill, *Medieval Irish annals*, p. 14.

examined because it seems likely from the extent of the similarities between them and AFM that the texts from which those translations derive were also consulted. While it has been noted that the exact relationship between AConn and the lost Ó Duibhgeannáin annalistic source used by the Four Masters cannot be definitively explained,[3] the extent of the parallels between AConn and AFM means that that text must also be included in this exploration into the methodology of the Four Masters. The loss of other collections of annals used by the Four Masters limits the scope of the analysis that can be undertaken here, so that the conclusions reached must be regarded as tentative. As has already been discussed in the preceding chapters, the Four Masters also drew on a range of non-annalistic sources.

The approach adopted by the Four Masters to the historical sources available to them is an important indicator of their aspirations and objectives as historians. From the evidence of the testimonies attached to the finished annals, it appears that the Four Masters assembled together a wide range of sources. That initiative, in itself, indicates that no one existing source was regarded by the compilers as comprehensively meeting their criteria as to what constituted a history of the kingdom of Ireland. Indeed, no pre-existing set of annals covered the full time-span from the biblical flood to the present. They regarded the contents of the earlier annals as the essential foundation on which to construct their history, but their working method necessitated the selection and re-ordering of that material. The objective was not transcription, therefore, but the creation of new annals from old.

The elements of the methodology of the Four Masters examined here will include the extent to which they systematically imposed a coherent pattern on the account presented of each year's events, through their selection and arrangement of entries, and thereby prioritized certain aspects of their story of the past. Their omission of many entries found in their source texts and the significance of the patterns of exclusion will be considered. At the level of individual entries the variety of ways in which the content of many entries differs from that found in the extant source texts will be examined. Some systematic changes in terminology, most notably in relation to politically significant words concerning kingship, have already been commented on by others,[4] and will be placed in context here.

While it can be shown clearly that the Four Masters deliberately excluded many entries found in their sources, the question of the extent to which they introduced new material is more problematic. The loss of many of their source

3 See above, pp 49–51.   4 F.J. Byrne, *Irish kings and high-kings* (London, 1973), pp 41–7; Donnchadh Ó Corráin, Review of Byrne, *Irish kings and high-kings*, *Celtica* 13 (1980), 50–68; Kenneth Nicholls, 'Introduction' to 1990 reprint of *AFM*; Katherine Megan McGowan, 'Political geography and political structures in earlier medieval Ireland: a chronicle-based approach' (PhD, University of Cambridge, 2003), pp 7–19.

texts means that it is not possible to present a comprehensive survey of the changes and additions the Four Masters may have made, even if that were desirable.

Overview of the relationship between AFM and the major extant late medieval annals

The extent to which the entries in AFM for the fifteenth and early sixteenth centuries track those found in AU varies very considerably from year to year. It is known that a manuscript of AU was available to the Four Masters when they were compiling their annals, and since they asserted that it contained entries down to the year 1532[5] it could be anticipated that it might have been used systematically in the compilation of entries prior to that date. Comparison of the entries in AU with those in AFM for the years 1401 to 1540, reveals a complex and sometimes haphazard relationship between the two sets of annals. There are a number of reasons for this complexity. First, it seems that it was rarely, if ever, the case that AU was the only source on which the Four Masters could draw for any given year. Secondly, even in those instances where AU was the predominant source used, the entries were frequently reordered by the Four Masters, and some entries recorded in AU were omitted. Thus, even though AU was evidently an important source for the post-1400 entries in AFM, they were not prioritized over other available sources, and the Four Masters freely selected from, adapted, and edited the entries they found in AU to suit their own purposes. Overall, AU contained 1,897 separate entries for the period 1401–1540, of which 1,148, or 60.5 per cent are matched by equivalent entries in AFM. The proportion varied over time, with a correspondence in excess of 70 per cent in the early fifteenth century, but below 60 per cent in the 1460s and 1480s.[6]

While the extant manuscript of AConn was almost certainly not available to the Four Masters, they did have access to a set of Ó Duibhgeannáin annals from which AConn probably derives.[7] As in the case of AU, the patterns of similarity and difference between AFM and AConn are complex. AConn contained 1,656 entries for the period 1401 to 1540, of which some 1,044 are matched by similar entries in AFM. At 63 per cent, this is marginally greater than the proportion of AU entries also found in AFM. The trend over time varied from as low as 40 per cent in the 1430s to over 80 per cent of entries in common between AConn and AFM in the 1460s and at certain dates after 1500.[8]

Another perspective on the relationship between AFM and earlier sets of annals, most especially AU and AConn, can be obtained by examining in some detail how particular sample years are treated in each set of annals. This

5 *AFM*, I, p. lxvi.   6 Bernadette Cunningham, 'The making of the Annals of the Four Masters' (PhD, UCD, 2005), p. 110, figure 5.1.   7 See above, pp 49–51.   8 Cunningham, 'The making of the Annals of the Four Masters', p. 110, figure 5.2.

approach gives a sense of the real extent of the process of selection and re-ordering of entries engaged in by the Four Masters.

Table 5.1: Correspondence between topics of entries in AFM,
AU and AConn for the year 1417[9]

Year	AFM	AU	AConn	Year	AFM	AU	AConn
1417	1	1	1416.28	1417	7		8
	2	5			8		9
	3	3	3		9		
	4	2	2		10		
	5	4	4		11		
	6		5				

In the sample year 1417, just five of the eleven entries contained in AFM are found in AU. There are differences in the level of detail recorded in each of those five entries, with AFM recording additional material not found in AU in two of those five (table 5:1).[10]

Both sets of annals, AFM and AU, open the year 1417 with an obituary for Art mac Airt mic Muirceartaigh. The AU version of the obituary is quite straight-forward. It records the man's name and status, mentions some praiseworthy attributes and concludes with a stock phrase referring to his having received the last sacraments.

AU 1417
Mac Murchadha, idon, ri Laighen, idon, Art, mac Airt Caemanaigh, idon, in coicedhach dobh' ferr einech 7 eaghnum 7 derc do bi i n-a aimsir fein, d'heg i n-a longport fein in bliadhain si, iar m-buaidh Ongtha 7 aithrighe.
(Mac Murchadha, namely, king of Leinster, that is, Art, son of Art Caemanach, to wit, the provincial who was best of hospitality and prowess and charity that was in his own time, died in his own stronghold this year after victory of Unction and penance.)[11]

Compared with this very standard obituary for a provincial king, the entry in AFM is more elaborate, and adds an unusual element of intrigue that is not mentioned in AU.

9 The entry numbers used in respect of AFM and AU are those assigned in the digitized edition of the Irish language version of the texts as published on the CELT website (www.ucc.ie/celt).   10 It should perhaps be restated that complete verbal equivalence is not implied here. Treatment of the same topic in broadly similar fashion is what is in question in these evaluations of similarity between different sets of annals.   11 *AU*, III, pp 72–3.

AFM 1417

Art mac Airt mic Muirceartaigh mic Muiris tighearna Laighen, fer do chosain a chuicceadh daimhdheoin Gall 7 Gaoídheal ó aoís a sé mbliadhan décc go cenn a thrí fichit bliadhan. Fer lán deineach, deolas, 7 deangnamh. Fer lán do rath, 7 do rioghacht, fer médaighthe ceall 7 mainistreach la a almsanaibh, 7 edhbartaibh do écc (iar na beith da bliadhain cethrachat i ttighearnus Laighen) sechtmain iar Nottlaicc atbath. Atberat araile gur bo do digh nimhe tucc ben hi Ross mic Briuin dósamh 7 dua dheórán breithemh Laighen dia ro eccsat ina ndísi. Donnchadh a mac do ghabhail a ionaidh dia éis.

(Art, the son of Art, son of Murtough, son of Maurice, lord of Leinster, a man who had defended his own province against the English and Irish from his sixteenth to his sixtieth year; a man full of hospitality, knowledge and chivalry; a man full of prosperity and royalty; the enricher of churches and monasteries, by his alms and offerings, died (after having been forty-two years in the lordship of Leinster) a week after Christmas. Some assert that it was a poisonous drink which a woman gave to him, and to O'Doran, chief brehon of Leinster, at Ros-Mic-Briuin, that both died. Donough, his son, assumed his place after him.)[12]

Although the death of Art Mac Murchadha is recorded in both AFM and AU, the entries appear to be independent of one another. The AConn version of this obituary, on the other hand, has strong similarities with that in AU, in terms of level of content and in the vocabulary of the attributes recorded, though it is entered at the year 1416.

AConn 1416

Art Caemanach ri Laigen mac Airt Chaemanaig meic Murcertaig Caemanaig meic Muiris Caemanaig 7 rl .i. cetroga Gaidel Erenn i nd-enech 7 i nd-engnam do ecc iar mbuaid n-aithrige ina longport fein anno Domini m⁰cccc⁰xvi.

(Art Caemanach, king of Leinster, son of Art Caemanach son of Muirchertach Caemanach son of Muiris Caemanach &c, first choice of the Gaels of Ireland for bounty and valour, died, after a victory of repentance, in his own stronghold in the year of our Lord 1416.)[13]

However, it must be concluded either that the source of the independent entry in AFM is no longer extant, or that the Four Masters themselves were responsible for the redrafting.

Three of the four remaining entries on subjects common to AFM and AU for the year 1417 are sufficiently different in content as well as vocabulary for it to be concluded that AU was probably not the source used by the Four Masters. One entry, the obituary of Diarmaid Laimderg mac Airt Caemanaigh, is identical in both annals, but since the entry merely contains the man's name and title and the fact of his death, there is little scope for variant renderings of the information recorded.[14]

12 *AFM*, IV, pp 830–1.   13 *AConn*, pp 432–3.   14 *AU*, III, pp 72–3; *AFM*, IV, pp 830–1.

Two of the entries included in AFM for the year 1417 relate to the Uí Néill. A short entry records the death of Úna, wife of Neill Óg Ó Néill, while a longer narrative describes an attack by Ó Néill on the Carn Glas stronghold of Neachtain Ó Domhnaill. Although Ó Néill was triumphant, AU, which usually gives prominence to Ó Néill activities, does not record the episode at all. The account presented in AFM ends the narrative from an Ó Domhnaill perspective, recording that although eleven men were killed or captured, *Neachtain budhdhein do thérnudh do thoradh a calmatais a engnamha 7 a eisiomail* ('Naghtan himself made his escape, by force of his valour, prowess and bravery').[15] Given that AU was apparently not the source of this episode involving Ó Néill, it seems possible that it was originally recorded by a historian with a special interest in the activities of Neachtain Ó Domhnaill, probably a member of the Ó Cléirigh school of history. Yet, an Ó Cléirigh source would probably not be sufficient to account for all eleven entries recorded by AFM for the year 1417, a year in which all four Irish provinces are represented in AFM. In that year, somewhat untypically, five of the entries in AFM relate to the province of Leinster, three to Ulster, two to Connacht and one to Munster. This balance suggests the significant influence of a Leinster source, but one that is no longer extant.

The record of events a century later, in the sample year 1517, adheres to a similar pattern in several respects. Just six of the twelve entries in AFM for 1517 are also recorded in AU, while four substantial entries for that year recorded in AU are omitted from AFM. All six entries in common relate to persons or events in Ulster. Yet no one entry in AFM for that year corresponds in every respect to an entry in AU.

Table 5.2: Correspondence between topics of entries in AFM,
AU and AConn for the year 1517

Year	AFM	AU	AConn	Year	AFM	AU	AConn
1517	1			**1517**	7		
	2	8	2		8		
	3	6	3		9		
	4	9	4		10		
	5	10			11	5	
	6	7&11	6		12		

The closest parallel is the 1517 record of the killing of Art son of Aodh Ó Néill, recorded as follows in AFM: *Art mac Aodha mic Domhnaill Uí Néill do mharbhadh lé Niall mac Cuinn, mic Airt Uí Néill* (Art, the son of Hugh, son of Donnell O'Neill, was slain by Niall, the son of Con, son of Art O'Neill).[16]

15 *AFM*, IV, pp 832–3.   16 *AFM*, V, pp 1338–9.

Curiously, this event is recorded in two separate entries in AU, in different wording; the annalist apparently not noticing the duplication. The entry in AFM closely resembles the second of the two versions recorded in AU, but omits the comment found in AU *Ocus do bo saí chinn-fedhna an t-Art sin* ('And an eminent leader was that Art').[17] The recording of the event in AFM is more closely matched by the version in AConn.[18] Of the four other obituaries common to AU and AFM for the year 1517, none of those in AFM could be said to have been modelled on the equivalent entry in AU. The obituary of Donnchadh Ó Baoighill, drowned at sea off Tory Island, is much abbreviated in AU compared with the entry in AFM and also in AConn.

Again, although both AU and AFM contain brief obituaries of Seán son of Conn Ó Néill, the terminology is so different that it is best to assume that the AFM entry was compiled with little regard for the version recorded in AU.

> AFM 1517
> *Sean mac Cuinn mic Enrí mic Éoccain í Neill, mac tighearna bá mó toice, 7 trom chonach i nUltaibh ina ré décc.*
> (John, the son of Con, son of Henry, son of Owen O'Neill, a son of a lord, the most affluent and wealthy of his time in Ulster, died.)[19]
>
> AU 1517
> *Seaan, mac Cuinn [U]i Néll, tánusti Tíre-nEogain 7 rídhamhna a cinidh gan chunntabairt 7 nech dob' ferr glicus 7 uaisli d'fhuil Eogain, d'fhagail báis Ongtha 7 aithrighi a Cend-airt an bliadhain si.*
> (John, son of Conn O'Neill, tanist of Tir-Eogain and royal heir of his own sept without dispute and one who was of most perspicacity and nobility of the blood of Eogan, died a death of unction and penance in Cenn-ard this year.)[20]

The death is also recorded in AConn, *Sean mac Cuinn meic Enri meic Eogain hI Nell d'ecc* ('Sean son of Conn son of Enri son of Eogan O Neill died'),[21] but in a very abbreviated form, lacking the level of detail found in AFM. In this, as in many other instances, therefore, the entry recorded in AFM does not correspond to any extant annalistic source. Thus, it may have been derived from an annalistic source that is no longer extant, but it is more likely that the Four Masters substantially redrafted it on the basis of the AU entry. Either way, it appears that the language and content of the AU entry was rejected by the Four Masters in favour of a more accessible, simplified, version that omitted terms such as *ridhamhna* and *tánuisti*, and chose a direct reference to Ulster rather than the more archaic allusion to *fuil Eogain*, which might not have been understood by their intended audience.

---

17 *AFM*, V, pp 1338–41; *AU*, III, pp 528–9. 18 *AConn*, pp 632–3. 19 *AFM*, V, pp 1338–9.
20 *AU*, III, pp 528–9. 21 *AConn*, pp 632–3.

Given its strong Franciscan associations, it is surprising that AFM excludes an entry recorded in AU concerning a General chapter of Friars Minor held at Rome in 1517 under the auspices of Pope Leo X.[22] A deliberate focus on affairs in Ireland to the exclusion of external events in AFM seems the best explanation for this editorial decision. Closer to home, some significant entries involving members of the Uí Dhomhnaill are also omitted from AFM for 1517. In particular, a narrative account of an attack by Ó Domhnaill on Ó Neill in which the town of Dungannon was burned and Aodh Dubh Ó Domhnaill emerged triumphant, is recounted in some detail in AU.

AU 1517

Sloighedh les O n-Domnaill, co maithibh Cini[ui]l-Conaill uima, d'ár'loisc Tír-Eóghain roimhe, no co ráinic an Coillichtarach. Ocus, ar m-beth coic oidchi annsin dó ag feithim ar mac Néll, mic Cuind 7 O Néll a cruinniugad t-slúaigh an fedh sin, loiscis O Domnaill an tír ag impód dó, no co rainic Dún-gheanaind. Ocus fácbais O Neill an baile dó 7 loiscter an baile iarum co him[sh]lán 7 assin astech co slíabh 7 tic slán d'á thigh. Ocus ar m-beth sechtmain do Cloinn-Aoda-buidhe a Tír-Conaill maille ris O n-Domnaill, téid annsein d'á n-innlacudh 7 teid gach cuid dib slán día tighibh.

(A hosting by O'Domnaill, with the nobles of Cenel-Conaill around him, whereon he burned Tir-Eogain before him, until he reached Coill-ichtarach. And, on his being five nights there waiting for [Aedh] the son of Niall, son of Conn and [on the same] O'Neill mustering a host during that space, O'Domnaill burns the country on his return, until he reached Dun-Genainn. And O'Neill abandons the town to him and the town is afterwards burned completely and from that inwards to the Mountain and he comes safe to his house. And after the Clann-Aedha-buidhe being a week in Tir-Conaill along with O'Domnaill, he proceeds then to escort them [home] and each part of them goes safe to their houses.)[23]

Numerous accounts of escapades similar to this, involving various members of the Uí Dhomhnaill, are recounted throughout AFM, and the omission of this one might be a simple oversight. However, it is perhaps better explained by the complex political alliances that evidently underpinned it. In north-west Tyrone, an alliance between Ó Domhnaill and the sons of Art Óg Ó Neill complicated the political situation prior to the death of Ó Néill in 1519. It is possible that the enthusiastic recording of an Ó Domhnaill success owed its origins to the supporters of Conn Bacach Ó Néill who succeeded to the lordship in 1519, or to the sons of Art Óg Ó Néill, who were in alliance with Ó Domhnaill in opposition to their father.[24]

In another instance, although AFM records the destruction of Dungannon under the year 1517, the involvement of Aodh Dubh Ó Domhnaill is not

22 *AU*, III, pp 526–7. 23 *AU*, III, pp 526–7. 24 D.B. Quinn, '"Irish" Ireland and "English" Ireland' in Art Cosgrove (ed.), *A new history of Ireland, II, medieval Ireland, 1169–1534* (Dublin, 1987), p. 624.

mentioned and the attack is attributed instead to the Lord Justice *ar tairraincc cloinne inghine an iarla* ('at the instance of the sons of the earl's daughter').[25] Precisely which sons are being referred to here needs to be established. The only earl in this scenario was Gerald Fitzgerald, ninth earl of Kildare, who was then lord justice.[26] He had close family links through marriage and fosterage with both Ó Néill and Ó Domhnaill. His son had been fostered with Aodh Ruadh Ó Domhnaill (d. 1505), while one of his sisters, Eleanor, later married Maghnus Ó Domhnaill in 1538. Eleanor subsequently married into the Uí Néill of Dungannon as did a daughter, Alice.[27] If Alice's sons are the conspirators in question, then the AFM account explains the episode entirely in terms of Ó Néill factionalism, with external support, but without any link to Ó Domhnaill. The prominence given by the Four Masters to the role of the earl of Kildare accords with later accounts of what transpired, so that the benefit of hindsight may be in evidence here.

Over half of the AFM entries for the sample year 1517 are not found in AU. The geographical distribution of these items is sufficient to explain the differences in most instances. The additional entries in AFM include three Leinster items, records of the deaths of Brian Ó Conchobhair Fáilghe, Art Ó Tuathail, and an account of the plundering activities of Maolruanaidh Ó Cearbhaill. One Munster entry records a defeat suffered by the family of Cormac Mac Carthaigh, while a Connacht entry records the last exploits and subsequent death of Tomás Burke. The only Ulster entry recorded in AFM not also found in AU for the year 1517 is a brief obituary for Pilib mac Toirrdhealbhaigh Méguidhir.[28] It is clear from this example that the geographical scope of AFM was generally more extensive than that of AU. The geographical spread of AConn for this sample year of 1517 is likewise narrower than AFM, with four Ulster entries, one north Leinster entry and one Connacht entry particularly close to home for the annalists in that it recorded the death of Matha Glas Ó Duibhgeannáin.[29] The geographical spread of entries recorded in ALec for the mid-fifteenth century appears to mirror that of AFM more closely than is the case with either AU or AConn.

The absence of evidence in AFM of a consistent pattern of reliance on either AU or the source from which AConn derived, has potentially very important implications for the assessment of the methodology of the Four Masters. The pattern of correspondence between these other annals and AFM suggests that the Four Masters selected and adapted material from a wider variety of annals than now survives.

25 *AFM*, V, pp 1340–1.   26 T.W. Moody, F.X. Martin and F.J. Byrne (eds), *A new history of Ireland, IX: maps, genealogies, lists* (Oxford 1984), p. 480.   27 Mary Ann Lyons, *Gearóid Óg Fitzgerald* ([Dublin], 1998), pp 18–19; Eleanor was widow of Mac Carthy Reagh (J.G. Simms, 'Manus O'Donnell, 21st lord of Tir Conaill', *Donegal Annual* 5:2 (1962), 118).   28 *AFM*, V, pp 1338–9. 29 *AConn*, pp 632–3.

Table 5.3: Relationship between topics of entries in AFM, AU and
AConn for sample year 1416[30]

Year	AFM	AU	AConn	Year	AFM	AU	AConn
1416	1		24	1416	14	5	13
	2		7		15		3
	3		4		16		15
	4		8		17		23
	5		9		18		
	6		5		19	1	1
	7		27		20		
	8	10	26		21		
	9		28		22	6	14
	10	9	22		23		
	11		10		24		16
	12	3	11		25		
	13	4	12		26	8	21

Comparison of how entries were arranged in AFM as compared with the older
extant annals, therefore, highlights the manner in which AFM differed from pre-
existing compilations in terms of both content and arrangement. Before the
implications of this can be discussed, however, it is necessary to consider the
textual evidence for the methodology adopted by the Four Masters.

The entries for the sample year 1416 can help clarify the relationship between
AFM and the other annals extant for that year, notably AU and AConn (table
5:3). The example suggests that the use made of AU was sporadic. Where
available, other annalistic compilations, among them the Ó Duibhgeannáin
source now represented by AConn, were preferred. For the year 1416, just eight
of the twenty-six entries in AFM have corresponding entries in AU, and even in
those eight instances where the same event is noted in both texts, there are
differences in the level of detail recorded. A further seven entries relating to the
year 1416 recorded in AU are omitted from AFM altogether, while AFM
contains eighteen entries for which there is no corresponding material found in
AU.

As can be seen from table 5:3, in the year 1416 all except five of the AFM
events were also recorded in AConn. The five items not found in AConn are not
in AU either. All of the topics common to both AU and AFM are also to be found
in AConn. However, this was not always the case, and in the year 1450, for

---

30 The entry numbers used in respect of AFM and AU are those assigned in the digitized edition
of the Irish language version of the texts as published on the CELT website (www.ucc.ie/celt).

Table 5.4: Relationship between topics of entries in AFM, AU and AConn for sample year 1450

Year	AFM	AU	AConn	Year	AFM	AU	AConn
1450	1			1450	9	4	
	2	7			10	5	
	3				11	6	
	4				12	8	
	5		2		13	10	
	6	3			14	11	
	7	1			15		
	8	2			16		

example, the correlation between AFM and AU was quite substantial, whereas that with AConn was negligible (table 5:4). This suggests that if the Four Masters were relying primarily on one annalistic source, then neither AU nor AConn can be described as consistently representing that source. Indeed, it seems unwise to postulate that any single source might have had a dominant influence on the material selected for inclusion in AFM. In the 1450 example, it is again apparent that AFM contains additional entries not found in either AU or AConn, a pattern that is sustained throughout most of the fifteenth- and sixteenth-century entries in AFM.

Evidence for use of Annals of Lecan and Annals of Clonmacnoise

The extent to which the so-called annals of Lecan (ALec) were used in compiling AFM is difficult to assess because only a brief extract survives. They are now represented by a mid-seventeenth-century translation into English prepared by Dubhaltach Mac Fhirbhisigh for Sir James Ware, covering the years 1443–68 only.[31] Mac Fhirbhisigh's exemplar probably originally covered a longer period, and a more extensive source known as the annals of Lecan was available to Roderic O'Flaherty when he annotated one of the AFM manuscripts, TCD MS 1301.[32] A comparison of AFM and ALec for the mid-fifteenth century reveals that the source from which ALec derives was used selectively by the Four Masters for those years. Significantly, it emerges that a very similar source was

31 John O'Donovan (ed.), 'The annals of Ireland, from the year 1443 to 1468, translated from the Irish by Dudley Firbisse … for Sir James Ware, in the year 1666' in *Miscellany of the Irish Archaeological Society* 1 (Dublin, 1846), 198–302.   32 Nicholls, 'Introduction' to 1990 reprint of *AFM*; see above, pp 59–60.

used by the compilers of AConn, but the pattern of use there was very different. Curiously, AConn shows little evidence of having made use of the source of ALec for the years 1443–55, whereas there is a strong, if partial, correspondence between AFM and ALec for the entire range of years (1443–68) for which the translation survives. It would also appear that during these years the version of events contained in ALec was preferred by the Four Masters to alternative accounts of the same events in at least some instances.

For the years 1456–68, years for which AConn contains virtually every entry recorded in the Lecan text, AFM continues with its selective use of the Lecan source. In the year 1463, for example, AConn contains versions of all but one of the annal entries recorded in ALec, whereas the correlation with AFM is much less pronounced. In the ten years from 1451 to 1460, ALec was a more significant source for the Four Masters than either AU or AConn. The manner in which Lecan entries appear to have been preferred to alternative available versions for these years in at least some instances indicates that their Lecan annals were not quite a last-minute acquisition but were already to hand as the fifteenth-century material was being finalized by the Four Masters.[33]

While the specific 'Lecan' annalistic source used by the Four Masters no longer survives, the English translation by Dubhaltach Mac Fhirbhisigh, together with Roderic O'Flaherty's annotations for some earlier years give an indication of its broad scope. Yet, despite the wealth of source entries known to have been available to the Four Masters from their Lecan source for the mid-fifteenth century, the compilers nonetheless chose to combine their selection from that source with further material from AU. In addition, there are a small number of entries in AFM not found in AU, ALec, or AConn for those years.

Another annalistic source that may have had an influence on the content and arrangement of AFM was the exemplar of the compilation known as the Annals of Clonmacnoise (AClon). This source now ends with the year 1408 and thus is only marginally relevant to an analysis of the fifteenth-and sixteenth-century portions of AFM. It is nonetheless apparent that for the sample decade 1351–60, there is a definite correspondence between AClon and AFM, where of the 104 entries in AFM, thirty-nine are found in AClon. Daniel Mc Carthy has proposed that AClon derives essentially from the source of AConn,[34] termed by Mac Eochagáin an 'olde Irish book'. However, this may apply only to the latter part of AClon, the work of translation having been completed in two stages from two different sets of sources.[35] It is certainly the case that the Four Masters were more likely to consult Conall Mac Eochagáin's 'olde Irish book' than his English translation.

33 See above, pp 58–60. 34 Mc Carthy, *The Irish annals*, p. 289. 35 The translator gives two dates of completion: 20 April 1627 in the dedication to his patron and 30 June 1627 at the end of the (unfinished) work (Murphy (ed.), *AClon*, pp 9, 328).

In the examples considered so far of the relationship between the entries recorded in AFM and the material available from other extant annals, no one set of source annals can be said to predominate. There are numerous instances where an earlier annalistic compilation had quite a comprehensive range of entries for a given year, but yet the Four Masters chose not to rely exclusively on that source but selected from a range of other sources also. It should also be noted that when versions of particular entries occur in multiple sets of annals and the Four Masters include the topic, it is not normally possible to establish which source was preferred. Many of their entries were composites, rewritten on the basis of the range of versions of the episode available to them.

Prioritization of ecclesiastical entries in AFM

At all times, the Four Masters were consciously editing their text, selecting, re-ordering, and occasionally omitting material from among the full range of available sources. The pronounced tendency of the Four Masters to place entries relating to ecclesiastical matters at the beginning of their records for most years is the most noticeable element of their re-ordering of material as compared with AU, AConn, ALec or AClon. Most commonly, obituaries of bishop or abbots are placed as the opening entry for the year in AFM, where AU and AConn would usually give pride of place to a prominent secular personality. Although not all years in AFM open with an ecclesiastical entry, instances abound from many different centuries where this is the case. A typical example is AFM 1443, which gives precedence to Aonghus Mac Gille Fhindéin, abbot of Lisgoole. A version of the 1443 item is recorded in AU at a later point in the entry for the year 1443, and in a different form.

> AU
> *An t-ab (idon, Aengus) Mac Gilla-Fhinnein do eg (15 Kalendas Octobris) an bliadain si: idon, ab Lesa-gabail for Loch-Eirne.*
> (The abbot (namely, Aengus) Mac Gilla-Finnein died (on the 15th of the Kalends of October) this year: to wit, the abbot of Lis-gabail upon Loch Eirne.)[36]

> AFM 1443
> *Aonghus mhac Gille Findéin abb Leassa Gabhail décc.*
> (Aengus Mac Gillafinnen, Abbot of Lisgool, died.)[37]

While it is clear that the Four Masters could have extracted the information that they record in this obituary from the more cumbersome AU entry, it is apparent that they preferred a simple, concise entry. Here too, as in many other instances,

---

36 *AU*, III, pp 150–3.   37 *AFM*, IV, pp 928–9.

they deemed the precise date of death as recorded in earlier annals to be superfluous information. Thus, they shortened the entry even while prioritizing it by placing it first in the sequence of entries for that year.

The AFM 1444 sample records as its first entry the death of Risterd Ó Fearghail, bishop of Ardagh, and secondly the death of a group of prominent north Connacht and Ulster clergy who had been on pilgrimage to Rome.[38]

> AFM 1444
>
> [1] *Risderd mac an deaganaigh mhoir mic Domhnaill mic Seaain Gallda Ui Fearghail, epscop Ardachaidh décc.*
>
> [2] *Uilliam Ua hEtigen epscop Oile Find do dhul do Roimh, 7 drong mór do clerchibh Connacht 7 a nécc durmhor .i. Tadhg mac Taidhg mic Diarmada iar ngnoughadh abdhaine na Búille, 7 Uilliam mac an decccanaigh Ui Fhlannagain prioir Commain, Mac Maoilechloinn mic Corbmaic mec Donnchaidh abb Baile Eassa Dara, 7 sochaidh oile do clerchib Uladh.*
>
> [1] (Richard, son of the Great Dean, son of Donnell, son of John Gallda O'Farrell, bishop of Ardagh, died.
>
> [2] William O'Hetigen, bishop of Elphin, and a great number of the clergy of Connaught, went to Rome, where the majority of them died, namely, Teige, son of Teige Mac Donough, who had been appointed to the abbacy of Boyle; William, son of the Dean O'Flanagan, prior of Roscommon; the son of Melaghlin, son of Cormac Mac Donough, abbot of Ballysadare; and many also of the clergy of Ulster.)[39]

These two ecclesiastical items in AFM for 1444 are not recorded at all in AU. A quite different account of the Rome pilgrimage in 1444 is found in AConn, close to the end of the record for that year.

> AConn 1444
>
> *Tadc mac Taidc Meic Diarmata proatsi Ola Finn do ecc ar sligid Roma.*
>
> (Tadc son of Tadc Mac Diarmata, provost of Elphin, died on the journey to Rome.)[40]

The version in AConn is much shorter, and without any indication that a large number of clergy were involved in the pilgrimage to Rome. It is noteworthy that the AFM detail of the account of the Roman pilgrimage and the deaths that ensued corresponds most closely to that in the surviving fragment of ALec. But again, AFM gives the entry priority in terms of the sequencing that it does not enjoy in ALec, where it appears as the twelfth entry for 1444.

> ALec 1444
>
> The bishop of Oilfinn, .i. William O-Etegen went to Rome, and many of the Connachtian clergy, and they for the most parte died, .i. Thady fitz Thady Mac

38 *AFM*, IV, pp 932–3. 39 *AFM*, IV, pp 932–3. 40 *AConn*, pp 486–7.

Diarmoda after obtaining the abbacie of the Boyle, and William son to the Deane O-Flannagan, .i. prior of Roscommon, and the son of Maelachlyn fitz Cormack McDonnaghy, .i. the abbot of Balaesadara, and John son to the Abbot McDavid, with many more of the clergy of Vlster and Connacht.[41]

A similar pattern is followed in AFM in subsequent years, with the 1445 annal opening with mention of the death of Tomas Ua Lennain, a canon of Lisgoole, and the 1446 annal recording the death of Eóin Ua Lennain, prior of the same monastery. The 1447 annal in AFM opens in the same style, recording the death of the coarb of Fenagh, following this with mention of the impact of plague on the priors of a number of monasteries in Meath, Leinster and Munster, and the reconstruction of a church in Fermanagh in the same year. In 1448, the first AFM entry records the continuing impact of plague on Longford monastery and follows this with entries relating to the death of Conor Mac Faolchadha, bishop of Ross, and the death of the abbot of the monastery of Holy Trinity on Lough Key. The death of the bishop of Ross is placed near the beginning of the AFM entry for 1448, even though it took place in December of that year.[42] This ecclesiastical prioritization is not paralleled in AU, AConn or ALec. The distinctive AFM pattern of allowing precedence to ecclesiastical entries is a clear indication of the annalists' judgment of the relative importance of the entries they recorded. They made no attempt to adhere to an internal chronology within a given year, any more than the earlier annals did, but chose instead to impose a systematic ordering of entries that emphasized their concern that ecclesiastical matters should enjoy due prominence in their annals of the Irish past.

Occasionally, more unusual religious themes are given precedence. In 1411, for instance, it is the miraculous crucifix at Raphoe that is given priority as the first entry for the year in AFM.

AFM 1411
Croch naomh Ratha both do tepirsin fola tar a créchtaibh galra. 7 tedhmanna iomdha do fhóiridhin las an bfuil hishin.
(The Holy Crucifix of Raphoe poured out blood from its wounds. Many distempers and diseases were healed by that blood.)[43]

A similar record is the final entry in AU for that year, and yet another version as the twenty-fourth item in AConn for the same year.[44] Similarly, in 1412, AFM gave precedence to an account of miracles wrought by the image of the Virgin Mary at Trim, an item placed seventh for that year in AU and as the twelfth of twenty entries in AConn.[45] The significance of the Four Masters' editorial policy of prioritizing ecclesiastical material is explored more fully in chapter eight below.

41 *ALec*, p. 206.   42 *AFM*, IV, pp 940–1; 944–5, 950–3, 957–8.   43 *AFM*, IV, pp 804–5.   44 *AU*, III, pp 60–1 (B. MacCarthy noted in his edition that the AU entry was copied corruptly by the Four Masters); *AConn*, pp 410–11.   45 *AFM*, IV, pp 808–9; *AU*, III, pp 62–6; *AConn*, pp 414–15.

Political terminology of kingship

One of the key characteristics of AFM remarked on by modern commentators is the manner in which the terminology of kingship differs between AFM and earlier annals. Thus, for example, F.J. Byrne has observed that AU restricts the title of 'king of Ireland' to eight Uí Néill kings and four from other dynasties, beginning with Domnall mac Aédo (AD628–42) and ending with Ruaidhrí Ó Conchobhair (1166–86, d. 1198). In most other instances, AU simply used a name and patronymic, or added the title 'king of the Uí Néill or 'king of Tara'. In most such instances, Byrne notes, the Four Masters use the term 'king of Ireland' instead.[46] Not only that, the whole format of AFM was structured around the idea of a kingship of Ireland dating back to AM3500. Donnchadh Ó Corráin supports Byrne's view that it was only in the ninth century that the Uí Néill can be said to have attained the 'kingship of Ireland'.[47]

The upgrading of certain kings was but one element of the Four Masters' modification of their sources in respect of kingship. The corollary was the downgrading of other petty kings, the rulers of individual *tuatha* in the Old Irish period, which the older annals had termed as kings. Examples abound, and since the phenomenon has already been commented on by others, two brief illustrations will suffice here, where the word *tigherna* is substituted for the word *rí*.

AFM 1172
Ticchernan ua Ruairce ticcherna Breifne agus Conmaicne
(Tiernan O'Rourke, lord of Breifny and Conmaicne.)[48]

AU 1172
Tigernan hUa Ruairc, ri Breifne 7 Conmaicne
(Tigernan Ua Ruairc, king of Breifni and Conmaicni.)[49]

AFM 1174
Maolruanaidh ua Ciardha tighearna cairpri
(Mulrony O'Keary, lord of Carbury.)[50]

AU 1174
Maelruanaigh hUa Ciardha, ri Cairpri
(Maelruanaigh Ua Ciarda, king of Cairpri.)[51]

Megan McGowan has shown that of 1,519 instances of the word *tigherna* in medieval Irish chronicles for the centuries before the coming of the Normans, 1,507 are found in AFM.[52] Byrne offers an explanation couched in terms of patriotic sentiment.

46 Byrne, *Irish kings and high kings*, pp 256–7; F.J. Byrne, *The rise of the Uí Néill and the high-kingship of Ireland* (O'Donnell lecture, Dublin, 1969). 47 Ó Corráin, Review of Byrne, *Irish kings and high-kings*, 166. 48 *AFM*, III, pp 4–5. 49 *AU*, II, pp 172–3. 50 *AFM*, III, pp 14–15. 51 *AU*, II, pp 178–9. 52 McGowan, 'Political geography and political structures in earlier medieval Ireland', p. 12.

In later ages, this multiplication of monarchies caused some embarrassment to patriotic Irishmen who had been brought up to believe in the glories of the high-kingship of Ireland centred in Tara. So, in the early seventeenth century the Four Masters, in their great compilation *The Annals of the Kingdom of Ireland (Annála Ríoghachta Éireann)*, consistently downgrade the kings of petty tuatha to the status of 'lord' or 'chieftain' –'*tigerna*' or '*taoiseach*'.[53]

Kenneth Nicholls has observed that the Four Masters' policy regarding the language of kingship was influenced by the fact that 'by the late sixteenth century the application of the term "king" in European usage, outside the national monarchies of Europe, was confined to the tribal chiefs of "barbarous" non-European peoples, such as the North American Indians'.[54] The Four Masters' controlled use of the language of kingship, therefore, was done to build up the prestige of the high kingship of Ireland. As well as indulging their enthusiasm for projecting the origins of the kingship of Ireland back into the prehistoric period, it also allowed them to emphasize the kingly status of men such as Ruaidhrí Ó Conchobhair, whose inauguration was recorded under the year 1166.

> AFM 1166
> *Slóighedh lá Ruaidhri Ua cConchobhair go Connachtaibh go bfearaibh Midhe, 7 go bferaibh Tethbha co hAth cliath, 7 go ríghadh ann Ruaidhri Ua Concobhair febh as onóraighe ro ríghadh rí riamh do Ghaoidhealaibh, 7 ro thíodhnaic siomh a ttuarastal do na Gallaibh do bhuar iomdha, uair ro sreathait da fichit céd bó for feraibh Ereann dóibh.*
>
> (An army was led by Ruaidhri Ua Conchobhair, with the Connaughtmen, the men of Meath and of Teathbha, to Atha-cliath; and Ruaidhri Ua Conchobhair was there inaugurated king as honourably as any king of the Gaeidhil was ever inaugurated; and he presented their stipends to the foreigners in many cows, for he levied a tax of four thousand cows upon the men of Ireland for them.)[55]

After his death Ruaidhrí Ó Conchobhair was remembered as *Rí Connacht 7 Ereann uile eittir ghallaibh 7 gaoidhelaibh* ('king of Connaught and of all Ireland, both the Irish and the English').[56] This contrasts with the treatment of the same king in Conall Mac Eochagáin's translation of AClon which records under the year 1164:

> AClon 1164
> Rory o'Connor king of Connaught succeeded in the monarchie. Rory more mcTerlagh o'Connor in the English Chronicles is called Rotherick, was the last king of Ireland of Irish blood, and raigned 10 years. Our Irish Chronicles for the most part call those seven and last kings imperfect and defective kings, because

---

53 Byrne, *Irish kings and high kings*, p. 41. 54 Nicholls, 'Introduction' to 1990 reprint of *AFM*. 55 *AFM*, II, pp 1160–1. 56 *AFM*, III, pp 112–15, s.a. 1198.

they raigned without a crown (as before is mentioned) since the raigne of Bryan Borowe and Moyleseachlin more o'Melaghlin.[57]

The passage is one of many in AClon that reads more like Conall Mac Eochagáin's own interpolation than a faithful translation of his source.[58] The text of AU is corrupt at this point[59] but the Cottonian annals, sometimes described as the Annals of Boyle, record the inauguration of Ó Conchobhair as king, in an entry that lacks the historical contextualization found in AFM. The Cottonian annals stated simply *Sluaged la Ruadri ua Conchobuir co Ath Cliath corarígsat gaill Atha Cliath he* ('Ruadri O Conchubair marched to Dublin and was made king by the foreigners there').[60]

Even after the end of the high-kingship of Ireland, the Four Masters continued to preserve the concept of kingship, and the praiseworthy attributes associated with the idea of kingship, particularly in obituaries of the Uí Chonchobhair. Thus the obituary for Fedhlimidh son of Cathal Crobderg Ó Conchobhair in 1265 described him as

AFM 1265
fear lan denech, deangnamh, 7 doirdercus, fear méadaighthe ord eccailseach, 7 ealadhan, deghadbhar rígh Éireann ar uaisli, ar cruth, or cródhacht, ar chéill, ar iocht, ar fhírinne.
(a man full of hospitality, prowess and renown; the exalter of the clerical orders and men of science; a worthy materies of a king of Ireland for his nobility, personal shape, heroism, wisdom, clemency and truth.)[61]

The equivalent obituary in AU simply noted that *Feidhlim[idh] hUa Chonchobuir, airdri Connacht, in t-aen Gaidhel rob' fherr maith[i]us dobí i n-Erinn i n-a réimheas fein, mortuus est* ('Feidhlimidh Ua Conchobuir, arch king of Connacht, the Gaidhel of most goodness that was in Ireland in his own period, died').[62] AConn described the same man as *fer lan d'oinech 7 d'engnam, fer lan d'urdercus 7 d'urrumus i nErinn 7 i Saxanaib* ('a man full of honour and valour, of respect and importance in Ireland and England'), but made no mention of the kingship of Ireland.[63]

In a later instance, in 1311, where Donnchadh Ó Briain, king of Munster, was described by the Four Masters as *adbhar rígh Éreann*,[64] there was a corresponding assertion in AConn, *rí Tuadmuman degadbar Rig Erenn* ('king of Thomond and good man for the kingship of Ireland'),[65] and also in AU.[66] However, this, and a

---

57 *AClon*, p. 206. 58 A little later in his text Conall Mac Eochagáin observes 'There are soe many leaves lost or stolen out of the ould Irish book which I translate, that I doe not know how to handle it' (*AClon*, p. 215). 59 *AU*, II, pp 150–7. 60 A.M. Freeman (ed.), 'The annals in Cotton MS Titus A XXV' [part 2], *Revue Celtique* 42 (1925), 289; 43 (1926), 371 (item 352). 61 *AFM*, III, pp 396–7. 62 *AU*, II, pp 334–5. 63 *AConn*, pp 144–5. 64 *AFM*, III, pp 498–9. 65 *AConn*, pp 226–7. 66 *AU*, II, pp 418–19.

later reference of the same type in respect of Conchobhar Ó Briain in 1328, was used more as a way of defining personal character than as a statement of political aspiration.[67] This is evident from the almost incidental manner in which the death of Conchobhar Ó Briain is recorded at the end of a short narrative that mentions related incidents also. The idea that certain individuals were contenders for the kingship of Ireland persisted for a time and was accepted by the Four Masters in respect of an Ó Néill in 1369, and again in 1397, but such references do not occur thereafter.[68]

The concept of provincial kings was retained by the Four Masters, however, and there are plentiful references from the tenth to the fifteenth centuries to kings of Ulster, Leinster, Munster and Connacht as well as of Meath or Tara. These provincial kings were an important element in sustaining the idea of continuity of kingship in Ireland after the end of the high kingship. Just very occasionally, a 'rí Desmumhan' ('king of Desmond') (1176, 1189),[69] or a Rí Chinél nEoghain ('king of the Kinel Owen'),[70] escapes the usually tight editorial control of Mícheál Ó Cléirigh and his chief editorial collaborator, Cú Choigcríche Ó Cléirigh. These stray references to local kings are the exceptions that prove the rule, and it is clear that the idea of the kingship of Ireland was carefully cultivated by the Four Masters through the controlled use of the language of kingship as well as through the structural framework of regnal years down to 1022. The annalists were carefully fulfilling Patrick Fleming's vision of a history de regibus hiberniae ('of the kings of Ireland'), the idea for which he had discussed with his fellow Franciscan, Hugh Ward.[71] They were systematically and comprehensively putting flesh on the bones of the history of Ireland as outlined by Donogh Mooney in 1617 as a preface to his history of the Franciscans in Ireland, where he observed that 'The government was always monarchical, but there were a number of subordinate kings, each of whom ruled in his own district'.[72] The Four Masters presented their material in a manner that enhanced the status of the kingship of Ireland, and the five provincial kings, by relegating all others to the lesser status of tighearna ('lord'), and by using regnal years as the basis of their chronology to create the impression of a kingdom of considerably antiquity.

67 AFM, III, pp 540–1; AU, II, pp 446–7; AConn, pp 264–5.   68 AFM, III, pp 648–9 (AD1369); AFM, IV, pp 750–1. The prophecy discussed below in respect of Aodh Ruadh Ó Domhnaill (d. 1602) might be deemed an exception, though he is not explicitly presented as 'king of Ireland' rather than a provincial king.   69 AFM, III, pp 28–9; 86–7.   70 AFM, III, pp 626–37; 642–3; IV, pp 750–1.   71 Fleming to Ward, 24 August 1624, printed in Jennings (ed.), 'Documents from of St Isidore's', 216.   72 Translated in Donagh Mooney, 'A history of the Franciscan Order in Ireland', Franciscan Tertiary 5 (1894–5), 324. Et licet unus eorum fuerit semper Monarcha, tamen multos regulos subordinatos Monarchae habuerunt antiquis saeculis, qui cum dividissent regnum, tot fecerunt territorian quot erant et comparticipantes (Brendan Jennings, (ed.), 'Brussels MS. 3947: Donatus Moneyus, De Provincia Hiberniae S. Francisci', Analecta Hibernica 6 (1934), 20).

Foreign kings

As already noted, the insertion of entries on the kings of England was a mere afterthought on the part of the Four Masters, although the actions of representatives of the king of England (*Rí Saxan*) emerge as a regular matter of record in the annals from the late fourteenth century.[73] It is noteworthy that, unlike his predecessors, the Stuart king, James I, did not merit the qualification 'Saxan', and the entry was worded so that the extent of his jurisdiction was not clearly defined.

AFM 1602
King Semus do ríoghadh i nionad na bainríoghna Elizabeth an cethramhadh lá fichet do Mharta, 1602, do réir airmhe na Saccsan, 7 do reir rímhe na Romhan as 1603. 7 as eisidhe an seiseadh Sémus do rioghaibh Alban.
(King James was proclaimed King in the place of the Queen, Elizabeth, on the 24th of March 1602, according to the English computation, or in 1603, according to the Roman computation. He was the sixth James of the Kings of Scotland.)[74]

A number of references to the king of Spain occur in the final pages of the annals in the section that derives in part from *Beatha Aodha Ruaidh*. Strong expressions of loyalty to the Spanish king are also found in the 1602 will of Aodh Ruadh Ó Domhnaill,[75] but these sentiments are not matched in the AFM account of his life. However, the annalists perceived it to be necessary to offer a historical explanation of Aodh Ruadh's alliance with the Spanish crown. Thus, in describing the aftermath of the battle of Kinsale, the Four Masters elaborated considerably on Lughaidh Ó Cléirigh's narrative, which had opened the account of 1602 with a statement of his intention to go to Spain:

BARUD 1602
Basí airle arriocht la hUa nDomhnaill íarsan dubha dermhair i mboí Ere do fhagbhail 7 dul don Spáinn do acaoine a imnidh frisan Righ an 3 Philip do chuingidh fuillidh slóicch 7 sochraide úaidibh.
(The plan which was arrived at by O Domhnaill after his great grief, was to leave Ireland and to go to Spain to complain of his distress to King Philip III and to ask for more forces and soldiers.)[76]

73 *AFM*, II, pp 1114–15 (AD1155); III, pp 88–9 (AD1189); III, pp 120–1 (AD1199); III, pp 190–1 (AD1216); III, pp 418–19 (AD1272); III, pp 488–9 (AD1307); III, pp 534 (AD1326); IV, pp 670–1 (AD1377); IV, pp 766–7 (AD1399); IV, pp 812–13 (AD1412); IV, pp 854–5 (AD1422); IV, pp 1008–9 (AD1460); IV, pp 1126–7 (AD1483); IV, pp 1136–7 (AD1485); V, pp 1302–3 (AD1509); V, pp 1498–9 (AD1547); V, pp 1528–9 (AD1553); V, pp 1568–9 (AD1558).   74 *AFM*, VI, pp 2322–3.   75 Silke, 'The last will of Red Hugh O'Donnell', 58.   76 *BARUD*, I, pp 340–2 (typographical errors in Walsh's edition of the Irish text of this passage have been amended here from RIA, MS 23 P 24, fo. 83v).

AFM 1602

Iar sraoinedh madhma Cinn tSáile lá Gallaibh for Gaoidhealaibh (amhaíl ro scriobhadh chena) an tres lá do mhí Ianuarii, 7 for an uathadh Spáinnech do muintir rígh na Spainne do rala a maille friú an tan sin, Ro ghabh deinmne, 7 dásacht, 7 utmoille mór menman Ua Domhnaill (Aodh Ruadh) co ná ro thuil 7 ná ro loing hi saimhe fri ré tri lá 7 teóra noidhche iaramh go ro ben ceill dia chabhair i nErinn conadh í airle ro chinn i necmhaing na ree sin (tre comhairle uí Néill gion gur bhó lainn lais-sidhe a comhairlécchadh dó) Ere d'faccbháil, 7 dol don Spainn d'ionnsaighidh an righ an 3. Pilip do chuinghidh fuilleadh sochraitte, 7 comhfhurtachta uadhaibh, uair ro badh dóigh laissiomh gur bhó hé rí na Spainne aon ro badh mó conicfeadh a fhóirithin, 7 lás ar lainne congnamh lás an ccách nó chathaighfeadh dar cenn an chreidimh catolice Rómhanaigh do gres 7 araill ele tria na bháidh fri Gaoidhealaibh ar a ttocht cétus do ghabháil Ereann as in Spainn amhail as follas isin leabhar dianidh ainm in leabhar gabhala.

(After this defeat of Kinsale had been given by the English (as has been already written), on the third day of the month of January, to the Irish and the few Spaniards of the King of Spain's people who happened to be along with them at that time, O'Donnell (Hugh Roe) was seized with great fury, rage and anxiety of mind; so that he did not sleep or rest soundly for the space of three days and three nights afterwards; so that he despaired of getting succour in Ireland. At the expiration of that time, the resolution he came to (by the advice of O'Neill, who, however, gave him this advice with reluctance) was to leave Ireland and go to Spain to King Philip III, to request more forces and succour from him; for he thought that the King of Spain was the person who could render him most relief, and who was the most willing to assist those who always fought in defence of the Roman Catholic religion; and moreover, on account of his [Philip's] attachment to the Gaels, from their having first come out of Spain to invade Ireland, as in manifest from the Book of Invasions.)[77]

This passage, evidently original to the AFM text, is interesting for the way its style imitates that of Ó Cléirigh's biography, but more so for the insights it offers into the political ideology of the Four Masters. Although these references to the Spanish king in AFM originated as an important element of the ideology that informed the narrative biography of Ó Domhnaill, as far as the Four Masters were concerned Aodh Ruadh's reliance on the Spanish monarchy was an issue that needed clarification because it did not fit easily with the idea of kingship that had informed their text to that point. There is no sense here of the Four Masters transferring allegiance from the Stuart king to the king of Spain, and there seems little doubt that it was the idea of the kingdom of Ireland and not any outside kingdom, whether English or Spanish, that was central to the political ideology of the Four Masters.

The question of support for Catholicism was highlighted in this passage, however, in a manner that Mícheál Mac Craith has traced in the writings of Irish

77 *AFM*, VI, pp 2290–1. The dating of the battle of Kinsale provides evidence of the Four Masters' use of the Gregorian calendar.

Franciscans in Europe in the aftermath of the death of Aodh Ó Néill in 1616. Mac Craith has shown that the more politicized 'faith and fatherland' ideology of *Beatha Aodha Ruaidh* contrasts with the writings of the Louvain Franciscans who had come to accept James I as legitimate monarch of Ireland. And although three instances of the 'faith and fatherland' terminology can be found in AFM in passages derived from *Beatha Aodha Ruaidh*, Mac Craith argues that the AFM version implies no hostility to the Stuart king. The phrase as used in AFM signifies a different set of loyalties: loyalty to Catholicism, loyalty to Ireland and loyalty to the Stuart monarchy.[78]

Evidence of the Four Masters' acceptance of the English monarchy is not confined to their record of the accession of James I. Each of his predecessors on the English throne, from Henry II to Elizabeth, was also recorded in AFM. These entries were a late insertion in the manuscripts, which means that their inclusion was the result of a conscious editorial decision.[79] It is possible that they were added as a kind of synchronism for foreign readers, but more likely in recognition of their royal status and consequent relevance to the history of the kingdom of Ireland. They are not merely there because they were recorded in the source annals from which the bulk of other entries derived.

Yet, the Four Masters' support for the Stuart monarchy may not have been unequivocal. Their use of a prophecy of Colum Cille as part of the annalistic commemoration of Aodha Ruadh Ó Domhnaill following his death in 1602 made specific allusion to kingship *is biadh .x. mbliadhna na rígh* ('and will be ten years king').[80] At the time of his death, Aodh Ruadh had indeed been lord of Tír Conaill for ten years.[81] The Four Masters' contextualization of kingship through the use of prophecy, at this point in the text, immediately followed by a lament on the state of the Gaeil after the death of Aodh Ruadh may be read as an expression of the annalists' view that the kingship of Ireland had come to an end with Aodh Ruadh's death in exile.[82]

The two thematic elements of comparison between AFM and the extant late medieval annals discussed so far, in terms of ecclesiastical prioritization and control of the political language of kingship, highlight significant aspects of the ideology of the Four Masters. It is evident that in terms of content and sequencing of entries, they systematically altered the arrangement of their sources as represented by older annals such as AU, AConn, ALec and AClon. Very many similarities in terms of general content can also be identified, of course, as might be expected in annals that claimed as the measure of their authenticity the fact that they were drawn from earlier, named, sources. Yet in

---

78 Mac Craith, 'Creideamh agus Athartha', pp 7–19.   79 The Four Masters' information about dates of inauguration of English kings derived from a source in which the year was deemed to commence on 25 March.   80 *AFM*, VI, pp 2298–9.   81 His inauguration was described by the annalists in their record of 1592 (*AFM*, VI, pp 1928–9).   82 Their source here was BARUD, but with considerable revision and adaptation. See above, pp 91–2.

analyzing the methodology of the Four Masters, the extent to which they deviated from those sources may be the most significant indicator of their objectives. While selecting the majority of their entries from the available sources, the Four Masters modified the content, style, language and sequencing of entries to produce a new compilation deemed appropriate to their intended audience. The content, political language and arrangement of entries in AFM reflect their concern to prioritize ecclesiastical matters, their concern not to trivialize Irish kingship, and also their concern to present the Uí Dhomhnaill in a favourable light. Even though some sources available to the Four Masters cannot now be identified, the range of innovative features in AFM is clear.

Patterns of omission in AFM

Another approach to assessing the nature of the relationship between AFM and the older extant annals containing late medieval entries is to consider the entries that the Four Masters chose to omit. As already seen, a range of source texts was usually available to the annalists when compiling the entries for any given year in the fifteenth- and early sixteenth-century sections of AFM. Conscious of the objective of producing a coherent set of annals that could be circulated in printed form, it proved necessary to condense the available material. This was achieved by abbreviating individual entries or by omitting them altogether.

One of the clearest ways in which entries recorded in AFM tend to differ from the equivalent entries in AU and AConn is the more concise wording of the AFM version. Entries were abbreviated in a variety of ways, as compared with the older annals. Though there is no consistency in the style of dating used for individual events, it is frequently the case that a dated event recorded in AU or AConn is given without a precise date in AFM. The 1414 obituary for Conchobhar Ó Flannagáin, for instance, is recorded with some very elaborate dating in AConn but in a simplified form in AFM. There is no corresponding entry in AU.

> AConn 1414
> *Conchabar mac Sefraid h. Flannacan damna taisig Clainni Cathail mortuus est vi. Calainn Nouimbir arai laithi mis greine, in uigilia Simionis 7 Iude, dia Sathairn arai laithi sechtmaine, an sesed la ria Samfuin e-sidein.*
> (Conchobar son of Sefraid O Flannacain, a possible chieftain of the Clann Chathail, died on the sixth of the Kalends of November by the day of the solar month, the vigil of SS Simon and Jude, Saturday by the day of the week, the sixth day before Samain.)[83]

---

83 *AConn*, pp 420–1.

AFM 1414

Concobhar mac Seffraidh uí Fhlannagáin adhbhar taoisigh Cloinne Cathail décc an seiseadh lá ria Samhain.

(Conor, son of Geoffrey O'Flanagan, heir to the chieftainship of Clann-Cathail, died six days before Allhallowtide.)[84]

A simpler obituary in AConn was recorded for an archbishop of Connacht under the year 1407, but again AFM omits details of the place and precise date of death.

AConn 1407

Murcertach h. Cellaig .i. ardespoc Connacht, sai na hErenn uli ind ecna 7 a nderc 7 i ndoennacht, in Christo quieuit i Tuaim Da Gualann fo feil Micheil.

(Muirchertach O Cellaig, archbishop of Connacht, eminent in all Ireland for wisdom, charity and humanity, rested in Christ at Tuam at the feast of Michael).[85]

AFM 1407

Muirchertach (.i. mac mic Maine) Ua Ceallaigh airdepscop Connacht, saoí i neccna, i neineach, 7 i crabaidh dég.

(Murtough, grandson of Maine O'Kelly, archbishop of Connaught, a man eminent for his wisdom, hospitality and piety, died.)[86]

There are two ways of interpreting the difference between AConn and AFM in the case of the obituary of this archbishop. It may be an instance where the source used by AFM and AConn differed, but it is not possible to know this for certain. An alternative interpretation of the difference largely circumvents the uncertainty over the precise sources available. Since the Four Masters had access to a range of source annals, they would have consulted more than one version of the obituary for the archbishop, and the entry in AFM was probably a composite, shaped to fit their view of what it was appropriate to record. In this instance, recording the place and precise date of death was of secondary importance as compared with presenting a version of the obituary that conveyed to readers the image of a wise, hospitable and pious archbishop.

There are many other instances where precise dates are deemed superfluous by the Four Masters. The record of the death in 1419 of Cú Choigcríche Ó Maoilmhuaidh is given in AConn with a note that he died on 25 June, but that dating is omitted in AFM.[87] It appears unwise, however, to conclude that the Four Masters adopted a consistent editorial policy as regards the omission or inclusion of references to exact dates. Many variations occur. If the internal dating of the 1420 entry on the killing of Cathal Mág Flannchadha in AFM is compared with the corresponding entry in AConn, the simplest explanation of

---

84 *AFM*, IV, pp 818–19. 85 *AConn*, pp 398–9. 86 *AFM*, IV, pp 790–1. 87 *AConn*, pp 444–5; *AFM*, IV, pp 840–1.

the difference is that the Four Masters' source was not used by the compilers of AConn. The event is dated *a tossach erraig* ('at the beginning of Spring') in AConn,[88] but as *im fél Brighde* ('about the festival of St Bridget') in AFM.[89] However, in the 1475 obituary of Eamonn Ó hAinlighe, AFM follows the style of dating found in AConn much more closely, referring both to the day of the week, Thursday, and the nearest feastday, Michaelmas.[90] Thus, while the number of instances where AFM adopts a more concise style of dating than either AConn or AU is considerable, the Four Masters are inconsistent in the matter, and it is possible that the level of variation in the style of dating found in entries in AFM may sometimes reflect the different source texts utilized. In their selection and adaptation of entries from the available sources, precision in the matter of dating appears to have been quite low in their priorities (though they make exceptions for saints and for many of the Uí Dhomhnaill).[91] Cumulatively, the impact of multiple obituaries of pious men was what mattered in their recall of the Irish past, and not the detail of the day or month on which individuals died.

Prayers and proverbs

The inclusion of incidental prayers or proverbs is a typical feature of obituaries in medieval Irish annals. However, the version of an obituary recorded in AFM normally omits such prayers. The obituary for Tadhg Ó Ceallaigh in 1410 is a case in point.

> AConn 1410
> *Esbaid bad mo ina cach esbaid do techt a ndered na bliadna-so coictigis tar es na feli Micheil .i. Tadc h. Cellaig ri h. Mane, int aenGaidel dobo mo tinnlaicti 7 taburtus do bai a nErinn ina aimsir 7 a nAlpain, do ecc iar mbuaidh ongtha 7 aithrige, et cur airchise Dia dia anmain in secula seculorum.*
> (A loss greater than all losses was suffered at the end of this year, a fortnight after the feast of Michael. Tadc O Cellaig, king of the Ui Maine, the most bountiful giver of all the Gaels of Ireland and Scotland in his time, died after a victory of Unction and Penance, and may God have mercy on his soul for ever and ever.)[92]

> AFM 1410
> *Tadhg mac Maoileachlainn mic Uilliam mic Donnchaidh Muimhnigh Uí Cheallaigh tighearna Ó Maine, flaithfhear dearcach daonnachtach do écc iar mbuaidh naithrighe.*
> (Teige, the son of Melaghlin, son of William, son of Donough Muimhneach O'Kelly, lord of Hy-Many, a charitable and benevolent chief, died, after the victory of penance.)[93]

---

88 *AConn*, pp 450–1. 89 *AFM*, IV, pp 844–5. 90 *AFM*, IV, pp 1092–3; *AConn*, pp 574–5.
91 These two categories of exceptions often appear as interlineations in the autograph manuscripts, indicating that they belonged to a phase of revision of the text by the compiler-editors rather than the initial phase of compilation. 92 *AConn*, pp 406–7. 93 *AFM*, IV, pp 802–3.

In this instance, the obituary is recorded in AU also, but is even more sparse in its content than AFM, and does not include the prayer found in the version preserved in AConn. It is noteworthy, however, that the genealogical detail incorporated into the AFM entry corresponds with the information supplied in AU. The usual change in terminology from *rí* to *tigherna* also occurs.

> AU 1410
> *Tadhg, mac Mail[-Sh]echlainn, mic Uilliam, mic Donnchadha Muimnigh hUi Ceallaigh, idon, ri hUa-Maine, d'eg in bliadhain si.*
> (Tadhg, son of Mail[-Sh]echlainn, son of William, son of Donnchadh Ua Ceallaigh the Momonian, namely, king of Ui-Maine, died this year.)[94]

The 1415 obituary in AFM for Éamonn Mág Findbairr also lacks the prayer, *bennachd De leis* ('God bless him'), which concluded the obituary for the same man in AConn.

> AFM 1415
> *Émann mag Findbairr prióir Insi Móire Locha Gamhna do ég an 27 April.*
> (Edmond Mac Finnvar, prior of Inis-Mor-Locha-Gamhna, died on 27 April.)[95]
>
> AConn 1415
> *Emand Mag Findbairr prior Insi Mori Locha Gamna in Christo quieuit sechtmain ria mBeltaine 7 bennacht De leis.*
> (Emann Mag Findbairr, prior of Inchmore in Loch Gowna, rested in Christ a week before May-day. God bless him.)[96]

In this, as in other cases, however, the style of dating also differs to the extent that it may be best to surmise that the Four Masters probably selected their entry from a source other than the Uí Dhuibhgeannáin annals. Comparison with the text of ALec likewise reveals that the prayers included in entries found in that source are not included in the corresponding entries in AFM.[97]

The prayers included in some records of death in AConn and ALec may have originated in obituaries compiled around the time of the death, as part of a public record of commemoration. The more detached historical form of such obituaries incorporated into AFM, omitting the prayer element, can be interpreted as evidence of the attempt by the Four Masters to present a formal record of the Irish past rather than serve as a vehicle for the preservation of social memory through local remembrance. It seems that such prayers were not deemed appropriate to a historical text intended for international publication.

As well as choosing to omit incidental prayers of the kind that feature in AConn and ALec, some of the more elaborate deathbed repentances recorded in

94 *AU*, III, pp 58–9. 95 *AFM*, IV, pp 820–1. 96 *AConn*, pp 426–7. 97 AFM 1454.4, 1452.19, 1452.20, 1458.3, 1458.9, 1458.20, 1460.6 are examples of entries in AFM that lack a prayer where a prayer forms part of the corresponding entry in ALec.

AConn are also absent from AFM. The obituary of Ruaidhri Ó Dubhda, who died in 1417, illustrates the point.

AConn 1417
Ruaidri mac Domnaill h. Dubda rex h. Fiachrach Muaide, tobar sonusa 7 saidbriusa Erenn uli 7 nar diult re dreich ndune riam im biad na im edach, in Christo quieuit iar n-ongad 7 aithrige ndingbala do Dia 7 don Eclais Catholecda 7 iar caithem Cuirp 7 a Fola ina longport budein hi tus Erraig do sundrad, 7 Tadc Riabach h. Dubda a derbrathair fein do gabail a inait iarom.
(Ruaidri son of Domnall O Dubda, king of Tireragh, well of prosperity and riches for all Ireland, one who never met any man's plea for food or clothing with a denial, rested in Christ after anointing and after repentance adequate in the sight of God and of the Catholic Church and after partaking the Body and Blood, in his own stronghold just at the beginning of Spring. Tadc Riabach his brother succeeded him.)[98]

AFM 1417
Ruaidhri (.i. ó Dubhda) mac Domhnaill mic Briain mic Taichligh Uí Dubhda tobar sonusa 7 saidhbriosa Ua fFiachrach dég ina bhaile fein iar ffél Bríghde i cind miosa dhErrach, 7 Tadhg Riabach a dearbhrathair do gabail a ionaidh.
(Rory, (i.e. the O'Dowda), the son of Donnell, son of Brian, son of Taichleach, Fountain of the prosperity and wealth of Tireragh, died in his own town, after the festival of St Bridget (at the end of the first month of Spring); and Teige Reagh, his brother, assumed his place.)[99]

The detail of the deathbed repentance is just one of several significant contrasts between these two entries. Other differences include the AFM omission of any reference to kingship, and the use of a local reference to Uí Fhiachrach rather than to all of Ireland as a measure of the significance of the deceased. As in the 1410 example noted earlier, the inclusion of additional genealogical detail in the AFM entry indicates that the AConn obituary alone could not have supplied all of the Four Masters' information. Yet the equivalence of the attributes recorded, *tobar sonusa 7 saidhbriosa*, hints at some connection between the sources of the two entries. An obituary for the same person is also found in AU, but in too cursory a form to be the source of the Four Masters' version.[100]

AU 1417
Ruaidhri, mac Domnaill hUi Dubhda, idon, ri hUa-Fiachrach, d'eg i n-a longport fein iar m-buaidh aithrighe.

98 *AConn*, pp 432–5.   99 *AFM*, IV, pp 830–1.   100 *AU*, III, pp 72–3. For further examples of the contrasting treatment of deathbed repentances in AFM and AConn see AFM 1464.3/AConn 1464.40. This is a particularly extreme example of abbreviation by AFM as compared with the elaborate death scene in AConn, which includes reference to the deceased O'Conor half-king having seen himself in a vision being snatched from Doom by Michael [the archangel]. See also AFM 1468.2/AConn 1468.2, and AFM 1499.3/AConn 1499.3.

(Ruaidhri, son of Domnall Ua Dubhda, namely, king of Ui-Fiachrach, died in his own stronghold after victory of penance.)[101]

Another feature of the entries in AConn that is rarely replicated in AFM is the occasional inclusion of a proverb, or other moralistic comment or colloquial saying, at the end of an entry. At the conclusion of the obituary for Ragnall Mág Ragnaill in 1410, for instance, AConn notes that his successor died within a fortnight of his installation and includes the comment *7 dob e sin int escur i mbeol airechtais*. ('This was "a fall in the doorway of the assembly".')[102] While AFM records the fact of Mág Ragnaill's successor having died within a fortnight, the colloquial phrase is omitted, perhaps merely to economize on words or perhaps out of consideration for those who might wish to translate the text into Latin. A similar phrase occurs in the AConn obituary of Eoghan son of Tigearnán Mór Ó Ruairc, who drowned while on his way to visit his father at his deathbed, *7 dob e sin ant escur i mbeol airechtais .i. a bathad a mbeol na rige* ('This was a "fall on the assembly threshold", his being drowned on the threshold of the kingship').[103] The AFM version of the obituary omits this comment, as does AU. Apart from wishing to omit these colloquial sayings, the Four Masters might also have wanted to exclude the reference to kingship in this context.[104]

As in other matters, however, the Four Masters are not entirely consistent in their treatment of proverbs and incidental comments. Their record of the death of the son of Mac William Burke of Clanricard in 1467 ends with the comment *as ni bhí glóir saogalda nach dubhachus a deiredh* ('There is no worldly glory but ends in gloom'). The corresponding entry in AConn simply records the sudden death of the individual concerned.[105]

Other omissions

It is also noticeable that many of the more unsavoury deeds recorded by earlier annalists were omitted from AFM. Thus, the obituary of Tadhg Ua Fallamhain as recorded under the year 1425 in AFM is a sparse, understated, record of an unlawful killing.

AFM 1425
Tadhg ua Fallamhain taoíseach Cloinne hUadach do mharbhadh i fell ina caislén fein dia bhraithribh.
(Teige O'Fallon, chief of Clann-Uadach, was treacherously slain by his kinsmen in his own castle.)[106]

---

101 *AU*, III, pp 72–3.   102 *AConn*, pp 406–7; *AFM*, IV, pp 800–3.   103 *AConn*, pp 436–7.
104 *AFM*, IV, pp 834–5; *AU*, III, pp 74–5.   105 *AFM*, IV, pp 1046–7; *AConn*, pp 538–9.
106 *AFM*, IV, pp 866–7.

The account of the same event given in AConn under the year 1424 offers a rather more lively account, though not one that reflects well on the participants in the event recorded. The reserved understatement of the AFM version conceals rather more than it preserves of the actuality of this episode.

> AConn 1424
> *Tadc h. Fallamain dux Clainni hUatach do marbad a mebail la Domnall nGlas h. Fallamain ina chaslen fein. Seaan Mag Ragallaig do cetbuail e do thuaid connaid bai aca ac scoltad ordan 7 do dibr-i [mac] maith in Taidc-sin 7 taisech do denam don Domnall-sin ina inad 7 dopo cloch a n-inad ugi sin.*
> (Tadc O Fallamain, chieftain of the Clann Uatach, was treacherously killed by Domnall Glas O Fallamain in his own castle. It was Seaan Mag Ragallaig who first struck him, with a wood-axe with which he was splitting sticks; and a well-qualified son of this Tadc was banished and this Domnall was made chieftain. That was 'a stone in place of an egg'.)[107]

The relative detachment of the AFM entry as compared with that found in AConn is matched by the description of the *creach* taken by Aodh Ó Máille in 1415. Where AFM gives a straightforward account of the encounter between Aodh and Diarmaid and the killing that ensued, the AConn comment contains a moralistic element lacking in the AFM rendering of the story *dar mo debrod do bad ferr doib na teccmad o shin* ('by Heaven it would have been better for them if they had not met any more').[108] Again, it would appear that the Four Masters' approach was to present a formal historical account devoid of the kind of personal comment earlier annalists were prone to use to enliven their narrative.

Other examples can be identified where it appears that the Four Masters deemed certain details found in other annals as inappropriate in tone for their chronicle. Thus, for example, their record of the death of Donnchadh Ó Conchobhair, in 1419, is considerably less informative than the equivalent entry in AConn. Whereas the AConn narrative casts light on a variety of aspects of life in their description of the circumstances surrounding the death of Ó Conchobhair, the objective of AFM again appears to be merely to record the fact of the death with just the minimum of concise comment about the cause thereof.

> AFM 1419
> *Donnchadh Mac Muircertaigh uí Concobhair do écc do easccar i ndorus chaisléin Sligigh.*
> (Donough, the son of Murtough O'Conor, died of a fall in the doorway of the castle of Sligo.)[109]

> AConn 1419
> *Dondchad mac Murcertaigh Baccaig meic Domnaill h. Conchobair do marbad do escur forind leic a ndorus caislein Slicig for bru na haband allabus don leith tes don drochet la*

107 *AConn*, pp 466–9.   108 *AConn*, pp 426–7.   109 *AFM*, IV, pp 840–1.

feli Mure tosaig fogmair for sucrad marcsluaig, 7 dob e sin an la tucad logad Slicig amach, 7 ranicc a les Dondchad a chuid don logad-sin oir ni rabi-sim beo acht oensechtmain iar mbrised a loargi in la-sin.

(Donnchad son of Muirchertach Baccach son of Domnall O Conchobair died from a fall on the flagstone in front of Sligo Castle, on the near side of the river, at the southern end of the bridge, at the cavalry sports on St Mary's day in the beginning of autumn. That was the day on which the Sligo Indulgence was proclaimed, and Donnchad stood in need of his share of that Indulgence, for he only lived a week after breaking his leg that day.)[110]

The omission of references to abnormal weather, plague, famine and other exceptional natural phenomena are all examples of the Four Masters' general tendency to condense the material found in earlier sources and to select for preservation the more significant entries relating to ecclesiastical and secular leaders, at the expense of the miscellaneous.[111]

Youths, women and minor families

In addition to these relatively minor omissions and editorial revisions that occur frequently if not always consistently in the fifteenth- and sixteenth-century sections of AFM as compared with other extant annals for the same period, other more coherent patterns of omission can also be detected. There are repeated instances where entries relating to certain categories of people are not just abbreviated but are excluded in their entirety from AFM. The three most significant categories are youths whose deaths occurred before they had achieved personal political prominence; women, especially those without a clear Ulster connection; and members of minor families who lacked significant political influence in the late medieval period. The most obvious common thread between these three categories of people is their relative lack of political importance, their lack of significance in the network of power relationships in Gaelic Ireland. It was not a case of the Four Masters consciously targeting the young, or women, or the lesser families for exclusion; rather these omissions were the incidental casualties in a work that sought to concentrate on what were perceived in the 1630s to be the ecclesiastical and political highlights of the Irish past that could be derived from the range of available historical sources.

Among the examples of entries on the deaths of young persons found in AConn being omitted from AFM in the years 1416–18 are *Aedh mac Uilliam meic Aeda h. Birn sarmac oclaich mortuus est ii. Kalendas Augusti* ('Aed son of Uilliam son of Aed O Birn, a brave young warrior, died on 31 July');[112] *Maelsechlainn mac Cormaic Meic Diarmata Ruaid mortuus est* ('Maelsechlainn son of Cormac Mac

---

110 *AConn*, pp 448–9.   111 Examples include AConn 1419.15, 1419.16, 1420.7, 1473.21; AFM 1471.12, 1471.34, 1492.24, 1497.28.   112 *AConn*, pp 432–3 (AD1416).

Diarmata Ruad died');[113] *Mailir a Burc .i. degmac Tomas a Burcc 7 ingine Remaind mortuus est in hoc anno* ('Mailir Burke, the good son of Thomas Burke and the daughter of Raymond, died this year').[114] In other instances, the records of the deaths of several youths are conflated into one entry in AFM. Thus in 1419, for example, the twentieth entry for that year records four deaths.

> AFM 1419
> *Murchadh Ua Concobair adhbar tigerna ua fFailge, Cathal mac Aodha még Uidhir, Diarmait Ruadh mac Uí Concobair Duinn, 7 Mac Muiris na mBrígh saoí i neaccna 7 i neolas do écc.*
> (Murtough O'Conor, heir to the lordship of Offaly; Cathal, the son of Hugh Maguire; Dermot Roe, the son of O'Conor Don; and Mac-Maurice-na-mBrigh, a man eminent for wisdom and knowledge, died.)[115]

Three of the deaths recorded were of individuals who apparently died before attaining political influence. The fourth was a member of the learned class, another group whose fortunes tended to be treated as peripheral to the core purpose of AFM. Two of these individuals merited obituaries in their own right in AConn. The Connacht annalist praised Cathal Mág Uidhir's character and also included a prayer for him.

> AConn 1419
> *Cathal mac Aeda Meg Uidir degadbar rig Fer Manach 7 fer a aesa dopo mo arim don taeb athuaid d'Erinn ule do ecc in hoc anno 7 bennacht lais.*
> (Cathal son of Aed Mag Uidir, a good man for the kingship in Fermanagh and the man of his age who was of highest standing of all the northern part of Ireland, died this year. A blessing on him.)[116]

The tendency in AFM to accord a low priority to entries relating to youth, to women, and to members of lesser families is not so much an innovation as an extension of a trend already discernible in the older annals. It is often the case in earlier annals also that records of the deaths of several young persons are condensed into one summary entry. Similarly, women were rarely accorded extensive obituaries in the annals, though there were exceptions, such as the lengthy entry in ALec for 1451 on the death of Maighread Ní Chearbhaill, wife of Ó Conchobhair Fáilghe.[117] An alternative, shorter version of that Ó Cearbhaill obituary is recorded in AConn, one shorter still in AU, but even that is surpassed in brevity by the Four Masters, in whose hands this exceptional obituary of a woman is made to conform to the standard pattern.[118]

---

113 *AConn*, pp 434–5 (AD1417).   114 *AConn*, pp 440–1 (AD1418).   115 *AFM*, IV, pp 840–3.
116 *AConn*, pp 448–9.   117 *ALec*, pp 227–9. The Annals of Lecan text is given in the appendix below, pp 305–6.   118 *AConn*, pp 492–3; *AU*, III, pp 170–1; *AFM*, IV, pp 972–3.

AFM 1451

Mairgrécc inghen ui Cherbhaill (Tadhg) bean Ui Conchobhair Failgigh (an Calbhach) bean as ferr baoí ina haimsir i nErinn uair as í tucc gairm enigh fá dhó i naoín bliadhain do lucht iarrata neth decc iar mbuaidh ongtha 7 aithright iar mbreath bhuadha ó domhan 7 o deaman.

(Margaret, daughter of O'Carroll (Teige), and wife of O'Conor Faly (Calbhach), the best woman in her time in Ireland, for it was she who had given two invitations of hospitality in the one year to those who sought for rewards, died, after the victory of Unction and Penance, triumphant over the world and the Devil.)[119]

The Four Masters included notice of the death of Lasarfina, daughter of Fearghal Mac Diarmada found in AConn for 1456, but found no space either for notices of the deaths of Donnchadh Mág Sgoloigi, a schoolmaster at Lisgoole, or Nicholas Mac Arachain recorded in AU for the same year.[120] Thus, the Four Masters' editorial policy was not simply one of excluding some women, but of excluding people whose careers apparently lacked power or influence.

More complicated is the matter of their exclusion of Gráinne [Mág Uidhir?], daughter of Aedh, whose obituary is recorded in AU for the same year 1456.

AU 1456

Graine, ingen Aedha, mic Ardghail, buime in abbaidh oig Lesa-gabail, idon, Briain, mic Gilla-Patraig, d'heg in bliadhain si.

(Graine, daughter of Aedh, son of Ardghal, nurse of the young abbot of Lis-gabail, namely, of Brian, son of Gilla-Patraig, died this year.)[121]

Another Gráinne, daughter of a different Aedh Mág Uidhir, whose death was recorded in AU in 1463 was likewise omitted from AFM.

AU 1463

Aedh, mac Gilla-Patraig, mic an Airchideochain Meg Uidhir, obiit. Graíne ballach, ingen Aedha Meg Uidhir, d'eg 13 Kalendas Aprilis.

(Aedh, son of Gilla-Patraig, son of the Archdeacon Mag Uidhir, died. Graine the Freckled, daughter of Aedh Mag Uidhir, died on the 13th of the Kalends of April.)[122]

In this latter instance, the record of the death of Gráinne's father is retained in AFM, though the mention that his grandfather was the renowned Archdeacon Mág Uidhir was silently omitted. Gráinne Mág Uidhir is one of many of that surname whose obituaries are omitted from AFM, not because of their gender but because of their descent from an Archdeacon.

Many women were recorded in AFM for achievements in their own right. Two examples of such women from Munster are Mór Ní Bhriain, who died in 1421, and Sláine Ní Bhriain, who died in 1481.

119 *AFM*, IV, pp 972–3.   120 *AFM*, IV, pp 996–7; *AU*, III, pp 188–9; *AConn*, pp 496–7. 121 *AU*, III, pp 188–9.   122 *AU*, III, pp 210–11.

AFM 1421

Mór inghen Briain Uí Bhriain bean Uater a Búrc, 7 do baoí ina mhnaoí ag Tadhg ua Chearbhaill én ben do bfearr aithne 7 oineach, ciall 7 crabhadh do bhaoi in aon aimsir ria illeth Mogha décc. Mór Mumhan na Muimneach atberthí fria.

(More, the daughter of Brian O'Brien, and wife of Walter Burke, and who had been married to Teige O'Carroll, the most distinguished woman in her time, in Leath Mogha, for knowledge, hospitality, good sense and piety, died. She was usually called Mor-Mumhan-na-Muimhneach.)[123]

AFM 1481

Sláine inghen Ui Bhriain ben Mec Uilliam Cloinne Riocaird soidhtheach lán do dheirc 7 dfhele, bean ro dearsccnaigh do mhnáibh a haimsire décc iar mbreith bhuadha ó dhomhan 7 ó demhan.

(Slaine, the daughter of O'Brien, and wife of Mac William of Clanrickard, a vessel full of charity and hospitality, and who excelled the women of her time, died, after having gained victory over the world and the devil.)[124]

In one of the rare instances where a woman featured as the first entry for a given year in AFM, it is no surprise to find an Ó Domhnaill connection. Thus, in 1494, the death of Inghen Dubh daughter of Aodh Ruadh Ó Domhnaill and wife of Niall Ó Néill was the first item recorded.[125] No special words of praise were added, however; it seems her family status alone – the importance of her male relatives – rather than her own personal achievements, won her this preferential treatment. Her death was recorded as the twentieth of twenty-two entries in AU for the same year, where the ancestry of her husband and father for three generations was recorded.[126]

There follows a sequence of sixteenth-century obituaries for women associated with the Uí Dhomhnaill either by birth or marriage, among them the wife and daughters of Maghnus Ó Domhnaill.[127] These obituaries of Ó Domhnaill women are unusual in that they record an exact date of death. The autograph manuscripts reveal that these dates were inserted at the revision stage. This shows that more than one source for the deaths of these women was available to the annalists. The dates that were added as editorial emendations probably derive from an obit book kept at the Franciscan house rather than from an Ó Cléirigh historical source.

For the near-contemporary period covered by the annalists, where earlier annalistic compilations were unavailable, other sources had to be used. In general, the sources used by the Four Masters for the mid-sixteenth century cannot now be identified. It is noteworthy that when Sir James Ware looked to native Irish sources for this period, AFM was among the sources he consulted.[128]

123 *AFM*, IV, pp 850–1 (typographical errors in the Irish text of O'Donovan's edition of this passage have been corrected here by reference to RIA MS 23 P 6). 124 *AFM*, IV, pp 1116–17. 125 *AFM*, IV, pp 1208–9. 126 *AU*, III, pp 384–5. 127 For examples, AFM 1521.9; 1524.6; 1544.6; 1544.7; 1549.2; 1551.4; 1553.3. 128 BL Add. MS 4784, fos 36–86; TCD MS 804. See below, pp 291–3.

The contemporary sources used by the Four Masters included the history of the Franciscan Order compiled in the early seventeenth century by Francis O'Mahony OFM, a work which Ó Cléirigh himself explained was compiled *as leabhraibh 7 as gnáthchuimhne bhráthar na ccoinveinnteach ccéadna* ('from books and from the recollections of brothers of the same convents').[129] It is likely that the Four Masters themselves drew on oral sources in a similar way for some of the secular entries relating to the mid-sixteenth century but, just as they did not cite their written sources in anything other than a very general prefatory statement, it is not to be expected that they would make special mention of their oral sources either. Indeed, they may have taken trouble to disguise the fact that some material was derived ultimately from oral sources. For example, there are instances where entries in ALec are paralleled by entries in AFM, but the phrases 'and we heard that' and '*ut audivimus*' given in ALec, implying an oral source, are silently omitted from the equivalent entries in AFM.[130]

Conclusion

Although AFM is partly derivative of earlier annalistic sources, it is evident from the extent of the editorial revision undertaken by the Four Masters that their annals are, in reality, a new historical text. Although the Four Masters preserve the conventional annalistic form – the simplest kind of historical writing – their work is far from being a simple transcription of entries found in earlier annals. Rather, their annals were the outcome of an extensive process of editing and revision of the available sources. This means that the annals reflect, to a greater or lesser extent, the interests and biases of the compilers, and through their selection and presentation of material from the evidence available to them, they presented readers with their version of the Irish past.

The adherence to a traditional annalistic form can be viewed as one element of the way in which the Four Masters sought to take control of the memory of the past, their texts gaining authority through conformity to accepted conventions. It can also be argued that their selection from the available sources was made with a view to remoulding that past so as to provide a blueprint for the future. In this way the methodology adopted by the Four Masters in their approach to their sources is an important indicator of their ideology.

129 Joseph Moloney (ed.), 'Brussels MS. 3410: a chronological list of the foundations of the Irish Franciscan Province', *Analecta Hibernica* 6 (1934), 192.   130 See appendix below, at ALec 1453.9 and 1460.3 (since the Four Masters presumably adapted these entries from a written source, presumably a set of Lecan annals, they may have felt justified in ignoring their oral origins).

CHAPTER SIX

Scribes at work

Introduction

In contrast to many other Irish texts in prose and verse from the early modern period, the autograph manuscripts of the Annals of the Four Masters have survived to the present day. In fact, not one but two sets of autograph manuscripts are in existence and they are currently divided among three separate archives in Dublin. It is now generally assumed that one set was the presentation set given to Fearghal Ó Gadhra, patron of the work, while a second set was taken to Louvain with the intention of preparing a text for printing, perhaps in Latin translation. There has been some debate in the course of the twentieth century as to which parts of the extant manuscripts should be regarded as comprising a complete set. A detailed analysis of the issue by Nollaig Ó Muraíle[1] has made a strong case for concluding that the breakdown of the extant manuscripts is as follows:

Louvain set:	UCD–OFM MS A 13 (formerly FLK A 13)	AM2242–AD1169
	RIA MS 23 P 6 (cat. no. 687)	AD1170–1499
	RIA MS 23 P 7 (cat. no. 688)	AD1500–1616
Ó Gadhra set:	RIA MS C iii 3 (cat. no. 1220)	AM2242–AD1171
	TCD MS 1301 (formerly H.2.11)	AD1334–1605

The 'Louvain set' survives essentially intact, and contains a complete set of the annals from their commencement with AM2242 through to the final entry for the year AD1616, lacking just one folio. The manuscript now known as UCD–OFM MS A 13 contains entries up to and including the year AD1169. This is followed, with minimal loss of text by RIA MS 23 P 6, which opens with the entry for AD1170 and concludes with AD1499. The scribe of the closing pages of A 13 is the scribe of the opening pages of 23 P 6. The foliation matches, in that A 13 ends on fo. 523 (and the entry for 1169), while 23 P 6 now opens with fo. 525, containing the latter part of the entry for 1170, and with the evident loss of fo. 524, which would have contained the opening part of 1170. Matching 'square' watermarks on the paper used at the end of one manuscript and the beginning

---

1 Ó Muraíle, 'The autograph manuscripts', 75–95.

of the other also support the conclusion that 23 P 6 is the continuation of A 13. RIA MS 23 P 6 is continued in turn by RIA MS 23 P 7, which opens with the entry for the year AD1500 and ends with AD1616. The division of RIA MSS 23 P 6 and 23 P 7 into two separate volumes for binding was done in the late 1830s after these manuscripts were acquired by the Royal Irish Academy. The presumed 'Ó Gadhra set' is less complete in that the section of TCD MS 1301 covering the years AD1172–1334 has been lost, and that manuscript now commences mid-way through the year 1334.[2] The lost portion was already missing in 1739.[3] Of the portions that survive of the autograph set presented to the patron of the work, RIA MS C iii 3 contains entries for the years AM2242 to AD1171, while TCD MS 1301 contains entries for the years AD1334 to AD1605, with further fragmentary headings for some years down to 1615. The surviving fragment of the 1616 entry containing the obituary of Aodh Ó Néill is now misplaced, being bound between fos 997 and 998.[4]

The autograph manuscripts were rarely consulted by researchers in the twentieth century because a printed edition with English translation and extensive historical and topographical notes has made the contents of the annals generally accessible since 1851. For over 150 years it has been John O'Donovan's landmark edition of the *Annals of the kingdom of Ireland* that has ensured the continued popularity of the work of the Four Masters as an encyclopedic guide to the early Irish past.[5] In the late 1830s and throughout the 1840s, however, when O'Donovan was preparing his edition for publication, he did not have access to all of the original autograph manuscripts of AFM now known to be extant. For the period up to 1169, O'Donovan had to rely on the edition published in 1826 by Rev. Charles O'Conor,[6] as well as on eighteenth-century transcripts,[7] because neither of the autograph manuscripts covering that period (UCD–OFM MS A 13 and RIA MS C iii 3) was in Ireland at that time.[8]

---

2 This led to the suggestion, first voiced in 1854 and more recently supported by Canice Mooney in *Cat. Ir. mss in FLK*, p. 25, that there was a 'lost volume' of the Annals of the Four Masters, believed to be lying unidentified in the Barbarini Archives in the Vatican Library. The suggestion was discounted by Paul Walsh, and has been effectively disproved by the researches of Nollaig Ó Muraíle into the extant autograph manuscripts (Ó Muraíle, 'The autograph manuscripts', esp. 86–8). 3 A preliminary note by John Fergus, dated 1739, now bound in to TCD MS 1301, observes that there was a hiatus in the volume from 1171 to 1335 and from 1606 to 1616. The hiatus was also commented on in Walter Harris, *The whole works of Sir James Ware concerning Ireland, revised and improved* (2 vols, Dublin, 1764), II, p. 117. 4 TCD MS 1301, fos 1150–1164, fos 997–998. O'Sullivan, 'The Slane manuscript', 84, n. 2. 5 O'Donovan (ed.), *Annála Ríoghachta Éireann: Annals of the kingdom of Ireland by the Four Masters from the earliest period to the year 1616*. 6 O'Conor (ed.), *Quatuor Magistrorum annales Hibernici*. 7 Particularly TCD MS 1300 and RIA MS 23 F 2. 8 John O'Donovan died in 1861. The Franciscan manuscript (UCD–OFM MS A 13) was in Rome through most of the nineteenth century. It was brought to Dublin (Merchant's Quay), in 1872, transferred to the Franciscan House of Studies at Killiney in 1946, and transferred again, this time to University College Dublin, in 2000. The Academy manuscript, C iii 3, was part of the collection in the library of the Marquis of Buckingham at Stowe in the early nineteenth century. The collection was later sold to the earl of Ashburnham, and the manuscripts were inaccessible to

Medievalists using O'Donovan's edition have repeatedly complained that the transcripts he used for the period prior to the twelfth century were not sufficiently accurate for the purpose for which O'Donovan relied on them. To date, however, there are no plans for a new edition based on the autograph manuscripts. A complete set of digitized images of all but one of the autograph manuscripts has now been published on the *Irish Script on Screen* website, making the preparation of a new edition less daunting perhaps.[9]

When editing the annals for the later period, covering the years 1171–1616, unlike the earlier part, O'Donovan had access to both sets of autograph manuscripts, RIA MSS 23 P 6 – 23 P 7[10] and TCD MS 1301. At the time of their acquisition by the RIA, O'Donovan reported that 'the manuscript … was a mere unbound roll, its margins worn away by damp'.[11] The manuscripts were promptly conserved and rebound in two volumes and it is from these that O'Donovan and O'Curry worked. O'Donovan also consulted the TCD manuscript, inserting occasional references in his footnotes to the 'college' copy. Essentially, O'Donovan's edition did not generally address the consequences of the fact that there were two autograph sets rather than just one, and his edition glosses over the differences between them. Thus, the occasional points at which the content of TCD MS 1301 differs in detail from RIA MS 23 P 6 are not noted systematically in O'Donovan's edition. Such an approach was largely justified from O'Donovan's perspective, since the differences between them are minor, and his primary concern was to make available the historical information recorded in the annals. It was not his intention to provide a critical edition. As will be shown below, the two sets of autograph manuscripts for the post-1170 period correspond very closely to one another in terms of layout, content, and degree of contemporary editorial revision by different scribal hands. Indeed, it is clear that, despite the comments of some scholars, the two sets of autograph manuscripts cannot easily be distinguished from one another in terms of one being a 'working draft' or 'normalized draft' and the other a 'fair copy' or 'final draft'. In reality, neither set qualifies as a 'fair copy', and because of this it is possible to analyze the contribution of the various scribes to each of the two sets of autograph manuscripts, thereby gaining insights into the working methods of the team of annalists.

researchers for some decades until they were purchased by the British government in 1883. Those of Irish interest were presented by the British Government to the Royal Irish Academy (Elizabeth FitzPatrick, *The catalogue of Irish manuscripts in the Royal Irish Academy: a brief introduction* (Dublin, 1988), p. 5). **9** Digital images of some of these manuscripts are currently available on the Irish Script on Screen website: www.isos.dias.ie. The three RIA autograph manuscripts of AFM were made available online in digitized format in 2003, followed by UCD–OFM MS A 13; which was made available in August 2004. At the time of writing (December 2008), the 'Ó Gadhra' manuscript covering the years 1334–1605 (TCD MS 1301) has not yet been made available in digitized form. **10** For a brief description of these manuscripts, see *Cat. Ir. mss in RIA*, nos 687 and 688. **11** It had been purchased for the Academy by Sir George Petrie in February 1831 at the sale of the manuscripts of Austin Cooper, having come from the library of William Burton Conyngham of Slane Castle. William O'Sullivan has suggested that the manuscript may have been brought back to Dublin from Louvain in the 1750s by Dominic McDevitt, guardian of Donegal,

No report of a detailed comparison of the two autograph sets of AFM has been published to date, though the issues involved in the existence of two sets have been variously discussed by Paul Walsh and Canice Mooney and have been revisited by Nollaig Ó Muraíle and Daniel Mc Carthy.[12] A posthumous publication in 1944 recorded Paul Walsh's opinion that the autograph set of the Annals of the Four Masters comprising RIA MS C iii 3 and its incomplete continuation TCD MS 1301 was the set presented to Fearghal Ó Gadhra and consisted of the 'draft from which the final copy was made for transmission to headquarters at Louvain.' He then added that the 'final copy now survives as the Franciscan MS [UCD–OFM MS A 13], and its continuation in the Academy MSS, 23 P 6 and 23 P 7'.[13] Walsh went on to assert that 'on examination considerable divergence will be found between the two scripts both in the matter recorded and in the order of the items under each year.'[14] The later history of the ownership of the manuscripts themselves is consistent with Walsh's assertion that the set of annals taken to Louvain comprised UCD–OFM MS A 13 and RIA MSS 23 P 6 and 23 P 7.

Two other assertions in the passages from Paul Walsh quoted above merit further investigation. The first of these is Walsh's distinction between a 'rough draft' and a 'fair copy'. Ó Muraíle similarly suggests that RIA MSS 23 P 6 and 23 P 7 seem more neatly written than TCD MS 1301, 'appearing to have less instances of rewriting, of later marginal and interlineal additions, and such like',[15] but he does not offer any illustrative examples as evidence. Mc Carthy's conjecture about the scribal process involved assumes that the various contributors to AFM undertook equivalent tasks, with 'six compilers excerpting and writing simultaneously' as they worked on a now lost initial draft.[16] While it is clear that the scribes of the extant manuscripts did indeed work from prior written entries,[17] the palaeographical evidence of the extant manuscripts does not support the idea that each of the annalists and their assistants did equivalent work. Rather, as will be seen below, there was a hierarchy of editors and scribes, with differentiated tasks. Accepting Walsh's view, Mc Carthy regards the 'Ó Gadhra set' as a 'normalized draft' and the 'Louvain set' as a 'final draft', but is unspecific as to the detail on this point. In contrast, it is argued here that the two extant sets of autograph manuscripts resemble one another far more closely than has been suggested by Walsh, Ó Muraíle or Mc Carthy.[18]

who was assembling a library at Stranorlar (O'Sullivan, 'The Slane manuscript', 82–3). O'Sullivan posits that the manuscript was subsequently obtained by Burton Conyngham by virtue of his Donegal connections.   12 Paul Walsh, *The Four Masters and their work* (Dublin, 1944), pp 10–14; Canice Mooney, 'Irish Franciscan libraries of the past', *Irish Ecclesiastical Record* 60 (ser. 5, 1942), 23–4, n. 4; *Cat. Ir. mss in FLK*, pp 24–7; Ó Muraíle, 'The autograph manuscripts', 75–95; Mc Carthy, *The Irish annals*, pp 298–301.   13 Walsh, *The Four Masters and their work*, pp 12–13.   14 Walsh, *The Four Masters and their work*, p. 13.   15 Ó Muraíle, 'The autograph manuscripts', 87.   16 Mc Carthy, *The Irish annals*, p. 300.   17 See discussion of homoeoteleuton below, p. 153.   18 A large amount of later annotation by Roderic O'Flaherty in TCD MS 1301 contributes to its general 'untidiness', but is ignored in this discussion.

6.1 Scribal hand A. RIA MS C iii 3, fo. 117v.

6.2 Scribal hand B. RIA MS C iii 3, fo. 311r.

6.3 Scribal hand C. RIA MS C iii 3, fo. 231r.

6.4 Scribal hand D. RIA MS C iii 3, fo. 387r.

6.5 Scribal hand E. RIA MS C iii 3, fo. 160v.

Perhaps the most significant point to emerge is that the two sets of manuscripts reveal consistently similar patterns of editorial revision by the scribal team, and this evidence will be discussed first. While Walsh, and even O'Donovan himself, made passing reference to the matter, the issue of whether the two autograph manuscripts of the Annals of the Four Masters covering the post-1170 period differed from one another in terms of content has not previously been addressed in any detail, and this will be analyzed in the following section. The treatment of the mid-fifth-century Patrician material in the two sets of manuscripts will be compared with the findings for the early fifteenth-century material. By way of conclusion, the relationship of both sets of manuscripts to O'Donovan's printed edition will be assessed.

The scribes

The basic working method adopted by the scribal team, as evidenced by the pattern of occurrence of different scribal hands in both manuscripts, is worth considering in some detail, because it can illuminate aspects of the process of compilation engaged in by the scribal team. Sample illustrations of the various hands are shown in figures 6.1–6.12. For the purpose of this discussion, the scribes are labelled A to K, and the probable identifications can be set out as follows.

A   possibly Muiris Ó Maoil Chonaire.[19]

B   probably Conaire Ó Cléirigh, tentatively identified on the basis of the statement in the *Testimonium* on the second vellum leaf of RIA MS 23 P 6 to the effect that the Ó Cléirigh scribes were entirely responsible for the post-1332 section of the text.[20]

C   Mícheál Ó Cléirigh.[21]

D   probably Cú Choigcríche Ó Cléirigh.[22]

E   probably Fearfeasa Ó Maoil Chonaire.[23]

[F]   by process of elimination, probably Cú Choigcríche Ó Duibhgeannáin.[24]

[G]   'hand 1'. A hand tentatively, but incorrectly, identified by the cataloguers of UCD–OFM MS A 13 as being that of Conaire Ó Cléirigh.[25] For Conaire Ó Cléirigh, see hand B above.

[H]   'hand 7'. Scribe of one substituted folio in UCD–OFM MS A 13, a hand that shares some of the characteristics of C.[26]

[J & K]   'hands 5 & 6', which are similar to one another, as described by the cataloguers of UCD–OFM MS A 13.[27]

19 A tall upright hand principally found in the first half of RIA C iii 3, ending at fo. 285v. 20 *AFM*, I, p. lxvi. 21 *Cat. Ir. mss in RIA*, p. 3277. 22 *Cat. Ir. mss in RIA*, p. 3278. 23 This identification is suggested on the basis of the evidence of BR MS 5100–4, fo. 124 (96), containing a *testimonium* signed by Fearfeasa Ó Maoil Chonaire and Cú Choigcríche Ó Cléirigh, with the text believed to be in the hand of Fearfeasa Ó Maoil Chonaire. 24 UCD–OFM MS A 13, fo. 303, for example. 25 *Cat. Ir. mss in FLK*, pp 24–5. 26 UCD–OFM MS A 13, fo. 231. 27 UCD–OFM

The most detailed analysis of the scribal hands published to date is that by Kathleen Mulchrone in respect of RIA MS C iii 3, one of the autograph manuscripts for the pre-1170 period, and her identifications of scribes A to E.[28] Her tentative identifications of the hands of the two Ó Maoil Chonaire scribes are supported by the sample of Fearfeasa's hand that survives in BR MS 5100–4, fo. 124.[29] The letters F–K have been assigned here to the additional hands tentatively identified in UCD–OFM MS A 13, but not identified in RIA MS C iii 3. The catalogers of UCD–OFM MS A 13 discerned up to eight different hands in that manuscript (figures 6.6–6.12), naming only Mícheál Ó Cléirigh with certainty, describing it as hand 2 and tentatively, but probably incorrectly, identifying a hand that closely resembled that of Mícheál as being that of his brother Conaire (hand 1). They avoided making any specific reference to the hand of Cú Choigcríche Ó Cléirigh,[30] and made no mention of the different suggested identification of the hand of Conaire Ó Cléirigh put forward by Kathleen Mulchrone.[31] It is not the purpose of the present discussion to provide a detailed palaeographical analysis of the manuscripts, but Mulchrone's scribal identifications appear correct, while those of the catalogers of UCD–OFM MS A 13 require modification.

Comparison of the autograph manuscripts for the years 1419–1454

The autograph manuscripts of AFM for the years 1334 to 1605, now preserved as TCD MS 1301, and its sister volumes RIA MS 23 P 6 and RIA MS 23 P 7, which together cover the years 1170 to 1616, are not always as aesthetically pleasing as their scribes had evidently planned them to be. However, for that very reason, both sets of manuscripts preserve very many clues as to the working method of the compilers. Both sets are heavily revised in places. The revisions and amendments made by the annalists in each set are the key to understanding how the team of scribes operated as the compilation progressed. They also present evidence that although neither TCD MS 1301 nor RIA MSS 23 P 6 and 23 P 7 can be clearly distinguished from one another in terms of one being a 'fair copy' and the other a 'rough draft', there is an occasional hint that the Louvain set is the more 'final' of the two, but the evidence on this matter is not consistent.

A comparison of the two sets, for a sample of forty-six years from 1419 to 1454 inclusive, can illuminate the issues. The start date of 1419 has been selected

MS A 13, fo. 448r; *Cat. Ir. mss in FLK*, p. 25.   **28** *Cat. Ir. mss in RIA*, pp 3276–82.   **29** The manuscript has two sets of foliation, the more recent in pencil; the relevant item is numbered fo. 96 in the older ink foliation.   **30** *Cat. Ir. mss in FLK*, pp 24–7.   **31** Given that the catalogers were working before any of these manuscripts were microfilmed, and that the custodianship arrangements under which the manuscripts are kept do not allow researchers to see the original manuscripts together in one place at one time, their reluctance to make comparisons between the two sets of manuscripts is understandable.

6.6 Scribal hand 1 [G]. UCD–OFM MS A 13, fo. 3r.

6.7 Scribal hand 2 [C]. UCD–OFM MS A 13, fo. 414r.

6.8 Scribal hand **3** [**B**]. UCD–OFM MS A 13, fo. 382r.

6.9 Scribal hand **4**. UCD–OFM MS A 13, fo. 301r.

6.10 Scribal hands 5 & 6 [J & K]. UCD–OFM MS A 13, fo. 448r.

6.11 Scribal hand 7 [H]. UCD–OFM MS A 13, fo. 231.

6.12 Scribal hand 8. UCD–OFM MS A 13, fo. xxiii.

here because this is the point at which Roderic O'Flaherty's extensive later annotations of TCD MS 1301 virtually cease, making it easier to study the scribal variations of that manuscript as originally completed. The closing date of 1454 was selected because after the mid-1440s both TCD MS 1301 and RIA MS 23 P 6 display much less evidence of additions and revisions by a second and sometimes a third scribe, so that both sets of manuscripts resemble a 'fair copy', rather than a first draft or 'working copy' of the annals for much of the later fifteenth century, as also for the fourteenth century.

The first point to observe is the remarkable degree of similarity between the two autograph manuscripts, TCD MS 1301 and RIA MS 23 P 6, for the years covered by this case study. Nollaig Ó Muraíle's assertion that RIA MSS 23 P 6–23 P 7 appear neater than TCD MS 1301 does not hold true for the years surveyed here.[32] In respect of the post-1170 annals, it is clear that the principal scribe, B (identified here as Conaire Ó Cléirigh), created a basic text from an earlier draft or comprehensive set of notes. He established the layout of the text on the pages by entering the annual headings and transcribing a number of entries for each year but also by leaving plenty of blank space for additions.[33] The entries in the hand of scribe B are not normally positioned on the page immediately following the heading for the year. Instead, it was usual for scribe B to leave some space between the heading and the first entry. He sometimes also left space in the middle of the year, before placing some final entries near the end of the space allocated for that year. He did this in both sets of manuscripts in a very similar way. Subsequently, a second and third scribe, normally either D (Cú Choigcríche Ó Cléirigh) or C (Mícheál Ó Cléirigh), revised the work, adding further entries, making occasional additions or corrections to the initial batch of entries, and supplying additional genealogical details about some of the people who featured in those entries.

In most instances, it is not possible to tell which of the two manuscripts might have been transcribed by scribe B first. Occasionally, however, minor variations between the two provide some clues. For the year 1421, for instance, it is clear that scribe B's entries in TCD MS 1301 were transcribed before RIA MS 23 P 6. The first eight entries for that year are transcribed by scribe B in both manuscripts. The AFM 1421.9 entry,[34] however, concerning Cormac Mac Carthaigh, is written in two different editorial hands, C and D, in TCD MS 1301, part of it in the margin, and subsequently partly deleted, whereas in RIA MS 23 P 6 it is entirely written in the hand of the main scribe B, suggesting that the latter was copied from the former. The wording of entry 1421.9 in RIA MS

---

32 Ó Muraíle, 'The autograph manuscripts', 87. 33 The practice of leaving space for later additions was a common one. The autograph manuscript of the Annals of Ulster preserved in TCD MS 1282 contains examples of the same practice from the fifteenth century. 34 Where reference is made to a specific entry within a given calendar year, the numbering system used is that of the digital edition on the CELT website (www.ucc.ie/celt).

23 P 6 was redrafted so that it is clear that the praise relates to the deceased and not to his killers.

TCD MS 1301
Corbmac na Coille mac Még Cartaigh Cairbrigh do marbadh lá cloinn Eogain Még Cartaigh 7 ba hesidhe mac tigerna ba ferr do Muimneachaibh ina ré.[35]
[Cormac na Coille, son of MacCarthy of Carbery, was slain by the sons of Owen MacCarthy and he was the best son of a lord of the Munstermen of his time.][36]

RIA MS 23 P 6
Corbmac na coille mac Még Cartaigh (Cairbrigh) mac tigherna ro ba ferr do Mhuimhneachaibh ina ré do mharbhadh lá cloinn Eoghain Még Cárthaigh.
(Cormac na Coille [son of] Mac Carthy of Carbery, the best son of a lord of the Momonians of his time, was slain by the sons of Owen Mac Carthy.)[37]

In addition to revision of the wording, the entire entry is neatly integrated into the body of the text of RIA MS 23 P 6 for that year, being placed at a slightly earlier point in the text than that at which it occurs in TCD MS 1301.[38] This is one of the very occasional indications in the early fifteenth-century material in AFM that RIA MS 23 P 6 is the more polished draft of the two. However, such evidence for one year cannot be taken as conclusive proof that scribe B wrote all of his allocation of entries in TCD MS 1301 before embarking on RIA MS 23 P 6.

Editorial revision of the manuscripts

In the case of the revisions and additions to the text made at a later stage than the initial transcription of both post-1170 manuscripts, the evidence is more complex, but several significant points emerge. The editorial revisions to both manuscripts are particularly extensive from 1419 up to the mid-1440s and are very similar in nature and content in both manuscripts. It is sometimes the case that editorial amendments made by C in one manuscript are made by D in the other. There are several different types of editorial intervention. They include the addition of new entries, at the beginning, middle and end of the space allocated for each year; the addition of extra genealogical details about many of the persons named – usually in the form of interlining in the text; the correction of scribal errors where the initial scribe had accidentally skipped a phrase; and the occasional deletion of a duplicated entry. Each of these kinds of editorial intervention reveals different aspects of the methodology of the Four Masters, and the nature of the input of each different scribal hand helps ascertain precisely how the work proceeded.

---

35 TCD MS 1301, fo. 753.   36 My translation.   37 *AFM*, IV, pp 850–1.   38 It is preceded by AFM 1421.10 and AFM 1421.11 in TCD MS 1301.

On the question of which of the two manuscripts was completed first, there are instances where the evidence of the scribal revisions, particularly those in the hand of scribe D, are at odds with the sequence suggested by the evidence discussed above in relation to the initial phase of the work by scribe B. This in itself is an indication that the two sets were worked on in tandem, through more than one phase of compilation and revision.

It was shown above that in the case of the 1421.9 entry, the more preliminary of the two autograph manuscripts was TCD MS 1301. However, when the editorial additions made in both manuscripts for that same year are compared (1421.12 to 1421.13), it emerges that the additions to TCD MS 1301 are in a neater and more final form than those in RIA MS 23 P 6. Apart from the neater general appearance of TCD MS 1301 at this point, the forename *Murcadh* that is interlined in RIA MS 23 P 6 at entry 1421.12 – *Ó Concobuir, .i. Murcadh* – is integrated into the text in TCD MS 1301. This detail suggests that TCD MS 1301 may have been the later of the two manuscripts to be revised in respect of the entries for 1421.

The most logical conclusion to be drawn from the examples of scribal differences between the two manuscripts discussed so far is that work on both manuscripts proceeded in two distinct phases: the initial transcription of basic entries for each year, usually by scribe B, though occasionally relieved by scribe C or D. As discussed above, there is some evidence that, in respect of some years at least, the first of the two to be worked on by scribe B was TCD MS 1301. There was then a phase of substantial editorial revision to both copies of the text, with numerous additions being made. There is some evidence that the first of the two to be revised was RIA MS 23 P 6, but it is also clear that the editorial hands made revisions to the text on more than one occasion. Occasionally, variations occur, some of which may be mere oversights. Thus, the evidence of the fifteenth-century entries strongly suggests that both manuscripts were essentially working copies; neither being a simple transcript of the other, and the nature and extent of the differences between the two are best accounted for by concluding that both manuscripts were worked on in tandem through more than one phase of compilation and revision.[39]

Content and arrangement of entries, and transcription errors

It seems clear that the preliminary work of scribe B in establishing the basic layout of both manuscripts was in accordance with a prior decision that provision should be made for substantial additions and revisions to be made later. A second

---

39 Examples from years outside the scope of the present case study reinforce the findings discussed here. AD1340, 1342, 1351 and 1368 contain material written in a more final form in RIA MS 23 P 6 than the interlining in TCD 1301, but AD1511 contains material interlined in RIA MS 23 P 7 (fo. 19) but integrated into the text in TCD 1301 (fo. 865).

6.13 AFM entry for AD1438. TCD MS 1301, fo. 767r.

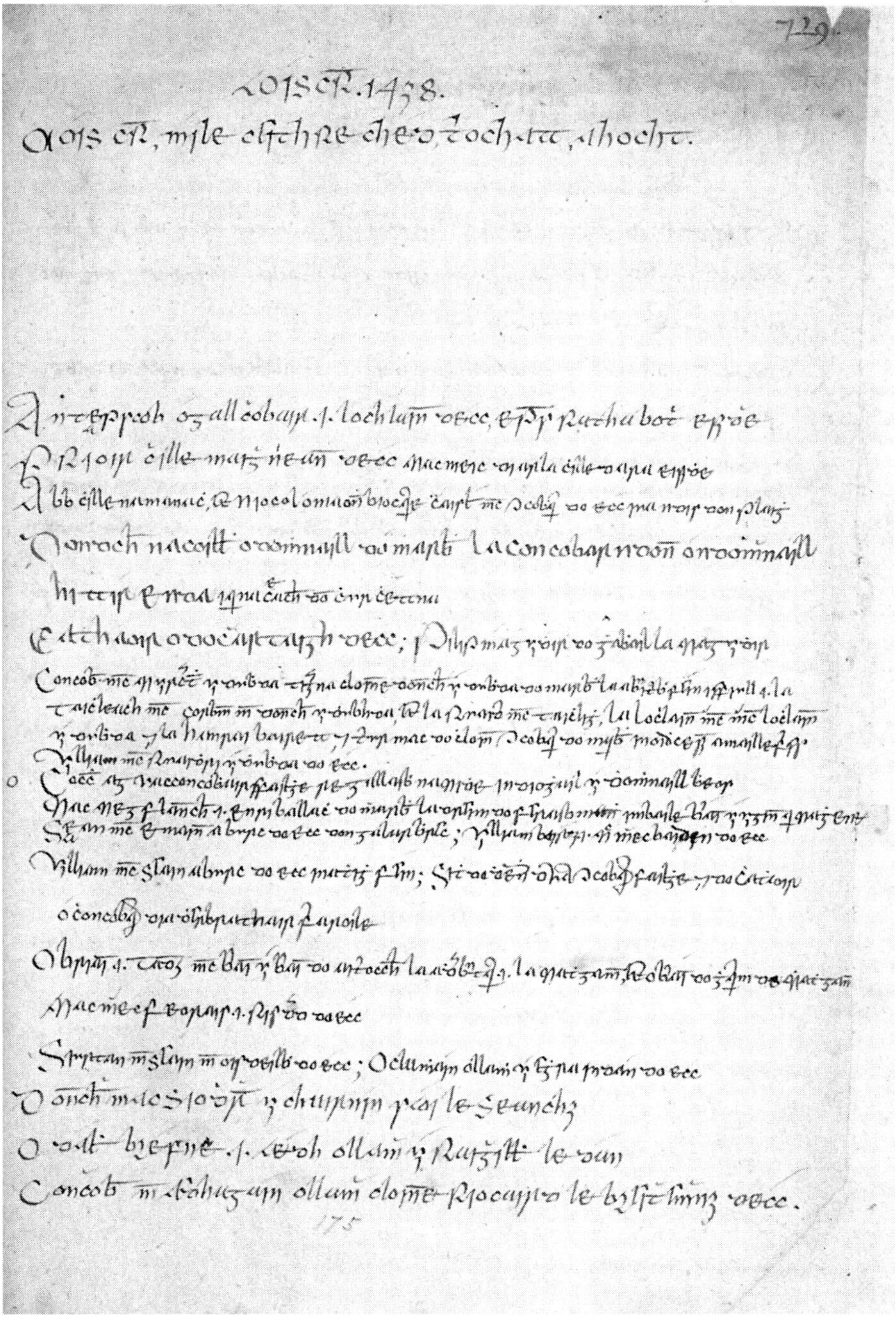

6.14 AFM entry for AD1438. RIA MS 23 P 6, fo. 175r.

key element of the editorial policy of the Four Masters concerns the sequence in which entries should be arranged within each year. Throughout AFM, certain kinds of entries are consistently placed at the beginning of the entry for the year, most especially those relating to ecclesiastical matters. Other kinds of entries, notably those relating to members of the learned class, and occasionally to the deaths of youths who have not yet attained political prominence, are positioned close to the end of the space allocated for the year in question. The evidence of the autograph manuscripts in respect of the work of scribe B indicates that he generally adhered to these basic editorial principles regarding the arrangement of entries within each year. For example, the sequencing of the entries for the year 1438 in both RIA MS 23 P 6 and TCD MS 1301, illustrate this clearly (figures 6.13 and 6.14). Scribe B placed the ecclesiastical entries at the beginning and the entries relating to learned men at the end. Further entries added by scribes C and D again adhered to the editorial practice of placing the ecclesiastical entries at or close to the beginning of the year, whereas other kinds of entries are placed further down the sequence. There are, nonetheless, minor variations in the sequencing of the entries added by the second and third hands for that year, for which the simplest explanation is that a dual set of manuscripts could not invariably achieve the uniformity of print.

At both phases of the work of compiling the final drafts of AFM – in the initial laying out of a basic number of entries for each year, and the subsequent revisions of the text – it appears that the scribes may have sometimes operated a rota system to advance the work, as was usual in major scribal undertakings of this kind. Although for these manuscripts covering the post-1171 period, scribe B did the bulk of the initial transcription and scribes C and D did the bulk of the editing and revision and insertion of additional entries, scribes C and D occasionally took over for a few years here and there, in either transcribing the basic text for the year or in the work of revision.

In TCD MS 1301, for example, there is a change from scribe B to scribe C half way through the year 1452,[40] and scribe C continues on to transcribe both the heading for the year and the entries for 1453 also, with scribe B then resuming with the second entry for the year 1454.[41] Something quite similar happens in the other copy of the annals for these years, RIA MS 23 P 6, where scribe C takes over for some of 1454 and 1455, before scribe B resumes work. Though far from conclusive, this might perhaps be interpreted as evidence that the two manuscripts were being worked on in tandem by scribe B, who took a break from the work of transcription and was temporarily replaced by scribe C when he had written as far as 1452 in one copy and 1454 in the other. The method points to the probability that the work was done under pressure of time and that they wished to complete the task as quickly as possible.

40 TCD MS 1301, fo. 779v, four lines from end of page.   41 TCD MS 1301, fo. 782, three lines from end of page.

One instance of an error in transcription in RIA MS 23 P 6 at the year 1461 hints at the human sensibilities behind the scribal task. Scribe B made an error of transcription – omitting three lines in mid-sentence from his exemplar.[42] Scribe B completed copying the entries for that year, but scribe C then took over and transcribed all of the entries for the following year, 1462. Having rested sufficiently, it might be supposed, scribe B then resumed his task, commencing with the year 1463.[43] Similarly, scribe C apparently took over from B to write the two-page entry for 1466 in TCD MS 1301.[44] The error in 23 P 6, incidentally, provides conclusive proof that the scribe was working from a written exemplar at this point, and was not transcribing material that was being dictated orally. Indeed, there are numerous examples in TCD MS 1301 also where transcription errors are corrected by careful revision of the manuscript. For example, in 1368.11, where the original scribe had inadvertently skipped from one instance of the name *Toirrdhealbhaigh* to the next in TCD MS 1301, the missing words were subsequently inserted by a colleague.[45] Apart from indicating that the work was carefully proof-read, the occurrence of this type of error provides a further insight into the Four Masters' working method. These instances of homoeoteleuton, where a passage between two instances of the same word was omitted, could occur when a scribe looked away from his exemplar so as to continue writing, and when he next looked at the exemplar his eye fixed on a different occurrence of the significant word or name. The result of this was that the intervening passage was either omitted or repeated.[46] The error indicates that the scribe was working from a written exemplar, most likely an early draft assembled on scraps of paper. Paul Walsh had suggested that the Four Masters team might have adopted a system where one scribe wrote a text while others dictated entries in turn. While they might occasionally have worked in this manner in the earlier part of the work (though perhaps with two scribes writing parallel texts simultaneously – a feature that would account for some of the orthographic differences between the two sets), the evidence of transcription errors, particularly in parts of TCD MS 1301, indicates that large parts of that manuscript were not produced through a process of dictation. Similarly, in RIA MS 23 P 7, on the fifth page of the lengthy entry for AD 1536, there is an error of transcription where a phrase was missed between two instances of *Conchobhair*.[47] This provides evidence that the entries in this manuscript too were transcribed from an earlier written exemplar.

42 RIA MS 23 P 6, fo. 196v.   43 RIA MS 23 P 6, fos 197r–199r.   44 TCD MS 1301, fos 795r–795v. 45 TCD MS 1301, fo. 710; *AFM*, III, p. 642.   46 Further examples of such transcription errors, or homoeoteleuton, that were noticed and corrected by the annalists as they checked the text, occur at TCD MS 1301, fo. 1012 (scribe had skipped from one '*Mac Cathaoir Mór*' to the next) *AFM*, V, p. 1838; TCD MS 1301, fo. 1080 (scribe had skipped from one '*Contae*' to the next), *AFM*, VI, p. 2082; TCD MS 1301, fo. 1087r (scribe had skipped from one '*Clár*' to the next), *AFM*, VI, p. 2104. These errors are not found in RIA MS 23 P 7.   47 RIA MS 23 P 7, fo. 51r. This corresponds to *AFM*, V, p. 1430, lines 16–17. No similar error is found in TCD MS 1301 (fo. 898r) at this point in the text.

While the scribal evidence suggests that the work was done with some speed, an urgency to complete the task was not the only, or even prevailing, concern of the compilers. In the sample year 1438, at least three scribes worked on the entries in each manuscript for that year, though the precise sequence in which they contributed to the text for that year is difficult to establish conclusively. In most but not all entries for that year, the scribe that contributed to one manuscript differed from the scribe that contributed the same entry to the other. It is also possible that individual scribes added material to the year 1438 on more than one occasion. The extent to which each year was worked and reworked by the team of compilers, and the fact that they worked on both sets of the annals in this way preserves first-hand evidence of the layered process of selection, arrangement and editing of both final versions of their text.

The comments of the guardian of the friary of Athlone in 1630, when four of the same team of scholars had completed an earlier project on the *Genealogiae regum et sanctorum Hiberniae*, gives an indication of their approach to their task.

> GRSH
> *criochnaicceadh an saothar so, da ngoirter rém rioghradh na hEreann 7 senchas a naomh, iar ccaitheamh mios go hiomlán les do laithibh 7 doidhcibh amaille le dícheall stuidér.*[48]
> (this work, entitled The Succession of the Kings and the Genealogies of the Saints of Ireland, was ended and completed with much industry, a whole month including days and nights having been occupied with it.)[49]

The rota system of editing in evidence in TCD MS 1301 and RIA MS 23 P 6 suggests that they approached their work on AFM with a similar degree of industry, and that the entire work was perhaps done in haste.

The analysis of the different scribal hands suggests that the initial phase of the work involved transcription (from an earlier outline draft) by the junior members of the team, principally scribe B, and similarly scribe A in respect of the early part of RIA MS C iii 3. As work proceeded, the senior contributors, Cú Choigcríche Ó Cléirigh (scribe D) and Mícheál Ó Cléirigh (scribe C), made substantial additions and revisions to certain sections of the text. The early fifteenth-century section was one of the most heavily revised sections of both sets of autograph manuscripts.

The scribal evidence, for the sample years examined, further indicates that the insertion of additional genealogical detail in many of the entries was done at an even later stage than the insertion of entire new entries by scribe D and another editorial hand. The evidence for this is that in both TCD MS 1301 and RIA MS 23 P 6, the interlining of genealogical information occurs not only in the sections of text transcribed by scribe B, but also in the sections that comprised later

48 *GRSH*, p. 9.   49 *GRSH*, p. 145.

additions by D and other scribes. Examples illustrating that the process of adding genealogical material was a late revision of the text can be found, for instance, in RIA MS 23 P 6, at the years 1421 and 1422. Refinements of genealogical detail (as italicized here) are added to 1421.3 (Tomaltach *óc*); 1421.9 (Még Cartaigh [.i.] *Cairbrigh*); 1421.12 (Ó Concobhair *.i. Murchadh*); 1422.1 (Rudhraidhe ua Conchobhair *.i. mac Concobair*); 1422.6 (lá hua nDomhnaill, *.i. Niall*). Again, in the year 1440, additional information concerning names of people is added to 1440.3 (dá ua nDochartaigh ... *.i. Emann mac Concobhair 7 Aodh mac Seain*), and 1440.10 (Maghnas Ó Domhnaill *.i. mac Domhnaill*). Some of these editorial interventions simply clarify which person is meant where the head of the lordship is mentioned. In other cases, however, there were evidently other reasons for supplying additional information about names, as in the case of the Ó Conchobhair and Ó Dochartaigh examples above. That revisions of this nature were made at all is evidence that the accuracy and clarity of such details were important to the annalists, and considerable care was taken to revise the text to ensure that the genealogical information supplied would be as comprehensive as was necessary. Incidentally, the fact that the genealogical material contained in AFM was evidently acquired piecemeal, and sometimes inserted into the text at a later stage, means that equivalence of genealogical detail cannot itself be used as a reliable guide when attempting to identify the principal sources used by the annalists.

The pattern revealed by the combined scribal evidence of the two sets of manuscripts in the case of the early fifteenth-century entries in AFM strongly suggests a clear division of labour between those whose role was that of copyist and those whose input was that of reviser and editor. The implications of the editorial role of scribes C and D have not been considered in discussions published to date. The evidence of the autograph manuscripts suggests that their work of revision must have taken place at quite a late stage in the overall project. Thus, for instance, where they state that a Lecan source was consulted after most of their own annals had been compiled and material was selected from the Lecan source where required,[50] it is notable that the autograph manuscripts reveal no correlation between the editorial additions to RIA MS 23 P 6 and TCD MS 1301 for the years 1443 to 1468 and the contents of such of the annals of Lecan as now survive in translation.[51] The manner in which the AFM entries for those 'Lecan' years are recorded in both RIA MS 23 P 6 and TCD MS 1301 is essentially a fair copy, in the hand of scribe B, with relatively little revision by hand C or D, suggesting that a set of Lecan annals was already available to the annalists before the mid-fifteenth-century material in either of the extant autograph manuscripts was recorded in its extant form. An alternative

---

50 *AFM*, I, p. lxv.   **51** Those annals are now extant for the years 1443 to 1468 only, and then only in Mac Fhirbhisigh's English translation. O'Donovan (ed.), 'The annals of Ireland from the year 1443 to 1468', 198–302.

explanation for the neat appearance of the post-1443 section of the two autograph manuscripts is that so much new fifteenth-century material came to hand that this section may represent a later draft as compared with the portion of the same two manuscripts covering the early fifteenth century. As noted above, Roderic O'Flaherty's annotations to TCD MS 1301 reveal that some of the additions made by the Four Masters in the early fifteenth-century portion of that manuscript (additions also made in RIA MS 23 P 6), were certainly drawn from a set of 'Mac Fhirbhisigh' annals.[52]

Variations in content between manuscripts

In terms of the content of the entries for each year, the differences that have been identified between TCD MS 1301 and RIA MS 23 P 6 are relatively minor. In five of the forty-six years sampled, there were minor variations in the sequence in which entries were arranged within a given year. The years in which there are variations in the sequence of entries are 1421, 1422, 1431, 1437 and 1438. In 1431, for example, where an entry on Moen Ó Gairmleadhaigh (1431.20) is placed slightly later in TCD MS 1301 than in RIA MS 23 P 6 (after 1431.22) the difference can probably be explained in terms of where blank space was available. In each of the two manuscripts it appears to be a late insertion, with the physical layout of the surrounding entries dictating where the scribe could insert it.

A more significant divergence of content occurs in the year 1419, when three entries found in RIA MS 23 P 6 are not recorded at all in TCD MS 1301 (1419.11; 1419.23 and 1419.24). Conversely, there are also instances when TCD MS 1301 contains an occasional detail not found in RIA MS 23 P 6. The entry at 1419.15 in RIA MS 23 P 6 omits a phrase referring to *an Justis*, so that it is more concise than the version in TCD MS 1301.

The year 1422 provides instances of some curious differences between the two sets of manuscripts. In that year, entries 1422.6, 1422.7 and 1422.10 as recorded in RIA MS 23 P 6 are not found under 1422 in TCD MS 1301. In two cases, there appears to have been confusion over the correct year under which to record the event described. Thus, the 1422.7 entry in RIA MS 23 P 6 concerning An Cosnamhach Óg Mac Aodhagáin, is placed instead at the end of the record for the year 1424 in TCD MS 1301. The entry recorded in RIA MS 23 P 6 at 1422.10, on the accession of Henry VI, is one of a series of entries on English monarchs that were added after the main text of each manuscript had been completed. From its position on the page and its relationship to preceding and subsequent entries in RIA MS 23 P 6 that entry was evidently made before the editorial hand D made other additions for that year. In RIA MS 23 P 6, it had originally been placed in 1421 but deleted and placed in 1422 instead. Apart from

52 O'Flaherty commences to identify a 'Mac Firbh' source beginning with the year 1361 (TCD MS 1301, fo. 704v–).

the case of Henry VI, in every other instance where this kind of entry concerning an English monarch was added to one manuscript it was also added to the other, and the 1422 omission was probably a simple oversight.[53] A final difference between the two autograph manuscripts in respect of 1422 concerns an entry describing an Ó Domhnaill attack on Sligo. It might be speculated that this was omitted from the Ó Gadhra copy of the work in deference to the Sligo allegiances of the patron, but this seems unlikely in the light of negative references to the family of Ó Gadhra preserved elsewhere throughout the text.

In TCD MS 1301 there is a marginal note at 1421.4 marking an obituary of Murchadh Ó Conchobhair, lord of Offaly, and making a cross reference to another more substantial entry relating to the same man, which scribe D had added on the following page near the end of the entry for the same year, and which is annotated in the margin *Sliocht Liubhair Lecain* ('extract from the book of Lecan').[54] This marginal note is not repeated in RIA MS 23 P 6, which likewise has two entries relating to the death of the same man (1421.4 and 1421.12).

AFM 1421.4

Murchadh ua Conchobhair tighearna Ua ffailghe fear ro bris iolchatha for gallaibh 7 gaoidhelaibh nó bhíodh ina aghaidh iar mbreith bhuadha ó dhomhan 7 o dhemhan do écc ina dhúnarus féin, 7 a adhnacal i mainistir Cille hAchaidh.
(Murrough O'Conor, lord of Offaly, a man who had gained victories over those English and Irish who opposed him, after vanquishing the world and the devil, died at his own mansion-seat, and was interred in the monastery of Killeigh.)

AFM 1421.12

O Concobhair (.i. Murchadh) do thecht dia thigh iarsin, 7 galar anbhail dia ghabhail, 7 a dhul is na bráithribh i ccill Achaidh, 7 aibitt brathar do ghabhail dó uimme, 7 a brathair fein do fhágbhail iona ionadh ria mbás .i. Diarmaitt Ó Conchobhair, 7 Ua Conchobhair do beith mí is na braithribh ria na écc, 7 atbath fo deóidh iar ndeghbhethaidh.
(O'Conor (Murrough) then returned home; but he was attacked by a dangerous disease, whereupon he retired among the friars in the monastery of Killeigh, and took the habit of a friar; but before his death he appointed his own kinsman, Dermot O'Conor, in his place. O'Conor was [only] a month among the friars, when he died, after a well-spent life.)[55]

The latter obituary is less formulaic than the former and records extra details, including an important mention of the appointment of Diarmait Ó Conchobhair

53 It appears that TCD MS 1301, fos 754–755v were rewritten by scribe C, perhaps because the earlier draft had so many revisions. These two folios in TCD MS 1301 are a fair copy entirely in the hand of scribe C, without any later additions. They contain the entries from 1422.8 to the end of 1424.   54 TCD MS 1301, fo. 752r. See also fos 752v and 753r.   55 *AFM*, IV, pp 848–9; 850–1.

as successor to the deceased. O'Donovan's printed edition records both obituaries of Murchadh Ó Conchobhair, noting that the language of the latter one is 'very rudely constructed'. O'Donovan even sought to improve on it in his translation.[56] Significantly, the marginal note, appended to 1421.4 in TCD MS 1301 only, appears to connect the subsequent obituary of the same person as recorded at 1421.12 with a Lecan source.

> TCD MS 1301
> *Fech an comardha eile atá andeireadh na duillinne thall amhail a deir leabur Lecáin bás í Concobhair Fhailge .i. Murchadh.*[57]
> [See the other symbol at the end of the opposite page as the Lecan book says the death of O'Conor Faly (Murchadh).][58]

This kind of duplication appears to have been something that the annalists generally wished to avoid, and the editorial hand that drew attention to it was perhaps marking it for revision before any final published edition would be produced. In this instance, it seems that the material came to hand from two quite different sources. Its inclusion may have been partly an oversight, something done in haste. It contrasts with the evidence encountered elsewhere in the early fifteenth century, where considerable redrafting of entries appears to have taken place as compared with such other annalistic sources as are extant.

Other variations between the two autograph manuscripts have also come to light. For example, the narrative entry at AFM 1423.5, telling of the exploits of a combined Ulster force against the English, varies between the two manuscripts, the sequence of the words having been altered, and RIA MS 23 P 6 omitting the specific mention of the killing of two hundred people recorded in TCD MS 1301: *ro marbadh dá céd do daoinibh don chur sin* ('two hundred people were killed on that occasion').[59] The explanatory clause recorded in RIA MS 23 P 6, *.i. la Maolmuire Mac Suibhne Connachtach consapal Ui Domhnaill 7 as laisidhe ro briseadh for ghallaibh* ('i.e. by Mulmurry Mac Sweeny Connachtach, O'Donnell's constable, and it was by him the English were routed') is presented differently in the corresponding entry in TCD MS 1301.[60]

Other variations between the two sets of autograph manuscripts include minor differences in the form of verbs used in 1424.4, and some rewording of the reference to Mac William Burke of Clanricard in 1424.8. Thus, TCD MS 1301 includes the word *tigearna* in his title, a word not found in RIA MS 23 P 6 at this point. Such differences are the exception rather than the rule, and may perhaps be best interpreted as spontaneous scribal decisions, curiosities without any major editorial or conceptual significance in the overall scheme of the annals.

---

56 *AFM*, IV, p. 851 n. i.   57 TCD MS 1301, at AD1421.   58 My translation.   59 TCD MS 1301, at fo. 755, lines 1–2.   60 *AFM*, IV, pp 858–9; TCD MS 1301, fos 754v–755r.

The variations provide evidence that the annalists were not mere copyists, but were still revising their text as they collaborated to produce the final drafts.

Patrician material in AFM

While the main focus of this study is on the post-1400 material in AFM, the scribal evidence of the autograph manuscripts covering the period before 1170 has a bearing on the discussion of the later period. A comparison of the Patrician material in the two autograph manuscripts offers an unexpected glimpse of the dilemmas faced by the annalists when coming to terms with external source material not derived from the native Irish hagiographical or historical tradition. Briefly stated, the evidence of the autograph manuscripts covering the earlier period, RIA MS C iii 3 and UCD–OFM MS A 13, provides some supporting evidence that the Louvain manuscript may represent the more final version of the text, but also some evidence that contradicts such a conclusion. In other words, it supports the argument presented here, that the two sets of manuscripts were worked on in tandem, through various stages of transcription and revision. In addition, there is evidence of a further phase of revision to the Louvain manuscript, not replicated in the Ó Gadhra set, a revision that was probably made after the manuscript had been taken to Louvain.

When comparing the two sets of autograph manuscripts, in respect of the presentation of fifth-century material, the first point to note again is the remarkable degree of similarity of layout between them. In the years AD457–9, for example, the general standardization of the layout of the two manuscripts is apparent, although the two copies are the work of different scribes (figs 6.15 and 6.16).[61] The headings and the text of the annual entries were neatly transcribed in each of the manuscripts by a main scribe – scribe G in the case of UCD–OFM MS A 13, and scribe A in the case of RIA MS C iii 3. The next significant feature to notice about the two manuscripts is that in both instances an additional passage has been added to the entry for AD457. There are two elements to the additional material. The first relates to the foundation of Armagh by Saint Patrick; the second is a reference to the death of *Sean Pattraic*.

AFM 457
Ard Macha d'fothuccadh lá Naomh Patraicc iarna edhbairt do ó Dhaire mac Fionnchadha mic Eoghain mic Nialláin. Ro hoirdnedh da fhir dhécc lais fri cumhdach an bhaile. Ro thionchoiscc dhóibh cetus, cathair airdepscoip do dhenamh isuidhe, 7 ecclus do mhanchaibh, 7 do chailleacha, 7 d'urdaibh oile archena doigh ro fhind-siomh combadh si budh cenn, 7 budh cleithe d'eccailsibh Erenn a coitchinne.
Sean-Patraicc do faoidhedh a spioraide.

---

61 RIA MS C iii 3, fo. 222r; UCD–OFM MS A 13, fo. 235r.

(Ard Macha was founded by Saint Patrick, it having been granted to him by Daire, son of Finnchadh, son of Eoghan, son of Niallan. Twelve men were appointed by him for building the town. He ordered them, in the first place, to erect an archbishop's city there, and a church for monks, for nuns and for the other orders in general, for he perceived that it would be the head and chief of the churches of Ireland in general.
Old Patrick yielded his spirit.)[62]

Prior to the insertion of this Patrician material, the original AFM entry had contained a brief description of the battle of Áth Dara, where king Laoghaire was in opposition to the Leinstermen – that entry made explicit reference to the king's pre-Christian character, mentioning his making oaths by the sun and wind – a reference also found in the Annals of Ulster under the year AD458.[63] The additional material on the foundation of Armagh is clearly propagandist in character, though its precise source is not identifiable from extant annals.[64] Given the patterns discernible elsewhere in these annals it is probably unwise to read the annals for AD457 as a deliberate juxtaposition of Christian missionary and pagan king. The normal practice in these annals of ignoring the connections between entries, and recording each discrete item on its own merits should be assumed to apply in this case also. The scribal evidence also probably argues against such subtlety of presentation or interpretation. It is more useful to concentrate on the basic conclusions about methodology to be drawn from an examination of scribal hands in the autograph manuscripts.

In this example of the annals for the 450s, the additions made after the basic text had been completed are inserted by scribe C in UCD–OFM MS A 13 and, unusually, partly by scribe B and partly by scribe C in RIA MS C iii 3. A basic point to note is that the additions are made to both manuscripts after the basic layout has been established. Thus, both sets of manuscripts can be described as working copies, and as elsewhere it is not realistic to draw a distinction between a draft and a fair copy.

Turning to the example of the corresponding entries in both manuscripts for the years AD493 and AD494, the overall similarity in terms of layout and changes between scribal hands is again clear. Here, it is evident that the headings for each year, and the text of the entry for AD494, were inserted first, by scribe G in UCD–OFM MS A 13 and by scribe A in the other manuscript, RIA MS C iii 3. Then a long entry on the death of Patrick was added to both manuscripts. This was done by scribe C in RIA MS C iii 3 and by scribe D in UCD–OFM MS A 13. As before, despite the involvement of different scribes, the editorial process to which the manuscripts were subjected was the same in each instance. The

62 *AFM*, I, pp 142–3.   **63** *AU*, I, pp 18–19. For an overview of the Patrician material in the older extant annals, see Liam Ó Buachalla, 'The construction of the Irish annals, 429–466', *Journal of the Cork Historical and Archaeological Society* 2nd ser., 63 (1958), 103–15.   **64** *AU*, I, pp 10–11. On Armagh see also Colgan, *Trias thaumaturga*, pp 164, 293.

scribal evidence again clearly indicates that work on both manuscripts proceeded in two distinct phases: the initial transcription of some entries for each year, followed by a phase of substantial editorial revision to both copies of the text with numerous additions being made.

Aside from the supporting evidence it provides concerning the working method of the scribes, there are some significant differences of detail in the presentation of Patrician material between the two manuscripts that require special notice. In the text as presented in RIA MS C iii 3, the year 430 is devoted to Palladius, who is presented as having arrived and left again within one year, his efforts being deemed a failure *o na fuair airmittin i nErinn* ('as he did not receive respect in Ireland').[65] This failed mission then sets the scene for the dispatch of St Patrick to Ireland in 431, and his arrival in 432. Further entries specifically relating to St Patrick are recorded for the years 438, 447, 448, 457 and 487, and finally his death is entered under the year 493. The entries are very basic, and may derive from a hagiographical rather than an annalistic source. The annalists do not usually cite their sources but, unusually, in the opening section of the entry for 432, they mention that material is derived from a life of the saint:

AFM 432
Pattraicc do theacht i nErinn an bliadhainsi, go ro gabh for baitseadh 7 beannachaigh eter[66] fiora, mna, maca, 7 ingena, cén mó tá uathadh na ro fhaomh baitsiodh na creideamh uadh, amhuil aisnedheas a bheatha.
(Patrick came to Ireland this year, and proceeded to baptize and bless both men, women, sons and daughters, except a few who did not consent to receive faith or baptism from him, as his Life relates.)[67]

It is significant that all of the stories in the various lives of Patrick about the miracle-working of the saint are consciously omitted by the Four Masters. They do not even incorporate the brief summary from the Martyrology of Donegal, which noted

MDon
As dírimh trá a nderna dfiortaibh, acus miorbhailibh, do thodhusccadh marbh a bas; díc clamh acus dall, acus bacach, acus aosa gacha tedmha arcena.
(Innumerable also was the number of signs and miracles he performed; by resuscitating the dead from death; by curing lepers, and the blind, and the lame, and people of every disease in like manner.)[68]

This editorial approach, paralleled in their treatment of other major saints such as Colum Cille,[69] is in direct contrast to the text in Conall Mac Eochagáin's

---

65 *AFM*, I, pp 128–9. 66 The O'Conor edition, on which O'Donovan probably relied here, read *Ereann* rather than *eter* here. 67 *AFM*, I, pp 130–1. 68 *MDon*, pp 78–9. 69 *AFM*, I, pp 214–17; compare with *MDon*, pp 150–63.

235.

Aoıs cr. 457.

[manuscript text in Irish Gaelic hand]

Aoıs cr. 458.

.30.

ɼ.

Aoıs cr. 459.

6.15 AFM entry for AD457–9. UCD–OFM MS A 13, fo. 235r.

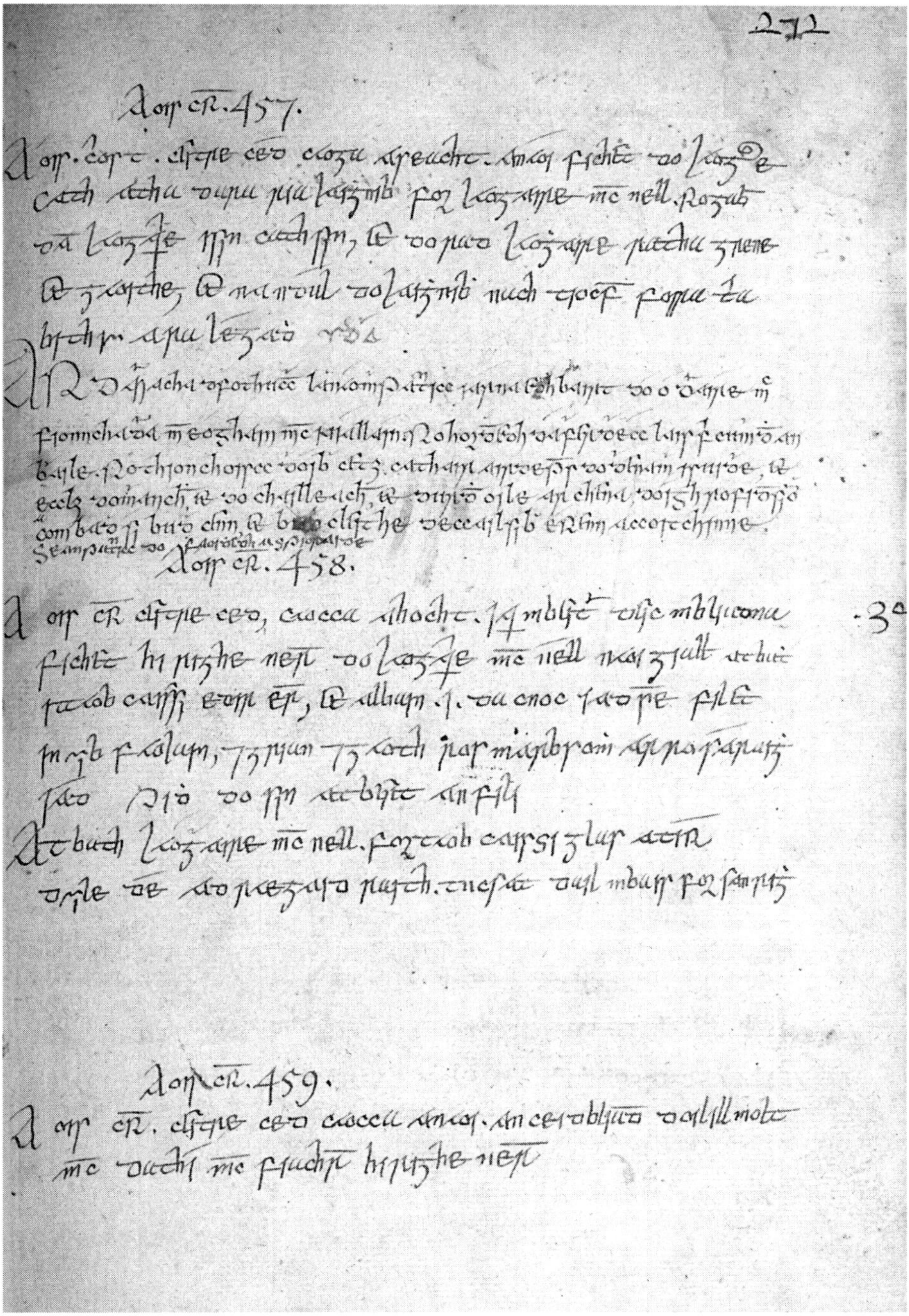

6.16 AFM entry for AD457–9. RIA MS C iii 3, fo. 222r.

translated annals, which relates Patrician miracles at some length.[70] It is clear from the treatment of the Patrician material that the Annals of the Four Masters were not designed to be hagiographical – rather they were conceived of as the secular history to complement the hagiographical works that were being separately compiled and prepared for publication.[71]

The two autograph manuscripts of AFM diverge significantly in respect of the contents of the entry for the years AD431 and AD432. The first point to note from the autograph manuscript RIA MS C iii 3 for the year 432 is that the verse extract attributed to Flann Mainistreach, which is printed in O'Donovan's edition of the text, is a later addition and must be disregarded here because it was not part of the work of the Four Masters.[72] O'Donovan prints all but the last two lines of this insertion – because it was included in the O'Conor edition derived from this manuscript.[73] However, if he had seen this autograph manuscript he would have known that it should be excluded. If O'Donovan had also seen the Franciscan copy of the autograph manuscript for the same year, AD432, he would have encountered a further puzzle. The entry bears no relationship to that found in RIA MS C iii 3 and appears to have been completely rewritten. Similarly, the preceding entry on Palladius was also redone. The entry relating to Palladius was redated to AD431 rather than AD430, and new material was added to the entry explaining the evidence for this new dating. Thus, the revised entry for AD431 in UCD–OFM MS A 13 ends as follows (unique material not found in RIA MS C iii 3 is given in bold):

> *Adeir an Cairdional Baronius, an té do sgriobh sdair na hEglaisi o bhliadhain go bliadhain ó ghein Criost gurab i so an bliadhain do chuir Celestinus Palladius go hÉirinn et go bfuair bas an bliadhain cedna so.*
> [**Cardinal Baronius, the one who wrote the history of the church from year to year from the birth of Christ, says that this was the year Celestinus sent Palladius to Ireland and that he died this same year.**][74]

Since Patrick had to be made to come later than Palladius, the entry that had been dated AD431 in RIA MS C iii 3 was moved to the year AD432 instead. The entry stated that in that year Saint Patrick was ordained bishop by Pope Celestine and ordered to go to Ireland to preach and teach faith and piety to the Gaeil. The revised entry for the year 432 in UCD–OFM, MS A 13 (with new material highlighted here in bold) reads:

70 *AClon*, pp 65–70. **71** For an overview of the related projects, see Jennings, *Michael O Cleirigh and his associates.* **72** The Ó Gadhra set of the autograph manuscripts, RIA MS C iii 3 and TCD MS 1301, have many additions of this kind in later hands, particularly those of Roderic O'Flaherty and Charles O'Conor. It may also be noted that the three-volume transcript of AFM (to 1171), made in the mid-eighteenth century by Maurice O'Gorman, does not contain the Flann Mainistreach passage (TCD MS 1279, pt I [formerly H. 1. 3], fo. 25v). The passage is likewise omitted from the 1734–5 transcript preserved in TCD MS 1300 (pp 147–8). **73** O'Conor (ed.), *Quatuor Magistrorum annales Hibernici*, pp 98–100. **74** UCD–OFM MS A 13, fo. 231v, with my translation.

UCD–OFM, MS A 13

As i so an bhliadhain do hoirdnedh náomh Patraig i n-easpugoide la Celestinus. Et do fhuráil air teacht go hEirinn do shioladh creidmhe et chrábhaidh do Ghaoidhealaibh et da mbaistedh. Tainicc iarsin Pátraig i n-Eirinn an bliadhain sin et do ghabh ag baistedh et ag bennughadh eter fiora, mna, maca et inghena genmotha uathadh beag nár fhaomh baistedh amhail aisneidhes a bheatha. Áth truim do fhothughadh la Patraicc íarna eadhbairt do Fheidhlim mhac Laoghaire mic Neill do Dhia, dhósomh, do Lomán et do Foirtchearn.

Adeir scribhneoir áiridhe don eaglais dárabh ainm Baronius, gurab é an seisead lá do mhí April na bliadhna so fúair Celestinus Pápa bás. Et go ndernadh Pápa do Shixtus a ccionn fhiched lá na dhíaidh sin. Et gurab é do chuir Patraig go hEirinn an bhliadhain si. Adeir an ghluais mhinighte atá ar moladh do rinne Fiach naomhtha espag slebhte do Phátraig, nach raibhe Celestinus beo, acht aoin tseachtmain iar ndol fo gradhaibh do Phatraig, et go ndernadh Papa do Shixtus 7 gur thaisbéin cennsa mór do Phátraig, et go ttug ní do thaisibh Póil 7 Pedair et liubhra iomdha dó ag teacht go hEirinn.[75]

[In this year Saint Patrick was ordained bishop by Celestinus. And he ordered him to come to Ireland to spread faith and piety to the Irish and to baptize them. After that Patrick came to Ireland that year and proceeded to baptize and to bless men, women sons, and daughters, except for a few who did not consent to receive faith or baptism from him, as his Life relates.

Ath-Truim was founded by Patrick, it having been granted to Fedhlim, son of Laeghaire, son of Niall, to God and to him, Loman and Fortchern.

According to a certain ecclesiastical writer, named Baronius, it was on the 6th day of the month of April in this year that Pope Celestine died. And that Sixtus was made pope twenty days after that. And that it was he who sent Patrick to Ireland in this year. According to an explanatory gloss in a praise poem [made] by holy Fiacc bishop of Slebhte, Celestine was alive for just one week after Patrick was ordained and Sixtus was made pope and showed great kindness to Patrick, and gave him relics of Paul and Peter and many books at his coming to Ireland.][76]

There were several matters at issue in the new material inserted here. First, there was the dating of the arrival of St Patrick to Ireland, and the related question of which pope, Celestine or Sixtus, had ordained him and had sent him to Ireland. It seems that the conflict in dating between evidence the Four Masters had drawn from native sources and that recorded in the prestigious publication of Caesar Baronius, a leading historian of the Counter Reformation, became a cause of concern.[77] For whatever reason, it was deemed necessary to cut out a page from the already completed manuscript and substitute a re-written one that accorded with the evidence documented by Baronius. The manner in which a substitute leaf, fo. 231, was pasted into the quire is clearly visible in UCD–OFM MS A 13.

---

75 UCD–OFM, MS A 13, fo. 231v.   76 My translation.   77 The ecclesiastical annals of Baronius were cited in Colgan, *Acta sanctorum Hiberniae*, pp 106, 432, 433, 448.

The further inclusion of material from the *Liber hymnorum* glosses to the poem *Génair Pattraic* attributed to Fiacc may well have been prompted by John Colgan and selected for inclusion because of the specific reference therein to Popes Celestine and Sixtus.[78] As was the norm for early modern chroniclers, the annalist left readers to decide for themselves which source to accept.

The fact that the Louvain set of the annals of the Four Masters was rewritten at this point – but the other set was not, suggests that the error may have been discovered, and the correction made, after the annals were taken to Louvain. The revision to the Louvain manuscript at this point is in a hand (figure 6.11) not found elsewhere in the autograph manuscripts.[79] Given what is known about the way corrections to one text were almost invariably replicated in the other, the fact that the other set, RIA MS C iii 3, was not amended in this case, suggests that the manuscripts had become separated before this correction was made.

If the revision was not done in Louvain, the next most likely place that the change might have been made was Dublin, where the manuscript was taken by Ó Cléirigh in 1637 to obtain approbations before taking his work to Louvain.[80] The Dublin Franciscans might have had a text of Baronius, which could have been consulted. The ecclesiastical annals of Caesar Baronius had been published in twelve volumes in the years 1588–1607. By the time of his death, in 1607, Baronius had brought his chronicle from the birth of Christ down to the year 1198. Others attempted to continue the work, but without much success.[81]

If the Dublin Franciscans themselves did not own a set of Baronius's *Annales ecclesiastici*, they may nonetheless have had access to the work. It is known, for example, that by the late 1630s James Ussher, the Protestant historian and archbishop of Armagh, consulted the ecclesiastical annals of Baronius, for he cites it in his 1639 work, *Britannicarum ecclesiarium antiquitates*.[82] It is also known that Ussher was in contact with the Dublin Franciscans concerning Irish manuscript sources and gave them access to items from his library in Drogheda.[83] Even the inclusion of material from the *Liber hymnorum* does not necessarily argue against a Dublin context for this revision. A copy of that text was one of two known to the Dublin antiquarian Sir James Ware, and was cited by both Ware and James Ussher, archbishop of Armagh.[84] On balance, however, it seems

---

78 The gloss appears in the second line of verse seven of the poem attributed to Fiacc, bishop of Sleghte in Colgan, *Trias thaumaturga*, p. 1; see also Colgan's 'note 14' to this at *Trias thaumaturga*, p. 5. This AFM material was presumably drawn from the copy of *Liber hymnorum* that was also available to Colgan, now UCD–OFM MS A 2.   79 It is hand 7 as described in *Cat. Ir. mss in FLK*, p. 25, a hand quite similar to that of Mícheál Ó Cléirigh himself.   80 The approbation of the Franciscan archbishop of Dublin, Thomas Fleming, was obtained on 8 February 1637 (*AFM*, I, p. lxx).   81 Cyriac K. Pullapilly, *Caesar Baronius: Counter-Reformation historian* (Notre Dame, IN, 1975).   82 See Elrington and Todd (eds), *The whole works of James Ussher*, VI, pp 356, 358, 362, for citation of Caesar Baronius among many other ecclesiastical writers in connection with the mission of Palladius the Greek to Ireland.   83 For these scholarly networks, see below, pp 289–93. 84 J.H. Bernard and R. Atkinson (eds), *The Irish Liber hymnorum* (2 vols, London, 1898), I, pp xiv–xv.

much more likely that Colgan would have been the person to influence the decision to amend the Patrician section of Ó Cléirigh's annals.

If the conclusion is reached that in this instance the text of AFM continued to be revised after it was taken to Louvain, this strengthens the view that the work was being prepared for publication there. The delay in publication can probably be attributed in part to the criticisms voiced by Tuileagna Ó Maoil Chonaire in respect of the way the province of Connacht was portrayed in Ó Cléirigh's work, and his insistence that revisions be made prior to publication.[85] However, there is no indication that any revisions were made to the text such as would answer the criticisms of Tuileagna.

The evidence of the autograph manuscripts indicates that great care was taken to enhance the accuracy of the text at all stages of production. And the evidence of the revisions to the Patrician material indicates that an attempt was made not merely to ensure that the annals accorded with the evidence of sources available in Ireland, but that it could also be reconciled with evidence from external sources. The decision to cite Baronius by name, when the annals so rarely cite their authorities – Bede was mentioned once – may have been taken so as to justify the deviation from the evidence of native sources. If the change was made in Louvain, then it was done after Tuileagna Ó Maoil Chonaire had begun to raise objections on points of detail and the reviser may have felt compelled to substantiate his case by citing his source. This may have been deemed particularly important given that evidence from a non-traditional source, which did not conform to the detail of the older annals, was being used. The revised passages are quite different from those they replaced. The difference is not the superficial one of redating Palladius from 430 to 431; rather the difference is in the attitude revealed to historical evidence, and the annalists' concession that, in this instance at least, the evidence from the printed work of Baronius was to be given at least as much credence as the indigenous sources on which their work had relied.

The more extensive revision of the Patrician material is not typical of the manuscript as a whole and must be regarded as exceptional. Its importance is that the attempt to alter the traditional chronology to accord with that contained in the printed ecclesiastical annals of Baronius provides evidence of changing attitudes to historical evidence. It marks a point where the native Irish historical record was modified in the light of the international standards dictated by Counter-Reformation historiography. When the entries in UCD–OFM MS A13 and RIA MS C iii 3 for the years AD431 and AD432 are compared, the revisions in the Louvain manuscript are evidence of something more than a manuscript being tidied up for publication. Rather, they record the moment when a trained scribe from the native Irish tradition was confronted with evidence from quite a

85 *GRSH*, pp 131, 147.

different tradition and adopted a pragmatic solution as to how best to enhance the accuracy of the work. It is first-hand evidence of an Irish historian at work at the very point where Counter-Reformation historiography directly influenced the Irish annalistic tradition.[86]

Other hagiographical material

While the revision of the Patrician material in one of the two autograph manuscripts of AFM provides an exceptional instance where the Louvain text is clearly a more polished version than the Ó Gadhra one, considerable caution should be exercised in extrapolating from one or two case studies about the nature of the entire manuscripts. Significantly, some examples drawn from the skeletal hagiographical material in AFM for the early Christian period contradict the evidence of the Patrician section about which manuscript is the closest to being a 'fair copy'. There is a clear correlation between the saints whose date of death is recorded in AFM and the saints included in the Martyrology of Donegal. Although the second recension of the Martyrology of Donegal had been completed by Mícheál and Cú Choigcríche Ó Cléirigh almost two years before the date they give for commencing work on the annals, the relationship between the two texts is not straightforward. In particular, the annalists showed no inclination to incorporate detailed hagiographical narratives from the martyrology into the annals in any systematic way. Rather, they were initially concerned only to fix the chronology of the Irish saints by recording their deaths under the appropriate year. However, it is clear from the autograph manuscripts of the annals that many of these very basic entries were subsequently revised to include the feast day, that is the day and month of death, in addition to the year, in instances where that information had been omitted originally. The dates supplied almost invariably correspond with dates given in the Martyrology of Donegal, by then the obvious and readily available source for such material.[87] Very occasionally, AFM gives date information not found in the Martyrology of Donegal, as in the case of Cuanna, 10 April 717, a saint for whom the Martyrology does not record the year of death.[88]

Curiously, however, some differences can be discerned between the two autograph manuscripts in the implementation of these revisions. For example, under the year AD652 in RIA MS C iii 3, the obit date *Maii 1* for Oisseine is

---

86 The corresponding manuscript that remained in Ireland was later augmented in a much more traditional manner by the addition of poetic material attributed to Flann Mainistreach (RIA MS C iii 3, fo. 218v). The untidy hand that adds the Flann Mainistreach material to the entry for AD432 also makes additions elsewhere in the same manuscript, some of which are signed Henry Burc and dated to the 1640s. 87 Very occasionally, the year given in the Martyrology of Donegal is as given in the Annals of Ulster rather than AFM, e.g. Fiodhmuine, 16 May 756, and one Suairleach, 23 April 774 (*MDon*, pp 130–1, 108–9; *AU*, I, pp 220–1, 242–3). 88 *AFM*, I, pp 314–15; *MDon*, pp 98–9.

added in a different hand from the remainder of the entry.[89] The date is not given at all in UCD–OFM MS A 13. In another editorial intervention in RIA MS C iii 3, at the year AD664, in relation to Saint Féchín, a reference to Fore is added and then cancelled. In the corresponding place in UCD–OFM MS A 13, the reference to Fore is not added at all.[90] In most other instances, however, where an obit date is added to one manuscript, there is a corresponding entry in the other. In several of these instances, however, where the day and month information in RIA MS C iii 3 is clearly an addition, it appears to be all in one hand and ink in UCD–OFM MS A 13.[91]

These variations in detail in the hagiographical entries in the early Christian section of AFM raise interesting questions about the Four Masters' use of the Martyrology of Donegal as a source. The added details regarding obits comprise material easily accessible in the Martyrology, especially since the autograph copy of that work contained extensive indices.[92] Yet, it appears that the annalists were not concerned to draw on the Martyrology in any detail beyond recording the basic chronological information about each saint, and even that was apparently something of an afterthought. It may be noted in passing that a somewhat similar exercise of adding obit dates to the entries on saints was also undertaken in respect of the Four Masters' other hagiographical work, the *Genealogiae regum et sanctorum Hiberniae*, after the basic text had been completed, though it was not done so comprehensively as in AFM.[93]

O'Donovan's edition of AFM

In comparing the two sets of manuscripts, and cross-checking them against O'Donovan's printed edition, the limitations of O'Donovan's edition become clear. The most serious problems relate to the pre-1171 material, for which O'Donovan did not have access to either set of autograph manuscripts, but relied on eighteenth-century transcripts of RIA MS C iii 3. O'Donovan had no access to the Franciscan manuscript, now UCD–OFM MS A 13, and therefore had no inkling of the differences between the two sets. Nor was O'Donovan aware that the transcripts of RIA MS C iii 3 available to him omitted numerous entries found in the original autograph manuscripts. In the case of the Patrician material, although O'Donovan's edition generally adheres to the content of RIA

89 RIA MS C iii 3, fo. 256r; UCD–OFM MS A 13, fo. 269r.   90 UCD–OFM MS A 13, fo. 272r; RIA MS C iii 3, fo. 259r.   91 For example, St Beoghna in AFM 605.2 (UCD–OFM MS A 13, fo. 259v; RIA MS C iii 3, fo. 246v); St Siollan, in AFM 606.2 (UCD–OFM MS A 13, fo. 260r; RIA MS C iii 3, fo. 247r); St Mochudu, AFM 636.2 (UCD–OFM MS A 13, fo. 266r; RIA MS C iii 3, fo. 253r).   92 BR MS 5095–6; *MDon*, pp 354–479.   93 For example, the entries on Bearchan, Becan, Baothan et al. in chapter thirteen *Do naomhaibh slechta Colla da Crioch*, all have information about the feast day inserted later (*GRSH*, p. 69; however, in the case of Saint Colman Eala, for example, no such information is supplied in GRSH even though the date (26 September) was added to AFM 610.1 (UCD–OFM MS A 13, fo. 260r), and was, of course, available in the Martyrology of

MS C iii 3 rather than UCD–OFM MS A 13, there are points where it does not fully reflect even the contents of RIA MS C iii 3. Thus, for example, the years AD429 and AD433 are entirely omitted from O'Donovan's edition. This feature represents a continuation of the practice noted earlier, where years containing little information other than the regnal year are omitted from the text.[94] Both of the autograph manuscripts RIA MS C iii 3 and UCD–OFM MS A 13 contain entries for these years, though they consist of merely a heading and a statement concerning the reign of the king. It should also be restated that the verse passage attributed to Flann Mainistreach in O'Donovan's edition of the entry for AD432 is an addition in a later hand in RIA MS C iii 3 and was not part of the text inserted by the Four Masters. Not surprisingly, this verse extract is not recorded at all in UCD–OFM MS A 13. But O'Donovan could not know this, and in his version of the entry for AD432, he presented the Flann Mainistreach material as though it was integral to the Four Masters' text.

This small Patrician sample lends some support, in this particular case, to Paul Walsh's statements that there are substantial differences in content between the two sets of autograph manuscripts, and that the Louvain set is a 'fair copy', as compared with the 'rough draft' that is the Ó Gadhra manuscript. However, the Patrician case is not typical of AFM as a whole, and it is the only instance where there is substantial revision of the text in one autograph manuscript not also found in the other set.

The Patrician case further highlights the shortcomings of O'Donovan's edition as revealed in the omission of some annals, and the inclusion of material extraneous to the original annals. The shortcomings of O'Donovan's edition of AFM for the years after 1171 are considerably less pronounced, because he was able to consult both of the extant sets of autograph manuscripts for these years. O'Donovan's edition was based on RIA MS 23 P 6–7 rather than on TCD MS 1301. However, the printed text does not invariably provide a complete transcript of everything in RIA MS 23 P 6–7. In the year 1420, for instance, both manuscripts have an additional two-line entry relating to Domhnall Ó Néill following 1420.3 that is not found in O'Donovan's edition. The two lines in question are marked in the left margin of both manuscripts with an asterisk in what may be contemporary ink, and in RIA MS 23 P 6 there is a note (evidently by scribe D) making reference to another related entry (1420.9), which is similarly

Donegal (*MDon*, pp 260–1). 94 As noted above, chapter four, on the form and structure of the annals, O'Donovan's edition, reliant on inadequate exemplars, omits very many entries in the pre-Christian and early Christian periods, so that the text up to AD653 is very substantially abridged in the printed edition. In general, the pattern of abridgment follows that in O'Conor's 1826 printed text, and that of the eighteenth-century transcripts found in TCD MS 1300 made for Dr John Fergus in 1734–5, and in RIA MS 23 F 2. In respect of years such as AD429, however, there is an entry in TCD MS 1300, p. 146, and also in O'Conor's edition, which O'Donovan opted to omit (O'Conor (ed.), *Quatuor Magistrorum annales Hibernici*, pp 96–7; *AFM*, I, pp 128–9). Thus, it appears that O'Donovan, like earlier transcribers, did not consider it necessary to include entries marked with an asterisk in both manuscripts.[95] As in the 1421 case discussed earlier, editorial revision of each of the two manuscripts highlighted duplication of content that had probably arisen when differently worded entries on the one topic were drawn from different sources. In the 1420 case, O'Donovan's edition omitted one of the duplicated entries whereas in another similar instance in 1422, O'Donovan reproduced the duplicated entries in their entirety.

An instance of repetition that was noticed by some reviser of the annals occurs in the entry for 1422, where both manuscripts contain two very similar but not identical entries relating to Eoghan Ó Néill, one in the hand of scribe B, the other in the hand of D (1422.3 and 1422.9), the first being marked by a marginal asterisk in each manuscript.[96] It is worth noting that in this instance O'Donovan commented on the duplication in a footnote, telling the reader that he left in the duplicated entry because the second was a stylistic improvement on the first.[97] The unstated implication is that in other instances O'Donovan silently omitted duplicated material, as happened in one of the examples noted above.

Conclusion

Paul Walsh's suggestion that when the two sets of autograph manuscripts of AFM are compared, 'considerable divergence will be found between the two scripts both in the matter recorded and in the order of the items under each year',[98] has been found to be overstated in respect of the fifteenth-century evidence. On the other hand, the distinctive treatment of the Patrician material in UCD–OFM MS A 13 may be the kind of discrepancy between the two sets of manuscripts that Walsh had in mind, but it is exceptional. In the case study of the entries for the years 1419 to 1454, significant variation in the sequence of entries within a year was found in respect of two of the forty-six years examined, 1422 and 1438. These were years in which three separate scribes contributed to both sets of manuscripts. Further very minor variations in the sequence of entries were identified in respect of the years 1421, 1431 and 1437. Variations in actual content between the two sets of manuscripts were noted in respect of 1419, 1424, 1436 and 1451. In the year 1419, three of the entries recorded in RIA MS 23 P 6 are not found in TCD MS 1301 under that year. In another three cases, there is an entry in TCD MS 1301 not recorded in RIA MS 23 P 6, though in two of these three instances a scribe subsequently deleted the entry from TCD MS 1301. Thus Walsh's observation is partly correct but the nature of the variation identified is rather less significant in respect of the post-1170 annals than Walsh's comment implies, and the Louvain set cannot be regarded

for years in which no specific events were recorded.   **95** *AFM*, IV, pp 842–7; RIA MS 23 P 6, fos 159–160. These asterisks may well be eighteenth-century or nineteenth-century insertions. **96** TCD MS 1301, fos 753v–754; RIA MS 23 P 6, fos 704v–705.   **97** *AFM*, IV, p. 854, note u. **98** Walsh, *The Four Masters and their work*, p. 13.

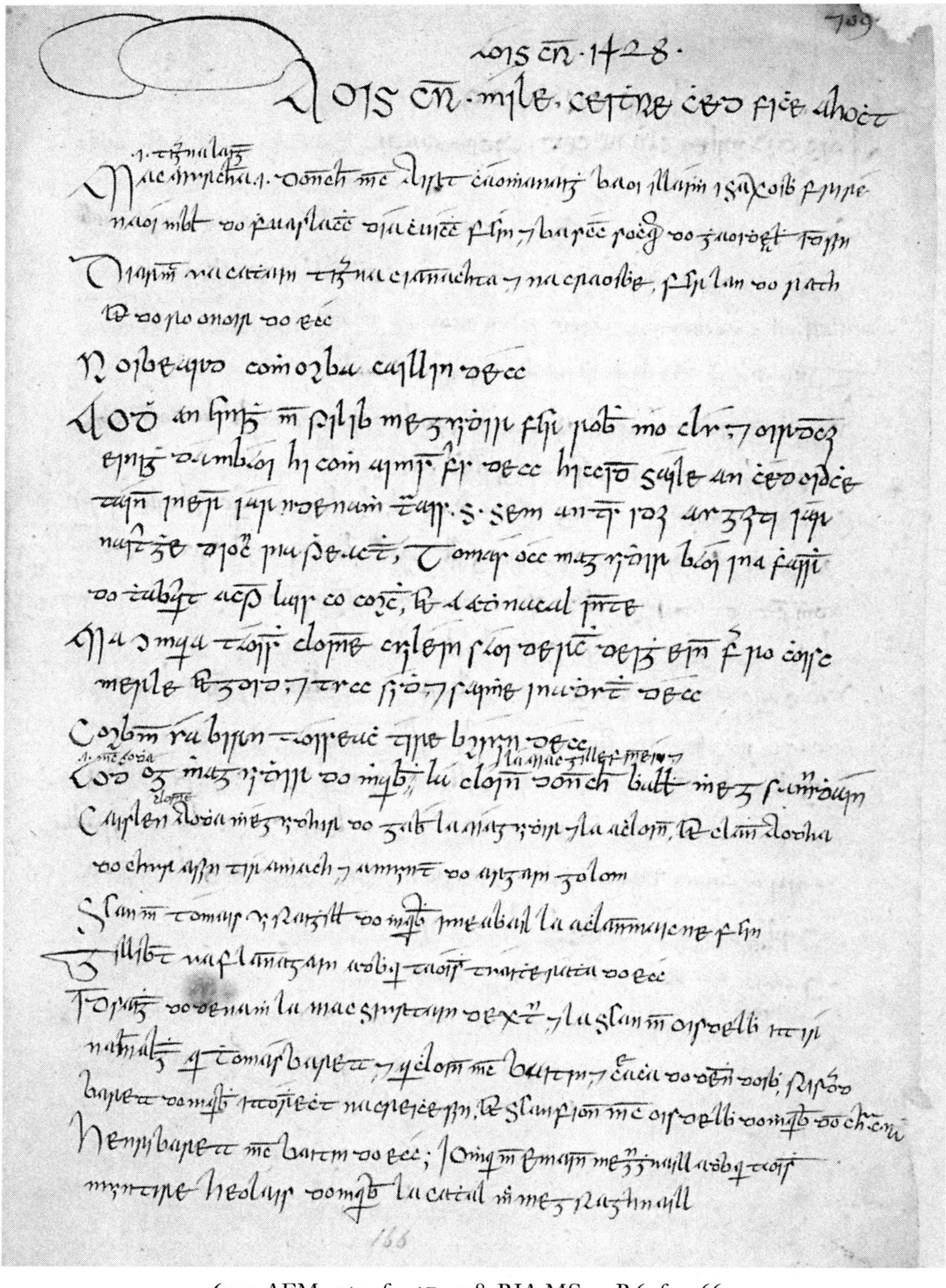
Aois Cr. 1428.

6.17 AFM entry for AD1428. RIA MS 23 P 6, fo. 166r.

6.18 AFM entry for AD1428. TCD MS 1301, fo. 758r.

as a 'fair copy'. There is occasional, if scant, evidence that where the two sets of annals differ, it is the Louvain set, RIA MSS 23 P 6–23 P 7, rather than the Ó Gadhra set, that represents the annalists' preferred form. Contrary evidence can also be found, as for instance in the first entry for AD1428, where RIA MS 23 P 6, fo. 166r is in a less finished form than TCD MS 1301, fo. 758r (figs 6.17–6.18).[99]

In addition to the differences noted above, there is another type of variation in the detail of some entries that may be significant. A small number of entries are drafted differently in RIA MS 23 P 6 than in TCD MS 1301, and when these differences are compared, it appears that the version in RIA MS 23 P 6 usually has greater clarity or is a stylistic improvement. Evidence from other texts of Cú Choigcríche Ó Cléirigh's skill as a textual editor, supports the conclusion that he would have had no reservations about continuing to make such revisions.[100] Mícheál Ó Cléirigh appears to have been equally inclined to redraft entries as he worked, as evidenced by occasional minor changes in fifteenth-century entries.

The sequences of change in scribal hands, though not identical, correspond very closely with one another in both manuscripts for the early fifteenth-century. The variations in the sequence of entries within a given year, and the occasional omission of a brief entry from one or other set are thus difficult to attribute to a firm editorial policy and are better accounted for by simple editorial oversight and the kind of variation between manuscripts inevitable where scribal hands fail to achieve the uniformity of print. The degree of similarity is very striking; the differences are quite minor.

The analysis presented here has sought to establish the extent of the variation between the two autograph sets of AFM, and to assess how closely the content of those manuscripts is reflected in O'Donovan's edition. The case studies have demonstrated that in addition to the minor orthographic and stylistic variations between the manuscripts that could be expected in any two versions of a text reproduced by hand, there are occasional variations in the structure of individual entries and some rare instances where an entry is recorded in one manuscript but not the other. Overall, however, the most striking finding is the degree of similarity between the two manuscripts, with the various scribes adhering to the same roles in terms of transcription or emendation in each instance.

The Patrician case study highlights the readiness of those associated with the annals to continue to improve the text when new evidence came to light. Thus, when confronted with documented evidence from Caesar Baronius that conflicted with the chronology derived from older Irish annals, the text was amended to accommodate the newly available evidence. Above all, the case study highlights the importance of examining both sets of autograph manuscripts in

---

99 The words .i. tighearna Liaghen are interpolated in MS 23 P 6 but integrated into the main text in MS 1301.　100 For analysis of Cú Choigcríche Ó Cléirigh's skills as a redactor of texts, see Breatnach, 'The methodology of seanchas', 1–18; Breatnach, 'A seventeenth-century abridgement of Beatha Aodha Ruaidh', 77–172.

tandem, since any differences between them can be important indicators of the intellectual approach of the compilers to their work.

Although John O'Donovan's edition of the text sometimes notices instances where the second autograph manuscript, TCD MS 1301, differs from his principal source, RIA MS 23 P 6, for the post-1170 period, his edition does not systematically record all the variations between the two sets of manuscripts. O'Donovan was concerned with recording the factual detail contained in his source manuscripts and not the detail concerning minor variations in the sequence of entries between the two sets. While the layout of the manuscripts themselves, of course, preserves evidence of the compilers' working method that O'Donovan's edition cannot be expected to convey, in general his edition of the post-1170 material records the content and arrangement of the annal entries as found in RIA MS 23 P 6 and 23 P 7 in an authoritative and readily accessible manner.

It is reasonable to conclude that the degree of variation between the two sets of autograph manuscripts of AFM for the period after 1170 generally falls within the range of what should be expected in a non-print environment. The full standardization achievable in print cannot be expected from these manuscripts. Although they are not identical, they probably resemble one another as closely as any two manuscript transcripts that are essentially working drafts can reasonably be expected to. The variations between the two sets that have been identified do not amount to evidence of a difference of editorial intent. Rather, they provide evidence of the compilers striving to apply the same editorial decisions to both sets of manuscripts in turn. Very occasionally, there is evidence of a small improvement in one that is not replicated in the other. Variations exist despite the compilers' meticulous efforts to achieve accuracy, consistency and completeness in both sets of autograph manuscripts. The Four Masters, and later John O'Donovan in editing their work, strove to meet exacting standards of scholarship, and while perfection eluded them both, the legacy of their work provides ample evidence of their careful scholarship.

CHAPTER SEVEN

Heroes, historians and political memory

The discussion of the methodology of the Four Masters in the preceding chapters has drawn attention to some of the ideological concerns underpinning the selection and arrangement of entries in the annals. The significance of those biases will now be investigated by examining the annalistic representation of particular political personages and events.

Introduction: heroes, historians and political memory

The key features of the kind of historical writing preserved in AFM can be illustrated through an analysis of the portrayal of the Uí Dhomhnaill in the annals for the years from 1500 to 1608. The first element to be considered is the obituaries of the Ó Domhnaill lords, a feature the Four Masters themselves evidently considered of special importance since they sometimes tagged them in their text by writing the name of the deceased in extra large letters.[1] The second kind of entry to be analyzed will be the narratives of Ó Domhnaill military exploits, which become increasingly discursive through the sixteenth century. In examining the nature and purpose of these military narratives, those relating to events prior to 1537 are considered first, this being the year the Four Masters identify as the latest year covered by their Ó Cléirigh source. The succeeding section discusses episodes from 1538 to 1587, a period for which no source manuscripts are named by the Four Masters. Finally, the post-1587 narrative entries are considered, most of which were derived from Lughaidh Ó Cléirigh's biography of Aodh Ruadh Ó Domhnaill.[2]

Behind all of these representations of the Uí Dhomhnaill in the sixteenth-century portion of the annals, there probably lies the work of successive Ó Cléirigh historians.[3] The work of specific individuals cannot normally be

1 See, for example, the 1505 and 1537 obituaries of Uí Dhomhnaill lords in RIA MS 23 P 7, fos 8v, 53r. The practice was not adopted by the scribe of the 1563 obituary for Maghnus Ó Domhnaill (RIA MS 23 P 7, fo. 98r). Other instances where large lettering is used include the return of Aodh Ó Domhnaill from Rome in 1512 (RIA MS 23 P 6, fo. 20), but otherwise that kind of scribal embellishment of the text is very rare.   2 Walsh (ed.), *Beatha Aodha Ruaidh*; P.A. Breatnach, 'Irish records of the Nine Years War: a brief survey with particular notice of the relationship between Beatha Aodha Ruaidh Uí Dhomhnaill and the Annals of the Four Masters' in Ó Riain (ed.), *Beatha Aodha Ruaidh*, pp 124–47; Damian McManus, 'The language of the Beatha' in Ó Riain (ed.), *Beatha Aodha Ruaidh*, pp 54–73.   3 Information on the origins of the family and an account of their coming to Tír Conaill, and the establishment of a house at Kilbarron in the time of Tadhg Cam

identified, and little more than genealogical and skeletal annalistic information is recoverable for most of the Ó Cléirigh scholars active in the fifteenth and sixteenth centuries. As historians to the Uí Dhomhnaill, prominent members of the learned family of Ó Cléirigh themselves usually earned a mention in AFM when they died. Thus, the death of Tadhg Cam Ó Cléirigh in 1492 was marked in the appropriate manner.

AFM 1492.23

Ua Cléiricch Tadhcc Cam ollamh Uí Domhnaill i neiccsi hi filidheacht 7 a senchus fer tighe aoidhedh coitchinn do thrénaibh 7 do truacchaibh décc iar mbreith buadha ó dhomhan 7 ó dhemhan.

(O'Clery, i.e. Teige Cam, ollav to O'Donnell in literature, poetry and history, a man who had kept a house of general hospitality for the mighty and the needy, died, after having gained the victory over the Devil and the world.)[4]

In 1527 the death of his son, Giolla Riabhach, was likewise noted:

AFM 1527.8

O Cléirigh .i. an Giolla Riabhach mac Taidhcc Caim saoi lé healadhain hi senchus, i ndán, 7 hi leighionn fer suim, saidhbhir, sochonáigh, 7 cumhaing móir éisidhe, 7 a écc in aibítt San Fronseis an 8. la do Mharta.

(O'Clery (Gilla-Reagh, the son of Teige Cam), a scientific adept in history, poetry and literature, and a man of consideration, wealth, prosperity and great power, died in the habit of St Francis, on the 8th day of March.)[5]

Although the position of *ollamh* in history to Ó Domhnaill remained within the Ó Cléirigh family throughout the sixteenth century, the office did not necessarily descend from father to son. Thus the obituary for Tadhg Cam's son, Giolla Riabhach, does not assert that he had been *ollamh* to Ó Domhnaill. Yet he nonetheless followed in the scholarly tradition of the family, successfully pursuing a career in history. He also established links with the Franciscans.

By the mid-sixteenth century, the position of *ollamh* to Ó Domhnaill was evidently held by Tadhg Cam, son of Tuathal Ó Cléirigh, who died in 1565. Again, this Tadhg Cam's learning and hospitality and also his association with the Franciscan convent at Donegal were noted by the annalists, in an obituary that displays none of the political ambivalence of the obituaries of the Ó Domhnaill lords that he may have been involved in drafting.[6] He is one of the few learned men whose obituary specifically describes his role as that of 'chronicler', a term which Mícheál Ó Cléirigh also applied to himself.[7]

and his sons, is provided in Pender (ed.), 'The O'Clery book of genealogies', 114–15. 4 *AFM*, IV, pp 1194–5. 5 *AFM*, V, pp 1388–9. 6 The ambivalence of the 1563 obituary of Maghnus Ó Domhnaill, for instance, is discussed below. 7 For Mícheál Ó Cléirigh's description of himself as being *dar duthchas 7 darb foghlaim croinic* ('a chronicler by descent and education', see *GRSH*, pp 7, 143.

AFM 1565.6

O Cleirigh Tadhcc Cam mac Tuathail ollamh Uí Dhomhnaill lé Senchus saoí hi ffilidheacht, 7 hi ccroinic, post congmala tighe naoidhedh do dhámhaibh, 7 do dheoradhaibh, 7 do fhealmacaibh foghlama na ccrioch báttar comhfoccus dó do écc (.i. an 20. la dOctober) iar sendataidh toghaidhe iar mbreith buadha o demhan 7 ó domhan, 7 a adhnacal i mainistir .S. Fronseis i nDún na nGall co nairmitin, 7 co nonoir nádhbhal.

(O'Clery (Teige Cam, the son of Tuathal), ollav to O'Donnell in history, a man learned in poetry and chronology, a prop who kept a house of hospitality for the learned, the exiled and the literary men of the neighbouring terrritories, died, on the 20th of October, at a venerable old age, after having gained the victory over the Devil and the world; and was buried with great respect and honour in the monastery of St Francis, at Donegal.)[8]

There was nothing exceptional about members of the Ó Cléirigh family being honoured with an obituary, as this form of commemoration was an honour accorded to members of many other learned families also. However, the real legacy of successive generations of Ó Cléirigh historians is not their own obituaries, but rather the historical records relating to the Uí Dhomhnaill generated by those historians. As historians to the Uí Dhomhnaill, their task was to record the lives and achievements of their patrons, and to publicize them in a manner appropriate to the political and cultural requirements of lordship society. There is plentiful evidence in the pages of AFM as to how they may have executed that task, even though their association with the contents of the annals can often only be inferred. Although it is difficult to estimate with any confidence how much of the Ó Domhnaill material in AFM derived ultimately from the work of earlier generations of professional historians of the Ó Cléirigh family, the likelihood that the Four Masters relied to a significant extent on that chronicling tradition is worth bearing in mind.[9]

Among the source manuscripts named in the Donegal approbation prefixed to AFM was 'a portion of the book of Cucogry, the son of Dermot, son of Tadhg Cam Ó Cléirigh', a work stated to have covered the years 1281 to 1537, but one that is not now known to exist.[10] It is possible that this historical book was mainly concerned with recording the activities of the Uí Dhomhnaill, but not necessarily so. Given the very precise dates at which it is said to have commenced

---

8 *AFM*, V, pp 1606–7.   9 There is also a substantial body of poetry on the Uí Dhomhnaill, much of it still unpublished, and which is generally outside the scope of this present study, including poems by an earlier Cú Choigcríche, son of Diarmaid Ó Cléirigh, on Maghnus Ó Domhnaill. The following five poems have been identified by Eóin Mac Carthaigh as dating from the 1540s: *Dlighidh file faghháil aisig*; *Fada a gcairt ó chloinn Dálaigh*; *Tréan ríogh uaisligheas ollamh*; *Truagh gan Maghnas 'na mhac ríogh*; *Deacair iomlaoid chlann gConaill* (Eoin Mac Carthaigh, 'Cú Choigcríche Ó Cléirigh', seminar paper, Mícheál Ó Cleirigh Insitute seminar, UCD, 20 February 2004). For Tadhg Mór Ó Cobhthaigh's poem *Cia ré gcuirfinn séd suirghe*, see P.A. Breatnach, 'In praise of Maghnas Ó Domhnaill', *Celtica* 16 (1984), 63–72.   10 *AFM*, I, p. lxvi.

and ended, it is likely that it took the form of annals. Although it apparently ended in 1537, its author was still alive in 1546.[11] Curiously, the Four Masters do not record the death of Cú Choigcríche, son of Diarmaid Ó Cléirigh, despite the fact that his historical work was known to them, and was directly relevant to their work.[12] Thus, where AFM contains Ó Domhnaill material not found in the other extant annals, these lost Ó Cléirigh annals seem an obvious source. However, as with other source annals drawn on by AFM, it is likely that their use of the Ó Cléirigh annals was selective and that it was combined with material from other sources and that it was rewritten as required. For these reasons any attempt to reconstruct those earlier Ó Cléirigh annals from the pages of AFM would be a futile exercise. Instead, the focus of this analysis of the late medieval Ó Domhnaill entries in AFM is on the nature of the finished product that emerged from that process of selection and editing of earlier historical texts.

The individual most likely to have come to own the Ó Cléirigh manuscript used as a source for AFM was Maccon Ó Cléirigh, son of its original compiler, Cú Choigcríche. Maccon died in 1595, at which time the manuscript may well have come, in turn, into the possession of his son, Lughaidh Ó Cléirigh, author of *Beatha Aodha Ruaidh*.

AFM 1595.6
Maccon mac Concoiccriche mic Diarmata mic Taidhg Caimm Ui Cleirigh ollamh Ui Domhnaill hi senchas, Saoí foirccthe, erghna, ealadhanta hi senchas, 7 i ndán, soerlabhraidh soingthe co mbuaidh ninnsgni, naitheisg 7 nerlabhra, fer craibhdeach caonduthrachtach diadha deshercach do écc i Leitir Maolain i tTuadhmumhain.
(Maccon, the son of Cucogry, son of Dermot, son of Teige Cam O'Clery, Ollav to O'Donnell in history, an erudite and ingenious man, professed in history and poetry; a fluent orator, with the gift of elocution, address and eloquence; a pious, devout, religious and charitable man, died at Leitir-Maelain, in Thomond.)[13]

A study of the Ó Domhnaill entries in AFM from 1500 provides a controlled context within which to evaluate how the leaders of one Gaelic lordship were perceived by the annalists from their early seventeenth-century viewpoint. At one remove, it also allows some glimpses of how they may have been represented by their own professional historians, members of the learned family of Ó Cléirigh. While most of AFM is sufficiently rooted in earlier sources for it to be argued that it preserves at least something of the values and attitudes of the earlier generations of chroniclers who compiled obituaries and narratives of the

---

11 Cú Choigcríche, son of Diarmaid Ó Cléirigh, was involved in a diplomatic role as protector of the son of Dónal, brother to Maghnus Ó Domhnaill, in 1546 (*AFM*, V, pp 1494–5 (1546.1)) He was the eldest of four sons; a younger brother, Cormac, being a Franciscan). He had six sons, MacCon, Cosnamhach, Dubthach, Tadhg, Corbmac and Muiris ballach. For this genealogical data, see Pender (ed.), 'O'Clery book of genealogies', 115, items 1573–4. 12 *AFM*, I, p. lxvi. 13 *AFM*, VI, pp 1960–1 (1595.6). On the Thomond connections of poets to Ó Domhnaill, including Maccon, see Brian Ó Cuív, 'The earl of Thomond and the poets, AD1572', *Celtica* 12 (1977), 125–45.

Ó Domhnaill leaders, the objective here is to try to discern the views and judgments of the Four Masters, even while conceding that those views may be derivative and unoriginal.

The focus of each of the three strands of this analysis – obituaries, the narratives of military exploits and the career of Aodh Ruadh – will be on how historical memorialization of the Ó Domhnaill kin group served the needs of society and politics in late medieval Ireland. Their obituaries offer evidence of the values and personal attributes that were most highly esteemed, while the narratives of their military exploits illuminate the political priorities and motivations of the leaders of Gaelic lordship society.

Obituaries

The death of a powerful overlord of the Uí Dhomhnaill was a milestone in the history of the lordship. It was normal for the death to be recorded in annals in an obituary that attempted to commemorate the lord's achievements. Despite the formulaic appearance of these obituaries, they vary in content over time, to an extent sufficient to argue that they were generally appropriate to the individual concerned and in tune with the evolving nature of the society from which they emanated.

The relatively concise obituary of Aodh Ruadh Ó Domhnaill (d.1505) is a good example of the formula generally adopted in the obituary of a significant Gaelic overlord in the late medieval period.

AFM 1505.5
O Domhnaill Aodh Ruadh mac Néill Gairbh mic Toirrdhealbhaigh an Fhíona ticcherna Tíre Conaill, Insi hEoghain, Cenél Moain, 7 Iochtair Chonnacht fer dár ghiallattar Fir Manach, Oirghialla, Clann Aodha Buidhe, an Rúta 7 Cathánaigh,[14] Ro ghiallsat dna Goill, 7 Gaoidhil Connacht ó Mac Uilliam Cloinne Riocaird anuas dó, 7 gidh eisidhe ann do dhioghail Ó Domhnaill a anumhla fair a leithre dol ina dhúthaigh dá aimhdheóin co meinic cona baí aen cethraimhe fherainn ó Shuca anuas 7 o Sliabh O nAedha don taoíbh thiar nach raibhe fó chíoschain dUa Dhomhnaill. An tUa Domhnaillsi tra escca iomlan einigh 7 uaisle an Tuaisceirt, fer bá mó grenn, 7 gaiscceadh, fer bá ferr ionnsaicchidh 7 anadh, fer rob ferr smacht, reacht, 7 riaghail baí i nErinn ina aimsir do Gaoidhealaibh, ar ní déntaoí do choimhéd i tTir Chonaill ré a linn acht iadhadh dorais na gaoithe nama, fer bá ferr do chiond ecclaisi, 7 eiccsi, fer ro thiodhlaic almsana aidhble i nonóir an choimdhe na ndul, fer las ro turccbhadh 7 las ro cumhdaighedh caislén cétus i nDun na nGall fó daigh gomadh inneoin fhosaighthi dia clannmaicne ina dheadhaidh, 7 mainistir bhrathar De obseruantia i tTír Conaill .i. Mainistir Dhúin na nGall, fer lasa ndearnadh iliomat do chreachsluaighedhaibh timchill fó Erinn, fer dár díles August Iarthair Thuaisceirt Eorpa do rádh fris,

---

14 The claim to overlordship over these areas was of interest to later readers and the five names of regions are underlined in a later hand in RIA MS 23 P 7.

*d'fhaghail bháis iar mbuaidh ó dhomhan 7 o dhemhan, iar nongadh, 7 iar naithrighe
tocchaighe ina longport fein i nDún na nGall dia hAoíne do shonnradh isin cuíccidh íd
Iulii, isin ochtmadh bliadhain sechtmoghat a aoisi, 7 isin cethramhadh bliadhain
cethrachat a fhlatha, 7 a adhnacal i Mainistir Dúin na nGall.*

(O'Donnell, Hugh Roe, the son of Niall Garv, son of Turlough of the Wine, Lord
of Tirconnell, Inishowen, Kinel-Moen and Lower Connaught, died; a man who
had obtained hostages from the people of Fermanagh, Oriel, Clannaboy and the
Route, and from the O'Kanes, and also the English and Irish of Connaught, with
the exception of Mac William of Clanrickard, who, however, did not go
unrevenged for his disobedience, for O'Donnell frequently entered his territory,
and left not a quarter of land from the River Suck upwards, and from Sliabh O n-
Aedha westwards, which he did not make tributary to him.

This O'Donnell was the full moon of the hospitality and nobility of the North, the
most jovial and valiant, the most prudent in war and peace, and of the best
jurisdiction, law and rule, of all the Gaels in Ireland in his time; for there was no
defence made [of the houses] in Tirconnell during his time, except to close the
door against the wind only; the best protector of the Church and the learned; a
man who had given great alms in honour of the Lord of the Elements; the man by
whom a castle was first raised and erected at Donegal, that it might serve as a
sustaining bulwark for his descendants; and a monastery for Friars de Observantiâ
in Tirconnell, namely, the monastery of Donegal; a man who had made many
predatory excursions around through Ireland; and a man who may be justly styled
the Augustus of the north-west of Europe.

He died, after having gained the victory over the Devil and the world, and after
[Extreme] Unction and good Penance, at his own fortress in Donegal, on Friday,
the 5th of the Ides of July, in the seventy-eighth year of his age, and forty-fourth
of his reign, and was interred in the monastery of Donegal.)[15]

The obituary is in three parts. The first part names the deceased and gives
sufficient genealogical detail to establish his identity clearly; it then records his
political status as 'Lord of Tirconnell, Inishowen, Kinel-Moen and Lower
Connaught', and follows this with a record of the neighbouring peoples over
whom he had succeeded in enforcing his overlordship. The second part of the
obituary focuses on the personal characteristics of the deceased, and notes his
special achievements. The third and final part gives details of the good death and
appropriate burial of the lord as a fitting end to a worthy life. A typical fourth
element, naming the successor of the deceased lord, is not found in the AFM
version of this particular obituary, though such a feature is not uncommon
elsewhere in AFM.

Each of the three key elements of the AFM 1505 obituary of Aodh Ruadh Ó
Domhnaill met a particular need. The first part was a quasi-official record of the
extent of Ó Domhnaill jurisdiction at the time of transition from one lord to the

15 *AFM*, V, pp 1282–3.

next. Given the constantly fluctuating nature of political power in late medieval Gaelic society, such jurisdiction was not a constant. Thus, in the 1505 obituary of Aodh Ruadh, it was claimed that Ó Domhnaill obtained hostages from the people of Fermanagh; in 1537 his son was described as lord of Fermanagh, perhaps suggesting a greater level of *de facto* power. On the other hand, where in 1505 some rights of overlordship were claimed over Oriel, that territory was not mentioned at all in the 1537 Ó Domhnaill obituary. In each obituary the contested nature of some of these assertions of overlordship was specifically alluded to. In 1505, the 'disobedience' of Mac William Burke of Clanricard in respect of Ó Domhnaill's claims to political overlordship was noted, together with Ó Domhnaill's assertive response, while in 1537 the fact that Aodh Ó Domhnaill had taken specific steps to safeguard the legality of his jurisdiction was given special mention. The Four Masters recorded under the year 1537 that Ó Domhnaill was the one who

AFM 1537.2

... *ro thabhaigh cartacha nuaa ar Inis Eocchain ar Cenel Moain, 7 ar Feraibh Manach (ar an ccethrar tighernadha bátar ré na linn i tTir Eoccain) do dhaingniucchadh ar na senchartachaibh baí accá shinnsearaibh ar na tíribhsin.*

(... compelled the four lords who ruled Tyrone during his time to give him new charters of Inishowen, Kinel-Moen and Fermanagh, as a further confirmation of the old charters which his ancestors had held [as a proof of their title] for these countries.)[16]

While those charters were a written legal record of the extent of the political jurisdiction of Ó Domhnaill, the record in the annals presumably originated in the work of the Ó Cléirigh ollamh in history to Ó Domhnaill, another formal written record of actual or perceived political jurisdiction at a given point in time. Their importance was probably all the greater because they related to critical points in the history of the lordship, on the death of its lord, and the appointment of a successor.

The personal attributes of Aodh Ruadh Ó Domhnaill as recorded in his 1505 obituary are typical of the kind of praise accorded to an effective Gaelic overlord. The opening statement had dealt in a general way with the *de facto* power and authority that the deceased had enjoyed, while the more personal description that followed was designed to pinpoint the specific achievements of the individual leader. The emphasis on nobility, hospitality, bravery, prudence in war and peace, effectiveness in law and rule, protection of the clergy and the learned class, and almsgiving is common to many other obituaries and is certainly influenced by the style and content of earlier obituaries. The affability ascribed to Aodh Ruadh should perhaps be interpreted as reflecting a dominant personal characteristic.

16 *AFM*, V, pp 1438–9.

Some specific building achievements are also noticed: the erection of Donegal Castle and the establishment of the Observant friary at Donegal, two milestones of particular interest to the Four Masters themselves, who had specific connections with that locality. The latter is also recorded in AU, but not the former. Indeed, while some details and even some phrases in the obituary of Aodh Ruadh are common to AFM and AU, the obit in AFM is quite different. The entire middle section of the AFM obituary dealing with Aodh Ruadh's personal attributes is not found in AU at all. On the other hand, a significant sentence from AU using heroic parallels to describe the high status and political influence enjoyed by Ó Domhnaill is omitted from AFM.

> AU 1505.4
> *Ocus ni thainig o Brian Borumha, no o Cathal Croibderg, anuas ri, no tigherna, dob' ferr smacht 7 riagail 7 do bo mo nert ina'n rí sin.*
> (And there came not from Brian Borumha, or from Cathal Red-hand [ob. 1224], down a king, or lord, that was of better sway and rule and was of more power than that king.)[17]

It appears that the Four Masters did not consider such allusions to heroes from Connacht or Thomond appropriate to their record of the life and achievements of the lord of Tír Conaill, and as discussed elsewhere, they were likewise unwilling to describe the overlords of Gaelic lordships at this period as kings.[18] However, the Four Masters chose to preserve an unusual phrase in this obituary, describing Aodh Ruadh as 'a man who may be justly styled the Augustus of the north-west of Europe', a phrase that occurs in the AU version of his obituary also.[19] In this, compilers may have been considering the intended European as well as Irish readers for their finished work.

While there are parallels between the AU version of this 1505 obituary and that of AFM, there is little in common between AFM and AConn in this instance.

> AConn 1505.2
> *Aodh Ruad mac Nell Gairb h. Domnaill, ant enGhaoidhel as mo do ghabh nert et tresi da tanic do slicht Nell Naíghiallaig 7 esga imlan enigh 7 uaisle an Tuaiscirt, fer dar ghiallador Fir Manach 7 Cenel Moain 7 Ichtur Connacht, do dul d'ecc an bliadain-si. Et ni ró linn re radha nac roibe a linn Gall na Gaoidel dobad tresi ar Leith Cuinn inas he. Et tri sechtmaine ria Lugnusa fuair bas ongtha et aitriighe a nDun na nGall, ar mbeith cetri bliadna ocus da xx. a righi Tire Conoill; et a mac do rigad ina inadh .i. Aodh mac Aodho Ruaid.*
> (Aed Ruad son of Niall Garb O Domnaill, the Gael, who achieved most power and might of all the posterity of Niall Noigiallach, full moon of the nobility and bounty

17 *AU*, III, pp 472–3.   18 See above, pp 117–20.   19 *AU*, III, pp 474–5.

of the North, the man to whom Fermanagh and Cenel Moain and Lower Connacht had submitted, died this year. And we do not think it too much to say that there was in his time no Gall or Gael who had more power in Leth Chuinn than he. Three weeks before Lammas he died, with Unction and Penance, in Donegal, having been for forty-four years king of Tir Conaill, and his son was made king in his stead, that is Aed son of Aed Ruad.)[20]

AConn, like AU, uses the language of kingship, but measures Ó Domhnaill's political stature in terms of Leath Cuinn rather than Ireland as a whole. AConn, too, names his successor, a significant detail omitted by both AU and AFM. While the phrase *esga imlan enigh 7 uaisle an Tuaiscirt* ('full moon of the nobility and bounty of the North') is found in AConn as well as AFM – indicating some influence of a shared source – it is only the AFM version that gives a detailed outline of his personal attributes and achievements sufficient to distinguish him from others of his contemporaries.

The natural harmony that prevailed in the lordship during the life of a lord is a frequent motif in obituaries. Thus, in the 1505 obituary of Aodh Ruadh, AFM notes that just rule was so effective under his leadership that *ní déntaoí do choimhéd i tTir Chonaill ré a linn acht iadhadh dorais na gaoithe nama* ('there was no defence made [of the houses] in Tirconnell during his time, except to close the door against the wind only').[21] The obituary of his son, Aodh, placed even more emphasis on harmony with the natural order. It described him as *[fear] gur bho toirtheach turchurthach muir 7 tír ina fhlaith* ('a man in whose reign the seasons were favourable, so that sea and land were productive').[22] These motifs traditionally associated with the literature of kingship,[23] were here intended to be read as indicators of good lordship.

The last part of the AFM version of the 1505 Ó Domhnaill obituary, on the actual death and burial of Aodh Ruadh, was its most formulaic element. Except in the case of death in battle, it was normal for the Four Masters to record that the deceased had died a good death after repentance for sin and after receiving the sacrament of Extreme Unction. It was also usual to state that the burial had been in an appropriately sanctified place, often a Franciscan monastery. In this instance the wording of the 1505 AFM entry closely follows that in AU, while the abbreviated version in AConn omits much of the detail that the northern annals chose to record.

Whereas the 1505 Ó Domhnaill obituary in AConn is otherwise less informative than the obits in AFM or AU, it does mention one important detail – that

20 *AConn*, pp 610–11.   21 *AFM*, V, pp 1282–3 (AFM 1505.5).   22 *AFM*, V, pp 1436–9 (AFM 1537.2).   23 Fergus Kelly, *Guide to early Irish law* (Dublin, 1988), 18; Kuno Meyer (ed.), *The instructions of King Cormac mac Airt* (RIA Todd Lecture series XV, Dublin, 1909); Breandán Ó Buachalla, 'Aodh Eangach and the Irish king-hero' in Donnchadh Ó Corráin, Liam Breatnach and Kim McCone (eds), *Sages, saints and storytellers: Celtic studies in honour of Professor James Carney* (Maynooth, 1989), pp 200–32; Katharine Simms, *From kings to warlords* (Woodbridge, 1987), pp 24–5.

Aodh Ruadh was succeeded as king by his son Aodh. The issue of succession is frequently mentioned in AFM obituaries, but not consistently so. When Aodh Ruadh's successor, Aodh Dubh, died in 1537, the obituary in AFM, following mention of the fact that he had died in the monastery of Donegal, recorded:

AFM 1537.2

... 7 a adhnacal isin mainistir chédna co nonóir 7 co nairmidin móir amhail ro ba dír. Maghnus Ó Domhnaill doirdneadh ina ionadh lá comharbaibh Choluim Chille do ched 7 do comhairle maithe Cenél cConaill etir thuaith 7 ecclais.

(... [and] he was buried in the same monastery with great honour and solemnity, as was meet; and Manus O'Donnell was inaugurated in his place by the successors of St Columbkille, with the permission and by the advice of the nobles of Tirconnell, both lay and ecclesiastical.)[24]

When the said Maghnus duly died in 1563, however, the honourable burial of the deceased lord was recorded in detail in the usual way, but again no successor was mentioned.[25] While the details of good death and honourable burial in a sanctified place were apparently essential elements of these obituaries, the recording of a successor was perhaps deemed less integral to the obituary. Nevertheless, the 1537 record of the accession of Maghnus Ó Domhnaill is an elaborate commemoration of the legitimacy of that event, and an indicator that such obituaries were designed to meet the needs of the living as well as the dead.

In contrast to the obituaries of Ó Domhnaill lords in 1505 and 1537, which are charged with political assertions of contemporary relevance, the obituary of Maghnus Ó Domhnaill, who died in 1563, seems to have been constructed with the benefit of hindsight, juxtaposing two contrasting aspects of his character, and explicitly relying on what was *amhail as reil acc senaibh 7 acc senchaidhibh* ('evident from the [accounts of] old people and historians') in doing so.[26] Apart from the detail regarding the place (Lifford) and date (9 Feb.) of Maghnus's death, which might well have been taken from an obit book of the Donegal Franciscans, the rest of the obituary could easily have been retrospectively compiled by the Four Masters themselves to the standard formula. Unlike the obituaries from 1505 and 1537, it makes no attempt to outline the territorial extent of his lordship. This may be another indication that the entry was not written by an official Ó Domhnaill chronicler. Alternatively, it may relate to the reality of his power having been usurped by his son some years prior to his death.

The obituary accorded Aodh Ruadh Ó Domhnaill following his death in exile in Simancas in 1602 is lengthier and more elaborate than most of those recorded for his ancestors who had held the title of Ó Domhnaill. It contains many of the same elements as earlier obituaries, but in a new sequence, so that it ends not

24 *AFM*, V, pp 1438–9.   25 *AFM*, V, pp 1594–7.   26 *AFM*, V, pp 1594–7.

with the burial of the lord or the naming of his successor in the lordship but with a lament for all the Gaeil of Ireland. In a closing paragraph, drawn from Lughaidh Ó Cléirigh's narrative biography, which clearly conveys his death as marking the end of an era, the annalists record:

AFM 1602.7

Bá trógh tra ro bás ag Gaoidhealaibh Ereann iar nécc Uí Domhnaill, doigh ro chlaochlaisiot a nairrdhe 7 a naigenta, oir do rattsat a milettacht ar miodhlachas, móirmhenma ar mheirtnighe, 7 uallcha ar inísle. Ro sgaith a ngráin, a ngaiscceadh, a ngal, a ngérraiteacht, a ccosgar, 7 a ccathbhuaidh iar ná oidheadh, Tallsatt céill dia ccabhair gur bhó heigen dia nurmhór dol for iocht eccrat, 7 ainffine, 7 araill ele for eisreidheadh 7 for sgaoíleadh, ní nama ar fud Ereann, acht seachnóin na ccennadhach go coitchend ina naittreabthachaibh bochta dinnime dearoile, 7 dronga ele ag creic a namhsaine lá hechtar chenelaibh go ro marbhaitt, 7 go ro mudhaighitt drechta dearmhara do shaorchlandaibh soichenelchoibh fer nÉreann i naile criochaibh cianibh comhaighthibh, 7 ro badh ádhbha aineoil 7 eccalsa andúthchasa robtar Rómha adhnaicthe dóibh, ar aba écca an aoín fhir sin do érna uadhaibh. Acht chena ro badh eimhilt, 7 ro badh diochumhaing ríomh nó aisnéis do na mór olcaibh ro shíolaidh, 7 ro shíorchlandaigh i ninis Ereann a los écca Aodha Ruaidh Uí Dhomhnaill an tan sin.

(Pitiable, indeed, was the state of the Gaels of Ireland after the death of O'Donnell; for their characteristics and dispositions were changed; for they exchanged their bravery for cowardice, their magnanimity for weakness, their pride for servility; their success, valour, prowess, heroism, exultation and military glory, vanished after his death. They despaired of relief, so that the most of them were obliged to seek aid and refuge from enemies and strangers, while others were scattered and dispersed, not only throughout Ireland, but throughout foreign countries, as poor, indigent, helpless paupers; and others were offering themselves for hire as soldiers to foreigners; so that countless numbers of the freeborn nobles of Ireland were slain in distant foreign countries, and were buried in strange places and unhereditary churches, in consequence of the death of this one man who departed from them. In a word, it would be tedious and impossible to enumerate or describe the great evils which sprang and took permanent root at that time in Ireland from the death of Hugh Roe O'Donnell.)[27]

While much of the obituary of this Aodh Ruadh (d. 1602) is derivative of *Beatha Aodha Ruaidh*, the Four Masters add some details of their own. Given their personal acquaintance with some of those present in Simancas at the time of Aodh Ruadh's death, the annalists were able to name the confessors who ministered to the dying leader.

AFM 1602.4

... an tAthair Flaithri Ua Maolchonaire (confessóir, 7 comhairleach spiratalta Ui Dhomhnaill, 7 rob Airdespuc Tuama iarttain cidh as a los) 7 an tAthair Muiris Ulltach

___

27 *AFM*, VI, pp 2298–9; see *BARUD*, I, pp 246–7.

mac Donnchaidh brathair bocht durd S. Fronseis a conueint mhainistre Duin na nGall, bá do longportaibh Í Dhomhnaill eisidhe.
(... Father Flaithri O'Mulconry (then confessor and spiritual adviser to O'Donnell, and afterwards archbishop of Tuam on that account), and Father Maurice Ultach [Donlevy], the son of Donough, a poor friar of the order of St Francis, from the convent of the monastery of [the town of] Donegal, which was one of O'Donnell's fortresses.)[28]

The Four Masters also added a telling sentence about those Irish who died abroad in the years after the death of their leader. The tragedy of their death in exile was encapsulated in the fact that they *ro badh ádhbha aineoil 7 eccalsa andúthchasa robtar Róma adhnaicthe dóibh* ('were buried in strange places and unhereditary churches').[29] Given the significance consistently attached to burial in monasteries throughout AFM, their augmentation of the *Beatha Aodha Ruaidh* text to mention specifically burial in 'unhereditary churches' emphasizes that the record of the place of burial in earlier obituaries was not merely formulaic. It was, rather, a reiteration of connection to a traditional family burial place, regarded as a fitting conclusion to the life of a lord. The perspective of the Four Masters regarding inappropriate foreign burial places reflected that of two early seventeenth-century poetic laments on the Ó Domhnaill lords who had died in exile, *A bhean fuair faill ar an bhfeart*, composed by Eoghan Ruadh Mac an Bhaird,[30] and *Truagh liom Máire agas Mairgrég*, composed by Fearghal Óg Mac an Bháird,[31] sentiments shared also by Geoffrey Keating.[32]

There is a clear sense of historical causality and irrevocable change in the Four Masters' 1602 obituary of Aodh Ruadh, quite unlike that which marked the annalistic commemoration of earlier Ó Domhnaill lords. The resort to prophecy likewise emphasizes the special significance attached to Aodh Ruadh. The annalists echo Lughaidh Ó Cléirigh's words from *Beatha Aodha Ruaidh* when describing Aodh Ruadh as *tairrngeartach tinghealltach ro fiorthiorchanadh lá fáidhibh ré chian ria na ghéin* ('a promised and prophesied one, who had been truly predicted by prophets a long time before his birth').[33] The Four Masters then cited a specific prophecy of Colum Cille about a noble man who would be ten years king.[34] This rare use of verse in the later part of the annals is a

---

28 *AFM*, VI, pp 2296–7 (AFM 1602.4). It is possible that both Muiris Ultachs were in Simancas at the time of Aodh Ruadh Ó Domhnaill's death in 1602 (see Silke, 'The last will of Red Hugh O'Donnell', 53). Both were present in the Donegal Franciscan convent in the mid-1630s when AFM was being compiled. They would have been able to supply their own personal memories of the death of Aodh Ruadh. Personal recollections were also used in the compilation of Irish Franciscan history (Jennings (ed.), 'Brevis synopsis', 139–91). 29 *AFM*, VI, pp 2298–9. 30 Eleanor Knott, 'Mac an Bhaird's elegy on the Ulster lords', *Celtica* 5 (1960), 161–71. 31 Osborn Bergin, *Irish bardic poetry* (Dublin, 1970), poem 8, pp 46–8, 230–1. 32 For the contemporary view of Geoffrey Keating on inappropriate burial practices, see Comyn and Dinneen (eds), *Foras feasa ar Éirinn*, III, pp 362–3. 33 *AFM*, VI, pp 2298–9. 34 *AFM*, VI, pp 2298–9; the verse was also used by Lughaigh Ó Cléirigh, but in a different way (*BARUD*, I, p. 4). For a much

conscious echo of the poetic material on early Irish kings incorporated in the early Christian section of the text. It may have been used to draw attention to Aodh Ruadh's qualifications for the kingship of Ireland.[35] Where the source texts available to the Four Masters included an element of historical causality, that was retained, and sometimes enhanced, in AFM, but yet there was no real attempt to adopt a similar method of historical explanation in the case of earlier material drawn from chroniclers for whom issues of causality were not part of their remit.

Prose narratives to 1537

The clear bias in favour of the Uí Dhomhnaill throughout the post-1200 section of AFM is given its clearest expression in the narratives of military exploits. These Ó Domhnaill narratives become increasingly discursive through the fifteenth- and sixteenth-century sections of the annals. They are often stylistically different from the other elements of the annals, and it is again tempting to speculate that they represent an aspect of the work of successive *ollamh*s in history to the Uí Dhomhnaill. It is possible that some of them were recorded, at least in part, in the Book of Cú Choigcríche Ó Cléirigh, which the Four Masters name as one of their sources for the years 1281 to 1537. However, as will be shown below, the Four Masters did not transcribe all of their Ó Domhnaill narratives from a single source. Some, but not all of them, occur in AU, though generally in somewhat different form.

Where the same episode is recorded in both AFM and AU, the entries sometimes have a quite different emphasis. The Uí Néill are sometimes prioritized in AU, while it is more usual for the Uí Dhomhnaill to be presented in the AFM version as having the leading role. An example from the mid-fifteenth century illustrates the contrasting presentations of the same episode:

AFM 1458.2
Sluaigheadh lá hUa nDomhnaill Toirrdealbhach Cairbreach, 7 tainicc Ua Néill Enrí dia chommoradh Rangattar cétus co hIochtar Chonnacht lotar iaromh don Bhrefne. Ro milleadh 7 ro loiscceadh leó o sliabh siar, 7 ro loiscceadh baile uí Ruairc druim dhá ethiar, 7 ro gabhsat braighde Iochtair Chonnacht, 7 do radadh illaimh Uí Domhnaill iatt. Tangattar iaromh dia ttighibh.
(A hosting was made by O'Donnell, Turlough Cairbreach; and O'Neill, Henry, came to join his muster. They first went to Lower Connaught, and from thence they proceeded into Breifny; and they spoiled and burned [that part of the territory lying] from the mountain westwards; and they also burned O'Rourk's town, Druim-da-Ethiar [Drumahaire]. They obtained the hostages of Lower

---

earlier occurrence of the same verse, in a different context, see Hennessy and Kelly (eds), *The book of Fenagh*, p. 152. This earlier use of the verse would also have been known to Mícheál Ó Cléirigh, who had access to the Book of Fenagh. **35** For discussion of the ideology of kingship in AFM, see above, pp 117–24.

Connaught, who were given into the hands of O'Donnell; after which they returned home.)[36]

AU 1458.4

Sluaghadh mor do dhenum do hUa Neill, idon, Enri 7 d'hUa Domnaill 7 do Mhag Uidhir i Connachtaibh 7 tuc braighdi Ichtair Connacht leis d'on turus sin. Ocus do loisc baile hUi Ruairc, idon, Druim-da-thigher 7 araile.

(A great hosting was made by Ua Neill, namely Henry and by Ua Domnaill and by Mag Uidhir into Connacht and he carried off the hostages of the Lower [northern] part of Connacht with him on that expedition. And he burned the town of Ua Ruairc, namely, Druim-da-thigher, and so on.)[37]

Though both texts recount the same episode, AFM gives the leading role to Toirrdhealbhach Ó Domhnaill, whereas AU is unequivocal that Ó Néill was no mere adjunct to Ó Domhnaill. As so often is the case, all mention of Mág Uidhir is omitted from the AFM account. Where the AFM version specifically states that Ó Domhnaill retained the hostages, the AU account implies that they were taken by Ó Néill. As is usual in the AFM descriptions of raids and hostings, the narrative is rounded off by a homecoming, whereas AU merely records key facts and leaves readers or listeners to finish the story for themselves.

In an earlier example, an encounter between Ó Néill and Ó Domhnaill is recorded in AFM under the year 1401 and in AU under the year 1402. The structure of the two stories is quite similar, and both are agreed that Ó Néill was the aggressor and was the one who ultimately suffered defeat.

AFM 1401.9

Coccadh deirghe eittir Ua nDomhnaill iaromh 7 Brian mac Enrí Uí Néill, uair tug Brian slógh lais go Tír Conaill, gur ro ionnsoigh longport Uí Dhomhnaill, 7 ro marbhadh mac Néill óig mic Neill Ghairbh mic Aedha mic Domhnaill Óig, 7 Maoileachloinn mac Flaithbertaigh Uí Ruairc 7 sochaidhe oile leo. Do deachaidh Ó Domhnaill co na cloinn, 7 Muintir Duirnín is in ló cedna illeanmhain Briain go ruccsat fáir, 7 creac Uí Gairmleadhaigh (.i. Enrí) roimhe iar marbhadh Énrí lais. Ro fígheadh iomaireg amhnus eidir ua nDomhnaill 7 Brian Ua Néill, 7 ro marbhadh Brian lais, 7 ro sraoineadh for a mhuintir iar bfágbhail creach cenél Moain. Ro marbhadh bheos sochaidhe oile imailli fri Brian ar an lathair sin. Soais Ua Domhnaill slán cona muintir co nedalaibh aidhblibh iar mbuaidh 7 cosccor.

(A war afterwards broke out between O'Donnell and Brian, the son of Henry O'Neill; for Brian had led an army into Tirconnell, and had attacked the fortress of O'Donnell, and killed the son of Niall Oge, son of Niall Garv, son of Hugh, son of Donnell Oge [O'Donnell], and Melaghlin, son of Flaherty O'Rourke, and many others. On the same day O'Donnell, his sons, and Muintir Duirnin, went in pursuit of Brian, and overtook him as he was driving off a prey taken from O'Gormly (Henry), whom he had slain. A fierce battle was fought between

36 *AFM*, IV, pp 1000–1.   37 *AU*, III, pp 194–7.

O'Donnell and Brian O'Neill, in which Brian was killed by O'Donnell, and his people were routed, leaving the spoils of Kinel-Moen behind them. Many others were slain along with Brian in this engagement. O'Donnell then returned home safely with his people, with great spoils, after victory and triumph.)[38]

AU 1402.4

Cogadh mor eter (Toirrdelbach) hUa n-Domnaill, ri Tiri-Conaill 7 Brian, mac Enri hUi Neill. Brian do chur sluaigh i n-ein inadh 7 indsoighidh do thabairt for foslongport hUi Domnaill 7 maidm do thabairt a tosach lai ar hUa n-Domnaill do 7 mac Neill, mic Neill hUi Domnaill, do marbadh ann 7 moran do Chonallchaibh 7 Mail[-Sh]echlainn, mac Flaithbertaigh hUi Ruairc, do marbadh ann. hUa Domnaill 7 a clann 7 Muinntir-Duirnin do tinol 'sa lo cetna 7 Brian hUa Neill do thegmail doib, becan fedhna, a n-diaigh a muinntiri d'inntogh o'n mhaidm 7 crech Enri hUi Gairmleghaidh roime 7 Enri fein do marbadh roime sin leis. Brian do beith, uathadh daine, annsin 7 hUa Domnaill, co n-a clainn 7 co n-a muinntir do marbadh Briain annsin 7 araile.

(Great war [arose] between (Toirdelbach) Ua Domnaill, king of Tir-Conaill and Brian son of Henry Ua Neill. Brian put his host in one place and delivered an attack upon the stronghold of Ua Domnaill and defeat was inflicted in the begin-ning of the day on Ua Domnaill. And the son of Niall, son of Niall Ua Domhnaill, was slain there and many of the Men of Tir-Conaill and Mail[Sh]echlainn, son of Flaithbertach Ua Ruairc, were slain there. Ua Domnaill and his sons and the Muinter-Duirnin mustered the same day and Brian Ua Neill met them, [with] a small force, in the rear of his people, [as he was] returning from the defeat, with the spoil of Henry Ua Gairmleghaidh [driven] before him and Henry himself was slain before that by him. Brian was [with but] a few persons there and Ua Domhnaill with his sons and with his people slew Brian there, and so on.)[39]

Where the AU version ends tamely, choosing not to dwell on an Ó Néill defeat, AFM avails of the opportunity to affirm the victory of Ó Domhnaill, rounding off the story with a typical statement of homecoming 'after victory and triumph'. If AU was the source for this AFM narrative, it is clear the Four Masters felt it appropriate to draw special attention to the successful outcome from an Ó Domhnaill perspective. Much the same story is recounted in AConn, in more colourful prose, but it too ends somewhat feebly, lacking the neat conclusion of the AFM version.[40]

It is also important to note that there is clear evidence that the pre-*Beatha Aodha Ruaidh* narratives of Ó Domhnaill exploits in AFM do not derive from a single prior manuscript source. Aside from the fact that some stories are common to AU and AFM while others are not, it is evident from the autograph manuscripts of AFM that some of the narratives are late additions – penned in the editorial hands C and D – while others are not. The 1422 and 1434 AFM entries on Niall Ó Domhnaill are two instances of late insertions in the text.[41] In

38 *AFM*, IV, pp 772–3.   39 *AU*, III, pp 46–9.   40 *AConn*, pp 380–3.   41 RIA MS 23 P 6, fos 162 (1422), 171v (1434).

the case of RIA MS 23 P 6, it is evident from the way the 1422 narrative on Niall Ó Domhnaill is inserted in very small script and partly written in the margin of the page that it was a late addition written after the main text for that year had been transcribed. The annalists had not anticipated the need to have space for a story of that length, but when it came to hand they chose to include it.

It is likely that these additions came from a different source from the main body of the text, where scribe B had transcribed other Ó Domhnaill narratives. In the case of the 1422 and 1434 examples, the narratives relate to the activities of Niall Ó Domhnaill in Sligo and north Connacht. Neither is recorded in AU. Whatever their source, it appears clear that not all the Ó Domhnaill narratives they record came to the attention of the Four Masters simultaneously, but were assembled incrementally from a range of sources.

It is quite uncertain whether the stories of the exploits of the Uí Dhomhnaill that are common to AFM and AU originated with AU. Many of them may have been in circulation in some form prior to their being incorporated into the annalistic record. It is certainly possible that some of the narratives were compiled by historians to the Uí Dhomhnaill and were adapted for inclusion in AU, and it is equally possible that some of them were the work of historians to the Uí Néill and subsequently adapted for inclusion in AFM. It is quite likely that many of them may have been recorded in the now lost Ó Cléirigh source which was stated to cover the three centuries up to 1537, but again may not have originated there. In the absence of definitive evidence as to the ultimate source of these narratives, the discussion here will focus on their purpose and content in the form in which they were incorporated into AFM. The evidence of the working method of the Four Masters is that it was normal for them to revise entries rather than transcribe material exactly as found in manuscript sources. Thus the biases of their sources would not necessarily be reflected in their rendering of an entry; they were well capable of retelling the episode as appropriate. For this reason, when considering the biases of AFM it is reasonable to accept that the Four Masters themselves were primarily responsible for those biases, either through selection or revision, the two main tools of editorial control.

Maghnus Ó Domhnaill

The early sixteenth-century entries in AFM preserve evidence of the influence of a historian writing from the perspective of Maghnus (son of Aodh) Ó Domhnaill, prior to 1537 when he attained the status of lord of Tír Conaill. When the Ó Domhnaill entries in AFM that mention Maghnus Ó Domhnaill are compared with the equivalent entries in AU (and AConn where applicable), the subtle editorial process emerges clearly.

Maghnus Ó Domhnaill first comes to notice in the annals in 1510 when he was left in charge of Tír Conaill while his father, Aodh son of Aodh Ruadh, went on pilgrimage to Rome. It was recorded soon afterwards that Maghnus had freed Art son of Conn Ó Néill from captivity 'without leave from Ó Domhnaill'.[42] When Art son of Aodh Ó Néill mustered an army to attack Tír Conaill in the absence of Ó Domhnaill, it was recorded that Maghnus, with the support of the Meic Shuibhne and the principal chieftains of Tír Conaill, 'proceeded to protect and defend the country as well as they could', so that Ó Néill's offensive proved ineffective.[43]

Following his father's return from Rome, Maghnus resumed a subsidiary role in support of his father against Ó Néill.[44] The AU narratives of Ó Domhnaill exploits at this time typically refer only to the chief and his followers *Ocus fostais O Domnaill coic ced déc túagh* ('and Ó Domnaill engages 1500 axes'); *Gluaisidh O Domnaill o Doiri* ('Ó Domnaill proceeds from Derry'), whereas the version in AFM inserts a specific reference to Maghnus into the narrative: *Ro fhost Ua Domhnaill cúicc céd décc tuacch ... do thaod somh iaramh 7 Maghnas cona sochraide amaille friu ó Dhoire* ('O Donnell hired fifteen hundred axe-men ... He and Manus afterwards marched with their forces from Derry').[45]

Maghnus is mentioned again four years later, and though the context is again a conflict between Ó Domhnaill and Ó Néill, Maghnus's actions are singled out for special mention along with those of his father. In this instance his activities are noticed in AU as well as in AFM.[46] Some further Ó Néill material recorded in AU for this year (AU 1516.3) is omitted from AFM. However, this material was contained in the 'B' text rather than the 'A' text of AU, which may be sufficient to explain why it was not used in AFM.[47]

In the major battle narrative in AFM 1522.4, Maghnus Ó Domhnaill is again given some prominence, though still within the context of assisting his father. At one stage in the narrative for this year, the AU annalist likewise makes special mention of Maghnus when the main supporters of Ó Domhnaill are named.[48] Indeed, on this occasion, AU adds extra detail on Maghnus, describing him as *rídhamhna in tíre* (royal heir of the territory), a description omitted from AFM. It is unclear whether this omission was because of the Four Masters' reluctance to use the term *rídhamhna*[49] in that context, or whether they simply regarded Maghnus's identity as obvious and not in need of further clarification. The continuation of this episode in AFM 1522.5 ends with Maghnus returning home 'in triumph'.

---

42 *AFM*, V, pp 1308–9.   **43** *AFM*, V, pp 1312–13.   **44** *AFM*, V, pp 1314–17.   **45** *AU*, III, pp 498–9; *AFM*, V, pp 1314–15; the corresponding narrative in AConn does not mention Maghnus Ó Domhnaill.   **46** *AFM*, V, pp 1332–5; *AU*, III, pp 520–1.   **47** On the probable use by the Four Masters of the 'A' text of AU, see above, pp 46–9.   **48** *AU*, III, pp 546–7.   **49** For discussion of this term, see Gearóid Mac Niocaill, 'The heir designate in early medieval Ireland', *Irish Jurist*, n.s. 3 (1968), 326–9; Mac Niocaill, 'A propos du vocabulaire social Irlandais du bas moyen age', *Études Celtiques* 12 (1970–1), 512–46.

AFM 1522.5

Iar ná cluinsin dUa Domhnaill na gniomha sin do denam lá hUa Neill ro forchongair
for Maghnus Ua nDomhnaill co ndruing dia sluaigh dol do creachlosccadh Tíre
hEoghain, 7 do deachaidh fein tar bernus gus an líon tarustair ina fharradh i
ndeadhaigh Í Néill dimdeaghail Tíre hAodha. Dála Maghnusa ro creachloiscceadh lais
ina mbaoí ina chomhfochraibh do Cenél Eocchain Ro Marbhait 7 ro mudhaighit daoíne
iomdha lais bheós, 7 soais go ccosccar.

(When O'Donnell heard that O'Neill had done these deeds, he ordered his son,
Manus O'Donnell, to proceed into Tyrone with a detachment of his army, and to
plunder and burn that country; and he himself, with the number of forces he had
kept with him, directed his course over Bearnas, in pursuit of O'Neill, and to
defend Tirhugh. As to Manus, he plundered and burned all the neighbouring parts
of Kinel-Owen; he also slew and destroyed many persons, and [then] returned in
triumph.)[50]

The entry is balanced in AFM by a follow-on description from the perspective
of Ó Néill:

AFM 1522.6

O Ro fidir Ó Neill (Maghnas do dhol hi tTir Eocchain) soais ina fhriting tar Finn, 7
ro mhill an tír roimhe go Cenn Maghair, 7 do bert creach a Cionn Maghair lais, 7 luidh
co ccosccar dia thír.

(When O'Neill discovered that Manus had gone into Tyrone, he returned across
the [River] Finn, and spoiled the country before him as far as Ceann-Maghair,
from whence he carried off a prey; and he then proceeded in triumph to his own
country.)[51]

In these narratives, the AFM version is more specific, not just in repeatedly
naming Maghnus, but also in its topographical detail – mentioning not just
general districts such as Tirhugh and Kinel-Owen, but also Bearnas, the river
Finn, and Ceann-Maghair. In contrast, the AU account is much less topo-
graphically specific.

AU 1522.3

Ocus do fhácbatur O Domnaill 7 cuid d'á ghalloglachaibh a foslongport 7 do ghlúais
Maghnus O Domnaill 7 an chuid eile do'n t-shluagh 7 Conn, mac Neill, mic Airt [U]í
Néll, a b-fhad amach a Tír-Eogain. Ocus fuaratur crecha 7 caóraighachta móra ré cur
rompa, indus nar'-b'urusa dóibh imáin dóibh ar mhed na boruma do bí and. Ocus
tancatur slán iar marbadh a lá[i]n do daínib 7 iar crechadh móráin do'n tír. Ocus ar n-
a cloistin sin d'U[a] Néll 7 d'á t-sluagh, do fhilletar fó tuaruscbáil na crech sin, ar
milliudh móráin do'n tír 7 can dít orrdairc do denamh dó do'n dul sin.

(And they left O'Domnaill and part of his gallowglasses in camp and Maghnus
O'Domnaill and the other part of the host and Conn, son of Niall, son of Art

50 *AFM*, V, pp 1354–5. 51 *AFM*, V, pp 1354–5.

O'Neill, marched far out into Tir-Eogain. And they found great spoils and herds to put before them, so that it was not easy for them to drive them, for the amount of the cattle-spoil that was there. And they came [off] safe, after killing a number of persons and after raiding much of the country.

And when Ua Neill and his host heard that, they turned on the track of those preys, destroying much of the country and without notable damage being done to him on that march.)[52]

It is evident that AFM favoured the storytelling device of the return home as an appropriate ending to these episodes, and in this instance applied it to Ó Néill's successful homecoming also. The Four Masters might possibly have been consciously writing for a wider readership when applying this more polished presentation of narrative episodes.

An unusual element of Maghnus Ó Domhnaill's role in inter-lordship politics is recorded in AFM 1522, when he was nominated by Ó Néill as an arbitrator, along with Ó Cearbhaill, in a dispute between the Uí Dhomhnaill and Mac William. Maghnus's arbitration appears to have been successful, so that a peaceful resolution was reached in this instance. AFM recorded that

> AFM 1522.9
> *... gér bhó hiongnadh 7 gér bhó deacair ionnsamhail an tslóicch baoí annsin ar líonmhaire a lérthionóil ar uaisle a naireach, 7 ar aidhbhle a neccrait fris an tí baoí for a cciont do shódh fón samhail sin co ro aithedh 7 co ro dioghladh cách díobh a ainninne for aroile.*
>
> (... though it was strange and wonderful that such an army as was there – so numerous, so complete, with leaders so noble, and with enmity so intense against the persons opposed to them – should have retreated in this manner, [and should not have waited] until each party had expended its fury, and wreaked its vengeance on the other.)[53]

Not content with merely recording a peaceful outcome, the Four Masters made specific reference to a separate major battle in which Ó Domhnaill had been victorious. It is as though there was such a demand for a story of bloodshed and heroism that a story of peace-making had to be presented in terms of triumph in violent battle. In contrast, AConn does not contain this 1522 episode, while the version in AU merely suggests that, given Ó Domhnaill's successes against Ó Neill, simply hearing of Ó Domhnaill's approach was enough to entice the Connachtmen to submit without a fight. The AU version of the victory does not glorify military triumph in the way AFM does.

> AU 1522.4
> *... Ocus o'tchúaladh an dá Mac Uilliam 7 an slúagh mór sin do bí ac freagra dóibh dáil [U]í Domnaill cuca 7 é ar n-denamh a áithir ar an t-sluagh sin eile, do elótar féin o'n*

52 *AU*, III, pp 542–3. 53 *AFM*, V, pp 1360–1.

*bhaile 7 do imghidhetar a cóir madhma, gen gur'-cuiredh chuca. Ocus tainic O Domnaill
7 a t-shlúagh slan can díghbail oirrderc do dhenam doib.*
(... And when the two Mac Williams and that large host that was responsive to
them heard of the march of O'Domnaill to them, and he after inflicting confusion
on that other host, they fled themselves from the town and went off in plight of
rout, without their having been attacked. And O'Domnaill and his host went
[home] safe, without notable damage being done to them.)[54]

AFM 1522.10
*As suaill má ro bá mó do clú nó do cosccar dUa Domhnaill ar fhud Ereann an maidhm
sin Chnuic Buidhbh in ro farccbadh ár daoine, 7 édála aidhbhle, iná an bánmaidhm sin
cen go ro fuiligheadh nó go ro fordhearccadh for neach etorra.*
(Scarcely did the defeat of Cnoc-Buidhbh, in which many men had been
slaughtered and vast spoils obtained, procure greater renown or victory for
O'Donnell throughout Ireland than this bloodless defeat, although no one among
them had lost a drop of blood or received a single wound.)[55]

Just how important the emphasis on heroism and bravery in battle was emerges
in the AFM narrative of the encounter between Ó Domhnaill and Ó Néill,
known as the battle of Cnoc Buidhbh, that preceded the Connacht arbitration of
Maghnus Ó Domhnaill and others. AU recorded that Ó Domhnaill and the
Cinéal Conaill had assembled: *Ocus, mar rugatur féin ar a chéle, is í comairle do
ronsat – iat féin do thabairt ar son a tíre 7 a talman* ('And, when themselves came
together, this is the counsel they adopted – to sacrifice themselves for the sake of
their territory and their land').[56] It was also noted that when attacking Ó Néill at
night, Ó Domhnaill's men had left their horses behind in a move of enforced
bravery, *ardaigh comad lughaiti no bíadh menma theithmi no fhillti tar a n-ais aca*
('in order that they should have less mind of flight or of turning back').[57] The
AFM account is similar, stating that Ó Domhnaill's men had decided to attack
Ó Néill despite being outnumbered, *uair roba lainne leo a mudhucchadh do
mhaighin oldas a mbiothfognamh do neoch isin mbith* ('choosing rather to be slain
on the field than to become slaves to any one in the world').[58] The same
sentiment is repeated soon afterwards

AFM 1522.9
*Iar nindeall, 7 iar norducchadh, iar ngresacht 7 iar ngérlaoidhedh a bhecc slóicch dUa
Dhomhnaill, Ro forcongair forra a neachra dfágbháil, ar ní baí menmarc aca a lathair
iombuailte diomghabhail munbhadh rempa bá raén.*
(O'Donnell, having arrayed and marshalled, excited and earnestly exhorted his
small army, commanded them to abandon their horses, for they had no desire to
escape from the field of battle unless they should be the victors.)[59]

54 *AU*, III, pp 546–9. 55 *AFM*, V, pp 1362–3. 56 *AU*, III, pp 544–5. 57 *AU*, III, pp 544–5.
58 *AFM*, V, pp 1356–7. 59 *AFM*, V, pp 1356–7. O'Donovan (*AFM*, V, p. 1357 note f) drew
attention to a similarity between features of this episode and one recounted in the tale known as the
battle of Magh Rath, found in the Yellow Book of Lecan. See also John O'Donovan (ed.), *The*

Defending one's honour, even to death, was a cornerstone of lordship. It was fundamental to the kind of leadership expected of a Gaelic lord. Heroism was not an optional virtue in these circumstances; the narrator was clear that history required honourable heroes, because therein lay the key to successful lordship.

A difference over strategy between Maghnus and his father in 1524 is noted in AFM in the course of a description of Ó Domhnaill resistance to an offensive by the lord justice allied with Conn Ó Néill. The Four Masters note that in attacking the forces of the earl of Kildare and Ó Néill at night, Maghnus had acted against the advice of his father.

> AFM 1524.4
>
> *Ro baí Maghnus Ó Domhnaill ag iarraidh an Iustis 7 Ó Néill dionnsaicchidh in adhaid sin 7 ní ro fhaomh Ó Domhnaill sin lá daingne an ionaidh ina rabhattar, 7 ar uamhan an ordanáis bátar lá muintir an Iustís. Do chóid tra Maghnus gan comharlécchadh dUa Dhomhnaill hi mescc na ngallócclach dia chois do chaithemh 7 do mhesccbhuaidhreadh tsluaigh an Iústís 7 Í Neill 7 ro gabhsat for a ndiúbhraccad do shaithibh saighitt conár leiccset tathamh nó tionnabradh dóibh.*
>
> (Manus O'Donnell was desirous of attacking the lord justice and O'Neill on that night, but to this O'Donnell would not consent, on account of the strength of the position of the enemy, and from a dread of the ordnance which the lord justice's people had with them. Manus, however, without consulting O'Donnell, set out on foot with a party of gallowglasses, to harrass and confuse the army of the lord justice and O'Neill, and commenced discharging showers of arrows at them, so that they neither allowed them to sleep nor rest.)[60]

In the peace negotiations that followed, the annalists record that:

> AFM 1524.4
>
> *... ar ro naidhm an Iustís sidh etir Ó nDomhnaill 7 Ua Neill, 7 é fein hi slánaibh etorra. Do rónadh bheós cairdes críost mar an ccédna etir an Iústis, 7 Ó Domhnaill co ro scarsatt fó sidh, 7 fó chaoincomrac tre mhíorbhailibh Dé don dul sin.*
>
> (... the lord justice confirmed a peace between O'Neill and O'Donnell, he himself being as surety between them. A gossipred was also formed between the lord justice and O'Donnell, so that on this occasion they parted from each other in friendship and amity, through the miraculous interposition of God.)[61]

The version of these events recorded in AU is much less focused on Ó Domhnaill and his son Maghnus, and merely records that *Maghnus O Domnaill 7 drong do na hAlbanachaibh do dhul do chaithimh airm ré sluagh an Iarla san oidchi* ('Maghnus O'Domnaill and a party of the Scots went to discharge weapons at the host of the earl in the night'). There is no mention of Maghnus acting

---

Banquet of Dun na nGedh and the Battle of Magh Rath, an ancient historical tale ... from a manuscript in the Library of Trinity College, Dublin (Dublin, Irish Archaeological Society, 1842), p. 202.
60 *AFM*, V, pp 1370–1.   61 *AFM*, V, pp 1370–1.

without his father's permission, and no mention that the peaceful outcome was divinely sanctioned. The AConn version of these events is close to that in AU; only AFM has the full detail from the perspective of the Uí Dhomhnaill.[62]

The Four Masters' account of the opposition to their father shown by two of Maghnus's brothers, Niall Garbh and Eoghan, in 1524, differs from that in AU and AConn in three significant details. First, AFM omits the explicit statement found in AU and AConn that the quarrel of these two was with Aodh Óg Ó Domhnaill himself.[63] Secondly, the Four Masters supply additional genealogical detail on the individuals involved.

AFM 1524
Dias Mac Í Dhomhnaill, Niall Garbh, 7 Eocchan Clann Aodha Óicc mic Aodha Ruaidh do cengal commbádha coccaidh ré roile.
(The two sons of O'Donnell, namely, Niall Garv and Owen, the sons of Hugh Oge, son of Hugh Roe, formed a confederacy to wage war.)[64]

AU 1524
Dis mac [U]í Domnaill, idon, Níall garbh 7 Eoghan, do chengal re céile do choccadh ar O n-Domnaill.
(Two sons of O'Domnaill, namely, Niall the Rough and Eogan, united with each other to war on O'Domnaill.)[65]

Thirdly, the closing sentence in the AFM entry, commenting on the deaths of the two sons of Ó Domhnaill as a result of their dispute, is deliberately equivocal: *Ro ba mór an techt rias an tan sin an dias torchair ann sin* ('The [loss of] two who fell there would have been the cause of great grief before this time').[66]

It appears that the annalists were reluctant to condemn the two sons of Ó Domhnaill outright, and to neglect to lament their passing, but they made it clear nonetheless that the two had destabilized the lordship at a time when Ó Domhnaill faced serious external challenges from the combined forces of Ó Néill and the lord deputy. AU and AConn agree on the wording to sum up the deaths of the two upstart sons of Ó Domhnaill: *ni hurusa co tanic lucht a n-aosa do Cenel Conoill doba mó d'echtaib ina [an] dis-sin* ('it is unlikely that there lived any of their years among the Cenel Conaill who were more deplored than these two').[67]

Maghnus was again cast in the role of arbitrator in the following year, when it was recorded that after a summer of disagreement and some aggression on the part of Aodh Óg Ó Domhnaill, a peace was concluded between Ó Néill and Ó Domhnaill, arranged by the lord justice and Maghnus Ó Domhnaill.[68] At no point did the annalists offer the information that Maghnus was married to Siubhán, daughter of Conn Ó Neill, as an explanation for his diplomatic role in maintaining peace between the two rival lordships.[69] That kind of historical

---

62 *AU*, III, pp 552–5 (AU 1524.5); *AConn*, pp 650–1.   63 *AFM*, V, pp 1368–9; *AU*, III, pp 550–1.
64 *AFM*, V, pp 1368–9.   65 *AU*, III, pp 550–1.   66 *AFM*, V, pp 1368–9.   67 *AConn*, pp 648–51.
68 *AFM*, V, pp 1328–9; *AU*, III, pp 556–7.   69 Siubhán Ó Néill's death, at the age of 42, is recorded

analysis would not have occurred to them – but they may well have taken the political context for granted.

Maghnus's role as a peacemaker was again noted in AFM 1526, but thereafter his portrayal is more typical of any heir apparent. However, the accounts of his exploits included in AFM are selective. His involvement with his father in raiding Tír Eoghain in 1526, an episode that reflects well on him from the perspective of those concerned about displays of Ó Domhnaill power, is recorded in AFM but not in AU.

> AFM 1526.5
> *Sluaiccheadh la hUa nDomhnaill (iar ttoidhecht Maghnusa ó Áth Cliath) 7 lá Maghnus feissin cona sochraide diblínibh hi ttús an Earraigh do shonnradh hi tTír Eogain. Creacha iomda 7 airccthe aidhble do dhénamh leó isin tír, 7 in init do dhénamh dhóibh fors na creachaibh sin hi cCoill na Lon hi Siol mBaoighill, 7 tangattar slán dia ttighibh iaromh co nedálaibh iomhdaibh.*
>
> (O Donnell (after the return of Manus from Dublin), and Manus himself, with the forces of both, marched, in the beginning of Spring, into Tyrone; they committed many depredations and great devastations in the territory. They feasted upon those preys during Shrovetide at Coill-na-lon, in Sil-Baoighill, and then returned home in safety, loaded with great booty.)[70]

In the following year, a less successful episode from the Tír Conaill perspective is recorded by AU but omitted from AFM.

> AU 1527.11
> *Maghnus O Domnaill do dol ar creich a n-Glenn-Eile ar Aod m-buidhe O n-Domnaill, 7 días ócmarcach do muinntir Maghnus[a] do marbadh, idon, mac Domnaill, mic Féi[dh]limthe, mic Aonghus[a] óic [U]i Gallcubuir 7 mac Briain caich, mic Domnaill Mic-an-decanaigh.*
>
> (Maghnus O'Domnaill went on a raid into Glenn-[Fh]eile on Aodh O'Domnaill the Tawny and two young horsemen of the people of Maghnus, namely, the son of Domnall, son of Feidhlimidh, son of Aenghus O'Gallcubuir junior and the son of Brian Blind[-eye], son of Domnall Mac-an-decanaigh, were slain.)[71]

The long entry at AFM 1531.20 is a significant one in tracing AFM's version of the career of Maghnus Ó Domhnaill. For the first time the contentious issue of the succession to the lordship is foregrounded. His brothers, rival contenders for the title, are unnamed, while AFM notes that:

> AFM 1531.20
> *Maguidhir do dhol sluagh hi tTír Conaill ar tarraing Uí Domhnaill ar ro bháttar clann Uí Dhomhnaill i frithbheart fria roile ar omhan nech uadhaibh do rochtain ria na roile*

in AFM 1535.3, two years before Maghnus Ó Domhnaill succeeded his father as head of the lordship of Tír Conaill. 70 *AFM*, V, pp 1380–1. 71 *AU*, III, pp 566–7. 72 *AFM*, V, pp 1404–7.

*i ccennus iar nécc a nathar ar ro leth ainm 7 eirdearcas Maghnusa Uí Domhnaill fó
Erinn uile, ní namá hi cCenel cConaill acht is na tíribh a neachtair, 7 ro baí acc forrán
for a bhraithribh sainnriudh. Bá himeccla lá hUa nDomhnaill gailfhine do dhénamh
dhóibh for aroile 7 a dhol fein i neineirte ass a los conadh aire ro thogairm Ua
Dhomhnaill Maguidhir dia shaighidh dus an ccaomhsattís Maghnus do chuibhdiughadh
fri tairisi 7 brathairsi fri a chomhfhuilidhibh. Do chóidh iaramh Maguidhir 7 Aodh
Buidhe Ua Domhnaill co na sochraide go rangattar co finn go ro chrechsat ina mbaoí fó
mhámus Mhaghnusa ó or co hor.*

(Maguire proceeded with an army into Tirconnell, at the instance of O'Donnell,
for O'Donnell's sons were at strife with each other, from fear that the one might
attain to the chieftainship in preference to the other, after their father's death; for
the name and renown of Manus O'Donnell had spread not only through all
Tirconnell, but through external territories; and he was oppressing his own
kindred. O'Donnell was afraid that they would commit fratricide upon each other,
and that his own power would, in consequence, be weakened, wherefore he had
invited Maguire to come to him, to see whether they could reconcile Manus with
his relatives through friendship and brotherly love. Maguire and Hugh Boy
O'Donnell afterwards marched with their troops until they arrived at the [River]
Fin; and they plundered all [the territory] that was under the jurisdiction of
Manus, from border to border.)[72]

The episode is not recounted from Maghnus's perspective, but rather from that
of his father, Aodh Ó Domhnaill, and his father's ally, Mág Uidhir, but yet
Maghnus is the one in the limelight throughout. Maghnus's brothers are
strangely invisible in this account.[73]

The same is true of a narrative in 1536, when Aodh Ó Domhnaill was
accompanied on an expedition to Connacht by some of his sons, though not
Maghnus on this occasion. Instead of naming and describing the activities and
achievements of those sons of Ó Domhnaill who participated in the expedition,
the Four Masters' account turns instead to explain why Maghnus was not
present. A plausible explanation of these entries, dominated as they are by the
person of Maghnus, whether or not he was part of the actions they describe, is
that they were assembled retrospectively to form a narrative of his life and
achievements prior to his attaining the title of lord of Tír Conaill. The
culmination of this is not the open hostility between Maghnus and his brother
Aodh Buidhe in 1537,[74] but rather the succession of Maghnus to the lordship
following the death of his father, Aodh, that same year. In an obituary that is
concerned about the successor as much as the deceased, it is recorded that
Maghnus was inaugurated *lá comharbaibh Choluim Chille do ched 7 do comhairle
maithe Cenél cConaill etir thuaith 7 ecclais* ('by the successors of St Columbkille,

73 The AU version of the same events (1531) omits mention of Ó Domhnaill's concerns over the
future of the lordship, arising from the dispute among his sons, and essentially tells the story from
the Mág Uidhir perspective (*AU*, III, pp 578–81). 74 *AFM*, V, pp 1436–7.

with the permission and by the advice of the nobles of Tir Conaill, both lay and ecclesiastical').[75] This was as unequivocal an endorsement of Maghnus's authority as could be drawn up. The contrast between the elaborate obituary followed by the record of inauguration in AFM and the corresponding entry in AU is quite marked:

> AU 1537.7
> *hUa Domnaill, idon, Aedh, mac Aedha ruaidh [U]i Domnaill, do dhul d'ég a ndheredh*
> *shamhraidh na bliadhna so. Ocus ní taníg o Bhrian Bhoraimhe anuas righ dob' fhearr*
> *smacht 7 riaghail 'nas e. Ocus hUa Domhnaill do dhenam d'a mac, idon, do Mhaghnas.*
> (Ua Domnaill, namely, Aedh, son of Aedh Ua Domnaill the Red, died in the end
> of summer of this year. And there came not from Brian Boruma downwards a king
> that was of better sway and rule than he. And his son, namely Maghnus, was made
> Ua Domnaill.)[76]

The Four Masters rejected this formulaic obituary, with its allusions to Brian Bóruma and kingship, in its entirety. They replaced it with a much more elaborate and discursive obituary, culminating in the inauguration of Maghnus as successor to the deceased lord. It is again tempting to speculate that the set of Ó Cléirigh annals that ended in 1537, and that was used as a source for AFM, may have been the source of this strong focus on the achievements of Maghnus up to the time of his succession to the lordship. That he employed a chronicler as propagandist in his campaign to ensure that he succeeded to the lordship at the expense of his brothers, is one likely explanation.[77] Even if he did so, perhaps this does not mean that such a chronicler engaged in much creative writing – he may have merely put a gloss on narratives so that they highlighted Maghnus's role.

The disappointing later career of Maghnus, particularly after his son, An Calbhach, succeeded in asserting his own authority and arranged for his father to be held in captivity for the last eight years of his life, is sufficient to account for the changing nature of the narratives involving Maghnus Ó Domhnaill through the 1540s and 1550s. However, it might also be at least partly accounted for by the ending of the Four Masters' Ó Cléirigh source in 1537. Thereafter, the increasing involvement of the Dublin government is mentioned but not analyzed and, even with the benefit of hindsight, its significance does not appear to have been noticed by the annalists. Their interest in these exploits seems to have been in matters of heroism, honour and lordship, and not least in their military expression, which gave scope for the assertion of true leadership. There is a central focus on personal leadership – culminating in the cult of the hero in the 1602 obituary of the later Aodh Ruadh. It could be argued that the kind of

75 *AFM*, V, pp 1438–9. 76 *AU*, III, pp 614–15. 77 As noted above, he employed poets as propagandists also. For a poetic description of Maghnus as *ardrígh chinidh Chuinn* ('high king of Conn's race') see Breatnach (ed.), 'In praise of Maghnas Ó Domhnaill', 70.

attitude to individual leaders evident in the Ó Domhnaill entries in AFM (and similarly in AU) is close to the attitude of a cult of leadership that led to the writing of *Beatha Aodha Ruaidh* also. For them, the subject matter of history comprised the lives of great men; particularly the men who had made the lordship of Tír Conaill great.

Post-1537 narratives in AFM

The descriptions of Ó Domhnaill exploits in AFM in the mid-sixteenth century are longer and more complex and adopt a more vivid narrative form so that they are much more akin to the style of *Beatha Aodha Ruaidh* than to older narrative episodes in the annals. None of the named source manuscripts for AFM cover the period between 1538 and 1587, and no extant manuscripts have been identified as a source for these mid-sixteenth-century stories of Ó Domhnaill exploits. It is possible that the annalists may have drawn on miscellaneous material compiled by historians to the Uí Dhomhnaill in the course of the sixteenth century and, since the era was within living memory, they may also have resorted to oral sources preserved within their own families. Some of their narratives have a retrospective gloss, and the possibility that they drew on now lost work by Lughaidh Ó Cléirigh cannot be discounted.

The accounts of events in the late 1550s involving An Calbhach, son of Maghnus, who eventually succeeded Maghnus Ó Domhnaill as head of the lordship in 1563, mark a new departure in terms of narrative style. An Calbhach was already exercising considerable power in the lordship in opposition to his father by the late 1540s, and by 1555 had placed Maghnus in captivity where he remained until his death in 1563.[78] The narrative relating to An Calbhach's actions in 1557 illustrates a vivid reporting style. The story has Seaán Ó Néill as its main focus, but An Calbhach is also given prominence, and the conclusion of the narrative emphasizes the Ó Domhnaill triumph. The story reads as a conflation of two stories, one told from the perspective of Seaán Ó Néill and the other from the perspective of An Calbhach Ó Domhnaill. Although the episode opens with the actions of Seaán Ó Néill, there are two lengthy passages devoted to the response and initiatives of An Calbhach Ó Domhnaill. Unusually, the story encompasses two endings, one narrating the fate of the loser, Seaán Ó Néill, followed by the triumphant account from the perspective of the victor.[79]

The description of An Calbhach's thought processes as he pondered in his mind what he should do, consulted his father, and arrived at a strategy whereby he thought that victory could be gained, focuses attention on the person of An Calbhach and his abilities as a leader, while being appropriately deferential to the

---

78 *AFM*, V, pp 1504–5 (AFM 1548.1); pp 1540–1 (AFM 1555.5).   79 *AFM*, V, pp 1550–9. The AFM text of this episode is reproduced in Cunningham, *O'Donnell histories*, appendix II, with sections told from an Ó Domhnaill perspective highlighted in italics.

wisdom and experience of Ó Domhnaill himself. Similar consultation between son and father, accompanied by strategic advice, is described in other such narratives – and was probably a necessary device to uphold the honour of the head of the lordship.[80] In the 1557 episode in AFM, there is much colourful detail about the actual military engagement: topographical detail of the location, and even a comment on the weather, elaborate descriptive detail on the appearance of the galloglasses, and a lively if verbose account of the attack on the Ó Néill camp. Despite the emphasis on An Calbhach's role, it is also emphasized that the strategy adopted was that agreed with his father who, despite his incapacity, was still portrayed as a competent military strategist, and at the conclusion, the victory is attributed to the Cinéal Conaill in general rather than An Calbhach. Significantly, the story ends with an allusion to another military triumph by an earlier Ó Domhnaill. Its form suggests that the story might possibly have originated in a composition intended for public performance at an Ó Domhnaill celebratory function rather than as a written annalistic record.[81]

It is not only An Calbhach's triumphs that are recorded, however. Two years later, in 1559, he was captured by Ó Néill and imprisoned, and in a further loss of honour, his wife was taken by Ó Néill.[82] Then in 1561 it was noted that his daughter, Máire, who was wife of Seaán Ó Néill, *dfabhail bháis dadhuath, 7 durghrain, do thruaighe, 7 do thromnemhele* ('died of horror, loathing, grief and deep anguish') in consequence of the severity of the treatment of her father, An Calbhach, by Ó Néill, in her presence.[83] While the military narratives can be imagined as being narrated in public, the less happy episodes may not have been presented in the same way. The political dominance of Ó Néill at this point, and the increasing involvement of the Dublin government in Ulster affairs can be detected in the AFM record, but only incidentally, as though, even with hindsight, they were unaware of its political significance. The ongoing focus on the local achievements of the Uí Dhomhnaill continued after the sudden death of An Calbhach in 1566, when he was succeeded by his brother, Aodh son of Maghnus (d. 1600), and some narratives of this Aodh's exploits were also recorded at length.

One such lengthy Ó Domhnaill narrative is recorded for 1567. It describes the new lord's encounter with the greater strength of Ó Néill's forces, itself a recurring motif in these narratives. As in some of the earlier episodes, the story opens with Ó Néill, but it is the response of Ó Domhnaill that is emphasized. There is much detail on topography, and the recording of specific details such as

---

80 See for instance *AFM*, VI, pp 2124–5 (AFM 1599.35), where Ó Domhnaill *Ro fhaccaibh Niall garbh Ó Domhnaill i ttoísighecht aésa an iomchoimhétta, 7 ro thioncoiscc dó gach ní bá dír do ghniomh* ('left Niall Garv O'Donnell in command of the besiegers, instructing him in everything that was proper to be done'). 81 For another lengthy narrative of an Ó Domhnaill triumph over Ó Néill that shares many of the characteristics of this one, see AFM 1567.2. 82 *AFM*, V, pp 1574–7 (AFM 1559.6). 83 *AFM*, V, pp 1584–5 (AFM 1561.2).

that the tide was out gives the impression of an eyewitness account of the encounter. However, the Four Masters were aware that there was more than one version of the events narrated, especially regarding the death of Niall son of Domhnall Cairbreach Ó Domhnaill. Having stated that he was killed by Ó Néill's army, they go on to add another sentence saying *Acht cena adbearad araile gur ab lá a mhuintir budhéin do cher Niall Ó Domhnaill* ('Some, however, assert that Niall O'Donnell was slain by his own people').[84] In the manner typical of chroniclers, they leave the reader to choose between these alternative scenarios, content merely to record the available versions.[85]

As before, the military encounter was presented as being essential to the defence of the honour of Ó Domhnaill. He had suffered the shame of being removed from his stronghold by Ó Néill. Essentially, this is heroic narrative rather than historical prose. The assembly of chieftains being addressed by Ó Domhnaill was described:

AFM 1567.2

... *7 atbert fríu gur bhó lainne 7 gur bhó maisi lais a écc, 7 a oittheadh do maighin, riasiú no fodaimhfedh an do radsat cenel eoccain do thár 7 do tarcasal fair budhein, for a dherbhfhine, 7 for a chomhfuilidhibh.*

(... and he protested to them that he would deem it more pleasing and becoming to fall and to die in the field, than to endure the contempt and dishonour with which he himself, his tribe, and his relations, had been treated by the Kinel-Owen.)[86]

This was presented in a manner that clearly affirmed Ó Domhnaill's status as leader. His words had proved persuasive, so that:

AFM 1567.2

Ro aontuighsiot na maithe sin uile fri haithescc an ardfhlatha, 7 atbeartsat gur bhó fíor na forchanta 7 na fuighle ro chan conadh fair deisidh oca Ua Neill co na slócch dionnsaicchidh.

(All the chieftains assented to the speech of their prince, and said that all the remarks and sentiments he had expressed were true, so that they resolved to attack O'Neill and his army.)[87]

The story continued in elaborate form, stressing the heroism that was required of those on the side of Ó Domhnaill:

AFM 1567.2

Bá dána dochoiscc, aindiuid, ecceilligh an comhairle do rónadh ann sin .i. saicchidh an mhór ghabhaidh 7 an mhór guasachta ro bhaoí for cionn dóibh. Ar a aoí bá mó ro

84 *AFM*, V, pp 1612–13. 85 On the typicality of this approach to conflicting evidence in a sixteenth-century English context, see F.J. Levy, *Tudor historical thought* (San Marino, 1967), pp 169–70. 86 *AFM*, V, pp 1612–13. 87 *AFM*, V, pp 1612–13.

fortamhluigh, gradh a neinigh, 7 a nathardha ina ccridhe oldás gradh a ccorp, 7 a ccaomhanmann. Ro asccnáttar iaramh co haoín mhenmnach for ccúla ina ninneall cróbecc bodhbha, 7 ina naonbhróin nathardha for amus longpoirt Uí Néill.

(The resolution here adopted, of facing the great danger and peril which awaited them, was bold, daring, obdurate and irrational; but the love of their protegees and inheritances prevailed in their hearts over the love of body and life, and they marched back with unanimous courage, in a regularly arrayed small body, and in a venomous phalanx, towards the camp of O'Neill.)[88]

Special emphasis was placed on the atmosphere of the battle and the heroism of the warriors who participated.

AFM 1567.2

Bá fiochdha forgranna an féccadh forniata forgruamdha do bert cach for aroile díbh dionnaibh a rosc rinnradharcach, do bertsat a ngáire catha os aird gur bhó lór dfurail time 7 teichmhe for fhiallach anbfann anarrachta an comhgáiriucchadh do rónsat ag rochtain hi ccenn aroile dóibh.

(Fierce and desperate were the grim and terrible looks that each cast at the other from their starlike eyes; they raised the battle cry aloud, and their united shouting, when rushing together, was sufficient to strike with dismay and turn to flight the feeble and the unwarlike.)[89]

As in an earlier narrative, it ended with Ó Néill slipping away unnoticed following the defeat. The encounter was formally named by the annalists as the defeat of Fersad Swilly [Farsetmore], which had occurred on 8 May 1567.[90] In structure, the account closely parallels the 1557 narrative discussed above.

Unlike the earlier episode, however, which had also involved Seaán Ó Néill in opposition to Ó Domhnaill, the 1567 narrative continues with a further account of Ó Néill, ending with his death at the hands of the Scots later the same year. A brief obituary is given. As is well known, the death of Seaán Ó Néill was of major significance for late sixteenth-century Ulster, and it is little surprise that it should be recorded in some detail in AFM, despite their Ó Domhnaill bias. The AFM obituary, however, is a brief and very traditional one, with allusions to legendary heroes, but bereft of any contemporary political comment other than the naming of Toirrdhealbhach Luineach as successor to Seaán Ó Néill.

AFM 1567

Ba doiligh do Cenel Eocchain mic Neill oidedh an ti torchair ann sin, ar bá hé a cConchobhar ar cóiccedhachas, a Lugh Lamhfhada ar laochdacht, 7 a ngreid gáidh 7 gaiscceadh an tUa Neill sin .i. Sean conadh dforaithmet a oidedha do raidhedh.

---

88 *AFM*, V, pp 1612–15.　89 *AFM*, V, pp 1614–15.　90 For a modern account of the battle of Farsetmore, see G.A. Hayes-McCoy, *Irish battles* (London, 1969), pp 68–86. Hayes-McCoy notes that the only contemporary account of the battle is that in AFM.

Secht mbliadhna Sesccatt cúicc céd,
míle bliadhain is ní brécc,
co bás tSeain mic mic Cuinn
ó thoidhecht Criost hi ccolainn.
O Neill do ghairm do Toirrdhealbhach Luineach mac Neill Conallaigh iar marbhadh
Sheain.
(Grievous to the race of Owen, son of Niall, was the death of him who was there
slain, for that O'Neill, i.e. John, had been their Conchobhar in provincial dignity,
their Lugh Longhanded in heroism, and their champion in [time of] danger and
prowess. The following [quatrain] was composed to commemorate his death:
Seven years, sixty, five hundred,
And a thousand years, it is no falsehood,
To the death of John, grandson of Con,
From the coming of Christ into a body.
After the murder of John, Turlough Luineach, the son of Niall Conallagh, was
styled O'Neill.)[91]

Given the significance of the event, it seems likely that this story was generally
narrated from an Ó Néill perspective, and it is possible that the AFM version
may have been adapted to highlight Ó Domhnaill's involvement. However, the
source of their account is unknown, and so the extent of their editorial work
cannot be fully evaluated.

Although at one level this narrative reads like an account of the battle of
Farsetmore, such as might have been subsequently retold at Ó Domhnaill
celebratory gatherings, there are indications that the version recorded in AFM
was constructed from more than one account, at some temporal remove from the
battle itself. Thus, for instance, when enumerating the numbers lost in battle, the
annalists give the number lost from Ó Néill's army as 1,300, but then add,
Atbearat araile liubhair gur bhó trí mhile fer co ttuilleadh easbhaidh shlóigh Í Néill
isin ló sin ('some books [however] state that O'Neill's loss in this battle was
upwards of 3,000 men').[92] In reality, the story is much more an Ó Néill defeat
than an Ó Domhnaill victory, and unusually for AFM it is Ó Néill's homecoming
that concludes the episode. It seems possible that the Four Masters may have
adapted this and some associated stories from a source dealing with the career of
Seaán Ó Néill, but if so, they did not deem it appropriate to name that source. It
is also uncertain whether the reference to 'some books' originates with AFM or
whether they adopted the entire account from a previous synthesis of the
exploits of Seaán Ó Néill. The reference confirms, at least, that the annalists had
some written sources available to them for these mid-sixteenth-century episodes,
though they do not itemize them among their source manuscripts.

91 *AFM*, V, pp 1618–23. The word 'sixty' has been substituted for O'Donovan's incorrect 'seventy'
in this translation.   92 *AFM*, V, pp 1616–17.

After this point, the Ó Domhnaill narratives in AFM cease for some years, the 1567 Ó Néill/Ó Domhnaill narrative having been an exceptional item. The next appearance of the Cineál Conaill is in the context of Sir Henry Sidney's arrival in Ulster in 1575, during his second term as lord deputy, and his attempted peace-making between Ó Néill and Ó Domhnaill.[93] While the episode includes some detail about the Uí Dhomhnaill, particularly the escape from prison in Dublin of Conn, son of An Calbhach Ó Domhnaill, it is essentially a narrative from the English perspective, and concludes with a description of the continuation of Sidney's circuit in Munster, visiting Waterford, Youghal and Cork.[94] There is no hint of the native perspective on events in the report that *Bá dírímh in ro mudhaigh do mheirleachaibh, 7 in ro díchend do drochdhaoínibh is na tíribh sin trias a ttudhchaidh gó sin* ('[He] suppressed countless numbers of rebels, and beheaded great numbers of bad men in these districts, as he passed along').[95] In the follow-up narrative of Sidney's further activities in Munster and Connacht in 1576, again it is Sidney rather than the Munster or Connacht lords who is the focus of attention. Sidney is favourably presented as *Ridire ar ainm, ar uaisle ar ghniomh, ar ghaiscceadh* ('a knight by title, nobleness, deed and valour').[96] While some others, such as Dónal Ó Briain in Clare, are also presented favourably, this is because *ro crochadh meirligh míbhésacha, 7 droch dhaoíne, 7 díbhearccaigh lais* ('he hanged refractory rebels, bad men and plunderers').[97] The terminology used is more typical of the English state papers relating to Ireland than of the annals, and the description might possibly have been adapted from an English account of the episode.

At points like this it emerges that, at times, the Four Masters were reluctant to deviate from the perspective of their sources. It is not so much that they were consciously striving to be objective, rather that they sometimes used the source material available to them in a simplistic way, in so far as they appear almost entirely oblivious to the partisan nature of those sources. Thus, in adapting these narratives involving Sir Henry Sidney, they essentially accept the standpoint of their source, rather than adopting a standpoint of their own. Why, when adapting an English source, were they content to present the world as much from an English perspective as their own? This question is important in attempting to understand the Four Masters' sense of history, and their overall objective in compiling the annals. Given their concern to ensure appropriate representation of the Uí Dhomhnaill in earlier episodes, why did they not feel it necessary to modify these Sidney narratives so that they adopted a Gaelic perspective? It seems that they did not perceive the actions of Sir Henry Sidney in terms of a wider 'Tudor conquest', as later generations did, but simply as a noble knight exercising power over his opponents. Their focus was on an individual noble leader and his achievements, not on broad national issues or allegiances. His

93 *AFM*, V, pp 1680–3.   94 *AFM*, V, pp 1680–3.   95 *AFM*, V, pp 1682–3.   96 *AFM*, V, pp 1684–5.   97 *AFM*, V, pp 1686–7.

respect for the law, as conveyed through his implementation of law and order, would have been acceptable to the annalists in that context. They appear to have lacked any sense of structured opposition between rival 'English' and 'Irish' power structures into which to fit their account of Sidney's exploits, and therefore presented the narratives in which he was involved as though he were the equivalent of a Gaelic nobleman. The annalists' approach mirrors that of the poets who were employed for Anglo-Irish patrons, and the sympathy for foreigners displayed by the fourteenth-century author of *Caithréim Thoirdhealbhaigh*.[98]

In contrast to the lack of a pre-existing political context in which to place their mid-1570s descriptions of Sidney's actions, the opposition between Cinéal Conaill and Cinéal Eoghain was a constant interpretative framework in the annals, recurring again in 1581 in a lengthy account involving Ó Néill and Ó Domhnaill, which opens with a reference to internal rivalry within the Cinéal Conaill.[99] When Conn, son of An Calbhach Ó Domhnaill, openly opposed his uncle, Aodh Ó Domhnaill, he sought assistance from Ó Néill. The annalists record that he persuaded Ó Néill to become involved by reminding him of past feuds between Cinéal Conaill and Cinéal Eoghain.[100] The response of Ó Domhnaill was expressed in consciously traditional terms, the annalists recording that Ó Domhnaill, though unprepared, *bá forrán lais sluagh eachtaircheneóil do thocht dia thír gan frithbert friú dia madh deimhin lais a oidheadh fo chedóir* ('he could not, however, brook that an extern army should come into his territory without opposing them, even though he was certain of meeting immediate death').[101] However, the circumstances were not quite traditional, for the annalists also record that the reason Ó Domhnaill was ill-prepared was because *baí sidhe fomhámaighthe do bainrioghain tSaxan, 7 robdar cairdi a [n-]eccraitte friss gó sin co na baoí hi foimhdin coccadh, no comhfuachadh* ('he was subject to the Queen of England, and his friends were till then at strife with him, so that he was not prepared for war or hostilities').[102] In the description of the military engagement that followed, the traditional opposition between Ó Néill and Ó Domhnaill was again alluded to.[103] The escapade ended in a defeat for Ó Domhnaill, and the annalists resorted to very traditional methods of explaining how that happened. First they attempted to universalize the event by reciting a proverb: *ro dearbhadh an dearbharuscc airdearc don chur sa (.i. beodha gach brathair fri aroile* ('the celebrated proverb was verified on this occasion, i.e. lively is each kinsman [when fighting] against the other.')[104]

98 Katharine Simms, 'Bards and barons: the Anglo-Irish aristocracy and the native culture' in Robert Bartlett and Angus Mackay (eds), *Medieval frontier societies* (Oxford, 1989) pp 177–97; Aoife Nic Ghiollamhaith, 'Dynastic warfare and historical writing in North Munster, 1276–1350', *Cambridge Medieval Celtic Studies* 2 (1981), 88; on the favourable representation of sixteenth-century English presidents of Connacht in the Irish annals, see Bernadette Cunningham and Raymond Gillespie, *Stories from Gaelic Ireland: microhistories from the sixteenth-century Irish annals* (Dublin, 2003), pp 179–202. 99 *AFM*, V, pp 1764–7. 100 *AFM*, V, pp 1766–7. 101 *AFM*, V, pp 1766–7. 102 *AFM*, V, pp 1766–7. 103 *AFM*, V, pp 1766–9. 104 *AFM*, V, pp 1766–9.

Next, they invoked an external, essentially supernatural, explanation, saying that the defeat was caused by the curse of an ecclesiastic.

AFM 1581.27
Ro badh tria easccaine an Epscoip Uí Fhirghil ro sraoíneadh an maidm sin uair ro sháraighsiot drong do Chenel cConaill Cill Mic Nenáin an lá rias an maidhm 7 ro ghuidh an tEpscop dóibh co nar bhó sóinmheach a tturas ittir.
(It was in consequence of the curse of Bishop O'Freel that they suffered this defeat; for a party of the Kinel-Connell had plundered Kilmacrenan the day before the battle, and the bishop had prayed that their expedition might not be successful.)[105]

Another Ó Domhnaill/Ó Néill narrative was recorded two years later. The scenario is familiar from many earlier episodes: Ó Domhnaill responds to attack, despite being unprepared, and repels the attackers. As before, the expectation of valour is affirmed: *Nir bo feich optha lá muintir Uí Dhomhnaill indsin go mbátar daoíne occá ndithiughadh etorra gach laoí* ('as O'Donnell's people would not refuse their challenge, great numbers were slain between them each day').[106] The episode ends in an Ó Domhnaill victory, though it lacks any eulogizing of Aodh Ó Domhnaill's leadership or achievements. A curious vignette in this narrative is the killing of Maolmhuire Ó Cléirigh, a supporter of Ó Néill, who was taken hostage by Ó Domhnaill. According to the annalists, Maolmhuire shared a mother with Toirrdhealbhach Luineach Ó Néill, and *bá for a chumas buí iolmhaoine Uí Neill ar aba a fhialusa fris* ('he had Ó Néill's various treasures under his control, on account of his relationship to him').[107] He was wounded and then drowned by Ó Domhnaill's followers *ro badh slán a menma, 7 roptar buidhigh dia thuitim leó* ('who were in high spirits, and who rejoiced at his falling by them').[108] Despite his tortuous death, at the hands of the Uí Dhomhnaill, the presence of this Ó Cléirigh character in the role of cultural custodian in the Ó Néill camp at this time may be a clue to the Four Masters' access to some of the narratives just discussed, which are essentially Ó Néill narratives that incorporate Ó Domhnaill elements also. This Maolmhuire was clearly of some interest to the annalists, for they took the trouble to record his ancestry in some detail.[109]

One can only speculate about the life of these stories before their inclusion as written narratives in the annals. In so far as any of this late sixteenth-century material might be attributed to the historian employed as *ollamh* to Ó Domhnaill, it could perhaps be identified as the work of Maccon Ó Cléirigh. The vivid narratives, which can be imagined as oral performances, might well have been the creation of Maccon, whose 1595 obituary made special mention of his

---

105 *AFM*, V, pp 1768–9.   106 *AFM*, V, pp 1812–13.   107 *AFM*, V, pp 1812–13.   108 *AFM*, V, pp 1814–15.   109 His ancestry, and also his association with Ó Néill is noted in Pender (ed.), 'O'Clery book of genealogies', 115, items 1569–70, *mac don Diarmait sin an Maol muire baoi ag úa Neill (: Toirrdelbach Luineach).*

oratorical skills: *soerlabhraidh soingthe co mbuaidh ninnsgni, naitheisg 7 nerlabhra* ('a fluent orator, with the gift of elocution, address and eloquence').[110]

Narratives adapted from Beatha Aodha Ruaidh Uí Dhomhnaill

Given the prominence accorded to narratives of Ó Domhnaill military exploits throughout the late medieval sections of AFM, the inclusion also in these annals of long passages of narrative prose recounting the military exploits of Aodh Ruadh Ó Domhnaill in the years 1587 to 1602 is easily understood. The text known as *Beatha Aodha Ruaidh Uí Dhomhnaill* was the source of much of this post-1587 material.[111] At the time the annals were being compiled, Lughaidh son of Maccon Ó Cléirigh's heroic biography of Aodh Ruadh was a very recent composition, having been written after 1616 and perhaps as late as 1627.[112] Its author was highly regarded by Mícheál Ó Cléirigh, who counted his older cousin Lughaidh among the experts in the language from whom he had learned most.[113] Its content was appropriate to AFM in that it told the story of a hero of the Uí Dhomhnaill; its political bias was in line with that of the annalists in that it deliberately emphasized Ó Domhnaill achievements at the expense of those of the Uí Néill. And in terms of the years it covered, it was a ready-made source that covered a period of recent history, 1587–1602, for which relatively few other Gaelic documentary sources appear to have been available. Just when the annals were in danger of petering out in the latter part of the sixteenth century for lack of source material, this comprehensive, learned account, written to the highest contemporary standards of scholarship by a historian of impeccable pedigree, must have seemed a godsend.

Perhaps the greatest difficulty with *Beatha Aodha Ruaidh*, from the perspective of the annalists, was that the text was quite different in scope to most of the other source material used by the Four Masters. Although Lughaidh Ó Cléirigh's text was arranged chronologically, with the events of each successive year dealt with in separate sections, its discursive style contrasted with most of the other material available to them, and considerable editing of the material was deemed necessary.[114] Nonetheless, to the modern reader, the material derived from *Beatha Aodha Ruaidh* incorporated into AFM is so extensive as effectively to alter the nature of the annals for the years after 1587. The juxtaposition of lengthy passages recounting the exploits of Aodh Ruadh Ó Domhnaill through the 1590s with very short annalistic entries on Thomond affairs, for instance, serves to emphasize the imbalances of the Four Masters' text. Yet, when the

---

110 *AFM*, VI, pp 1960–1. 111 Paul Walsh (ed.), *Beatha Aodha Ruaidh Uí Dhomhnaill* (2 vols, ITS XLII, XLV, Dublin, 1948–57). 112 Mícheál Mac Craith, 'The *Beatha* in the context of the literature of the Renaissance' in Ó Riain (ed.), *Beatha Aodha Ruaidh*, p. 53. 113 Mícheul O Cléirigh, *Focloir no sanasan nua* (Louvain 1643), preface. 114 The date headings for each year are in the form of marginal annotations in Cú Choigcríche Ó Cléirigh's copy of the text (RIA MS 23 P 24).

Beatha Aodha Ruaidh material is compared with the earlier narratives of Ó Domhnaill military exploits already considered in this chapter, the annalists' perception of the appropriateness of including most of the *Beatha Aodha Ruaidh* narrative is easier to understand. When looked at as discrete episodes, rather than as a continuous narrative, it is essentially a succession of chronologically arranged episodes not dissimilar to the earlier narratives of Ó Domhnaill exploits the annalists had already used. The Four Masters consciously segmented *Beatha Aodha Ruaidh* into separate episodes to adhere to their established annalistic style. The richness of the source in respect of the number and length of 'stories' it contained would not have been perceived by the annalists as a shortcoming.

Thus, the long AFM description derived from *Beatha Aodha Ruaidh* of an expedition to Connacht in 1595 is a typical narrative of a successful episode showing Ó Domhnaill's success, even when outnumbered by the opposition.[115] The corresponding passage in *Beatha Aodha Ruaidh* is considerably longer, and whole sections have been omitted from the version in AFM, though their account is still substantial.[116] It is much more heavily edited than were equivalent Ó Domhnaill narratives earlier adapted from AU or other annals. The important revisions are concerned with bolstering the role of Ó Domhnaill. Most obviously, where *Beatha Aodha Ruaidh* recounted the two sides of the story, detailing not just the actions and objectives of Ó Domhnaill, but also of Sir Richard Bingham, governor of Connacht, the AFM version concentrates almost exclusively on the achievement of Ó Domhnaill and his followers. Thus, the success of Ó Domhnaill's men in collecting large preys throughout mid-Connacht is at the core of the AFM narrative. In contrast, the *Beatha Aodha Ruaidh* narrative follows this episode with an account of Bingham's response, from which it is clear that Ó Domhnaill had no easy victory. Apart from greatly abbreviating the description of the strategy and actions of the English in this encounter, the Four Masters make a significant number of other changes to the text. When describing the raiding by Ó Domhnaill's followers, they insert a phrase, not found in *Beatha Aodha Ruaidh*, asserting that this was done on Ó Domhnaill's instructions, acting *amhail ro theccaiscc riumh dóibh ré ttocht an dú sin* ('as he [O'Donnell] had instructed them before they arrived at that place').[117] The annalists add details not in *Beatha Aodha Ruaidh* about the limited number of Ó Domhnaill's followers *uair nocha raibhe acht ceithre chéd nama fri hengnamh 7 fri hursclaighi* ('being only four hundred men fit for valour and action'), explaining that few had joined his muster apart from the Cinéal Conaill.[118] They draw particular attention to this, recounting that, at one point, Ó Domhnaill had halted his troops, arrayed and reviewed them. Again, in the description of their raiding, a reference is added to the manner in which the fewness of their number was

---

115 *AFM*, VI, pp 1960–5 (AFM 1595.8).   116 Walsh (ed.), *BARUD*, I, pp 80–5 (§40–§42).
117 *AFM*, VI, pp 1962–3 (AFM 1595.8).   118 *AFM*, VI, pp 1960–3.

disguised: *Ro badh lór do dhicleith an tslóigh íshin an dluimh-cheó diadh 7 dethaighe ro leth o na forloisccthibh in gach airm ro gabsat an slócch dá gach leth i nuirtimcheall Ratha Cruachan* ('The dense cloud of vapour and smoke which spread in every place where these forces passed, all around Rathcroghan, was enough to conceal their numbers').[119] The description of the less successful elements of Ó Domhnaill's expedition found in *Beatha Aodha Ruaidh* is curtailed in the AFM version, and the narrative hurries to its formulaic conclusion, where *Ar a aoí do deachattar Cenel cConaill tars an abhainn, 7 do chóttar dia ttighibh co na nédálaibh iar mbuaidh 7 cosgar* ('The Kinel-Connell, however, crossed the river, and went to their houses and carried off their spoils, after triumph').[120]

Aside from the changes in content, designed to enhance the image of Ó Domhnaill's leadership, the AFM version of this episode is altered in other ways too. As elsewhere, the language is modernized; the annalists choosing to dispense with most of Lughaidh Ó Cléirigh's archaisms.[121] Their revisions in this regard are not just orthographic; many of the surplus adjectives and descriptive phrases are omitted. They also chose to omit most of the archaic forms of place-names that Lughaidh Ó Cléirigh had inserted into his text. Thus, where the *Beatha Aodha Ruaidh* version has:

BARUD
Aissidhe dhóibh co taoi tóithenach tre Magh Luirg an Dághdha 7 tre Mhag Aoi an Fhinnbheandaigh go riachtatar la dobharshoillsi na maidne to Cruachanraith Aoi.
(From that silently through Moylurg of the Daghdha and through Magh Aoi Finnbendaig, till they came at the twilight of the morning to Cruachan, the fort of Aoi.)[122]

the corresponding narrative in AFM simplifies the place-names in this, to read *assaidhe dóibh tré Moigh Luircc, 7 tre Moigh Naoí co riachtattar lá dobharsoillsi na maidne co Ráith Cruachan* ('from thence they proceeded through Moylurg and Moy-Nai, and next morning, by break of day, arrived at Rathcroghan').[123] The allusions to heroic stories associated with each place mentioned in *Beatha Aodha Ruaidh* were deemed superfluous by the Four Masters. This may have been merely out of concern to avoid cluttering the text, but it this instance it might have been because the heroes alluded to could not be regarded as historical personages, or simply because those stories might be unfamiliar to their intended European audience.

The editorial process of the Four Masters in this instance is in accord with the evidence discussed by P.A. Breatnach in respect of a selection of other sample passages where the annalists' editorial process involved disgarding 'all but the

---

119 *AFM*, VI, pp 1962–3.   120 *AFM*, VI, pp 1964–5.   121 For further discussion of this feature, see Breatnach, 'Irish records of the Nine Years' War', 129–46, and McManus, 'The language of the *Beatha*', passim.   122 *BARUD*, i, pp 80–1.   123 *AFM*, VI, pp 1962–6.

factual record of significant events'.[124] As seen in the 1595 example considered above, they are, in addition, selective in their use of the facts available to them in *Beatha Aodha Ruaidh*. Some differences of emphasis emerge, and the annalists are rather more supportive of Donnchadh Ó Briain, earl of Thomond, than was Lughaidh Ó Cléirigh. Whereas Thomond was severely criticized in *Beatha Aodha Ruaidh* for his pro-English stance,[125] the AFM account merely recorded Ó Domhnaill's decision to plunder Thomond.[126]

Individuals whom the annalists regarded as peripheral to their chronicle were treated rather less sympathetically in AFM than was the central character. Thus, Fiach son of Aodh Ó Beirn, eulogized by Lughaidh Ó Cleirigh in his account of the events of 1592,[127] was merely mentioned in passing in AFM. The annalists simply recorded that he was at war with the English. Again, in keeping with their approach throughout their text, the Four Masters omitted many of the minor characters that had found a place in Lughaidh Ó Cléirigh's narrative.

The annalists added new material at the same time as omitting passages from their source text. The extent of their revisions indicates that the annalists had their own view of how the history of the exploits of Aodh Ruadh Ó Domhnaill should be recounted, and were prepared to adapt the content and perspective of their source text when creating their own narrative. This highlights again the extent to which the annalists were consciously presenting a new account of the Irish past, even while drawing extensively on pre-existing sources. Their selective and creative use of the material from *Beatha Aodha Ruaidh* illustrates that the Four Masters did have their own vision of the way the Irish past should be construed. That vision can be discerned in their pages, while the earlier layers on which they built have been altered and reshaped in the process.

Conclusion

Despite the strong editorial hand of the Four Masters, no single political outlook is consistently presented. The political sophistication of the Ó Domhnaill narratives, particularly those for the sixteenth century, is not always matched by other episodes. In some cases they appear to allow the sources to speak for themselves even to the extent of preserving the political bias of those sources (as suggested by the case of Sir Henry Sidney, discussed earlier). When the narratives recounted in the final years of the annals, after 1587, based on Lughaidh Ó Cléirigh's biography of Aodh Ruadh, are contrasted with the earlier Ó Domhnaill military narratives, the altered political outlook is particularly noticeable. The enemy is different, and the stakes are higher. There is a new emphasis on the religious faith of the protagonists, on the providence of God, and on the consequences of exile if they lose.

124 Breatnach, 'Irish records of the Nine Years' War', p. 146.   125 *BARUD*, i, pp 196–7.
126 *AFM*, VI, pp 2096–7.   127 *BARUD*, i, pp 22–3; *AFM*, VI, pp 1916–17.

AFM 1601

Ro badh daighlíon tabharta tachair 7 cloite catha dia neccraittibh cidh araill do na
fóirnibh báttar isin ffoslongport sin cen co mbittís féin uile ag congnamh fri aroile, dia
ndeonaiccheadh dia dóibh cathucchadh co séitreach síor chalma daoín mhenmain, 7 daon
aonta tar cend a nirsi, 7 a nathardha isin deidhendáil thennta i tecomnaccair a
mbiodhbhadha aca don chur sin.

(Efficient for giving the onset, and gaining the battle over their enemies, were the
tribes who were in this camp (although some of them did not assist one another),
had God permitted them to fight stoutly with one mind and one accord, in defence
of their religion and their patrimony, in the strait difficulty in which they had the
enemy on this occasion.)[128]

It is a life or death scenario, with the prospect of life in the aftermath of defeat
seeming worse than death itself.[129]

AFM 1601

Bá hádhbhal, 7 bá dírim in ro fáccbhadh isin maigin sin gér bhó dedhbal an líon do
rochrattar ann, uair ro fáccbhadh gérraideacht 7 gaiscceadh, 7 rath 7 roconach, uaisle
7 ionnsaicchidh, aireachas 7 airbeart, eineach, 7 eangnamh, cródhacht 7 cosnamh,
crábhad 7 caoín iris insi Gaoidheal isin iomairecc sin.

(Immense and countless was the loss in that place, although the number slain was
trifling; for the prowess and valour, prosperity and affluence, nobleness and
chivalry, dignity and renown, hospitality and generosity, bravery and protection,
devotion and pure religion, of the Island of the Gaeil, were lost in this
engagement.)[130]

Drawing on the political ideas of faith and fatherland evident in *Beatha Aodha
Ruaidh*, the annalists belatedly gave expression to an idea of Ireland that had
relevance to their circumstances in the 1630s. They did not, however, attempt a
systematic politicization of the detail of their earlier narratives in the light of that
new vision of Ireland. Because of this, when seeking to understand their political
reading of the present by reference to their representation of the past, it is not
enough to look at individual passages of the text in isolation; they should also be
viewed in the context of the complete work. While admitting the undoubted
inconsistencies of political perspective discernible between different parts of the
text derived from contrasting types of sources, it may be possible nonetheless to
discern the political meaning of the Four Masters' historical construct in its
entirety. The annals that ended with a politicized expression of loss, as
represented in the heroic life, exile and death of Aodh Ruadh Ó Domhnaill, were
the same annals that documented the continuity of the kingship of Ireland from
the beginning of recorded time. That was their essence.

128 *AFM*, VI, pp 2280–1.   129 *AFM*, VI, pp 2292–3.   130 *AFM*, VI, pp 2288–9.

The long and elaborate process of recalling and recording all of the narratives that were incorporated into the annals, in all their diversity, can be seen as the Four Masters' own contribution to counteracting the consequences of defeat and loss. The present was given meaning through its being contextualized by reference to past heroism, leadership and bravery. In their own act of heroism, the Four Masters had provided detailed documentary evidence regarding the patrimony of the Gaeil, of the ancestral territory that belonged to them, and of the heroic achievements of the leading families that had lived there through the ages. It was done according to the highest standards of scholarship within their profession, drawing its authority as well as its evidence from earlier sources, by being modelled on them. Their work was both an example and an expression of the value of cultural memory.[131]

In the face of the power vacuum in the Gaelic world after the deaths in exile of the northern lords, the annalists recalled many diverse stories of their ancestors within the setting of the Gaelic lordships in which they had lived over the centuries and down to their own day. The reality of lost political power and the failure of military strategy in their own generation made it imperative for them to preserve the memory of past honour and glory by recalling acts of valour and heroism by ancestral heroes. It is this elemental characteristic, the very existence of these annals as a scholarly record of the history of a people, written from their own perspective and in their own language, that contributed to their iconic status in the nineteenth and twentieth centuries.

The Four Masters did not include themselves in their chronicle, though some people personally known to them in the Donegal Franciscan convent were allowed cameo appearances. Yet, their engagement with, and influence over, communal memories of the past, through their scholarly activities, was not an exercise in detachment. The writing of Irish history did not happen outside of history, but within it, forming and being formed by the cultural and political context from which it emerged. There is a sense in which the very act of compiling these annals was the logical outcome of all that had gone before. The telling of these stories in one large-scale chronicle, that had its origins at the beginning of recorded time, was a statement of confidence in the power of the recall of the past. The annalists' achievement was to give voice to a continuing belief in the value of the memory of past heroism in the new Ireland that was being formed for the future out of the political and social upheaval experienced in their own lifetimes.

---

131 In his biographical narrative, Lughaidh Ó Cléirigh had made explicit reference to the importance of story and memory in the formation of Aodh Ó Domhnaill's character, and in directing his efforts against the English (*BARUD*, i, pp 12–13, 60–1). These allusions are diluted in AFM, being restricted to factual details (*AFM*, V, pp 1866–7), but as professional chroniclers the Four Masters would have had their own clear understanding of the power of story.

CHAPTER EIGHT

Holy men and holy places

Introduction: ecclesiastical bias

The Four Masters' political bias in favour of the Uí Dhomhnaill is one of the defining characteristics of the early modern section of their annals, but their interest in matters ecclesiastical permeates the text over a much longer time-span. Despite their secular focus, ecclesiastical topics feature prominently in AFM from the coming of Christianity to Ireland in the fifth century down to the sixteenth century. Since the annals were conceived as part of a wider research project, encompassing also the lives of saints and structured hagiological compilations such as the Martyrology of Donegal, the manner in which ecclesiastical material is presented in AFM is part of a bigger story.

Over time, the ratio of secular to ecclesiastical entries in AFM increases steadily. In the coverage of the seventh century, there were approximately one and a half times as many secular as ecclesiastical entries; by the fifteenth century there were more than ten times as many secular as ecclesiastical entries in AFM. This general trend is largely a reflection of the content of the sources from which the annalists derived their material, and in particular the ecclesiastical provenance of the earlier sources. A broadly similar trend is discernible in AU, particularly in the later middle ages.

While the proportion of ecclesiastical entries in AFM declines over time, there is nonetheless a strong religious dimension to the text throughout. Thus, in obituaries for secular personalities, their deaths are normally contextualized in religious as well as in secular terms. This is essentially a continuation of a practice that had become standard in earlier annals and owes much to the medieval Christian ethos of their source texts. The present discussion does not focus on that general Christian outlook in the secular obituaries but rather on the particular manner of presentation in AFM of historical material relating to ecclesiastical persons – saints, abbots, bishops, popes and other clergy – and also ecclesiastical establishments both monastic and secular.

While their late medieval annalistic sources shaped their text to a significant extent, the editorial influence of the Four Masters is clearly discernible in the selection, arrangement and omission of entries on ecclesiastical themes. A significant proportion of the ecclesiastical entries were later editorial additions to the autograph manuscripts of AFM, but such additions were almost invariably

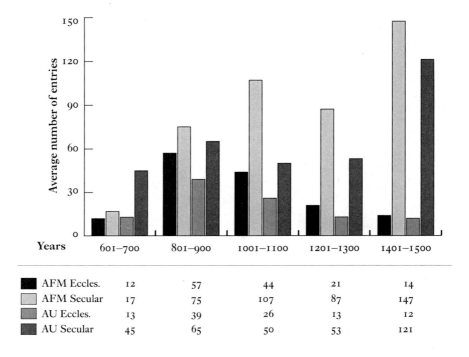

	AFM Eccles.	12	57	44	21	14
AFM Secular	17	75	107	87	147
AU Eccles.	13	39	26	13	12
AU Secular	45	65	50	53	121

8.1 Proportion of secular and ecclesiastical entries in AFM and AU, for sample dates from the seventh to the fifteenth century[1]

inserted at the beginning of the entry for a given year, which had the effect of prioritizing them.

The compilers cast their net widely, drawing on sources not included in earlier annals, as well as selecting and adapting ecclesiastical material from earlier annals to present it in a new way. Just as the Four Masters could simultaneously draw on medieval annals and contemporary Counter-Reformation histories of monastic foundations as source texts, so also did their intellectual approach to those sources combine aspects of the medieval and the modern.

The Counter-Reformation dimension

History was a tool of the Counter-Reformation, and among the objectives of the Four Masters was to supply a weapon in the armoury of Catholic Irish scholarly contributors to the debate over the true church.[2] It should come as no surprise,

1 Calculated from a sample of 10 per cent of annal entries recorded for each century. 2 Ó Buachalla, '*Annála ríoghachta Éireann* is *Foras feasa ar Éirinn*', 59–105; Cunningham, 'The culture and ideology of Irish Franciscan historians at Louvain', pp 11–30; 222–7; Momigliano, *Studies in historiography*, pp 1–39. At an international level, the annals of Caesar Baronius set the standard for

therefore, to find entries such as that recorded under the year 1537, describing the coming of religious reform to Ireland in terms quite new in the context of annalistic writing in Ireland.

The events recounted by the Four Masters concerning the impact of the Reformation had happened almost exactly one hundred years before the date of writing. The terminology of heresy and persecution they use is typical of continental Counter-Reformation writing of the seventeenth century.[3] The external English origin of the religious changes imposed in the 1530s is emphasized, and the focus is on the destruction of monasteries and of shrines and relics of saints, together with the attempted creation of an alternative ecclesiastical hierarchy. It is the contextual elements – the sentences with which the AFM description of the Reformation opens and concludes – that introduce the interpretive difference between these annals and earlier compilations such as AConn and ALCé.

AFM 1537

Eithriticceacht, 7 sechrán nua hi Saxaibh tria dhiumas, 7 ionnoccbháil tria accobhar, 7 antoil, 7 tré iomatt ealadhan néccsamhail co ndeachattar Fir Saxan i nacchaidh an Phapa 7 na Rómha acht atá ní chena ro adhrattar do bharamhlaibh examhlaibh, 7 do shenreacht Maoísi ar aithris an cinidh Iudaighe, 7 ro ghairsiot airdchenn ecclaisi Dé ina flaithes fein don righ. Do rónadh las an righ 7 las an ccomhairle dlighthe 7 statuiti nuaidhe iar na ttoil fein.

...

Do rónadh leó tra airdepscoip, 7 Suibepscoip aca fein, 7 ger mhor inghreim na nimpiredh Rómhanach i nacchaidh na heccailsi as suaill iná tainic a chomhmór so on Róimh anoir riamh conách eittir a tuaruscbháil, dfhaisneis nó dinnisin muna naisneidedh an tí do chonnairc í.

(A heresy and a new error [sprang up] in England, through pride, vain-glory, avarice and lust, and through many strange sciences, so that the men of England went into opposition to the pope and to Rome. They at the same time adopted various opinions, and [among others] the old law of Moses, in imitation of the Jewish people; and they styled the king the chief head of the Church of God in his own kingdom. New laws and statutes were enacted by the king and council [parliament] according to their own will.

...

They also appointed archbishops and sub-bishops for themselves; and, though great was the persecution of the Roman emperors against the Church, scarcely had there ever come so great a persecution from Rome as this; so that it is impossible to narrate or tell its description, unless it should be narrated by one who saw it.)[4]

The sixteenth-century narrative preserved in earlier annals, notably both AConn and ALCé, though itself second-hand, concentrates on the destruction of

Catholic history in the Counter-Reformation era. See Pullapilly, *Caesar Baronius*. 3 The changing terminology of persecution is discussed in B. Cunningham and R. Gillespie, '"Persecution" in seventeenth-century Irish', *Éigse* 22 (1987), 15–20. 4 *AFM*, V, pp 1444–9.

images, concluding with a vague reference to the implications for ecclesiastical politics.

> AConn 1538.6
>
> *Et ni hedh amain acht ni roibhe croch naomh na delp Mure na imáigh orrdeirc a nErinn ara ndechaid a cumachta nar loisced leo, et ni mo do bi ord dona vii. n-ordaib ara ndechaid a cumochta a nErinn nar sgrisadar 7 an Papa 7 an Eclais abus 7 toir ac coinnelbhathad na Saxanach trid sin. Et ni derbh lim nac arin mbliadain-si fúas da so.* (More than this, there was no holy Cross or effigy of Mary or famous image in Ireland which they did not burn if it fell into their power; nor was there one of the seven Orders which their power could reach in Ireland that they did not destroy; and on that account the pope and the Church both here and in the east were excommunicating the English. And I am not sure that this entry does not belong to the previous year.)[5]

The entry on the theme of the Reformation recorded under the year 1537 in AFM brings together in one succinct narrative a diverse range of religious themes that permeate the entire annalistic compilation: saints and their continuing influence in the world; the monastic structure particularly in its Franciscan expression; and the lives of worthy ecclesiastical personalities both secular and regular. The treatment of all three themes in AFM can be distinguished from the way similar material is presented in other extant annals, most particularly AU and AClon. A closer look at how these various kinds of ecclesiastical entries are handled allows the ethos of the AFM text emerge more clearly.

Hagiography

Since AFM was conceived in part as a secular historical framework to serve as a work of reference to complement the hagiographical texts that were being collected and prepared for publication at Louvain, it is not surprising that the cult of saints had a strong influence on the character of the text throughout. There is some evidence that the Louvain interest in particular saints, notably the three national patrons, Patrick, Colum Cille and Brigit, but also certain other key saints such as Malachy, prompted the Four Masters to give special attention to the entries on these saints in their annals. The annals were not, however, designed to incorporate lengthy entries on the lives of individual saints. Although the Four Masters appear to have recognized the significance of these key saints they carefully controlled the form and content of the obituary of each saint. Thus, for example, considering his significance for the Donegal-based compilers, the obituary of St Colum Cille is very restrained in terms of length, and is quite traditional in content. The inclusion of verse passages to supplement

---

5 *AConn*, pp 710–11. The entry in ALCé is virtually identical.

the prose summary is a feature of both secular and ecclesiastical obituaries in AFM down to the eleventh century, but is not an exclusive stylistic element of the compilers' own choosing. Generally, their inclusion of such material can be accounted for by its inclusion in conjunction with prose in their source texts.

AFM 592

Colum Cille, mac Feaidhlimidh, apstal Alban, ceann crabhaidh ermhoir Ereann, 7 Alban iar bPattraicc, décc ina ecclais fein in hI ind Albain, iars an ccúicceadh bliadhain triochad a oilithre, oidhce domhnaigh do shundradh an 9 lá Iunii. Seacht mbliadhna seachtmoghatt a aois uile an tan ro faoidh a spiorait dochum nimhe, amhail asberar isin rann:

> *Teora bliadhna bai gan lés*
> *Colum ina Duibhreglés,*
> *Luidh go haingli asa chacht*
> *iar seacht mbliadhna seachtmoghat.*

(Colum Cille, son of Feidhlimidh, apostle of Alba [Scotland], head of the piety of the most part of Ireland and Alba, [next] after Patrick, died in his own church in Hy, in Alba, after the thirty-fifth year of his pilgrimage, on Sunday night precisely, the 9th day of June. Seventy-seven years was his whole age when he resigned his spirit to heaven, as is said in this quatrain:

> Three years without light was Colum in his Duibh-regles;
> He went to the angels from his body, after seven years and seventy.)[6]

There was plentiful material on the life of Colum Cille available to the Four Masters, not least from Ó Cléirigh's earlier hagiological compilation, the Martyrology of Donegal. However, this material was scarcely used in the corresponding entry on Colum Cille in the annals; the only passage common to the Martyrology and AFM is the quatrain on the age of the saint at his death.[7] Whereas the Martyrology of Donegal contained extracts from descriptions of many episodes in the life of the saint, drawing in particular on the extensive treatment in the early sixteenth-century prose life of the saint, *Betha Colaim Chille*, the short obituary in AFM entirely omitted those narrative episodes.[8] And although *Amra Coluim Cille*, the hagiographical poem attributed to Dallán Forgaill, would have been familiar to the Four Masters, either from *Leabhar na hUidhre*[9] or at least from extracts in *Betha Colaim Chille*, they did not use it in this instance. The verse attributed to Dallán Forgaill, which follows on from this passage as though it was part of the obituary of Colum Cille in O'Donovan's

6 *AFM*, I, pp 214–17.   7 *MDon*, pp 152–3.   8 One point of difference between AFM and the Martyrology of Donegal is the date of death given for St Colum Cille, AFM entering the obituary under AD592, while the martyrology indicates AD599. This appears to be an error, as AFM normally follows the dates recorded in the Martyrology of Donegal in its obituaries of saints (*MDon*, p. 152n). *Betha Colaim Chille* is attributed to the initiative of Maghnus Ó Domhnaill, though it is probable that he was patron rather than compiler of the work.   9 Best and Bergin (eds), *Lebor na hUidre*, 11–41; Kenney, *The sources for the early history of Ireland*, pp 426–7, 716–18.

edition of the annals, is in fact an interpolation in the autograph manuscript by a later annotator, Henry Búrc, and is not part of the Four Masters' text.[10]

Another source of hagiological material well known to Mícheál Ó Cléirigh and his collaborator Cú Choigcríche Ó Cléirigh was the metrical version of *Naoimhsenchas naomh Insi Fáil.* Cú Choigcríche Ó Cléirigh had prepared a new recension of this work at the request of the Donegal Franciscans.[11] However, the stanzas on Colum Cille from this source were not used in AFM – a further indication that the Four Masters may have had no wish to occupy space in their annals with hagiographical material that they themselves had already incorporated into other manuscript compilations.

Colum Cille was one of the three saints given special attention by Thomas Messingham in his 1624 publication *Florilegium insulae sanctorum*,[12] by Robert Rochford in his 1625 compilation published at St Omer,[13] and of course by John Colgan who published five distinct lives of Colum Cille as part of his 1647 collection, *Trias thaumaturga*.[14] That the expanded emphasis on Colum Cille, together with Brigit and Patrick, is a feature of the seventeenth century is apparent from the references to saints in the religious poetry of the early modern period. While mid-seventeenth-century poetic compositions such as *An síogaí romhánach* invoke these saints, in fifteenth- and early sixteenth-century poetry on religious themes the saints invoked tend to be non-Irish ones such as St Catherine, St Margaret, St Dominic and St Francis.[15]

The AFM entry on St Colum Cille under the year AD592 could thus be interpreted as being consistent with the trend towards emphasis on Irish saints discernible in the religious poetry of the seventeenth century. It is considerably more substantial than the equivalent annalistic entries in AU and the Annals of Inisfallen, which merely record the vital dates of his life.

AU 594
Quies Coluim cille .u. idus iunii, anno aetatis sue lxx vi.
(The repose of Colum-Cille, on the 5th of the Ides of June, in the 76th year of his age.)[16]

---

10 RIA MS C iii 3, fo. 244. The same annotator, Henry Búrc, made a number of other signed additions to the manuscript in the 1640s. See, for example, RIA MS C iii 3, fos 1199, 220v–221, 226v. The corresponding entry on the death of Colum Cille in UCD–OFM MS A 13, fo. 257r contains no mention of Dallán Forgaill.   11 BR MS 2542–3, fos 1–20; Ó Riain (ed.), *Corpus genealogiarum sanctorum Hiberniae*, pp xl–xlii, 79–108.   12 (Paris, 1624). On Messingham's work, see O'Connor, 'Towards the invention of the Irish Catholic *natio*', 157–77.   13 R[ochford], *The life of the glorious bishop S. Patricke* (this work is signed merely 'Fr. B.B. one of the Irish Franciscan Friars at Lovain' (p. xvi), but since no Franciscan with those initials is known to have been in Louvain at the time it is now generally accepted as the work of Robert Rochford. The suggestion in Bianca Ross, *Britannia et Hibernia, Nationale und kulturelle Identitäten im Irland des 17. Jahrhunderts* (Heidelberg, 1998), p. 128, that the work might be attributed to Bonaventure Baron (b. 1610) is not sustainable, because he would have been merely 15 years old at the time of publication.   14 Colgan, *Trias thaumaturga*, pp 319–514.   15 For analysis of the representation of Irish and continental saints in late medieval Irish poetry, see Ryan, 'Popular religion in Gaelic Ireland, 1445–1645', I, pp 211–92.   16 *AU*, I, pp 74–7.

AI [597]

Quies Coluimb Cille nocte Dominica hi .ú. Íd Iúin anno .xxᵒx.u.ᵒ perigrinationis suae, aetate autem .lxxui.

(Repose of Colum Cille on Sunday night on the fifth of the Ides [9th] of June in the 35th year of his exile and in the 76th year of his age.)[17]

In contrast, Conall Mac Eochagáin's translation of AClon included an extended narrative of the life of St Colum Cille under the year 590, in a digression so long that it required 'But now to our History again' as a concluding phrase.[18] That some, at least, of the material on the life of St Colum Cille in the Mac Eochagáin text of AClon is a seventeenth-century insertion is obvious from the reference contained therein to Thomas Dempster's claim that both St Colum Cille and St Brigit were Scottish. Dempster's claims were first published in 1619, and reissued in 1627.[19] Mac Eochagáin, as translator, may well have been responsible for their inclusion here. The further account in AClon of a manuscript attributed to St Colum Cille being used to cure cattle, specifically stated to be an eyewitness account, might also be attributed to the translator. In addition, the occurrence of phrases such as 'as I said before' in relation to St Colum Cille's genealogy may also point to the mid-seventeenth-century translator being responsible for drafting most of this life of Colum Cille for inclusion in the AClon text.[20]

The AFM account of Colum Cille adopts a middle course between these extremes, being closer to the style of the Martyrology of Donegal than to that of other late medieval annals or martyrologies.[21] The extant annals that most closely resemble the general form of the AFM obituary of Colum Cille are those edited under the title *Fragmentary annals of Ireland* and thought to derive from the 'Book of Cluain Eidhneach'.[22]

FAI 595

Quies Coloim Cille .lxxui. anno aetatis suae. Unde Fedhelm cecinit:

> *Uch, iar fír,*
> *an th-e gabtha isin lín,*
> *h-e brecc baoi i mBoinn,*
> *Boand bruinnius in mur míl,*
> *Mur míl timcealla Iasconn,*
> *Iasconn do heimed a eithre;*
> *uch ar n-eccoibh mic an righ;*
> *uch iar ndith meic Eithne.*

---

17 *AI*, pp 80–1. 18 *AClon*, pp 91–6. 19 Dempster, *Scotorum scriptorum nomenclatura*; Dempster, *Historia ecclesiastica gentis Scottorum*. 20 *AClon*, pp 96, 92. There is no close association between the life of Colum Cille recorded in AClon and the material documented in the Martyrology of Donegal. 21 Their source was not the Martyrology of Gorman which merely records Colum Cille's death in three words '*Colum caemóg cille*' ('Dear and virginal Colomb cille'); see Stokes (ed.), *Félire hÚi Gormáin*, pp 112–13. 22 Joan N. Radner (ed.), *Fragmentary annals of Ireland* (Dublin, 1978), p. vii; the text is preserved in BR MS 5301–20. In this source the death of Colum Cille is

(The death of Colum Cille in the seventy-sixth year of his age; of which Fedelm sang:
>Alas, truly,
>for the salmon who was caught in the net;
>the speckled salmon that was in the Bóand,
>the Bóand that generates the wall of beasts;
>the wall of beasts that surrounds Iasconius,
>Iasconius who hides his fins;
>alas for the death of the king's son;
>alas for the destruction of Eithne's son.)[23]

Yet, the content of the AFM obituary appears to be entirely independent of the entry in the *Fragmentary annals*. It appears that the Four Masters were reluctant to rely on the obituaries of Colum Cille that might have been available to them in any of the secular annals.

While the AFM versions of the obituary of Colum Cille appear distinctive in an annalistic context, this is not always the case in respect of other saints. Thus, for instance, the Four Masters' AD1129 obituary of St Ceallach, archbishop of Armagh, corresponds quite closely to those in AU and ALCé.[24] The entry is a late insertion by the editorial hands in each of the autograph manuscripts of AFM, and was little modified as compared with older sources.[25] It is clear that only a small number of key saints were singled out for special treatment by the Four Masters. Predictably enough, in contrast to Colum Cille, the entry on Ceallach found in the Martyrology of Donegal is very insubstantial.[26]

Two national patron saints, Patrick and Brigit, whose lives were extensively publicized on the continent by Thomas Messingham and John Colgan in texts that also promoted the cult of Colum Cille, are given distinctive treatment in AFM. As already seen, there is clear evidence that the AFM obituary of St Patrick was enhanced as compared with the available annalistic sources covering the fifth century.[27] The enhancement seems to have been designed to make the entry more acceptable to those familiar with continental Counter-Reformation ecclesiastical history. The life of St Brigit, the third of the national patron saints, was likewise enhanced in AFM as compared with that found in older annals. Thus, under the year 523, AU simply recorded *Quies sanctae Brigitae anno lxx aetatis sue* ('Rest of Saint Brigit, in the 70th year of her age').[28] In contrast, a short, simple biography was included in AFM, one that clearly linked her to the founding of a religious house at Kildare and made specific reference to the availability of the text of her life and those of other saints.

---

recorded under the year 595.   **23** Radner (ed.), *Fragmentary annals*, pp 4–5.   **24** Ceallach features very prominently throughout his career in both AFM and ALCé, being mentioned in twelve entries between the years 1106 and his death in 1129; AU contains thirteen references to the same saint in the same period.   **25** UCD–OFM MS A 13, fo. 486r, RIA MS C iii 3, fo. 482r; *AFM*, II, pp 1032–5; c.f. *ALCé*, I, pp 126–7 and *AU*, II, pp 120–3.   **26** *MDon*, pp 92–93, entry for 1 April.   **27** See pp 159–68, above.   **28** *AU*, I, pp 40–1.

AFM 525

S. Brighit ogh, banab Chille dara [décc]. As disidhe cetus ro hiodhbradh Cill dara, 7 ba lé conrodacht. Así Brighit tra ná tucc a meanmain ná a hinntheifimh as in coimdheadh eadh naonuaire riamh acht a siorluadh, 7 a siorsmuaineadh do grés ina cridhe 7 menmain, amhail as errderc ina bethaidh fein, 7 i mbethaidh naoimh Brenainn, espucc Cluana ferta. Ro thochaith imorro a haimsir acc foghnamh go diochra don coimdhe, ag denomh fert 7 miorbhal, ag slánucchad gach galair 7 gach tedhma archena, amhail aisnéidhes a betha, go ro faoidh a spirat do chum nimhe, an céd lá do mí Febhru, 7 ro hadhnacht a corp i nDún i naon tumba la Patraicc, co nonoir 7 co nairmidin.

(Saint Brigit, virgin, Abbess of Cill-dara [died]. It was to her Cill-dara was first granted, and by her it was founded. Brigit was she who never turned her mind or attention from the Lord for the space of one hour, but was constantly meditating and thinking of him in her heart and mind, as in evident in her own Life, and in the Life of St Brenainn, bishop of Cluain-fearta. She spent her time diligently serving the Lord, performing wonders and miracles, healing every disease and every malady, as her Life relates, until she resigned her spirit to heaven, the first day of the month of February; and her body was interred at Dun, in the same tomb with Patrick, with honour and veneration.)[29]

While a vast amount of material on Brigit was available to John Colgan, some of it supplied by Mícheál Ó Cléirigh himself,[30] the Four Masters did not use that material in their annals. Their obituary of Brigit is much shorter even than the entry at 1 February in the Martyrology of Donegal.[31] The annalists were content simply to record the patron saint's association with the monastic foundation at Kildare, her piety, her miracle working, and the date and place of her burial. This was sufficient to establish her position in the chronology and topography of Irish ecclesiastical history, which may have been as much as the annals were concerned to achieve. The AFM entry itself made reference to the fact that the detail of Brigit's miracles and wonders was documented elsewhere 'as her life relates', a formula used in the Martyrology of Donegal also.[32]

The inclusion of the 1148 obituary of St Malachy is a particular instance where new material was deliberately incorporated into AFM. John Colgan highlighted the importance of Malachy in the story of Irish ecclesiastical life in his preface to *Acta sanctorum Hiberniae*, presenting the saint's career as one of the great turning points in the history of the Irish church. For Colgan, the key to the transformation of the Irish church in the twelfth century was not the institutional reform of Irish dioceses, but rather the example of the devout life of St Malachy.[33]

29 *AFM*, I, pp 170–3. 30 John Colgan published six lives of Brigit in Latin, including a verse life for which he also printed the Irish text (*Trias thaumaturga*, pp 515–634). Mícheál Ó Cléirigh's collection of saints' lives in BR MS 4190–200 includes part of a life of Brigit (fos 6–30v). 31 *MDon*, pp 34–7. 32 *MDon*, pp 36–7. 33 Colgan, *Acta sanctorum Hiberniae*, *prefatio ad lectorem*, sig. b 2. Since Malachy's feast day was in November, Colgan's published research, which included saints whose feast days fell in the months of January to March, did not include any lives

The events of 1148, the year of Malachy's death, are not recorded in any of the extant annals such as AU, AI or AClon, due perhaps to partial loss of texts, and so it cannot be established conclusively whether an obituary of Malachy was included in any earlier annals consulted by the Four Masters. Elements of the AFM obituary of Malachy, including the reference to the changes made regarding his feast day, may reflect seventeenth-century concerns about the commemoration of saints and their status within the church. It seems clear, therefore, that whether or not an obituary of St Malachy was available from an older annalistic source, the Four Masters deemed the model used in the Martyrology of Donegal more appropriate.

AFM 1148

Malachias .i. Maolmaedhócc Ua Morghair, airdepscop cathaoire Padraicc, airdcenn iarthair Eorpa, legaite comharba Petair aoin cheand ro riaraighset Gaoidhil, 7 Goill, ardshaoi in eaccna, 7 a ccrábhadh, lochrann solusta no shoillsighedh tuatha 7 eccalsa tria forcheatal, 7 chaoin gníomha, aoghaire tairisi na heccailsi co coitcend, iar noirdneadh do epscop 7 sacart, 7 aos gacha graidh archena, iar ccoisreagadh teampall 7 relgheadh niomdha, iar ndénamh gacha lubhra ecclastacdha sechnón Ereann, iar ttíodhnacal seód 7 bídh do thrénaibh 7 thruaghaibh, iar ffothughadh ceall 7 mainistreach, ar as leisiomh ro hathnuadhaighthe i nErinn, iar na ffailliughadh ó chéin mháir, gach eglais ro lécthi i faill, 7 i néislis, iar bfhághbhail gach riaghla 7 gach soibhésa in eaglaisibh Ereann archena, isin dara fecht a leccaidechta iar mbeith ceithre bliadhna décc ina priomhaidh, 7 iars an ceathramhadh bliadhain caeccat a aoisi, ro fhaidh a spirat do chum nimhe an dara lá do Nouember, 7 as ann cheleabraitt an eglais lith 7 sollamhain naomh Malachias ar an tres lá ar na claochlúdh las na sruithibh ó lá fhéle na marbh ar an lá na dhiaidh ar combadh usaide a erdach 7 a onóir, 7 ro hadhnacht, i mainistir S Bernard hi cClairualis hí fFrancoibh, go nonóir, 7 co nairmhittin.

(Malachias, i.e. Maelmaedhog Ua Morgair, archbishop of the Chair of Patrick, chief head of the west of Europe, legate of the successor of Peter, the only head whom the Irish and the foreigners obeyed, chief paragon of wisdom and piety, a brilliant lamp which illumined territories and churches by preaching and good works, faithful shepherd of the Church in general – after having ordained bishops and priests, and persons of every degree; after having consecrated many churches and cemeteries; after having performed every ecclesiastical work throughout Ireland; after having bestowed jewels and food upon the mighty and the needy; after having founded churches and monasteries (for by him were repaired in Ireland every church which had been consigned to decay and neglect, and they had been neglected from time remote); after leaving every rule and every good moral in the churches of Ireland in general; after having been the second time in the legateship; after having been fourteen years in the primacy; and after the fifty-fourth year of his age, resigned his spirit to heaven on the second day of

of St Malachy, but nonetheless Colgan commented on his significance in the preface to the first published volume of saints' lives. The other saints mentioned by Colgan in this regard were Celsius, Gelasius (Gilla Meic Liac) and Laurence (Lorcán Ó Tuathail).

November; and the Church celebrates the feast and solemnity of St Malachias on the third day, it having been changed by the seniors from the feast day of All Souls to the day after, in order that he might be the more easily revered and honoured; and he was buried in the monastery of St Bernard at Clarvallis, in France, with honour and veneration.)[34]

In essence, this corresponds to the entry on St Malachy recorded under 3 November in the Martyrology of Donegal, but with the addition of detail about the change in the saint's feast day; the clarification of the association of Clairvaux with St Bernard and the typical annalistic reference to burial *go nonóir, 7 co nairmhittin* ('with honour and veneration').[35] There is little that could not be regarded as pre-Tridentine about this entry, but the Four Masters were nonetheless keen to include in their secular annals due notice of St Malachy as a model among leaders of the medieval Irish church.

In contrast to the entries in AFM on the three national patron saints and on St Malachy, the obituary of St Ciarán is surprisingly short:

AFM 548
S. Ciarán, mac an tsaoir, ab Cluana mic Nóis, décc an naomhadh lá do September. Tri bliadhna triocha fot a shaoghail.
(St Ciarán, son of the artificer, abbot of Cluain-mic-Nois, died on the ninth day of September. Thirty-three years was the length of his life.)[36]

The detail regarding his genealogy and the name of his mother, along with a miracle story of his turning grain to gold recorded in the Martyrology of Donegal are omitted from AFM. Likewise, the parallel with the thirty-three years of the life of Christ, made explicit in the Martyrology of Donegal,[37] is left to the reader to discern in AFM. Other annals treat the saint rather differently. *Chronicum Scotorum* includes a stanza on his parentage, and combines the record of his death with a miracle story.[38] Not surprisingly, given his status as the founding saint of Clonmacnoise, a lengthy narrative on the life of St Ciarán is included in AClon. The entry intertwines the story of the secular patron, Diarmaid Ó Cearbhaill, with that of the saint.[39] The AClon narrative incorporates several stories of miracles associated with the saint, including one about king Diarmaid's sight being cured by the touch of clay from the grave of St Ciarán. None of the miracle stories found in AClon is documented in his obituary in AFM.

---

34 *AFM*, II, pp 1084–5.   35 *MDon*, pp 294–7.   36 *AFM*, I, pp 184–5. The obituary in AU 548 is even shorter, and calculated his life at 34 years. *Dormitacio filii artificis .i. Ciaraini, anno xxx iiii aetatis sue* 'The falling asleep of the son of the carpenter, i.e. Ciaran, in the 34th year of his age'. The 'A' manuscript of AU has an additional phrase referring to him having been seven years at Clonmacnoise.   37 *MDon*, pp 240–3.   38 *CS*, s.a. 544 (this story of the decapitation of Abacuc is found separately in AFM s.a. 539); see also UCD–OFM MS A 9, fo. 32b; Kenney, *Sources for the early history of Ireland*, p. 381.   39 *AClon*, pp 79–83.

As in other instances, details of the life and works of St Ciarán had been recorded by Mícheál Ó Cléirigh in the Martyrology of Donegal, according to the standard formula for such entries in the Martyrology, and the annalists did not attempt to replicate this work in AFM.[40] It seems that the Four Masters were concerned to give due recognition to major figures such as Patrick, Brigit, Colum Cille and Malachy, but in general they were careful to exclude the many miracle stories in circulation associated with Irish saints. Thus, the kind of hagiographical digression that occurs in AClon is not generally a feature of AFM, but on the other hand, the very cursory records of major saints found in AU were evidently deemed inadequate. No single extant source for the AFM versions of the lives of Patrick, Brigit, Colum Cille and Malachy has been identified, and it is probable that the material was assembled by the Four Masters from a variety of sources, including pre-existing martyrologies, as had earlier been done in the preparation of the Martyrology of Donegal.

Although the annalists did not usually reuse the hagiographical material presented in the Martyrology of Donegal, there is nonetheless a clear connection between the two texts. Firstly, the saints whose obituaries are recorded in AFM are the same saints that feature in the Martyrology and secondly, the two texts almost invariably agree on the basic chronological details of the day, month, and year of death of each saint.[41] Thus, Ermedhach (1 Jan. 681), Diomma Dubh (6 Jan. 658), Cronan Becc (7 Jan. 642), Laidhgenn (12 Jan. 660), Ite (15 Jan. 569) and Maedhóg (31 Jan. 624) are among the saints with January feast days for whom the obit information in the Martyrology and in AFM agree. While the feast day was the key to the sequencing in the Martyrology, the year of death being merely incidental, for the annalists it was the chronological arrangement by year that mattered, but they took special care also to incorporate information about the feast days of saints wherever possible. In some instances, the information regarding day and month of a saint's death are added in an editorial hand in both autograph manuscripts of AFM.[42]

If the lives of saints were perceived by seventeenth-century Catholic writers as 'a kind of ancillary scripture',[43] then Mícheál Ó Cléirigh and his associates may not have wished to trivialize those texts by adapting or summarizing them in their secular annals, and this may be part of the explanation as to why they generally omitted the traditional stories of miracles worked by the saints in the formal obituaries. This is not a fully satisfactory explanation, however, as the annalists were quite prepared to retain references to those saints at work in the

---

40 *MDon*, pp 240–3. 41 I am grateful to Prof. Pádraig Ó Riain for drawing my attention to this feature of the two texts. 42 There are very occasional instances where a date is inserted in one manuscript and not in the other. Thus, for instance, under the year AD652, the date 'Maii 1' for St Oisseine is interpolated in MS C iii 3, fo. 256r. The day and month information for Oisseine is not given in A 13 at all. 43 Catherine McKenna, 'Triangulating opposition: Irish expatriates and hagiography in the seventeenth century' in M. Tymoczko and C. Ireland (eds), *Language and tradition in Ireland: continuities and displacements* (Amherst, 2003), p. 149.

world when such incidents were found elsewhere in their sources. It appears that the annalists did not consciously compartmentalize sacred and secular material into separate categories, and the case of the representation of St Ciarán in the annals illustrates their approach. As has been seen, the obituary of St Ciarán under the year 548 in AFM is very cursory. Nevertheless, he features prominently in episodes from later centuries. Thus, for example, an entry for the year 1044 makes clear the continuing role of St Ciarán as protector of Clonmacnoise.

AFM 1044
Cluain mic Nóis do orgain do Chonmhaicnibh, 7 do rad Dia 7 Ciarán móirdhíoghail forra ind .i. tam anaithinidh co ffarccabhtha na buailte fása co na nindilibh iar nécc a ndaoineadh uile.
(Cluain-mic-Nois was plundered by the Conmhaicni, and God and Ciaran wreaked great vengeance upon them for it, i.e. an unknown plague [was sent among them], so that the booleys were left waste with their cattle after the death of all the [shepherd] people.)[44]

A more active role for St Ciarán and his clergy was conveyed in an entry for the year 1155, where the power of the saint as a force in secular conflict was emphasized.

AFM 1155
Ciarán dan ro bhris an cath sin for Bhreghmhainibh uair do chuatar somh co Cluain, 7 rugsat a coitedha leó, co ttuccsat ina bfuarattar do mhucaibh samhtha Chiaráin. Do chuattar dna, an samhadh co na scrín ina ndedhaidh go Lios an tsoiscela, 7 ní fuairset a riarucchadh. Ro briseadh maidhm forra arnabharach tria aimhreir Samhtha Chiaráin.
(It was Ciaran that turned this battle against the Breaghmhaini, for they had gone to Cluain, bringing with them cots, in which they carried off all they could find of the pigs of Ciaran's clergy. The clergy went after them with their shrine, as far as Lis-an-tsoiscela, but they were not obeyed. On the following day they sustained a defeat, in consequence of disobeying Ciaran's clergy.)[45]

Earlier in the same year, a more formulaic *tria mhiorbhail Dé 7 naomh Pattraicc, 7 na naomh archena* ('through the miracles of God and Patrick, and of the saints in general') had been invoked as an explanation of the triumph of Godfrey Ó Raghallaigh in restoring Donnchadh Ó Cearbhaill as lord of Oirghialla.[46]

That the incidental references to saints reflect the nature of the available sources as well as the particular preoccupations of the annalists is indicated by the proliferation of references to St Ciarán in entries relating to the twelfth and thirteenth centuries.[47] They presumably reflect the influence of a Clonmacnoise source on the contents of AFM.[48] The last such reference recorded in AFM to

44 *AFM*, II, pp 846–7.   45 *AFM*, II, pp 1116–17.   46 *AFM*, II, pp 1116–17.   47 AFM 1129, AFM 1178.8, AFM 1201.12; AFM 1210.6.   48 Mícheál Ó Cléirigh had collected materials relating

miracles worked by St Ciarán is dated 1210.[49] The pattern of references to miracles worked by St Colum Cille likewise suggests that they were probably drawn from a source that did not extend beyond the thirteenth century. Eleven separate stories in which a miracle is worked by Colum Cille are recorded in AFM between AD1172 and AD1296, but no further references to miracles by that saint are found after that date with the exception of one entry in AD1542.[50]

In a description of a quite different kind of episode in 1176, relating to the death of Richard de Clare, better known as Strongbow, St Brigit is given an influential role alongside Colum Cille.

> AFM 1176
> *An tiarla Saxanach (.i. Riocard) do écc in Áth Cliath do bainne aillsi ro gabh ar a chois do miorbailiph Bricchde Cholaim Chille 7 na naomh archena isa ceallu ro millead laiss. At connairc siumh féisin Brighit andarlais ag a mharbhadh.*
> (The English earl (i.e. Richard) died in Dublin, of an ulcer which had broken out in his foot through the miracles of SS Bridget and Columbkille, and of all the other saints whose churches had been destroyed by him. He saw, as he thought, St Bridget in the act of killing him.)[51]

Although a similar entry is found in AU, the final detail about the earl seeing St Brigit in the act of killing him is not mentioned there.[52] The death of Strongbow is not recorded at all in AClon. For the Four Masters, however, there was no doubt but that St Brigit was on the side of those whose churches had been destroyed by the Normans led by Strongbow, and that his death was directly attributable to the intervention of St Brigit as a saintly defender of the Irish church.

The hagiographical material preserved in AFM was part of a wider understanding of the world as a place where God's will is revealed through reward for the just and punishment for the unjust, and where saints and holy men continue to do God's work for the good of God's people. The representation of saints was influenced by a deep-rooted understanding of the supernatural at work in the natural world – something depicted also in annalistic descriptions of the miraculous either in the context of relics or of wonders in the natural world.[53] As an exercise in historical interpretation, the hagiographical material in AFM may well owe as much to the late medieval sources from which it derives much of its

---

to Ciarán of Clonmacnoise from a variety of sources, including the 'Red Book of Munster' and 'the book of Aodh óg Úa Dálacháin of Les Cluaine in Meath' (Kenney, *Sources for the early history of Ireland*, pp 378, 730).   **49** AFM 1210.6. These late Ciarán episodes are not found in ATig, CS or AU. Theoretically, they are consistent with the Four Masters' use of a 'Book of Clonmacnoise' ending in 1227, such as is listed in their preface, but if so that source cannot now be certainly identified (*AFM*, I, pp lxiv–lxv).   **50** For example, AFM 1172.8; AFM 1176.9; AFM 1178.7; AFM 1187.8; AFM 1197.1; AFM 1213.4; AFM 1214.4; AFM 1222.5; AFM 1261.2; AFM 1293.2; AFM 1296.2; AFM 1542.6.   **51** *AFM*, III, pp 24–5.   **52** *AU*, II, pp 184–5.   **53** For an overview of the late medieval Irish evidence on wonders and miracles, see Raymond Gillespie, *Devoted people: belief*

evidence as to the likely theological beliefs of the compilers and those for whom the finished work was intended. Nevertheless, as has been shown in this case study, the Four Masters appear to have augmented the available descriptions of certain key saints whose role in the early Irish church was seen as significant from a seventeenth-century perspective. These were the same saints who featured in Catholic polemic in catechetical and devotional works produced by Irish scholars on the continent, not least the Irish Franciscans at Louvain.[54] They included the three national patrons, Patrick, Brigit and Colum Cille, and also the lynchpin of the twelfth-century reform, St Malachy. Given Malachy's high profile in the universal church, vouched for by no less an author than St Bernard,[55] it was important that he should be presented appropriately as part of the Irish ecclesiastical story. And, in the light of the counter-arguments of Irish Protestant polemicists such as James Ussher, the reputation of the historic Catholic Church in Ireland relied quite heavily on the arguments for reform in the twelfth century. The point was emphasized by John Colgan in the preface to his lives of saints.[56] For the Four Masters, however, it was not necessary to labour the point of the reforms instituted by St Malachy, since the entire annals were a shrine to the continuity of the early church and the role of the Franciscans in its prosperity down to the annalists' own day.

Other ecclesiastical obituaries

One of the most noticeable features of the arrangement of entries in AFM when compared with other annalistic compilations is the manner in which ecclesiastical personalities are accorded priority throughout. Almost invariably, though there are exceptions, entries relating to abbots, bishops and other clergy are placed at the beginning of the AFM record for any given year. That this was an innovation is clear from a comparison of the format of a sample of entries in AFM with the material for the corresponding years in AU and ALCé. Thus, although the ratio of ecclesiastical to secular material may have declined by the late medieval period (figure 8.1, above, p. 216) the systematic prioritizing of such entries as were available on ecclesiastical themes allows AFM create the impression of annals in which the ecclesiastical material is of greater significance than the secular (table 8.1).

and religion in early modern Ireland (Manchester, 1997).   **54** Colgan, *Trias thaumaturga*; Thomas Messingham, *Florilegium insulae sanctorum*; Ó Maonaigh (ed.), *Scáthán shacramuinte na haithridhe*, lines 4137–274; for discussion of the polemical use of the cult of St Patrick in the seventeenth century, see B. Cunningham and R. Gillespie, '"The most adaptable of saints": the cult of St Patrick in the seventeenth century', *Archivium Hibernicum* 49 (1995), 82–104.   **55** H.J. Lawlor (trans.), *St Bernard of Clairvaux's Life of St Malachy of Armagh* (London, 1920).   **56** Colgan, *Acta sanctorum Hiberniae, praefatio ad lectorem*, sig. b1v–b2v.

Table 8.1: Percentage of annual entries that commence with an ecclesiastical theme[57]

Years sampled	AFM	AU	ALCé
1101–1200	93	31	21
1301–1400	57	8	8

Examples abound. An early instance of the Four Masters' editorial policy of placing entries concerning clergy at the beginning of the year, immediately following the statement of the regnal year, can be seen when the AFM entries for the year AD709 are contrasted with the corresponding entries in AU recorded under the year AD710 (entries common to the two texts are highlighted in bold in the extracts quoted below).

> AFM 709
> *1. An céid bhliadhain dFerghal mac Maoiledúin, mac Maoilefithrigh, hi righe uas Erinn.*
> *2. **Cendfaoladh, abb Fobhair, décc.***
> *3. Diccolan egnaidhe [décc].*
> *4. Tethghal, epscop ó Lainn Ela, décc 16 April.*
> *5. Ultan, mac Cummine, décc. Epscop Telcha Olaind.*
> *6. **Cath Slebhe Fuait ria fFerghal for Uibh Méith, in ro marbhadh Tnuthach, mac Mochloingsi, toisech Ua Méith, 7 Curoi, mac Aodha, mic Dluthaigh.***
> (1. The first year of Fearghal, son of Maelduin, son of Maelfithrigh, in sovereignty over Ireland.
> **2. Ceannfaeladh, abbot of Fobhar [Fore], died.**
> 3. Diccolan the Wise [died].
> 4. Tethghal, bishop of Lann-Ela [Lynally], died on the 16th of April.
> 5. Ultan, son of Cummine [died], bishop of Telach Olainn.
> **6. The battle of Sliabh Fuaid [was gained] by Fearghal over the Ui-Meith, wherein were slain Tnuthach, son of Mochloingi, chief of Ui-Meith, and Curoi, son of Aedh, son of Dluthach.)**[58]

> AU 710
> *1. Faelan nepos Silni moritur.*
> *2. **Bellum nepotum Meith ubi Tnuthach mac Mochloingse rex nepotum Meith et Curoi filius Aedho filii Dluthaig, ceciderunt.***
> *3. Strages Pictorum in campo Manonn apud Saxones, ubi Finnguine filius Deileroith inmatura morte iacuit.*
> *4. **Cennfaelad abbas Fobair moritur.***

---

57 The data in this table is presented in the form of percentages to allow for the missing years in ALCé (AD1138–70) and in AU (AD1133–55). 58 *AFM*, I, pp 308–11; O'Donovan's version of the Irish text has been revised here in line with the readings in RIA MS C iii 3, fo. 269r. In UCD–OFM MS A 13, fo. 282r, the words *easp[oc] telcha olaind* ('bishop of Telach Olainn') are interlined so as to explain the identity of Ultan.

5. *Congresio Britonum et Dal Riati for Loirgg ecclet, ubi Britones deuicti.*

6. *Murgal filius Noe moritur.*

7. *Coscrad nepotum Neill uc Cuinciu robairgi, in quo ceciderunt filius Condi et filii Dibcheini.*

8. *Diccolan sapiens 7 Ultan mac Cummeni epscop telcae Olaind mortui sunt.*
(1. Faelan Ua Silni dies.

2. **The battle of the Ui-Meith, wherein were slain Tnuthach, son of Mochloingse, King of the Ui-Meith, and Curoi, son of Aedh, son of Dluthach.**

3. A slaughter of the Picts in Magh-Manonn, by the Saxons, wherein Finnguine son of Deileroth was untimely slain.

4. **Cennfaeladh, abbot of Fobhar, dies.**

5. An encounter of Britons and Dalriata, on Lorgg-ecclet, where the Britons were defeated.

6. Murgal, son of Noe, dies.

7. The destruction of the Ui-Neill at Cuince-Robairgi, in which the son of Condi, and the sons of Dibhcein, were slain.

8. **Diccolan the Wise, and Ultan, son of Cummeni, bishop of Telach-Olaind, died.**)[59]

In the record of this year, AFM omits five of the entries recorded in AU. The remaining material is presented in a different sequence, so that the obituaries of clergy are grouped together at the beginning before the record of the battle. AFM also inserts a reference to Tethghal, bishop of Lynally, not recorded in AU or other extant annals.[60] Given that AFM records a precise date of death for Tethghal, it is no surprise to discover that the same bishop is also mentioned in the Martyrology of Donegal, although the year of his death is not given there.[61]

Another feature to note here is the insertion of details concerning the regnal year. This is a characteristic element of all AFM entries up to the year 1022. The Four Masters' omission of entries on Britons and on Picts may have been on the grounds that they were external events, though this does not explain the omission of the Ó Néill defeat. The omission of two minor personalities, Faelan Ó Silni and Murgal, son of Noe, is probably an example of another regularly recurring pattern throughout AFM of ignoring persons of lesser significance. Incidentally, the example also illustrates, yet again, that AU was neither the sole nor the principal source for AFM at this point. As elsewhere, the AFM material appears to have been assembled from a variety of sources, drawing on martyrologies as well as annals, and then arranged according to an editorial system that prioritized ecclesiastical material.

59 *AU*, I, pp 158–61. The first five entries in AU for this year correspond to the entries in the Annals of Tigernach and are in the same sequence (*ATig*, I, p. 222).   60 Entry not found in AClon or AI.   61 Entry for 16 April (*MDon*, pp 104–5). That martyrology does not, however, identify him as a bishop. He is also included in the *Martyrology of Tallaght* in the Book of Leinster in the form *Tetgall m[ac] Colbraind* (Anne O'Sullivan (ed.), *The Book of Leinster*, VI (Dublin, 1983), p. 1615,

The entries for a sample year from the thirteenth century further illustrate the annalists' working method. Five of the seventeen entries relate to ecclesiastical persons or places. Four are placed at the beginning of the AFM record of that year, while the fifth – relating to a building rather than a person – is placed as the final entry for the year. Only the ecclesiastical entries are quoted here:

> AFM 1266
> 1. *Gradha espuicc do tabairt ar brathair dord .S. Domenic (.i. ua Scopa) in Ard Macha do cum beith i Raith Both dó.*
> 2. *Tomas Ua Maolconaire aircideochain Tuama, 7 Maoilisu Ua hAnainn prioir Rosa Commain, 7 Atha Liacc, do écc.*
> 3. *Tomas Ua Miadachain do gabail espocóide Luigne.*
> 4. *Togha espuicc do tocht on Róimh go Cluain Ferta Brenainn, 7 gradha espuicc do tabairt do fein 7 do Tomas Ó Miadacháin in Ath na Ríogh an domnach ria Nodlaic.*
> . . .
> 17. *Maolpatraic ó Scandail Priomhaid Aird Macha do tabhairt brathar mionur go hArd Macha, 7 lethaindíog lándomhain do dénamh lais im an eacclais iaramh.*
> (1. The dignity of bishop was conferred at Armagh on a friar of the order of St Dominic (i.e. O'Scopa), and he was appointed to Raphoe.
> 2. Thomas O'Mulconry, archdeacon of Tuam, and Maelisa O'Hanainn, prior of Roscommon and Athleague, died.
> 3. Thomas O'Meehan became bishop of Leyny.
> 4. A bishop-elect came from Rome to Clonfert-Brendan, and the dignity of bishop was conferred on him, and on Thomas O'Meehan, at Athenry, on the Sunday before Christmas.
> . . .
> 17. Maelpatrick O'Scannal, primate of Armagh, brought the Friars Minor to Armagh, and afterwards cut a broad and deep trench around their church.)[62]

In contrast to the sequence in AFM, the AConn versions of all four entries on ecclesiastical personages for the year 1266 are recorded, but they are positioned well down the sequence as items 12, 14, 18 and 20 for that year. The final item in AFM for that year, concerning Ó Scannaill introducing the Order of Friars Minor to Armagh, is not recorded in AConn at all.[63] In AU it is recorded as the fourth of seven items under the year 1264.[64] The sequence in ALCé likewise contrasts sharply with that in AFM, so that of the four collections only AFM prioritizes ecclesiastical entries.

---

line 49506). **62** *AFM*, III, pp 398–401. **63** Its inclusion in AFM at this point may be an error, as a very similar entry is recorded in AFM under the year 1264. This latter date is the one supported by Mícheál Ó Cléirigh's own chronicle of Franciscan foundations in BR MS 3410, drawn from an Irish translation of Francis O'Mahony's '*Brevis Synopsis*'. Where O'Mahony had dated the foundation to 'before 1260' (Jennings (ed.), '*Brevis synopsis*', 150), Ó Cléirigh balanced this against the evidence of *sein leabhair* in opting for the year 1464 (Moloney (ed.), 'Brussels MS 3410', 194). **64** *AU*, II, pp 336–7. There are minor differences between the style of the entry in the 'A' and 'B' texts of AU. Related entries are found in AU in the years 1263 and 1266, *AU*, II, pp 334–5, 340–1,

The obituaries of ecclesiastics as recorded in AFM, though given pride of place within a given year, tend to be quite short. It is sometimes evident that the compilers had only scant information to hand. Thus the 1423 entry recording *Concobhar o Coineoil epscop do écc* ('Conor O'Coineoil, a bishop, died') suggests that the compilers probably did not know that this bishop was attached to the diocese of Killala.[65] The obituary of Conchobhar Ó Fearghail in 1424 is a typical example of a more elaborate record of the life of a cleric. Compared to those accorded to secular individuals, it is very brief, and merely lists some characteristic attributes, but without any detail about the achievements of the individual's career:

AFM 1424.1
Concobhar O Ferghail easpucc Conmaicne fer co nairmittin, 7 co nonoir, go naithne, go neolas go ndeserc, 7 go ndaonnacht do écc.
(Conor O'Farrrell, bishop of Conmaicne [Ardagh], a man of dignity, honour, intelligence, learning, charity and benevolence, died.)[66]

Occasionally, there are exceptional obituaries of clerics, such as that for Muiredhach Ua Cobhthaigh, bishop of Derry and Raphoe, who died in 1173.[67] Having described the many achievements of the bishop's life, the entry goes on to record a miraculous wonder that occurred on the night of his death, when *an oidhche dhorcha do shoillsiughadh o thá iarmeirge co muichdedoil ... agus ionnamhail chaoire moire tenedh do eirgi ós an mbaile agus a tocht soirdhes* ('The dark night was illumined from midnight to day-break ... and the likeness of a large globe of fire arose over the town, and moved in a south-easterly direction').[68] The linking of the death of the bishop with a natural wonder in this way greatly enhanced the annalists' attempt to convey a sense of the truly exceptional character of the deceased.

One further example may suffice to illustrate the editorial policy of the Four Masters in respect of ecclesiastics. There are twenty-one entries recorded for the year 1466. The year opens with a combined notice of the deaths of Brian Mág Uidhir, abbot of Lisgoole and of Domhnall Ua Leannain, a canon of Lisgoole.[69] These ecclesiastical entries are followed by nineteen entries on secular topics, including substantial narratives on military expeditions in Offaly and Munster. The year then concludes with mention of the burning of the monastery of Trinity Island in Lough Key and the image of the Trinity therein:

though there is some confusion over the dating of entries in AU for the 1260s.   65 *AFM*, IV, pp 856–8; the bishop was not mentioned by Sir James Ware in the original edition of his history of Irish bishops (James Ware, *De praesulibus Hiberniae commentarius* (Dublin, 1665), pp 269–73.   66 *AFM*, IV, pp 860–1; the word *ndonnacht* in O'Donovan's edition is a misprint for *ndaonnacht* in the manuscript (RIA MS 23 P 6, fo. 163r).   67 *AFM*, III, pp 8–11.   68 *AFM*, III, pp 10–11.   69 *AFM*, IV, pp 1040–1.

AFM 1466.21
Mainistir Oilein na Trinoide .i. for Loch Cé, co niomhaighin na Trinoide do losccadh lá coinnil.
(The monastery of Trinity Island in Lough Key, and the image of the Trinity there, were burned by a candle.)[70]

The effect of this structure to the year is to enclose the secular entries within a frame of ecclesiastical material, and the consistency with which such a framework is adopted, though bounded by the practicalities of manuscript production, suggests that it may have been a deliberate choice of the annalists.

The extent of editorial intervention by the Four Masters in respect of the ecclesiastical material does not end with the imposition of a pattern on the sequence of entries. The 1466 notice concerning the monastery of Trinity Island cited above is found in AConn also, where it reads as follows:

AConn 1466
Manestir na Trinoti for Loch Ce 7 imagin an Trinoti do loscad la connil bai ac mnai chanonaig ar lasad.
(The monastery of Holy Trinity Island in Loch Key and the image of the Trinity were burned by a lighted candle carried by a canon's wife.)[71]

In contrast to AConn, the presence of a woman in the monastery was silently omitted from AFM. The content of the ecclesiastical obituaries recorded in AFM for the same year was also subject to editing. The death of Brian Mág Uidhir, abbot of Lisgoole already mentioned, is the subject of a somewhat more informative notice in AU:

AU 1466
Brian, mac Gilla-Patraig, mic an airchideochain moir (Meg Uidhir), idon, abb Lesa-gabhail, d'heg 3 Idus Ianuarii.
(Brian, son of Gilla-Patraig, son of the great archdeacon (Mag Uidhir), namely, abbot of Lis-gabhail, died on the 3rd of the Ides [11th] of January.)[72]

The significant difference here is not the omission of the date of death from AFM, but rather the silence in the matter of genealogical pedigree. Here, and in numerous other instances, the offspring of the 'great archdeacon' are quietly ignored in AFM, either by omitting their obituaries altogether or else, as in this instance, omitting to mention that the deceased person was descended from a man in holy orders.

This editorial control appears to have been an entirely conscious and deliberate intervention, and one that is replicated elsewhere in AFM. Thus, in 1417, the death of John, son of the archdeacon, is recorded in AU, and is incorporated into AFM but without any reference to his parentage.

70 *AFM*, IV, pp 1044–5.   71 *AConn*, pp 534–5.   72 *AU*, III, pp 216–17.

AU 1417.5
Maighister Seoan, mac in Airchideochain móir, idon, persun Daim-innsi Locha-hErne, d'eg in bliadhain si, sexto Kalendas Octobris.
(Master John, son of the great archdeacon, namely, parson of Daim-inis of Loch-Erne, died this year on the 6th of the Kalends of October [Sep. 26].)[73]

AFM 1417.2
Maigistir Seon, persún Daimhinsi décc.
(Master John, parson of Devinish, died.)[74]

The death of the archdeacon himself, in 1423, is recorded in AFM, in a straightforward entry that appears to be copied from AU, but it is no surprise that the death of his wife in 1427, herself the daughter of a bishop, is not mentioned at all in AFM. She had received a substantial mention in AU:

AU 1427.11
Sibhan, ingen in espuic Mic Cathmhail, ben Muiris, idon, in Airchideochain mhoir, Mheg Uidhir, obiit 13 Kalendas Februarii, noch ig a raibh tech-aidhedh ic Clain-inis 7 i Ros-oirrtir re se bliadhna deg 7 da fichit co nosmur, daenachtach, dercech.
(Joan, daughter of the bishop Mac Cathmhail, wife of Maurice Mag Uidhir, that is, of the great archdeacon, died on the 13th of the Kalends of February [Jan. 20]; one that maintained a guest-house at Claen-inis and at Ros-oirther for six and fifty years reputably, humanely [and] charitably.)[75]

Similarly, the deaths of various of the offspring of Archdeacon Mág Uidhir through the fifteenth century, recorded with sufficient genealogical detail to identify them as children and grandchildren of the archdeacon, are entirely omitted from AFM.[76] These omissions from AFM contribute significantly to the under-representation of the family of Mág Uidhir in AFM as compared with AU. The omissions include individuals such as Seán Mág Uidhir, whose obituary was recorded in AU and who would most probably have been included in AFM were it not for his descent from an archdeacon:

AU 1495.12
Seaan, mac an espuicc Mheg Uidhir, idon, mac Piarais, mic Muiris airchideochain, d'heg in bliadhain si, ui die mensis Maii, scilicet, in festo Iohannis an[te] Portam Latinam, idon, persan Daire-Maela[i]n 7 aircindech Clain-indsi 7 fer tighi aidheadh gu coitchenn.
(John, son of the bishop Mag Uidhir, namely, son of Pierce, son of Archdeacon Maurice – to wit, parson of Daire-Maelain and herenagh of Claen-inis and a man of a general guest-house – died this year, on the 6th day of the month of May, namely on the feast of [St] John before the Latin Gate.)[77]

73 *AU*, III, pp 74–5.   74 *AFM*, IV, pp 830–1.   75 *AU*, III, pp 104–5.   76 They occur in AU as follows: AU 1419.6; AU 1421.11; AU 1439.4; AU 1441.11; AU 1450.9; AU 1463.10; AU 1466.10; AU 1478.13; AU 1481.13.   77 *AU*, III, pp 386–7.

Descendants of other men in holy orders whose obituaries are found in AU are likewise omitted from AFM, including a member of the family of Ó hÓgáin.

> AU 1416.14
> *Aedh bacach, mac in Aircinnich, idon, mac Nícoíl Fhinn, mic Conchobuir, idon, in Arcideochain, fer daennachta moire do Muinntir Innsi-cain Locha-hErne d'heg in bliadhain si, octauo Kalendas Septimbris.*
> (Aedh the Lame, son of the erenagh – namely, son of Nicholas the Fair, son of Conchobur, that is of the archdeacon – a man of great charity of the Community of Inis-Cain of Loch-Erne, died this year, on the 8th of the Kalends of September [Aug. 25].)[78]

Even after Mícheál Ó Cléirigh had made additions to the body of the text for that year, there was still space on the page at the beginning of the year 1416 where further entries could have been inserted. That he did not do so suggests that the entry on Aodh Bacach Ó hÓgáin as found in AU was deliberately omitted from the record of the year 1416 in AFM.[79] It appears, therefore, that it is not only the Meig Uidhir descendants of clergy that are excluded from AFM, but those of other lesser families also. The most likely explanation is a desire by the Four Masters team that aspects of Irish ecclesiastical history that did not accord with the teaching of the Catholic Church on celibacy, as promulgated at the Council of Trent,[80] should be passed over in silence.

Religious houses

Scattered throughout the late medieval section of AFM there are regular references to the building of religious houses and churches, and occasional mention of the burning or destruction of same. Some of the information is evidently derived from entries of this kind in AU and other annals, while others, particularly the entries concerning the foundation of many Franciscan friaries, are generally drawn from non-annalistic sources. The chronology of Franciscan foundations incorporated into AFM was largely taken from Francis O'Mahony's *Brevis synopsis Provinciae Hyberniae FF Minorum.*[81] An Irish translation of O'Mahony's work was prepared by Muiris Ulltach mac Seáin, Franciscan guardian of Donegal, and it was this Irish version that would have been available to the Four Masters in Donegal.[82] A summary chronology of Irish Franciscan

---

78 *AU*, III, pp 72–3; this Aedh Bacach is identified by Mc Carthy as a member of the family of Ó hÓgáin (*AU*, III, p. 72n). 79 RIA MS 23 P 6, fos 155r–156r. 80 Council of Trent, Session 24, Canon 9. J. Waterworth (ed. & trans.), *Canons and decrees of the sacred and ecumenical Council of Trent* (London, 1868), p. 195. 81 Jennings (ed.), 'Brevis synopsis', 139–91, edited from a manuscript in St Isidore's College, Rome. The author's name is variously translated as O'Mahony and Matthews (note that in this quotation Mícheál Ó Cléirigh gives the author's name in Irish as *an tAthair Proinsías ua Mathghamhna*). 82 Muiris Ulltach was guardian of Donegal between 1632 and 1635 (Jennings (ed.), 'Brevis synopsis', 142).

foundations copied by Mícheál Ó Cléirigh in 1641, now part of Brussels MS 3410, corresponds very closely with the content of the entries in AFM on the same theme, and probably represents Muiris Ulltach's work, at least in part. The source of the material in Mícheál Ó Cléirigh's 1641 transcript is documented in detail in the first paragraph, and it is clear from Ó Cléirigh's note that he was the scribe rather than the compiler of the material involved:

Ag so síos na bliadhna in ro tionnsgnadh mainstreacha uird S Froinséis in Érinn, do réir an chruinnighthe, 7 an teglamtha do rinne an tathair Proinsías ua Mathghamhna, an tráth do bhí na Phrovinnsial, as leabhraibh, 7 as gnáthchuimhne bhráthar na ccoinveinnteadh ccéadna. Agus do chuir an tathair Muiris Ulltach mac Seaain do bhí na ghairdían aimsear fhada a nDún [na] nGall an ní céadna a nGaoidhilcc. Agus do sgríobh an bráthair bocht túata le hughdarrdhás na naitreadh reumhráite, 7 fós le hughdardhás na leabhar airis, agus annalach, na neithe ceudna annso.[83]

[Here below are the years in which were founded monasteries of the Franciscan Order in Ireland, according to the collection and compilation done by Fr Francis O'Mahony when he was provincial, from books and from the recollections of brothers of the same convents. And Fr Muiris Ulltach mac Seáin, who was a long time guardian of Donegal, translated the same into Irish. And the poor lay brother wrote, with the authority of the fathers aforesaid, and also the authority of the books of history and annals, the same things here.][84]

While most of the material in this 1641 list transcribed by Mícheál Ó Cléirigh can be found almost word for word in AFM, it is uncertain whether the list reached its current form by being extracted from AFM or more directly from the translation of O'Mahony's work.

The point of most concern here, however, is the manner in which this material was originally incorporated into AFM. In most instances the entries on Franciscan monastic foundations in AFM are entered in the autograph manuscript by an editorial hand other than the main scribe for the year in question, suggesting that their insertion was an afterthought, albeit a deliberate and systematic addition. Though there are some exceptions, most of the entries on Franciscan monasteries in RIA MS 23 P 6 are added by Cú Choigcríche Ó Cléirigh (scribe D).[85] However, Mícheál Ó Cléirigh (scribe C) added the entries on the foundation of friaries at Killeigh (1393) and Quin (1402).[86] In one case, in RIA MS 23 P 6, the 1264 entry on Armagh friary was commenced by scribe C but completed by scribe D:

---

83 Moloney (ed.), 'Brussels MS 3410', 192.   84 My translation.   85 For example, the entries in RIA MS 23 P 6 on Youghal (AFM 1224.16), Cork (AFM 1229.1), Waterford (AFM 1240.1), Timoleague (AFM 1240.7), Galway (AFM 1247.13), Ennis (AFM 1247.14), Buttevant [Kilnamullagh] (AFM 1251.3) etc.   86 RIA MS 23 P 6, fos 135r, 140v.

AFM 1264.10

Airdepscop Ardamacha Maolpattraicc ó Sccannaill do thabairt na mbrathar minur go hArdmacha, 7 asé Mac Domhnaill Gallócclach (do reir gnatcuimne) do thionnsgain in mainestir sin do thógbhail ó thosach.

(The Archbishop of Armagh, Maelpatrick O'Scannal, brought the Friars Minor to Armagh; **and (according to tradition), it was Mac Donnell Galloglagh that commenced the erection of the monastery.)**[87]

Scribe D qualified the information supplied by Ó Cléirigh by adding a reference to conflicting evidence from 'tradition' (the addition by D being indicated in bold in the above citation).[88] In a few instances, the entries on Franciscan foundations are in the hand of the main scribe for the year, though this does not necessarily imply that they were written at the same time as the remainder of the entries for the year in question.[89]

Not all of the information derived from O'Mahony's history of the Franciscans agreed with information available in AU. Where a conflict occurred, the Four Masters appear to have preferred the evidence of AU to that of O'Mahony. Thus, for instance, O'Mahony's *Brevis synopsis* gives 1407 as the date of foundation of the Franciscan friary at Monaghan.[90] However, both AU and AFM record the foundation under the year 1462. The summary list subsequently transcribed by Mícheál Ó Cléirigh, in BR MS 3410, appears to attempt to reconcile the work of O'Mahony with the annalistic account in AU, as is clear from Ó Cléirigh's note concerning Monaghan friary. In typical chronicle style, he records both pieces of information, leaving it to the reader to draw his own conclusions:

AD1407. Mainistir do thógbháil a Muineachán in Oirghiallaibh, in easpuccóideacht Chlochair in Ulltoibh do Bhráithribh S. F. la Mág Mathghamhna tighearna Oirghiall. Agus do réir an leabhair annalach as re linn Fhéilim, mhic Bhríain, mhic Ardghail do tionnsgnadh an choinveint sin an bhliadhainsi d'aois Chr. 1462.[91]

[AD1407. A monastery was built in Monaghan in Oriel, in the diocese of Clogher in Ulster for the brothers of St Francis, by Mac Mahon lord of Oriel. And according to the book of annals it was in the time of Feilim son of Brian son of Ardall that that convent was begun this year of Christ 1462.][92]

It appears that the annalists did not draw directly on the earlier compilation on Franciscan history prepared by Donogh Mooney in 1616–17 when he had been

---

87 *AFM*, III, pp 394–5.   88 It is noteworthy that the material in scribe D's addition to AFM is incorporated into Mícheál Ó Cléirigh's 1641 transcript of a chronology of Irish Franciscan foundations. This appears to prove that the list in BR MS 3410 was compiled from AFM rather than adapted from the *Brevis Synopsis*.   89 RIA MS 23 P 6, fo. 227v (entry for 1486).   90 Jennings (ed.), 'Brevis synopsis', 155.   91 Moloney (ed.), 'Brussels MS 3410', 196 (since this note was transcribed in 1641, it is of course possible that the annals being referred to here were AFM, but it is more likely that Mícheál Ó Cléirigh would have regarded AU, being an older source, as authoritative).   92 My translation.

Franciscan provincial. That work was in Latin, and was apparently taken to Louvain and then given to Luke Wadding in Rome. It may not have been available to the Donegal Franciscans by the time work was in progress on the final volume of AFM.[93]

Aside from the material from contemporary Franciscan sources, the majority of other references to the building or destruction of monasteries, along with some obituaries of ecclesiastical patrons recorded in AFM, are not unique to those annals, but are to be found in AU or AConn also. However, the geographical spread of monasteries mentioned in AU is much more limited than in AFM, the former being largely confined to Ulster and north-east Connacht – locations such as Assaroe, Armagh, Boyle, Cavan, Clogher, Derry, Lisgoole, Roscommon and Sligo. The Four Masters on the other hand, largely because of their interest in Franciscan foundations, documented establishments in all parts of the country. Thus, AFM records the foundations at Athlone, Youghal, Cork, Waterford, Timoleague, Galway, Ennis, Ardfert, Kildare, Clane, Carrick-on-Suir and other places. The Four Masters' approach to ecclesiastical themes provides an indication of their desire that significant events from all parts of the island would be recorded in their history. Only occasionally was the source material to achieve this objective available to them, and in no case more comprehensively that through the Franciscan *Brevis synopsis* of Francis O'Mahony.

Table 8.2: *Number of entries in AFM and AU on the foundation, building, or destruction of churches and monasteries, 1201–1500*[94]

Years	AFM	AU	AConn*
1201–1300*	22	5	17**
1301–1400	11	5	8
1401–1500	27	7	7

* AConn commences in 1224
** Excludes 5 very general references in AConn to destruction in Connacht, including churches

The effect of their trawl through sources other than the secular annals is that there are rather more entries on ecclesiastical buildings in AFM than in other extant annals, particularly for the thirteenth and fifteenth centuries (table 8:2). However, this could be interpreted as merely an incidental characteristic of the annals. Ultimately, the concern of the annalists was not so much focused on church buildings as on the people, both ecclesiastical and lay, whose association

93 Brendan Jennings (ed.), 'Brussels MS 3947: *Donatus Moneyus, De Provincia Hiberniae S. Francisci*', *Analecta Hibernica* 6 (1934), 12–138. **94** These figures exclude the many incidental references to office-holders attached to and persons buried in monastic and other ecclesiastical establishments.

with those holy places was part of the historical record. Documenting that ecclesiastical association more systematically than had been achieved before, revising and restructuring the content of earlier annals to enhance the impact of the ecclesiastical entries, augmenting their text with new material, and continuing the chronology right down to the seventeenth century so that it became a text of contemporary relevance quite distinct from the 'old vellum books' on which it drew, all of these initiatives were inherent in the fundamental rationale for the compilation of AFM, which was the creation of a comprehensive record of the past appropriate to a Catholic kingdom.

Conclusion

The wider ecclesiastical context of the universal church, as represented by popes, synods and occasional visiting legates, seems to have been taken for granted throughout AFM, as in earlier annals, as a necessary element of the history of Ireland.[95] There were sufficient references to synods to indicate that the Four Masters regarded these as fairly routine events through which the guidelines of the universal church were implemented in Ireland. Occasionally, the contemporary views of the Four Masters on events of earlier centuries appear to be reflected in the text, as for instance in the comment added to an account of a synod held at Drogheda in 1152:

> AFM 1152
>
> *Coimhthionól seanaidh i nDroichet Atha ag epscopaibh Ereann im comharba Phátraicc imon cCairdional Iohannes Paprion, co ttribh mílibh mac neglastacda etir mhanchaibh 7 chananchaibh, co ro ordaighset araill do riaghlaibh ann. Atiad sídhe .i. mna cúil, 7 cairdeasa dionnarbhadh ó feraibh, gan lógh diarraidh ar ongadh, nó ar baisteadh. Acht chena ní maith gan a ttabhairt dia raibhe a ccumhang duine gan lóg do ghabháil ar domhan necclastucdha, 7 deachmhadh do ghabhail go hiondraic.*
>
> (A synod was convened at Droichet-atha by the bishops of Ireland, with the successor of Patrick, and the Cardinal Johannes Papiron, with three hundred ecclesiastics, both monks and canons; and they established some rules thereat, i.e. to put away concubines and lemans from men; not to demand payment for anointing or baptizing (though it is not good not to give such, if it were in a person's power); not to take [simonical] payment for church property; and to receive tithes punctually.)[96]

Given that the friars' rights to collect payments for sacraments was such a controversial issue in the early seventeenth century, it seems that the annalists

---

95 On synods, see AFM 1111.5; AFM 1134.13; AFM 1148.2; AFM 1151.4; AFM 1157.9; AFM 1158.3; AFM 1161.9; AFM 1172.12; AFM 1177.1; AFM 1201.3; AFM 1201.4. Among the synods referred to in AU that are omitted from AFM are AU 1175.7 (Birr); AU 1215.9 (Rome) and AU 1486.17 (Drogheda); the last of these dealt with issues involving an Observant friar's entitlement to be bishop of Derry. 96 *AFM*, II, pp 1100–3.

may have thought it unwise to record the decision of the synod on this issue without qualification. There is also a very significant contrast between the Four Masters' account of a synod at Drogheda in 1152 and the account offered by the secular priest, Geoffrey Keating, of a synod at Kells in the same year.[97] Keating's *Foras feasa ar Éirinn*, in contrast to AFM, draws attention instead to the decisions taken in 1152 concerning the diocesan structure of the country.[98] As a secular Catholic priest, Keating would have had far more interest in the formation of dioceses than would Mícheál Ó Cléirigh, and in each case these seventeenth-century historians were inclined to select for inclusion the evidence most pertinent to their own contemporary situations. In the case of another twelfth-century synod documented in AFM, the annalists' consciousness of an older order different to contemporary circumstances emerges. Under the year 1177 there is reference to a synod presided over by Cardinal Vivanus, at which *ro chinnsed deithide iomdha ná comhailtear* ('they enacted many ordinances not *now* observed'), a rare enough indicator of the annalists' sense of change over time.[99] The general tenor of descriptions of synods in AFM, however, conveys the sense that they were convened, as in the synod at Clane in 1162 *occ erail riaghla 7 soibhés, for feraibh Ereann, laechaibh cléirchibh* ('to establish rules and morality amongst the men of Ireland, both laity and clergy').[100] There is no suggestion that the Irish church or people were particularly in need of reform, and the comings and goings of various papal legates to these synods did not elicit any comment from the annalists to suggest that they regarded such events as unusual. Rather, in the view of the annalists, the Irish church, both clergy and laity, were fully integrated into the structures and systems of the universal church.

Of rather more immediate concern to the Four Masters than the authority of the universal church was the issue of the bonds of affinity between the Irish monastic church and the most prominent indigenous kin groups in Irish society. There was also a strong emphasis on the historic integration of the Irish monastic church with the secular families whose history was also recorded in the annals. This connection between the ecclesiastical and the secular is brought out most starkly in the summary list of Franciscan foundations transcribed by Mícheál Ó Cléirigh in 1641.[101] In that text, Ó Cléirigh records the lay patrons of the various Franciscan monastic foundations, and makes special mention of the families whose members were traditionally buried in those monasteries, sometimes remarking on the tombstones to be seen in them. Most, but not all, of this detail is also documented in AFM. There, its juxtaposition with the secular material of the bulk of the late medieval entries serves to entwine more fully the ecclesiastical with the secular in the historical record.

97 The synod convened at Kells subsequently transferred to Mellifont, and this latter venue, close to Drogheda, was probably what the Four Masters (and also AClon 1153) were referring to. 98 Comyn and Dinneen (eds), *Foras feasa ar Éirinn*, III, pp 312, 356; Cunningham, *World of Geoffrey Keating*, p. 43. 99 *AFM*, III, pp 28–9. 100 *AFM*, II, pp 1146–7. 101 Moloney (ed.), 'Brussels MS 3410'.

The precise contemporary purpose of this emphasis on the specific secular familial associations with the various Franciscan foundations is not made explicit. It may have been prompted by concern for the practicalities of Franciscan reliance on the charitable support of the wider community, already revealed in the comment concerning the 1152 synod. The ongoing patronage of those monastic institutions was still an issue, and a continuation of past traditions was the best guarantee for the future that the Franciscan community could hope for. Alternatively, it may be that the annalists wished to document the close historic links between Irish monastic foundations and noble families so as to enhance the perceived status of those foundations, not least those associated with the Franciscan community.

In treating of ecclesiastical topics, the Four Masters went well beyond what had been attempted in earlier secular annals such as AU or AConn that covered the late medieval period. Thus, for example, when Rev. John Lynch came to write his history of Irish bishops, he made systematic use of the *Annales Dungallenses*, as he termed the Annals of the Four Masters, and in so doing was able to supplement the information that James Ware had drawn from a range of older Irish annals, including AU, AI, ATig and ALCé.[102] The Four Masters did not merely preserve much of relevance to ecclesiastical history that could be found in the earlier annals, but enhanced it in a variety of ways. They augmented the ecclesiastical dimension of their work by restructuring the material extracted from older annals, by adding new material on selected saints and ecclesiastics, by omitting details that they judged were best forgotten and, finally, by integrating the history of monastic foundations, including the Observant reform, into the overall framework of Irish history. The result was a history that satisfied the requirements of John Colgan, the Franciscan hagiographer, who drew on the work of the Four Masters when researching the lives of Irish saints for his *Acta sanctorum Hiberniae* (1645) and *Trias thaumaturga* (1647).[103] In the preface to his 1645 collection of saints' lives, Colgan singled out the achievement of Mícheál Ó Cléirigh and his collaborators for special praise – applying the term the 'Four Masters' to them for the first time – in appreciation of their achievement. He acknowledged that they were 'pious men', men of 'approved faith', characteristics that he believed enhanced the value of their history.[104] They had provided a historical text appropriate to the needs of the Louvain research project in its quest to document the historical background from which Ireland's saints had emerged.[105] The historical detail documented in AFM allowed

102 Gwynn, 'John Lynch's *De praesulibus Hiberniae*', 48–9. 103 John Colgan footnotes the work of the Four Masters regularly in his annotations to the lives of Irish saints. For examples, see Colgan, *Acta sanctorum Hiberniae*, pp 437, 349, 453, 455, 456. The Four Masters' entries for the years AD489 and AD474 are cited by Colgan at length in Latin translation (Colgan, *Acta sanctorum Hiberniae*, p. 464). 104 Colgan, *Acta sanctorum Hiberniae*, preface, sig. b3–b3v. O'Curry, *Lectures on manuscript materials*, pp 143–5, provides an English translation of Colgan's comments on the Four Masters. 105 Colgan admitted that his interest in the annals, from the perspective of the

researchers to link those saints with the ecclesiastical history of Ireland, thereby strengthening the case for the Catholic Church in early seventeenth-century Ireland to be recognized as the true and worthy successor of the church of Patrick. The Four Masters' attention to detail regarding the presentation of ecclesiastical matters ensured that their finished work would meet the requirements of the Louvain project in a multiplicity of ways that set it apart from the older annalistic compilations it was designed to replace.

ecclesiastical material they contained, did not extend beyond the year 1267 (Colgan, *Acta sanctorum Hiberniae*, preface, sig. b3v).

CHAPTER NINE

Scholarly networks and patronage

Introduction

The collaboration among scholars from the three learned families of Ó Cléirigh, Ó Duibhgeannáin and Ó Maoil Chonaire, which resulted in the production of the Annals of the Four Masters and related texts in the early 1630s, was no mere chance encounter. All of those directly involved in the compilation of the annals were members of hereditary Gaelic learned families in the south-west Ulster/ north-Connacht region. Such families did not function in isolation. Rather, it was an established custom among them to share their scholarship. It was normal for members of learned families to receive training at a specialized centre of learning conducted by another scholarly family. In the absence of a university, these schools were Ireland's most advanced centres of higher learning, and they served as places in which scholars could establish and renew links with other scholars and arrange access to important manuscripts. Thus it was that the network of scholars with whom the Four Masters came into contact in the course of their researches extended well beyond their own regional context. This chapter traces the various scholarly networks through which Mícheál Ó Cléirigh and his collaborators operated, so as to understand better the immediate cultural context from which their historical writing emerged. It investigates the evidence for Ó Cléirigh's formal scholarly training as an historian; the network of contacts both Gaelic and Anglo-Irish he cultivated to achieve access to appropriate source manuscripts; the scholars who collaborated with him directly in his historical and genealogical endeavours; the senior scholars from whom he sought and was granted approbations asserting the quality of the finished work; the scholarly support available from within the Franciscan community; and finally the patrons from whom he received the necessary support to finance the research project.

In the first half of the twentieth century, both Paul Walsh and Brendan Jennings published significant pioneering studies concerning the scholars who were part of Ó Cléirigh's circle. The best known of these publications are Jennings's *Micheal O Cléirigh, chief of the Four Masters and his associates* (1936), Walsh's *The Ó Cléirigh family of Tír Conaill* (1938), and Walsh's essay collection published posthumously under the title *Irish men of learning* (1947), edited by Colm Ó Lochlainn. A welcome recent addition to this corpus is the collection of Walsh's previously published essays and notes published as *Irish leaders and learning through the ages* (2003), edited by Nollaig Ó Muraíle. This collection brings together seven short pieces on aspects of the work of the Four Masters, including Walsh's important revision of the chronology of Ó Cléirigh's work on saints' lives as documented by Jennings. The present chapter seeks to build on and extend the work of Jennings, Walsh and others, by drawing together such evidence as exists to assemble an integrated interpretation of the Irish cultural milieu within which the Four Masters carried out their historical and genealogical researches. It examines how and why overlapping cultural communities encompassing not just the Franciscans and the Gaelic learned class but also Old English Protestant scholars came to be connected with the research projects of the Four Masters. It considers how establishment figures such as Fearghal Ó Gadhra MP, Toirdhealbhach Mac Cochláin MP, James Ussher, Church of Ireland archbishop of Armagh, and Sir James Ware, auditor general for Ireland, were willing to cooperate on matters of scholarship with members of the Franciscan community and their lay collaborators. Given the traditional descriptions of the Franciscans carrying out their religious functions at a range of locations throughout the country quite openly in defiance of government orders, the fact that this community of scholars transcended confessional boundaries requires explanation. Finally, the chapter will assess how that complex cultural world, as well as the wider Louvain dimension, influenced the attitudes and methods of the annalists as they approached their task.

The evidence for the individual contributions of various historians and scribes to the AFM project has already been outlined.[1] This chapter seeks to illustrate how the various participants and those among whom they worked fitted into the wider world of Gaelic scholarship in the early seventeenth century, so as to understand more fully the nature of historical learning in early modern Ireland.

Learned families in the Ó Cléirigh circle

There were two important overlapping networks of people without whose support Mícheál Ó Cléirigh could not have conducted his researches throughout his eleven years in Ireland between 1626 and 1637. First, the Gaelic learned class into which he was born and among whom he had received his scholarly training continued to assist him and cooperate with his research. Simultaneously, the community of Observant Franciscans of which he was a member for the final twenty years of his life facilitated the practicalities of his scholarly work. The Franciscan community provided for his subsistence both at his Donegal base and at other Franciscan houses throughout Ireland, and presumably also facilitated his travels by accompanying him on his journeys between these various locations.

---

1 See chapter six, above.

The points at which the Franciscan community in early seventeenth-century Ireland intersected with the learned class were many and varied. In addition, there were obvious if superficial similarities between these two communities in that both had members throughout many different parts of Ireland, forming networks of like-minded professional men. Of more substance is the fact that links between the learned class and the Franciscan order can be traced back several generations before Ó Cléirigh.[2] However, it was in the early seventeenth century, as the secular patronage of the Gaelic learned class was undermined in changing social and political circumstances, that numerous members of learned families opted to join religious orders and found scope to pursue their life of learning within that alternative professional framework. Not least among those in Mícheál Ó Cléirigh's immediate circle of acquaintances who became Franciscans were his own elder brother, Fr Bernardinus (Maolmhuire) Ó Cléirigh, guardian of the Franciscan convent of Donegal, located at Bundrowes, at various times from 1629, the two men named Muiris Ulltach (Ó Duinnshléibhe) who were also attached to the Donegal convent in the 1630s, Hugh Ward (Aodh Buidhe Mac an Bhaird), appointed guardian of the Irish college of St Anthony at Louvain in 1626, Baothghalach Mac Aodhagáin, OFM, bishop of Elphin, Flaithri Ó Maoil Chonaire, archbishop of Tuam, and Ross Mac Eochagáin, bishop of Kildare.[3]

When Ó Cléirigh was engaged in scholarly research, and particularly when dealing with members of other learned families in Ireland, his credentials as a trained historian and as a member of the learned Ó Cléirigh family were probably more important than his status as a Franciscan in gaining him access to other scholars and to the manuscripts in their custody. It was his scholarly training as a member of the learned class that also ensured that he had the skills necessary to extract accurately from those manuscripts the saints' lives, genealogies and other historical material that he transcribed. As will be seen, his having studied under the guidance of learned men from the Mac Aodhagáin family was important in shaping the circle of scholars with whom he maintained contact. Because he was an Ó Cléirigh, from the renowned family of historians of that name, he was also recognized by Hugh Ward at Louvain in 1626 (and also by Luke Wadding), as a skilled historian whose talents could be directed towards research into Irish historical, genealogical and hagiographical manuscripts. In the equally close-knit world of the Irish in continental colleges, the fact that Ward had studied at Salamanca and there may have known Ó Cléirigh's brother, Maolmhuire, provided a further social bond that shaped the world of Mícheál Ó Cléirigh.[4] That same Maolmhuire later studied at St Anthony's College Louvain,

2 For example, Cormac Ó Cléirigh, OFM, grandson of Tadhg Cam, whose death at the Donegal convent is recorded in AFM for the year 1542 (*AFM*, V, pp 1466–7); his namesake, another Franciscan, was based at the nearby Franciscan house at Assaroe in 1597 (*AFM*, VI, pp 2046–7). 3 Ó Cléirigh, *Foclóir no sanasan nua*, dedication; UCD–OFM, MS A 13, fos xxiii, xxxii; BR, MS 4639, fo. 3. 4 O'Doherty (ed.), 'Students of the Irish College, Salamanca (1595–1619)', 28.

where he was received as a Franciscan novice on 15 August 1616.[5] Without the vision of Hugh Ward, and the encouragement and support of the Franciscan community, it is unlikely that Ó Cléirigh would have pursued the kind of hagiographical and historical scholarship for which he is now remembered.[6] To understand the scholarly networks within which Ó Cléirigh operated, therefore, it is necessary to consider both the traditional Gaelic learned families among whom he worked and also the Franciscan community which had many close connections with the learned class in the seventeenth century, and thus linked its members into a wider world of scholarship both in Ireland and abroad.

Mac Aodhagáin

The most direct personal evidence provided by Mícheál Ó Cléirigh concerning the key members of the scholarly circle in which he worked is contained in the preface he wrote for his Irish glossary, *Focloir no sanasan nua*.[7] This work, published late in 1643, was the only one of his works to be published in his own lifetime. Like so many authorial prefaces, it names the people who had most influenced him in his studies and those whose scholarly support he most valued. Members of the extended learned family of Mac Aodhagáin emerge as probably the most valued group of contacts from Ó Cléirigh's perspective. The dedication of his first book in print to his friend, Baothghalach Mac Aodhagáin, OFM, bishop of Elphin, suggests a probable longstanding association with this influential man, a Franciscan bishop and member of the learned family of Mac Aodhagáin.[8] The origins and extent of this friendship are not documented, but the possibility that these two men had studied together in Ireland in their youth cannot be discounted. Their other potential point of contact was, of course, the college of St Anthony at Louvain. The biographical account of Mac Aodhagáin compiled in the 1660s by Rev. John Lynch, archdeacon of Tuam, records the names of Baothghalach's parents as Tadaeus Eganus (Tadhg Mac Aodhagáin) of Parke, Co. Galway, and Margareta Kelly.[9] This identifies the Franciscan bishop of Elphin as a member of the Mac Aodhagáin family who had traditionally conducted a law school at Parke in Co. Galway, another instance of the many

---

5 Jennings (ed.), *Louvain papers, 1606–1827*, p. 55.   6 On Hugh Ward, see above, pp 27–8; see also Breatnach, 'An Irish Bollandus', 1–30; Hogan, 'Irish historical studies in the seventeenth century, II: Hugh Ward', 56–77.   7 Printed on the printing press in the College of St Anthony and published at Louvain, 1643. An edition, with translation of the prefatory material, is available in Arthur Miller (ed.), 'O'Clery's Irish glossary', *Revue Celtique* 4 (1880), 349–428; 5 (1881), 1–69.   8 Miller (ed.), 'O'Clery's Irish glossary', *Revue Celtique* 4 (1880), 351–2; on the distinction between the bishop of Elphin and his namesake, who was bishop of Ross at the same time, see Canice Mooney, *Boetius MacEgan of Ross* (Killiney, 1950), pp 9–10. Both men died in 1650.   9 For further biographical information, compiled by Rev. John Lynch, archdeacon of Tuam, on Baothghalach Mac Aodhagáin, bishop of Elphin, see J.F. O'Doherty, (ed.), *De Praesulibus Hiberniae* (2 vols, Dublin, 1944), II, pp 292–4. Writing in Latin, Lynch gives the bishop's name as *Boetius Eganus*, *vernaculae Bothalach Macaodhagan*, and also makes reference to Ó Cléirigh's dedication of his 1643

inter-connections between the learned class and the Irish Franciscans in the early seventeenth century.[10]

There is no specific evidence to connect Mícheál Ó Cléirigh with a Mac Aodhagáin school at Parke other than his stated friendship with the bishop. However, the likelihood that Ó Cléirigh had studied at some Mac Aodhagáin school is strongly suggested by a further acknowledgment, in his 1643 preface, of the influence of another Mac Aodhagáin scholar. Ó Cléirigh expressly states that he had personally learned much about the older forms of the Irish language from Baothghalach Ruadh Mac Aodhagáin. He alludes to this scholar being a namesake of the bishop without indicating any particular kin-relationship between the two men. In fact, any relationship may not have been a close one, the family being an extensive one with branches throughout north Munster and east Connacht, providing professional services to a wide range of Gaelic families in the region.[11] Naming Baothghalach Ruadh Mac Aodhagáin as the first of five learned scholars, Ó Cléirigh explains that:

> Giodh sáoi oirdheirc gach duine dhiobh sin, as é Baothghalach as mó do leanamar do bhrígh gurab uadha as mo do ghlacamar fein agas fuaramar ag cách eile míniughadh na bhfocal, ar a dtrachtmáoid, sgriobhtha agas fos gurbhó sáoi oirdheirc dearscaighthe é san cceirdsi.
>
> (Although each one of these was a distinguished scholar, it is Baothghalach whom we have chiefly followed, because it is from him that we have ourselves received and have found with all others the interpretation of the words of which we treat [written], and also because he was a distinguished and remarkable scholar in this profession.)[12]

Lambert McKenna has identified this Baothghalach Ruadh Mac Aodhagáin, one of the contributors to *Iomarbhágh na bhfileadh*, as 'master of the Bardic school in Ormond'.[13] This identification is supported by an *inquisition post mortem* dated 19 March 1629 at Clonmel, and referring to the death of Cairbre Mac Aodhagáin of Ballymacegan twenty-seven years previously, at which time his son and heir, Baothghalach, was of full age and married.[14] The inquisition also identifies William, Flann and Cornelius as brothers of Baothghalach. It is known from AFM that two other brothers, Cairbre Óg and Donnchadh, had predeceased

Foclóir to him. **10** Thomas B. Costello, 'The ancient law school of Park, Co. Galway', *Journal of the Galway Archaeological and Historical Society* 19 (1940), 89–100. The school was located approximately 10km east of Tuam, Co. Galway. **11** Caitilín Ní Maol-Chróin, 'Geinealaigh clainne Aodhagáin, AD1400–1500: ollamhain i bhféineachus is i bhfilidheacht' in O'Brien (ed.), *Measgra i gcuimhne Mhichíl Uí Chléirigh*, pp 132–9, and genealogical chart facing p. 136. **12** Miller (ed.), 'O'Clery's Irish glossary', 353. **13** Lambert McKenna (ed.), *Iomarbhágh na bhfileadh: the contention of the bards* (2 vols, ITS, XX, XXI (1920), I, p. xi. **14** National Archives (of Ireland) [NAI], Chancery inquisitions, Tipperary, Charles I, RC/4/10, pp 167–70, no. 74, 19 Mar. 1629. The inquisition is discussed in Conor MacHale, *Annals of the Clan Egan* (Enniscrone, Co. Sligo, 1990), p. 37. See also Dermot Gleeson, *The last lords of Ormond* (rev. ed., Nenagh, Co. Tipperary, 2001), p. 14.

their father in 1601 and 1602 respectively.[15] The details about the sons of Cairbre Mac Aodhagáin documented in a chancery inquisition relating to the family's title to the lands at Ballymacegan make sense in terms of the known association of both Baothghalach and Flann with the Ballymacegan school. However, the details are not fully consistent with the evidence of a Gaelic genealogy compiled in the 1640s which recorded just four sons of Cairbre Mac an Chosnaidhe, namely Flann, Uilliam, Donnchadh and Cairbre Óg, thereby omitting Baothghalach entirely.[16] Despite his omission from the 1644 genealogy, however, it can be accepted on the evidence of the chancery inquisition that Baothghalach Ruadh was indeed Cairbre's son and heir. It appears that after Baothghalach's death, his brother Flann took over the conduct of the Mac Aodhagáin school of learning at Ballymacegan. Meanwhile, through a complicated property deal, executed with the assistance of none other than the attorney general, Sir John Davies, the Mac Aodhagáin lands had been surrendered to the crown, and on 7 June 1611 they were granted to Cosnamach [Constance] Mac Aodhagáin, 'to hold for ever of the castle of Dublin in free and common soccage'. The elaborate legal transactions in which Sir John Davies became involved on behalf of the family of Mac Aodhagáin appear to have been designed to allow the family to circumvent the law in relation to inheritance. Though Cosnamach was the main beneficiary, the transaction secured the position of Flann and one Seán Mac Aodhagáin also.[17] The property deals involving the heirs to the lands of Cairbre Mac Aodhagáin in the years between 1602 and 1629 strongly indicate that the family was thoroughly versed in the niceties of common law in respect of land title. The involvement of the legal expert Sir John Davies therein suggests that they had cultivated contacts at the top level of the Dublin administration to ensure that the law could be used to the best advantage of the family.[18]

It is evident that Baothghalach Ruadh Mac Aodhagáin had been dead for quite a few years by the time Mícheál Ó Cléirigh wrote his 1643 preface, for he notes that Lughaidh Ó Cléirigh, another participant in the poetic dispute, had composed some verses in praise of the Mac Aodhagáin scholar after his death, and Lughaidh himself had died probably about 1630.[19]

> *Athairne athair na háoi,*
> *Dallán Forgaill an fpriomhsháoi,*
> *Do mheas rem cheile nír cheart,*
> *Neidhe ro feas, Feircheirt.*

---

15 *AFM*, VI, pp 2272–3; 2312–13.   16 RIA MS D i 3, fo. 62, a genealogy compiled by Pilib Ó Duibhgeannáin at Ballymacegan in 1644; see Ní Maol-Chróin, 'Geinealaigh Clainne Aodhagáin', 133–4.   17 NAI Chancery inquisitions, Tipperary, Charles I, RC/4/10, pp 167–70, no. 74, 19 Mar. 1629. See also below, n. 49.   18 Just as the Mac Aodhagáin lawyers were interested in the common law, so was Sir John Davies interested in Irish law. In the course of his researches he obtained some Irish manuscripts including an 'old chronicle', which was later acquired by Sir Robert Cotton (BL Harley MS 6018, fo. 174), (MacHale, *Annals of the Clan Egan*, pp 42–6).   19 See below, pp 268–70,

Seanchais diamhra, dlighthe ar sean,
Béurla foirtche na bfileadh,
Do bhí an éin mheidh gar naithnidh,
Clí an éirnidh an ionnaithmhigh.

(Athairne, father of learning,
Dallán Forgaill, the chief scholar,
To compare with my companion would be unjust,
Neide the learned, Feircertne.

Obscure history, laws of our ancients,
The dark language of the poets,
He in a word to our knowledge,
Had the power to explain and analyse.)[20]

Lughaidh, like Mícheál Ó Cléirigh, clearly regarded Baothghalach Ruadh as a 'father of learning', and it is possible that both Lughaidh and Mícheál Ó Cléirigh, who were themselves third cousins, had studied at the school conducted by Baothghalach Ruadh Mac Aodhagáin at Ballymacegan.[21]

The other prominent member of the Mac Aodhagáin family whom Ó Cléirigh names in his 1643 preface as being personally known to him is Flann mac Cairbre Mhic Aodhagáin who, he notes, was still alive at that time.[22] Aside from being acknowledged in the *Foclóir*, Flann Mac Aodhagáin's signature of approval is appended to three other works compiled by Ó Cléirigh and his team: the Martyrology of Donegal,[23] the *Genealogiae regum et sanctorum Hiberniae*[24] and AFM.[25] That his approbation was sought is an indication that Ó Cléirigh regarded him as one of the most learned Irish scholars of his day. When the Franciscan provincial, Rev. Valentine Browne, OFM, had instructed Mícheál Ó Cléirigh to have his historical compilations approved by the best scholars of Irish, Flann Mac Aodhagáin was one of those he sought out for this purpose. By the time the annals were completed, Rev. Joseph Everard had succeeded Rev. Browne in office as provincial, and he named Flann Mac Aodhagáin and Conchobhar Mac Bruaideadha as appropriate authorities to vouch for the worthiness of the work.[26]

The reputation of the family of Mac Aodhagáin was well documented in the pages of AFM, where the scholarly activities of no less than twenty-seven individuals of that surname were noted in the period between 1301 and 1550. The obituaries of seventeen of these learned men were recorded in the century

for discussion of Lughaidh Ó Cléirigh and the probable date of his death.   20 Miller (ed.), 'O'Clery's Irish glossary', 353–4, using O'Curry's translation.   21 McKenna (ed.), *Iomarbhágh na bhfileadh*, I, pp x–xi.   22 Miller (ed.), 'O'Clery's Irish glossary', 354.   23 *MDon*, pp l–li.   24 *GRSH*, p. 146.   25 *AFM*, I, lxviii–lxix.   26 For Everard, see *AFM*, I, lxviii–lxix, and also *MDon*, pp l–li.

from 1351 to 1450, with lesser numbers in the preceding and following centuries. Most were lawyers, but they also included poets and musicians.

In the 1620s and 1630s, when Mícheál Ó Cléirigh had contact with him, Flann Mac Aodhagáin, a lawyer and historian, lived at Ballymacegan, in the parish of Lorrha in north Co. Tipperary, and had responsibility for its school of law and history.[27] Ó Cléirigh's association with Flann and with Baothghalach Ruadh Mac Aodhagáin should not be considered unusual. A century earlier, for example, there was already a tradition of Ó Cléirigh and Mac Aodhagáin cooperation on historical projects, as evidenced by the manuscript miscellany now known as Bodleian Library MS Laud Misc 610, produced in the 1450s for Edmund Mac Richard Butler.[28]

An analysis of seventeenth-century landholding in Tipperary shows that the Mac Aodhagáin family held a very substantial 11.2 per cent of the land in the entire barony of Lower Ormond, and that the barony was the most stable in the region in terms of landownership in the early seventeenth century. While members of the Mac Aodhagáin family actively worked to establish individual title to particular portions of land, the traditional heartland at Ballymacegan, where the school was located, was still held in common by the leading members of the family.[29] According to the Civil Survey, in 1640 the proprietors of Ballymacegan were 'fflan mcEgan of BallymcEgan, Constance mcEgan of Killnalahagh and John mcEgan of Grainge, Irish Papists', and the lands were bounded on the north by the River Shannon. It was noted that 'The s[ai]d lands are not cleerely devided betweene the s[ai]d proprietors whereby each p[ro]prietors p[ro]portion may be p[ar]ticularly surrounded by its meares & bounds. The s[ai]d lands are totally wast[e] w[i]thout any improvem[en]t.'[30] In the same parish, the lands of 'Kearhuemota' were also held in common by Flann Mac Aodhagáin and others of the same surname. This property included one thatched house, the only building mentioned in the survey of the Mac Aodhagáin lands in Lorrha parish.[31]

The circumstantial evidence suggests that Flann succeeded his older brother Baothghalach Ruadh as head of the Mac Aodhagáin law school in Ormond. It is clear that Mícheál Ó Cléirigh cultivated his connection with Flann Mac Aodhagáin in the late 1620s, journeying specifically to visit him on a number of occasions. When Ó Cléirigh transcribed the text known as *Cáin Adamnáin* from

27 Bernadette Cunningham, 'Mícheál Ó Cléirigh and the Mac Aodhagáin school of law and history in Ormond' in George Cunningham (ed.), *The Roscrea Conference: commemorating forty conferences, 1987–2007, at Mount St Joseph Abbey* (Roscrea, 2007), pp 7–15. 28 The two main scribes were Seaán Buidhe Ó Cléirigh and Giolla na Naomh Mac Aodhagáin (*Cat. Ir. mss in Bodl.*, I, pp 62–3). See also Simms, 'Bards and barons', p. 191; Myles Dillon, 'Laud Misc 610, (continued)', *Celtica* 6 (1963), 135–55. 29 W.J. Smyth, 'Property, patronage and population: reconstructing the human geography of mid-seventeenth century County Tipperary' in William Nolan (ed.), *Tipperary: history and society* (Dublin, 1985), pp 117–18. 30 R.C. Simington (ed.), *The civil survey AD1654– 1656, county of Tipperary, vol. II: western and northern baronies* (Dublin, 1934), p. 318. 31 Simington (ed.), *The civil survey AD1654–1656, county of Tipperary, II*, p. 316.

an earlier source in May 1628, he made a note in another manuscript he was forwarding to Louvain that he wished to retain his transcript of this work because he hoped to consult Flann Mac Aodhagáin about some difficulties he had encountered with the text.[32]

> *Atá Cain Adhamnain agam … agus dá rabhtai aga hiarradh, cuirthear fios cugam ar a ceann, agus is aire atú aga congbhail an tanso deagla nach budh eidir do Bhaothghalach ó na sduidér aire do thabhairt dí, agus a muinighin go ffaicfeinn Flann mac Cairpri meic Aedhagain da fechain an ccuirfedh urlannacha ar na neithibh cruaidhe bhenus le breithemhnus filet innte.[33]*
> [I have Cain Adhamnain […] and if you should require it request it from me, and the reason I am retaining it at present is lest Baothghalach were unable because of his studies to take heed of it, and hoping to see Flann mac Cairbre Meic Aodhagáin to see if he could explain difficult things it contains relating to the law.][34]

This suggests that Flann Mac Aodhagáin was regarded by Ó Cléirigh as having particular expertise in analyzing such texts, and that he was one of the few to have such specialist knowledge. The identity of the Baothghalach mentioned in this passage whom Ó Cléirigh considered could advise him concerning the meaning of a legal text is uncertain. The memorandum could be interpreted as meaning that the man under whom Ó Cléirigh had studied was still alive in 1628, though this is unlikely as it also seems from the context of the colophon that the man in question was in Louvain rather than in Ireland at that time. He is thus probably to be identified as yet another Baothghalach Mac Aodhagáin, also known as Augustine, a Franciscan who taught theology at Louvain and worked on the compilation of an Irish dictionary. This man, one of several early seventeenth-century Irish Franciscans identified by Canice Mooney who were named Baothghalach Mac Aodhagáin, died at Louvain in January 1654.[35]

Given Mícheál Ó Cléirigh's focus on Flann Mac Aodhagáin as the source of expertise in such matters within Ireland by 1628, it is probably safe to assume that his former teacher, Baothghalach Ruadh, had died before that date. Ó Cléirigh visited Ballymacegan sometime late in 1628 or early in 1629, during which time he and Flann Mac Aodhagáin presumably discussed the finer points of the *Cáin Adamnáin* text that Ó Cléirigh had transcribed. While there, he also transcribed two further pieces relating to St Adamnán from a historical manuscript then in Mac Aodhagáin's possession.[36] Malachy Queely, vicar apostolic of Killaloe,

32 Jennings, *Michael Ó Cléirigh and his associates*, pp 60, 194–5. 33 BR MS 4190–200, fo. 46v; Jennings, *Michael Ó Cléirigh and his associates*, pp 194–5, n. 7; *DIL*, s.v. *airlann*. 34 My translation. 35 Jennings, *Michael Ó Cléirigh and his associates*, p. 60; Mooney, *Boetius MacEgan of Ross*, p. 10. 36 Nollaig Ó Muraíle, in his editorial notes to Paul Walsh's essay, 'The travels of Michael Ó Cléirigh', identifies the passages as nos 150 and 166 in Radner (ed.), *Fragmentary Annals of Ireland* (Walsh, *Irish leaders and learning*, p. 356n). This identifies Flann Mac Aodhagáin as the custodian of a copy of those annals in 1629, suggesting that Mícheál Ó Cléirigh might have been able to draw on them for other material besides the passages relating to Adamnán. This is discussed further below.

reported to Hugh Ward at Louvain on 30 January 1628/9 that he had sent Mícheál Ó Cléirigh into Ormond some time earlier.[37] The letter is dated 'Quinhy the 30 of Jan. 1628 according our computation', which meant that the year was 1629 new style:

> As I was teaching at Cassel uppon your patron his festivall daie [4 October], there I met your brother Clery who made a collection of more than three or four hundreth Lives. I gave him some Lives I collected, and sent him to Ormond parte of my diecese to write there for a time, from whence he promised to com to Thowmond wheare I undertook to get many things for him. And he came not since, soone I doe expect his comminge who shall be wellcom truely to me.[38]

Paul Walsh interpreted this winter sojourn by Ó Cléirigh in Ormond as the occasion of a visit to Flann Mac Aodhagáin.[39] This seems plausible as Queely's diocese of Killaloe extended east of the Shannon to encompass much of north Tipperary including Ballymacegan in the parish of Lorrha. Jennings likewise surmised that the visit to Mac Aodhagáin took place in the late autumn of 1628, around the same time as Mícheál Ó Cléirigh made other transcripts of hagiographical material at the Franciscan house at Cashel, also in Co. Tipperary.[40] It appears that Ó Cléirigh may have remained in the south during the entire winter of 1628–9, and so had the opportunity to undertake substantial research on the manuscripts available in the north Munster area, including those in the custody of Flann Mac Aodhagáin.[41] As will be seen below, it is possible that he also visited Conall Mac Eochagháin in nearby Lismoyny during that same winter.

On subsequent visits to the home of Flann Mac Aodhagáin, in August 1632 and in November 1636, Ó Cléirigh again brought with him manuscripts containing his own work. On these later occasions, he did not merely seek advice but requested and was granted Flann Mac Aodhagáin's written approbations for those works. Mac Aodhagáin's approbation of the *Genealogiae regum et sanctorum Hiberniae* is dated 31 August 1632 while his approbations for the Martyrology of Donegal and AFM are dated 1 and 2 November 1636 respectively.[42] In the

---

37 Jennings (ed.), 'Documents from St Isidore's', 217–18. The letter is written under the pseudonym David Rice. Jennings notes that Rice is identified with O'Queely in *Wadding Papers*, 372 (Jennings, *Michael Ó Cléirigh and his associates*, p. 195, n. 14).   38 Jennings (ed.), 'Documents from St Isidore's', 218.   39 Walsh, *Irish leaders and learning*, p. 356.   40 Jennings, *Michael Ó Cléirigh and his associates*, 66–7.   41 This conclusion accords with Paul Walsh's reading of the dates on the colophons to Ó Cléirigh's transcripts of saints' lives which substantially revise those of Brendan Jennings. The difficulty was that Jennings had assumed that Mícheál Ó Cléirigh consistently used new style dating, with the new year commencing on 1 January, as was the norm on the continent, and indeed in the annals. However, Walsh provided evidence that in his hagiographical manuscripts, though not normally in AFM, Ó Cléirigh used old style dating with the new year commencing on 25 March (Walsh, *Irish leaders and learning*, pp 351–3). Walsh made a convincing case, and his revisions have been adopted here.   42 *MDon*, pp l–liii; *AFM*, I, pp lxiii–lxix; *GRSH*, p. 146. The *Genealogiae regum et sanctorum Hiberniae* approbation by Flann Mac Aodhagáin, is found in RIA, MS 24 P 33, fo. 45, but this is not the earliest copy of that text.

following years, Flann Mac Aodhagáin continued to be held in high regard by the Franciscans and others. Among the correspondence addressed to Hugh Burke, superior of the Irish Franciscans in Belgium in 1642, is a letter dated 12 October from a traumatized Rev. Brendan O'Connor, who expressed regret at not having been able to visit Mac Aodhagáin.[43] A more upbeat letter, dated 20 September 1642, from Ruaidhrí Ó Mordha, expressed the hope that:

> If we may afore Flan Mac Egan dies, we will see an Irish school opened, and therefore could wish heartily that those learned and religious fathers in Lovayne did come over in hast with their monuments and with an Irish and Latin print.[44]

Ó Mordha's aspirations imply that Flann Mac Aodhagáin was now an elderly man, and that he was regarded as perhaps the last remaining scholar of the calibre required for such an initiative. Ó Mordha's comments also indicate that Mícheál Ó Cléirigh's high regard for Flann Mac Aodhagáin's exceptional learning, and his role as an important anchor in the world of Irish scholarship in the early seventeenth century, was widely shared. They reveal also, however, that by 1642 the world of Gaelic learning was perceived as in serious decline, such that the death of one man could be regarded as sounding the death knell for the profession.

Flann Mac Aodhagáin's involvement with Mícheál Ó Cléirigh's researches seems to have been primarily as scholarly consultant, and occasionally as source of manuscript materials – not just saints' lives, but secular history also. The fragments that Ó Cléirigh obtained from Mac Aodhagáin in 1628 comprised the story of Adamnán and Irgalach, and an account of the revision of the date of Easter in Ireland.[45] Joan Radner has argued the case for identifying the vellum manuscript containing historical annals that was in the possession of Flann Mac Aodhagáin when it was copied by Dubhaltach Mac Fhirbhisigh as deriving from the now lost Annals of Cluain Eidhneach. These annals were among the sources cited also by Geoffrey Keating, in his *Foras feasa ar Éirinn*. Keating also cited other manuscripts including *Leabhar ruadh Mic Aodhagáin* and *Leabhar breac Mic Aodhagáin*, which he may have consulted through contact with Flann Mac Aodhagáin.[46] Radner likewise presents the evidence for Sir James Ware having had access to material from the same lost annals. In the case of Ware's account of the Synod of Kells, which is almost identical to Keating's, the account is headed '*Ex Ms. Libro vetust. D. Flannani mac Aegain*' ['From the old manuscript book of Flann Mac Aodhagáin'].[47] Since neither Ware nor Keating appears to have

---

43 *HMC Franciscan MSS*, pp 192–3.   44 *HMC Franciscan MSS*, pp 193–4.   45 Jennings, *Michael Ó Cléirigh and his associates*, p. 67.   46 Comyn and Dinneen (eds), *Foras feasa ar Éirinn*, III, pp 24–5, 26–7, 48–9, 108–9, 294–5, 314–17, 362–3.   47 Radner (ed.), *Fragmentary annals of Ireland*, pp vii–viii; it is unclear how Ware obtained access to Flann Mac Aodhagáin's manuscript. The link was apparently not Mac Fhirbhisigh – the fragmentary transcript is not in Mac Fhirbhisigh's hand (BL Add. MS 4783, fos 34–35; Ó Muraíle, *Celebrated antiquary*, p. 93).

obtained more than scraps from the Annals of Cluain Eidhnech, and since those annals were not listed among the sources consulted by the Four Masters, it seems that they may not have been accessible in the 1630s, except perhaps in the most fragmentary form.

Among the other scholars who worked with Flann Mac Aodhagáin was Dubhaltach Mac Fhirbhisigh, who apparently spent time at Ballymacegan in 1643 and made transcripts of manuscripts there. Ó Muraíle notes that about a third of the text of Binchy's *Corpus iuris Hibernici*, an edition of Irish law tracts, comes from manuscripts that once formed part of the library of Dubhaltach Mac Fhirbhisigh, who had obtained his legal manuscripts from 'the law-schools of the MacEgans'.[48] Flann Mac Aodhagáin's reputation also reached the ears of Richard Bellings, later to be known as the historian of the Catholic Confederation. In 1640, when Bellings was still a young man and giving consideration for the first time to writing on the history of Ireland, he contacted the earl of Ormond concerning 'John Mac Regan', whom Bellings believed had 'certain books or papers which will much avail him in compiling the history of Ireland which he is about'.[49] The family may not have had the same prominence as they had enjoyed in earlier centuries, but it is evident that the name of Mac Aodhagáin still commanded respect. Though the evidence is fragmentary, it is clear that the Mac Aodhagáin school in Ormond continued to be a magnet for scholars of both Gaelic and Old English (Anglo-Norman) descent from all parts of the country down to the 1640s. The value placed by Ó Cléirigh on Flann Mac Aodhagáin's approbation is testament to the pre-eminence of the school's reputation. And at a less formal level the network of contacts that could be cultivated through association with the Mac Aodhagáin school may have been almost indispensable for those who sought to pursue Irish historical scholarship at the highest level.

Ó Maoil Chonaire

The second learned family to feature prominently in Mícheál Ó Cléirigh's acknowledgments in the preface to his 1643 *Foclóir* is that of Ó Maoil Chonaire. The family has been described by Katharine Simms as 'the most eminent of the native Irish historians'.[50] They were traditionally employed by the Síol

48 Ó Muraíle, *Celebrated antiquary*, p. 303; see also A. and W. O'Sullivan, 'Edward Lhuyd's collection of Irish manuscripts', *Transactions of the Honourable Society of Cymmrodorion* (1962), 57–76. 49 Bodl. Carte MSS, I, fo. 210v, cited in Raymond Gillespie, 'The social thought of Richard Bellings' in Mícheál Ó Siochrú (ed.), *Kingdoms in crisis: Ireland in the 1640s* (Dublin, 2001), p. 213; Kenneth Nicholls has suggested (pers. comm.) that it was almost certainly Flann Mac Aodhagáin that Bellings hoped to contact, despite the vagueness as to the man's forename. It should be noted, however, that a John/Seán was named along with Flann in the 1629 Chancery Inquisition and might possibly have been his son. See above, n. 17. 50 Simms, 'Bards and barons', p. 191. The family features particularly prominently in AConn.

Muireadaigh, a grouping that included the Uí Chonchobhair of Connacht, along with the families of Mac Diarmada and Mac Donnchadha. Among the lesser families associated with them were the Uí Bheirn of Connacht and the Uí Fhlannagáin.[51] By the fifteenth century, the Uí Mhaoil Chonaire were working well beyond their Roscommon home into Meath, Kildare and Longford,[52] but they also continued to maintain a school of history in Roscommon. Like other learned families, by the seventeenth century a number of their members had opted to join religious orders. Thus, in the years 1624–6, there were at least three of that surname in the Irish Franciscan college at Louvain. In addition to the well-known Flaithrí, archbishop of Tuam, who had founded the college of St Anthony, there were two others named Seán and Ferdinandus.[53] These men's time at Louvain would have coincided with the period that Ó Cléirigh himself spent there.

Those of the Uí Mhaoil Chonaire of whom Ó Cléirigh speaks in the past tense in his 1643 publication include Torna Ó Maoil Chonaire and Maoileachlainn Modartha Ó Maoil Chonaire. He notes that they had been distinguished scholars and were among *na maighistribh do ba foirtille agas dobadh foghlamtha an eolas chrúais na gáoidhilge in ar laithibh féin* ('the ablest and most learned masters of the knowledge of the difficulty of the Gaelic in our own days').[54] It is clear from the manner in which they are mentioned that these two members of the Ó Maoil Chonaire family, like Baothghalach Ruadh Mac Aodhagáin, were no longer living in 1643. Yet, their contribution to the study of the more obscure aspects of the language had been of assistance to Mícheál Ó Cléirigh in the past and was therefore acknowledged. Again, the possibility that there had at one time been a formal arrangement, whereby Ó Cléirigh studied at an Ó Maoil Chonaire school, cannot be discounted. However, that is not the sense of Ó Cléirigh's 1643 preface, where he indicates that his contact with their Irish language scholarship was not on such a personal basis as in the case of Baothghalach Ruadh Mac Aodhagáin. Paul Walsh has noted that Maoileachlainn Modartha was brother of the Franciscan archbishop of Tuam, Fláithrí Ó Maoil Chonaire, which suggests another possible route through which Ó Cléirigh might have established a connection with this branch of the Ó Maoil Chonaire family.[55] The Torna Ó Maoil Chonaire mentioned along with Maoileachlainn Modartha was probably his cousin, Torna mac Eóluis meic Muirghesa, both being grandsons of

51 Walsh, *Irish men of learning*, p. 34.   52 *AConn*, s.a. 1419, 1446, 1519; Simms, 'Bards and barons', 191–2, 196.   53 Correspondence (1624–5) preserved in the Roman archives of Propaganda Fide, from Thomas Fleming and Flaithrí Ó Maoil Chonaire, reporting on the progress of the Irish College at Louvain, printed in P. Moran, *History of the Catholic archbishops of Dublin since the Reformation* (Dublin, 1864), pp 300, 302; 'Relation of Rev Paul Raget, vicar-general of the Irish Cistercians to Cardinal De Sourdis, 12 February 1625' in *HMC Franciscan MSS*, p. 79.   54 Miller, (ed.), 'O'Clery's Irish glossary', 353; Paul Walsh notes that Maoileachlainn Modartha Ó Maoil Chonaire was scribe of an exemplar which Mícheál Ó Cléirigh copied into RIA MS B iv 2, in 1628. 55 Walsh, *Irish men of learning*, 41.

Muirgheas Ó Maoil Chonaire.[56] A seventeenth-century genealogy preserved in RIA MS E iv 4 identifies these two as members of Sliocht Pháidín, and therefore of the Ballymulconry (Cluain Plocáin) branch of the family. Their descent is traced in the genealogy from Páidín Ó Maoil Chonaire, who died in 1506.[57] Páidín was accorded a brief obituary in AFM: *Paidín ua Maolchonaire en rogha Ereann ina aimsir lé Senchus, 7 lé filidhecht décc.* ('Paidin O'Mulconry, only choice of Ireland in his time for history and poetry, died').[58] One of Paidín's sons, Muirgheas, who died in 1543, was scribe of the Book of Fenagh, and also copied a version of *Leabhar gabhála Éireann*, referred to by the Four Masters as being contained within 'The Book of Ballymulconry' when they consulted it in 1631 for their new recension of that text.[59] Ó Cléirigh also obtained copies of hagiographical texts from the Book of Fenagh, either directly or indirectly, from descendants of the same family.[60]

Ballymulconry, formerly known as Cluain Plocáin, was located in the parish of Kiltrustan, in the barony of Roscommon, close to an inlet from the River Shannon north of Strokestown.[61] By 1640, Sir Charles Coote had obtained possession of most of the townland of Ballymulconry, but Páidín Ruadh Ó Maoil Chonaire was still a significant landholder in the immediate neighbourhood at Rathmore and Cloneshannagh, and he also held land in the parish of Cloncraw.[62] Other members of the Ó Maoil Chonaire family were also recorded in the Books of Survey and Distribution as the holders of lands in the baronies of Roscommon and Boyle, though there was no Seán Ó Maoil Chonaire listed among them by 1640.[63] By the mid-sixteenth century, another branch of the same family, descendants of Torna Óg (d. 1532), had become established in the vicinity of Bunratty, Co. Clare.

Paul Walsh drew attention to some of the earlier scholarly contacts between Ó Cléirigh scholars and the Uí Mhaoil Chonaire of Corlios Conaill, when BL MS Harley 5280 was written there by Giolla Riabhach son of Tuathal Ó Cléirigh, in the early sixteenth century.[64] This is further proof, if such were needed, that

---

56 Walsh, *Irish men of learning*, p. 40.   57 RIA MS E iv 4, 13; Walsh, *Irish men of learning*, p. 40.
58 *AFM*, V, pp 1286–7.   59 The original copy of the dedication and preface to the Four Masters' recension of *Leabhar gabhála* is preserved in TCD MS 1286, and printed from that source in O'Curry, *Lectures on manuscript materials*, English translation, pp 168–73, Irish text in appendix LXXIV, pp 552–7; a fragment of the Ó Maoil Chonaire source manuscript, containing an incomplete copy of *Leabhar gabhála* transcribed by Muirgheas mac Pháidín Uí Mhaoil Chonaire and stated by the scribe to derive from *Leabhar na hUidhre*, is now RIA MS D iv 3. For Muirgheas's career, see Cunningham and Gillespie, 'Muirgheas Ó Maoilchonaire of Cluain Plocáin'.   60 The life of Caillín transcribed in BR MS 2324–40, fos 303–354v, is derived from this source. Colophon dated 21 Dec. 1629 is printed in Jennings, *Michael Ó Cléirigh and his associates*, p. 200, n. 5; for other manuscripts similarly sourced by Ó Cléirigh, see Walsh, *Irish leaders and learning*, p. 352.   61 M.J. Connellan, 'Ballymulconry and the Mulconrys', *Irish Ecclesiastical Record* 5th ser., 90 (1958), 322–30.   62 R.C. Simington (ed.), *Books of survey and distribution, Co. Roscommon* (Dublin, 1949), pp 73, 88.   63 Simington (ed.), *Books of survey and distribution, Co. Roscommon*, pp 29, 73–4, 83, 85, 88, 166.   64 Walsh, *Irish men of learning*, p. 48.

the kind of extensive scholarly network of which Mícheál Ó Cléirigh was a part was not a seventeenth-century innovation, but was built on a long tradition of association between these families in the cause of scholarship.

Separate acknowledgment was made by Mícheál Ó Cléirigh of Seán Ó Maoil Chonaire, whom he described as *priomhoide sgoile na druinge a dubhramar cheana agas fhear nEireann a seanchas, ina aimsir féin* ('the principal teacher of those whom we have mentioned, and of the men of Ireland [in history], in his own time').[65] This Seán Ó Maoil Chonaire is probably to be identified with the well-known historian, Seán son of Torna Ó Maoil Chonaire, whom Flann Mac Aodhagáin also mentioned explicitly in the course of his praise for AFM in 1636, asserting the pre-eminence that had been enjoyed by his school of history:

> ... *bhó líonmhar an nuimhir éccínte do leabhraibh aosda 7 nemhaosda, sgríobhtha, 7 acca sgríobhadh do connarc i scoil Seaain mic Torna Ui Mhaoilchonaire, oide fear nEreann hi ccoitchinne, hi senchus 7 hi ccroinic, 7 aga mbádar a raibh i nErinn ag foghlam na healadhna sin ga teaccasc aicce.*
> (... numerous the uncertain number of ancient and modern books which I saw written and being transcribed in the school of John, son of Torna Ua Maelchonaire, the tutor of the men of Ireland in general in history and chronology, and who had all that were in Ireland learning that science under his tuition.)[66]

Mac Aodhagáin, like Ó Cléirigh, writes of Seán Ó Maoil Chonaire in the past tense, but implies that he had been personally acquainted with him. Paul Walsh's suggestion that the scholar in question was the father of the two Ó Maoil Chonaire scribes who compiled the manuscript now known as BL Egerton MS 1782 in the second decade of the sixteenth century does not fit the evidence. Their father's death was recorded in the manuscript in 1517, at which time he was *ollamh* of Síol Muireadaigh.[67] If this is the man referred to by Ó Cléirigh, he had been dead for well over a hundred years, and the reference is an acknowledgment of a very abstract scholarly influence rather than personal acquaintance. It is the case that Flann Mac Aodhagáin's 1636 reference implies that he no longer presided over the activities of the industrious Ó Maoil Chonaire school, but Flann nonetheless claimed personal knowledge of the school run by Seán mac Torna, as though he were his own contemporary. Ó Cléirigh, too, contextualizes his reference to Sean Ó Maoil Chonaire by the phrase *fós san aimsir dheigheanaigh* ('even in the later time'), a clear indication that the man lived later than Baothghalach Ruadh Mac Aodhagáin, and that though Seán Ó Maoil Chonaire was no longer living, he was a near contemporary of Flann Mac Aodhagáin and of Ó Cléirigh himself. This being so, the identification with the father of the early sixteenth-century scribes of BL Egerton MS 1782 cannot be

65 Miller (ed.), 'O'Clery's Irish glossary', 354. 66 *AFM*, I, p. lxviii; Walsh, *Irish men of learning*, p. 37. 67 Flower, *Cat. Ir. mss in BL*, II, p. 262.

correct. Nor is he to be confused with a much later Seán mac Torna Uí Mhaoil Chonaire still alive and active as a scribe in the 1650s who transcribed, amongst other items, Keating's *Foras feasa ar Éirinn*.[68] This later scribe was most likely the son of Torna mac Muiris Uí Mhaoil Chonaire of the Thomond branch of the family, of Ceapach, Co. Clare, and was a generation too late to have been Ó Cléirigh's mentor.[69]

A possible candidate for acknowledgment as mentor to Mícheál Ó Cléirigh is the Seán Ó Maoil Chonaire who in 1575 facilitated the compilation of the manuscript now known as RIA MS 23 N 10, a manuscript usually regarded as a product of the same school as BL Egerton MS 1782.[70] This sixteenth-century vellum and paper collection of medieval tales was the work of three scribes, Aodh, Dubhthach and Torna, and was written in the house of Seán Ó Maoil Chonaire at *Baile Tibhaird* on *Bla Maige* and at *Baile in Chuimine* in Co. Roscommon.[71] A Seán Ó Maoil Chonaire active in 1560, perhaps the same man, was the scribe of an exemplar containing material derived from the renowned but long-lost historical manuscript, *Cín Dromma Snechtai*.[72] This was among the source manuscripts cited in the Book of Ballymote and the Book of Lecan, two major north Connacht manuscripts of the late fourteenth and early fifteenth centuries, but the original manuscript was apparently no longer extant by the seventeenth century. Despite the manuscript attributions associating Séan Ó Maoil Chonaire with the production of major manuscript compilations in the late sixteenth century, it is difficult to identify him from the extant genealogies of the family.[73] It is likely that Ó Cléirigh's mentor should be identified as the Seán Ó Maoil Chonaire who in 1566 wrote a lengthy poem in praise of Sir Brian na Múrtha Ó Ruairc (d. 1591) entitled *Fuair Breifne a díol do shaoghlonn* ('Breifne has obtained her due of a prince'). According to Tadhg Ó Rodaighe, the poet was a member of the Ardchoill, Co. Clare, branch of the family. He can thus

---

68 The following manuscripts contain transcripts prepared between the 1630s and 1650s by Seán mac Torna Uí Mhaoil Chonaire of some of Geoffrey Keating's works: King's Inns Gaelic MS 2; TCD MSS 1397, 1439; RIA MS 23 O 19.   69 RIA MS E iv 4, p. 12, cited in Walsh, *Irish men of learning*, p. 39. Another son of Torna mac Muiris Uí Mhaoil Chonaire, named Iollann, was also involved in making transcripts of Keating's history in the 1640s (RIA MS 23 O 19). The Co. Clare branch of the family is discussed in Brian Ó Dálaigh, 'The Uí Mhaoilchonaire of Thomond', unpublished lecture delivered at Tionól, School of Celtic Studies, Nov. 2008. I am grateful to Brian for providing me with a copy of this lecture in advance of publication.   70 Tomás Ó Concheanainn, 'A Connacht medieval literary heritage: texts derived from *Cín Dromma Snechtai* through *Leabhar na hUidhre*', *Cambridge Medieval Celtic Studies* 16 (1988), 1–40, passim.   71 *Cat. Ir. mss in RIA*, no. 967, pp 2769–80; 'Baile in Chuimine' has been identified by Kuno Meyer as Ballycumin, on Loch Bó Deirge, on the Shannon. According to the Books of Survey and Distribution, it was church land in the parish of Kilmore, barony of Ballintobber, Co. Roscommon (Simington (ed.), *Books of survey and distribution, Roscommon*, p. 31).   72 See title page of RIA MS 24 C 3, a mid-nineteenth-century manuscript; *Cat. Ir. mss in RIA*, p. 1883; see also Ó Concheanainn, 'A Connacht medieval literary heritage', 4–9.   73 There is no Seán named in the only Ó Maoil Chonaire genealogy recorded by Dubhaltach Mac Fhirbhisigh (Ó Muraíle (ed.), *Leabhar mór na ngenealach*, I, pp 402–3). Paul Walsh has printed a genealogy of Sliocht Páidín from RIA MS E iv 4, p. 12, in Walsh, *Irish men of learning*, pp 40–1.

be identified as son of Torna Óg, and a nephew of the Seaán mac Torna who had died in 1517.[74] Since Torna Óg had died in 1532, this Seán, who was certainly still alive in 1587,[75] would have been an elderly man in Ó Cléirigh's youth.

Mícheál Ó Cléirigh's 1643 acknowledgment of the influence of Seán Ó Maoil Chonaire on his own scholarship was unspecific. Though the two men appear to have come into contact with one another at some time, Ó Cléirigh did not elaborate on the precise nature of the association. In a curious way, too, the wording of the 1643 preface appears to echo Flann Mac Aodhagáin's 1636 description of the pre-eminent Ó Maoil Chonaire historian, as though Ó Cléirigh had Mac Aodhagáin's words of praise in mind as he recalled the influence of Seán Ó Maoil Chonaire on his own life's work.[76]

The 'fourth' master, Fearfeasa son of Lochlainn Ó Maoil Chonaire, was another member of Sliocht Pháidín, a relationship that further affirms Ó Cléirigh's ties with this particular branch of the extensive Ó Maoil Chonaire family.[77] Eoin Mac Cárthaigh has recently suggested that Fearfeasa's lands were in the modern townland of Creta, in Kiltrustan parish, and that his father, Lochlainn, had lived in the adjoining townland of Lisheen. The Páidín Ruadh Ó Maoil Chonaire who retained two thirds of his lands in Baile Uí Mhaoil Chonaire under the arrangements for the transplantation to Connacht in 1654–8, may have been Fearfeasa's brother.[78]

Paul Walsh notes that Fearfeasa Ó Maoil Chonaire lived for many years after his involvement with AFM and was the author of several poems, including *Mochean do[d] chuairt a Chalbhaigh*, addressed to An Calbhach Ruadh Ó Domhnaill.[79] It is therefore probable that Fearfeasa was a younger man than Ó Cléirigh when he worked on the AFM scheme. Fearfeasa also strenuously opposed Tuileagna Ó Maoil Chonaire's criticisms of the work of the Four Masters team well into the 1640s, which is itself an indication that his contribution was not just that of a scribe and that he is more appropriately regarded as a compiler.[80] Fearfeasa stated explicitly

---

74 Among the earliest extant manuscript copies of this poem are RIA MS 23 C 30 (a), pp 17–28, and RIA MS 24 C 55, [pp 687–95], the latter incorporating extensive notes in Irish and English. The copy of this poem preserved in BL MS Egerton 127 is accompanied by a note by Tadhg Ó Rodaighe associating it with Seán mac Torna Ó Maoil Chonaire of Ardchoill, Co. Clare (Flower, *Cat. Ir. mss in BL*, II, p. 67), though it should be cautioned that Tadhg Ó Rodaighe was not a contemporary of the poet. A version of the poem has been published in James Hardiman, *Irish Minstrelsy*, II (London, 1831), 286–305, 426–30. The Brian na Múrtha Ó Ruairc in question was a grandson of Maghnus Ó Domhnaill, his mother being Ó Domhnaill's daughter.   75 Pádraig Ó Fiannachta (ed.), *Táin Bó Cuailnge: the Maynooth manuscript* (Dublin, 1980), pp viii–ix.   76 Miller (ed.), 'O'Clery's Irish glossary', 354; *AFM*, I, p. lxviii.   77 Walsh, *Irish men of learning*, pp 40–1 (Fearfeasa son of Lochlainn son of Seán Ruadh son of Lochlainn son of Paidín); UCD–OFM MS A 13, fo. xxiii.   78 Eoin Mac Cárthaigh, 'Fearfeasa Ó Maolchonaire' in *DIB*.   79 Paul Walsh [Pól Breathnach], 'What we know of Cuchoigcriche Ó Cléirigh', *Irish Book Lover* 23 (1935), 63; Eoin Mac Cárthaigh, 'Three poems by Maol Muire Ó hUiginn to An Calbhach Ruadh Ó Domhnaill', *Ériu* 48 (1997), 59–82; Mac Cárthaigh, 'Fearfeasa Ó Maolchonaire'; NLI MS G 167, p. 339.   80 *GRSH*, appendix.

that only the Ó Cléirigh trio worked on the AFM material for the years after 1333,[81] and scribe E (tentatively identified as Fearfeasa) is associated with RIA MS C iii 3, one of the autograph manuscripts that contains pre-1170 material.[82]

The scribal assistant Muiris son of Torna Ó Maoil Chonaire who worked on AFM for one month was also from Co. Roscommon, and he may have owned land in the same parish of Kiltrustan.[83] In contrast to Fearfeasa Ó Maoil Chonaire, he appears to have been employed on the AFM project exclusively as a scribe. Much of the autograph manuscript of the first half of AFM now preserved in RIA MS C iii 3 is believed to be in his hand. Muiris Ó Maoil Chonaire had worked as a poet as well as a *seanchaidh* (historian/chronicler), composing poems in praise of Sir Lucas Dillon[84] and his wife, on Brian Mac Diarmada (d. 1636) and Aodh Ó Conchobhair (d. 1632).[85] It is possible, though not proven, that he was son of the Torna mac Eoluis Uí Mhaoil Chonaire whose influence Ó Cléirigh acknowledged in print in 1643. If so, this would mean that Muiris mac Torna was another member of Sliocht Pháidín, and also a direct descendant of the scribe of the Book of Fenagh.[86] Such a genealogical link would provide the context for Muiris's ownership of a vellum manuscript containing a text of *Naoimhsenchus naomh Insi Fáil* used as an exemplar by Mícheál Ó Cléirigh in April 1636.[87] On Muiris's death in 1645, a poem commemorating his life, *Máthair na horchra an éigsi* (Poetry is the mother of sorrow), was composed by Maolmhuire mac Eóghain Uí Uiginn.[88] The poem emphasizes his career as poet rather than historian; though his work as a genealogist and scribe is also mentioned:

> Tearc dá éis ar tí a dtarbha –
> corp, trácht, amhra, is agallmha,
> sgeóil ágha gan chomhdha a gcairt,
> tána, toghla, agus tochmhairc. …

---

81 *GRSH*, appendix, p. 150. 82 See chapter six, above. 83 Simington (ed.), *Books of survey and distribution, Roscommon*, p. 74. Eoin Mac Cárthaigh notes, however, that there were several others named Muiris Ó Maoil Chonaire living in the area in the early 1640s ('*Lúireach Chríosd fan gCalbhach Ruadh*', *Celtica* 24 (2003), 131–2). 84 Sir Lucas Dillon, brother to George Dillon OFM, belonged to the same circle of politically prominent patrons who had sponsored the historical works of the Four Masters. On Dillon family connections with the Franciscans and Poor Clares, see Bernadette Cunningham, 'The Poor Clare Order in Ireland' in Edel Breathnach, Joseph MacMahon and John McCafferty (eds), *The Irish Franciscans, 1540–1990* (Dublin, 2009), pp 159–74. 85 Eoin Mac Cárthaigh, 'Muiris Ó Maolchonaire' in *DIB*. 86 See genealogical information on this Torna of the principal Ballymulconry branch of the family in Walsh, *Irish men of learning*, p. 40. 87 *A cconveint Dhúin na nGall do sccríobh an bráthair Michel Ó Cleirigh an dhuan shencusa so da ngoirter Naoimhsencus naomh Innsi Fáil, 25 April 1636, as leabhar mheamruim le Muiris mac Torna ui Maoil Conaire* ('In the convent of Donegal brother Michael Ó Cléirigh wrote this historical poem called the history of the saints of Inis Fáil, 25 April 1636, from a vellum book of Muiris mac Torna Uí Mhaoil Chonaire'); Jennings, *Michael Ó Cléirigh and his associates*, pp 146, 204 (BR MS 5100–4, fos 230–238). The transcript is accompanied by an approbation from Conall Mac Eochagáin (BR MS 5100–4, fo. 232), dated 11 October 1636. The approbation is printed in *Cat. Ir. mss in BL*, II, p. 473. 88 Réamann Ó Muireadhaigh, 'Marbhna ar Mhuiris mac Torna Uí Mhaoilchonaire', *Éigse* 15:3 (1974), 215–21.

Filidheacht, fearacht dána,
sgéla trod as teagmhála,
's lorg gach aoin do leanmhuin leis,
's gach taoibh do mheabhruigh Muireis.

(After his death few will seek to profit from text, narrative, elegy, discourse, cattle raids, sackings, wooings – heroic tales are no longer preserved on paper.
... In every place Muiris committed to memory poetry, its practice, stories of fights and battle engagement, and the tracing of everyone's descent.)[89]

The elegy seems to have attached importance to his preserving the memory of the past by committing material to paper, though no particular allusion to his involvement with the AFM project can be read into this. Muiris mac Torna Uí Mhaoil Chonaire is the only one of the team of six named scholars known to have been commemorated by his own contemporaries with a traditional poetic lament.[90] That is an indication that Muiris had a successful scholarly career and is a reminder that his relatively minor role in the AFM project should not be interpreted as implying that his scholarship was in any way inferior to that of others of the 'Four Masters' team. Although his role was apparently confined to that of scribe, he was not a 'junior' member of the team, either in terms of age or experience, or as potential facilitator of access to important manuscript sources.

Ó Maoil Chonaire manuscripts

It has already been noted that Mícheál Ó Cléirigh and his AFM team had access to some manuscripts that were the property of the Ó Maoil Chonaire family. These included a transcript of *Leabhar gabhála Éireann*, taken from a manuscript known as *Leabhar Baile Uí Mhaoilchonaire* ('the Book of Ballymulconry'), copied by Muirgheas mac Phaídín Uí Mhaoil Chonaire from *Leabhar na hUidhre* and other sources.[91] The family also had a set of annals, ending in 1505, known to the Four Masters as *Leabhar Chloinne Uí Maoílconaire* (the Book of Clann Uí Mhaoil Chonaire).[92] The first of these two manuscripts, containing a transcript

89 Ó Muireadhaigh, 'Marbhna ar Mhuiris', 218, stanzas 11 and 13.   90 The poem itself records that the poet and the man who was the subject of the poem had entered into an agreement that the first to die would be commemorated in this way by the survivor (Ó Muireadhaigh, 'Marbhna ar Mhuiris', 220, stanza 22).   91 O'Curry, *Lectures on manuscript materials*, pp 171, 555. As noted above, Muirgheas's transcript of *Leabhar gabhála* is now partially preserved in RIA MS D iv 3, a vellum manuscript dating from the early sixteenth century. *Leabhar na hUidhre* was then more complete than it is now and only a small fragment of the *Leabhar gabhála* text now survives in the extant portion of the manuscript.   92 *AFM*, I, p. lxvi. Either one of these Uí Mhaoil Chonaire manuscripts might be the 'Book of Cluain Plocáin' cited as a source by Tuileagna Ó Maoil Chonaire in his attack on AFM (*GRSH*, pp 131–4). As Kenneth Nicholls has noted, there is no reason to assume that the Ó Maoil Chonaire manuscript partially preserved in RIA MS D iv 3 was the source known to the Four Masters in the seventeenth century as *Leabhar Chloinne Uí Mhaoilchonaire*

of *Leabhar gabhála* among other texts, was the work of Muirgheas mac Pháidín Uí Mhaoil Chonaire, grandfather of Torna and Maoileachlainn Modartha, the two whose influence Ó Cléirigh acknowledged in 1643, and a prominent early member of Sliocht Pháidín.[93] It is probable that the other Ó Maoil Chonaire book which included a set of annals was acquired from the same source, from a branch of the Uí Mhaoil Chonaire with which Mícheál Ó Cléirigh had an acknowledged link, and who had been known for their early sixteenth-century transcripts of older historical works. Ó Cléirigh had earlier worked with transcripts of manuscripts made by Maoileachlainn son of Fitheal son of Muirgheas Ó Maoil Chonaire, when transcribing sections of RIA MS B iv 2, in 1627 and 1628. This manuscript is a composite one, comprising mainly verse but also some historical prose tracts including one on the Christian monarchs of Ireland.[94] Ó Cléirigh names the scribe of his exemplar on three occasions throughout the manuscript.[95]

The pattern discernible here, in connection with the source manuscripts of AFM obtained from Ó Maoil Chonaire sources, is similar to that found in respect of other source manuscripts used by Mícheál Ó Cléirigh. It emerges that Ó Cléirigh's contacts in connection with the annals project had been established over the previous ten years when he worked on transcribing other texts. The learned families who had assisted his work on the lives of the saints by giving him access to manuscripts or making modern transcripts available to him, were the same people to whom he returned when he sought secular historical sources from which to compile the annals of the kingdom of Ireland. Indeed his associates in the secular historical projects, the 'Four Masters' team (all six of them that are named), were drawn from that same fairly tight network of learned families, Ó Cléirigh, Ó Duibhgeannáin and Ó Maoil Chonaire. They were scholars with whom Mícheál Ó Cléirigh had worked previously, and AFM was their final major collective historical undertaking under Franciscan auspices.

Tuileagna Ó Maoil Chonaire

There were others of the extended Ó Maoil Chonaire kin-group whose role in connection with Mícheál Ó Cléirigh's work was less positive than those discussed so far. Criticisms were voiced by Tuileagna Ó Maoil Chonaire in 1637 concerning four points of detail in the *Genealogiae regum et sanctorum Hiberniae* and AFM. The points at issue were said to cast a slur on the status of the province of

(Introduction to 1990 reprint of *AFM*, I, n. 11). Rather, the family probably had a range of historical manuscripts in their possession, including at the very least a set of annals and a transcript of *Leabhar gabhála*. **93** RIA MS E iv 4, p. 12; Walsh, *Irish men of learning*, p. 40. **94** RIA MS B iv 2, fos 10–11v. **95** RIA MS B iv 2, fos 124, 146, 156 as discussed in Walsh, *Irish men of learning*, p. 41. Other parts of this composite manuscript were transcribed at Kildare from the Book of Leinster or a transcript thereof. See *Cat. Ir. mss in RIA*, no. 1080, pp 3021–9.

Connacht. The ensuing controversy probably undermined plans for the publication of Ó Cléirigh's historical works. Tuileagna claimed that Conchobhar Mac Bruaideadha withdrew his approbation from AFM in a public manner following a general chapter of the Franciscans in Thomond in 1638, while Flann Mac Aodhagáin, more circumspectly, had temporarily withdrawn his approbation in 1637 until the points in dispute were resolved.[96] Discussion of the matter continued even after the death of Ó Cléirigh in 1643. The Four Masters' reply to Tuileagna was presented by Fearfeasa Ó Maoil Chonaire and Cú Choigcríche Ó Cléirigh. Fearfeasa's response, in prose and verse, has survived, but not that of Cú Choigcríche.[97]

The defence offered by Fearfeasa Ó Maoil Chonaire is revealing of his perception of the learned community. He argued that the matter should have been dealt with privately by *daoineadh ttromdha deagluis 7 dealadhuin* ('responsible men of the Church and the profession of History'), rather than in a public manner. He was concerned not just for Ó Cléirigh's reputation, and his own, but also for the reputation of all Ó Maoil Chonaire historians. He believed Tuileagna to be in error, and commented:

> ... *mur nár mhaith lemsa éiccert follus do dhul ós aird ar aon don chineadh dá bhfuil sean foillsighim go bráthardha fírcheart na cúisi go deiscréideach dhó re ndul dá haighneas do láthair a breithemhnais. Tugus mar chomhairle dhó go fiadhnach éisdeacht ris an cceirtshenchas do thrácht Míchél gona chomhoibrightheóiribh tre dhá adhbhur ionnus go ccuirtí ar a aghaidh é 7 a phuinc chethardha do ghairm ar ais nó do dhícleith as nach beithdís na siocair imresna o sin amach eidir uaislibh.*
>
> (... as I was unwilling that anyone of the name he bears should be publicly shown to be in manifest error, I charitably told him privately the rights of the case before going to plead it in the presence of the judges. I plainly advised him to accept the true history which Michel and his associates wrote, for two reasons, first that the work might go forward, and secondly, if he were to withdraw or suppress his four objections, that they would not henceforth lend matter for dispute among the nobility.)[98]

The controversy, and particularly the withdrawal of the approbations, suggests a controlled world of historical scholarship functioning in Ireland in the 1630s and 1640s, and a clear sense of collegiality expressed by Fearfeasa (which had been broken by the upstart Tuileagna Ó Maoil Chonaire). As in the case of another earlier scholarly controversy – *Iomarbhádh na bhfileadh* – neither would have happened without the existence of a tight-knit scholarly community aware

96 The text, with translation, of a letter from Br. Tuileagna Ó Maoil Chonaire to the Provincial of the Irish Franciscans is printed as an appendix to *GRSH*, pp 131, 147.   97 For Fearfeasa Ó Maoil Chonaire's prose reply to Tuileagna's criticisms, see *GRSH*, pp 134–8, with translation pp 150–3. His more comprehensive reply in a poem of 203 stanzas is published in Cuthbert Mhág Craith (ed.), *Dán na mBráthar Mionúr* (2 vols, Dublin, 1967), poem 39, text: I, pp 194–203; translation: II, pp 78–94; notes: II, pp 204–9.   98 *GRSH*, pp 135, 151.

of one another's strengths and weaknesses. The evidence points to a self-confident community, concerned with standards, with internal matters.

But even in this tight-knit world, it is interesting that authentication of the annals for the benefit of outsiders was also deemed necessary – one indication that this was an outward-looking rather than an inward-looking community. The annals, martyrology and genealogies of kings and saints were all prefaced with information designed to be useful to unknown external readers not just in Ireland but overseas. The influence of Counter-Reformation theological publications seems clear in these approbations, which were standard in theological works of the kind being produced in Louvain. It seems that it was considered inappropriate to publish Ó Cléirigh's annals without approbations from authorities of the highest calibre attached.

Precise details concerning the identity and the family connections of Tuileagna Ó Maoil Chonaire are difficult to trace. Fearfeasa's poem states that he was Tuileagna son of Seanchán. Thus he was not son of Torna as Paul Walsh had believed.[99] Of those named Tuileagna Ó Maoil Chonaire in contemporary documentation, he might possibly be identified either with a student at the University of Louvain in 1625 or alternatively with a student at the Irish College at Salamanca in April 1610, probably then aged 25.[100] He is usually identified as being the person of that name who was later living in Madrid. In March 1658, one Tuileagna Ó Maoil Chonaire authenticated a transcript of a genealogy, styling himself *seancha coitcheann Éireann* ('general historian of Ireland'),[101] and in September 1659, he transcribed a tract on grammar and prosody for Fr Patrick Tyrrell, OFM.[102] This indicates that the man in Madrid had close links with the Irish Franciscans there, and may well have been a member of the order. If he were to be tentatively identified as the person who was already a student at Salamanca in 1610, then he could hardly be the individual of that name (Tully Conry) who added a note to Laud Misc 610 in Oxford in 1673.[103] The student at the University of Louvain in 1625 (perhaps then under 20 years of age?) is a more likely candidate to have been still alive and in Oxford in 1673, but no evidence has been traced to establish such a connection. That the Tuileagna Ó

99 Mhág Craith (ed.), *Dán na mBrathar Mionúr*, I, pp 195, 222 (poem 39, verses 5 and 179); Walsh, *Irish men of learning*, p. 76.   100 Mhág Craith (ed.), *Dán na mBrathar Mionúr*, II, p. 205; O'Doherty, 'Students of the Irish College, Salamanca', 28; B. Jennings, 'The Irish students at the University of Louvain' in O'Brien (ed.), *Measgra i gcuimhne Mhichíl Uí Chléirigh*, p. 78.   101 OFM-UCD MS A 30, item 7; Walsh, *Gleanings from Irish manuscripts*, 2nd ed., 27–8. The identification has not been conclusively proven.   102 TCD MS 1431; see also TCD MS 804, pp 63–7, for a pedigree of Mac Raghnaill signed and sealed by Tully Conry, chronicler. The work was probably done for Sir James Ware, whose sister Russel married Humphrey Reynolds (Mac Raghnaill). See William O'Sullivan, 'A finding list of Sir James Ware's manuscripts', *Proceedings of the Royal Irish Academy* 97C2 (1997), 69; later in the same manuscript (TCD 804) there is a catalogue of Irish saints signed and dated 'D. Tulio O Conreo', 'chronicler of Ireland', Madrid 20 April 1658 (pp 75–8). This latter work appears to derive in part from the Four Masters' *GRSH*.   103 *Cat. Ir. mss in Bodl.*, I, p. 68.

Maoil Chonaire who criticized Ó Cléirigh's work was a Franciscan[104] would have made it relatively easy for him to have the matter of the accuracy of AFM and associated texts raised at no less than three formal Chapters of the order – at Thomond (1638), Multyfarnham (1641) and Dublin.[105]

His citation of manuscripts in his criticism of Ó Cléirigh's work is of interest. He claimed to have judged the work against authoritative sources including *Leabhar Chluana mac Nóis, Leabhar Chluana hEidhneach, Leabhar Leacain, Leabhar Chluana Plocáin* ('the Book of Cluain Mac Nois, the Book of Cluain Eidhneach, the Book of Lecan, the Book of Cluain Plocáin'),[106] a list not dissimilar to the authorities used by the Four Masters themselves – the Book of Cluain Plocáin probably being equivalent to the source they describe as the 'Book of Ballymulconry'. However, there is no clear evidence that the book of Cluain Eidhneach was used as a source for AFM though, as noted above, portions of it at least were apparently still extant in the hands of Flann Mac Aodhagáin. It is unlikely, though not impossible, that he had many of these manuscripts to hand at the same time as he had access to the text of AFM, but Tuileagna nonetheless felt able to be confident about their contents. At the very least, he must have moved in circles where he could claim to be familiar with such important manuscripts. It is most likely to have been when Ó Cléirigh was in Dublin in February 1637, obtaining the final approbations for his work from the archbishop Thomas Fleming, OFM,[107] and preparing to leave Ireland, that Tuileagna Ó Maoil Chonaire availed of the opportunity to examine the work. It is noteworthy that Tuileagna also had access to the work of another Franciscan historian, Flaithrí Ó Maoil Chonaire, together with the recently completed *Foras feasa ar Éirinn* of Geoffrey Keating – very probably the copy transcribed in part by Mícheál Ó Cléirigh, if not its exemplar.[108] He also claimed to be the recipient of a letter from Flann Mac Aodhagáin withdrawing his approbation.[109] The circumstances of the controversy demonstrate that there was a considerable degree of expert opinion available – within the Franciscan order as well as outside it – ready to comment on the quality of the historical research of Mícheál Ó Cléirigh and his team.

While the controversy may have helped undermine plans for publication of the annals, it nonetheless provided evidence of the importance attached to

---

104 *GRSH*, p. 134.   105 Mhág Craith (ed.), *Dán na mBrathar Mionúr*, II, p. 205. The Dublin chapter is undated but is mentioned by Fearfeasa Ó Maoil Chonaire in his poetic refutation of Tuileagna's criticisms (verse 16).   106 *GRSH*, pp 133, 149.   107 *AFM*, I, p. lxx.   108 *GRSH*, pp 132, 148. The historical work of Flaithrí Ó Maoil Chonaire is not known to be extant. The transcript of Keating's *Foras Feasa*, partly in Ó Cléirigh's hand, is now UCD–OFM MS A 14. These may be among the works alluded to by Fearfeasa as being not adequately informed (verse 145): *O do chuirsiom iad i gcúil leabhair nár lór linn a r<úis>, 'siad dhuitsi gidh aos grádha, treabh asda co <hedana>* ('Since we have put into a corner books considered by us to be inadequately informed, whilst they are favourites of yours, do not cultivate them rashly') (Mhág Craith (ed.), *Dán na mBrathar Mionúr*, I, p. 217; II, p. 90.)   109 *GRSH*, p. 131.

history, and the strong emotions it could engender among those who took part in the debate. It demonstrates that AFM was a work that emerged out of a vibrant scholarly environment, and was received by its earliest readers as such. Whether or not Tuileagna's criticisms were justified, they were debated in a professional manner by men of strongly-felt provincial and familial loyalties. The genealogical details of remote ancestors (whose very existence would now be doubted) still mattered, as did the precise nature of kingship and 'kingship with opposition' in early medieval Ireland. The participants in the debate were concerned with the nature of historical memory, not as a mere abstraction but as an element that mattered a great deal in their contemporary world. There is no hint in the controversy that the compilers and first readers of AFM perceived the annals to be a monument to a lost past.

While Tuileagna noted some points that he claimed were inaccurate, he did not offer to revise the text himself, as might theoretically have been expected of an Ó Maoil Chonaire Franciscan with a knowledge of the historical sources. Instead, he sought to delay the publication of Ó Cléirigh's work until it had been further assessed by one Rev. Brian Mac Aodhagáin and others.[110] That a Mac Aodhagáin should emerge as an authority in this context is no real surprise. The identity of Brian Mac Aodhagáin is uncertain, but it seems probable in the circumstances that he was a Franciscan.

Fearfeasa Ó Maoil Chonaire expressed annoyance that AFM had been kept from print because of Tuileagna's interference:

A chonnmhāil ō chlō Labhān
mairg nos iarr ar uachtarán.
(Woe to the man who asked superior to withhold it from print at Louvain.)[111]

There is no doubt that Tuileagna's views had considerable influence within the Franciscan community, perhaps because of his own status as a member of the learned family of Ó Maoil Chonaire. The close community of learned families within which the debate had arisen is also suggested by Fearfeasa Ó Maoil Chonaire's particular anguish that the criticism of the work he himself had done in association with Mícheál Ó Cléirigh came from a fellow Ó Maoil Chonaire historian.[112] His defence of the work and of the name of Ó Maoil Chonaire, in prose and verse, asserted the principles and standards of Ireland's professional historians, and affirmed, naively at times, that Ó Cléirigh and his team had striven at all times to adhere to those principles.

---

110 *GRSH*, p. 131.   111 Mhág Craith (ed.), *Dán na mBrathar Mionúr*, I, p. 197; II, p. 79 (poem 39, verse 19).   112 *GRSH*, pp 135–6; Mhág Craith (ed.), *Dán na mBrathar Mionúr*, I, p. 197 (poem 39, verse 21) recognizes Tuileagna as a historian, albeit in a back-handed way.

Extended Ó Cléirigh family

The third learned family to feature as part of the network alluded to by Mícheál Ó Cléirigh in his personal acknowledgment of the scholars who had influenced his work, is a related branch of his own family of Ó Cléirigh. The person acknowledged was Lughaidh Ó Cléirigh, best known to modern historians for his authorship of *Beatha Aodha Ruaidh Uí Dhomhnaill*.[113] He was son of Maccon son of Cú Choigcríche and, like Mícheál Ó Cléirigh himself, could trace his ancestry to the historian Tadhg Cam Ó Cléirigh, whose obituary was recorded to a standard formula in both AFM and ALCé under the year 1492.

> AFM 1492.23
> *Ua Cléiricch Tadhcc cam ollamh uí Domhnaill i neiccsi hi filidheacht 7 a senchus fer tighe aoidhedh coitchinn do thrénaibh 7 do truacchaibh décc iar mbreith buadha ó dhomhan 7 ó dhemhan.*
> (O'Clery, i.e. Teige Cam, Ollav to O'Donnell in literature, poetry and history, a man who had kept a house of general hospitality for the mighty and the needy, died, after having gained the victory over the Devil and the world.)[114]

As in the case of most of the others whose scholarly assistance was acknowledged by Mícheál Ó Cléirigh, it appears that Lughaidh Ó Cléirigh was dead by 1643. Recent research by Mícheál Mac Craith has made the case for dating Lughaidh Ó Cléirigh's life of Ó Domhnaill to 1627, and it is usually held that he died in 1630, though no contemporary record of his death has been traced.[115]

Prior to his composition of the prose biography of Aodh Ruadh Ó Domhnaill, Lughaidh Ó Cléirigh had come to prominence in the second decade of the seventeenth century as an active northern voice in the poetic dispute usually referred to as *Iomarbhágh na bhfileadh* (The contention of the bards).[116] Although he carefully defended the northern perspective in the poetic dispute, the reality was that it was probably because he and others had so much contact with their fellow poets in the southern half of the country that such a dispute could be engineered in the first place. As is recorded in the poems themselves, his own mother was a southerner. His active involvement in the *Iomarbhágh* is testimony to the fact that Lughaidh Ó Cléirigh was as well known in north Munster as he was in west Ulster. Like Mícheál Ó Cléirigh himself, Lughaidh's career provides evidence of the high level of contact maintained by members of the learned class with other scholars throughout the country, north and south. Nor was Lughaidh the first of his family to have made a name for himself in Thomond. His grand-

---

113 *BARUD*, II, pp 1–4.   114 *AFM*, IV, pp 1194–5.   115 Mac Craith, 'The *Beatha* in the context of the literature of the Renaissance', 53.   116 McKenna (ed.), *Iomarbhágh na bhFileadh*; Joep Leerssen, *The contention of the bards (Iomarbhágh na bhFileadh) and its place in Irish political and literary history* (London, 1994); Dooley, 'Literature and society in early seventeenth-century Ireland', pp 513–34.

father, Cú Choigcríche, had spent time in Thomond in 1546, and his uncle, Cosnamhach, maintained a *teach aoigheadh* (house of hospitality) in Thomond in the 1580s. His uncle, Muiris Ballach, described by the Four Masters as a man learned in history and poetry, had been one of the three poets executed by Conchobhar Ó Briain, earl of Thomond, in 1572. The incident was later condemned as *feillghníomh* (a treacherous act), in the entry for that year in AFM.[117] Lughaidh's father, Maccon, *ollamh* to Ó Domhnaill, died in Thomond in 1595.[118] Involvement with Thomond was the norm rather than the exception for this branch of the learned family of Ó Cléirigh.

Lughaidh Ó Cléirigh possessed an exceptional command of the older forms of the Irish language, to the extent that he succeeded in composing his biography of Aodh Ruadh Ó Domhnaill almost entirely in deliberately archaic language.[119] It was presumably this skill, well known to him because of the extensive use made of Lughaidh Ó Cléirigh's work in the closing section of AFM, that Mícheál Ó Cléirigh had in mind when naming Lughaidh among those from whom he had learned much about the Irish language. The absence of Lughaidh from any active participation in Mícheál Ó Cléirigh's work in the 1630s suggests that he was no longer alive. However, Muiris son of Lughaidh Ó Cléirigh was involved, at least peripherally, in Mícheál's work on the lives of saints. In August 1627 and again in February 1631, Mícheál copied texts from a manuscript provided by Muiris son of Lughaidh Ó Cléirigh:[120]

BR, MS 5100–4
I cconveint na mbráthar ind Áth Cliath ro scríobhadh riaghail Colaim Cille agus an méid fil ina diaigh anuasana, acht na ma riagail Corbmaic meig Cuileannáin ro scríobhadh as leabhar Muiris meig Lughaidh Í Clerigh i cconveint na mbráthar ag Drobhaois.[121]
[In the convent of the friars in Dublin the rule of Colum Cille was written and that which follows it, except that the rule of Cormac mac Cuileannáin was written from the book of Muiris son of Lughaidh Ó Cléirigh in the convent of the friars at Drowes.][122]

The Four Masters had access to two important source manuscripts that were the work of Ó Cléirigh historians. One of these, known to them as the 'Book of Lughaidh Ó Cléirigh', contained the narrative biography of Aodh Ruadh Ó Domhnaill. The autograph copy of the biography does not survive, but it

---

117 *AFM*, V, pp 1656–7; Ó Cuív, 'The earl of Thomond and the poets', 125–45.   118 Walsh, *The Ó Cléirigh family of Tír Conaill*, p. 13. The published poems of Maccon Ó Cléirigh include *Cionnus do mholfuinn mac ríogh* (James Carney (ed.), *Poems on the O'Reillys* (Dublin, 1950), poem 4) and *A bhean na lurgan luime* (Thomas F. O'Rahilly (ed.), *Dánta grádha* (Cork, 1925), poem 97).   119 McManus, 'The language of the Beatha', pp 54–73; Breatnach, 'Irish records of the Nine Years War', pp 124–47.   120 Jennings, *Michael Ó Cléirigh and his associates*, p. 193, n. 10; Walsh, *Irish leaders and learning*, p. 364.   121 Colophon printed in Jennings, *Michael Ó Cléirigh and his associates*, p. 193 (from BR MS 5100–4, fos 17–22v).   122 My translation.

appears that the work referred to by the Four Masters as the 'Book of Lughaidh Ó Cléirigh' did not contain anything other than the biographical narrative, since it was explicitly stated that the book covered the years from 1586 to 1602.[123] A second Ó Cléirigh manuscript source, the *Leabhar Choncoicccriche meic Diarmatta mic Taidhg caimm uí Clerigh* ('Book of Cú Coigcríche son of Dermot, son of Tadhg Cam Ó Cléirigh'), which covered the years 1281 to 1537, was also used as a source by the Four Masters.[124] This work, no longer known to be extant, was most probably the work of Lughaidh Ó Cléirigh's grandfather. As noted above, Lughaidh Ó Cléirigh was eldest son of Maccon, who was in turn eldest son of Cú Choigcríche.[125] The book of Cú Choigcríche Ó Cléirigh would most probably have stayed within the particular branch of the family in which it was first compiled, and in this way probably came into the hands of Lughaidh Ó Cléirigh, and subsequently of his son Muiris.

Lughaidh's grandfather, Cú Choigcríche, probable author of the 'Book of Cú Choigcríche Ó Cléirigh', was still alive in 1546,[126] but his date of death is not recorded in the annals. The AFM preface explicitly states that his book ended in 1537, so it may be that it formally closed with the end of the long reign of Aodh Dubh Ó Domhnaill, who died in that year.[127]

Cú Choigcríche Ó Cléirigh

Next to Mícheál Ó Cléirigh himself, the historian who probably contributed most to the form and substance of AFM was Cú Choigcríche Ó Cléirigh. It was most likely he, the northerner, that Fearfeasa Ó Maoil Chonaire had in mind when noting

> '< > *duine don triúr oile*
> *deimhin gur shaoi sheanchoidhe*
> *gan ghr<id>eacht thuaidh 'na aghoidh*
> *ag aoin fhior ré healadhain'*.
> ('One(?) of the other three was certainly an informed scholar without competition against him in the north from any learned man'.)[128]

There has been a certain amount of confusion in the secondary literature about Cú Choigcríche's family connections, not least the erroneous suggestion that he was son of Lughaidh, and brother of Cairbre.[129] The preface to the annals them-

---

123 *AFM*, I, p. lxvi.   124 *AFM*, I, p. lxvi.   125 Walsh, *The Ó Cléirigh family of Tír Conaill*, genealogical chart following p. 50.   126 *AFM*, V, pp 1494–5 (AFM 1546.1).   127 *AFM*, I, p. lxvi. 128 Mhág Craith (ed.), *Dán na mBráthar Mionúr*, poem 39, verse 169, I, p. 220; II, p. 92.   129 The errors in O'Donovan's identification of Cú Choigcríche have been addressed chiefly by Paul Walsh, *Irish leaders and learning*, pp 345–50 (repr. from *Irish Book Lover* 20 (1932), 105–6 and *Irish Book Lover* 22 (1934), 128–31). See also Walsh, 'What we know of Cuchoigcriche O Cleirigh', 60–6. O'Donovan also believed incorrectly that Cú Choigcríche Ó Cléirigh was the author of BARUD (on the basis of his having transcribed the text of same in RIA MS 23 P 24).

selves specifically state that Cú Choigcríche was son of Diarmaid Ó Cléirigh and the preface to *Genealogiae regum et sanctorum Hiberniae* states that he was from Baile Uí Chléirigh in Co. Donegal.[130] As noted earlier, he was already employed as a scholar by the Donegal Franciscans prior to the commencement of Mícheál Ó Cléirigh's project;[131] and he collaborated with Ó Cléirigh on the Martyrology of Donegal. Ó Cléirigh's unpublished preface to the 1628 recension of the Martyrology records Cú Choigcríche's involvement, on the initiative of the then guardian, Muiris Ulltach:

> *Iar na thuiccsin don athair Muiris Ulltach mac Seain robadh gairdian hi cconveint Dhúin na nGall an bliadainsi .1624. go rabhatar naoimh na hErenn arna ccuma go fordhorcha leis an easpucc naomhtha … ro chedaigh don athair Prouinnsi do bai isin cconveint cédnasin Dhúin na nGall (Muiris Ulltach eile a chomhainmsein) a thabhairt ar Chonchoicriche mac Diarmatta Uí Cleirigh aga mbáoi eolus maith isin nGaoidhilcc 7 aga mbaoi cuid dona seinleabhraibh do foghain don tsaotharso, na naoimh do chur ar an suidhuiccadh ara ffuilit sunna anosa fo chosmhailes na martarlaicci Romhanaighe amhail ro theccaisccsiot féin dó.*

(When Fr Muiris Ulltach son of Seán who was Guardian in the convent of Donegal in this year 1624 understood that Ireland's saints had been composed arcanely by the holy bishop … he requested the Fr Provincial who was in that same convent of Donegal (he was by name also another Muiris Ulltach) to prevail on [...] Cú Choigcríche son of Diarmaid Ó Cléirigh who was well versed in Irish and who had some of the old books required for this task to put the saints in the order in which they now are after the manner of the Roman Martyrology as they themselves instructed him.)[132]

His involvement in scholarly research commissioned by the Donegal friars two years before Mícheál Ó Cléirigh returned to Ireland is further evidence of the close links between the Franciscans and the learned families at this time. Cú Choigcríche was again part of the team of four who worked on the *Genealogiae regum et sanctorum Hiberniae* in 1630 and the new recension of *Leabhar gabhála Éireann* in 1631.[133] It appears that he was involved with the AFM enterprise from instigation to completion, and thus the only one of the team other than Mícheál Ó Cléirigh to be involved throughout the full duration of the project. His ownership of relevant books, commented on in 1628, was itself an indication of his importance to the research project. He continued to be active as a poet through the 1640s and later, enjoying the patronage, amongst others, of An

130 UCD–OFM MS A 13, preface; *GRSH*, pp 7–8. 131 BR MS 2542–3, fos 1–20, ed. Paul Grosjean, 'Naemhsenchus náemh nÉrenn' in J. Fraser, P. Grosjean and J.G. O'Keeffe (eds), *Irish Texts*, III (London, 1931), pp 40–80. 132 Printed and translated from BR MS 4639 in Breatnach, 'The methodology of *seanchas*', *Éigse* 29 (1996), 15. 133 UCD–OFM MS A 16, dedication to Toirrdhealbhach Mac Cochláin; TCD MS 1286, dedication to Brian Ruadh Mág Uidhir. See also Cú Choigcríche Ó Cléirigh's transcript of *Leabhar gabhála*, apparently for his own use, in RIA MS 23 K 32.

Calbhach Ruadh Ó Domhnaill, a status he had in common with his fellow annalist, Fearfeasa Ó Maoil Chonaire.[134] It is interesting to note, given their joint defence of the work of the Four Masters against the criticisms of Tuileagna Ó Maoil Chonaire at the Franciscan chapter, that their later poetry reveals contrasting political perspectives on issues that had been central to that debate, namely the right of the Uí Dhomhnaill, or An Calbhach Ruadh Ó Domhnaill in particular, to be present in Connacht.[135]

Pádraig A. Breatnach has identified Cú Choigcríche as the probable editor of an abridgment of Lughaidh Ó Cléirigh's life of Aodh Ruadh Ó Domhnaill and an abridgment of a chronicle poem, *Leanam croinic Clann nDálaigh*, first composed by Dubhthach Óg Ó Duibhgeannáin about the year 1600.[136] As previously discussed, there is also clear evidence that Cú Choigcríche undertook a major editorial role in the compilation of AFM. While Fearfeasa Ó Maoil Chonaire makes clear that the project was led by Mícheál Ó Cléirigh, it seems that Cú Choigcríche should be regarded as his principal assistant.[137]

Conaire Ó Cléirigh

The other scribal assistant to work on AFM for a brief period was Conaire Ó Cléirigh, an older brother of Mícheál Ó Cléirigh. Both men, together with Maolmhuire (Fr Bernardinus), who was head of the Donegal convent at the time the annals were completed in 1636, were sons of Donnchadh son of Uilliam Ó Cléirigh. Described in seventeenth-century genealogies as belonging to *Sliocht Tuathail*, the family were descendants of Tuathal son of Tadhg Cam (d. 1492), and quite distant cousins of Lughaidh son of Maccon Ó Cléirigh and his son Muiris, who belonged to *Sliocht Diarmada*.[138]

Both Conaire and Cú Choigcríche already had either professional or family links with the Donegal Franciscans, even before Mícheál Ó Cléirigh's arrival there in 1626, and they would have formed part of the scholarly circle which Mícheál Ó Cléirigh re-entered on his return to Donegal from the continent. It could even be argued that with Conaire's evident expertise as a scribe and Cú Choigcríche's proven skills both as a redactor of historical and hagiographical texts, and the interest displayed by the senior members of the Donegal convent in hagiographical work, there was scarcely any need for Mícheál Ó Cléirigh to

---

134 Eoin Mac Cárthaigh, 'Cú Choigcríche Ó Cléirigh' in *DIB*. 135 Mac Cárthaigh, 'Three poems by Maol Muire Ó hUiginn', 59–60. 136 Breatnach, 'A seventeenth-century abridgement of *Beatha Aodha Ruaidh*', 77–172; Breatnach, 'The methodology of *Seanchas*', 1–18. 137 Mhág Craith (ed.), *Dán na mBráthar Mionúr*, I, pp 210–11, 215, 217 (poem 39, verses 101, 104, 133, 135, 149, 169). Incidentally, the poem also makes clear that there were just four principal compilers – Mícheál, Fearfeasa and the two Cú Choigcríches – (Mhág Craith (ed.), *Dán na mBráthar Mionúr*, I, p. 221, verse 176). 138 Pender (ed.), 'The O'Clery book of genealogies', 116. The information is conveniently summarized in Walsh, *The Ó Cléirigh family of Tír Conaill*, genealogical chart following p. 50.

become involved at all. Nonetheless, it seems to have been Mícheál Ó Cléirigh's commitment and enterprise that provided the momentum for the project, sustaining a team of scholars over an extended period of time, and shaping the history to serve the needs of the hagiographical scholars at Louvain.

Mícheál Ó Cléirigh ends his preface to his 1643 dictionary by noting that there were 'others whom I do not mention' in the circle of scholars, living and deceased, who had influenced him in his study of the obscure elements of Irish manuscripts and 'the difficult words of our mother tongue'.[139] Among the learned families that could justifiably be counted among this wider circle, on the basis of their known involvement with the scholarly work of Ó Cléirigh, are the families of Ó Duibhgeannáin, Mac Bruaideadha, Ó Luinín, Mac Fhirbhisigh and Mac Eochagáin. The evidence for their association with the Four Masters circle will be briefly considered here.

Ó Duibhgeannáin

The learned family of Ó Duibhgeannáin of Castlefore, Co. Leitrim, had an input to the AFM project, both through the participation of Cú Choigcríche Ó Duibhgeannáin as one of the 'Four Masters', and also by facilitating access to manuscripts in their possession. There were two main branches of the family active in scholarly circles by the early seventeenth century, those based at Castlefore and the senior branch associated with Kilronan, in the northern extremity of Co. Roscommon, bordering on Co. Leitrim.[140] Cú Choigcríche Ó Duibhgeannáin is specifically stated to have been from *Baile Choille Foghar a ccontae Liattroma* (Castlefore in Co. Leitrim) in the prefaces to *Genealogiae regum et sanctorum Hiberniae* and *Leabhar gabhála*.[141] The precise nature of his contribution to the various collaborative projects in which he is named along with Mícheál Ó Cléirigh, Cú Choigcríche Ó Cléirigh and Fearfeasa Ó Maoil Chonaire is difficult to gauge, and the autograph manuscripts of AFM show little clear evidence of his contribution to the annals. His name is absent from the signatures appended to the preface to the Franciscan copy of the autograph manuscript, UCD–OFM A 13 (figure 9.1).[142] Yet, in Fearfeasa Ó Maoil Chonaire's poem in defence of the work of the Four Masters, the two Cú Choigcríches are specifically mentioned, meaning Ó Duibhgeannáin and Ó Cléirigh, and there is no suggestion by Ó Maoil Chonaire that Ó Duibhgeannáin was a less than active participant in the early part of the project – down to the completion of the annals for the year 1333.[143] It is unlikely, however, that he was in the Donegal friary

---

139 Miller (ed.), 'O'Clery's Irish glossary', 353, 354.   140 Walsh, *Irish men of learning*, pp 1–12; Bernadette Cunningham, 'The Ó Duibhgeannáin family of historians and the Annals of the Four Masters', *Breifne* 44 (2008), 557–72.   141 *GRSH*, pp 8, 143. Pól Ó Colla of Castlefore also added to the manuscript (UCD–OFM MS A 16; TCD MS 1286, preface).   142 UCD–OFM MS A 13, fo. xxiii.   143 Mhág Craith (ed.), *Dán na mBráthar Mionúr*, I, p. 221 (poem 39, verse 176); *GRSH*, pp 134, 150.

during the second phase of work on the annals in 1635–6. This would explain his absence when the other contributors signed the work, though it appears that when it came to the turn of Conaire to sign, he deferred to the seniority of Ó Duibhgeannáin, and left space for a name to be added above his own. Some six years earlier, in 1630, he had been present at Athlone when the *Genealogiae regum et sanctorum Hiberniae* was completed, and the dedication to the patron Toirdhealbhach Mág Cochláin is signed by all four masters, the last of the four signing his name simply *Cucoiccrici D* in what appears a rather feeble, possibly elderly, hand (fig. 9.2).[144]

In addition to the direct contribution of Cú Choigcríche son of Tuathal Buidhe Ó Duibhgeannáin of Castlefore[145] to the compilation of the annals themselves, the Four Masters were also able to draw on an important annalistic source owned by the Uí Dhuibhgeannáin of Kilronan. The preface to AFM specifically mentions *Leabhar muintere Duibgendáin chille Rónáin* ('Book of the O'Duigenans of Kilronan'), and states that it covered the years 900 to 1563, indicating that it was a set of chronological annals rather than a miscellany of texts.[146] The association between the Ó Duibhgeannáin scholars and the annals now known as the Annals of Connacht has already been discussed.[147] Although the annals were the property of the senior branch of the family at Kilronan, it is possible that Cú Choigcríche Ó Duibhgeannáin was instrumental in obtaining the manuscript on loan for the AFM project. Little manuscript evidence of the other activities of Cú Choigcríche Ó Duibhgeannáin survives, apart from an eighteenth-century transcript of a poem dated 1641 attributed to him. The poem, *Aoinsgiath cosnaimh na gceall*, was composed in praise of Tadhg Ó Rodaighe of Fenagh, Co. Leitrim, a likely patron of the Uí Dhuibhgeannáin.[148] However, other historical manuscripts survive that were produced by the Uí Dhuibhgeannáin at Castlefore in the mid-seventeenth century. They include a genealogical manuscript produced in 1644, at least partly the work of Pilib and Mathghamhain Ó Duibhgeannáin of Castlefore.[149] Meanwhile, another member of the extended family, Fearfeasa Ó Duibhgeannáin, made a transcript of Keating's *Foras feasa ar Éirinn* in 1646, though he was based at Tombrick in Co. Wexford at the time.[150] These chance survivals indicate that the learned family of Ó Duibhgeannáin was still actively involved in historical and genealogical scholarship in the seventeenth century. Like their neighbouring Uí Mhaoil Chonaire, their

---

144 OFM-UCD MS A 16, fo. ix.   145 Walsh, *Irish leaders and learning*, pp 345–7.   146 *AFM*, I, pp lxv–lxvi; Walsh, *Irish men of learning*, pp 22–4.   147 See above, pp 49–51.   148 The attribution is uncertain. A copy of the poem transcribed by Mícheál son of Peadair Ó Longáin is preserved in RIA MS 23 N 11, p. 166; another late seventeenth-century poem addressed to the same Tadhg Ó Rodaighe, this time by Seaán Ballach Ó Duibhgeannáin, and entitled *Beannacht uaim ó rún chroidhe*, has also survived in an eighteenth-century manuscript (TCD MS 1419, p. 82) (Tomás Ó Raghallaigh (ed.), *Filí agus filidheacht Chonnacht* (Dublin, 1938), pp xvi–xvii). The text of the poem was originally published by T. Ó Raghallaigh in *Ar Aghaidh* (Sept. 1931), 3.   149 RIA MS D i 3, part d; discussed in Paul Walsh, *Irish men of learning*, pp 4–5.   150 TCD MS 1394.

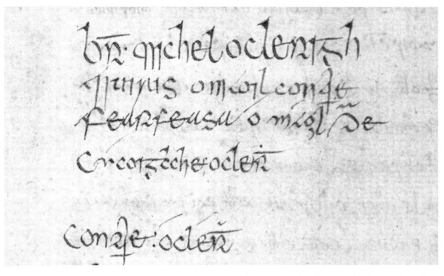

9.1 Signatures appended to autograph copy of AFM. UCD–OFM MS A 13, fo. xxiv.

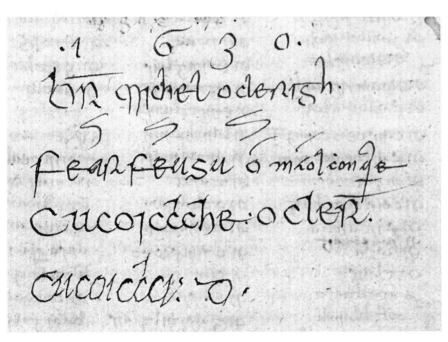

9.2 Signatures of Four Masters appended to *Genealogiae regum et sanctorum Hiberniae*, 1630. UCD–OFM MS A 16, fo. x verso.

activities cultivated an ongoing interest in historical scholarship, through to the 1640s and beyond, and shaped the cultural landscape that allowed projects of the scale embarked on by Mícheál Ó Cléirigh to prosper and come to fruition.

Ó Luinín

Further evidence that the AFM project was not an isolated enterprise in west Ulster in the 1630s comes from the activities of the learned family of Ó Luinín. The involvement of one Giolla Pádraig Ó Luinín, of Ard Uí Luinín, in the compilation of Mícheál Ó Cléirigh's new recension of *Leabhar gabhála Éireann* is well documented,[151] and is worth recalling here because it provides evidence of Ó Cléirigh contacts with the professional families employed by the dominant Fermanagh family of Mág Uidhir.[152] Ó Cléirigh also obtained information on Mág Uidhir genealogies from the same scholar.[153] Nollaig Ó Muráile has suggested that Ó Luinín was most probably the contact through whom the Four Masters gained access to the Annals of Ulster as a source for their own annals, and this certainly seems likely given his collaboration with the Four Masters immediately prior to their commencing the AFM project.[154] Earlier, when he was compiling the Martyrology of Donegal, Mícheál Ó Cléirigh drew extensively on a text of *Féilire Oengusso* transcribed by Ruaidhrí Ó Luinín for Cathal Mág Uidhir sometime before 1470, a transcript later made available to John Colgan.[155] Aside from the ready availability of source manuscripts and expert assistance, of particular interest in assessing the broader cultural context of west Ulster within which the AFM project took place is that the Ó Luinín historians were involved in their own major historical compilation in the late 1630s, producing the original 'Book of Knockninny' at the request of Mág Uidhir.[156] Although the 1630s 'Book of Knockninny' no longer survives, a good deal is known about it because it was

151 The preface to the Ó Cléirigh recension of *Leabhar gabhála* is printed in O'Curry, *Lectures on manuscript materials*, pp 86, 170, 553; see also Jennings, *Michael Ó Cléirigh and his associates*, pp 119–20.   152 The Mág Uidhir and Ó Luinín connections are recorded also in an eighteenth-century transcript of the work (RIA MS 23 K 45; *Cat. Ir. mss in RIA*, p. 1291).   153 RIA MS 23 K 45 (part b), p. 106.   154 Ó Muráile, 'Annála Uladh: the Annals of Ulster: Introduction to the 1998 reprint' in *AU*, 2nd ed., I [p. 20]. Ó Muráile indicates that a manuscript containing the Annals of Ulster remained in Ó Luinín hands until the early eighteenth century, when Charles Lynegar (Ó Luinín) may have sold it to John Conry (Ó Maoil Chonaire).   155 W. Stokes (ed.), *Félire Oengusso: the Martyrology of Oengus the Culdee* (London, 1905), pp xii–xiii. Stokes notes that Mícheál Ó Cléirigh also had access to a text of the Martyrology of Oengus preserved in a manuscript written by Siodrach Ó Maoil Chonaire in 1533, and that it was from this that the transcript in BR MS 5100–4, fos 94a–119b was made (Stokes (ed.), *Félire Oengusso*, viii). Ó Cléirigh also copied other hagiographical texts from an exemplar in the hand of the same Siodrach Ó Maoil Chonaire (Jennings, *Michael O Cleirigh and his associates*, p. 77; Charles Plummer (ed.), *Bethada Náem nÉrenn*, 2 vols (Oxford, 1922), II, p. 92). The scribe may be identified as Siodrach son of Seáan son of Maoilín Mór Ó Maoil Chonaire, who refurbished Bodl. Laud Misc. 610 before 1520 (Myles Dillon, 'Laud Misc. 610', *Celtica* 6 (1963), 136–7, 138–9, 146–7).   156 For discussion of the early eighteenth-century transcript of the Book of Knockninny and the cultural context in which it was created, see Cunningham and Gillespie, 'The purposes of patronage', 38–49.

reworked in the early eighteenth century by Toirrdhealbhach Ó Dóailen and Semus Mha Guidhir. The reworked manuscript is now RIA MS C vi 1.[157] Significantly, it was claimed that Páttraig Ballach Ó Luinín assembled a large number of manuscripts at Tulach Maol to assist in the compilation of the Mág Uidhir sponsored history, *áit ar chruinnidh sé leabhair Uí Chléirigh, Uí Dhuibhgeannan 7 Uí Mhaoilchonaire* ('where he assembled the books of Ó Cléirigh, Ó Duibhgeannáin and Ó Maoil Chonaire').[158] There is an unmistakeable echo here of the principal sources also available to the Four Masters through their own immediate scholarly circle. The reliability of the list of sources used by Ó Luinín is cast in doubt, however, by the inclusion of *Saltair Chaisil 7 Teamhrach*, since the Psalter of Tara, if it ever existed, was no longer extant by the seventeenth century.[159] It is certainly possible, however, that Ó Luinín could have obtained access to many of the sources that had been available to the Four Masters shortly after the AFM project had been completed. This might well have been arranged in return for Ó Luinín having facilitated access to the Annals of Ulster (*Leabhar Seanadh Mec Maghnusa*), though there is no definite evidence that this was the case. One clear link to Ó Cléirigh is acknowledged where the version of the *Leabhar gabhála* used in the Book of Knockninny is stated to be the Ó Cléirigh recension.[160]

There is some evidence detectible in the editorial method of the Four Masters that they were anxious not to stray into topics that were the preserve of the historians to the Méig Uidhir, and they may have been aware of Ó Luinín's own ambitions to assemble a major history of the Méig Uidhir.[161] The 1630s 'Book of Knockninny' was praised by its later copyists who asserted *gurab é aon leabhar bá mó meas fírine 7 glaneólais do raibhe san ccóige é* ('that it was the most respected, truthful and informed book in the province').[162] Such a claim may have been intended to imply that the work was a serious rival to the Annals of the Four Masters in terms of its scholarly achievement, though it may be observed that the geographical scope of the claim was limited to the province of Ulster.

157 *Cat. Ir. mss in RIA*, no. 936, pp 2697–705.   **158** *Cat. Ir. mss in RIA*, no. 936, p. 2699. **159** Cunningham, *World of Geoffrey Keating*, p. 64. Scribes continued to make reference to the 'Psalter of Tara' into the eighteenth century. Dermod O'Connor even mentioned it on the title page to his 1723 translation of Keating's *History of Ireland*, which led to mockery by Anthony Raymond and Thomas O'Sullevane of his claim to be the 'antiquary of Ireland' (Alan Harrison, *Ag cruinniú meala: Anthony Raymond, 1675–1726* (Dublin, 1988), pp 102–3).   **160** RIA MS C vi 1, book 1, p. 1; *Cat. Ir. mss in RIA*, no. 936, p. 2699.   **161** Quite a few entries concerning members of the Mág Uidhir family that feature in AU are omitted from AFM. Some of these can be explained by the concern of the Four Masters to omit the offspring and descendants of the 'Great Archdeacon'. However, it may indicate awareness of the need not to trespass on areas that were the preserve of other professional historians; the convention that historians should limit their area of interest was explicitly mentioned in *BARUD*, I, pp 170–3.   **162** RIA MS C vi 1, book 1, p. 1; *Cat. Ir. mss in RIA*, no. 936, pp 2699–700.

Mac Bruaideadha

It has already been noted that there were certain clear links between those scholars named by Mícheál Ó Cléirigh in the 1643 preface to his *Foclóir* and those whose names were appended not just to the annals but also to two of Mícheál Ó Cléirigh's other historical and hagiographical works, the *Genealogiae regum et sanctorum Hiberniae* and the Martyrology of Donegal, as testimony to the high standard he had achieved in his researches. The overlaps might have been greater had the scholars from whom he had learned most been still alive in the 1630s. The approbations, therefore, while necessarily confined to those members of Mícheál Ó Cléirigh's network of contacts who were personally accessible to him in the 1630s, are an important source of additional information about those networks.

In addition to Flann Mac Aodhagáin, and Baothghalach Mac Aodhagáin, bishop of Elphin, the name of Conchobhar Mac Bruaideadha was also appended to AFM. The signature was dated 11 November 1636.[163] Mac Bruaideadha added his signature to the *Genealogiae regum et sanctorum Hiberniae*[164] and the Martyrology of Donegal[165] on the same occasion. It appears that the visit to Thomond made by Mícheál Ó Cléirigh in 1636 was probably undertaken expressly to obtain these approbations, and that the opportunity to meet Conchobhar Mac Bruaideadha was a relatively rare one. By the mid-1630s, Conchobhar Mac Bruaideadha was head of the learned family of Mac Bruaideadha, traditionally poets to the Uí Bhriain of Thomond. It is almost certainly no coincidence that the scholar who was asked for his approbation for AFM was the probable custodian of one of the source manuscripts used in that work. The annals of Maoilín Óg Mac Bruaideadha, compiled by Conchobhar Mac Bruaideadha's father, were a significant supplementary source used by the Four Masters in their annals for the years after 1587. After the death of Maoilín Óg in 1602, his son, Conchobhar, presumably became custodian of his father's manuscripts. Maoilín Óg's scholarly interests had been diverse. He had assisted in revising Uilliam Ó Domhnaill's Irish translation of the New Testament, printed in 1595 though not issued until 1603.[166] His death is recorded in AFM under the year 1602, where it was asserted that *Ní bhaoí i nErinn i nén pearsain Senchaidh, file, 7 fer dána do bhferr inás* ('There was not in Ireland, in the person of one individual, a better historian, poet and rhymer, than he'). Unusually, the annalists also provided a list of six poems that had been composed by Maoilín Óg.[167] His work was also known to

---

163 O'Donovan may well have been correct in not reading '11' as though it were 'ii' in Roman numerals when he printed the date as 11 November 1636 (*AFM*, I, p. lxix), even though the date is spelt out as '*an dara lá do mhis November 1636*' in the transcript of *Genealogiae regum et sanctorum Hiberniae* contained in RIA MS 24 P 33, p. 45. Mícheál Ó Cléirigh could not have been with Mac Bruaideadha in Thomond on 2 November, as he was with Flann Mac Aodhagáin on that date (see n. 37 above). **164** *GRSH*, p. 146; RIA 24 P 33, p. 45. **165** *MDon*, p. li. **166** Osborn Bergin, 'A poem by Domhnall mac Dáire', *Ériu* 9 (1921–3), 160. **167** *AFM*, VI, pp 2320–1.

Geoffrey Keating, who made reference to a poem beginning *Cuirfead commaoin ar chloinn Táil* ('I will lay an obligation on the descendants of Tál'), which he attributed to Maoilín Óg. However, Keating did not always concur with Maoilín Óg's interpretations, and contrasted the genealogical information concerning Donnchadh son of Brian Bóruma as supplied by Maoilín Óg with that of earlier sources. He noted that only Maoilín Óg, his own contemporary, made any claim that the Powers, Eustaces and Plunketts could trace their ancestry to the said Uí Bhriain king.[168] An episode in which Maoilín Óg Mac Bruaideadha composed a poem for Aodh Ruadh Ó Domhnaill in 1599 is recorded at length by Lughaidh Ó Cléirigh, where Maoilín Óg is described as *file foircthi fíreolach* ('a well-read learned poet'). A much-shortened version of Lughaidh Ó Cléirigh's story of Maoilín Óg was incorporated into the AFM account of the year 1599.[169]

The annals of Maoilín Óg Mac Bruaideadha might have been borrowed in June 1634 around the time Mícheál Ó Cléirigh visited the Franciscan friary at Quin in Thomond.[170] While based in Thomond in that year, Ó Cléirigh had transcribed saints' lives from the Red Book of Munster and other sources.[171] No specific record of a visit to Mac Bruaideadha at this time has survived, however, and it seems that Ó Cléirigh may have obtained the Mac Bruaideadha annals from Conall Mac Eochagáin.[172] At any rate, the likelihood is that Ó Cléirigh was personally responsible for bringing the Mac Bruaideadha annals to Donegal at about that time. Since they related to the late sixteenth century only, these annals were probably used by the Four Masters in the later stages of their work, in late 1635 or early 1636. In November 1636, when Ó Cléirigh visited Conchobhar Mac Bruaideadha for the purpose of obtaining his approbation for AFM and other works, the purpose of the visit may have been twofold, the second task being the return of the Thomond annals of Maoilín Óg Mac Bruaideadha that had been obtained some time before.

Given that the poetic dispute that had taken place some twenty years earlier had involved poets from both the families of Mac Bruaideadha and Ó Cléirigh, it may be that Mícheál Ó Cléirigh's cultivation of an association with the Thomond family was a conscious attempt to demonstrate that the earlier rivalries between north and south were no longer an issue.[173]

Conall Mac Eochagáin and others of the circle of learned families

When in Dublin in 1627 transcribing texts associated with early Irish saints, Mícheál Ó Cléirigh had access to a vellum manuscript of Flann Mág Craith, a Munster scholar of some repute: *as seinleabhar membruim le Flann Mag Craith do*

---

168 Comyn and Dinneen (eds), *Foras feasa ar Éirinn*, III, pp 292–3.   169 *BARUD*, I, pp 208–9; *AFM*, VI, pp 2102–5.   170 Jennings, *Michael Ó Cléirigh and his associates*, pp 139, 203.   171 According to Ó Cléirigh, the Red Book of Munster had been written by Murchadh Ó Cuinlis (Jennings, *Michael Ó Cléirigh and his associates*, p. 139). It is not now known to survive.   172 *Cat. Ir. mss in BL*, II, 472.   173 Leerssen, *Mere Irish and Fíor Ghael*, p. 268.

scríobadh na riaglacha eile mar adubramar reime in Áth Cliath ('the other rules were written from the old vellum book of Flann Mac Craith in Dublin as we said before').[174] Closer to home, manuscripts were borrowed from the Mac Fhirbhisigh family of Lecan in Co. Sligo, including a source obtained after much of the work of compiling AFM had already been completed.[175] In return, Dubhaltach Mac Fhirbhisigh may have been allowed access to Ó Cléirigh's Martyrology of Donegal.[176] No matter how minor a role they played, all of these scholars who made sources available were part of an extended network that made it possible for Ó Cléirigh and his team to pursue their researches into the Irish past. In addition to the locations of the traditional schools, Dublin seems to have provided a further point of contact and Ó Cléirigh obtained access to a variety of material on his visits there.[177]

One other important point of contact among scholars for the loan and copying of manuscripts appears to have been the home of Conall Mac Eochagáin, at Lismoyny in the southern part of Co. Westmeath. Mac Eochagáin too had Dublin or Drogheda connections, since he had possession of the Great Book of Lecan in 1634, borrowed from James Ussher, archbishop of Armagh, and he may have made transcripts of material from it.[178] Mac Eochagáin had been an active facilitator of the Four Masters in their undertaking to compile the genealogies of Irish saints and kings. Their 1630 preface to the completed text records that it had commenced at Mac Eochagáin's house in Lismoyny. He was also one of those who provided a signed approbation for the completed work.[179] He did not feature, however, among those called on to approve AFM in 1636. This was despite Ó Cléirigh having been in contact with him in October 1636 to obtain written authentication for a transcript of the *Naomhsheanchas*.[180] Instead, another Mac Eochagáin, Ross [Rochus], Dominican bishop of Kildare from 1629 to 1644, authenticated the completed AFM manuscripts,[181] chosen no doubt because of his episcopal status.[182] The absence of a formal approbation from Conall Mac Eochagáin for AFM is best explained by the fact that he did not come from an established family of hereditary historians. This lack of hereditary status meant that whereas he was acceptable as authenticator of hagiographical transcripts of manuscripts in his possession, when it came to approving the

---

174 Jennings, *Michael Ó Cléirigh and his associates*, pp 55, 193. 175 *AFM*, I, p. lxv. 176 The martyrology was used by Dubhaltach Mac Fhirbhisigh in his research on Irish bishops, edited from Bodl. MS Rawl. 480 in Duald Mac Firbis, 'On some bishops of Ireland', *Proceedings of the Royal Irish Academy, Irish MSS series* 1, pt 1 (1870), 82–133. 177 Among those he encountered there were Francis O'Mahony, OFM, and Thomas Strange, OFM, who had contacts with James Ussher (Jennings, *Michael O Cleirigh and his associates*, pp 55–6, 61–2; Cunningham and Gillespie, 'James Ussher and his Irish manuscripts', 81–99. 178 King's Inns Gaelic MS 4, p. 54. 179 *DNB*, s.n. 'Conall Mageoghegan'; UCD–OFM MS A 16, fo. xiii. 180 BR MS 5100–4, fo. 232; extract printed in *Cat. Ir. mss in BL*, II, p. 473. 181 UCD–OFM MS A 13, fo. xxxii. 182 One Ross Mac Eochagáin, from Moycashel, Co. Westmeath, had been a student at the Irish college in Salamanca in 1600–1 (O'Doherty, 'Students of the Irish College, Salamanca', 11–12).

content of the annals, men from established learned families, Flann Mac Aodhagáin and Conor Mac Bruaideadha were selected in preference to him.

Despite his lack of pedigree – in 1566 his great grandfather had been unable to sign his name – Conall Mac Eochagáin was a prominent scholar by the 1630s.[183] In addition to his proven scholarly association with the Four Masters team, he also facilitated the work of other contemporary genealogists and historians including Dubhaltach Mac Fhirbhisigh, Geoffrey Keating and James Ussher.[184] His wide network of contacts meant that his collaboration would have been beneficial to any historical undertaking that relied on access to a broad range of manuscript sources.[185] He acted as an important link between the world of Gaelic scholarship and Dublin-based antiquarians.

The extent of Conall Mac Eochagáin's connection with the AFM project may have been greater than might at first appear. A comparison of the contents of the late fourteenth-century and very early fifteenth-century entries in AFM with material for the same period in the Annals of Clonmacnoise (AClon) reveals that the compilers of AFM had access to a source containing substantially the same material. AClon, which ends with the year 1408, now survives only in Mac Eochagáin's English version, which he had completed in 1627.[186] Obviously, he must have had access in the mid-1620s to the Irish source text or texts from which his AClon translation derives. Given his cooperation with the AFM team in 1630, it seems likely that Mac Eochagáin, if asked, would have facilitated access to the annalistic sources that had been available to him for translation. That material would have been known to Mícheál Ó Cléirigh by a name other than the modern name, the 'Annals of Clonmacnoise', a title first assigned to Mac Eochagáin's text by its nineteenth-century editor, Denis Murphy. As discussed earlier, the Four Masters used the name 'Book of Clonmacnoise' to refer to a quite different source, the identity of which is not now known with certainty, but which they assert did not contain material later than the year 1227.[187] Likewise, the source they identify as the 'Book of the Island of Saints' came to an end in the early thirteenth century, and so does not correspond to the scope of Mac Eochagáin's Clonmacnoise annals either.[188]

As in all other cases where AFM preserved echoes of other extant annals, the correspondence between the two texts is not complete. The Four Masters used AClon (or, potentially, the unidentified sources from which AClon derives) selectively, rather than transcribing all the material contained therein. Nonetheless,

183 Paul Walsh, 'Connla and Conall Mageoghegan' in *Irish leaders and learning*, pp 125–9. 184 Cunningham and Gillespie, 'James Ussher and his Irish manuscripts'. 185 For Mac Eochagáin's probable association with Geoffrey Keating at about the same time, see Cunningham, *World of Geoffrey Keating*, pp 60, 62, 77. 186 Denis Murphy (ed.), *Annals of Clonmacnoise from the earliest period to AD1408, translated into English by Conell Mageoghagan, AD1627* (Dublin, 1896); the earliest extant transcript of Mac Eochagáin's translation is in Armagh Public Library (unnumbered manuscript in safe), and is dated 1660. 187 *AFM*, I, pp lxiv–lxv; see above, pp 55–8. 188 *AFM*, I, pp lxiv–lxv.

the extent of the parallel is noteworthy.[189] The textual evidence suggests that Conall Mac Eochagáin may have given the annalists access to 'his' source annals at an early stage of the AFM project. Alternatively, Daniel Mc Carthy's suggestion that Mac Eochagáin's exemplar was a set of annals compiled c.1423 by Maoilín Ua Maoil Chonaire raises the possibility that the compilers of AFM and AClon independently accessed a set of Ó Maoil Chonaire annals.[190] Conall Mac Eochagáin must have had his exemplar for AClon to hand in the mid-1620s, and when Mícheál Ó Cléirigh spent the winter of 1628–9 in Ormond, he might well have made notes from or even a transcript of that exemplar at the house of Mac Eochagáin in Lismoyny. There is no hint in AFM, however, that the annalists used Mac Eochagáin's own translated work. As discussed above, the Four Masters did not use any of the extended passages on saints which Mac Eochagáin appears to have inserted into his translation.

Just as there was no shortage of source material from which the Four Masters could select entries for inclusion in their annals, so also there was no shortage of scholarly expertise and cooperation at the disposal of Mícheál Ó Cléirigh's team. Despite declining patronage, there was still enough of a scholarly network in place to ensure access to key manuscripts. Some of those manuscripts had been transferred out of the hands of their traditional owners into the hands of Old English and New English collectors. Yet, as the case of James Ussher illustrates, scholars drew a distinction between the issue of access to manuscripts and the nature of the historical or political arguments that were subsequently constructed on the basis of the available evidence. Old English and Gaelic scholars alike, interested in the Irish past, were drawn to the traditional centres of learning where those manuscripts were preserved, not as antiquarian artefacts, but as the living record of a valued culture and civilization. This scholarly collaboration can be taken as one of the defining characteristics of Ireland's early modern cultural 'Renaissance'.

The Franciscan connection

It is a common misapprehension that the Four Masters were all Franciscans, whereas in fact Mícheál Ó Cléirigh was the only Franciscan among the four historians and two scribes known to have actively worked on the AFM project. It is true, however, that the work of compiling the annals was carried out in the Donegal convent of the Franciscans[191] located at Bundrowes,[192] and that it would probably not have been begun or completed without the support of that religious community.

---

189 See analysis in chapter five, above. 190 Mc Carthy, *The Irish annals*, p. 289. 191 *AFM*, I, p. lxvii. 192 For Bundrowes as a base used by Aodh son of Maghnus Ó Domhnaill in 1567, see TNA, SP 63/20, no. 69, 28 April 1567.

The Donegal convent did not exist in isolation. Rather, its members were part of an extended and growing network by the 1630s, and the Donegal community had contacts with other Franciscans in many parts of the country and beyond. Some members of the Franciscan order had strong associations with many of the leading Gaelic learned families and, while their secular fortunes were on a less secure footing than in earlier centuries, those who joined the Franciscan community found that it provided an alternative professional network that supported scholarship.

The Donegal Franciscan community, based at Bundrowes in the extreme south of the county, provided Ó Cléirigh's base for most of the eleven years he spent in Ireland as a Franciscan friar between 1626 and 1637. His own brother, Fr Bernardinus, was serving as guardian of the Donegal convent during the period when the annals were completed in 1636.[193] Fr Bernardinus had lived at Salamanca and Louvain and would have had a network of contacts deriving from that experience.[194] Others who had similarly studied at Salamanca included, for example, Ross Mac Eochagáin, the Kildare bishop who later provided an approbation for AFM.[195] The Donegal friary had been a particularly important Franciscan novitiate. When Donogh Mooney spent time there as a novice in 1600, before the destruction of the monastic buildings in Donegal itself, he was one of a community of forty men. Mooney recorded that the building was taken over and then destroyed by fire shortly afterwards. Writing in 1617, Mooney noted that all of the Irish provincials of the Franciscan order over the previous twenty years, with the exception of Flaithrí Ó Maoil Chonaire, had made their novitiate at Donegal. By 1617, a community of twelve men was living near the old convent, while others had moved to other Franciscan convents.[196] The numbers in the Donegal convent in the late 1620s, when Mícheál Ó Cléirigh took up residence there, are unknown, but they had far-reaching connections. Among the prominent members of the Irish Franciscan community living there was Muiris Ulltach (son of Seaán) who had earlier re-established the Franciscan house at Drogheda when he was provincial of the order in 1609–10.[197] The same man also ensured that, even before Mícheál Ó Cléirigh arrived at the Donegal convent, the community there were engaged in research into the lives of Irish saints, and they had employed a lay scholar, Cú Choigcríche Ó Cléirigh, to assist in that research.[198] Their initiative was recorded by Cú Choigcríche in the preface to his recension of the *Naomhsheanchas*:

193 UCD–OFM MS A 13, fo. xxiii.   194 Jennings, *Michael Ó Cléirigh and his associates*, p. 17; O'Doherty (ed.), 'Students of the Irish College, Salamanca', 28.   195 Listed as 'Rossius ma Geoghagan' in O'Doherty (ed.), 'Students of the Irish College, Salamanca', 11.   196 Mooney, 'A history of the Franciscan Order in Ireland', *Franciscan Tertiary* 5 (1894–5), 129–32; for a description of the burning of the friary and Ó Domhnaill involvement in the episode, narrated from another perspective, see William Kelly (ed.), *Docwra's Derry: a narration of events in north-west Ulster, 1600–1604* (Belfast, 2003), p. 60.   197 Jennings (ed.), 'Brussels MS 3947', 28; Mooney, 'A history of the Franciscan Order in Ireland', *Franciscan Tertiary* 6 (1895–6), 2.   198 BR MS 2542–3, fo. 1. The manuscript is not in the hand found in other manuscripts usually identified as the work of Cú

ro fhorailset na braithre bochtacha dord S. Fr. .i. an da Muiris Ultacha ... ormsa Cucoiccriche Ó Clérigh an duansa do scríobhadh ... [199]
[the poor friars of the order of St Francis, i.e. the two Muiris Ulltachs ordered me, Cú Choigcríche Ó Cléirigh, to write this poem ... .][200]

Cú Choigcríche went on to explain that the task was not merely one of transcription, but that he had been instructed to insert additional hagiological material in accordance with the manuscript sources available to him, which included the Martyrology of Oengus, the Martyrology of Gorman and other manuscripts.[201] Given that work on the martyrologies was already in hand at the Donegal friary, and that the scholarly talents of the lay scholar Cú Choigcríche Ó Cléirigh were already being employed by the Franciscans there before Mícheál Ó Cléirigh came, his arrival in Donegal with instructions to conduct further research into Irish saints' lives was probably enthusiastically welcomed by many of the community there. Mícheál's family was well known to the Franciscans. His own mother, Onóra Ulltach, may possibly have been related to one or other of the two Muiris Ulltachs then living there. When he returned to Donegal in 1626, therefore, Mícheál Ó Cléirigh joined a Franciscan community that was in some respects an extension of the Ó Cléirigh family, and one that was already actively engaging in scholarly research on the lives of Irish saints, and cultivating current contacts with lay scholars who could assist in the research. Despite his lowly status as a lay brother, it is likely that Mícheál Ó Cléirigh's scholarly talents were fully appreciated within the Donegal convent and that he was allowed to devote a considerable amount of his time to the work of transcription and subsequently to more original historical research.

His personal genealogical pedigree would have undoubtedly compensated for any perceived lack of status within the Franciscan order. In addition to these contemporary associations, the Ó Cléirigh family could also trace older relationships with the Donegal convent.[202] Among those buried in the original convent at Donegal was Tadhg Cam mac Tuathail Uí Chléirigh, *ollamh* to Ó Domhnaill in history, who died in 1566, *7 a adhnacal i mainistir S. Fronseis i nDún na nGall co nairmitin, 7 co nonoir nádhbhal* ('and was buried with great respect and honour in the monastery of St Francis, at Donegal').[203] Some years earlier, in 1527, Giolla Riabhach, son of an earlier Tadhg Cam, likewise *a écc in aibítt San Fronseis* ('died in the habit of St Francis').[204] This Ó Cléirigh association with the

Choigcríche Ó Cléirigh, such as RIA MS 23 P 24. **199** BR MS 2542–3, fo. 1. **200** My translation. **201** BR MS 2542–3, fo. 1. Manuscripts such as the *Liber hymnorum* (now UCD–OFM MS A 2) had also been preserved in the Donegal friary. A copy of the *Liber hymnorum* that had once belonged to the Donegal friary was subsequently available for use by James Ussher, James Ware and John Colgan. For discussion of the use made of a Donegal copy of this work, see Bernard and Atkinson (eds), *The Irish Liber hymnorum*, pp xiv–xv. **202** Katharine Simms, 'Late medieval Donegal' in W. Nolan, L. Ronayne and M. Dunlevy (eds), *Donegal: history and society* (Dublin, 1995), pp 196–7. **203** *AFM*, V, pp 1606–7. **204** *AFM*, V, pp 1388–9.

Franciscans, and Mícheál Ó Cléirigh's precise genealogical link with those forebears, would have been well known to the community at Bundrowes when he arrived there in 1626. That he was a distant cousin to Cú Choigcríche Ó Cléirigh would also have been known to all concerned, and the scholarly collaboration between the two men may well have been initiated at the suggestion of Muiris Ulltach mac Seaáin.[205]

From his Donegal base, Ó Cléirigh was able to access a range of manuscripts owned by people in the locality. Thus, in the early part of 1627, he copied extracts from manuscripts of Tadhg Ó Cianáin and Cú Mumhan Ó Cléirigh.[206] The following January, and again in April 1629, he worked from a manuscript of Brian Mág Niallusa.[207] In the opening months of 1630, Ó Cléirigh had access to, and copied saints' lives from, manuscripts owned by members of the families of Ó Caiside, Ó Duibhgeannáin, Ó Maoil Chonaire, Mág Uidhir, Ó Maonaigh and Mac Suibhne.[208] Similarly, in February 1631 he again transcribed material from manuscripts of the Ó Maoil Chonaire and Ó Cléirigh families.[209] During his time in Bundrowes, Mícheál Ó Cléirigh also enjoyed access to *Leabhar na hUidhre*, one of the manuscript treasures then in the possession of the Uí Dhomhnaill, and he transcribed material from that source in May 1628.[210] While Ó Cléirigh may have been unusual in the extent of his meticulous recording of his source texts, the access to manuscripts he enjoyed in Donegal was probably not exceptional. Rather, his range of scholarly contacts within his own locality may well have fallen within the scope of normal scholarly collaboration within the learned professions.

By the time Mícheál Ó Cléirigh commenced his researches into the lives of Irish saints in 1626, the revival in the fortunes of the Irish Franciscan community had already been underway for almost twenty years. Although only three friaries – Donegal, Armagh and Multyfarnham – had regular communities at the time of the 1612 provincial chapter, between the commencement of Donogh Mooney's term as provincial in 1615 and his death in April 1624, additional Franciscan houses were established at Cavan, Clonmel, Dublin, Kinalehin, Limerick, Lisgoole, New Ross and Wexford. By 1629, there had been a very considerable expansion, with a total of thirty-two Franciscan houses re-established throughout the country. The most recent phase of expansion in the late 1620s had led to

205 BR MS 4639, fo. 3.   206 Jennings, *Michael Ó Cléirigh and his associates*, pp 52–3, 270–1, for Cú Mumhan Ó Cléirigh, see BR MS 2324–40, fo. 82v.   207 For Mág Niallusa, see BR 4190–200, fo. 270. Walsh, *Irish leaders and learning*, p. 354, interprets this as old-style dating, therefore indicating that the year in question in the first of these transcripts was 1628 rather than 1627, as stated by Jennings; see also Jennings, *Michael Ó Cléirigh and his associates*, pp 52, 77–8, and associated notes containing transcript of the second colophon, p. 197 (n. 25). As Paul Walsh notes, the same Brian Mág Niallusa was scribe of a seventeenth-century copy of Maghnus Ó Domhnaill's life of Colum Cille, now UCD–OFM MS A 19 (Walsh, *Irish leaders and learning*, p. 354).   208 Walsh, *Irish leaders and learning*, pp 364–9.   209 Jennings, *Michael Ó Cléirigh and his associates*, 95–6 (again, the February dates given by Jennings should be adjusted to read 1631, not 1630).   210 Jennings, *Michael Ó Cléirigh and his associates*, p. 60; Walsh, *Irish leaders and learning*, p. 355.

the re-opening of Franciscan houses at locations such as Galway, Ross, Quin, Timoleague, Athlone and Kildare.[211]

At another level, the success of the Franciscan Irish college of St Anthony at Louvain from its foundation in 1607 ensured that there was an adequate supply of educated clergy at these locations. As already seen, members of the learned class who could no longer find patrons to sustain them as secular scholars found an outlet for their talents within the revived Catholic Church in the early seventeenth century. Thus, for example, among the early students and staff at the Franciscan College of St Anthony at Louvain there were members of the learned families of Ó hEodhusa, Mac Aodhagáin, Ó Cléirigh, Mac an Bhaird and Ó Maoil Chonaire, as well as other prominent Gaelic families such as Ó Néill and Ó Domhnaill.[212] Bonaventure Ó hEodhusa, who compiled the first catechism printed in Irish at Louvain,[213] had earlier composed a bardic poem lamenting that the honour that formerly attached to the profession of poet had disappeared.[214] Nonetheless, many of the clergy returning from their continental education had significant family ties with the remaining members of the scholarly communities in the areas to which they returned to work. The Ó Cléirigh family in Donegal was just one of those families, and their members were prominent both in the Franciscan order and among the lay scholars still active in south-west Ulster in the early seventeenth century. Even for the lay scholars among them, such as Cú Choigcríche Ó Cléirigh, the role of the Franciscans was a significant one.[215]

This revival meant that by the 1620s a substantial network of Franciscan personnel was again in place throughout the country – despite government disapproval – and, as is well known, the existence of that network greatly facilitated the work of Mícheál Ó Cléirigh. The wider Irish Franciscan success in Louvain, Rome and elsewhere, as well as the progress at home in Ireland created the circumstances which made it possible for Mícheál Ó Cléirigh to pursue research into the manuscript heritage throughout Ireland in the 1620s and 1630s. As discussed in chapter two above, the influence of Louvain in guiding the direction of scholarly research was considerable. That ideological impetus was but one dimension of the Franciscan contribution to the AFM enterprise. There was also the practical support provided by those of the Franciscan community resident in Ireland. It is that aspect of the Franciscan contribution to the historical research of Ó Cléirigh and his fellow chroniclers that is being highlighted here.

During the twelve years (1626–37) in which he was attached to the Donegal convent, Ó Cléirigh also spent time in other friaries of the order in each of the four

---

211 Patrick Conlan, *Franciscan Ireland* (Dublin, 1978), pp 29–32. 212 Jennings (ed.), *Louvain papers*, pp 54–5; P.F. Moran (ed.), 'Mortuary book of the Irish Franciscan monastery in Louvain' in *Spicilegium Ossoriense*, 3rd ser. (Dublin, 1884), 46–55. 213 Mac Raghnaill (ed.), *An teagasc Críosdaidhe*. 214 *Slán agaibh, a fhir chumtha*, printed in Mhág Craith (ed.), *Dán na mBráthar Mionúr*, I, pp 25–7 (poem 5). 215 Much of the extant documentary material for the history of the Franciscans in Ireland in the early seventeenth century has been edited in *Analecta Hibernica* 6

Irish provinces. This extensive schedule of travel brought him to Multyfarnham, Drogheda, Dublin, Kildare, Athlone and Wexford in Leinster; Quin, Limerick, Cashel, Clonmel, Cork and Timoleague in Munster; Galway, Kinalehin and Rosserrilly in Connacht and Lisgoole in west Ulster.[216] Such travel was necessary to gain access to source manuscripts, some of them preserved in Franciscan houses, and others in the hands of laity and clergy throughout the country.

Mícheál Ó Cléirigh recorded the locations throughout Ireland in which he secured access to source manuscripts from which he transcribed historical and hagiographical material. It is clear from the colophons preserved in three manuscripts containing his fair copies of saints' lives, now Bibliothèque Royale MSS 2324–40; 4190–200; 5100–4, that many of the recently re-established Franciscan houses provided him with accommodation as the initial work of transcription proceeded. The colophons in these manuscripts provided much of the information used by Brendan Jennings in his 1936 account of Ó Cléirigh's work. Paul Walsh substantially revised the dating of some of the colophons, to allow for Ó Cléirigh having used the local calendar in these colophons and thus accepting 25 March as the beginning of a new year. However, Walsh agreed with Jennings's overall interpretation of the achievement of Ó Cléirigh as a scribe and historian, and the extensive travelling which he undertook in the course of his researches.[217]

The provincial of the order in the years after 1615, Donogh Mooney, had been round much the same circuit more than a decade earlier than Ó Cléirigh, working to promote the order and simultaneously writing his account of the history of each Franciscan establishment. Mooney's history was completed in 1617–18 at Louvain. In his address to his readers, he apologized for the shortcomings of his history and explained that:

> *meque excusatum habeat quod non meliora prestiterim, qui nimirum, eversa facie Ecclesiae et Reipublicae in hoc Regno, vix fragmenta eorum quae colligenda erant, percurrens regnum in visitationibus meis, et persecutionis furorem pertimescens, colligere potui.*[218]
>
> (The confusion of Church and State in this unhappy land is my apology. In making my visitations I have been compelled to hurry from convent to convent surrounded by the alarms of persecution, so that I have been unable to collect more than the fragments of the historical documents necessary for a work such as this.)[219]

Whatever about Mooney's experiences in the mid-1610s, Breandán Ó Buachalla rejects the notion that Ó Cléirigh's research, conducted in the late 1620s, was

(1934).   216 Jennings, *Michael O Cleirigh and his associates*, passim.   217 Jennings, *Michael O Cleirigh and his associates*, passim; Walsh, *Irish leaders and learning*, pp 350–70; Walsh's two articles, 'Travels of an Irish scholar' and 'The work of a winter', were originally published in *Catholic Bulletin* 27 (1937), 123–32, and 28 (1938), 226–34.   218 Jennings (ed.), 'Brussels MS 3947', *Analecta Hibernica* 6 (1934), 20.   219 Translated in Mooney, 'A history of the Franciscan Order in Ireland', *Franciscan Tertiary* 5:11 (1894–5), 323.

particularly dangerous.[220] Romantic notions of the dangers involved conveyed by earlier writers may have been somewhat exaggerated.[221] The suggestion that he was lucky to have escaped with his life first emerged in a Louvain context.[222] It may have been boring, tedious work, however, working under strict guidelines, and involving much travel, which may have been undertaken on foot. He sometimes complained about the tedium or the special demands of the work in the colophons he added to his transcripts of older texts, but he never complained about persecution. Though 1629–30 may have been a difficult year, things eased again after the arrival of Wentworth, who adopted a pragmatic approach in tolerating Catholic religious practice.[223] Incidentally, there is no evidence of Ó Cléirigh having been away from the Donegal friary between November 1629 and October 1630.[224]

While Ó Cléirigh did not repeat Mooney's comments concerning obstacles to travel or problems with access to manuscripts, it was the case in several friaries, particularly those in urban locations such as Dublin, Drogheda and Athlone, that the original monastic buildings were not in use, the friars residing instead in rented houses.[225] Franciscan reports of persecution persisted, such complaints emanating particularly from those familiar with events in Dublin.[226] Yet, regardless of the physical conditions in which they lived, and the political regime under which they operated, it is clear that a vibrant Franciscan community existed in the 1620s that provided an important nationwide network that could be availed of even by an un-ordained brother such as Mícheál Ó Cléirigh.

Some of the convents Ó Cléirigh visited were openly functioning for the previous twenty years – evidence of the revival of the Franciscan movement in Ireland – and there is no doubt that the convents of Athlone, Donegal and Lisgoole, though they may have been functioning in quite remote temporary locations, were in a position to provide adequate facilities for the research work of Ó Cléirigh and his collaborators.[227]

Although only a lowly brother himself, in the course of his visits to various Franciscan houses, Ó Cléirigh encountered some of the most influential members of the order in Ireland, including, at Cork, Francis O'Mahony (alias Matthews), who was appointed provincial in 1626. While engaged in transcription of saints' lives at the Franciscan convent at Timoleague in the summer of 1629, he took time out to travel to Cork to meet with Francis O'Mahony.[228] O'Mahony, too, was actively researching the Irish past, and his *Brevis synopsis Provinciae Hiberniae*

220 Ó Buachalla, 'Annála ríoghachta Éireann is Foras feasa ar Éirinn', 89–93.   221 For example, Ó Cléirigh, *Aodh Mac Aingil*, p. 4.   222 Nollaig Ó Muraíle, 'Míchél Ó Cléirigh' in *Oxford DNB*; Cainneach Ó Maonaigh, 'Franciscan Library MS A 30.4', *Irish Book Lover* 27 (1940), 202–4.   223 P.J. Corish, *The Catholic community in the seventeenth and eighteenth centuries* (Dublin, 1981), pp 39–41.   224 Walsh, *Irish leaders and learning*, p. 359.   225 Jennings (ed.), 'Brussels MS 3947', 28, 86–8.   226 For a description of events in Dublin in 1630, from a Franciscan perspective, see *HMC Franciscan MSS*, pp 17, 20.   227 On the conditions at Lisgoole, see Jennings, *Michael O Cleirigh and his associates*, pp 117–18.   228 Jennings, *Michael O Cleirigh and his associates*, pp 80–1.

FF Minorum was completed by 1629.[229] In August 1629, Rev. Thomas Strange, writing from Dublin, reported to Rev. Luke Wadding at Rome that 'the Father Provincial, that now is, has compiled a treatise on the convents of this Province, which I will send your Paternity after the chapter: it will afford Your Paternity much light as to the years when they were founded'.[230] Given his own scholarly interests, O'Mahony would certainly have encouraged Ó Cléirigh in his hagiographical research and the meeting at Cork may well have been arranged to allow Ó Cléirigh the opportunity to communicate with his superiors at Louvain on the progress of his work.

While staying at Cashel, Mícheál Ó Cléirigh would also have encountered Rev. John Goulde, guardian of the Franciscan convent there. Goulde was himself actively involved in research into the lives of Irish saints.[231] During time spent at the Franciscan house in Dublin in 1627 Ó Cléirigh would also have encountered Thomas Strange, guardian of the Dublin convent and a well-connected member of the Franciscan community in the city. Strange was in regular contact with other Irish Franciscan historians, not least his cousin Luke Wadding who was based at St Isidore's College, Rome, from 1625.

Thomas Strange also acted as the scholarly intermediary between Wadding and the Protestant archbishop of Armagh, James Ussher, and he reported to Wadding on more than one occasion that he enjoyed access to Ussher's collection of manuscripts: 'He has a famous library of manuscripts; let me know whatever you would have me search out in the said library, for he allows me access to it'.[232] In August 1629, Strange wrote to Wadding concerning the ecclesiastical history of Ireland, which Wadding planned to write, telling him that Ussher, the 'pseudoprimate', could be of more assistance than any other, 'inasmuch as he has made a complete collection of the antiquities of this country, which he has offered to lend me, being desirous that the book should see the light'.[233] Ussher was also in contact with other high-level Catholic ecclesiastical personnel, including David Rothe, bishop of Ossory, and the two men exchanged correspondence particularly on the history of St Patrick and the coming of Christianity to Ireland.[234]

Stephen White, an indefatigable researcher into the lives of Irish saints, also enjoyed the cooperation of James Ussher in his researches. White summarized the nature of that cooperation in a letter to Colgan in January 1640:

229 O'Mahony's history is published in Jennings (ed.), '*Brevis synopsis*', 139–91. As noted above, information from this source was incorporated into AFM, having first been translated into Irish by Muiris Ulltach.　**230** *HMC Franciscan MSS*, p. 14; Jennings, *Michael Ó Cléirigh and his associates*, pp 81–3.　**231** Jennings, *Michael Ó Cléirigh and his associates*, p. 66; for further details of Goulde's work, see UCD–OFM MS A 34.　**232** Thomas Strange to Luke Wadding, 20 Nov. 1629, in *HMC Franciscan MSS*, p. 16 (translated from Spanish by the editor).　**233** Thomas Strange to Luke Wadding, 4 Aug. 1629, in *HMC Franciscan MSS*, pp 12–13.　**234** For an edition of this correspondence, see William O'Sullivan (ed.), 'Correspondence of David Rothe and James Ussher, 1619–23', *Collectanea Hibernica* 36–7 (1994–5), 7–49.

I was invited by him, and three times I spent many hours with that Mr Ussher. He received me with the greatest affability and treated me with candour and unaffectedness, and bade me good-bye with the greatest politeness. Moreover, in person and by letter, he often invited me to his house, not only to dine, which I modestly declined, but to everything of his house, even to his most choice library, which is really of very great value. In that library I saw that catalogue and those Latin Lives of our Irish saints written at length in manuscript.[235]

Thomas Strange's influential contacts and his enthusiasm for research into Irish ecclesiastical history are sufficently well established for it to be accepted that, as a fellow Franciscan, he would have helped facilitate Ó Cléirigh's researches. Strange may have been instrumental in arranging access to the manuscript containing the Martyrology of Tallaght owned by Ussher when Ó Cléirigh consulted it in Drogheda in April 1627. Ó Cléirigh recorded that the manuscript – believed to be part of the Book of Leinster – had been brought from Dublin to Drogheda and described it merely as *seinleabar cianaosta dorcha* ('an extremely old and obscure book').[236] James Ussher was also in contact with the Franciscan provincial, Francis O'Mahony, and gave him permission to have a transcript made of saints' lives then in Ussher's library,[237] and Ó Cléirigh may have come to Dublin with a letter of recommendation from O'Mahony also. Paul Walsh pointed out that in the colophons attached to the four pieces Ó Cléirigh transcribed at Drogheda from this source, he did not state that he was in the Franciscan convent as was his wont. Walsh suggests that Ó Cléirigh may well have been working instead in Ussher's library, which was then located in Drogheda, in his palace near the east gate.[238] He may have thought it better to pass over in silence the fact that he was transcribing the material from a manuscript obtained from the Protestant archbishop, and perhaps even enjoying his hospitality. Ussher normally resided at Drogheda during the years he served as archbishop of Armagh.[239] Ó Cléirigh was subsequently allowed to take some vellum folios containing the Martyrology of Tallaght to Donegal, from where they were brought to Louvain for use by John Colgan. The manuscript was retained in Franciscan hands thereafter.[240] An earlier link between the Drogheda convent and that of Donegal might partially explain why this loan was permitted. Muiris Ulltach mac Seaáin, who had been instrumental in re-establishing the Franciscans at a rented house in Drogheda in 1609–10, when he served as provincial, was subsequently resident at Donegal during Mícheál Ó Cléirigh's

235 Cited in translation in Sharpe, *Medieval Irish saints' lives*, p. 59. 236 BR MS 5100–4, fo. 238; Jennings, *Michael O Cleirigh and his associates*, p. 57; Walsh, *Irish leaders and learning*, p. 353. 237 Colgan, *Trias thaumaturga*, ed. Pádraig Ó Riain (repr., Dublin, 1997), introduction, n. 36. 238 Walsh, *Irish leaders and learning*, p. 353; for evidence that Ussher's library was in Drogheda in 1641, see Nicholas Bernard, *The whole proceedings of the siege of Drogheda in Ireland* (London, 1642), p. 81. 239 C. Litton Falkiner, *Illustrations of Irish history and topography, mainly of the seventeenth century* (London, 1904), p. 375. 240 It is now UCD–OFM MS A 3.

time there, and served as guardian from 1632 to 1635.[241] In return, Ó Cléirigh or another of the Donegal Franciscans may have been the person who brought the Irish *Liber hymnorum* manuscript to Ussher either then or later, where it was consulted and cited by both Ussher and Sir James Ware.[242]

There are several proven connections also between Ó Cléirigh and Sir James Ware. Among the extant manuscripts formerly owned by Ware is one that includes a list in the hand of Mícheál Ó Cléirigh itemizing saints' lives.[243] A second Ware manuscript linked to Ó Cléirigh comprises a series of extracts in Irish from AFM. The manuscript, BL Add. 4784, is a composite one. The extracts from AFM that it contains are incorrectly described in O'Grady's catalogue entry as comprising 'rough material amassed from chronicles of the 5th–16th century for the Annals of the Four Masters'.[244] However, an analysis of the content of this annalistic miscellany reveals that the transcribed extracts in Ware's possession are later in date than the autograph manuscripts of AFM. Unlike either of the autograph manuscripts, the AFM extracts in Ware's manuscript are a fair copy, with no amendments or interlinings. There are even some minor stylistic improvements as compared with AFM, which support the case that Ware's manuscript is a later transcript. Thus, for instance in the entry for 1600, which is largely a verbatim transcript of the AFM text, the reference to the earl of Thomond is rendered simply as *iarla Tuadhmumhan* ('earl of Thomond') which is neater than the form *an tiarla (.i. tuadhmumhan)* ('the earl: i.e. Thomond') found in AFM.[245] Occasionally, the material in Ware's manuscript appears to have been customized for its intended recipient, as in the entry for 1545 relating to the earl of Ormond, where the last phrase *tre chomhairle na neitriticceadh* ('by the advice of the heretics') recorded in the autograph annals is silently omitted.[246] The scribe who copied the 1421 entry from AFM relating to Tadhg Mac Cárthaigh appears to have attempted to improve the style of the entry for Ware's manuscript but in the effort made an error by omitting the words *do mharbhadh*.[247]

The precise purpose of the AFM extracts transcribed for Ware is difficult to discern. A significant number of the entries relate to castles and other fortifications, and scarcely any obituaries are included. In geographical terms, the focus is on Munster and Leinster, with little of Ulster interest recorded. The most

241 Mooney, 'A history of the Franciscan Order in Ireland', *Franciscan Tertiary* 5:1 (1894), 2; Muiris Ulltach was one of the two Franciscans of that name in the Donegal friary who signed the completed manuscript of AFM in August 1636 (UCD–OFM MS A 13, fo. xxiii). 242 Bernard and Atkinson (eds), *The Irish Liber hymnorum*, I, p. xiv. The editors make the case that it was the Franciscan copy that Ussher and Ware cited and not the alternative text of *Liber hymnorum* now in TCD. It may have been the same Franciscan manuscript of *Liber hymnorum* that was subsequently taken to Louvain for Colgan's use, though this has not been proven; Colgan endorsed the copy he obtained *Ex libris de Conventus de Dunnagall* (p. 3); it is now UCD–OFM MS A 2. 243 Bodl. MS Rawl. B. 487, fo. 74v; *Cat. Ir. mss in Bodl.*, I, p. 141. 244 *Cat. Ir. mss in BL*, I, p. 20. 245 BL Add. MS 4784, fo. 43; *AFM*, VI, pp 2176–7. 246 BL Add. MS 4784, fo. 56; *AFM*, V, pp 1490–1. 247 BL Add. MS 4784, fo. 76v; *AFM* IV, pp 806–7.

curious feature of the AFM extracts as preserved in Ware's manuscript collection is that they are not in chronological order. For example, folio 238 contains entries for 1539, 1458, 1420 and 1540 in that order.[248] This is a characteristic that the text shares with other selected annalistic references elsewhere in Ware's manuscript. The same manuscript also contains annalistic material in English, extracted from a variety of named sources including patent rolls and Primate Swayne's Register. None of these collections of extracts is in chronological order. The recording of historical references in this manner suggests that Ware's interest was not in the general narrative or the precise chronology of events but rather in specific information of a broadly antiquarian nature about particular places. Elsewhere in the same manuscript is preserved the partial Latin translation of thirteenth-century material from AU, known as the 'D' text, the immediate Irish source of which may also have been known to the Four Masters. Since the manuscript is a composite one, however, no particular conclusion can be drawn from the juxtaposition of extracts from AFM placed in close proximity to the 'D' text of AU, other than that both were available to Sir James Ware.

Whatever Ware's purpose was in obtaining extensive transcripts from AFM, it can only have been done in conversation with the scribes, either directly or through an intermediary, so that he could specify which entries he required to be transcribed. The most likely occasion on which this work might have been undertaken was early in the year 1637. Mícheál Ó Cléirigh was in Dublin in February 1637, and had with him a copy of the annals for the purpose of obtaining the approbation of the Catholic archbishop, Thomas Fleming, for his work.[249] There may have been an opportunity at about that time for Ó Cléirigh personally to have done some work for Sir James Ware, and the finished text of the annals was ready to hand in Dublin, so that extracts could have been copied with ease. Ware, then or subsequently, annotated the extracts with his own comments in English, mostly by summarizing in the margin the subject matter of the Irish text.[250] Ware's interest in the work of the Four Masters did not end there. In addition to obtaining these extracts in Irish, he also arranged for all of the Four Masters' entries relating to the period from 1547 to 1558 to be translated into Latin.[251] This was probably because those years were not covered by other annals, such as AU, to which Ware had access, and he had a particular research interest in the reigns of Edward VI and Mary I.[252] The manuscript owned by Ware contained full translations of all entries in AFM for the eighteen years concerned.

248 BL Add. MS 4784, fo. 238. 249 *AFM*, I, p. lxx. 250 BL Add. MS 4784. 251 TCD MS 804. These Latin translations are given in the notes to O'Donovan's edition of AFM for the years covered (*AFM*, V, passim). 252 Ware's annalistic publications included *Rerum Hibernicarum Henrico octavo regnante annales nunc primum editi* (Dublin, 1662), and an extended edition, *Rerum Hibernicarum annales, regnantibus Henrico VII, Henrico VIII, Edwardo VI, et Maria ab anno scilicet Domini MCCCCLXXXV ad annum MDLVIII* (Dublin, 1664).

The idea of a senior government official, and even a Protestant archbishop, sharing historical manuscripts with the Donegal Franciscans seems at odds with the confessional and polemical objectives of the research in which each party was separately engaged. But yet the collaboration between Ware, Ussher and Ó Cléirigh may also be considered as part of an established tradition where historians from Gaelic learned families participated in historical projects on behalf of Anglo-Irish patrons. Katharine Simms has shown that the learned families engaged in such work in earlier centuries had included those of Mac Aodhagáin and Ó Cléirigh.[253] Scholarly collaboration continued to transcend ethnic and even religious divisions in later centuries. This established tradition of scholarly cooperation goes a long way to explaining how it was that the copying and exchange of texts and the sharing of scholarly expertise continued into the seventeenth century, at a time when conflicting confessional allegiances would have worked against such cooperation.

As a historian and manuscript collector himself, Sir James Ware also took a scholarly interest in the Irish monastic foundations, and noted that significant libraries had formerly been located at Donegal and Timoleague.[254] He included references from the *Liber hymnorum* formerly belonging to the Donegal library, printed as a marginal note in his *De scriptoribus* (1639)[255] and again in his *Opuscula S. Patricii* (1656).[256] In the second of these references, he stated that the manuscript was now in the library of James Ussher.[257]

Patrons

Each of Mícheál Ó Cléirigh's collaborative scholarly enterprises had a lay patron. That each separate project had a different patron is an indication that the agenda of research was driven by Ó Cléirigh and his assistants rather than by the patrons. It may also indicate that it was difficult to persuade individual patrons to provide financial support over an extended period. The precise nature of the working relationship between the various patrons and the scribal team is not easy to discern. Toirrdhealbhach Mág Cochláin was patron of the Four Masters while they worked on compiling the *Genealogiae regum et sanctorum Hiberniae*, commenced at the house of Conall Mac Eochagáin at Lismoyny. Aside from his involvement with the Four Masters in 1630, Mac Cochláin was also involved in supporting Conall Mac Eochagáin's translation of the Annals of Clonmacnoise. That work was dedicated to 'the worthy and of great expectacon young gentleman Mr Terenc Coghlan'.[258] It may well be that Mac Eochagáin was the

253 Simms, 'Bards and barons'. 254 Sir James Ware, *The history and antiquities of Ireland* [English translation] (Dublin, 1705), pp 76–116. 255 Ware, *De scriptoribus Hiberniae*, p. 15. 256 Sir James Ware, *Opuscula Sancto Patricio, qui Hibernos ad fidem Christi convertit* (London, 1656), p. 150. 257 ... *ex antiquo codice Ms. Hymnorum, olim ad conventum ordinis Minorum de observantia Donagalliae pertinente, nunc in Bibliotheca instructissima Usseriana asservato* (Ware, *S. Patricio*, p. 150). See also Bernard and Atkinson (eds), *The Irish Liber hymnorum*, I, p. xiv. 258 For the

intermediary who encouraged Mac Cochláin's sponsorship of Ó Cléirigh's genealogical research. Ó Cléirigh's dedication to Mac Cochláin notes that though many noblemen were approached with a request for assistance, Mac Cochláin was the only one he found who was willing to support the project. Though such statements regarding patrons were largely formulaic, there may have been some truth in the assertion that patrons such as Mac Cochláin were difficult to find.[259]

Some time later, Brian Ruadh Mág Uidhir was involved in sponsoring the Four Masters in preparing a new recension of *Leabhar gabhála Éireann*, which was completed at Lisgoole late in the year 1631.[260] The work contained a formal dedication to him, acknowledging his support and asserting, in a formulaic manner, that the work would exhalt his own ancestors as well as the saints, nobility and history of Ireland in general.[261] Brian Ruadh died in the following year but, as noted earlier, his interest in history was subsequently pursued by others of the Mág Uidhir family for whom a history, sometimes referred to as the 'Book of Knockninny', was compiled.[262]

Whereas Mac Cochláin and Mág Uidhir were involved as sponsors of other scholarly projects also, in the case of Fearghal Ó Gadhra, the annals are the only extant project with which he is known to have been associated. Of the three patrons, Ó Gadhra's background is the least well known. After the death of his father, he had been made a ward of court and was educated under the care of Theobald Dillon, an Old Englishman from Westmeath.[263] Dillon was a man who had made an enormous personal profit from the changes in landholding in late sixteenth-century Connacht.[264] Dillon and his wife, Eleanor Tuite, reared a large family, of whom two sons became Franciscan priests and two daughters were founding members of the Irish Poor Clares.[265] Fearghal Ó Gadhra grew up in that same household, one that included Edward and George Dillon, OFM, as well as the Irish privy councillor Sir Lucas Dillon. George Dillon subsequently served as guardian of the Athlone Franciscan friary, and together with Conall Mac Eochagáin provided a signed testimonial to the *Genealogiae regum et sanctorum Hiberniae* of the Four Masters in 1630.[266] The Mac Cochláin and Dillon families were interrelated through marriage, and this association may have helped draw Fearghal Ó Gadhra further into the circle of patrons that supported the scholarly activities of the Four Masters and their associates.

An important observation by Breandán Ó Buachalla in relation to all three major patrons of the Four Masters is that they were establishment figures within

dedication to 'Terenc Coghlan' prefixed to the Annals of Clonmacnoise, see *AClon*, pp 7–9. Mac Cochláin's sister, Margaret, married Conall Mac Eochagáin, who refers to him in the preface of AClon as 'his brother'.   **259** *GRSH*, pp 5–6, 142.   **260** RIA MSS 23 M 70; 23 K 32; see also Jennings, *Michael O Cleirigh and his associates*, pp 119–21.   **261** The text of the dedication is printed from TCD MS 1286 in O'Curry, *Lectures on manuscript materials*, pp 168–9, 552–4.   **262** See above, pp 276–7.   **263** *Irish patent rolls of James I* (Dublin, 1966), p. 311.   **264** Bernadette Cunningham, 'Theobald Dillon: a newcomer in sixteenth-century Mayo', *Cathair na Mart* 6 (1986), 24–32.   **265** Jennings, *Louvain papers*, 57, 72n; Cunningham, 'The Poor Clare order in Ireland'.   **266** *GRSH*, p. 9.

the new political order in Ireland in the 1630s.[267] Toirrdhealbhach Mac Cochláin was an MP with extensive lands in Westmeath and Offaly.[268] In 1636, his wife's relative, James Dillon, married a sister of the Irish lord deputy, Thomas Wentworth, earl of Strafford.[269] Brian Ruadh Mág Uidhir was baron of Enniskillen, a title he had acquired in 1628, shortly before he became involved in the cultural patronage of the Four Masters' historical researches. It is noteworthy that this anglicized title was specifically mentioned by Mícheál Ó Cléirigh in his dedication to the patron prefaced to *Leabhar gabhála*:

> *[Brian Ruadh] Meguidhir, a thigherna Insi Cethlionn, a chéidfir dar goireadh an tainm sin (do shiol Uidhir le mordhacht Righ Saxan, Franc, Alban, ocus Eireann, Carolus, an thaonmhadh la fichit Ianuaríi, an bhliadhain si, d'aois ar tTighearna Iosa Criost, 1627, ocus an treas bhliadhain do Righe an Righ).*
>
> (Brian Roe Maguire, Lord of Enniskillen, the first of the race of Odhar who received that title (which thou didst from his Majesty Charles, King of England, France, Scotland and Ireland on the 21st of January, in the year of our Lord Christ, 1627, and the third year of the king's reign.)[270]

Brian Ruadh was son of Conchobhar Mág Uidhir, known as 'the Queen's Maguire', who had fought on the English side, against Ó Domhnaill, at the battle of Kinsale. His branch of the family had taken over the headship of the Méig Uidhir after the departure of Cú Chonnacht Mág Uidhir to the continent in 1607 in the Flight of the Earls. He was known as Sir Brian Maguire before he acquired the title of Baron of Enniskillen in 1628 and he also held a pension from the crown.[271] Brian Ruadh and his cousin, another Brian, were among those appointed to raise money in Fermanagh for the army in 1627.[272] His son, Conchobhar, second baron of Enniskillen, sat in the Irish House of Lords in the 1640 parliament, and later became involved in the 1641 rising.[273]

Fearghal Ó Gadhra, like Toirrdhealbhach Mac Cochláin, was a member of the 1634 parliament, where he served as MP for Sligo. This fact is not glossed over by the Four Masters, rather it is specifically mentioned in the dedication that the

---

267 There may have been a conscious effort to move beyond the conservatism and resistance to change that had found expression by northern poets in the contention of the bards twenty years earlier, and to look to patrons that had achieved high political status in the changed political circumstances of the 1630s. See Ó Buachalla, 'Annála ríoghachta Éireann is Foras feasa ar Éirinn', 94. 268 *Calendar of state papers Ireland, 1633–47*, p. 65. 269 GEC, *Complete peerage* (London, 1910), XI, pp 125–6. Mac Cochláin's wife was Mary Dillon. See Kenneth Nicholls, 'The MacCoghlans', *Irish Genealogist* 6 (1983), 456, n.95. 270 TCD MS 1286, fos 1–4, O'Curry, *Lectures on manuscript materials*, pp 552–4, 168–9. 271 See *Calendar of state papers Ireland, 1625–32*, p. 306. The pension amounted to £100 per annum out of the revenues of Fermanagh; there was also what appears to be a 'surrender and regrant' type grant of his lands from the king at the same time as he acquired the title of baron of Enniskillen. This confirmed a grant to his father of lands to the value of £20 per annum, and was granted in recognition of his and his father's services to the crown. 272 *Calendar of state papers Ireland, 1625–32*, p. 254 (in the context of fear of a Spanish invasion, and the crisis which gave rise to the concessions in the Graces); see P. Ó Gallachair, 'The first Maguire of Tempo', *Clogher Record* 2:1 (1957), 469–89. 273 *Calendar of state papers Ireland*,

annalists prefixed to their text.[274] Those three patrons offer a context within which to view Ó Cléirigh's work, suggesting that he was functioning within the political system rather than outside it. His patrons were men of standing within the current political set up, their status resting on the grace of the king. That Ó Cléirigh was happy to choose these individuals to sponsor his major historical works, and that they were willing to do so is an indication of Ó Cléirigh's standing within that newly evolving society. Ó Buachalla points out that this is the context within which Mícheál Ó Cléirigh's references to Charles I should be read.[275] They occur in AFM, *Genealogiae regum et sanctorum Hiberniae* and *Leabhar gabhála*, and can be interpreted as evidence of a deliberate construction of these works as a history of the kingdom of Ireland, a kingdom that had Charles I as its king. Mícheál Mac Craith has also discussed the references to the Stuarts in the context of changing political ideology of 'faith and fatherland', emphasizing the loyalty inherent in the attitude towards the Stuart monarch displayed by the Four Masters.[276]

Although they appear formulaic, when taken together the various dedications to patrons place the works of history prepared by Mícheál Ó Cléirigh and his fellow chroniclers firmly within the Stuart polity of Charles I, in a manner that can only have been deliberate. The adoption of establishment figures from 1630s Ireland as patrons of the works of the Four Masters and the inclusion of formal dedicatory prefaces to those patrons, which drew attention to their political standing within the Stuart kingdom of Ireland, is an indication that the annals of the Four Masters and the ancillary works that preceded it were perceived by its compilers as formal contributions towards the history of that kingdom, based on the best available sources in the Irish language.

Unlike in the case of poetic patronage, the patrons of the chronicles, histories and genealogies of Mícheál Ó Cléirigh and his team appear to have had much less of a direct connection with the texts they sponsored – at least in these instances. It is noticeable that no effort was made to present Ó Gadhra's ancestors in a favourable light in AFM other than in the dedication, and the text is in no sense a laudatory history of his family. Likewise, there is no obvious association between Mac Cochláin and the text of *Genealogiae regum et sanctorum Hiberniae* or Mág Uidhir and *Leabhar gabhála*, other than the place in which the manuscript was written. Rather, the common link between these secular patrons may have been a broader general interest in scholarly patronage. Pádraig Ó Macháin has argued that this should be interpreted as patronage of learning for its own sake, evidence of 'Renaissance' patronage at work in an Irish context.[277]

1633–47, p. 343. **274** RIA MS C iii 3, p. iii. **275** Ó Buachalla, '*Annála ríoghachta Éireann* is *Foras feasa ar Éirinn*', 94; *GRSH*, p. 6; TCD MS 1286, 1–4 (preface to *Leabhar gabhála*). **276** Mac Craith, 'Creideamh agus Athartha'. **277** Pádraig Ó Macháin, '"A lleabraib imdaib": cleachtadh agus pátrúnacht an léinn, agus déanamh na lámhscríbhinní' in Ruairí Ó hUiginn (ed.), *Oidhreacht na lámhscríbhinní: Léachtaí Cholm Cille XXXIV* (Maynooth, 2004), p. 165.

That a man such as Ó Gadhra would have desired to have his pedigree recorded in detail – if only as an afterthought – reflects the political stance of Irish Catholics post-1603, where the antiquity of their association with the island of Ireland was a matter of political significance. It did not matter that the Ó Gadhra family had not been particularly prominent in the pages of the annals. That relative insignificance in the past could be rectified through cultural patronage in the present, so that the name of Fearghal Ó Gadhra, and by association those of his ancestors, could achieve retrospective distinction. The annalists did not feel it necessary to enhance the image of earlier members of the family of Ó Gadhra, their provision of a pedigree was evidently deemed prestige enough for their patron. They also went to some lengths to emphasize the importance of the work for Ireland, noting in their address to Ó Gadhra:

Do fhoillsighesa daoibhsi gur bhó doigh lem go ffuighinn cuidiucchadh na ccroinicighe ar ar mó mo mhes do chum leabhair Annaladh do sccríobhadh i ccuirfidhe i ccuimhne na neithe remraite, 7 da leiccthi ar cáirde gan a Sccriobhadh do lathair nach ffuighti iad doridhisi le a fforaithmet, 7 le a ccuimhniucchadh go crich, 7 go foircenn an betha. Do cruinniccheadh lem na leabhair Annáladh as ferr 7 as líonmhaire as mó do beidir lem dfághail i nErinn uile (biodh gur dhecair damh a ttecclamadh go haoin ionad) do chum an leabhairsi do sccriobhadh in bhar nainmsi, 7 in bhar nonóir óir as sibh tucc luach saothair do na croinicidhibh lás ro sccriobhadh é.

(I explained to you that I thought I could get the assistance of the chroniclers for whom I had most esteem, for writing a book of annals, in which the aforesaid matters might be put on record; and that, should the writing of them be neglected at present, they would not again be found to be put on record or commemorated to the end and termination of the world. There were collected by me all the best and most copious books of annals that I could find throughout all Ireland (though it was difficult for me to collect them to one place), to write this book in your name and to your honour, for it was you that gave the reward of their labour to the chroniclers, by whom it was written.)[278]

These words addressed to the patron have sometimes been misinterpreted to suggest that Ó Cléirigh regarded his work as a rescue mission to preserve the historical remnants of a lost civilization. It is useful to place this statement of purpose in the context of Ó Cléirigh's comments in the preface to his 1643 *Foclóir*, where he was concerned to cater for 'the young and ignorant who wish to read the old books (a thing which is not difficult for the educated of our country)'.[279] There was no sense there that the valued Irish manuscripts of historical significance were beyond reach. It was the unreliability of memory, not the permanent loss of manuscript sources, that was of concern to the Irish chroniclers who dedicated their work to Fearghal Ó Gadhra.

278 *AFM*, I, pp lvi–lvii.   279 Miller (ed.), 'O'Clery's Irish glossary', 355.

As Chris Given-Wilson has pointed out in the context of English medieval chronicles, 'references to *memoria* in chronicle prologues were generally couched in terms of the written word as a remedy for the corrosive force of forgetfulness'.[280] As Ranulf Higden had explained in the fourteenth century, in the preface to his *Polychronicon*, it was necessary to commit the record of the past to writing:

> For shortness of life, dullness of perception, numbness of the soul, weakness of memory and fruitless occupations prevent us from knowing many things, and forgetfulness is ever the stepmother and enemy of memory. At this present time, indeed, arts and the law would disappear entirely, examples of noble deeds would be unknown, and the eloquence and skills of speaking would utterly perish, were it not for the fact that divine mercy has provided a remedy for human imperfection in the use of letters.[281]

The act of writing history, as Given-Wilson explains, 'can be said to begin with an attitude towards what ought to be remembered',[282] and the Four Masters, too, had a clear sense of what they wished to preserve for the future from the varied record of the past.

Undoubtedly the circumstances of ownership and access to manuscripts were gradually changing, but the 'now or never' urgency of the address to the patron may also have been partly to convince Ó Gadhra that his financial support of the AFM project was money well spent. These were prestige products and the manuscripts were highly valued by those responsible for producing them.[283]

Conclusion

There is no doubt that the specific scholarly network within which AFM was compiled dictated the form and content of the work. The annalists made extensive use of a wide range of manuscript sources in the Irish language, made available to them by learned families and others from many parts of the country. It is noticeable however, that these south-west Ulster scholars rarely looked to east Ulster or to Scotland for their sources. While Ó Cléirigh was prepared to travel to the southern, south-eastern and eastern extremities of the country – to Timoleague and Wexford, for example, and also to Drogheda and Dublin, he makes no specific mention of manuscripts of Ó Néill provenance, either hagiographical or historical.

The Four Masters relied almost totally on Irish manuscript sources and evidently did not generally consider it appropriate to incorporate material from

280 Given-Wilson, *Chronicles*, p. 57. **281** C. Babington and J.R. Lumby (eds), *Polychronicon Ranulphi Higden Monachi Cestrensis*, by Ranulf Higden (9 vols, Rolls Series, London, 1865–86), I, pp 2–4; extract translated into English in Given-Wilson, *Chronicles*, p. 59. **282** Given-Wilson, *Chronicles*, p. 60. **283** Ó Macháin, 'A lleabraib imdaib', 155–8.

external printed sources. In this, they contrast with others of their Catholic contemporaries, such as the Munster historian Geoffrey Keating. That difference of approach is best explained not in terms of contrasting ethnic or political allegiances, but in terms of education. Keating's work displays the influence of his continental university education in theology and rhetoric, an experience not shared by any of the Four Masters whose scholarly training had taken place within the traditional schools of Gaelic learning.

That theirs was a history rooted in the manuscript sources was consistent with the Four Masters' objective of providing a secular chronicle to complement the ecclesiastical and hagiographical research in which the Irish Franciscans were involved, at home and abroad. The Four Masters' lack of overt engagement with current political issues in debate and the absence of a direct response to the polemic of other historians are among the characteristics that define their work. The annals were conceived as a 'true' history of Ireland, constructed in the traditional annalistic form from approved sources, with its authenticity and accuracy attested by senior scholars from the most respected learned families and by senior Catholic clergy. Where doubts existed about any factual detail, alternative versions were presented without judgment or preference being expressed. This was a well-established feature of chronicles, and one designed to enhance the reliability of the work. Neither the annalists, nor their most vocal critic Tuileagna Ó Maoil Chonaire, consciously entertained the notion of alternative readings of the past, in the manner so vividly expressed in the polemical preface to Keating's *Foras feasa ar Éirinn*.[284] Within their scholarly circle, the evidence of the source manuscripts was the key to truth. To deviate from that truth, as they perceived it, would be to depart from the ethos of the tradition of scholarship that formed their world. To deviate from the annalistic form would have been counter-productive. They sought to produce a coherent useable secular guide to the Irish past from earliest times to their own day. Given its ambitious scope, the annalistic form was the most practicable by far. Within this formal framework, as we have seen, there was still plenty of scope for manipulation of evidence through the process of selection, arrangement and omission of annalistic entries.

The work of the Four Masters was shaped by the traditions of the scholarly world of the learned families, not merely in terms of access to manuscripts, or technical skills in the Irish language, or the mechanics of manuscript production, but also in terms of their attitude to their source manuscripts and ultimately their concept of what constituted history. Any open admission that they had sometimes relied on oral sources would have been avoided. Their work emerged out of a particular cultural tradition at a time of transition. It enjoyed Renaissance-style patronage, which could be said to have given rise to a post-

284 Cunningham, *World of Geoffrey Keating*, pp 83–101.

Renaissance text. Given its emphasis on the exploits of the Uí Dhomhnaill, it was only slightly less dynastic in focus than the Annals of Loch Cé of fifty years before. And yet, there was no doubt that the status of the Uí Dhomhnaill as potential patrons in the 1630s was much diminished as compared to that of Brian Mac Diarmada in the 1580s.[285]

The annalists would have been well aware of that change in patronage in the recent past. It was something that determined the contemporary circumstances of their own lives and may well have provided the inspiration for them to record for posterity, on an ambitious scale, the story of their ancestors who had inhabited the kingdom of Ireland from the beginning of recorded time. They chose to do so in the most traditional way they knew, using the time-honoured chronicle form, knowing that it was a style likely to win the approbation of the most senior scholars then living, whose judgment and wisdom were highly valued.

285 On Brian Mac Diarmada's Annals of Loch Cé, see Cunningham and Gillespie, *Stories from Gaelic Ireland*, especially ch. 6, 'Remembering Ruaidhrí Mac Diarmada', pp 155–78; Bernadette Cunningham, 'The Annals of Loch Cé: scribes and manuscripts', *Irish Arts Review* (summer 2009), 92–5.

CHAPTER TEN

Conclusion: making history

We need as historians to consider myth and memory, not only as special clues to the past, but equally as windows on the making and remaking of individual and collective consciousness, in which both fact and fantasy, past and present, each has its part.[1]

The annals compiled by the Four Masters were designed to provide a new, accessible and comprehensive account of Irish history for seventeenth-century readers, yet they chose to present their record of the Irish past in a very conventional form, authenticated by tradition. It was not merely convention that prompted them to do so. The annalistic form was an appropriate one in which to pursue an interest in questions of chronology, and it was also suited to the kind of recall of the past that was possible in Gaelic lordship society. It catered for both the particular and the universal, incorporating details concerning many individuals from within many distinct Gaelic lordships set within the bigger picture of the kingdom of Ireland, dealing with the recent past set within the grand sweep of recorded time. The simplicity of form facilitated the efficient coordination of a team effort to produce a new set of annals. The annalistic form had a long pedigree, the very antiquity and familiarity of which would have enhanced its acceptability as an authentic account of the Irish past derived from ancient and authoritative sources. The conventional annalistic form of the work, no less than the impeccable hereditary credentials of the compilers, and the approbations from other respected learned men, nurtured a real sense of connection to the past and continuity from past to present. The written instruction to Mícheál Ó Cléirigh, from his then superior, Rev. Valentine Browne, issued in May 1632, that the finished annals should be submitted to 'the judgment of men skilful in the Irish tongue',[2] may also have encouraged a conservative approach to the task in hand. The professional Irish scholars who were asked to approve formally the work were themselves immersed in the same traditions of *seanchas* as were the compilers.

The discipline of Gaelic scholarship in which the annalists had been trained may have required practitioners to adhere to traditional forms and language, even where the political sentiments expressed were innovative. This was

---

1 Raphael Samuel and Paul Thompson (eds), *The myths we live by* (London, 1980), 'Introduction', p. 21. 2 Jennings, *The Four Masters and their associates*, p. 135.

particularly significant in a history that did not merely deal with the remote past but also incorporated very recent and very traumatic events. The annalistic form allowed the story of the past to be presented in a comfortingly familiar framework that evoked a sense of continuity from ancient times, while at the same time presenting a story of historical upheaval and change in the near contemporary accounts of late sixteenth- and early seventeenth-century Irish history.

Drawing the strands of their text from a range of earlier sources, comprising annals, prose narratives and occasional verse extracts, some recently composed, others with the sanction of antiquity, the Four Masters wove a new and coherent historical tapestry that preserved the essence of the *seanchas* tradition. It combined national origin legends with stories of kings, saints and secular heroes, within a framework of annals that took as its basis the idea of an ancient kingdom of Ireland, now addressed to a wider readership because of the potential of access to print. It has often been noted that the Annals of the Four Masters preserved information about past events that was not recorded in any other extant source, but the importance of the work transcends the minutiae of historical detail from which it was assembled. The Four Masters were not mere compilers of a miscellany of information about the Irish past. Rather, they took a time-honoured format for the recording of historical matter and constructed an elaborate extended overview, ranging broadly over time and space, in a systematic and controlled manner, documenting all that they deemed worthy of commemoration. Still rooted in local political allegiances, and informed by the religious values of its compilers and sponsors, it also served as a formal expression of the origins and history of the contemporary kingdom of Ireland.

Any attempt to categorize the Annals of the Four Masters by labelling the finished work a 'Counter-Reformation' or 'post-Renaissance' text, as an indigenous Irish work, or a by-product of the hagiographical researches of the Irish College of St Anthony at Louvain, probably does an injustice to the achievement of the annalists. The Annals of the Four Masters are all of these things, but those labels fall far short of explaining the totality of the achievement. Deceptive in its simplicity, the finished construct is an elaborate multi-purpose history that has been used in a myriad different ways in the four centuries since its completion. In its pages are woven together many of the essential elements of the Irish *seanchas* tradition, forming a richly textured expression of the collective historical consciousness of the Irish people in a form that has endured.

Commenting on the completed work, Ó Cléirigh's dedication to Ó Gadhra gave priority to the need to record the history of saints and ecclesiastics, placing secular leaders in a subsidiary role:

> *Do bhraithes ar bhar nonoir gur bhadbar truaighe, 7 nemhele, doghailsi, 7 dobroin libh (do chum gloire Dé 7 onora na hEreann) a mhed do dheachattar sliocht Gaoidhil meic Niuil fo chiaigh 7 dorchadas, gan fios ecca na oidhedha Naoimh, na bannaoimhe*

Airdepscoip, Epscoip, na abbad, na uasal graidh eccailsi oile, Righ, na Ruirigh, tigherna na toisicch, comhaimsir na coimhsinedh neich dibhsidhe fri aroile.

(I have calculated on your honour that it seemed to you a cause of pity and regret, grief and sorrow (for the glory of God and the honour of Ireland), how much of the race of Gaedhal son of Niul have gone under a cloud of darkness without a knowledge of the death or obit of saint or virgin, archbishop, bishop or abbot, or other noble dignitary of the Church, of king or prince, lord or chieftain, of the synchronism or connection of the one with the other.)[3]

This subtle prioritizing of ecclesiastical over lay is one of the elements that marks them out as different from the medieval Irish annals. It demonstrates that the compilers had consciously addressed the issue of the themes that should be prioritized in their history – issues that have been analyzed above in the case studies of ecclesiastical and secular themes. It was taken for granted that the history should consist of the doings of saints and ecclesiastics, kings and nobles. The common people had no place in the record of all that was honourable in the Irish past. That too, accorded with the European norm, and was part of a belief that the purpose of history was to enhance the honour of the nation. At the same time, the annals were not conceived by their creators as propaganda, but rather as the record of the truth of history. This inspiration to pursue the truth about the past through scholarly endeavour was shared by their fellow chroniclers in earlier generations both at home and abroad, seeking to record the facts as known to them as accurately as possible, and seeking to convey their understanding of the significance of the facts they recorded.[4] The text was crafted so as to be a formal, detached, non-polemical, matter-of-fact, account of historical truth.

In later generations, the Annals of the Four Masters were perceived as having captured the essence of Gaelic lordship society, recording in minute detail the personalities that had come to prominence in politics or the church, and placing them within a politically plausible framework of a kingdom of Ireland whose noble origins were as old as recorded time.

The Annals of the Four Masters drew their authority from the authenticity of their connection to the late medieval Gaelic manuscript tradition, and it was this authenticity that ensured that they came to form part of the cultural roots of modern Irish identity. The writing of history is a continuum, new texts emerging to reflect contemporary values but yet being formed out of, and influenced by, those narratives of the past that were created to serve the needs of earlier generations.

In the last analysis, what is the past but a once material existence now silenced, extant only as sign and as sign drawing to itself chains of conflicting inter-

---

3 *AFM*, I, p. lvi.   4 Given-Wilson, *Chronicles*, pp 1–20.

pretations that hover over its absent presence and compete for possession of the relics, seeking to invest traces of significance upon the bodies of the dead.[5]

5 Gabrielle M. Spiegel, *The past as text: the theory and practice of medieval historiography* (Baltimore, MD, 1999), p. 43.

APPENDIX

Annals of Lecan. Extract for the years 1451–1460[1]

[The sections of the Annals of Lecan text that correspond to passages in AFM are highlighted in **bold**.]

1451

1. A gracious yeare this yeare was, though the glory and solace of the Irish was sett by, the Glory of heauen was amplyfied and extolled therin, and although this is a yeare of grace or to with the Roman Church, it is an ungratious, and vnglorious yeare to all the Learned in Ireland, both philosophers, poets, guests, strangers, religious persons, souldiers, mendicant or poore orders, and to all manner and sorts of the poore in Irland also; for the generall support of their maintainances decease, to wit **Margarett daughter to Thady O-Carole King of Ely, O'Conner ffaly Calwaghs wife**, a woman that never refused any man in the world for any thing that shee might command, onely besides her own body. **It is shee that twice in one yeare proclaimed to, and comonly invited** (.i. in the darke dayes [of the] yeare) to wit, on the feast day of Dasinchell in Killaichy all persons both Irish and Scotish or rather Albians, **to two generall feasts** of bestowing both meate and moneyes with all other manner of guifts, wherinto gathered **to receue gifts** the matter of two thousand and seauen hundred persons, besides gamsters and poore men, as it was recorded in a Roll to that purpose, and that account was made thus, ut vidimus (viz.) the Chieftaine of each famelie of the Learned Irish, was by Gilla-na-naomh mac Ægans hand writen in that Roll, the chiefe Judg to O-Conner and his adherents, and kinsmen, so that the aforesaid number of 2700 was listed in that Roll with the arts of Dan or poetry, musick and Antiquitie. And Maelyn O-Maelconry one of the chiefe learned of Connaght, was the first writen in that Roll and first payed and dieted or sett to super, and those of his name after him, and so forth, every one, as he was payed, he was writen in that Roll, for feare of mistake, and sett downe to eate afterwards, and Margarett on the garretts of the greate church of Da Sinceall clad in cloath of gold, here deerest friends about her, her clergy and Judges too, Calwagh himselfe being on horseback by the churchs outwards side, to the end, that all things might be done orderly, and each one serued successiuely; and first of all she gave two chalices of gold as offerings that day on the Altar to God Almighty, and she also caused to nurse or foster two young orphans. But so it was, we never saw, nor heard the like of that day, nor comparable to its glory and solace. And she gaue the second inviting proclamation (to every one that came not that day) on the feast of the Assumpõn of our blessed Lady Mary in haruest at, or in Rath-Imayn. And so we haue been informed, that that second day in Rath-Imayn was

---

1 John O'Donovan (ed.), 'The annals of Ireland from the year 1443 to 1468 translated from the Irish by Dudley Firbisse, or as he is more usually called, Duald Mac Firbis, for Sir James Ware in the year 1666' in *Miscellany of the Irish Archaeological Society* 1 (Dublin, 1846), 227–42.

nothing inferiour to the first day, and she was the onely woman that has made most of preparing high-wayes, and erecting bridges, churches and mass-bookes, and all manner of things profittable to serue God, and her soule, and not that onely, but while the world stands, her very many gifts to the Irish and Scotish Nations shall never be numbred. God's blessing, the blessings of all saints, and every one, blessing from Jerusalem to Inis Glaaire be on her going to heauen, and blessed be he that will reade and heare this, for blessing her soule, and cursed be that sore in her breast, that killed Margrett.

2.   **Felim son to Calwagh O-Conner and to Margarett aforesaid,** the onely Kings son, **that has got most fame, reputation,** and notable name and that was most couragious, that liued of the Lagenians in later ages **died, and there was but one night betwixt his and his mothers death.**

3.   **Morragh O-Madagan** King **of Silnanmchada** a hospital man towards all men, and the onely man in all Ireland **that had best comaund, right and rule in his own land,** and a most couragious lord, and very good housekeeper was he also, **died.**

4.   **Ruairy son to Maelmordha Riavagh O'conner died.**

5.   Redmond Tirel Lord of Feara-tulagh, and his Cousins son, were murthered in Symonstown by the Barron of Delbhnas son, and by the sons of Garrett boy Tirel, and by the sons son of Sir Hugh Tirel. And the Earle of Ormond, made Richard son to Richard Tirel to be chiefe of the Tirels, nevertheles he was imediately slaine by Mac-eochagan and by Mac-eochagan's son, and by John Tirels son, and by the soÒs of Redmond Tirel, and John Tirels son was afterwards made Chiefetaine of the Tirels.

6.   The Castle of Balinua alias Newtowne was taken by the sonns of Brian Mageochagan, and by the son of Lysagh McRossa that was therin in restraint, and it was taken from y^m the same day, and Conner sons son to Brien Mageochagan was blinded and gelded afterwards by Mageochagans son.

7.   William Bulter went a preying to Maghery-Cuircney, and Fachtna fitz Lysagh fits Rossa was slaine in his pursuance.

8.   The Castle of Imper fell downe in the heads of Nicolas Dalton, and his wife Daniel boy o ffeargails daughter, so they were both slaine therein.

9.   **Greate warr in Maynagh and O-Conner Donn went to defend O-Kelly, so that he gaue him his son, and two other pledges prisoners, in pawn of twenty marks, to wit fourteen marks of the Lands of the Sithy, that those of Maynagh purchased from Torlagh oge afore that time (and Aedh O-Conner redeemed that or it) and six marks more on Mac-eochy by that warr; and so he defended O'Kelly from his adversaries, for that turne.**

10.   **The Castle of Corra-finny was built by Mac-william of Clanricard.**

11. Cathal Duffe fitz Tomalty oge mac Donnaghy being slaine.

12. Cathal fitz Brian mac Donnaghy slaine by his own father Brian aforesaid by the cast of a knife, he rescueing his protection.

13. Maeleachlyn O'Berns three sons, viz. Thady, William and Donnagh being slaine at once in Cluain-cremha, by Cormac O-Berns sept and by Maeleaghlyn Magranylls sept, and by Daniel fitz Brian O-Birn.

14. A prey taken by Felim O-Conner from O-Gara, and a prey taken by O-Gara from the people of Balimore-I-fflyn.

15. Macdermott taken with a heauy sicknes, so that the report of his death flew ouer all Irland, although he has recouered afterwards.

16. Calwagh O-conner went to the Ciuity of S. James in Spaine, and returned in health, after receuing indulgences in his sinns, and afterwards marryed he O-Kelly's daughter Catherine, O–Madadhans relict or widdow.

17. Diarmoid fitz Thady fitz Cormack Mac-Carthy, being slaine, and Diarmoid soÒ to O-Sullevane the greate was killed in revenge thereof.

18. Remond son to William Mac-ffeorius (Anglicé Bermingham), died on his journy from Rome after obtaining the Archbishoprick of Tuam.

19. Cathal roe fitz Cathal duffe O-Conner died on [his journey to or from] the way of Rome.

20. Gillepatrick oge O-Fialan a good Danmaker [i.e. poet], died.

1452

1. John mac Donnaghy, half King of O-Oilella died.

2. More daughter to O-Conner ffaly, Mac William of Clanricards wife killed by a fall.

3. Thady fitz Diarmoid roe I-conner Donn died.

4. Neachtyn O-Domnayll King of Tirconnell, was killed by the sons of Niall-Garw O-Donnell his own brother and Rory Neachtyns son was made King in his throne, and the one half of Tirconell was giuen to Niall Garws sons, and Kenel-moan and Inis-eogain taken from them by Clanna-Nell afterwards.

5. Torlagh roe son to Brian Ballagh O-Conner, and Thorlagh fitz Thady fitz Torlagh roe O-Conner, and Henry fitz-William Mac David, being killed on Corr-Sliaw-na-Seagsa by the Army of Clann Donnaghy in Sumer.

6. Maurice the Earl of Desmonds son being slaine on Vaithny by Conner O-maelrian, after the Castle of Vaithny was broken on Conner by the two Earls, Maurice, onely, returning against the pursuers, unknown to his own men, and one of the pursuers wounded his horse, and fell down and was killed. John Cleragh son to the said earl died.

7. A defeat giuen to Conner O-Maelrian after that by the sons of … and Conner escaped by the goodnesse of his horse, and there was killed his two sonns and 34 of the best men of their army, and all their foot were slaine too and he that has beaten the Earles son was cutt in pieces afterwards.

8. **Dauid O-mordha son to the King of Lysy, and one that ought to be king of Lysy was slaine by a fall.**

9. **Cathal-fitz-william, fitz John fitz Daniel O-Feargail, was killed by throwing a dart at him after they haue [*sic*] burned Fobhyr.**

10. **Gille-na-naemh fitz-Aedh O-hanly Dux of Kenel-Doffa died in Cluain-Corpey, he being blind therin for a long time after resigning his Lordship.**

11. Mac-Feorais his son, and Piers son to Meyler Mac-ffeorais haue taken O-Conner ffaly prisoner in the pursuance of their prey, which he tooke from them.

12. **A wonderfull presage happened this yeare afore the Earls decease, viz. the River Liffey being dry all ouer, for the space of two miles.**

13. **The Earle of Ormond, lord Deputy of Ireland** by the Authority of the King of England, and the best Captaine of the English nation that was in Irland and England in those ages, died in Ath-fir-dia-fitz-Daman **betwixt the two feasts of S. Mary in haruest,** after he has [*sic*] broken the Castle of Vaithny on Conner O-maelrian, and taken the Castle of Legey from the O-Dimasyes, vntil they licenced him to passe by, to Airemh to gett out Mac-ffeorais his son that was therin prisoner, so that he burned Aireamh afterwards, and marched thence to I-ffaly, and O-conner came he him as assurance of the releasement of Mac-ffeorais his son, and went thence to the Angaly, wherin O-ffeargyl came to him, and promised nine score beeues, for to graunt him peace, and thence marched they both to Magh-bregmany so that the Castle of Barrca was broken by them, and the most parte of the Countrymens corn was spoild, after y[t], and went from thence to Fobhar, and thence to Magh-many, so that Muintir-Reily came to his house and agreed with him, and thence to Maghery-orgiall, wherin the Mac-Mahons satisfied him, and thence to the meeting of Clanna-nell, and caused Henry O-nell to diuorce Mac-William Burkes daughter, whom he kept after O-Domnyll, and to take to him, his own married wife, Mac Morragh his daughter, sister to the selfe said Earl, and marched thence to Baliathafirdia mac Daman, wherin he died afterwards, after he has don theise journeyes within one moneth and a halfe.

14. The daughter of the Earl of Kildara the Countesse of Ormond, died three weeks before the Earles death.

15. Carbry fitz Lysagh fitz Rossa being prisoner to Thomas fitz Cathal O-Feargyl was gelded as revenge, in that he brought the Earl to breake Barrca.

16. The peace betwixt the English and Irish broke out into warrs after the Earls death, and Sir Edward Eustace was made Lord deputy. O-conner ffaley went out to the wildernesse of Kildare, wherein they lighted from their horses, expecting beverage, and the said new lord Deputy being informed therof, came with an army, vnawares to O-Conner, and O-Conner falling from his horse by mishap of his own horsemen, and Thady O-Conners son, most couragiously worked to rescue his father from the English horsemen, but O'Conners horse fell thrice down to the ground, and Thady put him upp twice, and O-Conner him selfe would not giue his consent the third time to goe with him, so that then O-Conner was taken prisoner, and his horsemen retired in safty towards their own houses afterwards.

17. Loughlin oge O-hanly the Chieftaine of Kenel-doffa was wickedly slaine vpon the Crannog of Logh-lesey, by the son of Morragh fitz Gille-na-naemh O-hanly, and by Vaithny fitz Gille na naemh O-Hanleys son, he being, but few men, and betrayed by his owne sargeants, viz. by Daniel Carragh O-maelbridy, and by his son, and by Thomas fitz Gillecrosach O-maelbridy; and Ruairy boy Gille na naemh O-Hanleys son was made Duke [i.e. Dux or chieftain] afterwards, and the three said sargents that comitted the murther was by him hanged.

18. William fitz Walter Mac-ffeory Laignagh died by the plague.

19. O-Conner ffaly was released by the English againe.

20. Nichol Dalton was killed by Mac herbertt.

21. Tegh-muÒa preyed, and burnt by Feargal Mageochagan.

22. Felim O-Conner roe his son, and Cathal roe son to the said O'Conner, became as souldiers to Lysagh fitz Rossa, to oppose Thomas fitz Cathal O-Feargyl that was enimy to them both, so that they burnt the Mothar first, and afterwards marched they together, to Kenel-fiagha and the sonns of the Barron of Dealbhna with them, to Baliatha-an-vraghyr, and … that town. But so it was, Fergal Mageochagan mett them at Bel-an-Atha-Soluis in Kenelenda, wherin some of their men was slaine, and many of them wounded, then the reare of that host, with its danger was left to the charge of O-conners sons, and the English fled. But that couragious Champion Felim, son to O-Conner, kept the rere of the English army, and forcibly brought them out of that danger, and two or three were slaine of the Army of O-Conners son about Æengus Carragh Mc Daniel Galloglagh and Felim being wounded escaped, neverthelesse, he died of his wounds and buried in Ath-lone.

23. A defeate called *maidhm-an-esg* (.i. the defeate of the fish) giuen to Feargal Mageochagan ag^t Lysagh fitz Rossa, and the Dillons, and the sons son of Art O-maelaghlyn, so it was, certaine English Marchants accompanying them, to be by the conweyed, haueing bigg packs of fish, carying them from Athlone to Athtrym, and to Athboy, and to Ath-cliath, .i. Dublin, and Mageochagans son mett them at the Leaccain of the Rubha, so that every one of the horsemen ran away and left all their foot behinde them, with their marchants also to Mageochagans sons mercy, so that they were slaughtered about Redmond Duffuylagh fitz Cormac more fitz william fitz Cathal O ffeargyl, and about the son of Vaithny fitz Rossa fitz Conner, and about Cathal fitz Many fitz Murchadh bane O-ffeargyl, and 14 of his own men with him, and noe man liuing shall giue a account of the multitude of eeles lost or left therein, wherefore that defeate was called *maidhm-an-esg* as aforesaid.

24. **Maelaghlyn fitz Irard O-maelconry died on the feast of S. Michael the Archangel, on fryday.** Michael helpe his soule.

25. Brian son to Calwagh O-Conner and to Margrett killed by a fall.

26. **O'Coffy, .i. Ædh son to the Classagh O'Coffy a good feardana and housekeeper died of the plague in Fera-Tulagh.**

27. **Cuconnacht O-Fialan, and Gille-iosa O-Fialan died.**

28. **O'Duibhgenan of Balicollyfower, .i. Magnus fitz Maelaghlyns son died.**

29. Warr in Maghery Connacht, and Tulagh-I-Maelbrenyn was preyed and burnt by Felim O'Connor. Aedh caech O-Conners sons were banished by Felim O-conner Donns son, lands taken from them, and to them giuen againe.

30. The Castle of Roscoman taken by the sons of Eogan fitz Ruairy O-conner, from Ruairy fitz Cathal fitz Ruairy more O-CoÒer by deceite.

31. **Feargal roe oge, fitz ffeargal roe, fitz Feargal roe fitz Donnagh, fitz Morthy more Mageochagan,** the onely **Captaine that was most famous and renowned** in all Irland, in his own dayes, **was slaine** in the later end of this yeare **by the Baron of Delbhnas sonn and by the sons of Piers Dalton,** he being by night time in the Sonnagh, so that, that night the English gathered against him, and the next day killed him, and [he] was beheaded, **and his head was carried to Athtrym, and to Athcliath,** viz. Dublin, and was caried back to the Lord Deputy, and many good peeces on its, and in its pores, **and afterwards, was buried in Durmay of Columb Killey, with its body,** and God be mercifull to his soule.

32. Mac-Carthy riavagh King of Carbry died.

1453

1. Ruairy fitz Aedh-O-Conner slaine by John Bourks son, in Conmacny de Dunmore.

2. Ruairy fitz Cathal fitz Ruairy O-conner died in the Castle of Rosscoman.

3. Aedh roe fitz Ruairy mag-mahon King of Orgiall died on Easter night.

4. O-Madadhan taken prisoner by William O-Kellyes sonns.

5. Walter fitz Tibott fitz Edmond Bourke slaine by Thomas Barrett.

6. Mortagh fitz Eoghan fitz Daniel o-coÒer was killed by his own kinsmen Daniel and Cathal.

7. Eoghan fitz Daniel bane-o-Reily, and Philipp fitz John O-Reily died.

8. Edmond fitz Terlagh O-Ruairc [*recte* O'Reilly] killed by the English.

9. A great defeate giuen to the sonns of Aedh boy O-nell, at Ardglassy by the Sauages, and by the English of Dublin. A greate fleet sayled on the sea northward after the skippers of the Britons by whom the shipps of Dublin were stolen, and by whom the Archbishop of Dublin was taken prisoner, vntill misfortune brought them in their vnhappy meeting to Ardglassy, wherin their Generall [i.e. the Generall of the Irish] was taken prisoner, viz. Henry sons son to O-nell boy, and wherin was slaine Cv-vladh fitz Cathbarr magenis that ought be King of Iuaagh in Vlster, Ædh magennis, and Macairtnen, and fourteen captains of Rowta Mac-evilin, with them also slaine, all their losses being 520 persons, ut audivimus.

10. Brian fitz Conner Mac Donnaghy tooke the whole domination of O-Oilella (viz. Tirerell), and Thady Mac Donnagh was forsaken by his owne friends.

11. A thunderbolt burnt the Church of Kill … ic nech.

12. An eclips of the sun, the last of November.

13. Mac Donnagh died in fine Anni.

1454

1. Isabell (daughter to Thady O-Carole whose first husband was James O-Kennedy, her second husband Mageochagan) died. God rest her soule.

2. Maelruany son to Magranyll (anglicÉ Reynolds) mortuus est.

3. Daniel O-Donell was made King against Rowry O-Donell, but O-Dogherty (by deceite) tooke the said Daniel prisoner in his own house after y[t]. Then Rowry gathered Mac Vgilin, and O-Cahan with their forces, and they altogether went, and besiedged O-Doghertyes castle [Inch], wherin the said Daniel O-Donell was kept, and few men (as keepers and wayters) with him, aboute Cathal O-Duffdirma. Rowry coming to the Castle did burne the tower dore, wherby the stayres was sett on fire so that the host could not enter the Castle; in the meane time Daniel desired Cathal O-Duffdirma to loose his fetters, saying, that it was more decent for him to so so slaine, than in his givves. Soe Cathal taking compassion on his cause, and certifying himselfe that he could not escape by any meanes, but that he should be slaine as soone as his enimyes should met him within the Castle, loosed his irons. Then imediately Daniel went to the topp of the tower, where he threw/gave the onely happiest throw or cast (that was ever cast in Irland, since Ludh lamoda cast the tathluibh) towards Rowry, and hit him with a great stone, so that he was instantly bruised all to the ground, so that neither Priest nor Clarke might find him aliue, and by that throw Daniel defended his own soule and body with the Lordship of Tirconnell to himselfe, and the Army that came full of pride and boasting retired with saddnesse and disdaine.

4. Brian Mac-Donnagh sole King of O-Oilealla died by stranguria on Friday before the Kalends of January in the subsequent yeare, and sure the yeare charged her due vnlookyly, thorough the decease of the only most hospital and valiantest man, that had best comaund, law and rule in all Connaght, and was buried in the Monastery of Sligo, after the extreame vnction, and due penance to God and to the Catholick Church. God's blessing be on him, to heauen.

5. Thomas fitz John fitz Meyler dexter Lord of Ath-Lehan, in senectute bona quievit.

6. Duffcawly daughter to Eogan fitz Daniel fitz Morthy O-Conner O-haras wife died, whose decease greeued many of the Irish.

7. Ædh son to Niall O-maelmoy King of Fer-kell, died, and his son Cu-cogry supplyed his place. An army made by the said Cucogry towards the east of Fer-kell, against Tibott O-maelmoy, another challenger of that Lordship of Fer-kell, and they took greate preyes, Tibott leauing his houlds and cowes to their pleasures, and the Army marched away with their booties, so that with O-maelmoyes son was left but few men on the tract of the preyes, his men being gone with too much pillage. Tibott O-Maelmoy, and Ædh boy Mageochagans sons, and the I-Riagans, pursueing the said preyes, ouertooke O-Maelmoyes son iust by a bogg, and killed him therin, and they took Thady O-Carole prisoner, and killed others. And afterwards the said Tibott, and the sons son of Cosny O-Maelmoy were proclaymed kings or lords, each against one another.

8. O-Domnallan, .i. Flann fitz Cormac O'Domnallan died.

9. Dunadhagh fitz Cathal O-Madadhan slaine by William O'Kelleys sons.

10. Sir Edward Eustace Deputy of Irland died, and Shane Cam the Earls son, took to Earldome of Kildare, and was made Deputy after the death of Sir Edward Eustace.

11. O-Broin slaine by deceit, thorough the malice of his own brothers son, he coming from Killmantan.

12. Daniel Bane O-Reily died.

13. Torlagh Dall fitz Torlagh oge O-conner died of a short sicknesse.

14. Terlagh fitz Morthy fitz Aedh O-Conner was killed by the Clann Kehernyes.

15. Feargal roe Mageochagan, resigning his Lordship, went to Durmagh of Colum-Killy, he being blind, and Niall Mageochagan in his seate.

16. Scor-mor sub advocatione Sanctissimae Trinitatis habetur in Registro Vaticano Bulla Nicholai 5, data Romae pridie idus Decembris anno 8 Pontificatus, atque adeo 1454, in qua Pontifex narratiuam supplicationem praemisit. Hi erant fratres, frater Eugenius O-Cormayn, et frater Thadaeus Mac Firbisis Eremitae Ordinis S Augustini qui terram quondam nuncupatam Scot-more a nobili viro Thadaeo O-Dovda Domicello Diocaesis Aladensis donatum ad erigendum Conventum sub titulo Sanctissimae Trinitatis, absque licencia Apostolicae Sedis acceptauerunt, eos absolutionem reatos comisit, et confirmationem donationis petentes Nicolaus exaudiuit, et Praeposito Ecclesiae Aladensis executionem remisit (in nomine Domini) Concedens fratribus, vt naviculam habere possent pro piscibus ex quodam flumine prope ipsum locum cursum faciente capiendis et salsandis, et per venditionem cponendis ad vsum et vtilitatem fratrum eorundem. Ita habetus in nostris Annalibus (inquit) frater Gvalelmus O-Meahayr.

1455

1. An eclips of the moone on the first day of May.

2. Torlagh Carragh fitz Daniel fitz Mortagh O-Conner lord of Sligo, died.

3. Caher fitz Murragh-I-Conner ffaly was killed by Thady fitz Calwagh-I-Conner, and Culen O-Dimosy was also by him slaine in the same day.

4. Eogan O-nell was deposed by his own son Henry O-nell. Henry sons son to O-nell boy escaped out of his giuues from the English.

5. The Castle of Athlone was taken from the English, it being betrayed by a woman therin.

6. The Castle of Sraide was broken by O-ffeargall, whereby Mac herberts son was killed.

7.   Mac Dermoda Gall Lord of Artagh died.

8.   **Thomas O-Carnen Prior of Athlone the chief in wisdome and knowledge of all Irland in Christo quievit.**

9.   **Jeffrey fitz Moragh oge fitz Moragh More fitz Cathal Lord of Clann-Aedha of the mountaine quievit.**

10.   **Eogan Mac Dermoda roe Lord of the woods was slaine by his own men.**

1456
1.   **Feargal fitz Conner Mac Dermoda, the second .i. tanista of Maghluyrg and Catharine[2] his daughter Carbry O-Conners wife both died,** in the beginning of this yeare.

2.   Jonyne fitz Thomas Burke died.

1457
1.   **Brian fitz Morthagh oge O-ffeargal, Dux of Clann-amly i-ffeargal, died.**

1458
1   **Tomaltagh fitz Conner Mac-Dermoda King of Magh Luyrg and Artagh,** and of Correnn, **and of Tirtuahayl,** and of a greate parte of Clan Cahyl, and a lord worthy of ye kingdome of Connaght, thorough **his great expences in Almesdeeds, hospitalitie, gifts, wages, or meanes to all manner of men in Irland** that pleased to accept it of him, **died, on the feast of S. Bartholomew in haruest, and his sonn Cahal Mac Dermoda died few dayes afore him, and they were both buried in the Abbey of Boyle.** The blessed, and holy Trinitie be mercifull to their soules in saecula saeculorum. Amen. **Aedh fitz Conner Mac Dermoda was made King in his throne.**

2.   **Calwagh the great fitz Morragh** *na madhmañ* **(.i. of the defeats) King of O-faly, who never refused any man living, died, and it was he** since Chaher the Great his Ancestor King of Ireland, **the onely King of the Lagenians, that tooke most from all such English and Irish his adversaryes,** and he also was the onely man that bestowed most, of both gold, silver, and broade cloath, to all men generally in Irland, and God (in whose power it is) rewarde his soule. Amen. And afore his death, he ordained **Conn O-Conner his own son to supply his place afterwards he was buried in Kill-aichy.** God rest his soule.

3.   **Edmond Burke Lord of the English of Connaght, and of many Irish men also, and the onely English man in Irland worthy to be chosen chiefe for his formositie and proportion of person** generosity, **hospitalitie,** constancie, **truth, gentilitie of blood,** martial feates, and for all qualities by which man might merit prayse **died in the later end of this yeare.** Gods blessing be on him.

2 AFM gives Lasarina instead of Catherine here.

4.   Feargal roe Mageoghagan Dux of Kenel fiacha xiiii° Kal. februarij died. God blesse his soule.

1459

1.   Cu-mara Mac Con-mara slaine thorough deceit.

2.   Muiredhach O-Daly, learned in his own art, died.

3.   Connla Mageoghagan Dux of Kenel fiacha, slaine by Art O-Maelaghlyns son.

1460

1.   The Monastery of Moyn in Tirawly, in the Bishoprick of Killala erected by Mac William Burke by the advise of Nehemias O-Donnaghada, the first provincial vicar of the order of S. Frances de Observantia in Irland.

2.   Thomas fitz Thomas Burke, that was Mac William Bourk after Edmond Bourke, died in hoc anno.

3.   Mac Caba, .i. Henry fitz Gille Christ came into the Angaly, with O-ffeargal, viz. Donell boy, and died a sudden death in Lis-ard-Aula, and was carried, to be buried in Cavan, and we heard, that there was the number of 280 axes or more about him going towards his buriall.

4.   Ruairy Ballagh Mortagh O'Conners son died.

5.   The Provost of Oil-finn, viz. Ruairy fitz Magnus O-Conner quievit.

6.   Daniel fitz Dermoid O-Mally, and William O-Manly, and John O-Manly sayled a fleet with O-Brians sons, to Corca-Baskyn, against Mac-mahon, and they were all three killed afore they might inter their shipps, and Daniel O-Brian was taken prisoner, and Mahon O-Brian was wounded goeing towards his shipp, and was drowned afore he could get therto, and their men were slaughtered, and the said Daniels death occasioned great griefe to all receuers of gifts in Irland. God reste his soule.

7.   Mac Magnusa de Tirthuathyl, .i. Ruairy fitz Eogan Roe mac magnusa fit chieftaine for that land, was killed by Conn O-Donell and by Thady fitz T. o Ruairk, in pursueance or rather tract of the preyes of the country after they have brought them as far as Argadgleann, wherin they were manfully rescued by the Clann Magnusa.[3]

---

3 AFM has more detail (*AFM*, IV, pp 1006–7). Entry also found in *AConn*, pp 500–1.

Bibliography

Reference works and guides to sources

Abbott, T.K., and E.J. Gwynn. *Catalogue of the Irish manuscripts in the library of Trinity College Dublin* (Dublin, 1921).

Calendar of State Papers relating to Ireland, 1509–73, etc. (24 vols, London, 1860–1903).

Dillon, Myles, Canice Mooney and Pádraig de Brún. *Catalogue of Irish manuscripts in the Franciscan Library, Killiney* (Dublin, 1969).

FitzPatrick, Elizabeth. *The catalogue of Irish manuscripts in the Royal Irish Academy: a brief introduction* (Dublin, 1988).

Gheyn, J. van den. *Catalogue des manuscrits de la Bibliothèque Royale de Belgique* (13 vols, Brussels, 1901–48).

Kenney, James F. *The sources for the early history of Ireland: ecclesiastical: an introduction and guide* (New York, 1929; repr. Dublin, 1979).

Moody, T.W., F.X. Martin and F.J. Byrne (eds). *A new history of Ireland, ix: maps, genealogies, lists* (Oxford, 1984).

Ní Mhurchú, Máire, and Diarmuid Breathnach. *1560–1781: Beathaisnéis* (Dublin, 2001).

Ní Shéaghdha, Nessa, et al. *Catalogue of Irish manuscripts in the National Library of Ireland*, fasciculi I–XIII (Dublin, 1967–96).

Ó Cuív, Brian. *Catalogue of Irish language manuscripts in the Bodleian Library at Oxford and Oxford College Libraries* (2 vols, Dublin, 2001–3).

Ó Fiannachta, Pádraig. *Lámhscríbhinní Gaeilge Choláiste Phádraig Má Nuad: clár, fascúl IV* (Maynooth, 1967).

O'Grady, S.H., and Robin Flower. *Catalogue of Irish manuscripts in the British Library* (3 vols, London, 1926–53; repr. Dublin, 1992).

O'Rahilly, T.F., Kathleen Mulchrone et al. *Catalogue of Irish manuscripts in the Royal Irish Academy*, fasciculi I–XXVII (Dublin, 1926–70).

Stephen, Leslie, et al. (eds). *Dictionary of national biography* (63 vols, London, 1885–1900).

Walsh, Paul, and Pádraig Ó Fiannachta. *Lámhscríbhinní Gaeilge Choláiste Phádraig Má Nuad*, fasciculi I–VII (Maynooth, 1943–72).

Primary sources

Manuscripts of the Annals of the Four Masters

Dublin: Royal Irish Academy

23 F 2 (988)   Abridged transcript of AFM AD76–946, with translation AM4547–AD946
23 F 3 (989)   Transcript of AFM (AD947–1171)

23 F 4 (990)   Transcript of AFM (AD1171–1397)
23 F 5 (991)   Transcript of AFM (AD1397–1556)
23 F 6 (992)   Transcript of AFM (AD1557–1611)
23 P 6 (687)   Autograph text of AFM (AD1170–1499)
23 P 7 (688)   Autograph text of AFM (AD1500–1616)
24 D 18 (1043) Abridged transcript of AFM (AD431–772), with translation
24 E 9 (1045) English translation of AFM (AD1180–1383)
24 E 10 (1046) English translation of AFM (AD1171–79; 1387–1513)
C iii 3 (1220) Autograph text of AFM (AM2242–AD1171)

Dublin: Trinity College Library

1279 (H.1.3–5) Abridged transcript of AFM (AM2242–AD1172) in three volumes, by Muiris Ó Gormáin
1300 (H.2.9–10) Abridged transcript of AFM (AM2242–AD1171) in two volumes, made in 1734–5 by Aodh Ó Maolmhuaidh for Dr John Fergus
1301 (H.2.11)   Autograph text of AFM (AD1334–1605, with fragment of AD1616)

Dublin: University College Dublin Archives

UCD–OFM MS A 13   Autograph text of AFM (AM2242–AD1169)

Other manuscripts

Armagh: Public Library

AClon   1660 transcript of Annals of Clonmacnoise

Brussels: Bibliothèque Royale

1569–72 *Cogadh Gaedhel re Gallaibh*, transcribed by Mícheál Ó Cléirigh
2324–40 Lives of Irish saints and also a chronological list of the foundations of the Irish Franciscan province, 1224–1632
2542–3   *Naomhsheanchas naoimh Inse Fáil*
2569–72 Historical poems and genealogies in Irish
3410   Chronology of Irish Franciscan foundations
4190–200 Lives of Irish saints
4241   *Acta sanctorum Hiberniae*, written in 1608
4639   Martyrology of Donegal, 1628 recension
5100–4   Lives of Irish saints, including a transcript of the Martyrology of Gorman
5095–6   Martyrology of Donegal, 1630 recension
5301–20 Historical compilation in Irish and Latin – extracts from annals, lives of saints, monastic histories, etc.

Dublin: Franciscan Library, Killiney

F 1   Hagiographical texts, transcribed by John Goulde

Dublin: King's Inns

Gaelic 2	*Foras feasa ar Éirinn*, 1657 transcript
Gaelic 4	Miscellany

Dublin: National Archives of Ireland

RC/4/10	Chancery Inquisitions, Tipperary, Charles I

Dublin: National Library of Ireland

G 131	Ó Cléirigh miscellany, *c*.1650–9
G 167	Poem book of the Uí Dhomhnaill
674	Summary biographies of Irish writers and lists of their works, *c*.1680

Dublin: Royal Irish Academy

12 N 22	Stokes' history of the Royal Irish Academy
14 C 17	Ordnance Survey letters, Co. Fermanagh
23 A 40 (427)	Transcript of *Genealogiae regum et sanctorum Hiberniae*
23 C 30 (783)	Miscellany
23 D 9 (148)	Genealogies
23 D 17 (790)	Ó Cléirigh book of genealogies
23 E 25 (1229)	*Leabhar na hUidhre*
23 F 7–8 (986–7)	Transcript of AConn, prepared by Muiris Ó Gormáin
23 K 32 (617)	*Leabhar gabhála*, seventeenth-century transcript
23 N 11 (487)	Miscellany
23 O 8 (167)	Transcript of *Chronicum Scotorum*
23 O 19 (142)	Transcript of *Foras feasa ar Éirinn*
23 P 2 (535)	Book of Lecan
23 P 16 (1230)	*Leabhar Breac*
23 P 24 (138)	*Beatha Aodha Ruaidh Uí Dhomhnaill*
23 M 70	*Leabhar gabhála*, transcribed by Mícheál Ó Cléirigh
24 G 16 (1136)	Kearney translation of *Foras feasa ar Éirinn*
24 C 55 (1185)	Miscellany
24 P 33 (1076)	Transcript of *Genealogiae regum et sanctorum Hiberniae*, with other texts
B iv 2 (1080)	Miscellany, mainly verse, in the hand of Mícheál Ó Cléirigh (1627–8)
C iii 1 (1219)	AConn, 1224–1544, written 1562, with genealogical papers on the Ó Conchobhair and Mac Diarmada families
C iv 3 (1192)	*Leabhar gabhála*
C vi 1 (936)	Book of Knockninny, 1718 transcript
D i 3 (539)	Genealogies
D iv 3 (1224)	*Leabhar gabhála*, transcribed by Muirgheas mac Pháidín Uí Mhaoil Chonaire

E iv 4 (621)   Genealogies
O'Curry catalogue of 'Academy' manuscripts (RR/67)

Dublin: Trinity College Library

574 (E.3.20)	Historical miscellany, including annals, assembled by James Ussher
804 (F.1.18)	Historical miscellany, including Irish hagiographical material compiled by Tuileagna Ó Maoil Chonaire, and James Ussher's notes from AFM
1282 (H.1.8)	AU, AD431–1504
1286 (H.1.12)	*Leabhar gabhála* (1631), Mícheál Ó Cléirigh recension
1292 (H.1.18)	Miscellany, including *Chronicum Scotorum*
1348 (H.4.6; H.4.7)	*Genealogium regum et sanctorum Hiberniae*, transcript by Muiris Ó Gormáin
1394 (H.5.22)	*Foras feasa ar Éirinn*
1397 (H.5.26)	*Foras feasa ar Éirinn*
1431 (D.4.35)	Tract on grammar and prosody, containing colophon by Tuileagna Ó Maoil Chonaire, Madrid, 1659
1439 (F.3.21)	*Foras feasa ar Éirinn*

Dublin: University College Dublin Archives

UCD–OFM A 2	*Liber hymnorum*
UCD–OFM A 16	Autograph text of *Genealogiae regum et sanctorum Hiberniae*
UCD–OFM A 30	Miscellaneous letters and documents
UCD–OFM A 33	Miscellany, including historical and hagiographical notes and transcripts in the hand of Mícheál Ó Cléirigh

London: British Library

Add. 4783	Historical miscellany, assembled by Sir James Ware
Add. 4784	Historical miscellany, including annals, assembled by Sir James Ware
Add. 4799	Autograph copy of Mac Fhirbhisigh translation of ALec
Cotton Vespasian MS E II	Abbreviated text of Book of Fenagh

Maynooth: Russell Library

R 70	Miscellany

Oxford: Bodleian Library

Rawl. B 487	Includes notes by Sir James Ware and hagiographical material in the hands of Mícheál Ó Cléirigh and John Colgan
Rawl. B 488	Includes fragment of Annals of the Island of Saints in Lough Ree
Rawl. B 489	AU, AD431–1541

Online versions of selected manuscript sources

http://image.ox.ac.uk   Early manuscripts in Oxford
http://www.isos.dias.ie   Irish Script on Screen

Printed primary sources

Baronius, Caesar. *Annales ecclesiastici* (12 vols, Mainz, 1601–8, another ed. Cologne, 1609, Antwerp, 1612).

Bergin, Osborn (ed.). 'A poem by Domhnall mac Dáire', *Ériu* 9 (1921–3), 160–74.

— *Irish bardic poetry* (Dublin, 1970).

Bernard, J.H., and R. Atkinson (eds). *The Irish liber hymnorum* (Henry Bradshaw Society, vols 13–14, London, 1898).

Bernard, Nicholas. *The whole proceedings of the siege of Drogheda in Ireland* (London, 1642).

Best, R.I., and O.J. Bergin (eds). *Lebor na hUidre: Book of the Dun Cow* (Dublin, 1929).

Best, R.I., M.A. O'Brien and A. O'Sullivan (eds), *The book of Leinster, formerly Lebar na Núachongbála* (6 vols, Dublin, 1957–83).

Bishop, William (ed.). *Relationum historicarum de rebus Anglicis*, by John Pits (Paris, 1619; repr. Farnborough, 1969).

Boece, Hector. *Scotorum historiae* (Paris, 1526).

Breatnach, Pádraig A. 'Marbhna Aodha Ruaidh Uí Dhomhnaill (+1602)', *Éigse* 15:1 (1973), 31–50.

— 'In praise of Maghnas Ó Domhnaill', *Celtica* 16 (1984), 63–72.

Buchanan, George. *De rerum Scoticarum historia* ([Antwerp], 1582).

Byrne, Matthew (ed.). *The Irish war of defence, 1598–1600: extracts from the De Hibernia insula commentarius of Peter Lombard* (Cork, 1930).

Carney, James (ed.). *Poems on the O'Reillys* (Dublin, 1950).

Colgan, John. *Acta sanctorum veteris et majoris Scotiae seu Hiberniae sanctorum insulae* (Louvain, 1645, repr. with introduction by Brendan Jennings, Dublin, 1948).

— *Triadis thaumaturgae, seu divorum Patricii, Columbae, et Brigidae … acta* (Louvain, 1647, repr. with introduction by Pádraig Ó Riain, Dublin, 1997).

Comóradh i n-onóir Mhichíl Uí Chléirigh, bráthair bocht, ceann na gCeithre Máistrí, Gaiety Theatre, Baile Átha Cliath (Dublin, 1944).

Comyn, David, and P.S. Dinneen (eds). *Foras feasa ar Éirinn: the history of Ireland*, by Geoffrey Keating (4 vols, ITS, IV, VIII, IX, XV, London, 1902–14).

Connellan, Owen (ed.). *The annals of Ireland translated from the original Irish of the Four Masters* (Dublin, 1846).

Dempster, Thomas. *Scotorum scriptorum nomenclatura* (Bologna, 1619).

— *Scotia illustrior, seu mendicabula repressa, modesta parecbasi Thomae Dempsteri* ([Lyon], 1620).

— *Historia ecclesiastica gentis Scottorum* (Bologna, 1627).

Elrington, C.R., and J.H. Todd (eds). *The whole works of … James Ussher* (17 vols, Dublin, 1847–64).

Fennessy, Ignatius (ed.). 'Printed books in St Anthony's College, Louvain, 1673 (FLK MS A 34)', *Collectanea Hibernica* 38 (1996), 82–117.

Fraser, J., and J.G. O'Keeffe (eds). 'Poems on the O'Donnells (1200–1600)' in *Irish Texts*, fasciculus II (London, 1931).

Freeman, A.M. (ed.). *Annála Connacht: the annals of Connacht, AD1224–1544* (Dublin, 1944, repr., 1970).

— *The annals in Cotton MS Titus AA XXV* (Paris, 1929) [repr. from *Revue Celtique* 41 (1924) 301–30; 42 (1925) 283–305; 43 (1926) 358–84; 44 (1927), 336–61. Annals of Boyle].

Grosjean, Paul (ed.). '*Naemhsenchus náemh nÉrenn*: Peregrine O'Clery's recension' in J. Fraser, P. Grosjean and J.G. O'Keeffe (eds), *Irish Texts*: fasciculus III (London, 1931), 40–80.

— 'Édition du *Catalogus praecipuorum sanctorum Hiberniae* de Henri Fitzsimon' in John Ryan (ed.), *Féilscríbhinn Eóin Mhic Néill* (Dublin, 1940), 335–93.

Hardiman, James. *Irish minstrelsy*, 2 vols (London, 1831).

Harris, Walter. *The whole works of Sir James Ware concerning Ireland, revised and improved* (2 vols, Dublin, 1764).

Hay, Denys (ed.). *The Anglica Historia of Polydore Virgil, AD1485–1537* (London, 1950).

Hayward, Sir John. *The lives of the three Normans, kings of England* (1613).

Hennessy, W.M. (ed.). *Chronicum Scotorum* (London, 1866).

— *The Annals of Loch Cé: a chronicle of Irish affairs from AD1014 to AD1590* (2 vols, London, 1871).

— and D.H. Kelly (eds). *The book of Fenagh, in Irish and English* (Dublin, 1875; repr., 1939).

— and Bartholomew MacCarthy (eds). *Annála Uladh: Annals of Ulster from the earliest times to the year 1541* (4 vols, Dublin, 1887–1901, repr. Dublin, 1998).

Historical Manuscripts Commission. 'The manuscripts of the former college of Irish Franciscans, Louvain' [by John T. Gilbert] in *Fourth report*, pt 1, appendix (London, 1874), 599–613.

— *Report on Franciscan manuscripts preserved at the convent, Merchant's Quay, Dublin* (Dublin, 1906).

Holinshed, Raphael. *Chronicles of England, Scotland and Ireland* (London, 1577).

Irish patent rolls of James I: facsimile of the Irish Record Commissioners' calendar prepared prior to 1830, with foreword by M.C. Griffith (Dublin, 1966).

Jennings, Brendan (ed.). 'Brevis synopsis Provinciae Hiberniae FF. Minorum', *Analecta Hibernica* 6 (1934), 139–91.

— 'Brussels MS 3947: Donatus Moneyus, De Provincia Hiberniae S. Francisci', *Analecta Hibernica* 6 (1934), 12–138.

— 'Documents from the archives of St Isidore's College, Rome', *Analecta Hibernica* 6 (1934), 203–47.

— *Wadding papers, 1614–1638* (Dublin, 1953).

— *Louvain papers, 1606–1827* (Dublin, 1968).

Keating, Geoffrey. *The history of the ancient Irish from their reception of Christianity till the invitation of the English in the reign of Henry the second, translated from the original Irish* (Newry, 1920).

Kelly, William (ed.). *Docwra's Derry: a narration of events in north-west Ulster, 1600–1604* (Belfast, 2003).

Knott, Eleanor. 'Mac an Bhaird's elegy on the Ulster lords', *Celtica* V (1960), 161–71.

Lawlor, H.J. (trans.). *St Bernard of Clairvaux's life of St Malachy of Armagh* (London, 1920).

Lizeray, Henri (trans.). *Le Livre des Quatre Maitres: annales du royaume d'Irlande depuis les origines jusqu'à l'arrivée de saint Patrice* (Paris, 1882).

Mac Airt, Seán (ed.). *Annals of Inisfallen (MS Rawlinson B.503)* (Dublin, 1951).

— and Gearóid Mac Niocaill (eds). *Annals of Ulster to AD1131: text and translation* (Dublin, 1983).

Macalister, R.A.S. (ed.). *Lebor gabála Érenn: the book of the taking of Ireland* (5 vols, ITS, XXXIV, XXXV, XXXIX, XLI, XLIV, Dublin, 1938–56).

— *Book of Fenagh: supplementary volume* (Dublin, 1939).

— and J. Mac Neill (eds). *Leabhar gabhála: the book of conquests of Ireland: the recension of Micheál Ó Cléirigh* (Dublin, 1916).

Mac Cárthaigh, Eoin. 'Three poems by Maol Muire Ó hUiginn to An Calbhach Ruadh Ó Domhnaill', *Ériu* 48 (1997), 59–82.

— 'Lúireach Chríosd fan gCalbhach Ruadh', *Celtica* 24 (2003), 131–2.

Mac Firbis, Duald. 'On some bishops of Ireland', *Proceedings of the Royal Irish Academy, Irish MSS series* 1:1 (1870), 82–133.

McKenna, Lambert (ed.). *Iomarbhágh na bhfileadh: the contention of the bards* (2 vols, ITS, XX, XXI, London, 1918).

Mac Raghnaill, F. (ed.). *An teagasc Críosdaidhe*, by Bonaventure Ó hEodhasa (Dublin, 1976) (Originally published Antwerp, 1611, 2nd ed. Louvain, 1614).

Mair, John. *Historia majoris Britanniae tam Angliae quam Scotiae* (Paris, 1621).

Messingham, Thomas. *Florilegium insulae sanctorum: seu vitae et acta sanctorum Hiberniae* (Paris, 1624).

Meyer, Kuno (ed.). *The instructions of King Cormac mac Airt* (RIA Todd Lecture series, XV) (Dublin, 1909).

Mhag Craith, Cuthbert (ed.). *Dán na mBrathar Mionúr* (2 vols, Dublin, 1967–80).

Miller, Arthur K.W. (ed. and trans.). 'O'Clery's Irish glossary', *Revue Celtique* 4 (1880), 349–428; 5 (1881), 1–69.

Moloney, Joseph (ed.). 'Brussels MS 3410: a chronological list of the foundations of the Irish Franciscan Province', *Analecta Hibernica* 6 (1934), 192–202.

Mooney, Donagh. 'A history of the Franciscan Order in Ireland', *Franciscan Tertiary* 5 (1894–5), 97–101, 129–34, 161–7, 193–7, 225–30, 257–60, 289–94, 321–6, 353–7; 6 (1895–6), 1–5, 33–40, 65–8, 97–101, 129–35, 161–5, 193–6, 225–8, 257–60, 289–93, 321–4, 353–7; 7 (1896–7), 1–4, 33–8, 65–7.

Moran, P.F. (ed.). *De regno Hiberniae, sanctorum insula commentarius*, by Peter Lombard (Louvain, 1632, Dublin, 1868).

— 'Mortuary book of the Irish Franciscan monastery in Louvain' in *Spicilegium Ossoriense, being a collection of original letters and papers illustrative of the History of the Irish church*, 3rd ser. (Dublin, 1884).

Mulchrone, Kathleen (ed.). *Book of Lecan: Leabhar Mór Mhic Fhir Bhisigh Leacain* (facsimile ed., Dublin, 1937).

Murphy, Denis (ed.). *Annals of Clonmacnoise from the earliest period to AD1408, translated into English by Conell Mageoghagan, AD1627* (Dublin, 1896).

Ó Briain, Felim (ed.). '*Elenchi conventuum in Hibernia fundatorum ac reformatorum et series ministrorum, auctore Michaele Ó Cléirigh, OFM*', *Archivum Franciscanum Historicum* 25 (1932), 349–77.

Ó Cléirigh, Michéul. *Focloir no sanasan nua* (Louvain, 1643).

O'Conor, Rev. Charles (ed.). *Quatuor Magistrorum annales Hibernici usque ad annum MCLXXII ex ipso O'Clerii autographo in Bibliotheca Stowense servato* (Rerum Hibernicarum Scriptores Veteres III, Buckingham, 1826).

Ó Cuív, Brian (ed.). 'The earl of Thomond and the poets, AD1572', *Celtica* 12 (1977), 125–45.

O'Doherty, D.J. (ed.). 'Students of the Irish College, Salamanca (1569–1619)', *Analecta Hibernica* 2 (1913), 1–36.

O'Doherty, J.F. (ed.). *De praesulibus Hiberniae potissimis Catholicae religionis in Hibernia serendae, propagandae et conservandae authoribus* (2 vols, IMC, Dublin, 1944).

O'Donovan, John (ed.). *The banquet of Dun na nGedh and the battle of Magh Rath, an ancient historical tale … from a manuscript in the library of Trinity College, Dublin* (IAS, Dublin, 1842).

— 'The annals of Ireland from the year 1443 to 1468, translated from the Irish by Dudley Firbisse, or as he is more usually called, Duald Mac Firbis, for Sir James Ware in the year, 1666' in *Miscellany of the Irish Archaeological Society* 1 (Dublin, 1846), 198–302.

— *Annála ríoghachta Éireann: annals of the kingdom of Ireland, by the Four Masters, from the earliest period to the year, 1616, edited from mss in the library of the Royal Irish Academy and of Trinity College Dublin, with a translation and copious notes* (1st ed., 7 vols, Dublin, 1848–51; 2nd ed., 7 vols, Dublin, 1856; repr. New York, 1966; Dublin, 1990 with introduction by Kenneth Nicholls).

— *Annals of Ireland: three fragments: copied from ancient sources, edited with a translation and notes from a ms preserved in the Burgundian library at Brussels* (Dublin, 1860).

Ó Fachtna, Anselm (ed.). *Parrthas an anma*, by Antoin Gearnon (Dublin, 1953).

Ó Fiannachta, Pádraig (ed.). *Táin Bó Cuailnge: the Maynooth manuscript* (Dublin, 1980).

Ó hInnse, Séamus (ed.). *Miscellaneous Irish annals (AD1114–1437)* (Dublin, 1947).

O'Kelleher, A., and G. Schoepperle (eds). *Betha Colaim Chille* (Illinois, 1918).

Ó Maonaigh, Cainneach (ed.). *Scathán shacramuinte na h-aithridhe*, Aodh Mac Aingil (Dublin, 1952) (originally published Louvain, 1618).

Ó Muireadhaigh, Réamann. 'Marbhna ar Mhuiris Mac Torna Uí Mhaoilchonaire', *Éigse* 15:3 (1974), 215–21.

Ó Muraíle, Nollaig (ed.). *Leabhar mór na ngenealach: the great book of Irish genealogies* (5 vols, Dublin, 2003).

Ó Raghallaigh, Tomás (ed.). *Filí agus filidheacht Chonnacht* (Dublin, 1938).

O'Rahilly, Thomas F. (ed.). *Dánta grádha* (Cork, 1925).

Ó Riain, Pádraig (ed.). *Corpus genealogiarum sanctorum Hiberniae* (Dublin, 1985).

O'Sullivan, Anne (ed.). *The Book of Leinster, formerly Lebar na Núachongbála*, VI (Dublin, 1983).

O'Sullivan, William (ed.). 'Correspondence of David Rothe and James Ussher, 1619–23', *Collectanea Hibernica* 36–7 (1994–5), 7–49.

Pender, Séamus (ed.). 'The O'Clery book of genealogies', *Analecta Hibernica* 15 (1951), xi–xxxiii, 1–198.

Plummer, Charles (ed.). *Vitae sanctorum Hiberniae* (2 vols, Oxford, 1910).

— *Bethada naem nÉrenn: lives of Irish saints* (2 vols, Oxford, 1922).

Radner, Joan N. (ed.). *Fragmentary annals of Ireland* (Dublin, 1978).

Rochford, Robert. *The life of the glorious bishop St Patricke ... together with the lives of the holy virgin S. Bridgit and of the glorious abbot Saint Columbe* (English Recusant Literature 210) (St Omer, 1625; repr. London, 1974).

Rothe, David. *Hibernia resurgens sive refrigerium antidotale, adversum morsum serpentis antiqui in quo modeste discutitur, immodesta parechasis Thomae Dempsteri a Muresck Scoti de represis mendicabulis* (Rouen, 1621).

Simington, R.C. (ed.). *The civil survey AD1654–1656, county of Tipperary, vol. II: western and northern baronies* (Dublin, 1934).

— *Books of survey and distribution, iii: Co. Roscommon* (Dublin, 1949).

Smith, Peter J. *Three historical poems ascribed to Gilla Cóemáin: a critical edition of the work of an eleventh-century Irish scholar* (Münster, [2007]).

Stanihurst, Richard. *De rebus in Hibernia gestis* (Antwerp, 1584).

Stokes, Whitley (ed.). *Félire hÚi Gormáin: the martyrology of Gorman, edited from a manuscript in the Royal Library, Brussels* (London, 1895).

— 'The Annals of Tigernach', *Revue Celtique* 16 (1895) 374–419; 17 (1896) 6–33, 116–263, 337–420; 18 (1897), 9–59, 150–303, 374–91 (repr. in 2 vols, Felinfach, 1993).

— *Félire Óengusso, The martyrology of Oengus the Culdee* (Henry Bradshaw Society) (London, 1905; repr. Dublin, 1984).

Todd, J.H. (ed.). *Cogadh Gaedhel re Gallaibh. The war of the Gaedhil with the Gaill, or the invasions of Ireland by the Danes and other Norsemen.* Rolls Series (London, 1867).

— and W. Reeves (eds). *The martyrology of Donegal: a calendar of the saints of Ireland: Féilire na naomh nErennach* (Dublin, 1864).

Ussher, James. *A discourse of the religion professed by the Irish and British* (Dublin, 1631).

— *Veterum epistolarum Hybernicarum sylloge, quae partim ab Hibernis, paratim ad Hibernos, partim de Hibernis vel rebus Hibernicis sunt conscriptae* (Dublin, 1632).

— *Britannicarum ecclesiarum antiquitates* (Dublin, 1639).

Walsh, Paul (ed.). *The flight of the earls*, by Tadhg Ó Cianáin (Dublin, 1916).

— 'Extracts from the Franciscan manuscripts of the Annals of the Four Masters', *Irisleabhar Muighe Nuadhad* (1916), 17–24.

— *Genealogiae regum et sanctorum Hiberniae, by the Four Masters, edited from the manuscript of Michél Ó Cléirigh* (Maynooth, 1918).

— 'O Donnell genealogies', *Analecta Hibernica* 8 (1938), 373–418.

— *Beatha Aodha Ruaidh Uí Dhomhnaill* (2 vols, ITS, XLII, XLV, London, 1948–57).

Ware, Sir James. *De scriptoribus Hiberniae, libri duo* (Dublin, 1639).

— *Opuscula Sancto Patricio, qui Hibernos ad fidem Christi convertit* (London, 1656).

— *Rerum Hibernicarum Henrico octavo regnante annales* (Dublin, 1662).

— *Rerum Hibernicarum annales, regnantibus Henrico VII, Henrico VIII, Edwardo VI, et Maria* (Dublin, 1664).

— *De praesulibus Hiberniae commentarius a prima gentis Hibernicae ad fidem Christianem conversione, ad nostra usque tempora* (Dublin, 1665).

— *The history and antiquities of Ireland* (Dublin, 1705).

Waterworth, J. (ed.). *Canons and decrees of the sacred and ecumenical Council of Trent* (London, 1868).

Secondary sources

Báiréad, Fearghus. 'Muintir Ghadhra' in O'Brien (ed.), *Measgra i gcuimhne Mhichíl Uí Chléirigh* (1944), pp 45–64.

Barnard, T.C. 'The purchase of Archbishop Ussher's library in 1657', *Long Room* 4 (1971), 9–14.

Baumgarten, Rolf. 'Kuno Meyer's Irish manuscript', *Newsletter of the Dublin Institute for Advanced Studies* 1 (1987), 23–5.

Bhreathnach, Edel, and Bernadette Cunningham (eds). *Writing Irish history: the Four Masters and their world* (Dublin, 2007).

Bieler, Ludwig. 'John Colgan as editor', *Franciscan Studies* 8 (1948), 1–24.

Boyle, Alexander. 'Fearghal Ó Gadhra and the Four Masters', *Irish Ecclesiastical Record* 5th ser., 100 (1963), 100–14.

Bradshaw, Brendan. '"Manus the magnificent": O'Donnell as renaissance prince' in A. Cosgrove and D. McCartney (eds), *Studies in Irish history presented to R. Dudley Edwards* (Dublin, 1979), pp 15–36.

— 'The English Reformation and identity formation in Ireland and Wales' in Brendan Bradshaw and Peter Roberts (eds), *British consciousness and identity: the making of Britain, 1533–1707* (Cambridge, 1998), pp 43–111.

— and Peter Roberts (eds). *British consciousness and identity: the making of Britain, 1533–1707* (Cambridge, 1998).

Brady, John. Review of Freeman's edition of the *Annals of Connacht*, *Irish Ecclesiastical Record* 5th ser., 65 (Jan. 1945), 64–5.

— 'The catechism in Ireland: a survey', *Irish Ecclesiastical Record* 5th ser., 83 (1955), 167–76.

Breatnach, Caoimhín. 'Rawlinson B 502, Lebar Glinne dá Lacha and Saltair na Rann', *Éigse* 30 (1997), 109–32.

— 'Manuscript sources and methodology: Rawlinson B 502 and *Lebar Glinne Dá Lacha*', *Celtica* 24 (2003), 40–54.

Breatnach, Pádraig A. 'The methodology of *seanchas*: the redaction by Cú Choigcríche Ó Cléirigh of the chronicle poem *Leanam croinic Clann nDálaigh*', *Éigse* 29 (1996), 1–18.

— 'An Irish Bollandus: Fr Hugh Ward and the Louvain hagiographical enterprise', *Éigse* 31 (1999), 1–30.

— 'An inventory of Latin lives of Irish saints from St Anthony's College, Louvain, c.1643' in Alfred P. Smyth (ed.), *Seanchas* (Dublin, 2000), pp 431–38 [on Bodl. MS Rawl. B 487]

— 'A seventeenth-century abridgement of *Beatha Aodha Ruaidh Uí Dhomhnaill*', *Éigse* 33 (2002), 77–172.

— 'Irish records of the Nine Years' War: a brief survey with particular notice of the relationship between Beatha Aodha Ruaidh Uí Dhomhnaill and the Annals of the Four Masters' in Ó Riain (ed.), *Beatha Aodha Ruaidh* (2002), pp 124–47.

Bruce, Gordon (ed.). *Protestant history and identity in sixteenth-century Europe, vol. 2: the later Reformation* (Aldershot, 1996).

Burke, Peter. *The Renaissance sense of the past* (London, 1969).

BIBLIOGRAPHY

— 'How to be a Counter-Reformation saint' in Kaspar Von Greyerz (ed.), *Religion and society in early modern Europe, 1500–1800* (London, 1984), pp 44–55.

Byrne, F.J. *The rise of the Uí Néill and the high-kingship of Ireland* (O'Donnell Lecture) (Dublin, 1969).

— *Irish kings and high kings* (London, 1973).

— 'Senchas: the nature of Gaelic historical tradition: approaches to history' in J.G. Barry (ed.), *Historical Studies* 9 (Belfast, 1974), pp 137–59.

Caerwyn Williams, J.E., and Patrick K. Ford. *The Irish literary tradition* (Cardiff, 1992).

Caerwyn Williams, J.E., and Máirín Ní Mhuiríosa. *Traidisiún liteartha na nGael* (Dublin, 1979).

Carey, John. '*Lebor gabála* and the legendary history of Ireland' in Helen Fulton (ed.), *Medieval Celtic literature and society* (Dublin, 2005), pp 32–48.

Cleary, Gregory. *Father Luke Wadding and St Isidore's College, Rome* (Rome, 1925).

Concannon, Helen. 'John O'Donovan and the annals of the Four Masters', *Studies* 37 (1948), 300–7.

Conlan, Patrick. *St Anthony's College of the Irish Franciscans, Louvain, 1607–1977* (Dublin, 1977).

— *Franciscan Ireland: the story of seven hundred and fifty years of the Friars Minor in Ireland* (Dublin, 1978).

Connellan, M.J. 'Ballymulconry and the Mulconrys', *Irish Ecclesiastical Record* 5th ser., 90 (1958), 322–30.

Corish, P.J. *The Catholic community in the seventeenth and eighteenth centuries* (Dublin, 1981).

Cosgrove, Art (ed.). *A new history of Ireland, II: medieval Ireland, 1169–1534* (Oxford, 1987).

Costello, Thomas B. 'The ancient law school of Park, Co. Galway', *Journal of the Galway Archaeological and Historical Society* 19 (1940), 89–100.

Cunningham, Bernadette. 'Seventeenth-century interpretations of the past: the case of Geoffrey Keating', *Irish Historical Studies* 25 (1986–7), 116–28.

— 'Theobald Dillon: a newcomer in sixteenth-century Mayo', *Cathair na Mart* 6 (1986), 24–32.

— 'The historical annals of Maoilín Óg Mac Bruaideadha, 1588–1602', *The Other Clare* 13 (1989), 21–8.

— 'The culture and ideology of Irish Franciscan historians at Louvain, 1607–1650' in Ciaran Brady (ed.), *Ideology and the historians: Historical Studies* 17 (Dublin, 1991), pp 11–30, 223–7.

— *The world of Geoffrey Keating: history, myth and religion in seventeenth-century Ireland* (Dublin, 2000).

— 'Colonized Catholics: perceptions of honour and history in Michael Kearney's reading of *Foras feasa ar Éirinn*' in V.P. Carey and U. Lotz-Heumann (eds), *Taking sides? colonial and confessional mentalités in early modern Ireland: essays in honour of Karl S. Bottigheimer* (Dublin, 2003), pp 150–64.

— '"An honour to the nation": publishing John O'Donovan's edition of the Annals of the Four Masters, 1848–56' in Martin Fanning and Raymond Gillespie (eds), *Print culture and intellectual life in Ireland, 1660–1941: essays in honour of Michael Adams* (Dublin, 2006), pp 116–42.

— *O'Donnell histories: Donegal and the Annals of the Four Masters* (Rathmullan, 2007).

— 'Micheál Ó Cléirigh and the Mac Aodhagáin school of law and history in Ormond' in George Cunningham (ed.), *The Roscrea Conference: commemorating forty conferences, 1987–2007, at Mount St Joseph Abbey* (Roscrea, 2007), pp 7–15.

— 'The Ó Duibhgeannáin family of historians and the Annals of the Four Masters', *Breifne* 44 (2008), 557–72.

— 'John O'Donovan's edition of the Annals of the Four Masters: an Irish classic?' in Dirk Van Hulle and Joep Leerssen (eds), *Editing the nation's memory: textual scholarship and nation-building in nineteenth-century Europe* (Amsterdam, 2008), pp 129–49.

— 'The Poor Clare Order in Ireland' in Edel Bhreathnach, Joseph MacMahon and John McCafferty (eds), *The Irish Franciscans, 1540–1990* (Dublin, 2009), pp 159–74.

— and R. Gillespie. '"Persecution" in seventeenth-century Irish', *Éigse* 22 (1987), 15–20.

— and — 'The purposes of patronage: Brian Maguire of Knockninny and his manuscripts', *Clogher Record* 13:1 (1988), 38–49.

— and — '"The most adaptable of saints": the cult of St Patrick in the seventeenth century', *Archivium Hibernicum* 49 (1995), 82–104.

— and — *Stories from Gaelic Ireland: microhistories from the sixteenth-century Irish annals* (Dublin, 2003).

— and — 'James Ussher and his Irish manuscripts', *Studia Hibernica* 33 (2004–5), 81–99.

— and — 'Muirgheas Ó Maoilchonaire of Cluain Plocáin: an early sixteenth-century Connacht scribe at work', *Studia Hibernica* 35 (2008–9), 17–43.

Curtis, Edmund. 'The O'Maolconaire family', *Journal of Galway Archaeological and Historical Society* 19 (1941), 118–46.

Davies, Ceri. 'Latin literature' in P.H. Jones and Eiluned Rees (eds), *A nation and its books: a history of the book in Wales* (Aberystwyth, 1998), pp 67–74.

Davis, Eugene. *Souvenir of Irish footprints over Europe* (Dublin, 1889).

de Blácam, Aodh. *Gaelic literature surveyed: from earliest times to the present* (Dublin, 1929, repr., 1973).

Dillon, Myles. 'Laud Misc 610', *Celtica* 5 (1960), 64–76; 6 (1963), 135–55.

Dooley, Ann. 'Literature and society in early seventeenth-century Ireland: the evaluation of change' in C. Byrne, M. Harry and P. Ó Siadhail (eds), *Celtic languages and Celtic peoples: proceedings of the second North American Congress of Celtic Studies* (Halifax, 1992), pp 513–34.

Ferguson, Samuel. 'The *Annals of the Four Masters*', *Dublin University Review* 31 (1848), 359–76.

— 'The *Annals of the Four Masters*: second article', *Dublin University Review* 31 (1848), 571–84.

Ford, Alan. 'James Ussher and the creation of an Irish Protestant identity' in Brendan Bradshaw and Peter Roberts (eds), *British consciousness and identity: the making of Britain, 1533–1707* (Cambridge, 1998), pp 185–212.

— 'James Ussher and the invention of Protestant history', unpublished lecture delivered at Mícheál Ó Cléirigh Institute, UCD, 8 April, 2005.

Giblin, Cathaldus. 'Father John Colgan, OFM (+1658) and the Irish school of hagiography at Louvain', *Franciscan College Annual* (1958), 23–32.

— 'The annals of the Four Masters' in Liam de Paor (ed.), *Great books of Ireland* (Dublin, 1967), pp 90–103.

Gillespie, Raymond. *Devoted people: belief and religion in early modern Ireland* (Manchester, 1997).

— 'The social thought of Richard Bellings' in Micheál Ó Siochrú (ed.), *Kingdoms in crisis: Ireland in the 1640s: essays in honour of Donal Cregan* (Dublin, 2001), pp 212–28.

Given-Wilson, Chris. *Chronicles: the writing of history in medieval England* (London, 2004).

Gleeson, D.F. *The last lords of Ormond* (revised ed., Nenagh, 2001).

Grabowski, Kathryn, and David Dumville. *Chronicles and annals of medieval Ireland and Wales: the Clonmacnoise-group texts* (Woodbridge, 1984).

Gwynn, Aubrey. Review of *Annals of Connacht. Studies: an Irish Quarterly Review* 33:131 (1944), 416–19.

— 'John Lynch's *De praesulibus Hiberniae*' [review article]. *Studies: an Irish Quarterly Review* 34:133 (1945), 37–52.

— 'Archbishop Ussher and Father Brendan O'Conor' in *Father Luke Wadding: commemorative volume*, ed. Franciscan Fathers (Dublin, 1957), pp 263–83.

— 'Cathal Mac Maghnusa and the Annals of Ulster', *Clogher Record* 2:2 (1958), 230–43; 2:3 (1959) 370–84; revised version, ed. Nollaig Ó Muraíle (Enniskillen, 1998).

Gwynn, E.J. 'On a source of O'Clery's glossary', *Hermathena* 14 (1907), 464–80; 15 (1909), 389–96.

— 'Miscellanea', *Ériu* 9 (1921–3), 27–30 [on verse fragments in AFM].

Harrison, Alan. *Ag cruinniú meala: Anthony Raymond (1675–1726): ministéir Protastúnach agus léann na Gaeilge i mBaile Átha Cliath* (Dublin, 1988).

Hayes-McCoy, G.A. *Irish battles* (London, 1969).

Henry, Gráinne. *The Irish military community in Spanish Flanders, 1586–1621* (Dublin, 1992).

Hogan, Edmund. 'Irish historical studies in the seventeenth century, I: The Franciscan college of St Anthony of Padua, Louvain', *Irish Ecclesiastical Record* n.s., 7 (1870–1), 31–43.

— 'Irish historical studies in the seventeenth century, II: Hugh Ward', *Irish Ecclesiastical Record* n.s., 7 (1870–1), 56–77.

— 'Irish historical studies in the seventeenth century, III: Patrick Fleming, OSF', *Irish Ecclesiastical Record* n.s., 7 (1870–1), 193–216.

— 'Irish historical studies in the seventeenth century, IV: The Four Masters', *Irish Ecclesiastical Record* n.s., 7 (1870–1), 268–89.

Huppert, George. *The idea of perfect history: historical erudition and historical philosophy in Renaissance France* (Urbana, 1970).

Hyde, Douglas. *A literary history of Ireland, from earliest times to the present day* (London, 1899, revised ed., 1967).

Jennings, Brendan. *The Irish Franciscan College of St Anthony at Louvain* (Dublin, 1925).

— 'The return of the Irish Franciscans to Louvain, 1606–1625', *Studies* 14 (1925), 451–8.

— *Michael O Cleirigh, chief of the Four Masters and his associates* (Dublin, 1936).

— 'The Irish students at the University of Louvain' in O'Brien (ed.), *Measgra i gcuimhne Mhichíl Uí Chléirigh* (1944), pp 74–97.

Kelley, D.R. *Foundations of modern historical scholarship: language, law and history in the French Renaissance* (New York, 1970).

— *Faces of history: historical inquiry from Herodotus to Herder* (New Haven and London, 1998).

Kelly, Fergus. *Guide to early Irish law* (Dublin, 1988).

Knowles, David. *Great historical enterprises* (London, 1963).

Leerssen, J. Th. *Mere Irish and Fíor Ghael: studies in the idea of nationality and its development and literary expression prior to the nineteenth century* (Amsterdam and Philadelphia, 1986; 2nd ed. Cork, 1996).

— *The contention of the bards: Iomarbhágh na bhFileadh and its place in Irish political and literary history* (London, 1994).

— *Remembrance and imagination: patterns in the historical and literary representation of Ireland in the nineteenth century* (Cork, 1996).

Lennon, Colm. *Richard Stanihurst, the Dubliner, 1547–1618* (Dublin, 1981).

Leslie, Shane. 'Some inscriptions from Louvain', *Irish Ecclesiastical Record* 5th ser., 5 (1915), 205–8.

Levy, F.J. *Tudor historical thought* (San Marino, 1967).

Litton Falkiner, C. *Illustrations of Irish history and topography, mainly of the seventeenth century* (London, 1904).

Lotz-Heumann, Ute. 'The Protestant interpretation of history in Ireland: the case of James Ussher's Discourse' in Gordon Bruce (ed.), *Protestant history and identity in sixteenth-century Europe, vol. 2: the later Reformation* (Aldershot, 1996), pp 107–20.

Lynch, Anthony, 'Scríbhinní foireann taighde Dhún Mhuire, 1945–1995' in Millett and Lynch (eds), *Dún Mhuire, Killiney* (1995), pp 14–36.

Lyons, Mary Ann. *Gearóid Óg Fitzgerald* (Dublin, 1998).

McCafferty, John. 'From manuscript to print: early modern receptions of the Patrician life', unpublished lecture delivered at Muirchú conference, Mícheál Ó Cléirigh Institute, UCD, 24 April, 2004.

Mac Cárthaigh, Eoin. Poems on the Uí Dhomhnaill, circa, 1641 (unpublished PhD thesis, University of Dublin, 1995).

— 'Cú Choigcríche Ó Cléirigh', unpublished lecture delivered at Mícheál Ó Cléirigh Institute, UCD, 20 February, 2004.

— 'Cú Choigcríche Ó Cléirigh' in *Dictionary of Irish biography* (9 vols, Cambridge, 2009).

— 'Fearfeasa Ó Maolchonaire' in *Dictionary of Irish biography* (9 vols, Cambridge, 2009).

— 'Muiris Ó Maolchonaire' in *Dictionary of Irish biography* (9 vols, Cambridge, 2009).

Mc Carthy, D.P. 'The chronological apparatus of the Annals of Ulster, AD431–1131', *Peritia* 8 (1994), 46–79.

— 'Collation of the Irish regnal canon', https://www.cs.tcd.ie/Dan.McCarthy/chronology/synchronisms/annals-chron.htm

— *The Irish annals: their genesis, evolution and history* (Dublin, 2008).

Mac Craith, Mícheál. 'Gaelic Ireland and the Renaissance' in Glanmor Williams and Robert Owen Jones (eds), *The Celts and the Renaissance: tradition and innovation: proceedings of the eighth international Congress of Celtic Studies, 1987* (Cardiff, 1990), pp 57–89.

— 'Scáthán shacramuinte na haithridhe: saothar reiligiúnda nó saothar polaitíochta', *Irisleabhar Mhá Nuad* (1993), 144–54.

— 'Beatha Aodha Ruaidh: beathaisnéis de chuid an Renaissance', *Irisleabhar Mha Nuad* (1994), 44–54.

— 'Creideamh agus Athartha: idé-eolaíocht pholaitíochta agus aos léinn na Gaeilge i dtús an seachtú haois déag' in Máirín Ní Dhonnchadha (ed.), *Nua-léamha: gnéithe de chultúr, stair agus polaitíocht na hÉireann*, c.*1600*–c.*1900* (Dublin, 1996), pp 7–19.

— 'The *Beatha* in the context of the literature of the Renaissance' in Ó Riain (ed.), *Beatha Aodha Ruaidh* (2002), pp 36–53.

— and David Worthington. 'Aspects of the literary activity of the Irish Franciscans in Prague, 1620–1786' in T. O'Connor and M. Lyons (eds), *Irish migrants in Europe after Kinsale, 1602–1820* (Dublin, 2003), pp 118–34.

McGowan, Katherine Megan. Political geography and political structures in earlier medieval Ireland: a chronicle-based approach (unpublished PhD thesis, University of Cambridge, 2003).

MacHale, Conor. *Annals of the Clan Egan: an account of the Mac Egan bardic family of Brehon lawyers* (Enniscrone, 1990).

McKenna, Catherine. 'Triangulating opposition: Irish expatriates and hagiography in the seventeenth century' in Maria Tymoczko and Colin Ireland (eds), *Language and tradition in Ireland: continuities and displacements* (Amherst, 2003), pp 139–55.

McKisack, May. *Medieval history in the Tudor age* (Oxford, 1971).

McManus, Damian. 'The language of the *Beatha*' in Ó Riain (ed.), *Beatha Aodha Ruaidh* (2002), pp 54–73.

Mac Niocaill, Gearóid. 'The heir designate in early medieval Ireland', *Irish Jurist* n.s., 3 (1968), 326–9.

— 'A propos du vocabulaire social Irlandais du bas moyen age', *Études Celtiques* 12 (1970–1), 512–46.

— *The medieval Irish annals* (Dublin, 1975).

Mac Suibhne, P. 'A great historical work: the Annals of the Four Masters', *Journal of the Ivernian Society* 7 (1915), 66–93.

Millett, Benignus, and Anthony Lynch (eds). *Dún Mhuire, Killiney, 1945–95: léann agus seanchas* (Dublin, 1995).

Momigliano, A. *Studies in historiography* (London, 1966).

Mooney, Canice. 'Irish Franciscan libraries of the past', *Irish Ecclesiastical Record* 5th ser., 60 (1942), 215–28.

— 'The golden age of the Irish Franciscans, 1615–50' in O'Brien (ed.), *Measgra i gcuimhne Mhichíl Uí Chléirigh* (1944), pp 21–33.

— *Boetius MacEgan of Ross* (Killiney, 1950).

— 'The Franciscan friary by the Drowes', *Donegal Annual* 3:3 (1957), 1–7.

— 'Father John Colgan' in T. O'Donnell (ed.), *Father John Colgan OFM* (Dublin, 1959), pp 7–40.

Moran, P.F. *History of the Catholic archbishops of Dublin since the Reformation* (Dublin, 1864).

Morét, Ulrike. 'An early Scottish national biography: Thomas Dempster's *Historia Ecclesiastica Gentis Scotorum* (1627)' in L. Houwen, A. Mac Donald and S. Mapstone (eds), *A palace in the wild: essays on vernacular culture and humanism in late medieval and Renaissance Scotland* (*Mediaevalia Groningana* 1) (Leuven, 2000), pp 249–70.

Murphy, Gerard. 'Royalist Ireland', *Studies: an Irish Quarterly Review* 24:96 (1935), 589–604.

Nicholls, Kenneth. 'The MacCoghlans', *Irish Genealogist* 6:4 (1983), 445–60.

Ní Maol-Chróin, Caitilín. 'Geinealaigh Clainne Aodhagáin, AD1400–1500: ollamhain i bhféineachus is i bhfilidheacht' in O'Brien (ed.), *Measgra i gcuimhne Mhichíl Uí Chléirigh* (1944), pp 132–9.

Nic Ghiollamhaith, Aoife. 'Dynastic warfare and historical writing in North Munster, 1276–1350', *Cambridge Medieval Celtic Studies* 2 (1981), 73–89.

O'Brien, Sylvester (ed.). *Measgra i gcuimhne Mhichíl Uí Chléirigh: miscellany of historical and linguistic studies in honour of Brother Michael Ó Cléirigh, OFM, chief of the Four Masters, 1643–1943* (Dublin, 1944).

Ó Buachalla, Breandán. '*Annála ríoghachta Éireann* is *Foras feasa ar Éirinn*: an comhthéacs comhaimseartha', *Studia Hibernica* 22–3 (1982–3), 59–105.

— 'Na Stíobhartaigh agus an t-aos léinn: Cing Séamas', *Proceedings of the Royal Irish Academy* 83C (1983), 81–134.

— 'Aodh Eangach and the Irish king-hero' in Donnchadh Ó Corráin, Liam Breatnach and Kim McCone (eds), *Sages, saints and storytellers: Celtic studies in honour of Professor James Carney* (Maynooth, 1989), pp 200–32.

— 'James our true king: the ideology of Irish royalism in the seventeenth century' in D.G. Boyce, Robert Eccleshall and Vincent Geoghegan (eds), *Political thought in Ireland since the seventeenth century* (London, 1993), pp 7–35.

— *Aisling ghéar: na Stíobhartaigh agus an t-aos léinn, 1603–1788* (Dublin, 1996).

Ó Buachalla, Liam. 'The construction of the Irish annals, 429–466', *Journal of the Cork Archaeological and Historical Society* 2nd ser., 63 (1958), 103–15.

Ó Catháin, Diarmaid. 'John Fergus MD, eighteenth-century doctor, book collector, and Irish scholar', *Journal of the Royal Society of Antiquaries of Ireland* 118 (1988), 139–62.

Ó Cléirigh, Tomás. *Aodh Mac Aingil agus an scoil Nua-Ghaedhlige i Lobháin* (Dublin, 1935, repr., 1985).

— 'A poem book of the O'Donnells', *Éigse* 1 (1939), 51–61, 130–42.

Ó Conchaneáinn, Tomás. 'A Connacht medieval literary heritage: texts derived from *Cín Dromma Snechtai* through *Leabhar na hUidhre*', *Cambridge Medieval Celtic Studies* 16 (1988), 1–40.

O'Connor, Frank. *The backward look: a survey of Irish literature* (London, 1967).

O'Connor, Thomas. 'Towards the invention of the Irish Catholic *natio*: Thomas Messingham's *Florilegium* (1624)', *Irish Theological Quarterly* 64 (1999), 157–77.

— 'A justification for foreign intervention in early modern Ireland: Peter Lombard's *Commentarius*' in T. O'Connor and M. Lyons (eds), *Irish migrants in Europe after Kinsale, 1602–1820* (2003), pp 14–31.

— (ed.). *The Irish in Europe, 1580–1815* (Dublin, 2001).

— and Mary Ann Lyons (eds). *Irish migrants in Europe after Kinsale, 1602–1820* (Dublin, 2003).

Ó Corráin, Donnchadh. 'Irish regnal succession: a reappraisal', *Studia Hibernica* 11 (1971), 7–39.

— 'Review of F.J. Byrne, *Irish kings and high kings*', *Celtica* 13 (1980), 150–68.

O'Curry, Eugene. *Lectures on the manuscript materials of ancient Irish history* (Dublin, 1861).

Ó Dálaigh, Brian. 'The Uí Mhaoilchonaire of Thomond', unpublished lecture delivered at Tionól, DIAS, 29 Nov. 2008.

O'Donnell, Terence (ed.). *Father John Colgan OFM, 1592–1658* (Dublin, 1959).

Ó Dúshláine, Tadhg. *An Eoraip agus litríocht na Gaeilge, 1600–1650: gnéithe den bharóchas Eorpach i litríocht na Gaeilge* (Dublin, 1987).

Ó Gallachair, P. 'The first Maguire of Tempo', *Clogher Record* 2:1 (1957), 469–89.

O'Halloran, Clare. *Golden ages and barbarous nations: antiquarian debate and cultural politics in Ireland, c.1750–1800* (Cork, 2004).

O'Leary, Philip. *Gaelic prose in the Irish Free State* (Dublin, 2004).

Ó Lochlainn, Colm. 'John O'Donovan and the Four Masters', *Irish Book Lover* 29 (1943–5), 4–8.

— Ó Domhnaill's claims for military service', *Irish Sword* 5 (1961–2), 117–18.

Ó Macháin, Pádraig. 'A lleabraib imdaib': cleachtadh agus pátrúnacht an léinn, agus déanamh na lámhscríbhinní' in Ruairí Ó hUiginn (ed.), *Oidhreacht na lámhscríbhinní: Léachtaí Cholm Cille XXXIV* (Maynooth, 2004), pp 148–78.

Ó Máille, Tomás. *An béal beo*, ed. Ruairí Ó hUiginn (Dublin, 2002).

Ó Maonaigh, Cainneach. 'Franciscan Library MS A.30.4', *Irish Book Lover* 27 (1940–1), 202–4.

Ó Muraíle, Nollaig. 'The autograph manuscripts of the Annals of the Four Masters', *Celtica* 19 (1987), 75–95.

— *The celebrated antiquary: Dubhaltach Mac Fhirbhisigh, c.1600–71: his lineage, life and learning* (Maynooth, 1996).

— 'Seán Ó Donnabháin: "an cúigiú máistir"', *Léachtaí Cholm Cille* 27 (1997), 11–82.

— 'Cathal Óg Mac Maghnusa: his time, life and legacy', *Clogher Record* 16:2 (1998), 45–64.

— (ed.), *Mícheál Ó Cléirigh, his associates and St Anthony's College Louvain* (Dublin, 2008).

O'Neill, Timothy. *The Irish hand: scribes and their manuscripts from the earliest times to the seventeenth century with an exemplar of scripts* (Mountrath, 1984).

O'Rahilly, T.F. *Early Irish history and mythology* (Dublin, 1946).

Ó Raifteartaigh, T. (ed.). *The Royal Irish Academy: a bicentennial history, 1785–1985* (Dublin, 1985).

Ó Riain, Pádraig. 'The Book of Glendalough or Rawlinson B 502', *Éigse* 18 (1981), 161–76.

— 'Rawlinson B 502 alias Lebar Glinne Dá Locha: a restatement of the case', *Zeitschrift für Celtische Philologie* 51 (1999), 130–47.

— 'The *Catalogus praecipuorum sanctorum Hiberniae*, sixty years on' in Alfred P. Smyth (ed.), *Seanchas: studies in early and medieval Irish archaeology, history and literature in honour of Francis J. Byrne* (Dublin, 2000), pp 396–430.

— (ed.). *Beatha Aodha Ruaidh: The life of Red Hugh O'Donnell, historical and literary contexts* (London, 2002).

— *Feastdays of the saints: a history of Irish martyrologies.* Subsidia Hagiographia 86 (Brussels, 2006).

O'Sullivan, Anne, and William O'Sullivan. 'Edward Lhuyd's collection of Irish manuscripts', *Transactions of the Honourable Society of Cymmrodorion* (1962), 57–76.

O'Sullivan, William. 'Ussher as a collector of manuscripts', *Hermathena* 88 (1956), 34–58.

— 'A finding list of Sir James Ware's manuscripts', *Proceedings of the Royal Irish Academy* 97C (1997), 69–99.

— 'The Slane manuscript of the Annals of the Four Masters', *Ríocht na Midhe* 10 (1999), 78–85.

Patterson, Annabel. *Reading Holinshed's Chronicles* (Chicago, 1994).

Petrie, George. 'Remarks on the history and authenticity of the Annals of the Four Masters', *Transactions of the Royal Irish Academy* 16 (1831), 381–93.

Plummer, Charles. 'On two collections of Latin lives of Irish saints in the Bodleian Library, Rawl. B. 485 and Rawl. B. 505', *Zeitschrift für Celtische Philologie* 5 (1904–5), 429–54.

Pocock, J.G.A. *The ancient constitution and the feudal law: a study of English historical thought in the seventeenth century* (Cambridge, 1957, new ed. 1987).

Pullapilly, Cyriac K. *Caesar Baronius: Counter-Reformation historian* (Notre Dame, Ind., 1975).

Quinn, D.B. '"Irish" Ireland and "English" Ireland' in Art Cosgrove (ed.), *A new history of Ireland, II: medieval Ireland, 1169–1534* (Dublin, 1987), pp 619–37.

Ranum, Orest. *Artisans of glory: writers and historical thought in seventeenth-century France* (Chapel Hill, 1981).

— (ed.). *National consciousness, history and political culture in early modern Europe* (Baltimore, MD, 1975).

Ross, Bianca. *Britannia et Hibernia: Nationale und Kulturelle Identitätion im Ireland des 17 Jahrhunderts* (Heidelberg, 1998).

Ryan, Salvador. Popular religion in Gaelic Ireland, 1445–1645 (unpublished PhD thesis, 2 vols, National University of Ireland, Maynooth, 2002).

Samuel, Raphael, and Paul Thompson (eds). *The myths we live by* (London, 1980).

Sharpe, Richard. 'The origin and elaboration of the *Catalogus praecipuorum sanctorum Hiberniae* attributed to Fr Henry Fitzsimon SJ', *Bodleian Library Record* 13:3 (1989), 202–30.

— *Medieval Irish saints' lives: an introduction to Vitae sanctorum Hiberniae* (Oxford, 1991).

Sheppard, Victor. *Michael O'Clery OFM, knight-errant of Irish history* (Dublin, 1944).

Silke, John J. 'Red Hugh O'Donnell, 1572–1601: a biographical survey', *Donegal Annual* 5 (1961), 1–19.

— 'Irish scholarship and the Renaissance, 1580–1673', *Studies in the Renaissance* 20 (1973), 169–206.

— 'The last will of Red Hugh O'Donnell', *Studia Hibernica* 24 (1984–8), 51–60.

Simms, J.G. 'Manus O'Donnell: 21st lord of Tir Conaill', *Donegal Annual* 5 (1962), 115–21.

Simms, Katharine. Gaelic lordships in Ulster in the later middle ages (unpublished PhD thesis, 2 vols, University of Dublin, 1976).

— 'Niall Garbh II O'Donnell, king of Tír Conaill, 1422–39', *Donegal Annual* 12:1 (1977), 7–21.

— *From kings to warlords: the changing political structure of Gaelic Ireland in the later Middle Ages* (Woodbridge, 1987).

— 'Bards and barons: the Anglo-Irish aristocracy and the native culture' in Robert Bartlett and Angus Mackay (eds), *Medieval frontier societies* (Oxford, 1989), pp 177–97.

— 'Late medieval Donegal' in W. Nolan, L. Ronayne and M. Dunlevy (eds), *Donegal: history and society* (Dublin, 1995), pp 183–201.

— 'Additional Ó Domhnaill entries in the D version of the Annals of Ulster' (unpublished typescript).

Skovgaard-Petersen, Karen. *Historiography at the court of Christian IV* (Copenhagen, 2002).

Smyth, A.P. (ed.). *Seanchas: studies in early and medieval Irish archaeology, history and literature in honour of Francis J. Byrne* (Dublin, 2000).

Smyth, W.J. 'Property, patronage and population: reconstructing the human geography of mid-seventeenth century County Tipperary' in William Nolan (ed.), *Tipperary, history and society* (Dublin, 1985), pp 104–38.

Spiegel, Gabrielle M. *The past as text: the theory and practice of medieval historiography* (Baltimore, MD, 1999).

Staunton, E. de Lacy. 'The O Maolconaire family: a note', *Journal of the Galway Archaeological and Historical Society* 20 (1942), 82–8.

Struever, Nancy S. *The language of history in the Renaissance: rhetoric and historical consciousness in Florentine humanism* (Princeton, 1970).

Trevor-Roper, Hugh. 'James Ussher, archbishop of Armagh' in Hugh Trevor-Roper, *Catholics, Anglicans and Puritans: seventeenth-century essays* (London, 1989), pp 120–65.

Walsh, Paul. *Gleanings from Irish manuscripts* (2nd ed., Dublin, 1933).

— 'The Four Masters', *Irish Book Lover* 22 (1934), 128–31.

— 'The convent of Donegal, 1632–36', *Irish Book Lover* 23 (1935), 109–15.

— 'The learned family of Ó Maelchonaire', *Catholic Bulletin* 26 (1936), 835–42.

— 'Manuscripts of the Four Masters, RIA 23 P 6 and 7', *Irish Book Lover* 24 (1936), 81–3.

— 'Slips in O'Donovan's Four Masters, vol. V', *Irish Book Lover* 25 (1937), 100–2.

— 'Travels of an Irish scholar', *Catholic Bulletin* 27 (1937), 123–32.

— 'The work of a winter', *Catholic Bulletin* 28 (1938), 226–34.

— 'The Book of Lecan in Ormond?', *Irish Book Lover* 26 (1938), 62.

— *The Ó Cléirigh family of Tír Conaill* (Dublin, 1938).

— *The Mageoghegans: a lecture … at Castletown-Geoghegan* (Mullingar, 1938).

— 'The dating of the Irish annals', *Irish Historical Studies* 2 (1940–1), 355–75.

— *The Four Masters and their work* (Dublin, 1944).

— *Irish men of learning*, ed. Colm Ó Lochlainn (Dublin, 1947).

— *Irish chiefs and leaders*, ed. Colm Ó Lochlainn (Dublin, 1960).

— *Irish leaders and learning through the ages*, ed. Nollaig Ó Muraíle (Dublin, 2003).

Woolf, D.R. *The idea of history in early Stuart England* (Toronto, 1990).

Index

Abraham, patriarch, 78

Act for the Kingly Title (1541), 87

Adam, 78

Adamnán, saint, 252

Amra Coluim Cille, 219

An síogaí romhánach, 220

'*Annales prioratus Insulae Omnium SS in Loughree*', 60

Annals of Boyle, *see* Cottonian annals

Annals of Clonmacnoise (AClon), 55, 56–7, 59, 77, 78, 80, 84, 102, 112–14, 118, 123, 221, 224, 225–6, 281–2, 293; word count, 76

Annals of Cluain Eidhneach, 254–5; *see also* Book of Cluain Eidhneach

Annals of Connacht (AConn), 15, 46, 49–51, 77, 93, 103–16, 119, 123, 124–34, 183, 184, 191, 194, 197, 217–18, 221, 232, 234, 239, 242, 274; word count, 76

'Annals of Donegal', 38

Annals of Inisfallen (AI), 77, 78, 89, 96, 220–1, 224; word count, 76

Annals of Lecan (ALec), 43n, 58, 102, 110, 112–16, 123, 127, 135, 305–15

Annals of Loch Cé (ALCé), 15, 49, 50, 51–4, 77, 96, 217–18, 229–30, 232, 242, 300; word count, 76

Annals of the Island of Saints, 43n, 49n, 60–1

Annals of Tigernach (ATig), 89, 231n, 242; word count, 76

Annals of Ulster (AU), 15, 45, 46–9, 89, 93, 96–7, 99, 102, 104–12, 113, 114–17, 119, 123, 124–34, 160, 183, 184, 188–201, 215, 220, 222, 224, 229–32, 234–6, 239, 242, 276; 'A' text, 46, 48, 225n; 'B' text, 46–8; 'C' text, 48; 'D' text, 48–9, 292 ; scribes of, 48; word count, 76

Aoinsgiath cosnaimh na gceall, 274

approbations, 69, 99, 278, 280, 294

Árd Uí Luinín, Co. Fermanagh, 276

Ardchoill, Co. Clare, 49n, 259, 260n

Ardfert, Co. Kerry, friary, 239

Armagh, Co. Armagh, 159–60; friary, 232, 237, 239, 285

Ashburnham, earl of, 137n

Atá sund forba feasa, 69, 89

Athlone, 274; friary, 67, 239, 286, 287, 288, 294

autograph manuscripts, *see* manuscripts of AFM

Baile in Chuimine, Co. Roscommon, 259

Baile Tibhaird, [Co. Roscommon], 259

Bale, John, 27

Ballymacegan, Co. Tipperary, 248, 249, 251, 253

Ballymacmanus, Co. Fermanagh, 47n

Ballymulconry (Cluain Plocáin), Co. Roscommon, 257, 260, 266

Baronius, Caesar, *Annales ecclesiastici*, 164–7, 174, 216n

battle of Áth Dara, 160

battle of Clontarf, 98

battle of Cnoc Buidhbh, 195

battle of Crinna, 90

battle of Cúil Dreimhne, 90

battle of Farsetmore, 204, 205

battle of Kinsale, 121–2, 295

battle of Magh Rath, 195n

battle of Ocha, 90

battles, *see also* military narratives

Beatha Aodha Ruaidh Uí Dhomhnaill, 44,
   54, 61–2, 63, 91, 93–4, 121–3, 176,
   187, 201, 209–12, 269–70
Becc mac Dé, poet, 90
Bede, Venerable, 167
Belleisle, Co. Fermanagh, 47n
Bellings, Richard, 255
Bergin, Osborn, 57
Bernard of Clairvaux, saint, 225, 229
Best, Richard I., 57
Bible, New Testament, 95; translation
   into Irish, 278
Bible, Old Testament, 95, as source, 78–9
Bignôn, Jérome, *De l'excellence*, 32–3
Binchy, Daniel, *Corpus iuris Hibernici*, 255
Bingham, Sir Richard, president of
   Connacht, 210
Birr, synod, 240n
Boece, Hector, 31
Bollandists, 38
Book of Ballymote, 259
Book of Clonmacnoise, 43n, 44, 55–8, 281
Book of Cluain Eidhneach, 221, 266; *see
   also* Annals of Cluain Eidhneach
Book of Cluain Plocáin, 266; *see also* Book
   of Ó Maoil Chonaire
Book of Cú Coigchríche Ó Cléirigh, 44,
   178–9, 188
Book of Fenagh, 55, 91–2, 188n, 257, 261
Book of Knockninny, 276–7, 294
Book of Lecan, 58, 70–1, 259, 266; loan
   of, 280
Book of Leinster, 65, 67, 69, 70n, 231n,
   290; *see also* 'Leabhar na hUachongbala'
Book of Lughaidh Ó Cléirigh, *see Beatha
   Aodha Ruaidh Uí Dhomhnaill*
Book of Ó Maoil Chonaire, 43n, 45, 54–5,
   257; *see also* Book of Cluain Plocáin
Book of Seanadh Mic Maghnusa, 45, 46,
   48, 102; *see also* Annals of Ulster
Book of the Island of Saints, 43, 44, 281
Book of the O'Duigenans of Kilronan,
   43n, 45, 49, 50
Boyle, Co. Roscommon, 52; barony, 257;
   monastery, 239
Brady, John, 51

Breatnach, Pádraig, 62, 211–2, 272
Brecan, saint, 88
Brendan of Clonfert, saint, 87, 223
Brian Bóruma, king, 98, 119, 183, 200, 279
Brigit of Kildare, saint, 35, 38, 87, 218–
   29; feastday of, 126
Britons, 231
Browne, Valentine, OFM, 250, 301
Buchanan, George, 31
Buckingham, Marquis of, 137n
Bundrowes, Co. Donegal, 246, 282, 285;
   see also Donegal
Bunratty, Co. Clare, 257
Búrc, Henry, 168n, 220
burial customs, 187
Burke, Hugh, OFM, 254
Burke, Mailir, son of Tomás, 132
Burke, Peter, 16, 21
Burke, Tomás, 110
Butler, Edmund Mac Richard, 251
Butler, James, ninth earl of Ormond, 291
Buttevant, Co. Cork, friary, 237n
Byrne, F.J., 117

Caillín, saint, 91
Cáin Adamnáin, 251–2
Caithréim Thoirdhealbhaigh, 207
Camden, William, *Annals of Queen
   Elizabeth*, 32; *Britannia*, 31–2
Canice, saint, 88
Carn Glas, 107
Carrick-on-Suir, Co. Tipperary, friary, 239
Cashel, Co. Tipperary, friary, 253, 287, 289
Castlefore, Co. Leitrim, 273, 274
catechisms, 38, 229
Catherine, saint, 220
Catholic Confederation, 255
Catholic University, Dublin, 19
Cavan, Co. Cavan, friary, 239, 285
Ceallach, saint, archbishop of Armagh,
   97, 222
Ceannfaeladh, poet, 90
Ceasair, 77
Celestine, pope, 164, 165
Charles I, king, 37, 296; as prince of
   Wales, 32

charters, 182
Christian IV, king of Denmark, 33
Chronicum Scotorum (CS), 55–8, 77, 78, 89, 225; word count, 76
chronology, 74, 81–4, 96–9
Ciaran, saint, 99–100, 225, 227–8
Cín Dromma Snechtai, 259
Cinéal Conaill, 195, 202, 206, 207, 210–11
Cinéal Eoghan, 203, 207; kings of, 120
Cinéal Fhiachach, 67
Cinéal Moain, 181
Clane, Co. Kildare, friary, 239; synod, 241
Clann Dálaigh, 24n
Clann Mhaolruanaidh, 51
Clann Mhíleadh, 78, 80, 99; kings, 65
Clanricard lordship, 129, 159, 182
Clare, county, 206
Cletty, Co. Sligo, 89
Clogher, Co. Tyrone, monastery, 239
Cloncraw parish, Co. Roscommon, 257
Cloneshannagh, Co. Roscommon, 257
Clonmacnoise, Co. Offaly, 99–100, 227; founder of, 225
Clonmel, Co. Tipperary, friary, 285, 287
Cluain Plocáin, *see* Ballymulconry
Cogagh Gaedhel re Gallaibh, 72
Colgan, John, OFM, 15, 19, 31, 38, 72, 167, 223, 229, 289–90; *Acta sanctorum Hiberniae*, 223, 242; *Trias thaumaturga*, 220, 242
Colum Cille, saint, 35, 38, 88, 161, 199–200, 218–29; prophecies, 91–2, 95, 187–8
Connacht, province, history of, 52, 107, 110, 118, 181, 183, 189, 191, 194–5, 199, 206, 207n, 210, 263–4; kings of 120; transplantation to (1654–8), 260
Connellan, Owen, 20n
Conry, John, 276n
Conry, Tully, 265; *see also* Ó Maoil Chonaire, Tuileagna
Conyngham, William Burton, 138n, 139n
Cooper, Austin, 138n
Coote, Sir Charles, 257
Cork, Co. Cork, 206, friary, 237n, 239, 287, 288

Corlios Conaill, 257
Cottonian annals (BL Cotton Titus A xxv), 119
Council of Trent, 34, 236
Counter-Reformation, in Ireland, 23, 35, 216–18, 302; in Europe, 34, 165, 167–8, 217, 222, 265
creach, 130
Creta townland, Co. Roscommon, 260
Crimhthann Niadhnair, king, 82
Cronan Becc, saint, 226
Cuanna, saint, 168
Cuirfead commaoin ar chloinn Táil, 279

Dallán Forgaill, 219, 220n
Darerca, saint, 90
Dathi mac Fiachrach, king, 82–3
Davies, Sir John, 249
Davis, Eugene, 14
de Blacam, Aodh, 13
de Courcy, John, 88
de Mariana, Juan, *Historia general de España*, 32
Dempster, Thomas, 27, 30–1, 221
de Ocampo, Florian, 32
Derry, Co. Londonderry, diocese, 240n, monastery, 239
Desmond, kings of, 120
de Valera, Eamon, taoiseach, 16
Diggenan, Dominick, 51n
Dillon, Edward, OFM, 294
Dillon, George, OFM, 67, 71, 294
Dillon, James, 295
Dillon, Sir Lucas, 261, 294
Dillon, Myles, 18
Dillon, Theobald, 294
Diomma Dubh, saint, 226
Domhnall mac Oédo, king, 117
Dominic, saint, 220
Donegal, Co. Donegal, castle, 183; Franciscan community in, 39, 43, 99, 214; friary at Bundrowes, 246, 273–4, 282–6, 285, 288, 290–1; friary at Donegal, 183, 184, 283n; monastic library, 45, 293
Donlevy, *see* Ó Duinnshléibhe

Drogheda, Co. Louth, 166, 237n, 290, 298; synod (1152), 240–1; friary, 283, 288; *see also* Ussher, James

Dublin government, 200, 202; *see also* lord justice of Ireland

Dublin, 266, 280, 292, 298; friary, 285, 287, 288; Franciscan Chapter at, 266

Du Chesne, André, *Les antiquitez et recherches*, 32

Dumoulin, Charles, 27

Dumville, David, 56

Dungannon, Co. Tyrone, 109, 110

Easter, date of, 254

ecclesiastical history, 215–43, 289–90

editions of AFM, by Rev Charles O'Conor, 20, 756, 82, 137, 164; by John O'Donovan, 18–20, 75–6, 137–42, 164, 169–71, 175

Edward VI, king, 292

Éire árd, inis na ríogh, 67, 69, 80–1, 89

Elizabeth I, queen, 123

Ennis, Co. Clare, friary, 237n, 239

Eochaidh Ollathair, king, 75

Erc, bishop, 90

Ermedhach, saint, 226

Eustace family, 279

Everard, Joseph, OFM, 250

exile, 213

Féchín, saint, 169

Féilire Oengusso, see Martyrology of Oengus

Fenagh, Co. Leitrim, 274

Ferghus Duibhdhedach, king, 90

Fergus, John, 37n, 76, 170n

Fermanagh, county, 116, 182, 183–4

Fiacc, bishop, 165

Fir Bolg, 80; kings, 65

Fitzgerald, Alice, 110

Fitzgerald, Eleanor, 110

Fitzgerald, Gerald, ninth earl of Kildare, 110

Fitzsimon, Henry, SJ, 30

Flann Mainistreach, 164, 168n, 170

Fleming, Patrick, OFM, 27–31, 38, 41, 120

Fleming, Thomas, OFM, archbishop of Dublin, 29, 71, 166n, 256n, 266, 292

Ford, Patrick, 15

Fore, Co. Westmeath, 169

Four Masters, *see* Ó Cléirigh, Cú Choigcríche; Ó Cléirigh, Mícheál, OFM; Ó Duibhgeannáin, Cú Choigcríche; Ó Maoil Chonaire, Fearfeasa; *see also* scribes of AFM

Fragmentary Annals of Ireland, 221–2

Francis of Assisi, saint, 48, 220

Franciscan friaries, in Ireland, 45, 67, 69, 157, 183, 184, 232, 237, 239, 273–4, 282–91, 194, 198; history of, 72; patronage of, 241–2; *see also names of individual friaries*

Franciscan Order, 16, 35, 36, 245–7; at Donegal, 39, 43, 99, 178, 181, 214, 245, 272–3, 293; at Dublin, 166; patrons, 241–2; historical sources, 109, 135, 185; general Chapters, 264, 272; research, 20–1; scholarly networks, 282–93; *see also* Louvain; St Anthony's College, Louvain, *and names of individual Irish friaries*

Freeman, A.M., 49–50

Fuair Breifne a díol do shaghlonn, 259

Gaiety Theatre, Dublin, 16

Gallagher, Rev., 29

galloglasses, 202

Galway, friary, 237n, 239, 286, 287

Gann, king, 65

Geanann, king, 65

Génair Pattraic, 166

Genealogiae regum et sanctorum Hiberniae, 45, 65–71, 80–3, 96–8, 154, 169, 250, 263–4, 271, 273, 278, 293, 296; approbations for, 253; signatures, 274, 275

Giblin, Cathaldus, OFM, 20–1

Gilla Cóemáin, 69, 81, 89, 92, 98

Given-Wilson, Chris, 298

Glen of Aherlow, Co. Tipperary, 15

Goulde, John, OFM, 61

grammatical tract, 265

Grange, Co. Tipperary, 251
Guicciardini, Francesco, 32
Gwynn, Aubrey, 46, 47–8

hagiography, 27–31, 38, 87–8, 218–29; *see also* Martyrology of Donegal; saints' lives
Hayward, Sir John, *Lives of the three Normans*, 32
Hennessy, William, 55
Henry II, king, 86, 123
Henry VI, king, 157
Henry VII, king, 32
Henry, prince of Wales, 32
heroes and heroism, 195, 196, 200, 203, 204, 211, 214
Higden, Ranulf, *Polychronicon*, 298
historical memory, 25, 100–1, 135, 180, 301–3
Holy Trinity monastery, Lough Key, 116, 233–4
honour, 26–7, 196, 200
Hyde, Douglas, 14

Inishowen, Co. Donegal, 181
Iomarbhádh na bhfileadh, 264–5, 268, 295n
Irish College, Paris, 30
Irish Texts Society, 20
Ite, saint, 226

James I, king, 36, 86, 98, 121, 123
Jennings, Brendan, OFM, 14–15, 20, 244–5, 253, 287
John Duns Scotus, 30

Kearney, Michael, 25n
Keating, Geoffrey, 15, 22–3, 29–30, 35, 41, 187, 299; *Foras feasa ar Éirinn*, 20, 22, 33, 79, 99, 241, 254, 266, 299
Kelley, D.R., 21
Kells, synod (1152), 241, 254
Kelly, Margareta, 247
Kilbarron, Co. Donegal, 176n
Kildare, county, 256; friary, 239, 286, 287; monastery, 222–3
Killeigh, Co. Offaly, friary, 157, 237

Kilnalahagh, Co. Tipperary, 251
Kilronan, Co. Roscommon, 273, 274
Kiltrustan parish, Co. Roscommon, 257, 260
Kinalehin, Co. Galway, friary, 285, 287
kings and kingship, 65–71, 80–7, 98, 100, 117–24, 128–9; inauguration, 200

Laidhgenn, saint, 226
Laoghaire, king, 65, 90, 160
Latin, 136, 239, 292; publications, 29–30, 41; translations from, 39; use of, 99, 129
'*Leabhar Airisin Meic Fhirbhisigh*', 56
'*Leabhar Baile Uí Cleirigh*', 53
'*Leabhar Baile Ui Mhaoil Conaire*', 53, 55, 262
Leabhar Breac, 70, 71
'*Leabhar breac Mic Aodhagáin*', 254; *see also* Mac Aodhagáin family
'*Leabhar Chloinne Uí Maoilconaire*', 43, 44, 45, 262–3, 277
'*Leabhar Chluana hEidhneach*', 221, 266
'*Leabhar Chluana mic Nóis*', 43, 57, 266
'*Leabhar Chluana Plocáin*', 266
'*Leabhar Choncoiccriche meic Diarmatta uí Clerigh*', 44, 54, 178–9, 270
Leabhar gabhála Éireann, 45, 85, 262, 263, 271; new recension, 52–3, 64–5, 69, 78–9, 80, 92, 273, 276, 296; sources of, 53; transcripts of, 257, 295
'*Leabhar Glinde da Lacha*', 53
'*Leabhar Leacain*', 266; *see also* Book of Lecan
'*Leabhar Lughach uí Clerigh*', 44; *see also* Beatha Aodha Ruaidh Uí Dhomhnaill
'*Leabhar Mec Bruaideadha*', 44; *see also* Mac Bruaideadha, Maoilín Óg
'*Leabhar muintere Duibgendáin Chille Rónáin*', 43, 45, 53, 274
'*Leabhar muintire Duibgendáin o Senchuaich ua nOilella*', 53
'*Leabhar na hUachongbala*', 53; *see also* Book of Leinster

Leabhar na hUidhre, 53, 55, 57–8, 219,
   257n, 262, 285
'*Leabhar Oiléin na Naemh*', 43
'*Leabhar oirisen Leacain meic Firbisicch*',
   43, 58; *see also* Annals of Lecan;
   Book of Lecan; Lecan; Mac
   Fhirbhisigh
'*Leabhar ruadh Mic Aodhagáin*', 254
'*Leabhar Sheanadh mhic Mhaghnusa*', 43,
   44, 45, 102, 277; *see also* Annals of
   Ulster
Leabhar, see also Book
Leanam croinic Clann nDálaigh, 272
Leath Cuinn, 63, 184
Leath Mogha, 63
Lecan, Co. Sligo, 280; manuscripts,
   112–14, 155–6, 157, 158; *see also*
   Annals of Lecan; Book of Lecan;
   Mac Fhirbhisigh
Leinster, province, history of, 107, 110,
   116, 291; kings of, 120
Liber hymnorum, 166, 284n, 291, 293
libraries, 45, 166, 290, 293
Limerick, Co. Limerick, friary, 285, 287
Lios Maighne, *see* Lismoyny, Co.
   Westmeath
Lisgoole, Co. Fermanagh, 133, 234, 294;
   friary, 239, 285, 288
Lisheen townland, Co. Roscommon, 260
Lismoyny, Co. Westmeath, 67, 253, 280
loan of manuscripts, *see* manuscripts, loan
   of
Lombard, Peter, archbishop of Armagh,
   28, 30
Longford, county, 256; friary, 116
lord justice of Ireland, 110, 197
lordship, characteristics of, 93–4, 182–4,
   196, 200–1
Lorrha, Co. Tipperary, 251
Lough Erne, Co. Fermanagh, 47
Lough Key, Co. Roscommon, 52, 116, 233
Louvain, Belgium, 14, 27–8, 29, 31, 33,
   35, 136, 139, 166, 167, 218, 239, 243,
   252, 265, 286, 287, 288; University,
   265; *see also* St Anthony's College,
   Louvain

Lynch, John, 56; *De praesulibus Hiberniae*,
   24, 247
Mac Aingil, Aodh, 30; *Scáthán
   shacramuinte na hAithridhe*, 36–7
Mac an Bhaird family, 286
Mac an Bhaird, Eoghan Ruadh, 187
Mac Aodhagáin family, 246, 247–55, 286,
   293; school of learning, 248–9, 251;
   lands, 251
Mac Aodhagáin, Baothghalach Ruadh,
   248–50, 251, 252, 256, 258
Mac Aodhagáin, Baothghalach, OFM,
   bishop of Elphin, 246, 247–8, 252,
   278
Mac Aodhagáin, Brian, 267
Mac Aodhagáin, Cairbre, 248, sons of,
   248–9, 50
Mac Aodhagáin, Cairbre Óg, 248, 249
Mac Aodhagáin, Cosnamhach
   (Constance; Cornelius), 248, 249, 251
Mac Aodhagáin, Donnchadh, 248, 249
Mac Aodhagáin, Flann, 69, 71, 99, 248,
   249, 250–5, 258, 260, 264, 266, 278,
   281
Mac Aodhagáin, Seán (John), 249, 251
Mac Aodhagáin, Tadhg, 247
Mac Aodhagáin, William, 248, 249
Mac Arachain, Nicholas, 133
Mac Bruaideadha family, 278–9
Mac Bruaideadha, Conchobhar, 69, 71,
   99, 250, 264, 278, 281
Mac Bruaideadha, Maoilín Óg, 279;
   annals, 62–3, 94, 278, 279
Mac Carthaigh, Cormac, 110, 147–8
Mac Cárthaigh, Eoin, 260
Mac Cárthaigh, Tadhg, 291
Mc Carthy, Daniel, 21n, 47, 51, 52, 56,
   59, 67, 68, 85, 98, 113, 139, 282
Mac Cathmhail, Siubhan, 235
Mac Cochláin, Toirrdhealbhach (patron),
   66, 80, 274, 293–4, 295–6
Mac Craith, Mícheál, OFM, 21, 35,
   122–3, 296
McDevitt, Dominic, 138n
Mac Diarmada family, 51, 256

Mac Diarmada, Brian (annalist), 51, 300
Mac Diarmada, Brian (d.1636), 261
Mac Diarmada, Lasarfina, daughter of Fearghal, 133
Mac Diarmata Ruadh, Maelsechlainn, son of Cormac, 131–2
Mac Donnchadha family, 256
Mac Eochagáin, Conall, 55, 56, 59, 66–7, 69, 71, 80, 113, 118–19, 161, 221, 253, 279–82, 293–4
Mac Eochagáin, Ross, OP, bishop of Kildare, 246, 280, 283
Mac Faolchadha, Conor, bishop of Ross, 116
Mac Fhirbhisigh family, manuscripts, 43, 56, 58, 59–60, 280; see also Book of Lecan
Mac Fhirbhisigh, Dubhaltach, 56, 58, 255 280; as scribe 254, translations by, 112–13
Mac Fir Bisich, Gilla Ísu, 58
Mac Gille Fhindéin, Aonghus, abbot of Lisgoole, 114
McGowan, Megan, 117
McKenna, Lambert, 248
Mac Lochlainn, Domhnall, king, 84
Mac Maghnusa, Cathal Óg, 47
Mac Murchadha, Art, son of Art, 105–6
Mac Niocaill, Gearóid, 47, 50, 51–2, 102
Mac Regan, John, 255
MacRory, Joseph, cardinal, 16
Mac Suibhne Connachtach, Maolmuire, 158
Mac Suibhne family, 192, manuscripts, 285
Mac William Burke family, 194–5
Mac William Burke, [Ulick], 181
Mac William Burke, [William], 158
Mac William Burke, son of, 129
Madrid, Spain, 265
Maedhóg, saint, 226
Mág Craith, Flann, 279–80
Mág Findbairr, Éamonn, 127
Mág Flannchadha, Cathal, 125–6
Mág Mathghamhna family, 93
Mág Niallusa, Brian, 285
Mág Raghnall family, 93

Mág Raghnaill, Ragnall, 129
Magraidhin, Auguistín, 60–1
Mág Sgoloigi, Donnchadha, 133
Mág Uidhir family, 48, 199n, 276; manuscripts, 276–7, 285, 294
Mág Uidhir, [Cú Chonnacht Óg], 198–9
Mág Uidhir, Aedh (d.1463), 133
Mág Uidhir, Aodh (d.1471), 97
Mág Uidhir, Brian, 295
Mág Uidhir, Brian, abbot of Lisgoole, 233, 234
Mág Uidhir, Brian Ruadh, baron of Enniskillen (patron), 58n, 294, 295, 296
Mág Uidhir, Cathal, 132, 27
Mág Uidhir, Conchobhar, 295
Mág Uidhir, Cú Chonnacht, 295
Mág Uidhir, Gráinne, daughter of Aedh, 133
Mág Uidhir, Muiris, Great Archdeacon, 234–5, 277n; wife of, 235
Mág Uidhir, Pilib mac Toirrdhealbhaigh, 110
Mág Uidhir, Semus, 277
Mág Uidhir, Seon, son of Great Archdeacon, 234–5
Mair, John, 31
Malachy, saint, 218, 223–6, 229
Malone, Fr, 37n
manuscripts
  BL Additional 4784: 48, 291
  BL Additional 4789: 48
  BL Additional 4792: 52
  BL Additional 4795: 48
  BL Cotton Vespasian E II, 91n, 92n
  BL Egerton 127: 260n
  BL Egerton 1782: 258, 259
  BL Harley 5280: 257
  BL Harley 6018: 249n
  Bodleian Laud Misc 610: 251, 276n
  Bodleian Rawl. B 480: 280n
  Bodleian Rawl. B 485: 61n
  Bodleian Rawl. B 488: 60–1
  Bodleian Rawl. B 489: 46–7, 48n, 77n
  Bodleian Rawl. B 505: 61n
  Bodleian Rawl. B 512: 53n
  BR 1569–72: 72n

manuscripts (*continued*)
  BR 2324–40: 45n, 287
  BR 2542–3: 271n, 283n
  BR 2569–72: 67, 69, 89
  BR 3410: 135n, 232n, 237, 238n
  BR 4190–200: 287
  BR 4639: 271n
  BR 5095–6: 71n
  BR 5100–4: 72n, 261n, 280n, 287
  NLI G 488: 62, 95n
  RIA 23 C 30: 260n
  RIA 23 D 17: 72
  RIA 23 E 25: 55
  RIA 23 F 2–3: 76n, 82n, 170n
  RIA 23 K 32: 64n, 271n
  RIA 23 K 45: 276n
  RIA 23 M 70: 64n
  RIA 23 N 10: 259
  RIA 23 N 11: 274n
  RIA 23 P 6: 18n, 67, 74–86, 136–58, 171–5, 191, 237–8; illustration of, 172
  RIA 23 P 7: 18n, 74–86, 95n, 136–58, 171–5
  RIA 23 P 24: 209n, 284n
  RIA 24 P 33: 69, 71n, 253n
  RIA B iv 2: 33n, 69, 263
  RIA C iii 1: 49, 50, 51
  RIA C iii 3: 19n, 74–84, 92, 136–43, 154, 159–71, 230n, 261; illustrations of, 140–1; 163
  RIA D i 3: 249n, 274n
  RIA E iv 4: 257, 259n
  TCD 804: 60n
  TCD 1282: 46–8, 77, 147n
  TCD 1286: 64n, 257n, 271n, 273n
  TCD 1292: 56
  TCD 1293: 52
  TCD 1300: 76n, 170n
  TCD 1301: 45n, 59, 74–86, 96n, 136–58, 171–5; illustration of, 173
  TCD 1318: 195n
  TCD 1348: 66n
  TCD 1394: 274n
  UCD-OFM A 2: 291n
  UCD-OFM A 13: 74–84, 136–43, 159–71, 230n; illustrations of, 144–6, 162, 273, 275; signatures, 275
  UCD-OFM A 14: 266n
  UCD-OFM A 16: 65, 66, 70, 80, 81n, 98n, 271n, 273n; illustration of, 275; signatures, 275
  UCD-OFM A 19: 285n
manuscripts of AFM, 21, 74–86, 136–75, 237–8, 261
manuscripts, loan of, 42, 71, 279–81, 291, 293
Maoilsechlainn, king, 66, 84, 119
Margaret, saint, 220
martyrologies, 221, 226, 231, 276, 284
Martyrology of Donegal, 57, 71–2, 88, 90, 92, 96–7, 161, 168–9, 215, 219, 221, 222–6, 231, 250, 271, 276, 278, 280; approbations for, 253
Martyrology of Gorman, 71, 97, 221n, 284
Martyrology of Oengus (*Féilire Oengusso*), 276, 284
Martyrology of Tallaght, 231n, 290
Mary, Queen, 86, 292
Máthair na horchra an éigsi, 261–2
Matthews, Francis, OFM, *see* O'Mahony, Francis, OFM
Meath, 116; county, 256; kings, 120
Méguidhir, *see* Mág Uidhir
Mellifont, synod, 241n
Messingham, Thomas, 30
Meursius, Johannes, *Historia Danica*, 33
Mha Guidhir, *see* Mág Uidhir
Míl, *see* Clann Mhíleadh
Milesians, *see* Clann Mhíleadh
military narratives, 92, 107, 188–214, 233
miracles, 116, 225, 227–9, 233
Mochean dod chuairt a Chalbhaigh, 260
Monaghan, Co. Monaghan, friary, 238
monasteries, foundation of, 236–40; destruction of, 217, 239; *see also* Franciscan friaries
Mooney, Canice, OFM, 17, 21n, 139

Mooney, Donagh, OFM, 35, 120, 238–9, 283, 285, 287
Moylurg, Co. Roscommon, 51, 211
Muircheartach, king, 89
Muiris Ulltach, *see* Ó Duinnshléibhe
Mulchrone, Kathleen, 50, 143
Multifarnham, friary, 287; Franciscan Chapter at, 266
Munemón, king, 81
Munster, province, history of, 107, 110, 116, 206, 233, 291; kings of, 119–20
Murphy, Denis, 281

Naomhsheanchas, 70, 85, 220, 280, 283–4; *see also* hagiography
national histories, 22, 27, 31–3
natural phenomena, 93, 131, 228–9, 233
New Ross, Co. Wexford, friary, 285
Ní Bhriain, Mór, 133–4
Ní Bhriain, Sláine, 133–4
Ní Chearbhaill, Maighread, 132–3
Nicholls, Kenneth, 118, 255n
Ní Dhomhnaill, Máire, 202
Ní Mhuiríosa, Máirín, 15
Nine Years War (1594–1603), 24, 28, 62
Noah, 77
Normans, coming of, 84; destruction of churches, 228

Ó Baoighill, Donnchadh, 108
Ó Beirn family, 256
Ó Birn, Aed, 131
obituaries, 92, 176–88, 215, 233–6, 250–1
Ó Briain family, 19, 63
Ó Briain, Conchobhar (d. 1328), 120
Ó Briain, Conchobhar, earl of Thomond, 269
Ó Briain, Dónal, 206
Ó Briain, Donnchadh, fourth earl of Thomond, 291
Ó Briain, Donnchadh, king, 119–20
Ó Briain, Muircheartach, king, 84
Ó Briain, Toirrdhealbhach, king, 83–4
O'Brien, Sylvester, 17
Ó Buachalla, Breandán, 21–2, 27, 37, 287, 294–5, 296

Ó Caiside family, manuscripts, 285
Ó Ceallaigh, Muircheartach, archbishop, 125
Ó Ceallaigh, Tadhg, 126–7
Ó Cearbhaill, Diarmaid, 225
Ó Cearbhaill, Donchadh, lord of Oirghialla, 227
Ó Cearbhaill, Maolruanaidh, 110
Ó Cianáin, Tadhg, 285
Ó Cléirigh family, 53, 54, 95, 168–73, 293; book of genealogies, 72; historians, 176–80, 191, 201, 244
Ó Cléirigh, Bernardinus (Maolmhuire), 39, 246, 272, 283
Ó Cléirigh, Cairbre, 270
Ó Cléirigh, Corbmac, 179n
Ó Cléirigh, Conaire (scribe), 142, 147, 149, 152–4, 160, 272–3, 274; signature, 275
Ó Cléirigh, Cosnamhach, 179n, 269
Ó Cléirigh, Cú Choigcríche (*floruit* 1546), son of Diarmaid, son of Tadhg Cam, 44, 54, 178–9, 270
Ó Cléirigh, Cú Choigcríche (annalist), 44, 45, 54, 69, 85, 120, 168, 264, 269, 270–2, 273, 286; and hagiography, 39, 283–4; as editor, 148–9, 152–5, 174; as scribe, 142, 147, 152–5, 160, 171, 237–8; manuscripts transcribed by, 61, 72, 209n; signature, 275
Ó Cléirigh, Cú Mumhan, 285
Ó Cléirigh, Diarmaid, 54
Ó Cléirigh, Dubhach, 179n
Ó Cléirigh, Giolla Riabhach (d.1527), 177, 257
Ó Cléirigh, Lughaidh, son of Maccon, 44, 54, 61–2, 63, 91, 95, 187, 201, 209, 211, 249–50, 254, 268–70; *see also Beatha Aodha Ruaidh Uí Dhomhnaill*
Ó Cléirigh, Maccon, son of Cú Choigcríche, 179, 208–9
Ó Cléirigh, Maolmhuire (d.1583), 208
Ó Cléirigh, Mícheál (annalist), 14, 22–3, 33, 38–40, 41, 54, 69, 78–9, 120, 168, 209, 241; as 'chronicler', 177;

Ó Cléirigh, Mícheál (annalist) (*continued*)
addresses to patrons, 26, 33, 74; as
editor, 148–9, 152–5, 174; as scribe,
142, 147, 152–5, 160, 237, 237, 246;
Foclóir, 247, 250, 255–6, 278, 297; in
Ormond, 251–3; manuscripts
consulted by, 57, 61, 67, 91–2, 285;
manuscripts penned by, 67, 70, 71,
72, 89, 136–75; networks, 42, 244–
300; saints' lives, 42, 223, 279; sent
to Ireland, 28, 72; modern legacy of,
13–22; signature, 275

Ó Cléirigh, Muiris Ballach, son of Cú
Choigcríche, 179n

Ó Cléirigh, Muiris, son of Lughaidh, 54,
269

Ó Cléirigh, Tadhg Cam (d.1492), 54,
176n, 177–8, 268

Ó Cléirigh, Tadhg, son of Cú
Choigcríche, 179n

Ó Cléirigh, Tadhg Cam (d.1566), son of
Tuathal, 177, 178, 284

Ó Cléirigh, Tomás, 14

Ó Cléirigh, Tuathal, 177, 178

O Coineoil, Concobhar, bishop of Killala,
233

Ó Colla, Pól, 71n, 273n

Ó Conchobhair Fáilghe, Brian, 110

Ó Conchobhair Fáilghe, Murchadh, 132,
157, 158

Ó Conchobhair family, 50, 51, 256

Ó Conchobhair, Aodh (d.1632), 261

Ó Conchobhair, Cathal Crobderg, 50, 77,
183; son of, 119

Ó Conchobhair, Donnchadh, 130–1

Ó Conchobhair, Fedhlimidh, 119

Ó Conchobhair, Ruaidhrí, king, 66, 83–4,
85, 117; inauguration, 118

Ó Conchobhair, Toirrdhealbhach Mór,
king, 85

O'Connor, Rev. Brendan, 254

O'Connor, Dermod, 277n

O'Connor, Frank, *The backward look*, 3

O'Conor, Charles, of Belanagare, 76n,
164n; *Rerum Hibernicarum scriptores*,
20, 75–6, 82, 137, 161n, 164

Ó Corráin, Donnchadh, 117

Ó Cuinlis, Murchadh, 279n

Ó Cuív, Brian, 47–8

O'Curry, Eugene, 18–19, 75, 138

Ó Dóailen, Toirrdhealbhach, 277

Ó Domhnaill family, 19, 24, 48, 49, 54,
92, 94, 126, 286; in European
armies, 34; histories of, 61–2, 124,
157, 176–214, 300; manuscripts
owned by, 57; marriages of, 110;
women, 134–5

Ó Domhnaill, An Calbhach (d.1566), 200,
201–3

Ó Domhnaill, An Calbhach Ruadh, 260,
272

Ó Domhnaill, Aodh (d.1600), 207

Ó Domhnaill, Aodh Buidhe (d.1538),
199

Ó Domhnaill, Aodh Dubh (Aodh Óg)
(d.1537), 109–10, 176n, 184–5,
191–2, 197, 199

Ó Domhnaill, Aodh Ruadh (d.1505), 110,
180–4

Ó Domhnaill, Aodh Ruadh (d.1602), 39,
61, 63, 91–2, 95, 96, 122, 209–12;
obituary of, 186–8; poem addressed
to, 279; will of, 121; *see also Beatha
Aodha Ruaidh Uí Dhomhnaill*

Ó Domhnaill, Conn, son of An Calbhach,
206, 207

Ó Domhnaill, Eoghan, son of Aodh Óg,
197

Ó Domhnaill, Inghen Dubh, daughter of
Aodh Ruadh, 134

Ó Domhnaill, Maghnus (d.1563), 176n,
185, 191–201, 219n, 260n; daughters
of, 134, 260n; wife of, 110, 134

Ó Domhnaill, Neachtain, 107

Ó Domhnaill, Niall Garbh, son of Aodh
Óg, 197

Ó Domhnaill, Niall Garbh, son of Con,
202n

Ó Domhnaill, Niall, son of Domhnall
Cairbreach, 203

Ó Domhnaill, Niall, son of
Toirrdhealbhach, 59, 190–1

Ó Domhnaill, Toirrdhealbhach Cairbreach, 188, 189

Ó Domhnaill, Uilliam, 278

O'Donovan, John, 13, 47n, 142; edition of AFM, 18–20, 75–6, 82, 137–42, 164, 169–71, 175

Ó Dubhda, Ruaidhrí, 128

Ó Duibhgeannáin family, 21n, 52–4, 244, 273–6, manuscripts, 43, 45, 49, 51, 52–4, 103, 104, 112, 127, 274, 285

Ó Duibhgeannáin, Cú Choigcríche, annalist, 54, 85; as scribe, 142–3; signature, 275

Ó Duibhgeannáin, Dubhthach óg, 272

Ó Duibhgeannáin, Matha Glas, 110

Ó Duibhgeannáin, Paitín, 50

Ó Duibhgeannáin, Pilib Ballach, 52

Ó Duibhgeannáin, Seaán Ballach, 274n

Ó Duibhgeannáin, Seán Riabhach, 50

Ó Duinnshléibhe, Muiris Ulltach, son of Donnchadh, 39, 186–7, 246

Ó Duinnshléibhe, Muiris Ulltach, son of Seaán, 39, 45n, 72, 246, 271, 283, 285, 290–1; as translator, 236–7, 289n

Ó Fearghail, Conchobhar, bishop of Ardagh, 233

Ó Fearghail, Risterd, bishop of Ardagh, 115

Offaly, county, 233, 295

O'Flaherty, Roderic, 59, 112, 113, 139n, 147, 156, 164n

Ó Flannagáin family, 256

Ó Flannagáin, Conchobhar, 124–5

Ó Gadhra family, 157

Ó Gadhra, Fearghal (patron), 26, 42, 74, 99, 136, 139, 294, 295–8, 302

Ó Gairmleadhaigh, Moen, 156

O'Gorman, Maurice, 164n

O'Gorman, Chevalier Thomas, 76

O'Grady, S.H., 291

Ó hAinlighe, Eamonn, 126

Ó hEodhasa, Bonaventure, 286; *Teagasc Críosdaidhe*, 36

Ó hÓgain family, 236

Ó hÓgain, Aodh Bacach, 236

Ó hUiginn, Maolmhuire mac Eoghain, 261

Oisseine, saint, 168–9, 226n

O'Leary, Philip, 17

Ó Lochlainn, Colm, 244

Ó Longáin, Mícheál, 274n

Ó Luinín family, 276–7

Ó Luinín, Giolla Pádraig, 276

Ó Luinín, Matha, 48

Ó Luinín, Páttraic Ballach, 277

Ó Luinín, Ruaidhrí, 47, 48, 276

Ó Macháin, Pádraig, 296

O'Mahony, Francis, OFM, 288, 290; *Brevis synopsis*, 72, 135, 232n, 236–9, 288–9; translation of, 236–7

Ó Máille, Aodh, 130

Ó Maoil Chonaire family, 21n, 50–2, 244; 255–67, 286; manuscripts 49n, 262–3; 263–8, 285; school of history, 256

Ó Maoil Chonaire, Fearfeasa (annalist), son of Lochlainn, 44n, 85, 260, 264, 267, 270, 272, 273; as scribe, 142–3; 261; signature, 275

Ó Maoil Chonaire, Ferdinandus, OFM, 256

Ó Maoil Chonaire, Flaithrí, OFM, 39, 186, 246, 256; *Desiderius*, 36, 37

Ó Maoil Chonaire, Lochlainn, 260

Ó Maoil Chonaire, Maoileachlainn Modartha, 256–7, 263

Ó Maoil Chonaire, Maoilín (*floruit* 1423), 282

Ó Maoil Chonaire, Muirgheas (d.1543), son of Páidín, 55, 91, 257, 262–3

Ó Maoil Chonaire, Muiris (scribe), son of Torna, 60, 142–3, 261, 262; signature, 275;

Ó Maoil Chonaire, Páidín (d.1506), 257

Ó Maoil Chonaire, Páidín Ruadh (*floruit* 1640), 257, 260

Ó Maoil Chonaire, Seán (d.1517), son of Torna, 260

Ó Maoil Chonaire, Seán (*floruit* 1560–70s), son of Torna Óg, 257–60

Ó Maoil Chonaire, Seán (*floruit* 1650s), son of Torna, 258

Ó Maoil Chonaire, Seán, OFM, 256
Ó Maoil Chonaire, Siodrach, 276n
Ó Maoil Chonaire, Torna, son of Eólus, 256–7, 261, 263
Ó Maoil Chonaire, Torna Óg (d.1532), *ollamh*, 257
Ó Maoil Chonaire, Tuileagna (Conry, Tully) (*floruit* 1673), 265
Ó Maoil Chonaire, Tuileagna, son of Seanchán, 167, 260, 263–7, 299
Ó Maoilmhuaidh, Cú Choigcríche, 125
Ó Maonaigh family, manuscripts, 285
Ó Mordha, Ruaidhrí, 254
Ó Muraíle, Nollaig, 56, 60, 136, 139, 245, 255, 276
Ó Néill family, 93, 107, 286; histories of, 188, 189, 192–7, 204–9; manuscripts, 298; marriages of 110; in European armies, 34
Ó Néill, Aodh (d.1616), 96, 123, 137
Ó Néill, Art, son of Aodh, 107–8, 192
Ó Neill, Art Óg, son of Conn, 109, 192
Ó Néill, Conn Bacach (d.1559), 109, 196; daughter of, 197
Ó Néill, Enrí, 188
Ó Néill, Eoghan, 171
Ó Néill, kings of, 117
Ó Néill, Néill Óg, 107
Ó Néill, Niall, wife of, 134
Ó Néill, Seaán (d.1567), son of Conn Bacach, 90–1, 201–2, 204–5; wife of, 202
Ó Néill, Seán (d.1517), son of Conn, 108
Ó Néill, Siubhán, 197
Ó Néill, Toirrdhealbhach Luineach, 204–5, 207, 208
Ó Raghallaigh, Godfrey, 227
oral sources, 63, 95, 135, 203
Ó Riain, Pádraig, 70, 72, 88, 226n
origin legends, 79
Ó Rodaighe, Tadhg, 259, 260n, 274
Ó Ruairc family, in European armies, 34
Ó Ruairc, Brian, 51
Ó Ruairc, Brian na Múrtha, 259, 260n
Ó Ruairc, Eoghan, son of Tigearnán Mór, 129

Ó Scanaill, Maolpatraic, 232, 238
Ó Tuathail, Art, 110
Ó, *see also* Ua
Oxford, England, 265

Palladius, 164, 167
Papiron, Johannes, cardinal, 240
Paris, France, 31
Parke, Co. Galway, 247–8
Parthalon, 77–80
Pasquier, Étienne, *Recherches de la France*, 32
patent rolls, 292
Patrick, saint, 34, 35, 38, 83, 84, 90, 98, 101, 159–68, 218–29, 243, 289
patrons and patronage, 26, 34, 66, 74, 225, 241, 245, 271, 293–8, 299–300; *see also* Ó Gadhra, Fearghal; Mac Cochláin, Toirrdhealbhach; Mág Uidhir, Brian Ruadh
persecution, 217n
Petrie, George, 18, 138n
Philip III, king of Spain, 122
Picts, 231
pilgrimage, 115, 192
Piton, Rotsel, 88
Pits, John, *De illustribus Angliae scriptoribus*, 31
Pius XII, Pope, 16–17
Plummer, Charles, 15
Plunkett family, 279
Pocock, J.G.A., 21
poetry, 67, 69, 79, 80–1, 89, 166, 187, 219, 220, 259, 260, 264–5, 272, 274; *see also first lines of individual poems*
political ideology, 212–14
Pontanus, Johannes, *Rerum Danicarum historia*, 33
postage stamps, 16
Power family, 279
prayers, 126–9
print, 34, 35, 41–2, 99
Prise, Sir John, *Historiae Brytannicae*, 32
prophecies, 91–2, 95, 123, 187–8
proverbs, 126–9

Psalter of Cashel, *see Saltair Chaisil*
Psalter of Tara, *see Saltair Teamhrach*

Queely, Malachy, 252–3
Quin, Co. Clare, friary, 237, 286, 287

Radner, Joan, 254
Raphoe, miraculous crucifix, 116
Rathcroghan, Co. Roscommon, 211
Rathmore, Co. Roscommon, 257
Red Book of Munster, 228n, 279n
Reformation, in Ireland, 22, 217–18; in
    Europe, 34, 42–3
Réim ríoghraidhe, 65, 66, 80, 85
relics, 217, 228–9
Renaissance in Ireland, 21, 282, 296,
    299–300, 301; in Europe, 34, 101
Reynolds, Humphrey, 265n
Rochford, Robert, OFM, 35, 220
Rome, 31, 35, 37, 217, 239, 286;
    pilgrimage to, 115, 176n, 192; synod,
    240n
Roscommon, barony, 257; county, 256;
    monastery, 239
Rosserrilly (Ross), friary, Co. Galway,
    286, 287
Rosweyde, Heribert, SJ, 38
Rothe, David, bishop of Ossory, 30, 289
royalism, 22, 37, 123
Rudhroighe, king, 65
Ryan, Salvador, 37–8

sacraments, 240–1
Saints' Island, Lough Ree, 60; *see also*
    '*Annales prioratus*'; Book of the Island
    of Saints
saints' lives, 27–31, 72, 218–29, 279, 290;
    see also hagiography, martyrologies
Salamanca, Spain, 31, Irish College, 39,
    265, 283
Saltair Chaisil, 277
Saltair Teamhrach, 277
scholarly networks, 244–300
Scotland, 30–1, 298; historians of, 31–2;
    saints, 221
Scots, 204

scribes of AFM, 136–75; *see also* Ó
    Cléirigh, Conaire; Ó Cléirigh, Cú
    Choigcríche; Ó Cléirigh, Mícheál,
    OFM; Ó Duibhgeannáin, Cú
    Choigcríche; Ó Maoil Chonaire,
    Fearfeasa; Ó Maoil Chonaire, Muiris
seanchas, 41–2, 50
Seangann, king, 65
Senmoigh elta Eadair, 79
Septuagint dating, 74
Sétna, king, 81
Shannon river, 251, 257
Sidney, Sir Henry, lord deputy of Ireland,
    206–7, 212
Sigonius, Carlus, 32
Silke, J.J., 21
Simancas, Spain, 185–6, 187n
Simms, Katharine, 46, 48, 255, 293
Síol Muireadaigh, 255–6, 258
Siorna Saoghlach mac Déin, king, 81
Sixtus, pope, 165
Sláinghe, king, 65, 74, 80
Sligo, Co. Sligo, 157, 191, 295; friary, 239
Sliocht Diarmada, 272
Sliocht Pháidín, 260, 261, 263; *see also* Ó
    Maoil Chonaire family
Smith, Peter, 69
sources of AFM, 41–74
Spain, kings of, 121–2
Spanish Flanders, 34
Speed, John, *History of Great Britaine*, 32
St Anthony's College, Louvain, 14, 27–8,
    39, 41, 99, 246–7, 256, 283, 286, 302;
    and publishing, 35–9, 247n; *see also*
    Louvain
Stanihurst, Richard, 31n
St Isidore's College, Rome, 236n, 289
St Omer, France, 220
state papers, 206
Strange, Thomas, OFM, 289–90
Strokestown, Co. Roscommon, 257
Strongbow (Richard de Clare), 228
Struever, Nancy, 101
Swayne, John, archbishop of Armagh,
    292
synods, 240–2, 254

Tara, kings of, 117, 118, 120
Tethghall, bishop, 231
Thomond, 253, 268–9, 278, 279
Thomond, annals, 209; king of, 119;
    lordship, 183, 212; see also Mac
    Bruaideadha, Maoilín Óg; Ó Briain
    family
Thomond, Franciscan Chapter at, 264
Timoleague, Co. Cork, friary, 237n, 239,
    286, 287, 298
Tír Conaill, 48, 92, 123, 180–1, 191, 192,
    198, 199–201; see also Donegal,
    county
Tír Éoghain, 198; see also Ó Néill
Tombrick, Co. Wexford, 274
topographical detail, 193–4, 202, 203
Tory Island, 108
translations, 113, 129; see also Annals of
    Clonmacnoise; Mac Fhirbhisigh,
    Dubhaltach
Trent, Council of, see Council of Trent
Trim, Co. Meath, 116
Trinity Island, see Holy Trinity
    monastery
Truagh liom Máire agus Mairgrég, 187
Tuatha Dé Danann, 80; kings, 65
Tuathal Techtmar, king, 90
Tuite, Eleanor, 294
Tulach Maol, 277
Tyrone, see Tír Éoghain
Tyrrell, Patrick, OFM, 265

Ua Caiside, Ruaidhrí, 47
Ua Comhthaigh, Muiredhach, bishop of
    Derry and Raphoe, 233
Úa Dálacháin, Aodh óg, book of, 228n
Ua Fallamhain, Tadhg, 129–30
Ua Lennain, Domhnall, canon of
    Lisgoole, 233
Ua Lennain, Eóin, prior of Lisgoole, 116
Ua Lennain, Tomas, canon of Lisgoole,
    116
Ua Maeileoin, Gillachrist, 56

Ua Maoil Chonaire, see Ó Maoil Chonaire
Ua Maoil Doraigh, Flaithbeartach, 88
Ua, see also Ó
Uí Fhiachrach, 128
Ulster, history of, 107, 277, 291, 298;
    kings of, 120
universities, 34, 38, 244
Ussher, James, archbishop of Armagh,
    89n, 229; 289; Britannicarum, 99,
    166; A discourse, 34, 35; library at
    Drogheda, 166, 290, 293; loan of
    manuscripts, 71, 281, 293

Valdez, Diego, 33
Vatican Library, 137n
Virgil, Polydor, Anglica historia, 32
Vivanus, cardinal, 241

Wadding, Luke, OFM, 35, 239, 246, 289
Walsh, Paul, 20, 21n, 51, 64, 65, 96, 139,
    142, 170, 171, 244–5, 253, 256, 258,
    260, 287
Ward, Hugh, OFM, 27–8, 31, 38, 39, 41,
    120, 246–7, 253
Ware, Sir James, 24, 58, 60, 61, 112, 134,
    166, 233n, 254–5, 265n, 291, 293;
    annals, 292; De scriptoribus, 293;
    Opuscula S. Patricii, 293
Waterford, Co. Waterford, 206; friary,
    237n, 239
watermarks, 137
weather, 202
Wentworth, Thomas, earl of Strafford,
    288; sister of, 295
Westmeath, county, 295
Wexford, friary, 285, 287, 298
White, Stephen, SJ, 289–90
Williams, J.E. Caerwyn, 15
women, 131–4, 234

Yellow Book of Lecan, 195n
Youghal, Co. Cork, 206; friary, 237n, 239
youths, 131–3